HANDBOOK OF
MATHEMATICAL
COGNITION

HANDBOOK OF MATHEMATICAL COGNITION

EDITED BY
JAMIE I.D. CAMPBELL

PSYCHOLOGY PRESS
NEW YORK AND HOVE

Published in 2005 by
Psychology Press
270 Madison Avenue
New York, NY 10016
www.psypress.com

Published in Great Britain by
Psychology Press Ltd.
27 Church Road
Hove, East Sussex
BN3 2FA
www.psypress.co.uk

10 9 8 7 6 5 4 3 2 1

Library of Congress Cataloging-in-Publication Data
    Handbook of mathematical cognition / edited by Jamie I. D. Campbell.
        p. cm.
    Includes bibliographical references and index.
    ISBN 1-84169-411-8 (hard cover : alk. paper)
    1. Mathematics–Study and teaching–Methodology. 2. Mathematical ability.
I. Campbell, Jamie I. D.

QA11. 2.H37 2005
510'.71–dc 22

                                                    2004009847

Contents

Part 1: Cognitive Representations for Numbers and Mathematics

Part 5: Neuropsychology of Number Processing and Calculation

About the Editor

Jamie Campbell is a Professor of Psychology at the University of Saskatchewan, Canada. He earned a B.A. in Psychology from Queen's University in Kingston and a Ph.D. from the University of Waterloo. He has published numerous scientific articles in the area of mathematical cognition and previously edited *The Nature and Origin of Mathematical Skills* (1992). His main research area is cognitive arithmetic, including computational modeling of memory for arithmetic facts, cross-cultural differences in arithmetic skills, and issues of cognitive architecture for calculation and number processing. Other research interests include processes of visual attention, memory inhibition, perception without awareness, and development of procedures and software for statistical power analysis. To contact the editor, send email to jamie.campbell@usask.ca or visit http://www.usask.ca/~Jamie.Campbell. Professor Campbell's research is funded by the Natural Sciences and Engineering Research Council of Canada.

Contributors

Dor Abrahamson
Northwestern University, USA

Mark H. Ashcraft
Cleveland State University, USA

Marcia A. Barnes
University of Guelph, University of Toronto, Canada

Talia Ben-Zeev
San Francisco State University, USA

Jeffrey Bisanz
University of Alberta, Canada

Julie L. Booth
Carnegie Mellon University, USA

Elizabeth M. Brannon
Duke University, USA

Marc Brysbaert
Royal Holloway University of London, United Kingdom

Brian Butterworth
University College London, United Kingdom

Jamie I. D. Campbell
University of Saskatchewan, Canada

Laurent Cohen
Service Hospitalier Frédéric Joliot, France

Benjamin Coleman
Carleton University, Canada

Sara Cordes
Rutgers University, USA

Stanislas Dehaene
Service Hospitalier Frédéric Joliot, France

Margarete Delazer
Universitätsklinik für Neurologie, Innsbruck, Austria

Diana DeStefano
Carleton University, Canada

James A. Dixon
University of Connecticut, USA

Frank Domahs
Universitätsklinik für Neurologie, Innsbruck, Austria

Seth Duncan
San Francisco State University, USA

Sandrine Duverne
CNRS and Université de Provence, France

Lynette J. Epp
University of Saskatchewan, Canada

Michel Fayol
Université Blaise Pascal, France

Wim Fias
Ghent University, Belgium

Martin H. Fischer
University of Dundee, United Kingdom

Chad Forbes
San Francisco State University, USA

Karen C. Fuson
Northwestern University, USA

Dana Ganor-Stern
Ben-Gurion University of the Negev, Israel

David C. Geary
University of Missouri-Columbia, USA

Rochel Gelman
Rutgers University, USA

Elaine Ho
University of Alberta, Canada

Mary K. Hoard
University of Missouri-Columbia, USA

Melissa Kelly
University of Illinois at Urbana-Champaign, USA

George Lakoff
University of California at Berkeley, USA

Susan H. Landry
University of Texas-Houston Health Sciences Center, USA

Jo-Anne LeFevre
Carleton University, Canada

Patrick Lemaire
CNRS and Université de Provence, France

Aliette Lochy
*Universitätsklinik für Neurologie, Innsbruck, Austria; and
Université Catholique de Louvain-la-Neuve, Belgium*

Gordon D. Logan
Vanderbilt University, USA

Michèle M. M. Mazzocco
Johns Hopkins University, USA

Michael McCloskey
Johns Hopkins University, USA

Kevin F. Miller
University of Illinois at Urbana-Champaign, USA

Christophe Mussolin
Université Catholique de Louvain, Belgium

Marie-Pascale Noël
Université Catholique de Louvain, Belgium

Rafael Núñez
University of California, San Diego, USA

Mauro Pesenti
Université Catholique de Louvain, Belgium

Manuela Piazza
Service Hospitalier Frédéric Joliot, France

Philippe Pinel
Service Hospitalier Frédéric Joliot, France

Carmen Rasmussen
University of Alberta, Canada

Kelly S. Ridley
Cleveland State University, USA

Laurence Rousselle
Université Catholique de Louvain, Belgium

Xavier Seron
Université Catholique de Louvain, Belgium

Tina Shanahan
Carleton University, Canada

Jody L. Sherman
University of Alberta, Canada

Robert S. Siegler
Carnegie Mellon University, USA

Brenda Smith-Chant
Trent University, Canada

Ivilin Stoianov
Università di Padova, Italy

Joseph Tzelgov
Ben-Gurion University of the Negev, Israel

Carlo Umiltà
Università di Padova, Italy

N. Jane Zbrodoff
Vanderbilt University, USA

Xiaobin Zhou
University of Illinois at Urbana-Champaign, USA

Marco Zorzi
Università di Padova, Italy

Preface

How does the mind represent number and make mathematical calculations? What underlies the cognitive development of numerical and mathematical abilities? What factors affect the learning of numerical concepts and procedures? What are the biological bases of number knowledge? Do humans and other animals share similar numerical representations and processes? What underlies numerical and mathematical disabilities and disorders, and what is the prognosis for rehabilitation?

These questions are the domain of mathematical cognition, the field of research concerned with the cognitive and neurological processes that underlie numerical and mathematical abilities. Mathematical cognition research intersects a wide array of subfields including: cognitive development; neurological development; computational science; cognitive and educational psychology; animal cognition; cognitive and clinical neuropsychology; neuroscience; and cognitive science.

This volume is a collection of twenty-seven essays by leading researchers in the field, and constitutes a comprehensive survey of state-of-the-art research on important facets of mathematical cognition. Anyone interested in any aspect of numerical or mathematical cognition will find pointers to all the major issues, methods, phenomena, and theories in any major research subarea of the field. The book thereby provides a general reference for mathematical cognition research, and is intended for academics, scientists, clinicians, and senior students who want a definitive, comprehensive survey of the field.

The volume is divided into five parts.

Part 1 (Cognitive Representations for Number and Mathematics) addresses diverse representational issues of numerical and mathematical thinking. Fayol and Seron (Chapter 1) review neuropsychological, experimental, and developmental research into the cognitive representations that mediate elementary number processing. Many important insights have been gained, but the authors also identify shortcomings of extant theories of number representation. Brysbaert (Chapter 2) summarizes research on the recognition of numbers presented in various surface forms (e.g., verbal, Arabic, and analog). A comprehensive model of the functional relations among the underlying symbolic and semantic codes is proposed. Fias and Fischer (Chapter 3) review evidence that components of the number processing system (e.g., visual Arabic number form, and magnitude representations) are linked with spatial processing. Spatial coding of numbers occurs automatically. Its characteristics are determined by task-dependent numerical and spatial parameters. Tzelgov and Ganor-Stern (Chapter 4) focus on automatic processing of numerical information and, in particular, on ordinal relations. Zorzi, Stoianov, and Umiltà (Chapter 5) provide a critical review of existing computational models of number processing and simple arithmetic. They present simulations of number comparison, number priming, and simple arithmetic based on a new connectionist theory of numerosity representation. Brannon (Chapter 6) describes the numerical abilities of nonhuman animals and shows that species as diverse as pigeons, rats, cats, and monkeys are capable of representing numbers and performing operations on numerical representations.

There are both important commonalities and differences between non-human and human number processing. To conclude Part 1, Núñez and Lakoff (Chapter 7) explain how conceptual metaphor provides the inferential organization and structure of mathematical ideas. Everyday cognitive mechanisms operating in special ways underlie the inferential organization that makes mathematics what it is.

In Part 2 (Learning and Development of Numerical Skills), the focus turns to the acquisition of numerical and mathematical abilities. Cordes and Gelman (Chapter 8) present research and arguments that development of counting skills is based on a domain-specific, nonverbal counting, and arithmetic structure. These nonverbal mechanisms provide young learners with a basis for understanding the cardinal counting principle, and the framework to acquire a verbal count routine. Bisanz, Sherman, Rasmussen, and Ho (Chapter 9) review research on the development of procedures and concepts related to mathematical cognition in preschool children, with a focus on knowledge and skills underlying basic arithmetic. Miller, Kelly, and Zhou (Chapter 10) explore the nature of cross-national differences in mathematics acquisition by preschoolers. Cross-national comparisons are essential to distinguish universal problems children face in acquiring mathematical competence from those that are consequences of linguistic conventions or of a particular cultural context. Noël, Rousselle, and Mussolin (Chapter 11) review research on the development of number-magnitude representation in children, including studies of both normal and dysfunctional development. Siegler and Booth (Chapter 12) examine definitional and conceptual issues of numerical estimation and its development. Their overlapping waves model provides a unified theory of the development of computational numerosity and number line estimation skills. Fuson and Abrahamson (Chapter 13) describe the theoretical background and framework for a model-based approach to the design of curricular units in mathematics education, and illustrate this approach with research on fifth graders' understanding of ratio and proportion. The final chapter in this section by Ben-Zeev, Duncan, and Forbes (Chapter 14) explores how stereotype threat (when individuals are targets of stereotypes alleging intellectual inferiority) can contribute to underperformance in math. They develop the case that stereotype threat contributes to males outperforming females on standardized mathematics achievement tests such as the SAT-M and the GRE-Q.

Part 3 of the book (Learning and Performance Disabilities in Math and Number Processing) deals with troubled numerical cognition. Geary and Hoard (Chapter 15) provide a review of prevalence, diagnostic issues, and cognitive correlates of mathematical disabilities (MD). The authors describe how children with MD differ from their academically-normal peers, and provide a general framework for the study of the cognitive deficits that underlie various forms of MD. Mazzocco and McCloskey (Chapter 16) describe mathematical deficits associated with two genetic disorders: Fragile X Syndrome and Turner Syndrome. The research reviewed illuminates the cognitive dysfunctions that give rise to math disabilities and may also shed light on the biological basis of mathematical ability. Barnes, Smith-Chant, and Landry (Chapter 17) describe a series of studies of preschoolers, children, and young adults with spina bifida myelomeningocele (SBM), a congenital malformation of the spine and brain associated with impairments in math skills. Their focus is on the early motor and cognitive origins of deficits in emerging number skills, and the relation of neuropathological variables to math skills in SBM. Ashcraft and Ridley (Chapter 18) review research showing that math anxious individuals experience disruption of cognitive processes during math performance, particularly for tasks that rely on working memory. The authors outline future directions for math anxiety research in the context of the strong co-variation of math achievement with math anxiety.

Part 4 (Calculation and Cognition) presents a series of reviews of basic issues and phenomena of calculation and mathematical problem solving. Zbrodoff and Logan (Chapter 19) review research on the ubiquitous problem-size effect in basic calculation, tracing the greater difficulty of numerically large, simple arithmetic problems to factors that affect both associative memory for number facts and algorithmic processes for calculation. Campbell and Epp (Chapter 20) review evidence that memory for basic number facts is affected by the format in which problems appear (Arabic digits vs. written number words). They conclude that numeral encoding processes and mechanisms of calculation are more integrated and interactive than is commonly assumed. LeFevre, DeStefano, Coleman, and Shanahan (Chapter 21) present a comprehensive survey of extant research on working memory and cognitive arithmetic, and evaluate it with respect to current models of mathematical cognition. Dixon (Chapter 22) presents a theory of mathematical problem solving that merges analogical problem solving research with recent work on representing the functional relations of arithmetic. As people work with mathematics, they create both contextually rich problem categories and representations of the relational structure inherent in each operation. Duverne and Lemaire (Chapter 23) present a review of research on age-related changes in arithmetic. Their review illustrates both the contributions of studies of aging for understanding cognitive arithmetic, and the contributions of cognitive arithmetic research for understanding cognitive aging. Pesenti (Chapter 24) summarizes what is known about calculating prodigies and reviews evidence that calculation expertise entails a large repertoire of memorized number facts, complex calculation algorithms, as well as increased number-specific memory capacities. He reviews related behavioral and neuroanatomical data both from healthy individuals and people suffering neurological disorders.

Part 5 (Neuropsychology of Number Processing and Calculation) concludes the volume with a focus on neuropsychological issues of mathematical cognition. Dehaene, Piazza, Pinel, and Cohen (Chapter 25) review neuropsychological evidence and describe corresponding fMRI activations during a variety of numerical tasks to identify the organization of number-related processes in the parietal lobe. Butterworth (Chapter 26) reviews developmental disorders of arithmetic and of reading and writing numbers. He proposes, on the basis of genetic and neuroanatomical evidence, that developmental mathematical disorders are due to a congenital deficit in understanding the core concepts of numerosity. In the concluding chapter, Lochy, Domahs, and Delazer (Chapter 27) review research on the rehabilitation of disorders of number processing and calculation after brain lesions, with a focus on methodological principles for effective design of rehabilitation attempts.

As the contents of this volume illustrate, mathematical cognition research subsumes a broad, interdisciplinary spectrum of theoretical and practical issues. Yet, there is a strong cohesiveness, because the research conducted within these diverse areas mutually informs and reinforces developments across areas. The multidisciplinary interest in mathematical cognition reflects the central place of mathematics in commerce, education, science and technology; and also indicates that questions about the nature of mathematical skills have far reaching implications for psychological science and society.

Acknowledgments

Creating a large volume of edited chapters such as this involves the efforts and cooperation of many people. I want to especially thank the authors for the very fine quality of their chapters and for their sincere efforts to meet deadlines. The excellence of the work presented here also owes a great debt to the many people who provided careful, thorough, and insightful reviews of the chapters. Paul Dukes and Stacy Malyil at Psychology Press offered much valuable advice and encouragement throughout the project. Lynette Epp, who coauthored a chapter with me in this volume, and Jody Shynkaruk provided acute and very valuable proofreading for several chapters. Finally, I want to thank my great friend and partner in life, Valerie Thompson, for innumerable insightful observations related to the book, life, and everything else.

Jamie Campbell
January 29, 2004

Part 1

Cognitive Representations
for Numbers and Mathematics

1

About Numerical Representations
Insights from Neuropsychological, Experimental, and Developmental Studies

Michel Fayol
Xavier Seron

Research into cognitive number processing has made considerable progress over the last twenty years (Dehaene, 1997; Butterworth, 1999). These advances have been the result of both work on acquired (Seron & Deloche, 1994) and developmental disorders in number computation and processing (Temple, 1997) and on adults' and children's performances during different phases of learning (Ashcraft, 1992; Fayol, 1990; Geary, 1994). Although there is an impressive volume of data providing us with valuable information, this sometimes makes it difficult to gain a global view of what has been learned, particularly in regard to the different types of representations involved in number processing. In this chapter, we shall address the question of the relations between the different mental representations, the existence of which have been postulated in order to account for number skills in human beings, whether innate or acquired, approximate or precise, symbolic or nonsymbolic. Within this perspective we shall, on the one hand, list the most important insights gained into the mental representations that underlie the elementary processing of numbers and, on the other, stress the shortcomings of the available theoretical proposals relating to these various representations and their functions, interrelations, and origins.

Below, we distinguish between different interpretations of the concept of number representations and, in particular, (a) *numerosity,* which designates the numeric properties of a set of items in the real world; (b) the *numerical notations* or *symbolic codes* used in order to represent numerical information, which correspond to realities that are external to the subject and which have historically been constructed and organized in the form of systems (i.e., Arabic numerals, spoken numbers, and Roman numerals); and finally (c) the *internal or mental numerical representations* which correspond to entities that are internal to the subject and which refer both to systems of numerical notation and to the numerosity of sets of objects or real or mental events. In the remainder of this text, whenever we talk about the semantic representation of numbers, we are referring to the mental representation of numerosity.[1]

The authors are ranked by alphabetic order but they have equally contributed to the writing of this chapter.

THE TYPES OF MENTAL REPRESENTATION: CHARACTERISTICS, DEVELOPMENT, AND DISORDERS

The Preverbal Representations

In Animals

The performances of animals in tasks requiring them to compare or discriminate between quantities of objects or events reveal that they are able to do so, but only to a limited extent. Although their choices are not random, they simultaneously vary around a mean from one trial or quantity to the next. This variability increases with the size or magnitude of the entities that are to be compared. The data collected for different species (monkeys, Brannon & Terrace, 1998; rats, Meck & Church, 1983; pigeons, Roberts & Mitchell, 1994) have shown that the dispersal ratio of evaluations of the size of the quantity for estimation is a constant. This corresponds to a classic finding in the field of psychophysics, namely Weber's law. Animals are thus thought to possess a mental representation of magnitude, which is formally analogous to spatial locations on a continuous line. This representation is thought to be fuzzy given that, even after a long period of training, animals are not able to distinguish the precise numerosity of a set or series (e.g., hit a lever an exact number of times). They would thus appear to be unable to represent quantities such as 4, 6, or 8 in a discrete or digital manner. However, Hauser, Carey, and Hauser (2000) have shown that rhesus macaques are able to choose precisely which of two sets (½, ⅔, ¾, but not greater) is the larger. To summarize, the animals that have been studied may be able to form analogous and approximate representations of continuous (distance, surface, intensity, etc.) and discrete quantities (objects, events) and may also be capable of accurately processing small, discrete sets (fewer than five).

In Infants

Infants are known to become sensitive to quantity at a very early age. For example, they can discriminate between groups of objects or counters provided that the quantities involved are small (1, 2, or 3 items; Antell & Keating, 1983; Starkey & Cooper, 1980; Strauss & Curtis, 1981). They might even possess an amodal representation of quantity since they are able to discriminate and match numbers of events (Canfield & Smith, 1996; Sharon & Wynn, 1998; Wynn, 1996) and sets of sounds (Bijeljac-Babic, Bertoncini, & Mehler, 1993) based on their quantity.

One important question to which there is as of yet no satisfactory answer is whether or not the identified representations are numerical in nature. Are these representations specifically numerical, and therefore discrete, from the outset, thus supporting the hypothesis of an innate system dedicated to number processing (Wynn, 1998; Butterworth, 1999)? Or is there a system for the processing of continuous quantities in which the inherent discrete, numerical nature of such processing is absent and emerges only later? Or is it instead a general system (i.e., not specifically dedicated to either number or quantity) which processes discrete objects and possesses certain properties which might prompt observers to believe that they are witnessing numerical processing (Simon, 1997)?

A number of sets of research claim to have found that preverbal infants possess a mental representation of small quantities. The data comes from habituation tasks and tasks in which the subjects' expectations are violated. Generally, the experiments have employed material which combines the number of items with various continuous dimensions which are closely correlated with numerosity (e.g., contour length, surface area, volume; Starkey & Cooper, 1980). This observation prompted Feigenson, Carey, and Spelke (2002) to manipulate both the numerical and continuous dimensions in order to study the comparison of the quantities 1 versus 2 and 2 versus 3, their hypothesis being that the pair 1 2 should be easier to discrimi than the 2 versus 3, as in previous studies. The results showed that children did not specifica. respond to numerosity either in a habituation or a transformation task. The authors therefore suggested that when infants observed an event which involved a limited number of objects, they opened an *object file*, i.e., a sort of mental model, for each of the objects in question. This object file is thought to store the concrete characteristics of the represented item (color, shape, identity etc.). Separate object files would represent multiple distinct objects or multiple objects with different trajectories. This would not only be possible for numerosities of two or three objects but also for larger quantities which exceed infants' parallel processing capabilities, for example, five or six items. The processing system for small numerosities would, therefore, not be specifically dedicated to the processing of number. Feigenson, Carey, and Hauser (2002) used a new paradigm (asking children to choose which of two boxes contains more biscuits) to show that infants aged 10 to 12 months possessed a very early understanding of the more than/less than relation. In general terms, these data showed that young children were able to discriminate very precisely between small numerosities (1/2, 2/3) and that these discriminations were associated at an early age with the more than/less than relation. However, the data also cast some doubt on the specificity of a system dedicated solely to number processing.

When the sets contained more than four or five objects, very young children were thought to refer to an analogue representation, which yields an approximate quantification. In this case, number processing might depend on another type of process which is associated with an analogue number line (Mix, Huttenlocher, & Levine, 2002). Two series of experiments have yielded unequivocal data in support of this hypothesis. In the first one, Xu and Spelke (2000) have shown that six-month-old infants exhibit dishabituation when the set size changes from 8 to 16 counters (but not from 8 to 12), when the surface area, density, brightness, etc. are kept constant across the sets. And in a second series of experiments, Xu (2000) has extended this conclusion to the difference between 16 and 32.

To summarize, both newborns and animals seem to be able to mobilize two different systems for the processing of quantities (Brannon & Roitman, 2003). One of these is precise and is limited by its absolute set size (e.g., 1, 2, and 3), while the other is extensible to very large quantities, operates on continuous dimensions, and yields an approximate evaluation in accordance with Weber's law. The question of the specifically numerical character of these modes of processing remains to be answered, as does that of the characteristics of the representations to which they might be applied.

Given that most researchers believe that there is an innate cognitive system which is specifically dedicated to the processing of quantities and even to that of numerosities (Gallistel & Gelman, 1992; Spelke & Dehaene, 1999), the question of the development of the abilities to discriminate small quantities and to estimate larger ones has not been raised. However, one vital question remains: do these preverbal competencies constitute the basis from which symbolic arithmetic emerges and, if so, do they undergo any transformation as a result of this association? Or is it more appropriate to consider that the acquisition of language and systems of symbolic notation brings about new representations which are not contiguous with the earlier ones (Carey, 2001), thus raising the question of the relations between these later representations and the former ones?

The Persistence and the Development
of the Preverbal Representations in Adults

The question of further development of these initial proto-numeric competencies has been addressed in three ways. Researchers have attempted to identify traces of these competencies in adults either (a) by confronting them with tasks which prevent the use of symbolic representations; (b) by searching for traces of these preverbal representations within symbolic number tasks;

or, more rarely, (c) by examining the later development of arithmetic abilities in children exhibiting an impairment in their preverbal representations.

Non-Linguistic Processing of Numerosity in Adults

To test the maintenance of preverbal representations of quantities in adults, Whalen, Gallistel, and Gelman (1999) asked literate adults to produce tapping movements or to evaluate series of tones corresponding to different numerosities in situations in which the high speed of responding and stimuli presentation did not permit the use of verbal counting strategies. The psychophysical function of the subjects' performances showed that mathematically educated adults possess an analog representation of quantity which has the same characteristics as that observed in animals and infants. Whatever the task, either in estimation or production, the quantities provided corresponded approximately to the required or presented numerosity and, in the same way as in animals, the coefficient of variation (i.e., the ratio of the standard deviation to the mean) remained constant, regardless of the quantities involved. In another study, Barth, Kanwisher, and Spelke (2003) suggest that this representation is an abstract one. These authors have indeed shown that normal subjects were able to perform approximate comparisons of sets of numerosities within and across the visual and auditory modalities and within and across formats (simultaneous versus temporal sequences) at comparable levels of efficiency in tasks that also prevented the use of symbolic notations or language. Taken together, these studies strongly suggest that when human adults have to process numerosities in situations that prevent them from using symbolic representations, they use an analogue representation of numerosity. Furthermore, their ability to compare numerosities across modalities indicates that their judgments do not rely on modality and format-specific attributes (e.g., duration, rate, texture, density, contour length, or area). However, these attributes may act as cues in the formation of an abstract representation.

Thus, adults may be able to represent discrete quantities nonverbally in a way which is qualitatively and quantitatively similar to that which has been adduced in order to explain the performances observed in animals and infants. Within this perspective, the number semantics would be provided by the process which associates the numerosity and the symbolic notations with these internal, nonsymbolic representations as well as by the processes which operate on these representations.

Activation of the Preverbal Representations by the Symbolic Systems

The existence of analogue representations of numerosity is further supported by the observation of *distance effects* (number comparisons are faster and more accurate as the numerical distance between the items in a pair increases) and *size effects* (at the same numerical distance, performance decreases as the size of the numbers increases). These effects indicate the mobilization of an analogue representation and have been observed in adults performing comparisons on the basis of symbolic notations (Brysbaert, 1995; Dehaene, 1989; Dehaene & Akhavein, 1995; Dehaene, Dupoux, & Mehler, 1990). The distance effect is already present in 6-month-old infants (Xu & Spelke, 2000), since it has been observed in children aged 3 to 5 years old (Huntley-Fenner & Cannon, 2000). At 5 years old, response times and error distributions have been observed as being the same as those seen in adult participants (Duncan & McFerland, 1980; Huntley-Fenner, 2001; Sekuler & Mierkiewicz, 1977; Siegler & Robinson, 1982). Furthermore, the cerebral activity observed in 5-year-old children and adults in number comparison tasks is the same (Temple & Posner, 1998).

Moreover, some neuroimaging studies even point to the existence of different representations of small and large numbers, echoing the distinction observed in children. In a related vein, Gobel, Walsh, and Rushworth (2001a) have shown that the comparison of two-digit Arabic numbers is disrupted when the angular gyrus is stimulated by means of the transcranial magnetic stimulation (TMS), but not when the stimulation is applied to the more anterior supramarginal gyrus. In contrast, the comparison of single-digit numbers (Gobel, Walsh, & Rushworth, 2001b) is disrupted when the supramarginal gyrus is stimulated. Other cerebral imaging data provide further support for these findings, suggesting that anterior regions tend to be activated in the case of single-digit numbers (Pinel, Dehaene, Rivière, & Le Bihan, 2001; Fias, Lammertyn, Reynvoet, Dupont, & Orban, 2003), whereas more posterior regions are activated in the presence of two-digit numbers (Naccache & Dehaene, 2001; Pesenti, Thioux, Seron, & de Volder, 2000). Similarly, research involving various number tasks designed to investigate the habitual signature of the analogue continuum in adults, (i.e., the size effect, the distance effect, and the SNARC effect[2]), indicate that some of these effects differ for large and small numbers (Verguts, Fias & Stevens, submitted). For example, Brysbaert (1995) obtained a size effect in the naming of numbers from 11 to 90, whereas no size effect was observed by Reynvoet, Brysbaert, and Fias (2002) in the naming of Arabic numerals from 1 to 9 or by Butterworth and colleagues in the naming of Arabic numerals from 1 to 18 (Butterworth, Zorzi, Girelli, & Jonckeere, 2001). These discrepancies led Verguts, Fias, and Stevens (submitted) to suggest that there are actually two numerical systems in the human brain, one corresponding to a discrete and exact representation which is used for small numbers, while another approximate one is involved in the representation of large numbers. Thus, even when they are processing symbolic codes, the performances observed in adults exhibit effects similar to those observed in children and animals. These data reinforce the idea that the preverbal internal representations continue to be activated even when symbolic arithmetic is employed but do not allow us to assert that the preverbal representations are not modified by the acquisition of symbolic codes.

Premature Impairment of the Preverbal Representations

If we adopt the developmental continuum viewpoint which considers that the preverbal number representation constitutes the base on which the symbolic system of number representation is constructed, then we would expect to observe difficulties in the development of symbolic arithmetic following the premature impairment of the preverbal representations. In fact, very little work has been devoted to this question. To our knowledge, the only study of this issue is the one conducted by Paterson (2001; see also Ansari & Karmiloff-Smith, 2002). This author investigated the developmental paths exhibited by participants. In particular, he was concerned about the relations between early performances in quantity discrimination and the later performances observed in certain arithmetical and/or language tasks. Following a familiarization phase, children aged 30 months who exhibited symptoms of Down's or Williams' syndrome and two groups of normal children, one group matched on IQ and the other on chronological age, were subjected to a task in which they were required to differentiate between 2 and 3. Their performances were then compared with those of adults exhibiting the same disorders. The reported data revealed an interesting paradox. Whereas the children suffering from Down's syndrome manifested a disorder in numerical discrimination, this was not observed in the Down's syndrome adult group. On the other hand, although the William's syndrome children were able to discriminate correctly between 2 and 3, no distance effect was observed in the William's syndrome adults. This research therefore indicates the value of conducting a longitudinal study of the development of performances in children whose preverbal number representations appear to be impaired and raises (but does not answer) the question of how these representations are related to adult numerical abilities. Working within the same perspective, Ta'ir, Brezner, and Ariel (1997) described a child aged 11 years (YK) suffering from a profound acalculia even though his IQ and language capabilities were normal. They believed that YK might have suffered from a difficulty in constructing analogue number representations which was sufficiently severe to prevent later symbolic learning. Although this interpretation is speculative, it does indicate the value of studying anarithmetic individuals in order to come to a thorough assessment of their disorders (see also Chapter 17 by Barnes, Smith-Chant, & Landry in this volume).

The question of the relationship between the preverbal number and the symbolic ones remains unanswered. However, before examining this question further, we shall present a brief review of the current state of knowledge concerning symbolic representations followed by an examination of the issue of what it is to which they may be related.

The Symbolic Representations

Any model of number processing must account for the fact that educated adults are able to recognize and produce numbers in the Arabic code and the verbal code. It is therefore necessary to postulate that adults possess mental representations which are able to guide these recognition and production operations. However, researchers disagree as to the role and the format of these representations and their interrelations. It now appears to be well established that the symbolic representations are functionally independent and that they may undergo isolated impairment or be degraded in accordance with specific patterns in brain-damaged patients. More precisely, when considering the manipulation of symbolic representations, dissociations have been observed between the comprehension and production mechanisms (Benson & Denckla, 1969; McCloskey, Sokol, & Goodman, 1986, case of HY); between the Arabic code and the verbal code (Noël & Seron, 1993, case of NR); and, finally, between the lexical and syntactic mechanisms within each code (Cipolotti, Butterworth, & Warrington, 1994, case of DM; Noël & Seron, 1995; Sokol & McCloskey, 1988). Evidence for the existence of some of these dissociations is also provided by cerebral imaging data which suggests that the verbal and Arabic codes are not processed in the same regions (Pinel et al., 1999). We shall examine the Arabic and verbal representations separately, starting with a presentation of the structure of the notational systems corresponding to each of them.

The Verbal Codes for Naming Quantities

The verbal systems for naming quantities vary significantly from one culture to another (Hurford, 1987). However, behind this cultural diversity lie a number of organizational principles which appear to be universal.

The linguistic organization of the verbal system is manifest at different levels: the size of the lexicon (e.g., the units, the teens, the decade names, and, in certain languages, multipliers such as hundred, thousand and million) and the complexity of the syntax in which the order of the items reveals their relations which are either additive (twenty-four, fifty-six) or multiplicative (three thousand; two hundred). Importantly, these lexical and syntactic variations may make the base-ten structure of the number verbal system more or less transparent.

Specifically, the base-ten structure of the system is not immediately evident at the beginning of the number verbal sequence. This fact becomes clear if we compare verbal numbering in German, English, Spanish, French, Italian, and Chinese. In the Chinese system, the numbers above the base are constructed according to very regular additive, multiplicative, and power rules (i.e., eleven is spoken as "ten one," twenty-three as "two ten three," etc.). This is clearly not the case for most western languages, which are not regular base-10 systems. As a result, young westerners have to learn by heart the sequence of number names extending above ten (such as in English: eleven, twelve, thirteen, and so on). In consequence, English (or German or French) children perform equally well as their Chinese counterparts on the verbal names up to ten (i.e., up to the age of about three years) which demand the memorization of the number words and their sequence. In contrast, their performances at age four or five are considerably worse than those of young Chinese children when asked to count beyond 10 (Fuson & Kwon, 1991; Miller, Smith, Zhu, & Zhang, 1995). This superiority persists throughout elementary school and beyond (Geary, Salthouse, Chen, & Fan, 1996; Stevenson et al., 1985; Stevenson, Lee, & Stigler, 1986), but the question of its impact on later learning remains unanswered. However, the syntactico-lexical structure of the verbal numeral system also has an influence on the naming errors made by brain-damaged patients. Some patients primarily made lexical errors (e.g., saying sixty-*three* instead of sixty-*five*), whereas others made syntactic errors which affect the size (e.g., 10023 instead of 123) or the order of the components (e.g., vingt quatre instead of quatre-vingt) (Seron & Noël, 1995).

The Arabic Code

The written numbering that developed from Indo-Arabian origins possesses only a limited number of digits (10: from 0 to 9) and uses positional notation to encode the powers of 10. It offers many advantages for encoding numerosity. It is easy to interpret and write, it can be easily generalized to very large numbers, and its structure is readily conducive to the development of computational procedures (Nickerson, 1988; Zhang & Norman, 1995). The acquisition and use of this notational system tend to have been studied to a lesser extent than the acquisition of the verbal system. This is probably due to the fact that Arabic numerals are taught and are therefore explicitly learned.

The data revealed by developmental studies (Hughes, 1986) indicate that the learning of the series of digits (from 1 to 9) is unproblematic. The zero, as a digit, causes more difficulties (Wellman & Miller, 1986), although we do not know exactly why. It may simply be because there is no habitual correspondence in verbal numbering. It should also be noted that zero requires *abnormally* long reading times in adults (Brysbaert, 1995). However, the most significant difficulties in handling Arabic numerals result from the use of positional notation and, in particular, from the fact that the value of a digit changes depending on its position within a number (e.g., 1 may be worth a unit, ten, a hundred, etc., depending on the position it occupies). In the writing of multiple digit numbers, the 0 again causes particular difficulties which, in children, result in the appearance of errors in the writing of numbers containing an interposed zero as well as in a modification to the kinematics of the handwriting (Lochy, Pillon, Zesiger, & Seron, 2002). Finally, in brain-damaged patients, the 0 is the object of selective errors depending on whether it occupies a syntactic or lexical role in the number (Granà, Lochy, Girelli, Seron, & Semenza, 2003).

Relations between the Arabic and Verbal Codes

In terms of ontogeny, verbal numerals are used before arabic numerals. In addition, the latter are the object of explicit teaching. At least in western societies, tuition is conducted in such a way that the verbal code is systematically used to introduce the arabic code. The former therefore precedes and, at least initially, takes precedence over the latter. However, the observation of double dissociations between the two codes in brain-damaged patients suggests that they are relatively independent of one another in adults (Anderson, Damasio, & Damasio, 1990; Cipolotti, 1995; McCloskey, 1992). This double observation—initial dominance of the verbal code and later independence of the two codes—raises questions concerning their interrelations in adults on the one hand and the development of learning and the subsequent representations on the other. The task that has been used most frequently to examine this question is the transcoding task. This consists of asking subjects to transform a form presented in one code (the source code) into another code (the target code; i.e., reading aloud or writing under dictation arabic numerals).

Some studies have investigated the hypothesis that the processing of the arabic code is systematically mediated by the verbal code. The question addressed is as follows: do tasks such as magnitude comparison, reading, or calculation with arabic numerals induce the systematic activation of the verbal code? The hypothesis that the verbal code is automatically activated was suggested by Noël and Seron (1993), who described a patient who compared two numbers not on the basis of the arabic numerals (e.g., 3) presented to him but on their verbal counterparts (e.g., /trwa/). The authors suggested that some subjects might employ a "preferred code" to access number-related knowledge. The possible activation of verbal representations when processing arabic numbers is also suggested by the observation of code intrusion errors in transcoding tasks. For instance, Thioux and his coworkers (Thioux, Ivanoiu, Turconi, & Seron, 1999) observed a patient with an Alzheimer's dementia (AD) who exhibited systematic intrusions of verbal numerals when she had to produce arabic forms, whatever the task (calculating, transcoding, delayed copy). These intrusions gave rise to mixed errors such as "3 mille" instead of "3000" (trois mille/three thousand) or "15ZE" instead of 15 (quinze/fifteen) or even "h8t" instead of 8 (huit/eight). However, in group studies, intrusion errors have been observed in both directions (Arabic to verbal and vice versa), mainly in AD patients (Tegnèr & Nybäck, 1990; Kessler & Kalbe, 1996) but also in normal elderly subjects (Della Sala, Gentileschi, Gray, & Spinnler, 2002). These errors have been interpreted as the result of an impairment in the transcoding mechanism itself as well as in inhibitory processes which are postulated to be necessary to inhibit one code when the task requires the production of the other. In such a view, when subjects have to process a number in one code, the other code is automatically activated but is not produced thanks to the inhibitory processes.

In other transcoding studies, researchers have examined whether there are any traces of the activation of the verbal code in tasks soliciting the arabic code. The initial studies investigated the reading of Arabic numbers (e.g., 90), the length in syllables and in phonemes of the corresponding verbal number being controlled. The various authors either asked their subjects to read numbers aloud (Eriksen, Pollack, & Montague, 1970) or made use of eye movement analysis techniques during silent reading. Pynte (1974) found that the fixation time for numbers presented in arabic format increased as the number of syllables that the corresponding verbal form possessed increased (for example, this time was longer for 82 (quatre vingt deux– 3 syllables) than for 28 (vingt huit–2 syllables). Gielen, Brysbaert, and Dhondt (1991, Experiment 1) have replicated this result. These data support the hypothesis of systematic verbal mediation during the processing of arabic numbers. However, when a motor (nonverbal) task was used to indicate whether one number was located between two others, all three being presented in arabic format, no phonological length effect was observed but a size (magnitude) effect emerged (Gielen et al., 1991, Experiment 2). This last result shows that the processing of arabic numbers does not systematically and automatically give rise to phonological recoding and that arabic numbers may directly activate the analogue semantic representation since a magnitude effect is observed.

The data relating to development and learning, in particular those drawn from interlanguage comparisons, favor the idea that, in the first acquisition stages, the arabic code is dependent on the verbal code. Thus, children from Southeast Asia whose verbal system for number naming is decimal based (e.g., twelve is spoken "ten two"; twenty-eight is rendered as "two ten eight") learn the arabic code better and more quickly than their western counterparts, who are generally confronted with nontransparent verbal systems in which the base-ten organization is less clearly perceptible (onze, douze; eleven, twelve; elf, zwölf) (Miura, Okamoto, Kim, Steere, & Fayol, 1993; Miura, Okamoto, Kim, Chang, Steere, & Fayol, 1994). These interlanguage comparisons suggest that the transparency of the verbal system, that is, the fact that the base-ten is clearly apparent, facilitates the acquisition of the arabic code, thus providing support for the position of those who believe that the latter is dependent on the former (Bialystok, 1992; Bialystok & Codd, 1997).

Starting from this conception, Seron, Deloche, and Noël (1992) have shown that the errors of children aged seven and nine years in tasks requiring transcoding from the verbal to the arabic code (e.g., 10013 for "mille treize/one thousand and thirteen" or 10030 pour "mille trente/one thousand and thirty"; i.e., the so-called syntactic errors) are due to the induction and application of an asemantic transcoding mechanism which permits the direct transition, by means of formal rules, from the verbal code (first) to the arabic code (second) (Power & Dal Martello, 1990). By comparing the transcoding performances of Walloon and French children, the former being faced with a simpler number naming system than the latter,[3] Seron and Fayol (1994) have been able to show that the difficulties are primarily located in the production phase, that is to say at the point where the sequence of digits is produced. Here again, the earlier, dominant verbal format guides the processing of the arabic format.

However, other data yielded by studies of normal or pathological development/learning support arguments contrary to this hypothesis. Jarlegan, Fayol, and Barrouillet (1996) asked French second-graders attending normal schools to transcode quantities of varying levels of difficulty (see Seron & Fayol, 1994). These quantities were presented in three formats (analogue: cubes-units, bars-tens, plates-hundreds, etc.; written verbal: sixty-three, eight hundred and four, etc.; arabic: 97, 630, etc.) and the children had to transcode them into the two other formats (e.g., from verbal to analogue and arabic; from arabic to written verbal and analogue). The results revealed that the performances were significantly better when transcoding was performed from the arabic code to the analogue format (and vice versa) than when the verbal code was involved (it should be remembered that the French verbal code is particularly difficult). Such a result is difficult to reconcile with the idea of systematic mediation by the verbal code. As of second grade, children appear to be able to establish a direct relation between the analogue format and the quantities expressed in arabic code without needing to perform any verbal recoding. Finally, Donlan (1993) has also suggested the independence of the codes. While dysphasic children exhibit verbal performances which are generally about two standard deviations below those of normal children, thus resulting in a failure to accomplish certain verbal number tasks, their understanding of quantities, in particular as revealed by comparison tasks, is unaffected. Furthermore, the dysphasic children succeed in these same tasks when they relate to continuous quantities (e.g., surface area) just as well as when these quantities are presented in arabic format (Donlan, Bishop, & Hitch, 1998).

To summarize, the currently available data suggests that, in western cultures, the arabic code is initially learned in relation to the verbal code. However, the arabic code very quickly becomes independent of the verbal code. In normal subjects, this independence is manifested in the ability to perform better, or differently, with the former compared to the latter. It can also be seen in the vastly superior performances achieved by dysphasic children when using the arabic code. It has been shown to exist in adult patients through the presence of double dissociations.

These conclusions lead us to raise two issues. The first relates to the possibility that the arabic code is, from the outset, associated with the analogue representation without any mediation via the verbal code. If this is the case, it would be conceivable to design a specific mode of teaching the arabic code for dysphasic children who would then no longer be hampered by the effects induced by their language problems. The second issue bears on the relations between the verbal code and the arabic code. In effect, even if access to the verbal code appears to be neither automatic nor indispensable in certain tasks (Brysbaert, 1995), we know that it plays a role in others, particularly in the transcoding tasks. One possible hypothesis is that during the transcoding of the verbal code into the arabic code, the retention of the verbal form (e.g., one thousand two hundred and ninety-seven) at the very same time that transcoding is to be performed tends to induce performance errors without, however, affecting number understanding or the number processing mechanisms (Fayol, Barrouillet, & Renaud, 1996). Empirical research will be necessary to fully address this question and to achieve a better understanding of the errors described in the literature which may be due not to a deterioration of the numerical representations but to the fragility of the phonological information or to a problem in keeping this information activated during transcoding.

Verbal Code and Semantic Representations

Some hypotheses have supported the idea that language might have a major impact on the way arithmetic cognition proceeds (Brysbaert, Fias, & Noël, 1998). Indeed, differences in performance in arithmetical tasks, which are associated with language differences, have been reported in a number of studies. However, very few of these have established a relation between these differences and a theory of arithmetical cognition (Fayol, 2002), thus making it difficult to determine the stage in processing at which the variations in performance have their origin. For example, the differences may not be due to any change in the numerical representations as a function of the language in question but, more simply, to the fact that the cognitive cost involved in the transition from the verbal format specific to any given language to the abstract or analogue format may vary from language to language.

The Question of the Possible Impact of Language on Mental Arithmetic

Some theories postulate that language exerts an influence on mental arithmetic only at a peripheral encoding stages, whereas others propose that the language representations intervene at more central processing stages. McCloskey (1992), like Gallistel and Gelman (1992), considers that numerical processing is performed on mental representations that are independent of language, the input and output formats therefore having no influence on the representations or on the arithmetical processing performed. Other theories hold that numerical processing is totally or partially dependent on language and more generally on the modality and the format of the input stimulus and response. Campbell and Clark (1988), for example, postulate that arithmetical-fact retrieval is mediated by format-specific representations; therefore, they predict the existence of language-related effects in mental arithmetic when problems and/or answers have to be produced in the verbal code. Finally, other authors propose that some number processing is independent of language, whereas some is critically dependent on verbal representations. This is the case of Dehaene's triple code model (Dehaene & Cohen, 2000), which postulates the existence of three interconnected systems of numerical representation, each of which is associated with certain numerical activities. Some activities, such as the comparison or estimation of numbers, are performed on an analog format and are thus language-independent, whereas others, such as arithmetical-fact retrieval, are stored in auditory-phonological representations and are thus language dependent. Such a model is thus compatible with the idea that language has either a central (i.e., affecting the form of the representations) or peripheral (i.e., affecting only the modes of access to the representations) impact on arithmetical cognition.

In mental arithmetic, many studies have been conducted to determine the nature of the underlying representations. These have taken two different directions: some have tried to demonstrate the impact of stimulus formats on arithmetical-fact retrieval by contrasting verbal and arabic codes—or even the Roman one (Gonzales & Kohlers, 1987; Noël & Seron, 1992, 1997)—whereas others have contrasted the performances of bilingual subjects by varying the first or second language used when resolving simple arithmetic problems (Marsh & Makki, 1976; Frenck-Mestre & Vaid, 1993; Brysbaert, Fias, & Noël, 1998). The majority of this research has identified language- or format-related effects in arithmetic although their interpretation remains controversial. Some authors (Brysbaert et al., 1998; McCloskey, 1992), hold that the majority of the effects could be due to the transition from the input formats (e.g., verbal or arabic) to the abstract (or analogue) format which is used for processing. Others (Campbell, 1994), in contrast, believe that at least the numerical facts are stored in a linguistic format. It is currently difficult to come to a decision between these two views. However, a consideration of the developmental and learning data could help us to constrain the models and interpret the phenomena that have been identified in adult subjects. Working within this perspective, Spelke and Tsivkin (2001) used a bilingual (Russian/English) learning study to explore the role of a specific language in human representations of number. Adults were taught new arithmetical operations, arithmetic equations, and new historical or geographic facts in one language. After learning, they were tested in both languages. Results indicated that adults retrieved information about exact numbers more effectively in the language of training but retrieved information about approximate numbers and non-numerical facts with equal efficiency in either language. These results suggest that the representation of large, exact numbers is language dependent, whereas that of approximate number representations is not. However, we have to be prudent about generalizing such data to the representation of arithmetical facts. Indeed, in a recent study, Whalen and his collaborators (Whalen, McCloskey, Lindenmann, & Bouton, 2002) have described the performance of two brain-damaged patients who, although unable to generate the phonological representation of arithmetic problems, could nevertheless retrieve their correct answer in the arabic code. Such patterns of performance do not negate the possibility that arithmetical facts are stored in a phonological form but are incompatible with the hypothesis that this phonological form is the unique stored representation.

The Question of the Development of the Relations between Preverbal and Verbal Representations

The identification of very early abilities to compare and evaluate quantities has led researchers to believe that the first numbers are probably acquired very quickly and easily. It would then appear to be sufficient to establish simple associations between the verbal labels and small quantities (e.g., one, two and three) which are known to be discriminated at a very early age. However, developmental studies indicate that this phase poses particular problems. There is indeed a period during which children know that number words refer to cardinality but do not know which. Wynn (1992) presented children between two and a half and three and a half years old with number tasks in which the children had to choose which of two cards (containing drawings of objects or sets of objects) corresponded to which cardinality. The data, and in particular that obtained from the longitudinal study, suggest that a considerable period of time is necessary before children move on from the knowledge that a number word refers to a quantity to the knowledge of precisely to what quantity "3" or "4" refers. This phenomenon is difficult to explain within an empiricist perspective, which conceives of learning in terms of associations between quantities and names. The same holds for the theory proposed by Gelman and Gallistel (1978), which postulates that children possess a set of innate counting-related principles and that these principles underpin the routines implemented during the activity of counting.

   The acquisition of the cardinal meaning of number names raises two problems that have been underestimated: the abstract nature of the encoding of quantities in terms of names and the categorical nature of the number lexicon (Fayol, 2002). The use of verbal numbering to determine the cardinal value of a set presupposes the understanding of the principle according to which language represents quantities. In an analogue mental representation, an increase in quantity is reflected by an increase in length, density, or volume (English & Halford, 1995). In verbal numbering, quantity is represented in a conventional, nontransparent way in terms of the rank occupied by the signs in the verbal sequence (one, two, three, four, five, etc.). "Six" refers to a larger quantity than "five" does because it comes in the sequence after "five."

However, there is nothing in the term "six" to indicate that the cardinal value to which it refers is greater than "five." The name provides no information about the increase in the quantities. It therefore makes it necessary for the number names to evoke cardinal values in a precise and automatic fashion. It is, without doubt, that the evocation of cardinal values constitutes the most serious problem confronting young children (aged 18 months to four or five years), and the problem is related to the question of categorization.

The ability to recognize equivalence is a key cognitive ability which in the numerical domain presupposes the capacity to recognize sets as being equivalent although they differ on numerous dimensions apart from one: cardinality. Two opposing ideas have been put forward in this regard: According to the first, the construction of numerical equivalence classes obeys the general principles of categorization. If this is the case, then judgments of similarity should be sensitive to the same factors as those that have been identified in the similarity judgment tasks used in other fields, for example, the degree of similarity relating to irrelevant dimensions or the knowledge of number words. If knowing the number words has an impact, then children who know the number names should achieve better performances due to the fact that they are able to perform categorizations on the basis of these words. According to the second approach, learning in the numerical field is guided by innate, specific principles (Gallistel & Gelman, 1992; Gelman & Gallistel, 1978). If this is indeed the case, then the development of numerical equivalence should not exhibit the same difficulties as have been observed in other fields, especially in relation to categorization.

Mix (1999) has reported a series of nonverbal experiments in which children aged between two and one-half and four and one-half years had to choose which of two sets differing in the nature, density, and length of the items corresponded to the number of items depicted in a target set. Before doing this, the children were asked to perform counting tasks, which made it possible to assess their level of numerical performance. The results revealed a gradual progression between the ages of three and four and one-half years from the recognition of equivalence in comparisons bearing on identical objects to the recognition of equivalence in comparisons involving relatively homogenous sets and then onto heterogeneous sets. They also revealed a weak impact of the knowledge of the number words. The children who could count furthest were also those who were best able to recognize the equivalence of heterogeneous sets. However, the data reported by Starkey (1992) indicated that, at 18 months, children understand that a transformation (e.g., adding or taking away) modifies the quantity even if they err as to the precise result of the operation. This data also revealed that such performances were not dependent on the prior acquisition of verbal counting. Therefore, the problem of the relation between the preverbal and verbal codes is as yet unresolved.

The transition from the preverbal representations to the verbal code is a difficult step during which children have, on the one hand, to acquire the ability to mentally evoke quantities on the basis of names and to do so independently of the concrete characteristics involved and, on the other, to understand that the order of the number names indicates, in a conventional way, an increase in quantity. These two dimensions each raise specific problems which as yet have been poorly identified and insufficiently studied but which exist in all languages, as the comparable slowness in learning the first section of the verbal number sequence (i.e., from one to ten) in both western and eastern cultures attests (Miller & Paredes, 1996). Furthermore, the establishment of associations between cardinalities and values seems to be based on the same mechanisms that are involved in the other types of categorization. In particular, the availability of a lexicon makes it possible to consider sets whose appearance would tend to cause them to be processed separately as equivalent in terms of their cardinality. During this stage, language would thus act as a cognitive tool facilitating the formation of cardinality. To our knowledge, no one has systematically addressed this question in research.

The most important question remains that of the initial establishment of a relation between the preverbal representation and the verbal code. In effect, even in the case of very small quantities (i.e., 1, 2, and 3) which, according to many studies, are acquired at a very early age, the observed learning difficulties lead one to suspect that the preverbal representations might not be specific to numbers but, instead, have to be constructed—including in the form of discrete, preverbal representations. Indeed, in a study of children aged between 30 and 47 months, Jordan, Huttenlocher, and Levine (1992, 1994) obtained performances which suggest the existence of a precise computational mechanism which can be applied to small quantities independently of the acquisition of language and even of cultural experience. This mechanism could be based on the mental manipulation of object files or on that of more abstract representations such as the *numerons* initially referred to by Gallistel and Gelman (1978) as a sort of nonconventional, discrete, symbolic code.

Fingers as the Missing Link?

To summarize so far, the acquisition by children of the first number words and their matching to numerosities appear to be a long and hesitant process which does not seem to lead on naturally from the preverbal skills that are already in place in infants. The experienced difficulty in documenting such a relationship could be due to the fact that this relationship is only an indirect one. It could indeed be that the linkage between preverbal number knowledge and language is in fact mediated by the relations children establish between number concepts and the use of their fingers and hands.[4] As rightly noted by Butterworth (1999), in all human cultures, children use their fingers to count before they are systematically taught arithmetic in school. At the developmental level, bi-directional links have been established between the presence of digital agnosia and an arithmetical deficit, in group studies (Kinsbourne & Warrington, 1962, 1963; Strauss & Werner, 1938; Rourke, 1993) as well as in single case study (Pebenito, 1987). Furthermore, in a longitudinal study, Fayol and his coworkers (Fayol, Barrouillet, & Marinthe, 1998; Marinthe, Fayol, & Barrouillet, 2001) have shown that the perceptuo-tactile performances of children evaluated at age five are better predictors than the general development scores of subsequent arithmetical performance at six and then eight years of age. This reinforces the hypothesis of a functional link between digital representations and numerical representations. These results confirm the link that exists between the perceptivo-tactile skills and the ability to represent and manipulate quantities and suggest their long-term predictive character. In a similar vein, Barnes and her collaborators have shown in a study on children with the neurodevelopmental spina bifida myelomeningocele (SBM) that some tests on fine motor skill (implying the fingers) predict significant and unique variance in tasks measuring counting concept competencies, whereas visuo-spatial competence appears to be unrelated to this specific number competence (Barnes, Smith-Chant, & Landry, Chapter 17, this volume). These data are also supported by some neuroanatomical data. First, brain-damaged adult patients suffering from severe acalculia after a left brain parietal lesion exhibit a set of associated disorders (the Gertsmann syndrome), a key element of which is the loss of the finger sense (digital agnosia) (Gertsmann, 1940; Cipolotti, Butterworth, & Denes, 1991; Mayer et al., 2000). Second, in various functional imaging studies (Pinel et al., 1999; Dehaene et al., 1996; Pesenti et al., 2000), the involvement of the left precentral gyrus and close areas in the frontal lobes has been repeatedly observed when subjects are asked to perform simple arithmetical tasks. Third, anatomical magnetic resonance images in children with SBM have shown that the posterior regions of the brain in these children have reduced volumes of gray and white matter. However, the relationship between these volume changes and math and fine motor control skills is still to be quantitatively examined.

Although these associations are correlational and cannot thus be used to infer that finger use is critical for the acquisition of counting and other basic computational abilities, some of the characteristics of finger-based representations and finger use make these a powerful candidate for the establishment of such a link. At a representational level, fingers, like language, have an abstract dimension since the same pattern of raised fingers can equally well represent three giraffes, three toys, or three elements in an argument. However, whereas language permits the same type of abstraction, finger representations exhibit an iconic relation to numerosities, since they preserve the one-to-one matching relation between the represented set and the fingers used to represent it. Fingers also possess the advantage of exceeding in magnitude the span limitation of the object files (i.e., three or four items; Feigenson et al., 2002). They also have the advantage that they may support children's actions when adding items to, or removing them from, small sets to which the raising or lowering of fingers can be made to correspond. In this way, finger actions can reproduce additive or subtractive compositions (Brissiaud, 2003). Later, when children begin to count, the fingers might act as an anchor point or memory aid in the realization of the counting procedures, with the order of the fingers constituting a conventional sequence which children might associate with the verbal labels (Fuson, 1988). Finally, it is perfectly conceivable that the joint use of the fingers and the hands also constitutes a useful representation that plays a mediating role in the understanding of the number concept of base. Children may indeed discover that one hand raised and one finger raised on the other hand makes six fingers and that there is, therefore, a way of counting units by making use of higher-order units.

Relations between Preverbal Representation and Arabic Code

Whereas the study of the relations between the verbal code and preverbal representations has been frequently addressed, less attention has been paid to the relations between preverbal representations and the arabic code.

As a matter of fact, quantities are not necessarily compared in the same way when they are presented in arabic or verbal format. For example, the decision may be made either sequentially by processing the different digits one after the other until a decision is possible or holistically by taking account of the overall quantity (i.e., the magnitude). The data available regarding the comparison of large numbers (i.e., of three or more digits) suggest that adults use a sequential procedure and therefore successively take account of the different digits (Hinrichs, Berie, & Mosell, 1982; Poltrock & Schwartz, 1984). In contrast, comparisons of one- or two-digit numbers tend to support the theory that numbers presented in arabic format directly activate the analogue representation and are therefore processed on the basis of this representation rather than by means of a comparison of the digits they contain as a function of their position in the number. Thus, Dehaene and his collaborators (Dehaene, Dupoux, & Mehler, 1990) as well as Brysbaert and colleagues (Brysbaert, 1995; Reynvoet & Brysbaert, 1999) found a general distance effect but no decade break effect in number comparisons involving two-digit numerals (but see Nuerk, Weger, & Willmes, 2001, for a different point of view).

In accordance with this theory, at least as far as the quantities corresponding to units and certain Decade-Unit (DU) combinations are concerned, numbers in arabic format activate the corresponding analogue representation (i.e., the number line) and are therefore processed holistically. However, numbers larger than two-digit numbers are compared by means of a left-to-right serial procedure for establishing correspondences between their components. This corresponds to an analytical processing mode. What is yet unknown is whether the transition from a holistic processing mode to an analytical processing mode occurs systematically as of a certain quantity (e.g., 99) or whether interindividual variations exist. We also do not know whether there are some numbers that give rise to both analytic and holistic processing. Finally, we do not know whether holistic processing is strategic (i.e., under the participant's control) and, if so, what factors prompt its application.

The unsolved question is to determine the extent to which the presentation of numbers in arabic numerals automatically activates the corresponding analogue representations, even when these representations are not relevant for the task in question. Dehaene, Bossini, and

Giraux (1993) made use of a Stroop-type task, in which they asked adults to decide which of two numbers was the larger while presenting them with pairs of digits whose physical size was either congruent ($_5$ 3) or not congruent (5 $_3$) with the magnitude. They observed a size congruity effect which indicated the existence of automatic processing of the irrelevant dimension (as the physical size). Importantly, this congruence effect was observed both when the judgments related to digits and to physical sizes. This led the authors to conclude that access to numerical information is autonomous in adults such that it starts and continues through to its conclusion without any intentional action (Zbrodoff & Logan, 1986).

Duncan and McFerland (1980) have reported a distance effect in magnitude comparison tasks involving pairs such as (2,3) or (2,8) in both children and adults. This result suggests that access to the analogue representation of quantity is available at an early age. However, it is not possible to determine whether this access is automatic or strategic (i.e., intentional). Girelli, Lucangelli, and Butterworth (2000) used a Stroop-type paradigm to trace the developmental changes in the automatic and intentional processing of arabic numerals. University students, as well as first-grade, third-grade, and fifth-grade children compared the numerical or physical size of arabic numerals varying along both these dimensions. In the numerical comparison task, a size congruity effect was found at all ages, whereas in the physical comparison task, the incongruity between physical and numerical size affected only older children and adults. These findings strongly suggest that the automatization in number processing is achieved gradually as numerical skills progress and that six-year-old children do not automatically access the analogue representation of quantity when confronted with digits. Rubinsten, Henik, Berger, and Shahar-Shalev (2002) have confirmed the key elements of these conclusions. The arabic code becomes established rapidly as a structure—easy to learn and use, at least for small quantities—and is relatively slow in acquiring the capacity to activate the precise quantities with which it is associated quickly. However, we do not possess the longitudinal studies required in order to specify the course of this acquisition and determine whether and to what extent the associations between the arabic numerals and quantity representations are dependent on the verbal code. Nevertheless, it seems clear that the establishment of a precise relation between the arabic code and the analogue representation occurs rapidly during the period between six and nine to ten years of age.

CONCLUSIONS AND OUTLOOKS

The domain of number and calculation processing is still confronted with many open questions concerning the nature of the representations and processes that underlie arithmetic and number cognition. As we conclude this chapter, we stress two main challenges for the future. From the developmental point of view, it will be necessary to explain how preverbal representations of numerosities, and even the simple additive and subtraction processes that they seem able to sustain, are connected to (or transformed into) symbolic representations. This is a somewhat complex question since the literature indicates that children probably possess two different systems for representing numerosities: the object-file system and the analogue-magnitude system. Both these systems exhibit some important limitations compared to symbolic representations. On the one hand, object-file representations are limited to small sets and cannot represent cardinal values. On the other, analogue magnitude representations have no upper extension limit. However, in line with Weber's law, numbers become more imprecise as their magnitude increases. Furthermore, the analogue medium, at least as it is presently conceived,[5] is unable to represent the equidistant property of the number system and does not constitute a useful medium for precise calculation (even if addition has been described as iterative jumps on the number line and multiplication as surface areas determined by the length of the multiplicands; Gallistel & Gelman, 1992). It is also clear that the passage from the protonumeric representations to the symbolic ones is not rapid or straightforward. On the contrary, the time asynchrony between the age at which children master the recitation of the verbal number sequence and the age at which this sequence is used for cardinality judgments and calculation is so large that it seems implausible that the protonumeric system implicitly contains all the core principles of symbolic number and arithmetic processing. This asynchrony has even led some authors to suggest the hypothesis of a partial discontinuity between these different systems. It should be stressed here that the use of fingers as a representative medium may play an intermediary role, permitting the connection between the object-file representations and the symbolic ones. Fingers, as used by children in number and calculation activities, do indeed constitute a system that shares some properties with both preverbal and symbolic systems. Specifically, fingers and the preverbal systems share an analog (or iconic) relation to the numerosities that makes it possible, as in the object-file system, to establish a one-to-one correspondence between them and a set of numerosities. On the other hand, fingers and the verbal system share some abstract properties, since the same collection of fingers can represent any set of numerosities and, more importantly, the raising of fingers in a regular order can be matched with the order of the number names in the verbal number sequence. Finally, fingers may also be used to realize addition and multiplication and, in combination with the hands, they could act as a mediating representation for the understanding of the concept of base. It is necessary, however, to recognize that although these particular structural and processing aspects of fingers use make them plausible candidates for the missing link in a continuity hypothesis, their precise role in math development still has to be empirically established.

In the study of math cognition, a considerable amount of time is currently devoted to checking, in human symbolic arithmetic, for the signature behind the symbolic systems of the preverbal ones. We think that this effort has been detrimental to the study of the properties of the symbolic number system. Currently, there are only two main proposals concerning the number representations associated with the symbolic systems: the McCloskey's (1992) base ten-semantic system and the verbal semantic system developed by Power and Longuet-Higgins (1978; Power & Dal Martello, 1990). A good deal of work remains to be done before we understand how the human brain is able to represent many of the properties of the symbolic number systems per se.

NOTES

1. However, in some contexts, the activated semantic representations are encyclopaedic in nature.
2. The SNARC effect, first described by Dehaene, Bossini, & Giraux (1993), expresses a spatial-numerical relationship between the space of the responses and the size of the numbers: small numbers elicit shorter RTs on the left side than on the right, whereas the reverse holds for large numbers.
3. In French from France, some ten names are composed of two or three words (quatre-vingt (80), soixante-dix (70), and quatre-vingt-dix (90)), whereas in French from Wallonia 70 and 90 are simple one-word numerals.
4. For a very similar perspective, see Remi Brissiaud (2003) and Butterworth (1999).
5. Actually, this question is complicated by the fact that there are currently a number of different proposals regarding the structure of the preverbal number representations. Alongside the logarithmically compressed number line (Dehaene, 1992) and the linearly organized number line (Gallistel & Gelman,1992), new propositions are currently emerging (see Zorzi and Butterworth, 2001, and Verguts, Fias, and Stevens, submitted). These new propositions tend to reconcile the main psychophysical functions of number processing (size, distance, and SNARC effects) with discrete and precise number representations.

REFERENCES

Anderson, S. W., Damasio, A. R., & Damasio, H. (1990). Troubled letters but not numbers. Domain specific cognitive impairments following focal damage in frontal cortex. Brain, 113, 749–766.

Ansari, D., & Karmiloff-Smith, A. (2002). Atypical trajectories of number development: A neuroconstructivist perspective. Trends in Cognitive Sciences, 6, 511–516.

Antell, S. E., & Keating, D. P. (1983). Perception of numerical invariance in neonates. Child Development, 54, 695–701.

Ashcraft, M. H. (1992). Cognitive arithmetic: A review of data and theory. Cognition, 44, 75–106.

Barnes, M.A., Smith-Chant, B., & Landry, S. (in press). Number processing in neurodevelopemental disorders: Spina bifida myelomeningocele. In J. I. M. Campbell.

Barth, H., Kanwisher, N., & Spelke, E. (2003). The construction of large number representations in adults. Cognition, 86, 201–221.

Benson, D. F., & Denckla, M. B. (1969). Verbal paraphasia as a source of calculation disturbance. Archives of Neurology, 21, 96–102.

Bialystok, E. (1992). Symbolic representation of letters and numbers. Cognitive Development, 7, 301–316.

Bialystok, E., & Codd, J. (1997). Cardinal limits: Evidence from language awareness and bilinguism for developing concept of number. *Cognitive Development, 12,* 85–106.

Bijeljac-Babic, R., Bertoncini, J., & Mehler, J. (1991). How do four-day-old infants categorize multisyllabic utterances. *Developmental Psychology, 29,* 711–721.

Brannon, E. M., & Roitman, J. D. (2003). Nonverbal representations of time and number in animals and human infants. In W. H. Meck (Ed.), *Functional and neural mechanisms of interval timing.* Boca Raton, FL: CRC Press.

Brannon, E. M., & Terrace, H. S. (1998). Ordering of the numerosities 1 to 9 by monkeys. *Science, 282,* 746–749.

Brissiaud, R. (2003). *Comment les enfants apprennent à calculer.* Paris: Retz.

Brysbaert, M. (1995). Arabic number reading: On the nature of the numerical scale and the origin of phonological recoding. *Journal of Experimental Psychology: General, 124,* 343–447.

Brysbaert, M., Fias, W., & Noël, M. P. (1998). The worfian hypothesis and numerical cognition: Is "twenty-four" processed the same way as "four-and-twenty." *Cognition, 66,* 51–77.

Butterworth, B. (1999). *The mathematical brain.* London: Macmillan.

Butterworth, B., Zorzi, M., Girelli, L., & Jonckeere, A. R. (2001). Storage and retrieval of addition facts: The role of number comparison. *The Quarterly Journal of Experimental Psychology, 54,* 1005–1029.

Campbell, J. I. D. (1994). Architecture for numerical cognition. *Cognition, 53,* 1–44.

Campbell, J. L. D., & Clark, J. M. (1988). An encoding-complex view of cognitive number processing: Comment on McCloskey, Sokol, & Goodman (1986). *Journal of Experimental Psychology: General, 117,* 204–214.

Campbell, J. I. D., & Clark, J. M. (1992). Cognitive number processing: An encoding-complex perspective. In J. I. D. Campbell (Ed.), *The nature and origins of mathematical skills* (pp. 457–492). Amsterdam: Elsevier Science Publishers B.V.

Canfield R. L., & Smith E. G. (1996). Number-based expectations and sequential enumeration by 5-month-old infants. *Developmental Psychology, 32* (2), 269–279.

Carey, S. (2001). Bridging the gap between cognition and developmental neuroscience: The example of number representation. In C. A. Nelson & M. Luciana (Eds.), *Handbook of developmental cognitive neuroscience* (pp. 415–431). Cambridge, MA: MIT Press.

Cipolotti, L. (1995). Multiple route for reading words, why not numbers? Evidence from a case of Arabic numeral dyslexia. *Cognitive Neuropsychology, 12,* 313–342.

Cipolotti, L., Butterworth, B., & Denes, G. (1991). A specific deficit for numbers in a case of dense acalculia. *Brain, 114,* 2619–2637.

Cipolotti, L., Butterworth, B., & Warrington, E. (1994). From one thousand nine hundred and forty-five to 1000,945. *Neuropsychologia, 32,* 503–509.

Clark, J. M., & Campbell, J. I. D. (1991). Integrated verus modular theories of number skills and acalculia. *Brain and Cognition, 17,* 204–239.

Dehaene, S. (1989). The psychophysics of numerical comparison: A reexamination of apparently incompatible data. *Perception and Psychophysics, 45,* 557–66.

Dehaene, S. (1992). Varieties of numerical abilities. *Cognition, 44,* 1–42.

Dehaene, S. (1997). *The number sense: How the mind creates mathematics.* New York: Oxford University Press.

Dehaene, S., & Akhavein, R. (1995). Attention, automaticity, and levels of representation in number processing. *Journal of Experimental Psychology, Learning, Memory and Cognition, 21,* 314–326.

Dehaene, S., Bossini, S., & Giraux, P. (1993). The mental representation of parity and numerical magnitude. *Journal of Experimental Psychology: General, 122,* 371–396.

Dehaene, S., & Cohen, L. (1995). Towards an anatomical and functional model of number processing. *Mathematical Cognition, 1,* 83–120.

Dehaene, S., & Cohen, L. (1997). Cerebral pathways for calculation: Double dissociations between Gerstmann's acalculia and subcortical acalculia. *Cortex, 33,* 219–250.

Dehaene, S., & Cohen, L. (2000). Un modèle anatomique et fonctionnel de l'arithmétique mentale. In M. Pesenti & X. Seron (Eds.), *Neuropsychologie des troubles du calcul et du traitement des nombres.* Marseille: Solal.

Dehaene, S., Dupoux, E., & Mehler, J. (1990). Is numerical comparison digital-analogical and symbolic effects in 2-digit number comparison. *Journal of Experimental Psychology, Human Perception and Performance. 16,* 626–641.

Dehaene, S., Tzourio, N., Frak, V., Raynaud, L., Cohen, L., Mehler, T., & Mazoyer, B. (1996). Cerebral activations during number multiplication and comparison: A PET study. *Neuropsychologia, 34,* 1097–1106.

Delazer, M., & Denes, G. (1998). Writing arabic numerals in an agraphic patient. *Brain and Language, 64,* 257–266.

Della Sala, S., Gentileschi, V., Gray C., & Spinnler, H. (2002). Intrusion errors in numerical transcoding by Alzheimer patients. *Neuropsychologia, 38,* 768–777.

Donlan, C. (1993). Basic numeracy in children with specific language impairment. *Child Language Teaching and Therapy, 9,* 95–104.

Donlan, C. V., Bishop, D. V. M., & Hitch, G. J. (1998). Magnitude comparisons by children with specific language impairments: Evidence of unimpaired symbolic processing. *International Journal of Language and Communicative Disorders, 33,* 149–160.

Duncan, E. M., & McFerland, C. E. (1980). Isolating the effects of symbolic distance and semantic congruity in comparative judgments: An additive-factors analysis. *Memory & Cognition, 8,* 612–622.

English, L. D., & Halford, G. S. (1995). *Mathematics education.* Mahwah, NJ: L.E.A.

Eriksen, C. W., Pollack, M. D., & Montague, W. E. (1970). Implicit speech: Mechanisms in perceptual encoding? *Journal of Experimental Psychology, 84,* 502–507.

Fayol, M. (1990). *L'enfant et le nombre.* Lausanne: Delachaux et Niestlé.

Fayol, M. (2002). Le facteur verbal dans les traitements numériques: Perspective développementale. In J. Bideaud & H. Lehalle (Eds.), *Le développement des activités numériques* (pp. 151–173). Paris: Hermès.

Fayol, M. Barrouillet, P., & Renaud, A. (1996). Pourquoi l'écriture des grands nombres est-elle aussi difficile? *Revue de Psychologie de l'Education, 1,* 109–132.

Fayol, M., Barrouillet, P., & Marinthe, C. (1998). Predicting arithmetical achievement from neuropsychological performance: A longitudinal study. *Cognition, 68,* B63–B70.

Feigenson, L., Carey, S., & Hauser, M. (2002). The representations underlying infants' choice of more: Object files versus analog magnitudes. *Psychological Science, 13,* 150–156.

Feigenson, L., Carey, S., & Spelke, E. (2002). Infants' discrimination of number vs. continuous extent. *Cognitive Psychology, 44*, 33–66.

Fias, W., Lammertyn, J., Reynvoet, B., Dupont, P., & Orban, G. A. (2003). Parietal representation of symbolic and non-symbolic magnitude. *Journal of Cognitive Neuroscience. 15*, 47–56.

Fuson, K. C. (1988). *Children's counting and the concepts of number.* New York: Springer.

Frenck-Mestre, C., & Vaid, J. (1993). Activation of number facts in bilinguals. *Memory and Cognition, 21*, 809–818.

Fuson, K., & Kwon, Y. (1991). Systèmes de mots-nombres et autres outils cultturels. In J. Bideaud, C. Meljac, & Fischer, J. C. (Eds.), *Les chemins du nombre.* Lille: Presses Universitaires de Lille.

Gallistel, C. R., & Gelman, R. (1978). *The child's understanding of number.* Cambridge, MA: Harvard University Press.

Gallistel, C. R., & Gelman, R. (1992). Preverbal and verbal counting and computation. *Cognition, 44*, 43–74.

Geary, D. C., Salthouse, T. A., Chen, G., & Fan, L. (1996). Are East Asian versus American differences in arithmetical ability a recent phenomenon? *Developmental Psychology, 32*, 254–262.

Geary, D. G. (1994). *Children's mathematical development, research and practical applications.* Washington, DC: American Psychological Association.

Gerstmann, J. (1940). Syndrome of finger agnosia, disorientation for right and left, agraphia, and acalculia. *Archives of Neurology and Psychiatry, 44*, 398–408.

Gielen, I., Brysbaert, M., & Dhondt, A. (1991). The syllable-length effect in number processing is task dependent. *Perception and Psychophysics, 50*, 449–458.

Girelli, L., Lucangelli, D., & Butterworth, B. (2000). The development of automaticity in accessing number magnitude. *Journal of Experimental Child Psychology, 76*, 104–122.

Gobel, S., Walsh, V., & Rushworth, M. F. S. (2001a). rTMS disrupts the representation of small numbers in supramarginal gyrus. *Neuroimage, 13*, S409.

Gobel, S., Walsh, V., & Rushworth, M. F. S. (2001b). The mental number line and the human angular gyrus. *Neuroimage, 14*, 1278–1289.

Gonzalez, E. G., & Kolers, P.A. (1982). Mental manipulation of arithmetic symbols. *Journal of Experimental Psychology, Learning, Memory and Cognition, 4*, 308–319.

Granà A., Lochy A., Girelli L., Seron X., & Semenza C. (2003). Transcoding zero within complex numerals. *Neuropsychologia.*

Hauser, M. D., Carey, S., & Hauser, L. B. (2000). Spontaneous number representation in semi-free-ranging rhesus monkeys. *Proceedings of the Royal Society of London Series B-Biological Sciences, 267*(1445), 829–833.

Hinrichs, J. V., Berie, J. L., & Mosell, M. K. (1982). Place information in multidigit number comparison. *Memory & Cognition, 10*, 487–495.

Hughes, M. (1986). *Children and number: Difficulties in learning.* New York: Basic Blackwell.

Huntley-Fenner, G., & Cannon, E. (2000). Preschoolers' magnitude comparisons are mediated by a preverbal analog mechanism. *Psychological Science, 11*, 147–152.

Huntley-Fenner, G. (2001). Children's understanding of number is similar to adults' and rats': numerical estimation by 5–7-year-olds. *Cognition, 78*, B27–B40.

Hurford, J. R. (1987). *Language and number.* Oxford: Basil Blackwell.

Jarlegan, A., Fayol, M., & Barrouillet, P. (1996). De soixante douze à 72, et inversement: Une étude du transcodage chez les enfants de 7 ans. *Revue de Psychologie de l'Education, 1*, 109–131.

Jordan, N. C., Huttenlocher, J., & Levine, S. C. (1992). Differential calculation abilities in young children from middle- and low- income families. *Developmental Psychology, 28*, 644–653.

Jordan, N. C., Huttenlocher, J., & Levine, S. C. (1994). Assessing early arithmetic abilities: Effects of verbal and nonverbal response types on the calculation performance of middle- and low-income children. *Learning and Individual Differences, 6*, 413–432.

Kessler, J., & Kalbe, E. (1996). Written numeral transcoding in patients with Alzheimer's disease. *Cortex, 32*, 755–761.

Kinsbourne M., & Warrington, E. (1962). A study of finger agnosia. *Brain, 85*, 47–66.

Kinsbourne, M., & Warrington, E. (1963). The developmental Gerstmann syndrome. *Archives of Neurology, 8*, 490–501.

Lochy, A. Pillon, A., Zesiger, P., & Seron, X. (2002). Verbal structure of numerals and digits handwriting: New evidence from kinematics. *The Quarterly Journal of Experimental Psychology, 55A*, 263–288.

Marinthe, C., Fayol, M., & Barrouillet, P. (2001). Gnosies digitales et développement des performances arithmétiques. In A. Van Hout & C. Meljac (Eds.), *Les dyscalculies* (pp. 238–254). Paris: Masson.

Marsh, L. G., & Makki, R. H. (1976). Efficiency of arithmetical operations in bilinguals as a function of language. *Memory and Cognition, 4*, 459–464.

Mayer, E., Martory, M. D., Pegna, A. J., Landis, T., Delavelle, J., & Annoni, J. M. (2000). A pure case of Gerstmann syndrome with a subangular lesion. *Brain, 122*, 1107–1120.

McCloskey, M. (1992). Cognitive mechanisms in numerical processing: Evidence from acquired dyscalculia. *Cognition, 44*, 107–157.

McCloskey, M., Sokol, S. M., & Goodman, R. A. (1986). Cognitive processes in verba–number production: Inferences from the performance of brain-damaged subjects. *Journal of Experimental Psychology: General, 115*(4), 307–330.

Meck, W. H., & Church, R. M. (1983). A mode control model of counting and timing processes. *Journal of Experimental Psychology: Animal Behavior Processes, 9*, 320–334.

Miller, K. F., & Paredes, D. R. (1996). On the shoulders of giants: Cultural tools and mathematical development. In R. Sternberg & T. Ben Zeev (Eds.), *The nature of mathematical thinking* (pp. 83–117). Hillsdale, NJ: Erlbaum.

Miller, K. F., Smith, C. M., Zhu, J., & Zhang, H. (1995). Preschool origins of cross-national differences in mathematical competence: The role of number-naming systems. *Psychological Science, 6*, 56–60.

Miura, I. T., Okamoto, Y., Kim, C. C., Steere, M., & Fayol, M. (1993). First graders' cognitive representation of numbers and understanding of place value: Cross-national comparison—France, Japan, Korea, Sweden, and the United States. *Journal of Educational Psychology, 85*, 24–30.

Miura, I. T., Okamoto, Y., Kim, C. C., Chang, C. M., Steere, M., & Fayol, M. (1994). Comparisons of cognitive representation of number: China, France, Japan,

Korea, Sweden, and the United States. *International of Behavioral Development, 17,* 401–411.

Mix, K. S. (1999). Similarity and numerical equivalence: Appearances count. *Cognitive Development, 14,* 269–297.

Mix, K. S., Huttenlocher, J., & Levine, S. C. (2002). Multiple cues for quantification in infancy: Is number one of them? *Psychological Bulletin, 128,* 278–294.

Moyer, R. S., & Landauer, T. K. (1967). Time required for judgements of numerical inequality. *Nature, 215,* 1519–1520.

Naccache, L., & Dehaene, S. (2001). The priming method: Imaging unconscious repetition priming reveals an abstract representation of number in the parietal lobes. *Cerebral Cortex, 11,* 966–974.

Nickerson, R. S. (1988). Counting, computing, and the representation of numbers. *Human Factors, 30,* 181–199.

Noël, M. P., & Seron, X. (1992). Notational constraints and number processing: A reappraisal of the Gonzalez and Kolers (1982) study. *Quarterly Journal of Experimental Psychology: Human Experimental Psychology, 45,* 451–478.

Noël, M. P., & Seron, X. (1993). Arabic number reading deficit: A single case study. *Cognitive Neuropsychology, 10,* 317–339.

Noël, M. P., & Seron, X. (1995). Lexicalization errors in writing arabic numerals: A single case study. *Brain and Cognition, 29,* 151–179.

Noël, M. P., & Seron, X. (1997). On the existence of intermediate representations in numerical processing. *Journal of Experimental Psychology, Learning, Memory and Cognition, 23,* 697–720.

Nuerk, H.-C., Weger, U., & Willmes, K. (2001). Decade breaks in the mental number line? Putting the tens and units back in different bins. *Cognition, 82,* B25–B33.

Paterson, S. (2001). Language and number in Down syndrome: The complex developmental trajectory from infancy to adulthood. *Down Syndrome Research and Practice, 7,* 79–86.

Pebenito, R. (1987). Developmental Gerstmann syndrome: Case report and review of the litterature. *Developmental and Behavioral Pediatrics, 8,* 229–232.

Pesenti, M., Thioux, M., Seron, X., & de Volder, A. (2000). Neuroanatomical substrates of arabic number processing, numerical comparison, and simple addition: A pet study. *Journal of Cognitive Neuroscience, 12*(3), 461–479.

Pinel, P., Dehaene, S., Rivière, D., & Le Bihan, D. (2001). Modulation of parietal activation by semantic distance in a number comparison task. *Neuroimage, 14,* 1013–1026.

Pinel, P., Le Clec'h, G., van de Moortele, P.-F., Naccache, L., Le Bihan, D., & Dehaene, S. (1999). Event-related fMRI analysis of the cerebral circuit for number comparison. *NeuroReport, 10,* 1473–1479.

Poltrock, S. E., & Schwartz, D. R. (1984). Comparative judgments of multidigit numbers. *Journal of Experimental Psychology: Learning, Memory, and Cognition, 10,* 32–45.

Power, R. J. D., & Dal Martello, M. F. (1990). The dictation of Italian numeral. *Language and Cognitive Processes, 5,* 237–254.

Power, R. J. D., & Longuet-Higgins, F. R. S. (1978). Learning to count: A computational model of language acquisition. *Proceedings of the Royal Society of London, B200,* 391–417.

Pynte, J. (1974). Readiness for pronunciation during the reading process. *Perception and Psychophysics, 16,* 110–112.

Reynvoet B., & Brysbaert M. (1999). Single-digit and two-digit Arabic numerals address the same semantic number line. *Cognition, 72,* 191–201.

Reynvoet, B., Brysbaert, M., & Fias, W. (2002). Semantic priming in number naming. *Quarterly Journal of Experimental Psychology-A, 55,* 1127–1139.

Roberts, W. A., & Mitchell, S. (1994). Can a pigeon simultaneously process temporal and numerical information. *Journal of Experimental Psychology: Animal Behavior Processes, 20,* 66–78.

Rourke, B. P. (1993). Arithmetic disabilities, specific and otherwise: A neuropsychological perspective. *Journal of Learning Disabilities, 26,* 214–226.

Rubinsten, O., Henik, A., Berger, A., & Shahar-Shalev, S. (2002). The development of internal representations of magnitude and their association with arabic numerals. *Journal of Experimental Child Psychology, 81,* 74–92.

Sekuler, R., & Mierkiewicz, D. (1977). Children's judgments of numerical equality. *Child Development, 48,* 630–633.

Seron, X., Delòche, G., & Noël, M. P. (1992). Number transcribing by children. In J. Bideaud, C. Meljac, & J. P. Fisher (Eds.), *Pathways to number.* Hillsdale, NJ: Erlbaum.

Seron, X., & Deloche, G. (1994). Les troubles du calcul et du traitement des nombres. In X. Seron & M. Jeannerod (Eds.), *La neuropsychologie humaine.* Liège: Mardaga.

Seron, X., & Fayol, M. (1994). Number transcoding in children: A functional analysis. *British Journal of Developmental Psychology, 12,* 281–300.

Seron, X., & Noël, M. P. (1995). Transcoding numbers from the Arabic code to the verbal one or vice versa: How many routes? *Mathematical Cognition, 1,* 215–235.

Sharon, T., & Wynn, K. (1998). Infants' individuation of actions from continuous motion. *Psychological Science, 9,* 357–362.

Siegler, R. S., & Robinson, M. (1982). The development of number understanding. In H. W. Reese & L. P. Lipsitt (Eds.), *Advances in child development and behavior. Vol. 16.* New York: Academic Press.

Simon, T. J. (1997). Reconceptualizing the origins of number knowledge: A non-numerical account. *Cognitive Development, 12,* 349–372.

Simon, T. J. (1999). The foundation of numerical thinking in a brain without numbers. *Trends in Cognitive Sciences, 3,* 363–365.

Sokol, S. M., & McCloskey, M. (1988). Levels of representation in verbal number production. *Applied Psycholinguistics, 9,* 267–281.

Spelke, E., & Dehaene, S. (1999). Biological foundations of numerical thinking. *Trends in Cognitive Sciences, 3,* 365–366.

Spelke, E. S., & Tsivkin, S. (2001). Language and number: A bilingual training study. *Cognition, 78,* 45–88.

Starkey, P. (1992). The early development of numerial reasoning. *Cognition, 43,* 93–126.

Starkey, P., & Cooper, R. G. (1980). Perception of numbers by human infants. *Science, 210,* 1033–1034.

Stevenson, H. W., Lee, S. Y., & Stigler, J. W. (1986). Mathematics achievement of Chinese, Japanese, and American children. *Science, 231,* 593–599.

Stevenson, H. W., Stigler, J. W., Lee, S. Y., Lucker, G. W., Kitamura, S., & Hsu, C. C. (1985). Cognitive performance and academic achievement of Japanese, Chinese and American children. *Child Development, 56,* 718–734.

Strauss, A., & Werner, H. (1938). Deficiency in the finger schema in relation to arithmetic disability (Finger agnosia and acalculia). *The American Journal of Orthopsychiatry, 8,* 719–725.

Strauss, M. S., & Curtis, L. E. (1981). Infant perception of numerosity. *Child Development, 52,* 1146–1152.

Ta'ir, J., Brezner, A., & Ariel, R. (1997). Profound developmental dyscalculia: Evidence for a cardinal/ordinal skills acquisition device. *Brain and Cognition, 35,* 184–206.

Tegnér, R., & Nybäck, H. (1990). "Two hundred and twenty 4our": A study of transcoding in dementia. *Acta Neurologica Scandinavia, 81,* 177–178.

Temple C. M. (1997). *Developmental cognitive neuropsychology.* London: Psychology Press.

Temple, E., & Posner, M. I. (1998). Brain mechanisms of quantity are similar in 5-year-old children and adults. *Proceedings of the National Academy of Sciences (USA), 95,* 7836–7841.

Thioux, M., Ivanoiu, A., Turconi, E., & Seron, X. (1999). Intrusions of the verbal code during the production of arabic numerals: A single case study in a patient with probable Alzheimer's disease. *Cognitive Neuropsychology, 16,* 749–773.

Verguts, T., Fias, W., & Stevens (submitted). A model of exact small-number representation.

Walsh, V. (2003). Cognitive neuroscience: Numerate neurons. *Current Biology, 23,* 447–448.

Warrington, E. K. (1982). The fractionation of arithmetical skills: A single case study. *The Quarterly Journal of Experimental Psychology, 34A,* 31–51.

Wellman, H. M., & Miller, K. F. (1986). Thinking about nothing: Development of concept of zero. *British Journal of Developmental Psychology, 4,* 31–42.

Whalen, J., Gallistel, C. R., & Gelman, R. (1999). Nonverbal counting in humans: The psychophysics of number representation. *Psychological Science, 10,* 130–137.

Whalen, J., McCloskey, M., Lindemann, M., & Bouton, G. (2002). Representing arithmetic table facts in memory: Evidence from acquired impairments. *Cognitive Neuropsychology, 19,* 505–522.

Wynn, K. (1992). Addition and subtraction by human infants. *Nature, 358,* 749–750.

Wynn, K. (1996). Infants' individuation and enumeration of actions. *Psychological Science, 7,* 164–169.

Wynn, K. (1998). Psychological foundations of number: Numerical competence in human infants. *Trends in Cognitive Sciences, 2,* 296–303.

Xu, F. (2000). *Numerical competence in infancy: Two systems of representation.* Paper presented at the 12th Biennial International Conference on Infant Studies.

Xu, F., & Spelke, E. S. (2000). Large number discrimination in 6-month-old infants. *Cognition, 74,* B1–B11.

Zbrodoff, N. J., & Logan, G. D. (1986). On the autonomy of mental processes: A case study of arithmetic. *Journal of Experimental Psychology: General, 115,* 118–130.

Zhang, J., & Norman, D. A. (1995). A representational analysis of numeration systems. *Cognition, 57,* 271–295.

Zorzi, M., & Butterworth, B. (2001). A computational model of number comparison. In M. Hahn & S. C. Stones (Eds.), *Proceedings of the twenty-first annual conference of the cognitive science society* (1999) (pp.778–783).. Mahwah, NJ: Erlbaum.

2

Number Recognition in Different Formats

Marc Brysbaert

An interesting aspect of numbers is that they can be presented in different formats. Although numbers are associated spontaneously with arabic digits, they can also be represented as Roman numerals (e.g., MMIV), sequences of words (both spoken and written), or in an analogue form (e.g., dots on a die, tallies on a sheet of paper, or bar graphs). This raises the question of how numbers in the different formats are processed. What are the commonalities and what are the differences? I will first deal with the analogue displays, which have a meaning both for humans and animals, and I will then continue with the verbal and the arabic numerals, which are uniquely human achievements. In line with McCloskey and Macaruso (1995), I will use the term *number* for format-independent aspects of numerical cognition and the term *numeral* to refer to modality-specific representations (i.e., analogue, verbal, and arabic numerals).

PERCEIVING ANALOGUE DISPLAYS OF NUMBERS

The basic function of numbers is to represent quantities (also called numerosities when the elements are clearly separated). By counting how many similar elements there are in a scene, we can assess their number. Because five-year-olds regularly make errors in their counting (e.g., Gelman & Gallistel, 1978), for a long time it was thought that knowledge of numerosities required formal education to be mastered. However, research in the 1980s and 1990s has indicated that this is not true for the apprehension of small numerosities. It is now well established that young babies, just like many kinds of animals (rats, pigeons, pigs, etc.), can easily discriminate numerosities smaller than four (see Chapter 6). In addition, they can compare two quantities when the differences between the quantities are large. For instance, Antell and Keating (1983) reported that newborns who were habituated to successive displays with two elements each (and, therefore, barely looked at them anymore), showed increased interest when a display with three elements was presented. Using a similar habituation technique, Xu and Spelke (2000) reported that 6-month-olds can discriminate between 8 and 16 items but not between 8 and 12.

Human adults also show a distinction between the perception of a small number of items and the perception of a large number. Whereas it only takes some 50 milliseconds (ms) longer to decide that a display contains three dots than to decide that it contains one dot, the time needed to detect nine dots is more than 600 ms longer than the time to detect seven dots. The difference is even consciously felt by the participants. Whereas they *see* the numerosity directly when the display contains less than four items, they have to *count* in order to correctly assess larger numbers. In addition, the assessment of larger numerosities is easier when the items are presented in a canonical form (e.g., a six represented by two rows of three dots, as on a die) than when they are presented in a random configuration (Mandler & Shebo, 1982; Wender & Rothkegel, 2000). The immediate apprehension of small numerosities (up to three to four elements) has been called *subitizing* (Kaufman, Lord, Reese, & Volkman, 1949; Jensen, Reese, & Reese, 1950). Figure 2.1 shows the typical results of a study on subitizing.

Further interesting observations are made when numerosities larger than four are presented and mathematically literate participants are prevented from counting them (e.g., by a brief display of the stimulus pattern). Under these circumstances, participants have to come up with an educated guess, and they again show behavior that very much resembles that of animals.

A first finding is that participants spontaneously underestimate the number of elements in the display. The underestimate increases as the numerosity grows. For instance, Krueger (1982) showed each participant one sheet of paper with some Xs on it. Participants were asked to give an estimate of the number of Xs on the page. When 50 Xs were present on the sheet, participants estimated them to be around 40; when 100 Xs were shown, estimates hinged around 75; when 200 were shown, the average estimate was some 135; and when 300 Xs were shown, participants estimated them to be around 200. There was a compressive function between the estimates given by the participants and the actual number presented (the former increased less rapidly than the latter). The compressive function was best captured by a power function with an exponent of .8 (i.e., in between a linear function—exponent 1—and a square root function—exponent .5).

A second finding when adults estimate numerosities on the basis of analogue displays is that the estimates show variability. For instance, van Oeffelen and Vos (1982) showed participants tachistoscopic displays with random configurations of dots and asked them to estimate whether

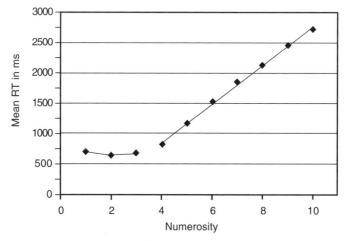

Figure 2.1. Mean reaction time needed by participants to say how many white asterisks are presented on a computer screen, as a function of numerosity. The points represent the observed data. The lines represent linear regression functions relating reaction time to numerosity within the subitizing range (1–3) and the counting range (4–10). Notice that the lack of a difference between the enumeration of 3 vs. 1 dots, shown in Figure 1, is not always present. Usually, there is a small positive slope of some 50 ms in the subitizing range (partly dependent on whether or not the numerosity 4 is included in the range). Also notice the slope of more than 300 ms in the counting range. (From Logan & Zbrodoff, 2003.)

or not there were exactly 12 dots in the display. The interesting variable was how often the participants would think there were 12 elements given that another number had been presented. The results of this study are shown in the lower left part of Figure 2.2. When the number of elements presented was 11 or 13, participants made some 35% false alarms. When 10 or 14 elements were on the display, participants made some 24% errors. For a distance of 3, they made 17% errors, and for a distance of 4 they made 8% errors. This pattern of mistakes is very similar to the patterns of errors shown by animals in similar designs (see the two upper parts of Figure 2.2).

A third finding with numerosity estimates shows that the variability in estimates increases with growing target numbers. This was particularly clear in an experiment reported by Whalen, Gallistel, and Gelman (1999). Participants were presented with a dot that repeatedly flashed on and off in one location and were asked to say approximately how many times the dots flashed, without verbal counting (special precautions were taken to prevent the counting). Both the response means and the standard deviations increased in direct proportion to the target number, which ranged from 7 to 25. Again, these findings were very similar to previous results obtained with rats and are shown in Figure 2.3.

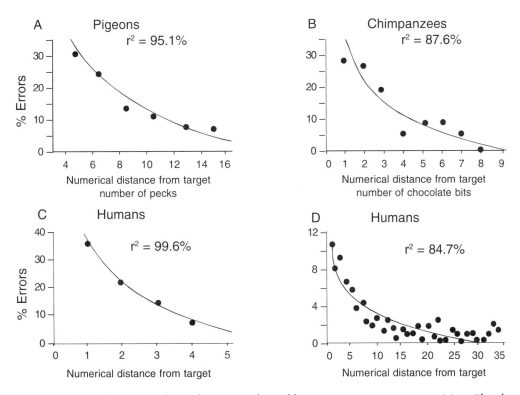

Figure 2.2. The distance effect when animals and humans compare numerosities. The data discussed in the text are those of the lower left part (panel C). This panel shows how many times participants wrongly indicated that 12 elements were presented on the screen as a function of the actual number presented. As can be seen, the percentage of errors dropped systematically from a distance of 1 (i.e., when 11 or 13 elements were presented) to a distance of 4. The upper panels show data of animals in similar situations: (A) the deviation between the actual number of pecks made by pigeons and the fixed standard of 50, (B) chimpanzees selecting the larger of two small numbers of chocolate bits. Finally, panel D shows the number of errors students make when they compare arabic numerals to a fixed standard of 65 (see also Figure 2.8). Figure copied from Dehaene et al. (1998).

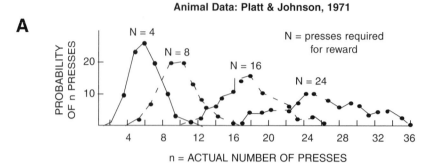

Figure 2.3.   These data show the actual number of lever presses made by rats after they had learned that a certain number (4, 8, 16, or 24) was required for a reward (part A). Notice that in this situation, the average number matches the required number quite well but that the data vary from trial to trial. The variability increases with increasing average number. The increase in variability is a linear function of the average (and required) number, as shown in part B. Very similar data are found with humans when they are prevented from counting the actual number and have to rely on rough estimates. Figure copied from Whalen et al. (1999).

On the basis of these findings, a considerable number of researchers now assume that animals and humans are born with a *preverbal numerical system* (based on analogue magnitudes) that is capable of apprehending small numerosities precisely and larger numerosities approximately (e.g., Butterworth, 1999; Dehaene, Dehaene-Lambertz, & Cohen, 1998; Gallistel & Gelman, 1992; Wynn, 1998).

Gallistel and Gelman (1992), for instance, hypothesized that subitizing is nothing else than fast counting, based on the preverbal representations. In their model, each time an element of a display is encountered, a quantity is added to an accumulator (the authors compare this process to pouring cups of water in a bucket). At the end of the count, the accumulator is emptied into memory and the total quantity is read. However, because there is some noise in the unit quantities added and/or in the reading from memory, there will be variability in the outcomes. This variability grows as the number of units (cups) increases. Therefore, only for small numbers of units is it possible to rapidly assess the exact quantity. For larger numbers, either mistakes are made, or a more laborious process must be used that consists of verbal counting.

The idea of an innate, preverbal numerical system has also been defended by Dehaene and colleagues (e.g., Dehaene, 1992; Dehaene, Dehaene-Lambertz, & Cohen, 1998). They use the metaphor of a number line for this system. Numerical representations are thought to be ordered from small to large, and numbers are recognized by looking at which part of the number line is activated. The number line is thought to be compressed (e.g., according to a logarithmic function or a power function), so that the part of the line devoted to the number 1 is larger than the part devoted to the number 2, which in turn is larger than the part devoted to the number 3, and so on. Because of this characteristic, the representations of small numbers are more easily discernable than those of large numbers and from a certain magnitude on the numerical representation can no longer be determined with certainty. It can only be estimated, unless an explicit verbal counting process is initiated.

This interpretation, however, is not shared by everyone (e.g., Mix, Huttenlocher, & Levine, 2002; Simon, 1997). There are two main points of contention. First, there is the question to what extent the empirical evidence of numerical knowledge in children and animals is due to the numerosity of the items (i.e., to the abstract notion of number: "two-ness, three-ness") or to some confounded perceptual factor, such as the area covered by the items, the duration of the stimulus display (when the items are presented in time), or the density of the elements in the display. Feigenson, Carey, and Spelke (2002) replicated Antell & Keating's (1983) experiment with the use of animal-like objects made of Lego bricks: infants of seven months old who were habituated to successive displays of one object showed increased interest when a display with two objects was shown, and vice versa. However, in four subsequent experiments, the authors failed to find the dishabituation effect when the front surface area of the objects was controlled, so that the task could not be explained on the basis of the total size of the stimulus configuration. For instance, the infants did not show renewed interest when in the habituation phase two small objects were presented and in the test phase one double-sized object. Apparently, the infants' behavior was more influenced by the size of the total stimulus configuration than by the number of elements in the display.

The second point of contention is whether one really needs numerical knowledge to perceive numerosities up to 4. It is generally assumed that humans (and animals) can keep 3–4 chunks of information simultaneously in short-term memory. Maybe this is the reason why infants and animals can perceive the difference between 2 and 3 elements and why human adults show the subitizing effect. All they have to do is to match the second perceptual stimulus to the information of the first stimulus stored in short-term memory (Simon, 1997). This could be done by a simple one-to-one matching process, without any requirement of numerical knowledge (see also Logan & Zbrodoff, in press, for a recent perceptual interpretation of both the subitizing effect and the counting effect shown in Figure 2.1). One specific prediction of the short-term memory account is that infants and animals must not be able to compare numerosities larger than 4 (when perceptual factors are controlled), because these numerosities lie outside the short-term memory span. Needless to say, this is currently a matter of strong debate in the literature (see Feigenson, Carey, & Hauser, 2002 versus Xu & Spelke, 2000; Xu, 2003).

In summary, when mathematically literate humans are confronted with numbers shown in an analog format, they have no problems perceiving numerosities smaller than 4 (subitizing). For larger numerosities, they either start to count or they make a rough estimate. Because the subitizing effect and the rough estimates resemble characteristics of animal cognition (accurate perception of small numerosities, a tendency to underestimate large numerosities, and an increased variability in the estimates of larger numerosities), some authors have suggested that they are based on an innate, preverbal numerical system, which humans share with animals. Other researchers question such a nativistic view of numerical cognition and point to the fact that much empirical evidence can be explained by perceptual factors unrelated to numerical cognition.

The finding that people spontaneously start to count numerosities larger than 4 shows how important symbolic representations are for human numerical cognition. In the following sections, I review the main findings on the processing of these symbolic representations.

RECOGNIZING VERBAL NUMERALS

The words for the small numbers are among the first acquired, and research has shown that nearly half of the three-year-olds are capable of using the words up to seven in a sensible way (e.g., to count a row of objects; Gelman & Gallistel, 1978). Needless to say, knowledge of number words dramatically facilitates the mathematical competence of humans, and a look at the number words themselves reveals some of the hurdles that had to be overcome in inventing them (Ifrah, 1998). For instance, the fact that the words "one," "two," and "three" have the same stem in German and Roman languages indicates that they have a common, more ancient origin. Similarly, nearly all Western languages have a number word related to "new" (nine, neuf), presumably because this number marked a discovery at some moment in our history; and the words for 11 and 12 betray that the base-ten structure of our number system was not yet well established by the time they were coined (although "eleven" and "twelve" originate from the sayings "one-left" and "two-left"–after you've counted all 10 fingers/digits; the fact that our number system has a base 10 also originates from the widespread use of fingers to count).

There are no reasons to assume that the perception and the production of verbal numerals would be any different from that of other words. Thus, we can take inspiration from the more general models of visual and auditory word recognition and production. Because not everything can be covered in the space of a chapter, I will limit myself to the recognition of printed words. Readers interested in an introduction to spoken word recognition may want to see McQueen (2004). Those interested in spoken word production are referred to Levelt, Roelofs, and Meyers (1999) and the following commentaries. Finally, those interested in written word production may want to read Bonin, Peereman, and Fayol (2001).

There are three discussions within the literature of visual word recognition that are particularly interesting for number recognition. The first deals with the question of whether or not a mental lexicon is needed for the recognition of word forms, the second concerns the question of how the meaning of words is accessed, and the third addresses the question of how morphologically complex words are recognized.

In models of word recognition, it has been customary to make a distinction between a so-called word-form level and a word-meaning level (e.g., Balota, 1994; see Figure 2.4 for an example of such a model). The flowcharts of these models usually capture the former under the term "lexicon" and the latter under the term "semantic system." At the lexical level, a match is made between the incoming perceptual information and word-form knowledge stored in memory to determine whether a given stimulus (either visual or auditory) refers to a known word or not. At the semantic level, the meaning of a known word is derived. Several reasons have been given for the distinction between the lexical and the semantic level. A first reason is that many researchers believe that the lexical level is more differentiated than the semantic level. For instance, many authors are convinced that a distinction should be made between a visual and an auditory lexicon. Some arguments for this distinction are related to the nature of the input (e.g., the letters of short written words are probably processed in parallel, whereas there is a clear serial component in the phonemes of spoken words, which typically take hundreds of milliseconds to be pronounced). Other arguments are derived from priming studies. It has been shown that within-modality repetition of a word (e.g., visual–visual) results in larger facilitation effects than cross-modality repetition (e.g., auditory–visual; Morton, 1979).

A second reason for separating lexical from semantic representations has to do with the lack of one-to-one mappings between words and meanings. For example, the meanings of words to some extent depend on the context: the word *big* has a different meaning in the phrase *the big ant* than in *the big rocket* (Harley, 2001). Also, many words have different meanings (polysemy) or share their meaning with other words (synonyms). It is difficult to explain the resolution of these ambiguities in the mappings from form to meaning within a single layer of representations.

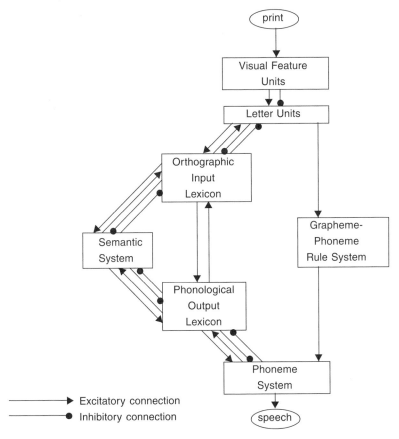

Figure 2.4. Coltheart et al.'s (2001) dual-route cascaded model of visual word recognition and reading aloud. This model is exemplary of many traditional models of visual word recognition, based on localist representations. First, the letters of the presented words are identified. These letter representations then activate entries in the orthographic lexicon and are converted simultaneously into their most likely sounds (phonemes). The phonemes feed into a phonological lexicon, which contains the spoken representations of all known words. Reading aloud of words occurs through a combination of direct grapheme-phoneme conversions and the activation of known word forms in the lexicons. Lexical decision is based on activation within the orthographic and/or the phonological lexicon. Notice that although the model contains a third route through the semantic system, this route is not believed to be fast enough to influence word naming or lexical decision times. For this reason, it has not yet been implemented in the working, computational model. Copyright © 2001 by the American Psychological Association. Reprinted with permission.

A third reason for separating the lexical from the semantic system is that humans can do quite some processing of words without understanding them. For instance, a long series of neuropsychological patients have been described who had severe difficulties matching visually presented words to pictures but who nonetheless knew very well which letter sequences formed existing words and which formed nonwords. In addition, they could read the words aloud, even when the words contained irregular letter sound correspondences, as in *blood, climb,* and *come* (Coltheart, in press; Gerhand, 2002).

Although the distinction between word form and word meaning is still dominant in models of visual word recognition, it has been criticized by Seidenberg and McClelland (1989). In their distributed model of visual word recognition (see Figure 2.5), word knowledge no longer begins when the activation of an entry in the orthographic lexicon exceeds a certain threshold but consists of the co-activation of processing units that encode the orthographic, phonological, and semantic properties of a word (see also Van Orden, Pennington, & Stone, 1990). A visual word activates a number of orthographic units representing the sequence of input letters. This activation spreads to the semantic and the phonological units that are connected to the activated orthographic units and feeds back until a stable state is reached. In addition, the various units are no longer devoted to single words (i.e., there are no localist representations). Each unit is activated by many words, and the identity of a word is determined by a pattern of activation across multiple units. Seidenberg and McClelland (1989) showed that many features of human visual word recognition can be simulated with such a model that no longer contains a visual lexicon.

With respect to the recognition of number words, the large majority of existing models have taken inspiration from the Coltheart et al. model (Figure 2.4) and, therefore, contain an orthographic lexicon with localist representations (for a review, see Campbell's chapter in this book). A major exception has been Campbell (1994) who defended a view very similar to Seidenberg and McClelland's. According to his multiple encoding view, numbers are simultaneously encoded in multiple ways (analogue, verbal, arabic) through a process of activation that automatically dissipates. In this model, number recognition depends on the pattern of co-activation of the different codes rather than on the activation of one particular, localist code.

The second discussion within the literature of visual word recognition that is pertinent to number recognition, has to do with the question of how central the meaning system is within

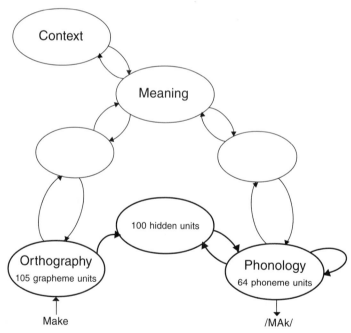

Figure 2.5. Seidenberg and McClelland's (1989) triangular model of visual word processing (as implemented by Plaut et al., 1996). In this model, there is no longer a lexicon, where all known word forms are stored in dedicated (localist) units. Instead, information about words is stored in collections of units in the orthographic, the phonological, and the meaning layers that are co-activated. The individual units are activated (to a different extent) by many different words. In this model, the activation of the meaning of words is thought to be central in word processing. However, this part of the model has not yet been implemented and does not seem necessary to simulate the basic findings of word naming and lexical decision.

the language architecture. To an outsider, this may seem a strange discussion, because what else is (visual) word recognition for than to access the meaning of a written message? However, researchers discovered that for the two tasks they usually ask participants to perform, meaning can be more or less discarded to explain the results. These tasks are the naming of visually presented, isolated words (word naming) and deciding whether or not a presented string of letters forms a correct English word (lexical decision). For word naming, traditionally three routes have been postulated (see Figure 2.4; but also see Seidenberg & McClelland (Figure 2.5) who distinguished between two routes only). First, there is a direct conversion from letters to sounds, making it possible to name unknown sequences of letters, such as nonwords. The second route goes from the orthographic input lexicon to a phonological output lexicon, enabling the reader to correctly pronounce irregular words such as *come*. Finally, the third route goes from the orthographic input lexicon, through the semantic system, to the phonological output lexicon. However, it is usually assumed that this route is too slow to affect performance. Hence, this route has not been implemented in any of the existing computational models of word naming. Similarly, lexical decision times have been explained by focusing on the activity within the word-form lexicon, with little or no contribution from the words' meanings.

In general, findings with verbal numerals are well in line with the assumption of asemantic routes in visual word processing. Fias, Reynvoet, and Brysbaert (2001), for instance, presented a verbal numeral and an arabic numeral on the same display. Participants were asked to name the verbal numeral and to ignore the arabic numeral. They were perfectly capable of doing so, as evidenced by the fact that the naming latencies were the same when the arabic numerals referred to different magnitudes than the verbal numerals (e.g., *six*–5) as when they referred to the same magnitudes (e.g., *six*–6). In contrast, when the participants had to make a response that involved the meaning of the verbal numerals (i.e., indicate whether the verbal numeral was odd or even), they showed faster responses when both numbers referred to the same magnitude than when they referred to different magnitudes. Other evidence for the existence of nonsemantic processing routes for verbal numerals comes from the finding that participants do not need more time to indicate that *eight* is written in small letters and *two* in large letters than to indicate that *eight* is written in large letters and *two* in small letters, whereas they do show such a magnitude-size congruity effect with arabic numerals and other types of nonalphabetic stimuli (e.g., Ito & Hatta, 2003; see the section on arabic numerals for more information about this task).

On the other hand, research on the processing of verbal numerals has also shown that although the semantically mediated route is slightly slower in the naming of words, its importance must not be underestimated within the traditional three-route model. Reynvoet, Brysbaert, and Fias (2002), for instance, showed that the naming of verbal numerals was primed by arabic numerals with a close value. That is, participants named the target word *five* faster when 115 ms before the arabic primes *4* or *6* had been presented tachistoscopically than when the arabic primes *2* or *8* had been presented (see the section on arabic numerals for more information about this distance-related priming effect). Subsequent research showed that the same effect was obtained with masked primes presented a mere 43 ms before the targets (Reynvoet & Brysbaert, in press). This cross-notation priming effect suggests that it does not take much to preactivate the number magnitude route enough to find semantically mediated effects in the naming of verbal numerals.

Other evidence of the importance of the semantically mediated route in the naming of verbal numerals comes from Cappelletti, Kopelman, and Butterworth (2001). They reported the case of a semantic dementia patient who could hardly read words any more (21% of the words with regular letter-sound mappings, such as *must*; and 12% of the words with irregular mappings, such as *pint*) but who was flawless at reading verbal numerals, due to spared numerical knowledge. Spared numerical knowledge is also often reported in Alzheimer's disease and is in line with the finding that numerical knowledge is represented separately from many other types of semantic knowledge in the brain (e.g., Pesenti et al., 2000; see also Chapter 25 of this book).

Finally, the third discussion in the visual word recognition literature that has a particular bearing on number processing, is the question of how morphologically complex words are recognized. In number reading, only the verbal numerals from *zero* to *twelve* are without question monomorphemic (i.e., consisting of one meaning unit only). In contrast, words like *twenty-one* and *one-hundred twenty-six* are clearly polymorphemic (i.e., contain at least two morphemes). Inbetween, there are some number names for which it is not clear whether they can be considered as polymorphemic because their constituents are different from the original words (e.g., *thirteen, twenty, fifty, . . . [instead of threeten, twoty, and fivety]*). There are two types of clear polymorphemic number words. The first are derivations obtained by adding a suffix to a simple number word (e.g., *sixty, seventy*). The second are compound words that are obtained by combining two or more words (e.g., *twenty-one*). Theoretically, morphologically complex words can be processed in two ways (see, e.g., Bertram & Hyona, 2003). Either they can be decomposed into their constituents which are then used to compute the meaning, or they can be stored as a whole in the mental lexicon. Researchers have offered quite divergent ideas about the relative importance of the two processing pathways and the factors that determine the balance. Variables that have been proposed are semantic transparency, word frequency, and the length of the constituting words. Morphologically complex words are more likely to be stored and retrieved as a whole when the semantic relation between the word and the constituents is unclear (i.e., more likely for *honeymoon* than for *honeybee*), when the complex word is frequently encountered (i.e, more likely for *honeybee* than for *honeyfungus*), and when the complex word is short (i.e., more likely for *eyelid* than for *watercourse*). These factors allow us to predict that verbal numerals like *fifteen* and *twenty* (high-frequency, short, no clear relationship between the constituents and the complex word) are more likely to be recognized as a whole than numerals like *seventy* and *ninety* (lower-frequency, semantically transparent) and that words like *ninety-eight* (long, low-frequency) are bound to be processed through decomposition. However, thus far, virtually no research has been done on this topic.

All in all, research on the processing of written verbal numerals, even though limited, has returned findings that are well in line with what can be expected on the basis of what is known about the processing of visually presented words in general. Most importantly, there is evidence that for many tasks (e.g., number naming and decisions about the size of number words) the meaning of verbal numerals is not activated fast enough to influence the response. This is in line with the assumption of nonsemantically mediated routes in models of word processing, an assumption made by both localist (Figure 2.4) and distributed (Figure 2.5) models. As the majority of verbal numerals consist of more than one morpheme, any comprehensive theory of verbal numeral recognition will have to address the question of how morphologically complex words are recognized, an issue that has been overlooked so far.

RECOGNIZING ARABIC NUMERALS

The invention and application of arabic (actually Hindi) numerals has further advanced the human numerical competence (Ifrah, 1998). It is widely assumed that the use of roman numerals prevented the Romans from attaining a mathematical sophistication that matches the sophistication they reached in other knowledge areas (just try to solve the problem CMIX times LI). Interesting features of arabic numerals are the use of a base 10 throughout (remember that the base-ten structure is not completely present in many verbal number systems; see Miller's Chapter 10 for the implications of this) and the use of place coding. Units are always written rightmost, tens are second, hundreds third, and so on. This way of coding required the invention of the digit 0, for instance, to represent *909* (nine hundreds and nine units, no tens). The power of the arabic notation can be seen in the fact that even for simple arithmetic problems involving the addition or multiplication of single digits, participants are much faster and more accurate when the numerals are presented as digits rather than as words (Campbell, 1994; Noel et al., 1997), even when the words are spoken (LeFevre et al., 2001).

The existence of arabic numerals begs the question of how they are recognized. As for the verbal numerals, a distinction must be made between small numbers and large numbers. Nearly all numerals with three digits or more require a decomposition (parsing) process. There is nobody defending the idea that a numeral like 4253 with its associated magnitude is stored as a whole in the human brain. The only known exception to this parsing requirement is when a complex numeral is frequently used as a nominal label to refer to a particular entity (e.g., when the participant's car is a Peugeot 206, when the participant is heavily interested in Boeing 747, or when the participant is a postman working near the Belgian village of Darion, which has the postal code 4253). For these familiar complex numbers, there is some evidence that they may be stored holistically, as it is possible to prime them with their associated words (e.g., the number 206 is recognized faster after the tachistoscopically presented prime Peugeot than after the tachistoscopically presented prime Boeing; Alameda, Cuetos, & Brysbaert, 2003; Delazer & Girelli, 1997). In general, however, complex numbers must be decomposed into their constituents, and this is a process that is prone to brain damage (due to a stroke or to dementia). Many patients with numerical problems have difficulties reading and writing complex arabic numerals correctly (e.g., writing three hundred and four as 3004).

Researchers largely agree that small numbers are recognized as a whole but disagree about (1) whether these small numbers are limited to single digits or whether they also include two-digit numbers (12, 20, 88) and (2) whether semantic activation is pivotal for the processing of arabic numerals. Before homing in on these two discussions, I will first review the major empirical findings about the processing of small arabic numerals.

A first robust finding is that the processing is more demanding for larger numbers than for smaller numbers. This is already true for digits. It is easier to indicate which is the smaller of the pair 2–3 than to indicate which is the smaller of the pair 8–9. It is also easier to calculate 2 + 3 and 2 × 3 than 8 + 9 and 8 × 9. Brysbaert (1995) even found a robust number magnitude effect in a short-term memory experiment. In this experiment, participants first had to read three arabic numerals going from 0 to 99, and then to look at a fourth arabic numeral and to decide whether this fourth numeral was part of the initial set: yes or no. Eye movements of the participants were tracked, and the time participants needed to store the numeral in short-term memory before they proceeded to the next numeral was measured. Figure 2.6 shows the average reading time for the first numeral seen by the participants as a function of number magnitude. The most important variable to predict the reading times turned out to be the logarithm of the number magnitude, in line with the predictions of the compressed number line model (Dehaene, 1992).

A second robust finding in arabic numeral processing is that when two numbers are processed together, processing times are influenced by the distance between the numbers. This is particularly clear when both numbers have to be compared, as it is much easier to say which digit is the smaller for the pair 2–8 than for the pair 2–3. More precisely, decision times are a function of the logarithm of the distance between the two numbers (see Figure 2.7). Another distance-related effect that has been described is the number priming effect. A target digit is recognized faster when it follows a (tachistoscopically presented) prime with a close value than when it follows a prime with a more distant value. Figure 2.8 shows data obtained by Reynvoet and Brysbaert (1999) with a number naming task and masked primes. Response latencies were fastest when prime and target were the same (e.g., 5 and 5; the font size was manipulated in order to diminish the physical overlap of the stimuli). They were significantly slower when prime and target differed by one unit (e.g., 4 or 6 and 5) and again significantly slower when the distance was 2 or 3. With non-tachistoscopic presentation of the prime, the priming is obtained over a range of more than 10 units (Brysbaert, 1995); with tachistoscopic presentation

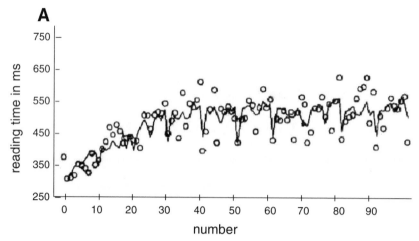

Figure 2.6. Reading times for arabic numerals ranging from 0 to 99 in a short-term memory task. Circles indicate the observed data; lines indicate the predicted times on the basis of the logarithm of number magnitude, number frequency, and the number of syllables in the number name. Figure copied from Brysbaert. Copyright © 1995 by the American Psychological Association. Adapted with permission.

of the prime, it usually ends at a distance of 3. A further intriguing aspect of the distance-related priming effect is that it is symmetric. That is, the priming is equally strong from 6 on 5 as from 4 on 5, despite the fact that the associative strength between 4 and 5 is stronger than between 6 and 5 (when asked to say the first word that comes to mind, participants are more likely to say *five* after hearing *four* than after hearing *six*). A last interesting aspect about the priming effect is that it is equally strong across notations as within notations (Reynvoet et

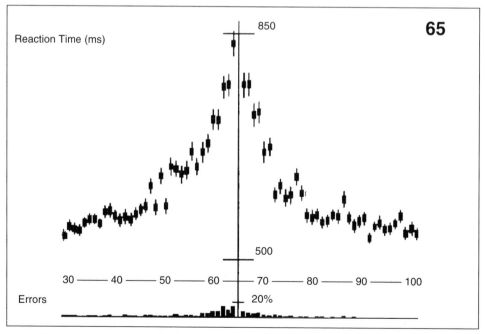

Figure 2.7. Time mathematically literate adults need to indicate whether a two-digit arabic numeral is larger or smaller than a fixed standard of 65. Figure copied from Dehaene et al. Copyright © 1990 by the American Psychological Association. Adapted with permission.

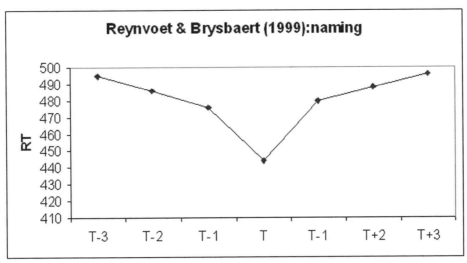

Figure 2.8. Time participants need to name an arabic numeral as a function of the value of the preceding prime. Naming latencies are fastest when prime and target have the same value (e.g., 9–9). They are slightly slower when the prime is one unit less than the target (e.g., 8–9) or one unit more (e.g., 10–9). Reaction times are again slower when the distance between prime and target is 2 and when it is 3 (at which point the priming effect for tachistoscopically presented primes levels off). The extra priming effect observed when prime and target have the same value (identity priming) is present only when prime and target are displayed in the same modality (e.g., prime and target in arabic notation). When prime and target are presented in different formats (e.g., prime is verbal, target is arabic), the net priming effect reduces to what can be expected solely on the basis of the distance between prime and target. Data from Reynvoet & Brysbaert (1999).

al., 2002). The effect of the prime 6 on the arabic target 5 is the same whether the prime is presented in arabic notation or in verbal notation. This finding has been interpreted as evidence that the interaction between prime and target occurs at an abstract, notation-independent level. The most often cited candidate is the number line of analog magnitudes.

A third major finding about the processing of arabic numerals is that the semantic magnitude information of the numeral is activated more rapidly than is the case for verbal numerals. Because of this feature, it is nearly impossible to design a task with arabic input that is not affected by the meaning of the numeral. Henik and Tzelgov (1982) designed one of the first studies that demonstrated this aspect of arabic numeral processing. They asked participants to indicate which numeral of a presented pair of digits had the larger physical size (see also Ito & Hatta, 2003, discussed above). Participants found it more difficult to indicate that 2 was the larger in the pair 2–8 than to indicate that 8 was the larger in the pair 2–8, thereby effectively showing a Stroop-like interference effect between the numerical size (which was to be ignored) and the physical size. Similar findings have been reported in a counting task. It is easier to say that four digits are present in the stimulus *4 4 4 4* than in the stimulus *3 3 3 3* (Pavese & Umilta, 1998).

People in western cultures have a strong tendency to associate small numbers with left and large numbers with right (Dehaene et al., 1993; see also the chapter by Fias & Fischer). When participants have to indicate whether a number is odd or even, they can do so faster with the left hand to small numbers (e.g., 1, 3) and with the right hand to large numbers (e.g., 6, 8; see Figure 2.9). This effect has been linked to the reading direction of the participants and/or to the way in which ordered continua (such as the number line) are taught in school. In the parity judgment task, there is an additional tendency to associate odd numbers with left-hand responses and even numbers with right-hand responses (Nuerk et al., 2004).

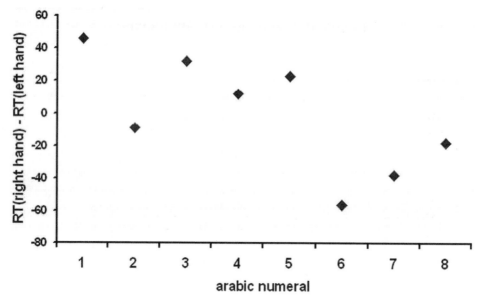

Figure 2.9. Figure illustrating the findings that in western cultures (1) small numbers are preferentially associated with left-hand responses and large numbers with right-hand responses and (2) that odd numbers are preferentially associated with left-hand responses and even numbers with right-hand responses. The figure shows the results of an experiment in which participants had to indicate whether a presented arabic numeral ranging from 1 to 8 was odd or even by pressing with the left or the right hand. The figure shows the differences in RT of right-hand responses minus that of left-hand responses. When left-hand responses were faster than right hand responses, this difference score is positive, which was the case for the small numbers. For the numbers 5–8, the right-hand responses were faster than the left-hand responses, giving rise to negative difference scores. The difference scores in general were also more negative for the even numbers (2, 4, 6, and 8) than for the odd numbers, indicating that the right-hand responses were faster for these numbers. Data from Nuerk et al. (2004).

Some of the above effects have been used to try to find out whether two-digit arabic numerals are processed as a whole or as a syntactic combination of tens and units (see the first issue of discussion mentioned at the beginning of this section). If these numbers are processed as a whole, one would expect them to form some kind of continuous number line as a function of their magnitude. On the other hand, if they are stored as combinations of tens and units, one would expect discontinuities at the transition from one ten to the next. As it has turned out, researchers have observed evidence for both views.

Brysbaert (1995) argued that the reading times shown in Figure 2.6 strongly suggested that all numerals between 1 and 99 are part of a single compressed number line. Similarly, Dehaene et al. (1990) obtained a logarithmic distance effect in a magnitude comparison of two-digit numbers (in which participants had to indicate whether numerals like 60 and 59 were smaller than 65; see Figure 2.7) and argued on the basis of this that two-digit numbers were compared by looking at the analog magnitude they represented and not by looking at the individual digits (in which case it would be much easier to decide that 59 is smaller than 65 than that 60 is smaller than 65, because the former pair of numbers starts with different digits). Reynvoet and Brysbaert (1998) wondered whether they would find the same priming effect from 10 on 9 as from 8 on 9 and, having found so, also concluded that units and teens were part of the same continuum. Finally, Dehaene et al. (1993) noted that the small-left and large-right association extended over the boundary of units and teens and also concluded that they were part of the same number line.

On the other hand, there are findings that cannot easily be explained by the assumption of a single number line going from 1 to 99 and that seem to indicate that two-digit arabic numerals are rapidly decomposed into a syntactic structure of tens and units (a view most strongly defended by McCloskey [1992]). Nuerk, Weger, and Willmes (2001) showed that in the comparison of two-digit number pairs, not only the distance between the numbers (Dehaene et al. 1990) but also whether or not both numbers are unit-ten compatible count. A number pair was defined as compatible if the magnitude comparison of the tens and the magnitude comparison of the units led to the same response (e.g., 52 and 67 are compatible because 5 < 6 and 2 < 7) and as incompatible if this was not the case (e.g., 47 and 62 are incompatible because 4 < 6 but 7 > 2). Nuerk et al. (2001) observed a significant compatibility effect. Participants were faster to indicate that 52 < 67 than that 47 < 62, even though the distances between the numbers are the same. This compatibility effect suggests that the tens and the units were compared in parallel, a finding which is more in line with the view that number magnitudes are represented as composites of powers of 10 (i.e., the meaning of the numeral 28 is represented as $\{2\} \times \{10^1\} + \{8\} \times \{10^0\}$). Other evidence for a rapid decomposition of two-digit arabic numerals into powers of 10 was recently reported by Ratinck, Brysbaert, and Fias (in press). These authors asked participants to name two-digit arabic numerals, which were preceded by tachistoscopically presented primes. They not only observed the expected distance-related priming effect (e.g., prime 37 and target 38) but also priming when the prime and the target shared a single digit in the tens or the units position (e.g., primes 28 and 34 for target 38). In addition, there was an *interference* effect when prime and target shared a digit on different positions (e.g., primes 82, 43, and 83 for target 38).

One way of interpreting the divergent findings on the processing of two-digit arabic numerals (recognized as a whole or as a combination of powers of 10) is to assume that both types of processing occur in parallel. Such a model has been proposed by Dehaene and colleagues (e.g., Dehaene, 1992; Dehaene & Cohen, 1995). In this model, arabic numerals simultaneously activate an analogue magnitude representation on the number line and a visual arabic number form in which numbers are represented as strings of digits on an internal visuo-spatial scratchpad. Another idea could be that simultaneously with the analogue magnitude, a more precise semantic representation consisting of powers of ten is built. This representation is needed, anyway, for the processing and storing of more complex numbers (i.e., integers with more than two digits and real numbers with multidigit precision; see the parsing process mentioned above).

Dehaene's model brings us to the second point of discussion in the literature: whether there exists a lexicon for arabic numerals similar to the orthographic lexicon for visual word recognition, so that quite some processing of arabic numerals can be done before the meaning is fully activated. Dehaene and colleagues claim there is.

For instance, Cohen et al. (1994) described a patient who had difficulties reading complex numbers, except when they were highly familiar (e.g., 1945). They attributed this spared capacity to the existence of an input lexicon for familiar arabic numerals, which has direct, nonsemantic connections to the speech output. Similarly, Dehaene and Cohen (1977) described a patient who could name digits, despite the fact that her number understanding was impaired (she made 20% errors when asked to indicate whether digits were larger or smaller than a standard). Also in the literature of visual word recognition, it had been claimed that digits, just like all other logographic symbols in texts (abbreviations, punctuation marks, special characters), are part of the orthographic input lexicon used for text reading (e.g., Coltheart, 1978). On the other hand, there is very little empirical support for nonsemantically mediated processing in arabic numerals. As reviewed above, the meaning of a number can easily be ignored in a font-size judgment task when the number is presented as an alphabetic word (i.e., deciding which is the physically smaller stimulus is not more difficult for the pair eight-two than for the pair eight-two). However, this is much less easy (and maybe impossible) when the numbers are presented in arabic format or in another logographic script (Henik & Tzelgov, 1982; Ito & Hatta, 2003 (arabic numerals and Kanji words); Pansky & Algom, 1999). Similarly, Fias et al.

(2001) reported that verbal numerals could be read without any interference from an arabic distractor on the same display. However, the very same study showed that this was not true for the naming of digits: naming latencies to the numeral 5 were longer when the distractor was *four* than when it was *five*.

Because of the rapid and omnipresent activation of the semantic information, it has been claimed that the processing of arabic numerals resembles more the processing of pictures than the processing of words (e.g., Brysbaert, Fias, & Reynvoet, 2000; Fias, 2001; Fias et al., 2001; McCloskey, 1992). In theories of picture processing, it is widely assumed that some perceptual form processing is needed before the meaning can be activated, but the idea of an independent picture lexicon directly connected to the speech output has not found empirical support (e.g., Hodges & Greene, 1998). In this respect, it is important to keep in mind that the meaning of arabic numerals need not be confined to magnitude information (although this obviously is the most important semantic attribute of numbers). It can also be encyclopedic or episodic information related to the arabic numeral, certainly when the numeral is often used as a non-quantitative label (as in Boeing 747 or in the number year 1992). This could explain some of the remaining abilities of neuropsychological patients to name arabic numerals of which they no longer know the exact magnitude (Cohen et al., 1994; Dehaene & Cohen, 1997).

Brysbaert, Fias, and Reynvoet (2000) listed some reasons why they thought the creation of a full-fledged lexicon was less compelling for the recognition of arabic numerals than for the recognition of visual words (see also Seidenberg & McClelland [1989] for the reasons why they claim a lexicon is not needed, not even for the recognition of words). For a start, printed words are quite long combinations of letters, which nevertheless have to be read within roughly a third of a second. Indeed, one of the most striking characteristics of the visual word recognition system is that it does not take notably longer to read a nine-letter word than a three-letter word (e.g., compare *lucrative* and *rat*). The same is not true for arabic numerals: as soon as the number length exceeds two digits, response latencies increase dramatically, indicative of a cumbersome parsing process (e.g., compare *582617493* and *617*). Second, all combinations of arabic digits have a meaning, as opposed to only a very few of all possible letter combinations. Third, the meaning of arabic numerals is always the same, independent of the context (as opposed to words; see the previous section). Fourth, arabic numerals only exist in one visual form, whereas words can both be written and spoken and are language-dependent (for those who master more than one language). Finally, more information is attached to words than simply their meaning. In many languages, words have a gender, can differ in number, and can only take certain syntactic roles within a sentence. Many authors believe this word-form related information is stored in the lexicon. For these reasons, the creation of a lexical system next to a word-meaning system seems more compelling for verbal numerals than for arabic numerals. Arabic numerals can in principle be recognized like objects (or pictures of them): the stimulus is decomposed into a structural description of perceptual features, which activates the corresponding semantic information.

The difference between word and digit processing has also been documented in the neuropsychological literature, in which patients have been described who could no longer read printed words (alexia) but could still recognize arabic numerals and do some rather sophisticated processing on them (e.g., Cohen & Dehaene, 2000). Intriguingly, Pesenti et al. (2000) also described a patient who had major difficulties identifying visually presented objects (visual agnosia) but who nevertheless read arabic numerals fluently. Apparently, the similarities in the processing of pictures and arabic numerals do not imply that they are functionally identical (maybe because the meaning of numbers and the meaning of visual objects are different sources of knowledge?).

All in all, recent research on the recognition of small arabic numerals has revealed a rather intriguing picture. First, digits activate their meaning faster than words and also seem to require semantic mediation for further processing. In this respect, their processing is closer to that of picture recognition than to that of word processing. The meaning primarily refers to the magnitude of the numeral, but can also involve encyclopedic and episodic knowledge associated with the numeral certainly if the numeral is frequently used in a nonquantitative way. Arabic numerals of three digits and more virtually always need to be parsed (unless they are familiar labels), a process that is rather demanding and highly susceptible to brain damage. Two-digit numbers form a kind of in-between category with quite some evidence for holistic processing but also some signs of decomposition into tens and units.

CONCLUSION

I have reviewed the basic findings in number recognition and their implications for our views of what is happening. Rather than giving a personalized and simplified account, I have tried to keep an eye for the major discussions that are going on, although inevitably I biased the text toward my own convictions. A summary of these convictions is shown in Figure 2.10. For each of the three types of input, I have tried to sketch a general outline of the steps that are likely to be involved. Attentive readers can, on the basis of the various uncertainties that have been discussed, build their own version of the model (and test this).

A first choice is to divide the semantic number system in a part dedicated to the processing of the magnitude of the numerical input, and a part dedicated to the encyclopedic and episodic knowledge associated with numbers. In the number magnitude system, as before (Brysbaert, 1995), I make a distinction between the recognition of the core numbers and the precise representation of each and every possible number (simple and complex), probably in a base-10 format. The core numbers consist of the integers 1–99 (the number line) and some basic multipliers (hundred, thousand, etc.).

For the perception of numerosities in analogue displays, I postulate a visual feature detection stage (needed for the separation of the stimulus from the background) directly connected to the compressed, analogue number line. This is a simplification, as it does not deal with the processes needed for the sequential counting of the elements in a display that is shown long enough. Another extension of the model would be the addition of a connection between the visual feature units and stored mental images of triangles, faces of dice, and so on, which are probably involved in the apprehension of numerosities presented in a familiar, canonical form.

For the recognition of verbal numerals, I have copied the Coltheart et al. (2001) model and connected it to the semantic system. As individual number words always represent core numbers, only connections between the orthographic input lexicon and the core numbers are postulated. For the same reason, no direct connections between the orthographic input lexicon and the encyclopedic/episodic information are accepted (e.g., the stimulus "two hundred and six" is not directly associated with a Peugeot car; this requires mediation of the number magnitude system). Another choice that has been made is to postulate the feedback mechanisms not from the number line but from the extended number system (which has more precise representations, certainly for numbers beyond the subitizing range). Because the verbal output for many numbers requires a sequence of multiple words, I have included Levelt et al.'s (1999) stage of lemma retrieval and syntactic parsing between the number magnitude system and the phonological output system.

Arabic numerals are encoded in two different ways: as a sequence of position-specific digits and as a percept of the complete numeral (probably limited to numerals of four digits, the maximum capacity of visual short-term memory). The position-specific digits activate the number line and the extended number magnitude system in parallel (in line with the finding that all types of numerical tasks are easier with arabic input than with verbal input). In addition, the mental images of familiar numbers activate associated information in semantic and episodic memory.

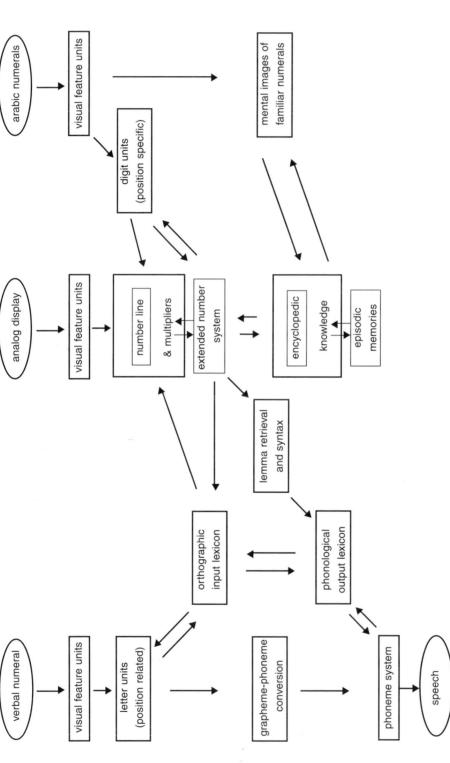

Figure 2.10. A model of number recognition in verbal, analog, and arabic format. Note that the three boxes with visual feature units refer to the same perceptual processes. This box has been drawn anew for each input format to increase the clarity of the graph. Also note that the verbal system is the same as in Figure 2.4. This is a choice for localist representations (against the model presented in Figure 2.5). Other noteworthy choices are: (1) verbal numerals do not activate representations in the extended number system directly; (2) arabic numerals do, but this is probably limited given the laborious parsing that is needed for numerals of more than 2 digits; (3) there is no feedback from the number line; (4) there is no lexicon for arabic numerals; but (5) there is a store of percepts of arabic numerals similar to the images we have of other visual pictorial stimuli. This store (6) can activate associated memories in semantic and episodic memory.

A justified criticism against the box-and-arrow type of model proposed in Figure 2.10 is that it offers little explanation of the specific processes involved. There is a big gap between a general, verbal description of the processes in the different boxes and arrows and the actual implementation of them, which would make the model detailed enough to quantitatively simulate the various empirical benchmarks that have been listed in the present chapter. This will be the major challenge for the coming years.

REFERENCES

Alameda, J. R., Cuetos, F., & Brysbaert, M. (2003). The number 747 is named faster after seeing Boeing than after seeing Levis: Associative priming is the processing of multi-digit Arabic numerals. *Quarterly Journal of Experimental Psychology, 56A,* 1009–1019.

Antell, S. E., & Keating, D. P. (1983). Perception of numerical invariance in neonates. *Child Development, 54,* 695–701.

Balota, D. A. (1994). Visual word recognition: The journey from features to meaning. In M. A. Gernsbacher (Ed.), *Handbook of psycholinguistics* (pp. 303–358). San Diego: Academic Press.

Bertram, R., & Hyona, J. (2003). The length of a complex word modifies the role of morphological structure: Evidence from eye movements when reading short and long Finnish compounds. *Journal of Memory and Language, 48,* 615–634.

Bonin, P., Peereman, R., & Fayol, M. (2001). Do phonological codes constrain the selection of orthographic codes in written picture naming? *Journal of Memory and Language, 45,* 688–720.

Brysbaert, M. (1995). Arabic number reading: On the nature of the numerical scale and the origin of phonological recoding. *Journal of Experimental Psychology: General, 124,* 434–452.

Brysbaert, M., Fias, W., & Reynvoet, B. (2000). The issue of semantic mediation in word and number naming. In F. Columbus (Ed.), *Advances in psychological research, Volume I* (pp. 181–200). Huntington, NY: Nova Science Publishers.

Butterworth, B. (1999). *The mathematical brain.* London: Macmillan.

Campbell, J. I. D. (1994). Architectures for numerical cognition. *Cognition, 53,* 1–44.

Cappelletti, M., Butterworth, B., & Kopelman, M. (2001). Spared numerical abilities in a case of semantic dementia. *Neuropsychologia, 39,* 1224–1239.

Cohen, L., & Dehaene, S. (2000). Calculating without reading: Unsuspected residual abilities in pure alexia. *Cognitive Neuropsychology, 17,* 563–583.

Cohen, L., Dehaene, S., & Verstichel, P. (1994). Number words and number non-words—A case of deep dyslexia extending to Arabic numerals. *Brain, 117,* 267–279.

Coltheart, M. (1978). Lexical access in simple reading tasks. In G. Underwood (Ed.), *Strategies of information processing* (pp. 151–216). London: Academic Press.

Coltheart, M. (in press). Are there lexicons? *Quarterly Journal of Experimental Psychology (A).*

Coltheart, M., Rastle, K., Perry, C., Langdon, R., & Ziegler, J. C. (2001). DRC: A dual route cascaded model of visual word recognition and reading aloud. *Psychological Review, 108,* 204–256.

Dehaene, S. (1992). Varieties of numerical abilities. *Cognition, 44,* 1–42.

Dehaene, S., Bossini, S., & Giraux, P. (1993). The mental representation of parity and number magnitude. *Journal of Experimental Psychology: General, 122,* 371–396.

Dehaene, S., & Changeux, J. P. (1993). Development of elementary numerical abilities: A neuronal model. *Journal of Cognitive Neuroscience, 5,* 390–407.

Dehaene, S., & Cohen, L. (1995). Towards an anatomical and functional model of number processing. *Mathematical Cognition, 1,* 83–120.

Dehaene, S., & Cohen, L. (1997). Cerebral pathways for calculation: Double dissociation between rote verbal and quantitative knowledge of arithmetic. *Cortex, 33,* 219–250.

Dehaene, S., Dehaene-Lambertz, G., & Cohen, L. (1998). Abstract representations of numbers in the animal and human brain. *Trends in Neurosciences, 21,* 355–361.

Dehaene, S., Dupoux, E., & Mehler, J. (1990). Is numerical comparison digital? Analogical and symbolic effects in two-digit number comparison. *Journal of Experimental Psychology: Human Perception and Performance, 16,* 626–641.

Delazer, M., & Girelli, L. (1997). When "Alfa Romeo" facilitates 164: Semantic effects in verbal number production. *Neurocase, 3,* 461–475.

Feigenson, L., Carey, S., & Hauser, M. (2002). The representations underlying infants' choice of more: Object files versus analog magnitudes. *Psychological Science, 13,* 150–156.

Feigenson, L., Carey, S., & Spelke, E. (2002). Infants' discrimination of number vs. continuous extent. *Cognitive Psychology, 44,* 33–66.

Fias, W. (2001). Two routes for the processing of verbal numerals: Evidence from the SNARC effect. *Psychological Research, 65,* 250–259.

Fias, W., Brysbaert, M., Geypens, F., & d'Ydewalle, G. (1996). The importance of magnitude information in numerical processing: Evidence from the SNARC effect. *Mathematical Cognition, 2,* 95–110.

Fias, W., Reynvoet, B., & Brysbaert, M. (2001). Are Arabic numerals processed as pictures in a Stroop interference task? *Psychological Research, 65,* 242–249.

Gallistel C. R., & Gelman, R. (1992). Preverbal and verbal counting and computation. *Cognition, 44 (1–2),* 43–74.

Gelman, R. & Gallistel, C. R. (1978). *The child's understanding of number.* Cambridge, MA: Harvard University Press.

Gerhand, S. (2001). Routes to reading: a report of a non-semantic reader with equivalent performance on regular and exception words. *Neuropsychologia, 39,* 1473–1484.

Harley, T. A. (2001). *The psychology of language: From data to theory* (2nd ed.). Hove: Psychology Press.

Henik, A., & Tzelgov, J. (1982). Is 3 greater than 5: The relation between physical and semantic size in comparison tasks. *Memory & Cognition, 10,* 389–395.

Hodges, J .R., & Greene, J. D. W. (1998). Knowing about people and naming them: Can Alzheimer's disease patients do one without the other? *Quarterly Journal of Experimental Psychology (A)*, *51*, 121-134.

Ifrah, G. (1998). *The universal history of numbers: from pre-history to the invention of the computer*. London: Collins and Harvill Press.

Ito, Y. & Hatta, T. (2003). Semantic processing of Arabic, Kanji, and Kana numbers: Evidence from interference in physical and numerical size judgments. *Memory & Cognition*, *31*, 360-368.

Jensen, E. M., Reese, E. P., & Reese, T. W. (1950). The subitizing and counting of visually presented fields of dots. *Journal of Psychology*, *30*, 363-392.

Kaufman, E. L., Lord, M. W., Reese, T. W., & Volkmann, J. (1949). The discrimination of visual number. *American Journal of Psychology*, *62*, 498-525.

Krueger, L. E. (1982). Single judgments of numerosity. *Perception & Psychophysics*, *31*, 175-182.

Lefevre, J. A., Lei, Q. W., Smith-Chant, B. L., & Mullins, D. B. (2001). Multiplication by eye and by ear for Chinese-speaking and English-speaking adults. *Canadian Journal of Experimental Psychology*, *55*, 277-284.

Levelt, W. J. M, Roelofs, A., & Meyer, A. S. (1999). A theory of lexical access in speech production. *Behavioral and Brain Sciences*, *22*, 1-75.

Logan, G. D., & Zbrodoff, N. J. (2003). Subitizing and similarity: Toward a pattern-matching theory of enumeration. *Psychonomic Bulletin & Review*, *10*, 676-682.

Mandler, G., & Shebo, B. J. (1982). Subitizing: An analysis of its component processes. *Journal of Experimental Psychology: General*, *111*, 1-22.

McCloskey, M. (1992). Cognitive mechanisms in numerical processing: evidence from acquired dyscalculia. *Cognition*, *44*, 107-157.

McCloskey, M., & Macaruso, P. (1995). Representing and using numerical information. *American Psychologist*, *50*, 351-363.

McQueen, J. M. (2004). Speech perception. In K. Lamberts & R. Goldstone (Eds.), *The handbook of cognition*. London: Sage Publications.

Mix, K. S., Huttenlocher, J., & Levince, S. C. (2002). Multiple cues for quantification in infancy: Is number one of them? *Psychological Bulletin*, *128*, 278-294.

Morton, J. (1979). Facilitation in word recognition: Experiments causing change in the logogen model. In P. A. Kolers, M. E. Wrolstad, & H. Bouma (Eds.), *Processing of visible language* (pp. 259-268). New York: Plenum.

Noël, M. P., Fias, W., & Brysbaert, M. (1997). About the influence of the presentation format on arithmetical-fact retrieval processes. *Cognition*, *63*, 335-374.

Nuerk, H. C., Iversen, W., & Willmes, K. (2004). Notation modulation of the SNARC and the MARC (linguistic markedness of response codes) effects. *Quarterly Journal of Experimental Psychology*, *57A*, 835-863.

Nuerk, H, C., Weger, U., & Willmes, K. (2001). Decade breaks in the mental number line? Putting the tens and the units back in different bins. *Cognition*, *82*, 25-33.

Pansky, A., & Algom, D. (1999). Stroop and Garner effects in comparative judgment of numerals: The role of attention. *Journal of Experimental Psychology: Human Perception and Performance*, *25*, 39-58.

Pavese, A., & Umilta, C. (1998). Symbolic distance between numerosity and identity modulates Stroop interference. *Journal of Experimental Psychology: Human Perception and Performance*, *24*, 1535-1545.

Pesenti, M., Thioux, M., Samson, D., Bruyer, R., & Seron, X. (2000). Number processing and calculation in a case of visual agnosia. *Cortex*, *36*, 377-400.

Pesenti, M., Thioux, M., Seron, X., & De Volder, A. (2000). Neuroanatomical substrates of Arabic number processing, numerical comparison, and simple addition: A PET study. *Journal of Cognitive Neuroscience*, *12*, 461-479.

Plaut, D. C., McClelland, J. L., Seidenberg, M. S., & Patterson, K. (1996). Understanding normal and impaired word reading: Computational principles in quasi-regular domains. *Psychological Review*, *103*, 56-115.

Ratinck, E., Brysbaert, M., & Fias, W. (in press). The mental representation of two-digit Arabic numerals examined with masked priming: 28 rapidly activates {{2} × {10}} + {8} in number naming.

Reynvoet, B., & Brysbaert, M. (1999). Single-digit and two-digit Arabic numerals address the same semantic number line. *Cognition*, *72*, 191-201.

Reynvoet, B., & Brysbaert, M. (2004). Cross-notational number priming investigated at different stimulus onset asynchronies in parity and naming tasks. *Experimental Psychology*, *51*, 81-90.

Reynvoet, B., Brysbaert, M., & Fias, W. (2002). Semantic priming in number naming. *Quarterly Journal of Experimental Psychology*, *55A*, 1127-1139.

Seidenberg, M. S., & McClelland, J. L. (1989). A distributed, developmental model of word recognition and naming. *Psychological Review*, *96*, 523-568.

Simon, T. J. (1997). Reconceptualizing the origins of number knowledge: A "non-numerical" account. *Cognitive Development*, *12*, 349-372.

Van Oeffelen, M. P., & Vols, P. G. (1982). A probabilistic model for the discrimination of visual number. *Perception & Psychophysics*, *32*, 163-170.

Van Orden, G. C., Pennington, B. F., & Stone, G. O. (1990). Word identification in reading and the promise of subsymbolic psycholinguistics. *Psychological Review*, *97*, 488-522.

Wender, K. F., & Rothkegel, R. (2000). Subitizing and its subprocesses. *Psychological Research*, *64*, 81-92.

Whalen, J., Gallistel, C. R., & Gelman, R. (1999). Nonverbal counting in humans: The psychophysics of number representation. *Psychological Science*, *10*, 130-137.

Wynn, K. (1998). Psychological foundations of number: Numerical competence in human infants. *Trends in Cognitive Sciences*, *2*, 296-303.

Xu, F. (2003). Numerosity discrimination in infants: Evidence for two systems of representation. *Cognition*, *89*, B15-B25.

Xu, F., & Spelke, E.S. (2000). Large number discrimination in 6-month-old infants. *Cognition*, *74*, B1-B11.

3

Spatial Representation of Numbers

Wim Fias
Martin H. Fischer

INTRODUCTION

Intuitively, we think of number processing as an abstract and nonspatial cognitive activity. Apart from those skills necessary for mental symbol manipulation, no spatial processing seems to be involved in numerical operations. A closer inspection, however, shows that spatial and number processing are intimately connected. A link between mathematical abilities and spatial skills has been anecdotally reported in the past. Great mathematicians like Einstein explicitly emphasized the role of visuo-spatial imagery for the development of their mathematical ideas (cf. Hadamard, 1945/1996). About 15% of normal adults report visuo-spatial representations of numbers (Galton, 1880a,b; Seron et al., 1992). This suggests that the integration of number representations into visuo-spatial coordinates is not a rare phenomenon. The reported spatial layouts were predominantly oriented from left to right, were mostly automatically activated, were stable in time and had emerged in childhood.

More systematic studies have supported these anecdotal reports by demonstrating a tight correlation between mathematical and visuo-spatial skill. In the clinical field, learning disorders establish a similar association between visuo-spatial and mathematical disabilities (e.g., Rourke & Conway, 1997). Evidence from brain imaging provides further support for a link between numbers and space. Tasks that require either number processing or spatial transformations tend to activate structures within the parietal lobes (Milner & Goodale, 1995; Dehaene et al., 2003). Using transcranial magnetic stimulation in healthy participants, Göbel et al. (2001) showed that stimulation of the left and right parietal cortices leads to decreased performance in both visuo-spatial search and number comparison tasks. This suggests that the processing of numerical magnitudes and of visuo-spatial information are functionally connected. Patient studies further confirm the close link between visuo-spatial processing and basic number processing. A particular example is Gerstmann syndrome, which is characterized by the co-occurrence of left–right confusion, finger agnosia, and dyscalculia (e.g., Dehaene & Cohen, 1997).

Thus, there appears to be a convincing case for a link between numbers and space. None of the above reports does, however, force the conclusion that truly numerical representations or processes are associated with spatial representations. The observed correlation could instead reflect the involvement of shared peripheral support structures. For example, visuo-spatial working memory is engaged in symbol manipulation during mental arithmetic (Lee & Kang, 2002). In this chapter we will report evidence that semantic representations of number magnitude are indeed spatially defined and can be conceptualized as positions on an oriented *mental number line*. The idea of a linear analogue representation of numbers in the mind has been proposed (e.g., Moyer & Landauer, 1967; Restle, 1970) to account for some basic performance patterns in numerical cognition. More recently, this useful metaphor has been augmented by postulating that the hypothetical mental number line also has a spatial orientation. We will also show that this spatial cognitive representation of numbers should not be considered as fixed and unchangeable, by demonstrating that the characteristics of spatial number coding are largely determined by numerical and spatial parameters specific to the task at hand. Moreover, the spatial coding of numbers is not under strategic control but rather occurs automatically.

MENTAL REPRESENTATION OF NUMBER MAGNITUDE IS SPATIALLY CODED: THE SNARC EFFECT

Mental chronometry involves the timing of behavioral responses in simple cognitive tasks. Using this approach, Dehaene et al. (1990) asked their participants to indicate with a left or right key press whether a visually presented probe number was smaller or larger than a previously announced reference number. For example, randomly drawn probe numbers from 1 to 99 (but excluding 55) would be compared against the fixed reference number 55. The decision speed in this *number comparison task* with fixed reference was recorded and analyzed as a function of the probe number's magnitude and the response side. Participants who had to press the left key to indicate a "smaller" response and the right key to indicate a "larger" response were faster than those who had to respond left for "larger" and right for "smaller" probe numbers. This response side effect suggested that number magnitude is represented on a left-to-right oriented mental number line, with small numbers on the left side and larger numbers further on the right side. In a seminal paper, Dehaene et al. (1993) further explored this observation.

Dehaene et al. (1993) asked their participants to decide, by using a left or right key, whether a single number was odd or even. In the basic version of this *parity task*, the digits from 0 to 9 appeared repeatedly in a random order in central vision. Different response rules (odd number—left button, even number—right button; or even number—left button, odd number—right button) were tested in counterbalanced blocks. In this way, each participant's response speed as a function of number magnitude could be evaluated. Statistical analysis of the reaction times (RT) revealed that small numbers were responded to faster with the left key, whereas large numbers consistently showed a right key advantage. Dehaene et al. (1993) named this association of numbers with spatial left–right response coordinates the *SNARC effect* for Spatial–Numerical Association of Response Codes.

The SNARC effect is of key importance for the current issue of spatial coding of numbers. It unequivocally demonstrates that numerical magnitude information is spatially coded in most people. The SNARC effect, as an index of the spatial attributes of number representations, has led to several studies into the nature of the mental number line. Below, we will review these studies and their implications. But first we discuss the measurement of the SNARC effect.

Figure 3.1a shows that the SNARC effect can be expressed as a statistical interaction between number magnitude and response side. But because the SNARC effect reflects an association between the position of a number on the mental number line and the position of a response key, we can assess this spatial association more effectively with a statistical regression

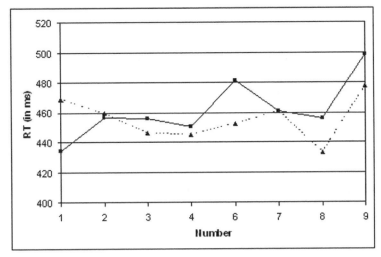

Figure 3.1a. Typical SNARC effect presented as an interaction between number magnitude and side of response (dotted line: right-hand responses; full line: left-hand responses).

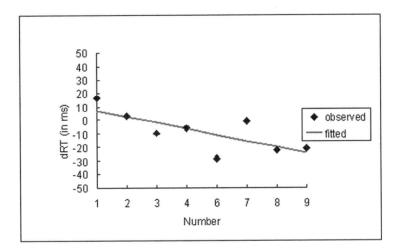

Figure 3.1b. The same SNARC effect presented as a linear regression line with negative slope that is fitted through the difference scores dRT for each stimulus digit.

analysis (Fias et al., 1996). Specifically, the difference in RTs (dRT) for right minus left key responses will be positive for small numbers and negative for larger numbers (see Figure 3.1b). The most straightforward way to capture this negative correlation between numbers and space statistically is to regress dRT on number magnitude for each participant and to then test the slope coefficients against zero (Lorch & Myers, 1990).[1]

There are several advantages related to this regression-based analysis of the SNARC effect. First, the presence of a SNARC effect is judged by a main effect (does the averaged slope coefficient obtained from individual regression equations differ from zero?) rather than by the presence of an interaction between magnitude and side of response. Second, number magnitude is considered as a continuous variable. Third, the regression analysis allows a straightforward

---

[1] A participant's hand dominance has no effect on the overall pattern but can affect the intercept of the regression line.

quantification of the size of the effect (how steep is the slope?) rather than a mere qualitative judgment about the presence or absence of an interaction. Fourth, the effect of additional variables can easily be partialed out through statistical techniques. Fifth, the method evaluates the linear relation between number magnitude and dRT for each participant, reducing the chance of misestimating the SNARC effect due to group averaging. This also allows researchers to explore the influence of individual-specific variables such as gender or handedness on the association between numbers and space. Finally, the method is more flexible than other approaches because it does not require an orthogonal combination of the experimental factors. This is of interest when investigating other tasks than parity judgments that do not rely on the sequential alternation between number magnitudes and response codes.

SPATIAL NUMERICAL CODING IS DYNAMIC: NUMERICAL AND SPATIAL DETERMINANTS OF THE SNARC EFFECT

To obtain a detailed understanding of the association between numbers and space and, by extension, the properties of the mental number line, it is important to know which numerical and spatial variables determine the SNARC effect. We therefore review the recent literature from this perspective.

Numerical Determinants of the SNARC Effect

Several studies have shown that the spatial coding of numbers depends on the task context. The SNARC effect has most frequently been studied in parity tasks with Arabic digits from 0 to 9. An important observation emerged from manipulating the range of stimulus digits: when the *range* of digits was either 0–5 or 4–9 in separate conditions (Dehaene et al., 1993, Experiment 3; see also Fias et al., 1996), the digits 4 and 5 were associated with right responses when they were the largest digits but with left responses when they were the smallest digits to be judged. This shows that the spatial association for a given number is between its *relative* magnitude and space.

An obvious extension is to ask whether the spatial associations also hold for multi-digit numbers. Dehaene et al. (1993) used digits from 0 to 19 and found that the SNARC effect did not clearly extend toward the two-digit numbers. This suggests that the mental number line might be restricted to the representation of single-digit numbers. However, before accepting this conclusion, it is important to realize that the parity status of a two-digit number is determined by the rightmost digit. Parity judgment RTs in Dehaene et al.'s (1993) experiment were indeed largely predictable from the rightmost digit, indicating that the participants had adopted this selective attentional strategy. More informative with regard to the issue of multi-digit spatial representations is the earlier magnitude comparison study of Dehaene et al. (1990), in which probe numbers smaller than the reference were responded to faster with the left hand than with the right hand and vice versa for larger numbers, indicating spatial coding of two-digit numbers. Using another variant of the SNARC effect, Brysbaert (1995) also found a SNARC effect for two-digit numbers, which were processed more quickly when the smaller number was to the left of the larger number compared to a display with the larger number on the left.

Together, these results indicate that number meanings conveyed by single-digit as well as by two-digit numbers are spatially coded. It remains, however, unclear whether the mental number line is a single, analogue continuum onto which various number intervals can be projected as required or whether there are separate mental representations for single- and multi-digit numbers. At this point, it is also unresolved whether two-digit numbers are processed holistically or compositionally. Initially, holistic processing was assumed (Brysbaert, 1995; Dehaene et al., 1990; Reynvoet & Brysbaert, 1999), but recently evidence is accumulating for a separate representation of decade and unit magnitudes during the processing of two-digit numbers (Fias et al., 2003; Nuerk et al., 2001). How both separate and holistic effects should be incorporated into a single processing model is not clear at present. At the very least, effects of stimulus manipulations in number tasks point to a considerable flexibility in accessing the cognitive representation of numbers.

Related to the issue of two-digit processing is the possible extension of the mental number line to *negative numbers*. In western cultures, negative numbers are frequently displayed to the left of positive numbers on the abscissas of statistical graphs. As a consequence of this, we might develop an association of negative numbers with left space. On the other hand, one could argue that negative numbers can be represented more economically on the basis of positive entries alone. The empirical evidence on this issue to date is inconsistent. Fischer (2003a) asked participants to select the numerically larger of a pair of digits ranging from –9 to 9 and measured their decision times in this magnitude comparison with variable reference. Negative numbers were associated with left responses and positive numbers with right responses, supporting the learned association hypothesis. However, pairs of negative digits incurred additional processing costs when compared to mixed or positive pairs, thus suggesting that an additional processing step might have been involved. Moreover, Nuerk et al. (2004) found no reliable spatial association with negative numbers in a parity task. Finally, Fischer and Rottmann (2004) found that large negative magnitudes were associated with right and not left space when a parity task was used but that negative numbers became associated with left space when digits from –9 to 9 had to be classified relative to zero as the fixed reference value. Thus, the spatial associations of negative numbers may be less automatized compared to those of positive numbers.

We now turn to a discussion of the role of number *format* for the spatial association of numbers. Numerical information can be conveyed in many ways, e.g., with Arabic or Roman symbols; in the form of finger postures, dot patterns, or number words; and using either the visual, auditory, or tactile modality. If the SNARC effect indicates access to the abstract representation of number magnitude then it should be insensitive to these variations (see also chapter 2 on this issue). Several studies have obtained SNARC effects when numbers were presented either as Arabic digits or as written words (e.g., Fias, 2001; Dehaene et al., 1993; Nuerk et al., 2004). The slopes of the SNARC functions had similar magnitudes (although sometimes they tended to be smaller for number words), in agreement with the idea that the spatial association reflects access to an abstract representation of number magnitude. Although we know of no published SNARC studies with other number formats (e.g., Roman or Chinese numerals, dot patterns, counting fingers, auditory or tactile magnitude information), further support for a supramodal number representation comes from priming studies, where in each trial a task-irrelevant prime appears before the task-relevant probe number. The typical finding is that decision speed is fastest when the prime and probe are identical, and RT gradually increases with increasing numerical distance between prime and probe. Importantly, this distance effect is not affected by whether the prime and probe numbers are presented in the same or in different formats (Reynvoet et al., 2002).

Finally, it is worth considering whether spatial associations are exclusively numerical or whether they can occur with *non-numerical stimuli* that are sequentially ordered (e.g., letters of the alphabet, days of the week, months of the year). An initial study (Dehaene et al., 1993, Experiment 4) found no reliable associations between letters and space when participants classified letters from the beginning or end of the alphabet as vowels or consonants (see also Fischer, 2003b). However, a statistically more powerful study (Gevers et al., 2003) found that both letters of the alphabet and months of the year can exhibit a SNARC effect. This raises the question: Which aspect of numerical information is spatially coded? Numbers do not only convey quantity information (three buses), but also ordinal information (the third bus) or even nominative information (Bus line 3). It is possible that these different number meanings are conveyed by different representational systems. Given that both numbers and ordered sequences can elicit a SNARC effect, one could argue that it is the ordinal property and not the quantitative property of numbers that is spatially coded. Alternatively, ordinal and quantitative information may be represented separately but characterized by similar internal properties (chapter 4 discusses the processing of ordinal information). Another possibility is that a shared representation can handle numerical or ordinal information, depending on the task context, because quantitative information hierarchically implies ordinal information. In support of this possibility, Marshuetz et al. (2000) found that brain areas which responded to ordinal attributes of non-numerical stimuli were also engaged during number-processing tasks.

Spatial Determinants of the SNARC Effect

In general, spatial information can be coded with respect to a variety of *reference frames*: either centered on part of an observer's body (egocentric coding) or on some non-bodily object (allocentric coding). To investigate the reference frame(s) involved in the SNARC effect, Dehaene et al. (1993, Experiment 6) asked participants in a parity task to respond with crossed-over hands, the left hand pressing the right key and the right hand pressing the left key. Large numbers were classified faster with the right key/left hand and small numbers were classified faster with the left key/right hand. This shows that the relative position of the response, and not the responding hand, determines the SNARC effect. This conclusion is supported by studies involving unimanual responses. Kim and Zaidel (2003) obtained a SNARC effect when participants responded with two fingers of one hand. Fischer (2003b) obtained a SNARC effect when participants classified digits as odd or even by pointing with one hand to a left or right button.

The SNARC effect can be obtained for *effectors* other than the hand and in tasks other than selecting one of two buttons. For example, the time to initiate eye movements away from centrally presented digits to the left or right side (as a function of parity status) depends on the relation between the digit's magnitude and the direction of the eye movement (Fischer et al., 2004; Schwarz & Keus, 2004). Two further results from these oculomotor studies suggest that the SNARC effect emerges at a processing stage prior to effector selection. First, Fischer et al. (2004) showed that the saccadic amplitude is not influenced by the magnitude of the presented number. Second, Schwarz and Keus (2004) found equally sized SNARC effects when comparing manual and oculomotor versions of the parity task.

Bächtold et al. (1998) demonstrated that not only the spatial coordinate system of the response but also the *internal representation* of the numerical information is important. They instructed participants to think of the digits as either lengths on a ruler or times on an analogue clock face. The same digits were then associated with either left or right space, depending on the ruler or clock face condition. For instance, a small number was preferentially responded to with the left hand in the ruler condition but with the right hand in the clock face condition. A similar conclusion can be drawn from two descriptions of brain-damaged patients with hemi-neglect whose impairment to attentively process left space was reflected in their mental representation of numbers. In the first study, Zorzi et al. (2002) observed a systematic representation-based midpoint shift toward the right in a number interval bisection task. For instance, their patients named 6 as the number in the middle between 3 and 7. Apparently, because they were neglecting the left side of their mental number line, these patients positioned the midpoint of a verbally presented interval towards the right. In the second report, Vuilleumier et al. (2004) studied how a group of patients neglecting the left side of space compared numbers to a fixed reference. The patients were selectively slow in responding to the number just smaller than the reference, indicating difficulties in orienting attention towards the left on their mental number line. This selective difficulty was observed for different references (5 and 7). When asked to imagine whether the presented target number was earlier or later than 6 o'clock, the patients showed the reverse effect, a selective slowing of numbers larger than 6, thereby further confirming the dynamic and representational nature of the association between numbers and space

To conclude, the SNARC effect does not seem to tap into a fixed component of the long-term representation of numbers. Rather, numerical information can be dynamically allocated to different representationally defined reference frames, with the left–right line-like spatial coding being merely a default.

A BROADER PERSPECTIVE: THE SNARC EFFECT IN RELATION TO OTHER SPATIAL COMPATIBILITY EFFECTS

Generally speaking, the SNARC effect is the result of joint activation of the spatial components of the cognitive representation of number meaning (magnitude) and of spatial task requirements. More specifically, both the mental number line and the response requirements of certain number tasks share a left–right code. Its congruent activation seems to cause the effect. This makes the SNARC effect a special instance of a *spatial compatibility* effect. Spatial compatibility refers to the fact that lateralized responses can be emitted faster and, less error prone when the trigger stimulus is lateralized to the same side (Fitts & Seeger, 1953). Various types of spatial compatibility can be distinguished as a function of the involvement of spatial aspects in relevant and irrelevant stimulus attributes and in response components of the task (see Kornblum et al., 1990, for a taxonomy). The SNARC effect seems structurally similar to the established Simon effect (Simon, 1969). To obtain the *Simon effect,* participants are asked to give a left- or right-key response to a nonspatial task-relevant attribute of a stimulus (e.g., its color) which is presented randomly either left or right of fixation. This task-irrelevant spatial information contained in the stimulus position then influences the response: right-key presses are slowed down when stimuli appear on the left compared to the right side, and vice versa for left key presses. In SNARC experiments, stimuli are presented centrally and the task-relevant information (typically parity status or magnitude) is also nonspatial in nature. Nevertheless, a task-irrelevant spatial attribute seems to become activated from the internal number representation and to then either facilitate or interfere with the spatial processing required to respond.

The compatibility effects obtained with internally represented spatial dimensions and externally presented spatial stimulus attributes seem to have a similar origin. For instance, Masaki et al. (2000) showed that the compatibility effect with centrally presented arrows (conveying spatial information symbolically) evoked a pattern of electrophysiological brain potentials that highly resembled the pattern obtained with the traditional Simon paradigm (e.g., De Jong et al., 1994). This interpretation is, however, not supported by a recent study of Mapelli et al. (2003). To look for interactions between the SNARC and the Simon effect, they presented digits to the left or right of fixation for parity classification. Thus, they introduced a numerical version of the Simon task, in which the spatial position of the number stimulus was task irrelevant. If the SNARC effect, like the Simon effect, is indeed originating from a common processing stage, then one would expect a statistical interaction between magnitude and position of the digits (Sternberg, 1969). Mapelli et al. (2004), found no such statistical interaction. On the other hand, researchers recently demonstrated interactions between the SNARC and the Simon effects (e.g., Caessens et al., 2003; Wood et al., 2004), suggesting that, like the Simon effect, the SNARC effect results when selecting a spatial response on the basis of task-relevant information and an automatically induced spatial bias. Moreover, in a recent study, Gevers et al. (2004) demonstrated that the SNARC effect was characterized by the same electrophysiological correlates of response selection as observed by Masaki et al.

However, to consider the SNARC effect as an instance of the Simon effect, it is important to demonstrate that the spatial coding of numerical information occurs automatically. We now turn to evidence supporting such automaticity.

Although the SNARC effect has been primarily investigated with the parity task and to a lesser extent with magnitude comparison, the effect is clearly not specific to these tasks. Participants in the study by Fias et al. (1996), for instance, indicated whether the name corresponding to a visually presented digit contained an/e/-sound or not by pressing a left or right response key. Fias et al. found a robust SNARC effect in this phoneme monitoring task. Huha et al. (1995) also observed a SNARC effect when participants evaluated the appearance of visually presented digits. Fischer (2001) reported that the perception of the midpoint of long strings made from small or large digits was shifted to the left or right, depending on the digit magnitude. Finally, participants respond faster with a left button to 1 than to 100 and faster with a right button to 100 than to 1 (Tlauka, 2002), again illustrating how perceptual tasks induce spontaneous semantic processing that is then reflected in a SNARC effect.

Some of the tasks reviewed above required no explicit number-related information to be performed. However, despite the fact that number magnitude was not needed, the numbers had to be processed to some degree. The SNARC effect, however, has also been obtained in studies in which the visually presented numbers were completely irrelevant. For instance, using digits as a background upon which oriented lines or triangles were superimposed for classification, Fias et al. (2001) found that participants' manual responses were influenced by the spatial–numerical association evoked by the background. This is a strong argument in favor of automatic spatial coding. Also, in Fischer et al.'s (2003b) study of visual–spatial attention allocation, the digits served merely as a fixation point but did nevertheless influence speed of target detection. The fact that the SNARC effect emerges when information about numbers is not required for correct performance, and may even interfere with performing the task, suggests that a high degree of automaticity is involved in the processes that give access to the magnitude representation and its spatial association (cf. chapter 4).

To sum up, the SNARC effect in its pure form expresses an overlap in the cognitive representations of the spatial left–right dimensions from the irrelevant number magnitude and the required response and thus fits the category of Simon-like effects in Kornblum et al.'s (1990) taxonomy of compatibility effects. We believe that it is a theoretically fruitful approach to put the investigation of the spatial coding of numerical information within the theoretical frameworks developed to understand general spatial compatibility effects. This leads to two advantages. First, by understanding the domain-general components of the SNARC effect, the number-specific components can be isolated and therefore better understood. Second, a framework is provided to understand spatial coding of numbers in its different manifestations.

DEVELOPMENTAL AND CULTURAL DETERMINANTS

If we want to understand how the association between numbers and space comes about, it makes sense to look at the way children deal with magnitude information.

Developmental studies have shown that very young infants can discriminate numerosities and continuous magnitudes and even perform simple additions and subtractions (Wynn, 1998; see also chapter 9). Following these findings, a debate arose about the functional origin of this precocious numerical ability. Some authors adhere to the idea that these abilities reflect the operation of a "number sense" (e.g., Dehaene, 1997), whereas others suggest that these abilities are not truly numerical in nature but reflect the operation of early visuo-spatial abilities (Newcombe, 2002).

Further evidence for the involvement of spatial cognition in numerical abilities can be obtained at later stages of a child's development. From the work of Rourke and Conway (1997), it is known that visuo-spatial learning disorders correlate with a delayed or abnormal development of mathematical skills. The same correlation has been observed in genetic disorders like velocardiofacial syndrome (Simon et al., 2003) and Williams syndrome (e.g., Ansari et al., 2003; see also chapter 17). These observations demonstrate a prominent role of visuo-spatial abilities in number processing, but they do not clarify how numerical representations become spatially coded. We must therefore turn to the available evidence from developmental and cross-cultural studies on the SNARC effect. Berch et al. (1999) investigated the onset of the SNARC effect with the parity task. They found that the SNARC effect appeared from third grade. However, given the evidence for well-developed spatial and numerical skills in much younger children (see above), it could be argued that the parity task is not sensitive enough to discover the presence of such associations in younger children; they may be unable to respond consistently in this speeded task. The use of behaviorally simpler tasks such as detection (Fischer et al. 2003b) or bisection (Fischer, 2001) may reveal spatial–numerical associations even in such special populations. Alternatively, it might also be that the number line is spatially coded from an earlier age but that it is not yet automatically activated. Remember that the parity task does not necessarily require magnitude information. Consistent with this idea, Girelli et al. (2000) showed that number magnitude is only activated automatically from third grade onward. In sum, further research is needed to establish the critical developmental period for the SNARC effect.

What determines the left–right orientation of the mental number line? One prominent proposal has been that the effect reflects acquired reading habits (Dehaene et al., 1993). Western participants in number studies typically read from left to right, and this cognitive strategy may transfer from the domain of letter, word, and sentence processing to the processing of digits, numbers, and equations. In support of this view, the association of numbers with space tended to be weaker in a group of Iranian participants who normally read from right to left and who probably would associate small digits with right space and larger digits with left space (see Dehaene et al., 1993, Experiment 7, for details of this trend). A recent series of studies by Zebian (2001) strengthens this conclusion. She found that monolingual Arabic speakers in Beirut process two numbers more easily when the larger number is placed to the left of the smaller number, compared to a display with the larger number on the right. This effect decreased for a group of bilingual Arabic–English speakers (see also Maass & Russo, 2003).

Of course, these studies do not demonstrate directly that writing direction itself is the crucial determinant of the orientation of the number line. With the currently available data, any variable that is correlated with it can have a decisive impact. For instance, one might suspect that the association of numbers with spatial positions is a reflection of early training with number lines in school. Poster boards with printed left-to-right-oriented number lines have been used to teach generations of school children the principles of addition and subtraction (Fueyo & Buschel, 1998). Or it could be an expression of culture-specific general exploration strategies (Dehaene et al., 1993). It may also be worthwhile considering finger-counting habits as a reason for the emergence of associations between numbers and space. Several arguments can be made in support of this hypothesis. First and foremost, finger counting is a universal means of learning to deal with numbers (see Butterworth, 1999, chapter 5). Specifically, it could then be argued that the majority of children in Western countries prefer to enumerate objects on the fingers of their left hand and that this brings about the association of small numbers with left space and larger numbers with right space. Conant (1896/1960, p. 437f) reported that from 206 U.S. school children almost all began to count with their left hand. Clearly more up-to-date and cross-cultural data are needed to evaluate this possibility further.

Having discussed these possible candidates for the acquisition of associations between numbers and space, we wish to briefly draw the reader's attention to one further proposal. In an impressive analysis of mental arithmetic from the viewpoint of embodied cognition, Lakoff and Nunez (2000) show how numerical abilities can emerge from ordinary behavior and daily experiences in a physical world. These become cognitively represented in schemas and are then transferred from their source domain to the target domain of arithmetic through the use of metaphor. To illustrate, consider how basic facts about any object collection (its size and how it is modified by removing and adding elements) can be mapped onto statements about numbers. This has also been illustrated by Cooper (1984, p. 158):

> "Consider number development as learning about the space of number. In this space, one must learn where things are and how to get from one place to another. For purposes of the analogy the locations are specific numerosities and the actions to get from one place to another are additions and subtractions. How do you get from two to five? You must start in a particular direction (increasing numerosity) and go past certain landmarks (three and four) until you arrive at five (having gone a certain distance). Points in this space capture the cardinal characteristics of number: direction and landmarks, their ordinal properties . . . It is through experiences of moving in this space that children learn its ordinal structure, which is the primary content of early number development."

Lakoff and Nunez (2000) elaborate how such concrete experiences yield all the laws of arithmetic, such as preservation of equality, symmetry, transitivity, and inverse operations. Their theory, primarily based on arguments from structural and logical analysis, may become a promising avenue for further theory development if put in an empirically testable theoretical framework. We refer the reader to chapter 7 by Nunez and Lakoff for more details.

In sum, there is now good evidence that the direction of the number line is culturally determined, although it remains unclear what the crucial variables are. Further developmental research in a cross-cultural perspective can increase our understanding of the developmental trajectory and the cultural determination of how space is integrated in our internal mental representations of numbers.

CONCLUSIONS

We hope that this chapter has convinced the reader that the meaning of numbers is indeed spatially coded and that the mental number line is a useful metaphor to capture this surprising fact. However, this metaphor should not be taken literally, as there is no sign of a topographic organization of number-selective neurons in the brain (Nieder et al., 2003; Verguts & Fias, 2004). Rather, spatial associations are attached to numbers as part of our strategic use of knowledge and skills, and, as a result, these associations are highly task-dependent. Further evidence of this flexibility of spatial associations challenges the appropriateness of the number line metaphor. Examples include the existence of vertical as well as horizontal spatial associations (Schwarz & Keus, 2003) and the systematic association of odd numbers with left space and even numbers with right space (Nuerk et al., 2003). Future research will have to determine the extent to which the wide range of spatial numerical associations can help us understand the cognitive representation of numbers.

REFERENCES

Ansari, D., Donlan, C., Thomas, M. S. C., Ewing, S. A., Peen, T., & Karmiloff-Smith, A. (2003). What makes counting count? Verbal and visuo-spatial contributions to typical and atypical number development. *Journal of Experimental Child Psychology, 85*(1), 50–62.

Bächtold, D., Baumüller, M., & Brugger, P. (1998). Stimulus-response compatibility in representational space. *Neuropsychologia, 36*(8), 731–735.

Berch, D. B., Foley, E. J., Hill, R. J., & Ryan, P. M. (1999). Extracting parity and magnitude from Arabic numerals: Developmental changes in number processing and mental representation. *Journal of Experimental Child Psychology, 74*(4), 286–308.

Brysbaert, M. (1995). Arabic number reading: On the nature of the numerical scale and the origin of phonological recoding. *Journal of Experimental Psychology: General, 124*, 434–452.

Butterworth (1999). *The mathematical brain*. London: Macmillan.

Caessens, B., Gevers, W., & Fias, W. (2003). *Spatial code activation in conflict paradigms: Insights from number processing*. Paper presented at the 13th Conference of the European Society for Cognitive Psychology, Granada/Spain, 17–20 September.

Conant, L. L. (1896/1960). Counting. In J. R. Newman (Ed.), *The world of mathematics, Vol. I* (pp. 432–441). London: George Allen & Unwin Ltd.

Cooper, R. G. (1984). Early number development: Discovering number space with addition and subtraction. In C. Sophian (Ed.), *Origins of cognitive skills* (pp. 157–192). Hillsdale, NJ Erlbaum.

Dehaene, S. (1997). *The number sense: How the mind creates mathematics*. New York: Oxford University Press.

Dehaene, S., Bossini, S., & Giraux, P. (1993). The mental representation of parity and number magnitude. *Journal of Experimental Psychology: General, 122* (3), 371–396.

Dehaene, S., & Cohen, L. (1997). Cerebral pathways for calculation: Double dissociation between rote verbal and quantitative knowledge of arithmetic. *Cortex, 33*(2), 219–250.

Dehaene, S., Dupoux, E., & Mehler, J. (1990). Is numerical comparison digital? Analogical and symbolic effects in two-digit number comparison. *Journal of Experimental Psychology: Human Perception and Performance, 16*(3), 626–641.

Dehaene, S., Piazza, M., Pinel, P., & Cohne, L. (2003) Three parietal circuits for number processing. *Cognitive Neuropsychology, 20*(3/4/5/6), 487–506.

De Jong, R., Liang, C., & Lauber, E. (1994). Conditional and unconditional automaticity: A dual-process model of effects of spatial stimulus–response correspondence. *Journal of Experimental Psychology: Human Perception and Performance, 20,* 731–750.

Fias, W. (2001). Two routes for the processing of verbal numbers: Evidence from the SNARC effect. *Psychological Research-Psychologische Forschung, 65*(4), 250–259.

Fias, W., Brysbaert, M., Geypens, F., & d'Ydewalle (1996). The importance of magnitude information in numerical processing: Evidence from the SNARC effect. *Mathematical Cognition, 2* (1), 95–110.

Fias, W., Lammertyn, J., Reynvoet, B., Dupont, P., & Orban, G. A. (2003). Parietal representation of symbolic and nonsymbolic magnitude. *Journal of Cognitive Neuroscience, 15*(1), 47–56.

Fias, W., Lauwereyns, J., & Lammertyn, J. (2001). Irrelevant digits affect feature-based attention depending on the overlap of neural circuits. *Cognitive Brain Research, 12*(3), 415–423.

Fischer, M. H. (2001). Number processing induces spatial performance biases. *Neurology, 57*(5), 822–826.

Fischer, M. H. (2003a). Cognitive representation of negative numbers. *Psychological Science, 14*(3), 278–282.

Fischer, M. H. (2003b). Spatial representations in number processing—Evidence from a pointing task. *Visual Cognition, 10*(4), 493–508.

Fischer, M. H., Castel. A. D., Dodd, M. D., & Pratt, J. (2003b). Perceiving numbers causes spatial shifts of attention. *Nature Neuroscience, 6*(6), 555–556.

Fischer, M. H., & Rottmann, J. (in press). Do negative numbers have a place on the mental number line? *Psychology Science.*

Fischer, M. H., Warlop, N., Hill, R. L., & Fias, W. (2004). Oculomotor bias induced by number perception. *Experimental Psychology, 51*(2), 91–97.

Fitts, P. M., & Seeger, C. M. (1953). S–R compatibility: Spatial characteristics of stimulus and response codes. *Journal of Experimental Psychology: General, 46,* 199–210.

Fueyo, V., & Bushell, D., Jr. (1998). Using number line procedures and peer tutoring to improve the mathematics computation of low-performing first graders. *Journal of Applied Behavior Analysis, 31,* 417–430.

Galton, F. (1880a). Visualised numerals. *Nature, 21,* 252–256.

Galton, F. (1880b). Visualised numerals. *Nature, 21,* 494–495.

Gevers, W., Ratinckx, E., Debaene, W., & Fias, W. (2004). *The functional locus of the SNARC effect investigated with event-related brain potentials.* Manuscript submitted for publication.

Gevers, W., Reynvoet, B., & Fias, W. (2003). The mental representation of ordinal sequences is spatially organized. *Cognition, 87*(3), B87–B95.

Girelli, L., Lucangeli, D., & Butterworth, B. (2000). The development of automaticity in accessing number magnitude. *Journal of Experimental Child Psychology, 76*(2), 104–122.

Göbel, S., Walsh, V., & Rushworth, M. F. S. (2001). The mental number line and the human angular gyrus. *Neuroimage, 14*(6), 1278–1289.

Hadamard, J. (1996). *The mathematician's mind: The psychology of invention in the mathematical field.* Princeton, NJ: Princeton University Press. Originally published in 1945.

Huha, E. M., Berch, D. B., & Krikorian, R. (1995). *Obligatory activation of magnitude information during nonnumerical judgments of Arabic numerals.* Paper presented at a meeting of the American Psychological Society, New York, 29 June–2 July.

Kim, A., & Zaidel, E. (2003). Plasticity in the SNARC effect during manipulation of order in response conditions. *Journal of Cognitive Neuroscience,* (Suppl.), 134.

Kornblum, S., Hasbroucq, T., & Osman, A. (1990). Dimensional overlap: Cognitive basis for stimulus-response compatibility—A model and taxonomy. *Psychological Review, 97,* 253–270.

Lakoff, G., & Nunez, R. (2000). *Where mathematics comes from: How the embodied mind brings mathematics into being.* New York: Basic Books

Lee, K.-M., & Kang, S.-Y. (2002). Arithmetic operation and working memory: Differential suppression in dual tasks. *Cognition, 83*(3), B63–B68.

Lorch, R. F., & Myers, J. L. (1990). Regression analyses of repeated measures data in cognition research. *Journal of Experimental Psychology: Learning, Memory, and Cognition, 16,* 149–157.

Maass, A., & Russo, A. (2003). Directional bias in the mental representation of spatial events. *Psychological Science, 14*(4), 296–301.

Mapelli, D., Rusconi, E., & Umilta, C. (2003). The SNARC effect: An instance of the Simon effect? *Cognition, 88,* B1–B10.

Marshuetz, C., Smith, E. E., Jonides, J., DeGutis, J., & Chenevert, T. L. (2000). Order information in working memory: fMRI evidence for parietal and prefrontal mechanisms. *Journal of Cognitive Neuroscience, 12*(Suppl. 2), 130–144.

Masaki, H., Takasawa, N., & Yamazaki, K. (2000). An electrophysiological sudy of the locus of the interference effect in a stimulus–response compatibility paradigm. *Psychophysiology, 37*(4), 464–472.

Milner, A. D., & Goodale, M. A. (1995). *The visual brain in action.* Oxford: Oxford University Press.

Moyer, R. S., & Landauer, T. K. (1967). Time required for judgments of numerical inequality. *Nature, 215,* 1519–1520.

Newcombe, N. S. (2002). The Nativist–Empiricist controversy in the context of recent research on spatial and quantitative development. *Psychological Science, 13*(5), 395–401.

Nieder, A., Friedman, D. J., & Miller, E. K. (2003). Representation of the quantity of visual items in the prefrontal cortex. *Science, 297* (6 September), 1708–1711.

Nuerk, H. C., Weger, U., & Willmes, K. (2001). Decade breaks in the mental number line? Putting the tens and units back in different bins. *Cognition, 82*(1), B25–B33.

Nuerk, H. C., Iversen, W., & Willmes, K. (2004). Notational modulation of the SNARC and the MARC (Linguistic markedness of response codes) effect. *Quarterly Journal of Experimental Psychology, 57A,* 835–863.

Restle, F. (1970). Speed of adding and comparing numbers. *Journal of Experimental Psychology, 83,* 274–278.

Reynvoet, B., & Brysbaert, M. (1999). Single-digit and two-digit numerals address the same semantic number line. *Cognition, 72,* 191–201.

Reynvoet, B., Brysbaert, M., & Fias, W. (2002). Semantic priming in number naming. *Quarterly Journal of Experimental Psychology–A, 55A*(4), 1127–1139.

Rourke, B. P., & Conway, J. A. (1997). Disabilities of arithmetic and mathematical reasonning. Perspectives from neurology and neuropsychology. *Journal of Learning Disabilities, 30,* 34–46.

Schwarz, W., & Keus, I. (2004). Moving the eyes along the mental number line: Comparing SNARC Effects with manual and saccadicresponses. *Perception and Psychophysics, 66*(4), 651–664.

Seron, X., Pesenti, M., Noel, M.-P., Deloche, G., & Cornet, J.-A. (1992). Images of numbers, or "when 98 is upper left and 6 sky blue." *Cognition, 44,* 159–196.

Simon, J. R. (1969). Reaction toward the source of stimulation. *Journal of Experimental Psychology, 81,* 1974–1976.

Simon, T. J., Bearden, C. E., McDonald Mc-Ginn, D., & Zackai, E. (2004), Visuospatial and numerical cognitive deficits in children with chromosome 22q11.2 deletion syndrome. Cortex, in press.

Sternberg, S. (1969). The discovery of processing stages: Extensions of Donders' method. In W. G. Koster (Ed.), *Attention and performance II: Acta Psychologica, 30,* 276–315.

Tlauka, M. (2002). The processing of numbers in choice-reaction tasks. *Australian Journal of Psychology, 54*(2), 94–98.

Vuilleumier, P., Ortigue, S., & Brugger, P. (2004). The number space and neglect. *Cortex, 40,* 399–410.

Wood, G., Nuerk, H. C., & Willmes, K. (2004). *Responding to visual numbers guided by mental numbers: multiple frames of reference and the SNARC effect.* Paper submitted for publication.

Wynn, K. (1998). Psychological foundations of number: Numerical competence in human infants. *Trends in Cognitive Sciences, 2,* 296–303.

Zebian, S. (2001). *Influences of cultural artifacts and social practices on number conceptualization: Experimental and ethnographic approaches to everyday numeric cognition.* Unpublished doctoral dissertation. University of Western Ontario: Ontario, Canada.

Zorzi, M., Priftis, K., & Umiltà, C. (2002). Neglect disrupts the mental number line. *Nature, 417*(6885), 138–139.

Automaticity in Processing Ordinal Information

Joseph Tzelgov
Dana Ganor-Stern

Ordinality, a critical component of numerical competence (Davis & Perusee, 1988), refers to the order of the quantities corresponding to the number labels. These quantities are aligned along a single line–the mental number line (Restle, 1970). In this chapter we discuss the automaticity of the ordinal processing. Automatic processing is important because it provides a picture of the internal representation, which is relatively uncontaminated by intentional operations. We start with a brief review of the various definitions proposed in the literature for the concept of automaticity, followed with a presentation of the definition posed by the authors of this chapter. We continue with a critical evaluation of the experimental phenomena that have been assumed by researchers to be evidence for the automaticity of ordinal processing, namely, interference effects, distance effect, and SNARC (Spatial–Numerical Association of Response Code) effects. Next, we discuss the conditions leading to automatization of the processing of ordinal information. We conclude the chapter by discussing the implications of the existing data for the emerging picture on the automatization of ordinal relations.

DEFINING AUTOMATICITY

Automaticity has been most frequently defined in terms of a list of features (e.g., Hasher & Zacks, 1979; Posner, 1978), but, as pointed out by Logan (1992), these definitions state what automaticity is not rather than what it is. The three features common to most definitions of automaticity are the absence of (a) attentional limitations, (b) consciousness, and (c) intentionality. Previous research, however, has shown not only that it is rarely the case for the three criteria to hold simultaneously (Carr, 1992; Neumann, 1984), but that the validity of each feature as a criterion of automaticity is also questionable (e.g., Kahneman & Chajczyk, 1983; Logan & Zbrodoff, 1979; Tzelgov, Henik, & Berger, 1992a). This has led some (e.g., Pashler, 1998) to conclude that the concept of automatic processing is not useful and should be abandoned. Others (e.g., Bargh, 1997) believe that the notion of automaticity is important for explaining human behavior and, therefore, other ways to define it should be pursued.

Logan (1989, 1992) argued that the definition of automaticity should specify the learning mechanisms that lead to automaticity. Logan's (1988) instance theory and connectionist/controlled architecture of Schneider and Detweiller (1987, 1988) are good examples for such a "construct-oriented" approach. Another "minimalist approach," by contrast, defines automatic processing by a single feature common to all automatic processes. Following Bargh (1989), Tzelgov has proposed using processing without monitoring as the defining feature of automatic processing, where monitoring means an intentional setting of the goal of behavior, and a continous intentional evaluation of the output of the process, as long as it takes place (Tzelgov, 1997; Tzelgov, Yehene, & Naveh-Benjamin, 1997).

Tzelgov et al. (2000; 1997) distinguished between two modes of automatic processing (i.e., processing that occurs without monitoring). The first is intentional automatic processing, in which automatic processing is part of the task requirement but the monitoring is set on a higher superordinate level (Vallacher & Wegner, 1987). Processing the individual words when a sentence is read for meaning is a good example. The second is autonomous automatic processing, in which automatic processing takes place when it is not part of the task requirement. The Stroop effect (Stroop, 1935) that indicates reading a word when a person is asked to name its color exemplifies this mode of automatic processing. Although both cases are considered to be automatic, when a process is part of the task requirement it is not always possible to tell whether it runs with or without monitoring. Diagnosing of automatic processing in the autonomous mode is in most cases unequivocal. To diagnose a process as automatic, therefore, it is necessary to show that it can run when it is not part of the task requirement. It should be noted that, even in this mode, it is unclear if a process occurs with or without monitoring when the processing of the irrelevant dimension might be beneficial for the task. In such a case, one cannot be sure if participants were not processing the irrelevant dimension intentionally. We therefore call processing conducted under such conditions "incidental" and consider as markers for automatic processing only experimental phenomena that provide evidence for the occurrence of a process, although it was neither part of the task nor beneficial for the task.

In their analysis of markers of automaticity, Ganor-Stern, Tzelgov, and Deutsch (submitted) introduced the notion of triggering (i.e., activation of the irrelevant dimension provided by the experimental task). The level of triggering depends on the relationship between the processing of the relevant and irrelevant dimensions: the more related the two processes, the more triggering is provided. For example, when studying automatic processing of numerical magnitude by using a task that involves a numerical parity task, it might be argued that, since both dimensions are numerical, the processing of the relevant dimension (parity) might have triggered the processing of the irrelevant dimension (magnitude).

Tasks vary with the amount of triggering that they provide for the processing of the irrelevant dimension. Minimizing triggering allows one to see the extent to which it is necessary for the occurrence of the automatic process. Consequentially, it helps to distinguish between the two types of automatic processing proposed by Bargh (1996, 1992): "unconditioned automatic processes," which require only information and skill in order to occur (Neumann, 1984) and take place even if no triggering is provided by the task, and "conditioned automatic processes," which depend upon some level of triggering from the task in addition to information and skill.

In the next section we describe three possible markers for automatic processing of ordinal relations: interference effects, distance effects, and the SNARC effect. For each effect we discuss the following three questions: Is there evidence that the effect reflects automatic processing? To what extent does such automatic processing depend upon triggering from the task? What can be learned from each marker about the nature of the automatic numerical processing taking place and the representations that underlie it?

MARKERS OF AUTOMATICITY
IN PROCESSING ORDINAL INFORMATION

Interference Effects

In the interference paradigm, the participant is presented with an object to process. The experimental task specifies which aspect of the object is relevant for the task, and therefore should be processed. The purpose of this paradigm is to look for indications for the automatic processing of an irrelevant dimension, which was not part of the task requirement. In studies that used the interference paradigm to tap automatic ordinal processing, digits or verbal numerals were presented for processing, but the numerical magnitude was always the irrelevant dimension. In one line of studies (e.g., Henik & Tzelgov, 1982), the physical size was the relevant dimension; digits that varied in physical and numerical magnitude were presented for a physical size comparison task ("choose the physically larger digit"). In another line of studies (e.g., Pansky & Algom, 2002; Pavese & Umilta, 1998), displays of identical digits were presented and the relevant dimension was the number of digits in the display ("choose the display that contains more digits"). In both lines of research, automatic processing of numerical magnitude was indicated by poorer performance in the incongruent trials, in which the information in the relevant and irrelevant dimensions was inconsistent, compared to congruent trials, in which the information in the relevant and irrelevant dimensions was consistent. Specifically, performance was poorer when the physically larger digit was numerically smaller compared to when it was numerically larger. This effect is known as the Size Congruency Effect (SiCE). In a similar manner, performance was poorer when the number of digits was large but the numerical magnitude of each digit was small, compared to when the number of digits in the display and the numerical magnitude of each digit were large (e.g., Pansky & Algom, 2002). Since, in these studies, processing of numerical size was not part of the task and it could not be beneficial for the task, it meets our criterion for a marker for automatic processing. It was argued by Pansky and Algom (1999, 2002) that because the magnitude of those interference effects is affected by contextual characteristics, they reflect only partially automatic processing. We disagree. Although we are aware that automatic processes can be more or less visible depending on the context, as is shown, for example, by Pansky and Algom (1999, 2002) and by Schwarz and Ischebeck (2003), there is nothing in our approach to automaticity that requires that the indications for automatic processes will stay unaffected by context.

In the studies described so far, the level of triggering was not minimal. Thus, the processing of numerical information could, in principle, be triggered by the task; that is, the physical size comparison task might have activated the processing of numerical size, and, in a similar manner, the processing of numerical size might have been activated by counting. As of this writing, there are no interference studies that used lower levels of triggering.

As to the underlying representations, Tzelgov et al. (1992b) suggested that interference effects, and in particular SiCE, reflect two components: an activation of the number line and the tagging of each number larger than 5 as "large" and each number smaller than five as "small." The first component is apparently responsible for the increase in the magnitude of SiCE as a function of intrapair distance found in many studies (e.g., Cohen-Kadosh, Henik, & Rubinsten, submitted; Henik & Tzelgov, 1982; Tzelgov et al., 2000). The second component might explain why the size of SiCE for pairs of numbers equal in intrapair distance was smaller where the two members were on the same side of 5 as compared to when they were on the two sides of 5 (Tzelgov et al., 1992b).

In sum, the following two conclusions can be drawn from the present section. First, interference effects reflecting ordinal processing can be considered markers for automatic ordinal processing, and second, there is not enough empirical evidence to evaluate the role of triggering in such effects.

Distance Effect

The term "distance effect" refers to the effect of the numerical difference between two numbers in the time to process them. In the present context, we examine if and under which conditions it may be seen as a marker for automatic ordinal processing. It should be noted that the term "distance effect" was used in the past with regard to two manifestations of intrapair numerical difference. In the first, the larger the difference between the two numbers, the better the performance. This is found when two numbers are presented for a numerical comparison task, and for this reason it is called here "comparative distance effect." In the second, the smaller the difference, the better the performance. This effect is found when one number is processed in the context of another number (e.g., Brysbaert, 1995; Reynvoet & Brysbaert, 1999) and is similar to the priming effect found in the verbal domain. We thus refer to it as "priming distance effect." Next, we review separately the existing evidence for the automaticity of the two manifestations of the distance effect.

Some researchers (e.g., Rubinsten, Henik, Berger, & Shahar-Shalev, 2002) view the "comparative distance effect" found in numerical comparison tasks as an indication for automatic processing of ordinal information. We disagree. In such a case, the distance effect is a product of the task requirement. According to our approach to automaticity, to view the distance effect as a marker for automaticity, it should be present when it is not part of the task. Dehaene and Akhevein (1995) generated conditions in which the comparative distance effect can serve as a marker of automaticity. They presented pairs of either two digits or two verbal numbers, or one digit and one verbal number. In the numerical same–different task, participants had to decide if the two stimuli were numerically the same or different. In the physical same–different task, participants had to decide if the two stimuli were physically the same or different. While the former task involves intentional numerical processing, the latter does not, and therefore a distance effect found in the physical identity task might be seen as an indication for the automaticity of numerical processing. Moreover, since physical comparison is unrelated to numerical processing, the physical comparison task of Dehaene and Akhavein (1995) may be seen as providing weak triggering for numerical processing. The presence of a distance effect under such conditions could be seen as evidence for an unconditioned automatic numerical process. Dehaene and Akhavein (1995), however, obtained the effect only for pairs of the same notation (such as 1 8, or one eight) and not in pairs of different notations (such as 1 eight). Because in pairs of the same notation the numerically identical numbers were always physically identical, and the numerically different numbers were always physically different, numerical processing could thus be beneficial in the physical identity task. Thus, the comparative distance effect found under these conditions cannot be seen as unequivocal evidence for automatic processing.

The priming distance effect found in Morin, Derosa, and Stultz (1967) was taken by Dehaene and Akhavein (1995) as indicating automatic processing. Morin, Derosa, and Stultz (1967) asked participants to memorize a set of consecutive digits and to decide if a probe digit was in the set or not. The priming distance effect was reflected in slower responses when the probe was outside, but close to the set, than when it was more distant. Although this task provides relatively weak triggering for numerical processing, the participants still might have used the number line as an aid for the memorizing task, and, thus, we view it as evidence of incidental, and not automatic, processing.

The priming distance effect could be taken as a marker of automatic processing only if shown when the processing of the prime is clearly not beneficial to numerical processing of the target. Currently, such evidence is missing. Neely (1977) used the primed lexical decision task paradigm in the verbal domain to provide evidence of processing the prime when it was clearly not beneficial to task performance. In one of the conditions when the prime was the name of category A, it was followed by an item from category B as a target and the participants were so told. Under this condition, monitored action that is aimed to optimize performance in the task should lead to facilitated response to items from category B and to inhibition of items from category A, following the presentation of the name of category A. However, when the target appeared less than 250 ms after the appearance of prime, presenting the name of category A as a prime facilitated the processing of items from Category A when they appeared as targets. Facilitation of processing of unexpected stimuli was not beneficial to the task, and therefore it indicates automatic processing. One possible way to obtain evidence of the automaticity of the priming distance effect could be by applying a similar paradigm in the numerical domain.

It should be noted that although there is no doubt that the distance effect in its two manifestations reflects numerical processing, it cannot be interpreted exclusively in terms of the numerical relations between the numbers. It might also reflect the associative relations between the lexical entries of the numbers (e.g., Brysbaert, 1995; Dehaene & Akhavein, 1995; Reynvoet & Brysbaert, 1999; Reynvoet, Brysbaert, & Fias, 2002). The distance effect can be seen as a measure of numerical (semantic) relations only, and not also associative (lexical) processing, when processing of remote numbers is compared to processing of close but non-consecutive numbers.

To sum up, although the distance effect is usually seen as a marker for numerical processing and is consistent with the notion of processing in terms of a mental number line, there is not enough evidence showing that it can be taken as a marker for automaticity of numerical processing for the following reasons. First, there is not sufficient evidence for its existence when it is not beneficial for the task. Second, the distance effect obtained in most studies is not a pure measure of numerical processing, since it also reflects associative lexical relations between the numbers.

SNARC Effect

The SNARC effect was originally reported by Dehaene and colleagues (Dehaene, Bossini, & Giraux, 1993). When participants were presented with a single digit for a binary parity judgment, reaction times to relatively small numbers were faster with the left hand than with the right hand, whereas reaction times to relatively large numbers were faster with the right hand than with the left hand. This corresponds to the idea that the mental number line spreads from left to right with small numbers at its left end. The effect seems to be a product of the association of numerical magnitude to space and not a product of the association of numerical magnitude to hand, since it was obtained with the participants' hands crossed (Dehaene et al., 1993, Experiment 6). Since ordinal processing was not part of the requirement of the parity judgment, it meets our criterion for automatic processing.

The parity judgment task is a numerical task, and it might have activated the numerical features of the number, including its magnitude; it therefore might be considered as providing strong triggering. The question is whether the SNARC effect occurs also when the experimental task requires non-numerical processing (i.e., under conditions of weak triggering). Fias et al. (2001, 1996) demonstrate that a SNARC effect also emerged when participants were performing a non-numerical phoneme-monitoring task on the names of the numbers ("Is there an e-sound in the name of the number presented?") and an orientation task ("Is the stimulus pointing upward or downward?"). Thus, these findings indicate that automatic activation of the number line also occurs under conditions of minimal triggering. Fias et al. (2001) have also shown that not all non-semantic tasks produce the SNARC effect. The authors argue that the presence of a SNARC effect was dependent on the amount of overlap between the neural circuits activated by the processing of the relevant dimension (orientation, color, or shape) and the irrelevant ordinal dimension. When such overlapping existed (as in the case of an orientation task), the SNARC effect was present. When there was no such overlap, however (as in the case of a color or a shape decision), the SNARC effect was absent. These findings suggest that triggering reflects not only similarity between cognitive processes but also overlapping in the underlying neural circuits.

Recent findings of Fischer, Castel, Dodd, and Pratt (2003) also support the conclusion that the SNARC effect requires only minimal triggering. They presented a large (8 or 9) or a small (1 or 2) number in the center of the screen followed by a target in a box to the left or to the right of fixation. Responses in a detection task were faster for small numbers than for large numbers when the target appeared to the left of fixation, and for large numbers as compared to small numbers when the target appeared to the right of fixation. This indicates that numbers were mapped onto their spatial locations on the number line even without triggering.

In sum, the SNARC effect meets our criterion for automaticity, and it seems to suggest an automatic activation of the whole number line. In addition, its occurrence under minimal triggering conditions (Fias, 2001; Fias et al., 2001) suggests that processing of ordinal information is an "unconditioned automatic process" that occurs given the skill and the information (Neumann, 1984).

The following conclusions can be drawn from the present discussion on each of the three markers of automatic ordinal processing. First, interference effects are robust and replicable markers for automaticity. Studies that used this experimental paradigm, however, did not reduce the level of triggering sufficiently to allow for the conclusion that automatic processing of ordinal magnitudes is unconditioned. Second, the distance effect was found when numerical processing was not part of the task requirement. In most cases, however, this effect was found under conditions in which numerical processing was beneficial to task performance and therefore, according to our view, could indicate only incidental, and not automatic, processing. Another limitation of the use of distance effect as a marker for automatic processing of ordinal information is that it is contaminated by associative relations on the lexical level. Third, the SNARC effect was found when ordinal processing was not part of the task requirement and was not beneficial for the task therefore suggesting that ordinal processing is an automatic process. Moreover, because it was also obtained under minimal triggering conditions (Fias, 2001; Fias et al., 2001) suggests that processing ordinal information is an "unconditioned automatic process."

Although there is evidence that processing ordinal information is an unconditioned automatic process, it should be clear that it will take place only given skill and information (Neumann, 1984). Previous findings have shown that the indications for the automatic numerical processing may disappear when the information is either presented for too short a time or in an unfamiliar format. Distance effect in the same–different physical task of Dehaene and Akhavein (1995) was not found for different-notation pairs. This was probably due to the very fast responses for these highly dissimilar pairs. As shown in a recent study by Schwarz and Ischebeck (2003), the visibility of the automatic process depends on the speed of processing of the relevant dimension. Interference effects, which indicate automatic processing of numerical magnitude, were observed when the experimental task required comparisons between the physical sizes of the stimuli, but only when the stimuli were Arabic digits and not when they were number words (Cohen-Kadosh et al., submitted). Similarly, the SNARC effect was observed under both strong and weak triggering when the stimuli were Arabic digits. However, when the stimuli were number words, the effect was found only under strong triggering conditions. This is apparently due to the participants' being more skilled in extracting numerical information from Arabic digits than from number words (Cohen-Kadosh et al., submitted; Dehaene & Akhavein, 1995; Dehaene et al., 1993; Koechlin, Naccache, Block, & Dehaene, 1999). In the next section we discuss the acquisition of such skill.

SOME ASPECTS OF THE ACQUISITION AND AUTOMATIZATION OF ORDINAL RELATIONS

The acquisition and automatization of ordinal relations can be investigated from at least two perspectives. The developmental perspective is the one taken by some scholars (e.g., Girelli, Lucangeli, & Butterworth, 2000; Rubinsten et al., 2002), and it raises questions such as at what age children demonstrate automaticity of numerical processing. For example, Rubinsten et al. (2002) found that children demonstrated intentional ordinal processing at the beginning of first grade but that they did not show evidence for automatic ordinal processing until the end of first grade. The second perspective, which was pursued in our laboratory, is experimental, and it attempts to specify what kind of training is needed to acquire the ordinal relations of symbols and to automatize such knowledge.

Tzelgov, Yehene, Kotler, and Alon (2000) were interested to see if it is necessary to encounter all possible pairs of symbols during study for the acquisition and automatization of ordinal relations among all possible pairs, or if a subset of pairs that provides all the relevant order information (i.e., pairs of symbols representing adjacent magnitudes) is sufficient. In the experimental paradigm that was used, college students were trained with arbitrary symbols (Gibson figures) that represent a series of consecutive numbers. The study phase included several thousand trials, in each of which a pair of figures was presented and participants were asked to decide which figure corresponded to a larger (or smaller) magnitude. Feedback was provided after each trial. Two groups of participants were used. The "all pairs" group was trained on all possible pairs of symbols, whereas the "adjacent pairs" group was trained only on pairs of symbols representing adjacent numbers. The test phase included two tasks performed on all pairs of symbols. In the "numerical size comparison task" that was aimed to estimate intentional ordinal processing, participants were presented with pairs of symbols, differing only in numerical size. Participants had to decide which symbol was numerically larger. In the "physical size comparison task" that was aimed to estimate automatic ordinal processing, participants were presented with pairs of symbols differing in physical and numerical sizes and had to decide which symbol was physically larger. Automatic processing was indicated by SiCE—the difference in response latency between congruent and incongruent trials. In the numerical-size comparisons, both groups showed distance effects. Thus, the "adjacent pairs" group could numerically process pairs that were never seen during training. These participants demonstrated transitivity, which, according to Brainerd (1979) and Hulse and O'Leary (1982), is the marker for ordinal knowledge. More importantly, in a physical comparison task, participants from both groups demonstrated SiCE that increased with intrapair distance, indicating automatic processing of ordinal relations. These findings demonstrate that performance during a test was not based exclusively on retrieval of the binary order relation encoded during training. It follows that if the training provides all the relevant information, experiencing all possible binary relations during training is not necessary to form a representation of the number line—a representation that can be automatically activated.

Consistency of mapping during acquisition is usually considered critical for automatization (Schneider, Dumais, & Shiffrin, 1984). In visual search experiments, automatization was achieved only under conditions of consistent mapping (CM), where the mapping of items to targets and distractors as such was constant across trials, and not under varied mapping conditions (VM), where the mapping of items to targets and distractors changed between trials (Schneider & Shiffrin, 1977; Shiffrin & Schneider, 1977). In such experiments, automatization was indicated by a reduction or elimination of the set size effect (i.e., the positive correlation between the number of items in the display and RT). Fisk, Oransky, and Skedsvold (1988) applied the notion of CM to processing numerical relations. In their study, an array with a varying number of digits was presented in each trial. Participants had to search for the numerically largest digit in the display. Consistency was defined in terms of response requirements. In the CM group, the instructions were constant across training: the participants had to select the largest (or the smallest) digit in all trials. In the VM group, the instructions changed randomly from trial to trial between selecting the largest and selecting the smallest digits. Because the set size effect was reduced more in the CM than in the VM conditions, the authors argued that only such conditions lead to automatization. Aviv (2003) manipulated response consistency in a similar way when training participants, using a procedure similar to the one used in Tzelgov et al. (2000). There was response consistency for half of the participants—those who had to select the figure representing either the larger or the smaller magnitude. For the other half, the instructions alternated across trials between select smaller and select larger. Automaticity as measured by SiCE was achieved under both CM and VM conditions. Consistency of response mapping had no effect on SiCE, either by itself or in interaction with any other variable, suggesting that such consistency is not necessary for automatization. Thus, automatization does not simply mean that a person trained by being presented with a pair of symbols (Sj on the right and Si on the left; Sj representing a larger magnitude than Si) and asked which member of the pair is larger stores "for the pair (Sj Si) press Left" and retrieves this response when presented with the same pairs even when this is not part of the task requirement. Rather, these results, together with those of Tzelgov et al. (2000), suggest that there is more to automaticity than just retrieving the responses or even retrieving the binary relations between the magnitudes corresponding to pairs of symbols. Rather, it seems that exposure to the binary relations of a series of pairs results in the mapping of each symbol to its relative location on the number line.

AUTOMATIC PROCESSING OF ORDINAL INFORMATION: THE EMERGING PICTURE AND SOME SPECULATIONS

We started this chapter by presenting our approach to automatic processing as processing without monitoring. We made a distinction between intentional and autonomous modes of automatic processing and suggested that automaticity of a process, and in particular automaticity of processing numerical information, can be diagnosed only in the autonomous mode (i.e., when it is not part of the task requirement) and when it is not beneficial to the task. In addition, we also introduced the concept of triggering to differentiate between conditioned and unconditioned automatic processing. Taking this as a starting point, we discussed three possible markers of automatic processing of numerical information. Although the distance effect was reported under conditions of autonomous processing, it was, in many cases, contaminated by associative relations at the lexical level (Dehaene & Akhavein, 1995). In addition, distance effect found when not being part of the task requirement happened, in most cases, under conditions when numerical processing was beneficial to task performance, and therefore it could indicate only incidental, and not automatic, processing. Thus, although the distance effect may be a promising candidate for a marker of automatic processing of numerical information, additional data are needed to allow such a conclusion. Interference effects are robust, replicable, and they do not suffer from the limitations of the distance effect; that is, they were also found when numerical processing was not beneficial for the task, and they did not reflect any associative relations. They are, thus, reliable markers of automaticity of numerical processing. Studies that used this experimental paradigm did not reduce the level of triggering sufficiently to allow for the conclusion that automatic processing of numerical ordinal magnitudes is unconditional. By contrast, the SNARC effect was obtained when it was not part of the task requirement and when the task provided minimal triggering (Fias, 2001; Fias et al., 2001). Thus, we may conclude that the processing of numerical information is an "unconditioned automatic process," which meets Neumann's (1984) definition of automatic processing as one in which parameters for performance are fully specified by skill (procedures stored in memory) and input information.

As previously mentioned, automatic processing provides a picture of an internal representation that is relatively uncontaminated by intentional operations. This leads to the question of how ordinal information is represented. It should be noted that the answer to this question is not independent of the experimental paradigm used. In most cases, the SNARC effect seems to be consistent with the notion of internal representation in terms of location on a mental number line. The increase of SiCE with intrapair distance and indications (still requiring additional empirical support) of the distance effects under conditions of autonomous processing are also consistent with this conclusion.

Tzelgov et al. (1992b) proposed a hybrid representation of numerical information, suggesting that—in addition to the representation of order on a mental number line—numerical representation also includes a crude binary classification of numbers as large or small. In their two experiments, Girelli et al. (2000) obtained a pattern that was similar to that of Tzelgov et al.— larger SiCE for bilateral pairs (i.e., pairs in which both numbers are from the same side of 5) than for unilateral pairs (i.e., pairs in which the two numbers are from different sides of 5). Yet, in their case, SiCE was not significant for unilateral pairs (Experiment 1) or the difference between bilateral and unilateral pairs was not significant (Experiment 2).

It should be noted that the data from some studies most frequently interpreted as supporting the notion of a mental number line are also consistent with binary representation. This applies to studies in which the argument supporting the number line interpretation was based on the use of numbers 1, 2, 8, 9 (Dehaene & Akhavein, 1995; Fischer et al., 2003). In such cases, the numerical distance is confounded with small/large tagging. For example, the pair 1, 8 represents not only large numerical distance but also a small number and a large number. Results obtained under such conditions do not differentiate between the possible binary and linear (number line) representations. It seems that additional research is needed in order to decide if a crude large/small classification is part of the internal representation of numbers. Specifically, if such a crude classification exists, it should affect the distance effect obtained when numerical processing is not part of the task requirement. Keeping distance constant, the distance effect should be larger when it involves numbers on the two sides of five compared to numbers on the one side of five.

We have already pointed out automatization of ordinal relations cannot be based on encoding and retrieval of instances of binary relations between pairs of stimuli compared in the past. We believe that automatization of ordinal processing might be based on associative learning, as suggested by Perruchet and Vinter (in press), who recently proposed the notion of a "self-organizing consciousness" that argues for emergence of conscious representations on the basis of associative learning. Automatic processing is conceived as direct readout from these representations. The framework proposed by Perruchet and Vinter (2002) is similar to Logan's instance theory in that it attributes automatic processing to readout from memory, but, unlike Logan, it allows for automatization of relations that were not encoded as instances during practice. Because automaticity is viewed by Perruchet and Vinter as a direct readout from memory that does not involve any additional processing, it is consistent with the idea that automatic processing provides a picture of internal representation that is relatively uncontaminated by the applications of intentional operations. Furthermore, it explains quite naturally why one cannot describe the logical procedure or the "algorithm" employed in performing the task. Such a description cannot be provided simply because such an algorithm has not been applied. The automatic processing affecting performance is due to readout from the representation activated in a bottom-up manner by the appearance of the relevant stimuli, perhaps with the help of triggering by the intentionally performed task, or in a top-down manner by the task requirement set in terms of a superordinate unit of behavior (Vallacher & Wegner, 1987).

The model of Leth-Steensen and Marley (2000) provides an example of how associative learning could lead to representation of ordinal information. The authors emphasized the importance of activation of the end points of the scale, which serve as anchors. In all the comparisons, the lowest end point is small and the highest endpoint is large. The other points, in contrast, are not consistently mapped, as they are large in some of the comparisons and small in others. It should be noted, however, that this model describes performance after training only in intentional magnitude comparisons. Thus, in this case the processing of numerical information is part of the task requirements and, as such, does not model automatization of ordinal processing. To show that the model leads to automatization of numerical information would require showing the effects indicating automatic processing, for example, the SNARC effect, interference effects, moderation of SiCE by distance, and perhaps the distance effect. This was done by Cohen, Dunbar, and McClleland (1990) and Roelofs (2003) with respect to the Stroop effect, a marker of the automatic activation of word meaning. Both of these models of the Stroop task exemplify how an automatic process (reading) becomes activated when the task requirement is to do something else (to name the color) given the information presented and the skill level. In the model of Cohen, Dunbar, and McClleland (1990), instructions are represented by "task input nodes," and there is an indication of automatic reading, as reflected by the Stroop effect, when the "name the color" node, rather than "read the word" node, is activated. Suppose now that the model of Leth-Steensen and Marley is extended to include modules for processing the physical size of the presented stimuli or their parity as well as task nodes (e.g., numerical comparison node, physical size node, parity decision node). That would allow (by external activation) "to instruct the model which task to perform." One could then instruct the model to perform physical size comparisons or parity decisions in order to see whether, under such conditions, the SiCE or the SNARC effect were obtained. If, under such conditions, the model showed the SNARC effect or the SICE, it would support the idea that learning binary order relations, as conceptualized by the model, leads to automatization of ordinal relations. Working out the details of such a framework awaits further research.

REFERENCES

Aviv, H. (2003). *Can automatic processing occur in varied mapping?* Unpublished Master's thesis, Ben Gurion University of the Negev, Beer-Sheva, Israel.

Bargh, J., Chaiken, S., Raymond, P., & Hymes, C. (1996). The automatic evaluation effect: Unconditionally automatic attitude activation with a pronunciation task. *Journal of Experimental Social Psychology, 32*, 185–210.

Bargh, J. A. (1989). Conditional automaticity: Varieties of automatic influence in social perception and cognition. In J. S. Uleman & J. A. Bargh (Eds.), *Unintended thought* (pp. 3–51). New York: Guilford Press.

Bargh, J. A. (1992). The ecology of automaticity: Towards establishing the conditions needed to produce automatic processing effect. *American Journal of Psychology, 105*, 181–199.

Bargh, J. A. (1997). The automaticity of everyday life. In R. S. Wyer (Ed.), *Advances in social cognition* (vol. 10, pp. 1–63). Mahwah, NJ: LEA.

Brainerd, C. (1979). *The origins of the number concept.* New York: Praeger.

Brysbaert, M. (1995). Arabic number reading: On the nature of the number scale and the origin of the phonological recoding. *Journal of Experimental Psychology: General, 124*(4), 434–452.

Carr, T. (1992). Automaticity and cognitive anatomy: Is word recognition automatic? *Americal Journal of Psychology, 105*, 201–237.

Cohen, J., Dunbar, K., & McClleland, J. (1990). On the control of automatic processes: A parallel distributed processing account of the Stroop effect. *Psychological Review, 97*, 332–361.

Cohen-Kadosh, R., Henik, A., & Rubinsten, O. *Are arabic and word numbers processed in different ways?* Manuscript submitted for publication.

Davis, H., & Perusee, R. (1988). Numerical competence in animals. *Behavioral and Brain Sciences, 11*, 564–579.

Dehaene, S., & Akhavein, R. (1995). Attention, automaticity, and levels of representation in number processing. *Journal of Experimental Psychology: Learning, Memory, and Cognition, 21*(2), 314–326.

Dehaene, S., Bossini, S., & Giraux, P. (1993). The mental representation of parity and number magnitude. *Journal of Experimental Psychology: General, 122*(3), 371–396.

Fias, W. (2001). Two routes for the processing of verbal numbers: evidence from the SNARC effect. *Psychological Research, 65*, 250–259.

Fias, W., Brysbaert, M., Geypens, F., & d'Ydewalle, G. (1996). The importance of magnitude information in numerical processing: Evidence from the SNARC effect. *Mathematical Cognition, 2*(1), 95–110.

Fias, W., Lauwereyns, J., & Lammertyn, J. (2001). Irrelevant digits affect feature-based attention depending on the overlap of neural circuits. *Cognitive Brain Research, 12*, 415–423.

Fischer, M. H., Castel, A. D., Dodd, M., & Pratt, J. (2003). Perceiving numbers causes spatial shifts of attention. *Nature Neuroscience, 6*, 555–556.

Fisk, A., Oransky, N., & Skedsvold, P. (1988). Examination of the role of "higher-order" consistency in skill development. *Human Factors, 30*, 561–581.

Ganor-Stern, D., Tzelgov, J., & Deutsch, A. *The interference paradigm as a tool for studying automatic processing: The case of sentence processing.* Manuscript submitted for publication.

Girelli, L., Lucangeli, D., & Butterworth, B. (2000). The development of automaticity in accessing number magnitude. *Journal of Experimental Child Psychology, 76*, 104–122.

Hasher, L., & Zacks, R. T. (1979). Automatic and effortful processes in memory. *Journal of Experimental Psychology: General, 108*(3), 356–388.

Henik, A., & Tzelgov, J. (1982). Is three greater than five: The relation between physical and semantic size in comparison tasks. *Memory & Cognition, 10*, 389–395.

Hulse, S., & O'Leary, D. (1982). Serial position learning: teaching the alphabet to rats. *Journal of Experimental Psychology: Animal Behavior Processes, 8*, 260–273.

Kahneman, D., & Chajczyk, D. (1983). Test of automaticity of reading: Dilution of the Stroop effect by color-irrelevant stimuli. *Journal of Experimental Psychology: Human Perception and Performance, 9*, 497–509.

Koechlin, E., Naccache, L., Block, E., & Dehaene, S. (1999). Primed numbers: Exploring the modularity of numerical representations with masked and unmasked semantic priming. *Journal of Experimental Psychology: Human Perception and Performance, 25*(6), 1882–1905.

Leth-Steensen, C., & Marley, A. (2000). A model of response-time effects in symbolic comparison. *Psychological Review, 107*, 62–100.

Logan, G. (1988). Toward an instance theory of automatization. *Psychological Review, 91*, 295–327.

Logan, G. (1989). Automaticity and cognitive control. In J. Neuman & J. Bargh (Eds.), *Unintended thought* (pp. 52–74). New York: Guilford Press.

Logan, G. (1992). Attention and preattention in theories of automaticity. *Americal Journal of Psychology, 105*, 317–339.

Logan, G., & Zbrodoff, N. F. (1979). When it helps to be misled: Facilitative effects of increasing the frequency of conflicting stimuli in a Stroop-like task. *Memory & Cognition, 7*, 166–174.

Morin, R. E., Derosa, D. V., & Stultz, V. (1967). Recognition memory and reaction time. *Acta psychologica, 27*, 298–305.

Neely, J. H. (1977). Semantic priming and retrieval from lexical memory: Roles of inhibitionless spreading activation and limited capacity attention. *Journal of Experimental Psychology: General, 106*, 226–254.

Neumann, O. (1984). Automatic processing: A review of recent findings and a plea for an old theory. In W. Prinz & A. F. Sanders (Eds.), *Cognition and automatic processing* (pp. 255–293). Berlin: Springer-Verlag.

Pansky, A., & Algom, D. (1999). Stroop and Garner effects in comparative judgment of numerals: The role of attention. *Journal of Experimental Psychology: Human Perception and Performance, 25*(1), 39–58.

Pansky, A., & Algom, D. (2002). Comparative judgment of numerosity and numerical magnitude: Attention preempts automaticity. *Journal of Experimental Psychology: Learning, Memory, and Cognition, 28*(2), 259–274.

Pashler, H. (1998). *The psychology of attention.* Cambridge, MA: MIT Press.

Pavese, A., & Umilta, C. (1998). Symbolic distance between numerosity and identity modulates Stroop interference. *Journal of Experimental Psychology: Human Perception and Performance, 24*(5), 1535–1545.

Perruchet, P., & Vinter, A. (2002). The self-organizing consciousness. *Behavioral and Brain Sciences, 25*, 297–330.

Posner, M. (1978). *Chronometric explorations of mind.* Hillsdale, NJ: Erlbaum.

Restle, F. (1970). Speed of adding and comparing numbers. *Journal of Experimental Psychology, 91*, 191–205.

Reynvoet, B., & Brysbaert, M. (1999). Single-digit and two-digit arabic numerals address the same semantic number line. *Cognition, 72*, 191–201.

Reynvoet, B., Brysbaert, M., & Fias, W. (2002). Semantic priming in number naming. *The Quarterly Journal of Experimental Psychology, 55A*(4), 1127–1139.

Roelofs, A. (2003). Goal-referenced selection of verbal action: Modelling attentional control in the Stroop task. *Psychological Review, 110*, 88–125.

Rubinsten, O., Henik, A., Berger, A., & Shahar-Shalev, S. (2002). The development of internal represensations of magnitude and their association with arabic numerals. *Journal of Experimental Child Psychology, 81*, 74–92.

Schneider, W., & Detweiler, M. (1987). A connectionist/controlled approach to working memory. In G. H. Bower (Ed.), *The psychology of learning and motication* (vol. 21, pp. 53–119). New York: Academic Press.

Schneider, W., & Detweiler, M. (1988). The role of practice in dual task performance: Toward workload modeling in a connectionist/control architecture. *Human Factors, 30*, 539–566.

Schneider, W., Dumais, S. T., & Shiffrin, R. M. (1984). Automatic and control processing and attention. In R. Parasurman & R. Davies (Eds.), *Varieties of attention.* New York: Academic Press.

Schneider, W., & Shiffrin, R. M. (1977). Controlled and automatic human information processing. I. Detection search and attention. *Psychologival Review, 84*, 127–190.

Schwarz, W., & Ischebeck, A. (2003). On the relative speed account of number–size interference in comparative judgments of numerals. *Journal of Experimental Psychology: Human Perception and Performance, 29*(3), 507–522.

Shiffrin, R. M., & Schneider, W. (1977). Controlled and automatic human information processing. II. Perceptual learning, automatic attending, and a general theory. *Psychological Review, 84*, 127–190.

Stroop, J. R. (1935). Studies of interference in serial verbal reactions. *Journal of Experimental Psychology, 18*, 643–662.

Tzelgov, J. (1997). Automatic but conscious: That is how we act most of the time. In R. S. Wyer (Ed.), *Advances in Social Cognition.* Mahwah, NJ: Erlbaum.

Tzelgov, J., Henik, A., & Berger, J. (1992a). Controlling Stroop effect by manipulating expectation for color related stimuli. *Memory and Cognition, 20*, 727–735.

Tzelgov, J., Meyer, J., & Henik, A. (1992b). Automatic and intentional processing of numerical information. *Journal of Experimental Psychology: Learning, Memory, and Cognition, 18*(1), 166–179.

Tzelgov, J., Yehene, V., Kotler, L., & Alon, A. (2000). Automatic comparisons of artificial digits never compared: learning linear ordering relations. *Journal of Experimental Psychology: Learning, Memory, and Cognition, 26*(1), 103–120.

Tzelgov, J., Yehene, V., & Naveh-Benjamin, M. (1997). From automaticity to memory and vice versa: On the relations between automaticity and memory. In J. Brezezinski, B. Krause, & T. Maryszewski (Eds.), *Idealization in psychology: Poznan studies of the sciences and the humanities* (vol. 55, pp. 239–261). Amsterdam: Rodopi.

Vallacher, R. R., & Wegner, D. M. (1987). What do people think they're doing? Action identification and human behavior. *Psychological Review, 94*, 3–15.

5

Computational Modeling of Numerical Cognition

Marco Zorzi
Ivilin Stoianov
Carlo Umiltà

INTRODUCTION

Numerical cognition has been studied in both human and animal species for a long time. However, the computational basis of number representation and numerical skills has received very little attention, as compared with the computational basis of language processing, for example, reading (see Zorzi, 2004, for a review). In general, computational modeling is a powerful tool in cognitive science to evaluate or compare existing verbal theories (e.g., box-and-arrows models) and to make novel experimental predictions. In contrast to the loose formulation of traditional verbal theories, computational models need to be explicit in any implementational detail and can produce highly detailed simulations of human performance (e.g., they can be explicitly tested on any number of stimuli). Moreover, the performance after a "lesion" to the model can be readily compared to the behavior of neuropsychological patients.

In this chapter we review recent progress in developing computational (connectionist) models of numerical cognition. We focus on three main issues: (a) number representations, (b) basic numerical skills (number comparison, subitizing, counting), and (c) simple mental arithmetic. We first review the previous attempts to model human numerical skills. We then present our comprehensive theoretical proposal, which revolves around the notion of *numerosity* representations.

THE REPRESENTATION OF NUMBER CONCEPTS

The issue of what is the nature of the mental representation of cardinality is of paramount importance. Cardinal meanings are distinctive to numbers, since the other functions of numerical expressions—ordering, labeling, and measuring—can be carried out by different means (Butterworth, 1999). Since cardinality entails size, it has been frequently maintained that its mental representation is an analogue code. Dehaene and Cohen (1995) and Campbell (1994) have proposed models of arithmetic that combine an analogue code with representations of Arabic and verbal numerical expressions. Complex tasks such as multidigit arithmetic and symbolic mathematical reasoning are developmentally based on simpler tasks such as number comparison and simple addition. Hence, in order to understand our capacity to deal with numbers, it is crucial to identify the type of number representations that our brain uses for performing these simple tasks.

Theories of number representation place particular emphasis on accounting for the distribution of reaction times (RTs) and errors in the comparison of numerical magnitudes. As with many other stimulus dimensions, it is easier and quicker to select the larger of two numbers when they are numerically dissimilar than when they are similar (the *distance effect*; Moyer & Landauer, 1967). Moreover, for a given distance, pairs of small numbers are compared faster than pairs of large numbers (the *size effect*). This led to the widely shared assumption that number magnitudes are encoded as points (or regions) on a continuous, analogue *number line* (e.g., Dehaene, 2003, for review). In one proposal, the number line is held to be compressive so that larger numbers are closer together on the line than smaller numbers. Accordingly, the subjective difference between two numbers depends on their positions on the line; that is, the subjective difference between N and $N + 1$ is smaller as N increases (Dehaene, 1992; Dehaene, Dupoux, & Mehler, 1990). A different conception of number line is that of Gallistel and Gelman (1992, 2000). First, they propose that the mapping from the number symbol (word or numeral) is onto a line segment defined from the origin, not a point. Second, the mapping is linear, not compressive, but the variability of the mapping increases in proportion to the magnitude (scalar variability).

In most computational models, number semantics have been typically encoded as magnitude information, with various schemes that were considered as an instantiation of number line representations. As we shall see, the choice of representation can strongly influence the success or failure of a model. The comparison and theoretical analysis of the various schemes are postponed to a later section of this chapter.

MODELS OF SIMPLE ARITHMETIC

Simple arithmetic is a fundamental human numerical ability, thought to have a phylogenetic origin (Butterworth, 1999). For example, pigeons can subtract the numerosity of two sets of objects (Brannon, Wusthoff, Gallistel, & Gibbon, 2001), and human infants can sum and subtract small numerosities even before knowing number words (Wynn, 1992). The basic phenomena of single-digit arithmetic performance are robust, widely replicated, and well known (for instance, the effect of problem size; see below), yet there has been much controversy as to the psychological processes involved and as to how arithmetic facts are represented and organized in memory. For instance, one major controversy is whether skilled arithmetic performance (e.g., simple addition and multiplication) is built upon abstract semantic representations (e.g., McCloskey, 1992) or on verbally stored facts (e.g., Dehaene & Cohen, 1995). Nonetheless, it is generally agreed that competent adults use some mixture of fact retrieval from memory and procedures for transforming the problem if memory search fails (Cambell & Xue, 2001; Groen & Parkman, 1972; LeFevre, Sadesky, & Bisanz, 1996).

Simple arithmetic is systematically affected by the "difficulty" of the problem, indexed by its numerical size. Thus, the *problem-size effect* indicates that larger problems take longer to solve and are more prone to errors. For skilled adults, correlations from 0.6 to 0.8 are observed between mean RTs for correct responses and the sum of the operands or the square of the sum, with the latter accounting for a larger proportion of variance (e.g., Butterworh, Zorzi, Girelli, & Jonckheere, 2001, for addition).

Historically, simple mental arithmetic has been the focus of the earliest attempts to simulate human numerical abilities using neural network models. However, the number of connectionist simulations of simple mental arithmetic is quite modest in comparison with most other cognitive domains (for instance, consider the large number of papers on modeling reading aloud; see Zorzi, 2004, for a review). All connectionist simulations of mental arithmetic take the *associative* approach of Ashcraft (1992), among others, that mental arithmetic is a process of stored facts retrieval. We will distinguish two types of modeling approaches: (a) learning models, in which the knowledge about arithmetic facts is acquired through a learning algorithm and stored in a distributed form, and (b) performance models, in which the architecture is hard-wired and set up by the modeler(s) according to specific representational and processing assumptions (as it is typical, for instance, in localist interactive-activation models; McClelland & Rumelhart, 1981).

Learning Models

The models of Viscuso, Anderson, and Spoehr (1989; also Anderson, Spoehr, & Bennett, 1994) and McCloskey and Lindemann (1992) are based on *associative-memory* neural networks that store in their memory a set of patterns representing entire arithmetic facts—the two arguments and the result—and solve arithmetic problems by exploiting the ability of these networks to complete partial or noisy patterns. After training, arithmetic problems are solved by presenting to the network partial arithmetic facts, that is, their two arguments, which is followed by retrieval of a stored pattern that most closely matches the input. Both models learned single-digit multiplication facts. In the model of Viscuso et al. (1989), numbers were represented both as magnitudes (see section 5 below) and with a further set of units representing the number name, whereas McCloskey and Lindemann's (1992) MATHNET model used only the magnitude representation.

The Viscuso et al. (1989) model could only learn about 70% of the problems, and its performance was not quantitatively matched against human RT data. MATHNET, which used a more powerful learning algorithm (the Boltzmann Machine; Ackley, Hinton, & Sejnowski, 1985) but had the same basic properties, was shown to account for the problem-size effect: the correlation of the response time with the sum of the arguments was 0.69. However, the authors found that this result could be entirely attributed to the way in which arithmetic facts were presented to the network during training. The network experienced the arithmetic problems with a schedule claiming to be similar to the experience of children learning arithmetic: small facts in the beginning, all facts later. Fact frequency was also manipulated: smaller problems were presented up to seven times as often as larger problems. However, this ratio turns out to be highly implausible when compared to fact frequencies in mathematic textbooks as tabulated by Aschraft and Christy (1995). Moreover, control simulations showed that presentation frequency was entirely responsible for the problem-size effect: when frequency was held constant, the network failed to show the effect.

In later simulations with MATHNET, Lories, Aubrun, and Seron (1994) studied the effects of artificial lesions to the model and found a reasonable match to neuropsychological data of brain-damaged patients.

Performance Models

The model of Campbell (1995), known as the network-interference model, aimed to quantitatively account for skilled performance. Arithmetical knowledge was represented as both a physical code and a magnitude code. The physical code is simply an ordered set of elements (e.g., <{6 3}{+}{9}>), and the magnitude code is specified as a logarithmic function of the numbers. Problems with their solutions are "reactivated" over a series of cycles; variance in RTs is determined by the competing activation of problems similar in terms of their physical and magnitude codes. All parameters in the model were chosen to provide the best fit to empirical data. The problem-size effect arises because larger-number problems are more similar in magnitude to their neighbors than are smaller-number problems (i.e., because the number line is compressive). This causes larger problems to activate neighbors more strongly, which turns into more interference by way of inhibition from neighbors.

Another model based on a hard-wired architecture is that of Whalen (1997). This model is a connectionist implementation of the localist associative model of Aschraft (1992), in which number facts are represented by dedicated problem nodes. Both arguments and results are semantically represented, using a compressed (logarithmic) magnitude representation. However, the model was used to simulate an artificial mathematical operation—"diamond arithmetic"—of complexity similar to that of multiplication but in which the results were not systematically related to the arguments. The network exhibited growing retrieval times as one the argument increased, which was explained with the increasing similarity among the arguments that in turn resulted in a larger number of competing problem nodes.

Summary

The computational models of simple arithmetic reviewed above share some important features that can be summarized as follows:

1. All models are based on associative neural networks, either with distributed or localistic encoding of number facts.
2. All models use semantic representations of numbers, sometimes paired with a "physical" or "verbal" code. However, in all cases the semantic representations appear to be crucial.
3. All models have used magnitude information as number semantics (see section 5 below). The various schemes have been considered as an instantiation of number line representations.
4. The connectionist learning models have shown limited ability to account for the pattern of empirical data. The success of MATHNET (McCloskey & Lindemann, 1992) was entirely the result of an implausible frequency manipulation.

MODELS OF ELEMENTARY NUMERICAL ABILITIES

Number comparison is a core numerical skill. McCloskey (1992) takes the ability to select the larger of two numbers to be the criterion of understanding numbers. Neurological patients who perform abnormally on this task turn out to be profoundly acalculic (e.g., Cipolotti, Butterworth, & Denes, 1991; Delazer & Butterworth, 1997). Developmental psychologists following Piaget (1952) regard the ability to order number by size as indicating that the child now possesses the concept of number. However, there have been very few attempts to simulate number comparison with computational models. One problem faced by connectionist modelers is that it would make little sense to train a neural network on all possible bigger-smaller relationships, even for single digits. Number comparison is certainly not learned in the same way we learn mental arithmetic. Moreover, it is frequently assumed that the key parametric findings (i.e., distance and size effects) should be attributed to the nature of the representation into which the numerical symbols are mapped (that is, the mental number line).

Dehaene and Changeux (1993) were the first to investigate the development of elementary numerical abilities using a complex connectionist architecture. Of particular importance is their numerosity detection system, depicted in Figure 5.1. In this system, visual objects (presented as simplified one-dimensional input) are first normalized to a size-independent code. Activations are then summed to yield an estimate of input numerosity and finally sent to numerosity detectors that are tuned to a specific numerosity through a center-on, surround-off pattern of connectivity. The activity peaks for these latter units become lower and wider for larger numbers, which implies a logarithmic coding (Dehaene, 2003). It should also be noted that the numerosity detection system was hardwired, reflecting the assumption that it is

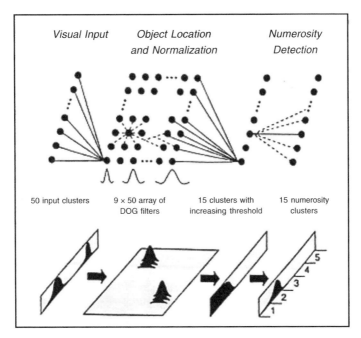

Figure 5.1. The numerosity detector network of Dehaene and Changeux (1993). The visual input is sent to a normalization layer encoding the objects in a size-independent code, which in turn activates a layer of "summation clusters" that yield an estimate of input numerosity. Finally, numerosity clusters are activated only in response to their preferred numerosity. Reprinted with permission from S. Dehaene and J-P. Changeaux, Development of elementary numerical abilities: A neuronal model, *Journal of Cognitive Neuroscience*, 5, 4 (Fall, 1993), 390–407. © 1993 by the Massachusetts Institute of Technology.

present at birth. Dehaene and Changeux augmented the basic architecture to simulate numerosity discrimination and comparison. To perform the comparison task, the model had to match the currently detected numerosity against a numerosity stored in short-term memory. Note, however, that the model was only concerned with preverbal elementary abilities, so it could only operate on small sets of objects (up to 4–5). After training the system, the distribution of errors in both the discrimination and the comparison tasks showed size and distance effects.

The ability to detect the numerosity of a small group of objects with a parallel process is known as *subitizing*. However, humans can also detect numerosity by means of *counting* (a slow sequential process reporting the exact number of visually presented objects, the number of single tones heard, etc.) or *estimation* (fast approximate detection of large numerosities). Subitizing and counting were specifically investigated in the computational study of Petersen and Simon (2000). While the model of Dehaene and Changeux (1993) assumes an innate parallel mechanism for the detection of small numerosities, Peterson and Simon proposed that subitizing is a learned recognition process, with a teaching signal provided by a more general counting mechanism. In their simulation, based on the ACT-R cognitive architecture of Anderson (1993), the counting procedure was implemented as a set of production rules that used the number facts to successively assign numbers to objects in a display. Recognition was implemented as a simple pattern-matching procedure that could match a given configuration of objects to a remembered configuration with known numerosity. In this case, the numerosity of the current display was directly retrieved from memory.

In Peterson and Simon's (2000) ACT-R simulations, learning to recognize (i.e., subitize) the patterns was fast and accurate for one to three items, more difficult for four-item patterns, and virtually impossible for five–six objects. In the latter case, the system always enumerated by means of the counting mechanism. Therefore, the enumeration latencies in the model showed a discontinuity in the slope at the numerosity of 3, in line with the empirical data. The gradual transfer from counting to recognition for a maximum of four items was taken as evidence that the subitizing limit derives only from the exponentially increasing complexity of the spatial combinatorics involved in the recognition process. This account was also tested in simulations with simple multilayer feed-forward networks (using backpropagation as learning algorithm; Rumelhart, Hinton, & Williams, 1986) that were trained to recognize the numerosity of the input patterns. Performance of the networks showed (although with some variability) an emergent limited capacity of numerosity recognition. However, this theoretical position apparently presumes that enumeration by counting is already developed when learning to subitize takes place, which is in contrast with experimental data showing that infants can discriminate numerosity (with a precision that increases over development) prior to the emergence of language or symbolic counting (Lipton & Spelke, 2003; Wynn, 1998; Xu & Spelke, 2000).

Ahmad, Casey, and Bale (2002) developed a more elaborated connectionist system that learned both to subitize and count, using two different mechanisms organized in a modular architecture. The subitizing module consisted of two connected parts: (a) a detector of the number of objects represented on an input "visual field" and (b) a one-dimensional SOM (self-organizing map; Kohonen, 1995) neural network of ordered numerosity detectors that self-organized into a compressive number line. After training, the winning nodes in the SOM network for each input pattern were ordered topologically in a way resembling Fechner's law: they were closer to each other as the numerical size increased and farther apart as the numerical difference increased. However, it is likely that these effects do not depend on the properties of the system (e.g., the learning properties of the SOM network, as claimed by the authors) but rather on the encoding of the input. That is, the input to the map, representing activity accumulated over the visual scene, was implemented as a "thermometer" representation, which has been shown to produce size and distance effects in connectionist simulations of number comparison (Zorzi & Butterworth, 1999; see below). The counting module, on the other hand, sequentially enumerated each of the visually presented objects by means of two basic networks that were synchronously running: (a) a "pointing next object" feed-forward neural network and (b) a counting recurrent neural network that "verbally" produced the name of the numerosity. The subitizing and counting modules were combined by means of a "gating" neural network that selected the response of either of them. However, enumeration RTs were not simulated and the model does not directly address human skilled performance.

COMPUTATIONAL APPROACHES FOR REPRESENTING NUMERICAL MAGNITUDE

One important aspect of computational modeling is that theorists are forced to make a number of formal assumptions about the representations on which the computations are carried out. In the context of number processing, numbers need to be turned into patterns of activation over a set of elementary processing units. As previously discussed, most computational models use a representation of numbers that includes magnitude information. Various schemes have been proposed, but they were typically considered as instantiations of the number-line hypothesis. An alternative proposal, built upon the constraint that magnitude information should encode cardinal meaning, is the numerosity code of Zorzi and Butterworth (1997, 1999).

Number Line Codes

The analogue "number line" hypothesis has been implemented in most neural network models of arithmetic (Anderson et al., 1994; McCloskey & Lindemann, 1992; Viscuso et al., 1989) as an ordered sequence of input nodes, where each node stands for a particular number. In this scheme, a number is encoded by activating the corresponding node together with the two immediate neighbors: thus, 5 was represented as the activation of the node labeled "5" plus activation of "4" and "6" (see Figure 5.2, panel A). Although this provides some ordering of numbers, "8" and "4," with no overlapping neighbors, would activate orthogonal representations (i.e., nodes 7-8-9 for "8" and nodes 3-4-5 for "4"). This kind of coding scheme has been described as *barcode magnitude representation* (Anderson, 1998, for review) because number magnitude is coded as a moving "bar" of activation on a topographic scale. It should be pointed out, however, that this scheme does not correspond to either a compressed number line (Dehaene, 2003) or to a linear number line with scalar variability (Gallistel & Gelman, 2000).

In Whalen's (1997) model of arithmetic, numerical magnitudes were encoded as patterns of activation over a set of 250 nodes, such that 100 nodes were active for each number. The total activation across nodes for each magnitude summed to 1. Numerals with similar magnitudes shared nodes with one another, and the closer the magnitudes, the more similar the representations. Crucially, the representations were designed so that larger magnitudes shared more nodes than smaller magnitudes. Moreover, the differences between magnitude decreased in a logarithmic fashion as the numbers increased. Therefore, the representation implements the assumption of a compressed number line.

Dehaene (2001) implemented number line representations, both in the compressive version (Dehaene, 1992) and in the linear version with scalar variability (Gallistel & Gelman, 1992) to simulate the animal data of Brannon, Wusthoff, Gallistel, and Gibbon (2001). The representation of a number *n* was a Gaussian, centered according to a logarithmic scale and with fixed variance (compressed version; see Figure 5.2, panel C) or to a linear scale with variance proportional to *n* (scalar variability version; see Figure 5.2, panel D). The important conclusion was that the two different implementations led to the same metric of number similarity and therefore to the same behavior.

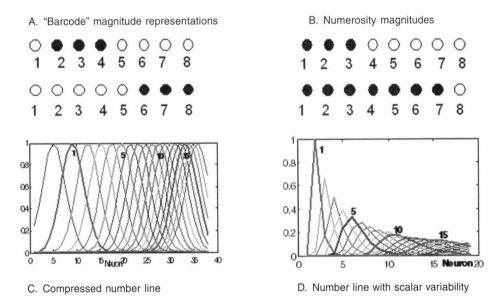

Figure 5.2. Alternative schemes for representing numerical magnitude. A. Barcode magnitude representation (Viscuso et al., 1989; Anderson et al., 1994; McCloskey & Lindemann, 1992). B. Numerosity code (Zorzi & Butterworth, 1999). C. Compressed number line (logarithmic scale and fixed variance, e.g., Dehaene, 2001, 2003). D. Linear number line with scalar variability (e.g., Gallistel & Gelman, 2002; Dehaene, 2001). A color version of this figure can be viewed at www.psypress.com/campbell.

The Numerosity Code

A radically different approach was taken by Zorzi and Butterworth (1997, 1999; also Zorzi, Stoianov, Becker, Umiltà, & Butterworth, submitted). They proposed to represent *numerosity magnitude* straightforwardly as the number of units activated, such that bigger numbers include smaller numbers; therefore, for $N > M$, a set with M members can be put in 1-1 correspondence with a proper subset of the set with N members. This representational scheme is also known as a "thermometer" representation (see Figure 5.2, panel B). The numerosity representation has several advantages. First, it readily maps onto lower-level perceptual processes (e.g., object identification) and enumeration procedures (e.g., subitizing, counting). That is, each magnitude increment in the numerosity representation corresponds to the enumeration of a further element in the to-be-counted set. Second, it entails that larger numbers are more similar to each other than smaller numbers, without assuming a logarithmic compression, since large numbers share more active nodes. For example, 9 and 8 would share 8 nodes, whereas 1 and 2 would share only 1 node. This can also be formalized in terms of the cosine of the angle formed by the vectors coding the two numbers. Finally, it is important to note that Zorzi and Butterworth's (1999) scheme does not assume that the variability of the mapping from symbols to magnitude representation increases with size, as Gallistel and Gelman (1992) proposed. Rather, the mapping is linear and not noisy.

It is interesting that the model of Dehaene and Changeux (1993) appears to contain both a numerosity code and a number line code. The final level of representation (numerosity detectors) is based on a logarithmic coding of numbers (i.e., detectors have Gaussian tuning curves with fixed variance when plotted on a logarithmic scale), an assumption that has recently received support from a study of single-cell recordings in behaving monkeys (Nieder, Freedman, & Miller, 2002). The preceding level of representation in the model (summation clusters; see Figure 5.1), however, is very similar to the numerosity code. These units sum the total activation of a normalized visual input and have increasing thresholds. Therefore, if a given unit receives sufficient input to exceed its threshold, it will be active together with all other units with lower thresholds. In other words, the representation produced by a set of n objects includes the representations of all smaller sets.

In the remainder of this chapter, we will discuss how the numerosity code accounts for the main empirical phenomena that are observed in number comparison, simple arithmetic, and number priming.

THE NUMEROSITY CODE FOR NUMBER COMPARISON

Zorzi and Butterworth (1999) defended the properties of the numerosity code in the context of number comparison. They showed that the distance and magnitude effects can be readily simulated in a model in which a simple nonlinear decision system operates on numerosity codes to select the larger of two numbers.

The model (see Figure 5.3) has two sets of nine input nodes (one set for each of the two numbers to be compared) that are activated according to the numerosity scheme. The representation of the two possible responses (left or right button-press, to indicate which of the numbers is the larger) consists of two nodes, which form a nonlinear response system that exhibits winner-takes-all behavior by means of competitive interactions (lateral inhibition). The decision system is not specific to number processing; rather, it is a general mechanism for response selection that has been previously employed in modeling cognitive domains as different as attention (e.g., Zorzi & Umiltà, 1995) and language processing (e.g., Zorzi, Houghton, & Butterworth, 1998). Activation of the magnitude nodes propagates gradually to the response nodes, and the model is allowed to cycle until a response criterion is reached, which consists of the difference threshold for the activations of the two response nodes.

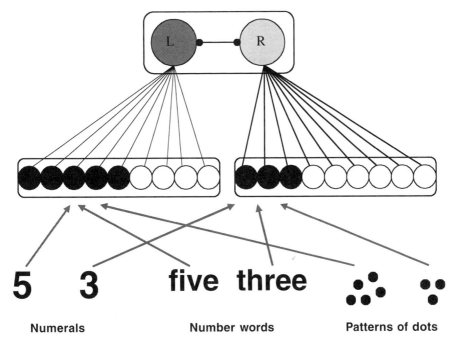

Figure 5.3. The model of number comparison of Zorzi and Butterworth (1999). The numerosity representations of the two input numbers send their activations to the decision system, which selects the response corresponding to the larger number through competitive interactions.

The comparison between two close numbers (e.g., 4 vs. 5) produces longer model RTs than the comparison between more distant numbers (e.g., 2 vs. 5). In both cases, the response node for the larger number needs to inhibit the alternative, incorrect response node to reach response threshold. The stronger competition produced by two close numbers turns into longer latencies (i.e., distance effect). Moreover, a sensitivity to number size emerges in the model through the nonlinearity that is intrinsic to the decision process. The response nodes in the decision system use a sigmoidal output function that bounds activation in the [–1;1] range, as is common in connectionist networks. This results in a compression of the output activation for larger numbers, because their stronger input will correspond to the saturated portion of the sigmoidal curve. In other words, the activation difference between 6 and 8 will be smaller than the difference between 2 and 4.

When run on the entire set of comparisons between two single-digit numbers (n = 72), the model shows an impressive match to human data, both qualitatively (size and distance effects) and quantitatively (the model latencies account for 42% of the variance when regressed onto human comparison RTs; Zorzi et al., submitted).

The model of Zorzi and Butterworth (1999) represents a very important demonstration that analogue representations of number magnitudes are not necessary to fit the data from comparison tasks, as has been often claimed. Moreover, magnitude representations need not be compressed in order to observe a Weber-Fechner logarithmic effect in number comparison, contrary to the claims of Dehaene (e.g., Dehaene, 1992; Dehaene, 2003). In Zorzi and Butterworth's model, numerals are mapped linearly onto magnitude representations, and the compressive effect on the comparison times emerged by virtue of the interactions of the numerosity code with a nonlinear decision process. It is also not necessary to postulate that magnitude representations have the property of scalar variability, that is, that the standard deviation of mapping from numerals to magnitudes increases with the mean magnitudes of the numbers, as claimed by Gallistel and Gelman (1992).

THE NUMEROSITY CODE FOR SIMPLE ARITHMETIC

Stoianov, Zorzi, Becker, and Umiltà (2002) contrasted symbolic codes, number line codes, and the numerosity code in a series of neural network simulations of simple addition. Four different types of representation were contrasted:

- *Symbolic Code.* Symbolic number encoding was abstracted to a simple localist scheme, which was independent from the numerical meaning. Each number was encoded by the activation of a dedicated node. Therefore, this simulation examined a model in which simple arithmetic facts are stored in a verbal form (e.g., Dehaene & Cohen, 1995).
- *Number Line Codes.* Following Dehaene (2001), two versions of number line were implemented. In the compressed number line, the representation of a number n was a Gaussian, centered according to a logarithmic scale and with fixed variance (see Figure 5.2, panel C), whereas in the linear number line with scalar variability, the Gaussian was centered according to a linear scale with variance proportional to n (see Figure 5.2, panel D).
- *Numerosity Code.* Numbers were encoded using the numerosity scheme of Zorzi and Butterworth (1999) (see Figure 5.2, panel B).

To assess independently the computational properties of the representations, all simulations used exactly the same network architecture and fact frequency was not manipulated. Therefore, each network was simply exposed to all simple addition facts, from 1 + 1 to 9 + 9. Each addition fact consisted of the representation of the two addends and of their sum (encoded according to one of the schemes).

In line with previous connectionist attempts to model mental arithmetic, Stoianov et al. (2002) used an associative-memory neural network, the Boltzmann Machine (Ackley et al., 1985), trained with the contrastive divergence mean field learning algorithm (Welling & Hinton, 2002). Training patterns are encoded by visible units, whereas hidden units capture high-order statistics. The update of a weight connecting two units is proportional to the difference between the average of the correlations between these two units, computed at time zero (positive, or fixed phase) and after reconstructing the pattern (negative, or free-running phase). This learning algorithm is neurobiologically plausible, as it uses only local signals and Hebbian rules.

Thus, arithmetic facts are learned and stored as attractor states in the recurrent neural network. After successful learning, if some of the visible units are clamped with a part of a learned pattern (input), the network should iteratively activate the rest of the units according to the data distribution learned (retrieval). In particular, fixing the two arguments (e.g., 7 + 5 = ?), the network will retrieve the result of the corresponding arithmetic operation (here, 12), since in the learning data it would have been the only correct completion to this input. The number of cycles to settle is taken as a measure of the network RT for the stimulus.

The results of the simulations were straightforward. First, numerosity representations made learning arithmetic facts easier than any other scheme. That is, the network using the numerosity code took a lower number of epochs (i.e., passes through the training set) to learn the addition facts. Second, and more crucial, only the network using the numerosity code exhibited the problem-size effect. The RT distributions for the other codes ranged from uniform to U-shaped and thus did not resemble the pattern of human RTs. Stoianov et al. (2002) also carried out a formal analysis of the statistical properties of the various representational schemes. This showed that the pattern of network RTs was produced by the joint effects of (a) the empirical distribution of active bits (i.e., a bias toward smaller numerosities) and (b) the degree of pattern overlap among arithmetic facts. These properties "conspire" toward a problem-size effect only in the case of the numerosity code. Further simulations with the numerosity code (Zorzi et al., submitted) show that both qualitative and quantitative fits to the human data can be further improved when fact frequency (manipulated according to frequency tables reported in Ashcraft & Christy, 1995) and the size of the arithmetic table (i.e., extending the table up to 12 + 12) are taken into account.

THE ROLE OF SEMANTIC AND SYMBOLIC CODES IN SIMPLE ARITHMETIC

Building upon the results of Stoianov et al. (2002), Stoianov, Zorzi, and Umilta (2003) expanded the model with a symbolic component. The aim of the study was to establish how symbolic representations of numbers would interact with the semantic representations. The network could in principle use either type of information, or at least differentially weight them, in learning simple arithmetic. Humans deal with more than one type of symbolic representation of numbers–verbal numerals (both spoken and written), Arabic digits, Roman numbers, etc. However, symbolic number encoding was abstracted to a simple two-digit code, which is independent from the numerical meaning, with the exception of the two-digit syntactic structure (the right digit stands for the units and the left one stands for the decades). Thus, each number was encoded by the activation of a dedicated node and an additional "ten" unit allowed the representation of two-digit numbers (for encoding sums up to 18).

Thus, representations of arithmetic facts integrated both symbolic and semantic (i.e., numerosity) components (see Figure 5.4). Children usually study arithmetic facts in verbal or Arabic notations (but also semantically, e.g., by finger counting or by observing set relations in the visual input). When pupils begin to learn arithmetic, they have already developed, or would shortly develop, associations between symbolic forms and semantic representations of the numbers. Hence, both the semantic and the symbolic codes would be activated during learning or practicing arithmetic. Accordingly, the network was trained on both symbolic and semantic input. As previously described, the network after learning can retrieve the result of an arithmetic operation as the best completion to the two input arguments. In the extended model, this can be achieved by activating the arguments in both symbolic and semantic forms, but, importantly, it can also be done by clamping the symbolic arguments only. The latter testing mode makes the retrieval objectively more difficult, but it is the best approximation to the task faced by humans when presented with arithmetic problems.

When provided with symbolic input only, the network had virtually the same success in retrieving the correct sum as when both symbolic and semantic inputs were present. However, it turned out that in both testing conditions the network relied upon the semantic representa-

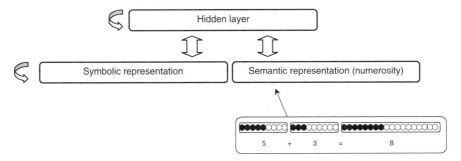

Figure 5.4. The model of simple arithmetic of Stoianov et al. (2003). Arithmetic facts (the two arguments and their result) are encoded in the visible layer using both symbolic and semantic representations. The structure of the semantic representation, based on the numerosity code, is shown in the call-out box. Note that the network is fully recurrent (each unit is bidirectionally connected to all other units in both the visible layer and the hidden layer).

tions to solve the task. The analysis of the dynamics of retrieval showed that the network had developed a very specific procedure for retrieving the arithmetic facts, comprising three parallel stages: (a) activating the associated semantic arguments, (b) retrieving the result corresponding to the current semantic arguments, and (c) activating the symbolic result corresponding to the current semantic result. This procedure contributed to producing a better match to the problem-size effect, because the time to access the semantic arguments increases with numerosity, adding up to the time to retrieve semantic facts. In a network trained with fact frequencies manipulated according to Ashcraft and Christy's (1995) frequency tables, the model RTs accounted for over 50% of the variance (N = 72) when regressed onto the human addition latencies of Butterworth et al. (2001).

The idea that semantic processing is central to mental arithmetic is certainly not new (e.g., McCloskey, Aluminosa, & Sokol, 1991). However, the model of Stoianov et al. (2003) shows that a network provided with both semantic and symbolic codes self-organizes its functioning to exploit the properties (and systematicity) of the semantic representations. It is important to stress that this division of labor is purely data driven.

To further investigate the division of labor between semantic and symbolic codes, Stoianov, Zorzi, and Umiltà (2004) carried out a series of simulations of acquired dyscalculia using the dual-code model just described. Acquired dyscalculia is a condition of impaired arithmetic performance in brain-damaged patients. If simple arithmetic is indeed reliant on semantic representations, damage to the semantic component of the network should affect addition performance to a greater extent than damage to the symbolic component.

Acquired dyscalculia was simulated by damaging the connections between the arguments and the result (*direct* pathway among visible units) or the connections between the hidden units and the visible units encoding the result (*mediated* pathway). To address the symbolic/semantic issue, Stoianov et al. (2004) selectively damaged (a) the *semantic* or (b) the *symbolic* components of the network. Damage consisted of random elimination of 20%, 50%, or 80% of the connections in (a) the *direct* pathway or (b) the *mediated* pathway between the hidden units and the result (see Figure 5.5). As expected, the more extensive the damage, the worse was the

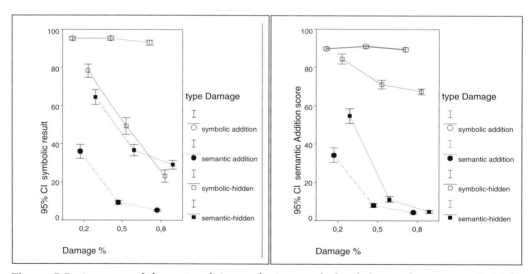

Figure 5.5. Accuracy of the network in producing symbolic (left panel) or semantic (right panel) responses after artificial lesions (adapted from Stoianov et al., 2004). Filled and outline marks represent the network performance after damage to semantic and to symbolic connections, respectively. Circles and squares represent damage to direct and to mediated connections, respectively. The x-axis shows the percentage of damage applied. Notably, performance is strongly affected by semantic damage.

network performance. However, damage to the semantic component had a stronger effect on performance than damage to the symbolic part did: removing even a small percentage of the semantic links was followed by loss of almost 50% of the learned facts and the responses significantly deviated from the results. This held independently of the input condition and output type tested (symbolic or semantic). In contrast, damage to the symbolic part typically produced few errors, with responses being very close to the correct results. Importantly, removing direct semantic connections resulted in greater damage than removing mediated semantic connections, whereas damage to the direct symbolic links did not affect performance.

Note that semantic damage can be assumed to correspond to lesions of the inferior parietal lobule (IPL), which causes impairments in addition and subtraction (e.g., patient MAR, Dehaene & Cohen, 1997; patient SS, van Harskamp, Rudge, & Cipolotti, 2002). Damage of the links between the hidden units and the symbolic result disrupted the production of symbolic responses but only weakly affected the retrieval of the semantic result (see Figure 5.5, right panel). This appears to mimic the behavior of patients with impairments in the language areas and preserved IPL, e.g., patients SAM (Cipolotti & Butterworth, 1995), ATH and VOL (Cohen et al., 2000). Arithmetic in these patients was generally preserved, but output deficits prevented them from reporting the results.

PRIMING THE NUMEROSITY CODE

The phenomenon of priming refers to a temporary change in the ability to identify perceptual objects as a result of a specific prior experience. When the effect is semantic (*semantic priming*), as opposed to perceptual, it allows one to establish the strength of the relations among items belonging to the same or to different categories. Several studies have found semantic priming effects for numbers (e.g., den Heyer & Briand, 1986; Koechlin, Naccache, Block, & Dehaene, 1999; Reynvoet & Brysbaert, 1999; Reynvoet, Brysbaert, & Fias, 2002). These studies show that the priming effect is inversely proportional to the numerical distance between the prime and the target (*distance-priming effect*). Moreover, the effect is symmetric with respect to the priming direction and additive to the effect of repetition priming (Reynvoet et al., 2002).

The symmetry of the semantic priming effect has a theoretical relevance. The size of the priming effect for a given target, say 5, is the same for both larger (e.g., 6) or smaller (e.g., 4) primes. This finding is difficult to reconcile with the compressed number line model, whereby the distance between two neighboring numbers depends on their numerical size: if the target 5 is closer to 6 than to 4, priming with 6 should produce stronger priming. It is therefore important to establish whether the numerosity code can account for the priming data. *Prima facie*, the structure of the numerosity code and, in particular, the fact that larger numbers include smaller numbers, might suggest that it predicts an asymmetric priming effect. However, this conclusion is incorrect because the numerosity code is linear. In recurrent neural networks, the priming effect is inversely proportional to the length of the trajectory in the unit's state space between initial state (prime) and final state (target). Regardless of whether the prime is 4 or 6, settling to target 5 requires changing the state of one unit: in one case the unit must be switched on (from 4 to 5), whereas in the other case it must be switched off (from 6 to 5). Since there is no reason to expect that one of these two operations takes a longer time to be completed, the priming should be symmetric.

Zorzi, Stoianov, Priftis, and Umiltà (2003) tested this prediction in a simulation. A network was trained to transcode symbolic codes to semantic (numerosity) codes, for numbers ranging from 1 to 18. Architecture and learning algorithm were identical to those of the addition simulations (Stoianov et al. 2003), with the exception that hidden units were not used (the task is much simpler). After training, the priming task was simulated as follows: (a) the network was primed by activating the semantic units representing the prime numerosity, and (b) the symbolic representation of the target was then activated and the network was allowed to

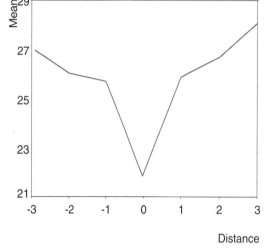

Figure 5.6. Mean network RTs (in number of cycles) in the priming simulation of Zorzi et al. (2003). The x-axis shows the distance between prime and target.

transcode it to the corresponding numerosity representation. As in the Reynovoet et al. (2002) study, target numbers n ranged from 4 to 9 and primes ranged from $n - 3$ to $n + 3$. The simulations showed an excellent fit to the human data. The network transcoded symbolic numbers faster when semantically primed with the same numerosity as that of the target (repetition effect), and the transcoding time gradually increased when the distance between the two of them increased (distance-priming effect). Moreover, the distance effect was symmetric (see Figure 5.6).

CONCLUDING REMARKS

The numerosity code proposed by Zorzi and Butterworth (1999; Zorzi et al., submitted) is a linear, discrete representation of cardinal meaning. Indeed, an exact representation of numerosity seems to better capture our intuitive understanding of integer numbers. What is more important, however, is that network models based on the numerosity code account for a wide range of empirical data: distance and size effects in number comparison, the symmetric distance effect in number priming, and the problem-size effect in simple arithmetic. Notably, phenomena that have been typically attributed to nonlinear (Dehaene, 2003) or noisy (Gallistel & Gelman, 2000) analogue magnitudes can be readily simulated with network models that operate on the numerosity code. On the other hand, recent empirical findings such as the symmetry of the distance-priming effect (Reynvoet et al. 2002) and the absence of a size effect in number bisection (Zorzi, Priftis, & Umiltà, 2002) are difficult to reconcile with nonlinear coding schemes but fit well with the linear nature of the numerosity code. Thus, this novel perspective offers a unitary and comprehensive account of the diverse phenomena that characterize numerical cognition in humans.

Nonetheless, this theoretical framework would seem to face a potential difficulty if we turn to the issue of the neuronal correlates of number representations. The numerosity code seems to be at odds with the recent finding that the tuning functions of "number neurons" in the monkey brain (Nieder et al., 2002) fit the logarithmic coding of Dehaene and Changeux's (1993) model. That is, the neurons studied by Nieder and colleagues have Gaussian tuning curves with fixed variance when plotted on a logarithmic scale. However, as previously discussed, the number neurons in Dehaene and Changeux's model ("numerosity detectors") are activated by a preceding layer of neurons ("summation clusters") that instantiate a numerosity code. In other words, the numerosity code appears to be a prerequisite for developing numerosity detectors. This view is supported by a recent study of Verguts and Fias (in press), which addressed the issue of how the numerosity detectors can be learned in response to a non-symbolic input (note that the numerosity detection system was hard-wired in Dehaene and Changeux's model). Verguts and Fias showed that number neurons with the characteristics described by Nieder et al. (2002) may develop through unsupervised learning in response to the activity of a layer of summation nodes. Notably, the summation nodes were activated according to the numerosity code (with the small variation of using two nodes for each numerosity increment instead of one).

Therefore, the question of whether neurons with tuning functions resembling a numerosity code will ever be found using single-cell recordings remains an empirical issue, but their existence is predicted not only by our model but also by all models containing a neuronal pool that accumulates activity over the visual scene (i.e., "summation neurons"; Ahmad et al., 2002; Dehaene & Changeux, 1993; Verguts & Fias, in press). The same reasoning applies to the issue of the neuroimaging correlates (e.g., brain activation as measured through the fMRI BOLD signal) of numerosity representations. Finally, it should be noted that the number neurons described by Nieder and colleagues (2002) were located in the primate lateral prefrontal cortex rather than in the parietal regions that have been classically associated to magnitude representations in both neuropsychological and neuroimaging studies in humans (Dehaene, Piazza, Pinel, & Cohen, 2003, for a review).

Much modeling work remains to be done. The picture that is likely to emerge is one in which multiple representations of numerical quantity coexist and are differentially used or weighted on the basis of specific task demands (e.g., Siegler & Opfer, 2003). Moreover, the way in which the development of numerical representations is influenced by the acquisition of the symbolic number system needs to be systematically explored (e.g., Verguts & Fias, in press). Finally, extending the models of mental arithmetic (e.g., Stoianov et al., 2003) to deal with multiple operations (addition, subtraction, multiplication) might be crucial for understanding the neuropsychological and neuroimaging patterns of association and dissociation among different arithmetic operations (see Dehaene et al., 2003, for a review).

The simulations of simple arithmetic using different input representations (Stoianov et al., 2002) also speak to the issue of adjudication between models. Adjudication can be a difficult and delicate enterprise (see, e.g., Zorzi, 2000), but the comparison between networks that differ only for the input coding scheme is a strong formal test of the different theories. The results of these simulations have far-reaching implications: together with the fact that the numerosity code is crucial for observing the problem-size effect, they show that domain-general learning systems come to exhibit human-like performance only if they operate on domain-specific representations.

REFERENCES

Ackley, D., Hinton, G., & Sejnowski, T. (1985). A learning algorithm for Boltzmann Machines. *Cognitive Science, 9,* 147–169

Ahmad, K., Casey, M., & Bale, T. (2002). Connectionist simulation of quantification skills. *Connection Science, 14,* 165–201.

Anderson, J. A. (1998). Learning arithmetic with a neural network: Seven times seven is about fifty. In Scarborough & S. Stenberg (Eds.), *An invitation to cognitive science: Methods, models, and conceptual issues* (vol. 4, pp. 255–300). Cambridge, MA: MIT Press.

Anderson, J. A., Spoehr, K. T., & Bennett, D. J. (1994). A study in numerical perversity: Teaching arithmetic to a neural network. In D. S. Levine & M. Aparicio

(Eds.), *Neural networks for knowledge representation and inference.* Hillsdale, NJ: Erlbaum.

Anderson, J. R. (1993). *Rules of the mind.* Hillsdale, NJ: Lawrence Erlbaum.

Ashcraft, M. (1992). Cognitive arithmetic: A review of data and theory. *Cognition, 44,* 75–106.

Ashcraft, M., & Christy, K. (1995). The frequency of arithmetical facts in elementary texts: addition and multiplication in grades 1–6. *Journal for Research in Mathematical Education, 26,* 396–421.

Brannon, E., Wusthoff, C., Gallistel, C. R., & Gibon, J. (2001). Numerical subtraction in the pigeon: Evidence for a linear subjective number scale. *Psychological Science, 12,* 238–243.

Butterworth, B. (1999). *The mathematical brain*. London: McMillan.

Butterworth, B., Zorzi, M., Girelli, L., & Jonckheere, A. R. (2001). Storage and retrieval of addition facts: The role of number comparison. *Quarterly Journal of Experimental Psychology, 54A*, 1005–1029.

Campbell, J. I. D. (1994). Architectures for numerical cognition. *Cognition, 53*, 1–44.

Campbell, J. I. D. (1995). Mechanism of simple addition and multiplication: a modified network–interference theory and simulation. *Mathematical cognition, 1*, 121–164.

Campbell, J. I. D., & Xue, Q. (2001). Cognitive arithmetic across cultures. *Journal of Experimental Psychology: General, 130*, 299–315.

Cipolotti, L., & Butterworth, B. (1995). Toward a multiroute model of number processing: Impaired number transcoding with preserved calculation skills. *Journal of Experimental Psychology: General, 124*, 375–390.

Cipolotti, L., Butterworth, B., & Denes, G. (1991) A specific deficit for numbers in a case of dense acalculia. *Brain, 114*, 2619–2637.

Cohen, L., & Dehaene, S. (2000). Calculating without reading: Unsuspected residual abilities in pure alexia. *Cognitive Neuropsychology, 17*, 563–583.

Dehaene, S. (1992). Varieties of numerical abilities. *Cognition, 44*, 1–42.

Dehaene, S. (2001). Subtracting pigeons: Logarithmic or linear? *Psychological Science, 12*, 244–246.

Dehaene, S. (2003). The neural basis of the Weber–Fechner law: A logarithmic mental number line. *Trends in Cognitive Sciences, 7*, 145–147.

Dehaene, S., & Changeux, J. P. (1993). Development of elementary numerical abilities: A neuronal model. *Journal of Cognitive Neuroscience, 5*, 390–407.

Dehaene, S., & Cohen, L. (1995). Towards an anatomical and functional model of number processing. *Mathematical Cognition, 1*, 83–120.

Dehaene, S., & Cohen, L. (1997) Cerebral pathways for calculation: double dissociation between Gerstmann's acalculia and subcortical acalculia. *Cortex, 33*, 219–250.

Dehaene, S., Dupoux, E., & Mehler, J. (1990). Is numerical comparison digital? Analogical and symbolic effects in two-digit number comparison. *Journal of Experimental Psychology: Human Perception and Performance, 16*, 626–641.

Dehaene, S., Piazza, M., Pinel, P., & Cohen, L. (2003). Three parietal circuits for number processing. *Cognitive Neuropsychology, 20*, 487–506.

Delazer, M., & Butterworth, B. (1997). A dissociation of number meanings. *Cognitive Neuropsychology, 14*, 613–636.

den Heyer, K., & Briand, K. (1986). Priming single digit numbers: Automatic spreading activation dissipates as a function of semantic distance. *American Journal of Psychology, 99*, 315–340.

Gallistel, C. R., & Gelman, R. (1992). Preverbal and verbal counting and computation. *Cognition, 44*, 43–74

Gallistel, C. R., & Gelman, R. (2000). Non-verbal numerical cognition: from reals to integers. *Trends in Cognitive Sciences, 4*, 59–65.

Groen, G. J., & Parkman, J. M. (1972). A chronometric analysis of simple addition, *Psychological Review, 79*, 329–343.

Koechlin, E., Naccache, L., Block, E., & Dehaene, S. (1999). Primed numbers: Exploring the modularity of numerical representaions with masked and unmasked priming. *Journal of Experimental Psychology: Human Perception and Performance, 25*, 1882–1905.

Kohonen, T. (1995). *Self-organizing maps*. Berlin: Springer-Verlag.

LeFevre, J., Sadesky, G. S., & Bisanz, J. (1996). Selection of procedures in mental addition: Reassessing the problem size effect in adults. *Journal of Experimental Psychology: Learning, Memory, and Cognition, 22*, 216–230.

Lipton, J. S., & Spelke, E. S. (2003). Origins of number sense: Large-number discrimination in human infants. *Psychological Science, 14*, 396–401.

Lories, G., Aubrun, A., & Seron, X. (1994). Lesioning McCloskey and Lindemann's (1992) MATHNET: The effect of damage location and amount. *Journal of Biological Systems, 2*, 335–356.

McClelland, J. L., & Rumelhart, D. E. (1981). An interactive activation model of context effects in letter perception: Part 1. An account of basic findings. *Psychological Review, 88*, 375–407.

McCloskey, M. (1992). Cognitive mechanisms in number processing: Evidence from acquired dyscalculia. *Cognition, 44*, 107-157.

McCloskey, M., & Lindemann, M. (1992). MATHNET: preliminary results from a distributed model of arithmetic fact retrieval. In J. Campbell (Ed.), *The nature and origin of mathematical skills* (pp. 365–409). Amsterdam: Elsevier.

McCloskey, M., Aliminosa, D., & Sokol, S. (1991). Facts, rules and procedures in normal calculation: Evidence from multiple single-patient studies of impaired arithmetic fact retrieval. *Brain and Cognition, 17*, 154–203.

Moyer, R., & Landauer, T. (1967). Time required for judgements of numerical inequality. *Nature, 215*, 1519–1520.

Nieder, A., Freedman, D. J., & Miller, E. K. (2002). Representation of the quantity of visual items in the primate prefrontal cortex. *Science, 297*, 1708–1711.

Peterson, S. A., & Simon, T. J. (2000). Computational evidence for the subitizing phenomenon as an emergent property of the human cognitive architecture. *Cognitive Science, 24*, 93–122.

Piaget, J. (1952). *The Child's Conception of Number*. London: Routledge & Kegan Paul.

Reynvoet, B., & Brysbaert, M. (1999). Single-digit and two-digit Arabic numerals address the same semantic number line. *Cognition, 72*, 191–201.

Reynvoet, B., Brysbaert, M., & Fias, W. (2002). Semantic priming in number naming. *Quarterly Journal of Experimental Psychology, 55A*, 1127–1139.

Rumelhart, D. E., Hinton, G. E., & Williams, R. J. (1986). Learning internal representations by error propagation. In D. E. Rumelhart, & J. L. McClelland (Eds.), *Parallel distributed processing: Explorations in the microstructure of cognition* (Vol. 1: Foundations). Cambridge, MA: MIT Press.

Siegler, R. S., & Opfer, J. E. (2003). The development of numerical estimation: Evidence for multiple representations of numerical quantity. *Psychological Science, 14*, 237–243.

Stoianov, I., Zorzi, M., Becker, S., & Umiltà, C. (2002). Associative arithmetic with Boltzmann Machines: The role of number representations. In J. Dorronsoro (Ed.), *ICANN 2002, Lecture notes in computer science, 2415*, pp. 277–283. Berlin: Springer.

Stoianov, I., Zorzi, M., & Umiltà, C. (2003). A connectionist model of simple mental arithmetic. In F. Schmalhofer, R. M. Young, & G. Katz (Eds.), *Proceedings of EuroCogSci03* (pp. 313–318). Mahwah, NJ: Erlbaum.

Stoianov, I., Zorzi, M., & Umilta, C. (2004). The role of semantic and symbolic representations in arithmetic processing: Insights from simulated dyscalculia in a connectionist model. *Cortex, 40,* 194–196.

Van Harskapm, N., Rudge, P., & Cipolotti, L. (2002). Are multiplication facts implemented by the left supramarginal and angular gyrus? *Neuropsychologia, 40,* 1786–1793.

Verguts, T., & Fias, W. (in press). Representation of number in animals and humans: A neural model. *Journal of Cognitive Neuroscience.*

Viscuso, S. R., Anderson, J. A., & Spoehr, K. T. (1989). Representing simple arithmetic in neural networks. In G. Tiberghien (Ed.), *Advances in cognitive science* (Vol. 2, pp. 141–164). Chichester, UK: Ellis Horwood.

Welling, M., & Hinton, G. (2002). A new learning algorithm for mean field Boltzmann Machines. In J. Dorronsoro (Ed.), *ICANN2002, Lecture notes in computer science, 2415,* pp. 351–357. Berlin: Springer.

Whalen, J. (1997). The influence of semantic magnitude representations on arithmetic: Theory, data, and simulation. In M. G. Shafto & P. Langley (Eds.), *Proceedings of the nineteenth annual conference of the Cognitive Science Society* (pp. 814–819). Mahwah, NJ: Erlbaum.

Wynn, K. (1998) Psychological foundations of number: numerical competence in human infants. *Trends in Cognitive Science, 2,* 296–303.

Wynn, K. (1992). Addition and subtraction by human infants. *Nature, 358,* 749–751.

Xu, F., & Spelke, E. S. (2000). Large number discrimination in 6-month-old infants. *Cognition, 74,* B1–B11.

Zorzi, M. (2000). Serial processing in reading aloud: No challenge for a parallel model. *Journal of Experimental Psychology: Human Perception and Performance, 26,* 847–856.

Zorzi, M. (2004). Computational models of reading. In G. Houghton (Ed.), *Connectionist models in cognitive psychology.* London: Psychology Press.

Zorzi, M., & Butterworth, B. (1997). On the representation of number concepts. In M. Shafto & P. Langley (Eds.), *Proceedings of the nineteenth annual conference of the Cognitive Science Society* (p. 1098). Mahwah, NJ: Erlbaum.

Zorzi, M., & Butterworth, B. (1999). A computational model of number comparison. In M. Hahn & S. C. Stoness (Eds.), *Proceedings of the twenty first annual conference of the Cognitive Science Society* (pp. 778–783). Mahwah, NJ: Erlbaum.

Zorzi, M., & Umiltà, C. (1995). A computational model of the Simon effect. *Psychological Research, 58,* 193–205.

Zorzi, M., Houghton, G., & Butterworth, B. (1998). Two routes or one in reading aloud? A connectionist dual-process model. *Journal of Experimental Psychology: Human Perception and Performance, 24,* 1131–1161.

Zorzi, M., Priftis, K., & Umiltà, C. (2002). Neglect disrupts the mental number line. *Nature, 417,* 138–139.

Zorzi, M., Stoianov, I., Becker, S., Umiltà, C., & Butterworth, B. (2004). *The numerosity code for the representation of numerical magnitude.* Manuscript submitted for publication.

Zorzi, M., Stoianov, I., Priftis, K., & Umiltà, C. (2003, January). *Semantic priming with the numerosity representations: Connectionist simulation.* Presented at the Twenty-first European Workshop on Cognitive Neuropsychology, Bressanone, Italy.

6

What Animals Know about Numbers

Elizabeth M. Brannon

Adult humans use number to categorize, quantify, and measure almost every aspect of our environment—be it serial numbers, football jerseys, addresses, shoe sizes, weights, heights, spatial coordinates, grocery prices, batting averages, or the Dow Jones Industrial Average. This book documents the vast research that has addressed how the human mind represents number and makes mathematical calculations, the biological bases of the human number sense, and the development of both nonverbal and verbal mathematics. Although humans alone are capable of complex and abstract mathematics, a Darwinian perspective predicts that even the most complicated and impressive human cognitive capacities should have precursors in the minds of nonhuman animals. In accord with this prediction, researchers of the animal mind have made it increasingly difficult to argue that any particular complex human behavior is uniquely human. Over the last few decades, precursors of language (e.g., Savage-Rumbaugh, Shanker, & Taylor, 1998), culture (e.g., Whiten et al., 1999; Van Schaik et al., 2003), tool use (e.g., Boesch, 1995), theory of mind (e.g., Tomasello, Call, & Hare, 2003), metacognition (e.g., Shields, Smith, & Washburn, 1997), and even music appreciation (Wright, Rivera, Hulse, Shyan, & Neiworth, 2000) have been found in nonhuman primate species. Likewise, researchers of the animal mind have developed many different experimental paradigms to test the numerical capacities of animals and found that a wide variety of species possess numerical competence. The goal of this chapter is to summarize the main findings that a century of study of animal numerical competence has revealed and to highlight the similarities and differences between human and nonhuman numerical abilities.

It would be impossible to review all of the many paradigms that have been used to study animal numerical competence or each numerical feat that animals have mastered in the laboratory, so instead I will review the most important conclusions that can be drawn from this rich literature with a few key examples. First, I review the evidence that animals represent number abstractly, independently of superficial features or continuous stimulus attributes such as surface area. Second, I describe the support for the claim that animals not only represent number but also operate on their numerical representations by performing arithmetic calculations. Third, I review the evidence that an animal number sense is likely to be an evolutionary adaptation rather than a fancy circus act with no biological function. Fourth, I review data that address how number is represented in the animal mind, both in terms of the format of the representation and the process by which the representations are formed. The fifth section summarizes a burgeoning new area of research that is uncovering the neural basis of numerical ability in animals. Finally, I offer some conclusions about the similarities and differences between animal and human numerical capacities.

ABSTRACT NUMBER

What kind of evidence is required to claim that an animal holds an abstract number concept? First, we must be sure that the concept is truly numerical in nature and not a mere by-product of an ability to attend carefully to correlated stimulus features such as brightness, density, or surface area. In fact, the study of numerical competence in animals is a particularly difficult endeavor because there is a multitude of continuous variables that typically covary with number. For example, ten acorns are more numerous than five acorns but also have a greater volume and surface area, two bananas are more numerous than one but also have a greater caloric content and hedonic value, and three alarm calls are more numerous than two but are also typically longer in duration. To demonstrate an abstract number concept it is necessary to control for all of these many continuous variables (time, perimeter, area, volume, hedonic value, energetic effort, etc.) and research to date has had variable success in eliminating these confounds.

Flexibility is another important aspect of an abstract number concept. For example, if trained to numerically discriminate geometric shapes, will animals numerically discriminate collections of fruits or conspecifics? A truly abstract number concept should also allow animals to recognize the equivalence between stimuli presented in different modalities. A young child uses the same word to describe the numerosity of two dogs, two barks, and two dog biscuits. Does the dog also appreciate the profound equivalence between these numerical sets?

A nice demonstration that rhesus monkeys represent number independently of continuous dimensions comes from a recent study by Jordan and Brannon (2003). Three rhesus monkeys were trained in a delayed match-to-sample task in which the monkeys were required to match stimuli based on numerosity and ignore the color, size, density, or cumulative area of the elements. In initial training the sample stimulus contained 2 or 8 elements. After the monkey touched the sample stimulus, it disappeared and the monkey was presented with a choice between a stimulus that contained two elements and a second stimulus that contained eight elements. Element, size, color, configuration, cumulative surface area, and density were all controlled (see Figure 6.1). Performance did not vary systematically with cumulative surface area, element size, or density. Subsequently, monkeys were tested in a bisection procedure in which the sample contained anywhere from 1 to 9 elements and the choices again contained 2 or 8 elements. The monkeys' job was to choose the test stimulus that was most similar in number to the sample. As can be seen in Figure 6.2, the probability with which the monkeys chose 8 varied systematically as a function of stimulus numerosity.

Another example of abstract numerical ability in monkeys comes from an experiment in which two rhesus monkeys were trained to respond to exemplars of the numerosities 1–4 in ascending numerical order (Brannon & Terrace, 1998, 2000, 2002). On each trial, four stimuli were presented in a random spatial configuration on a touch-sensitive video monitor with each stimulus containing 1, 2, 3, or 4 elements (see Figure 6.3b). The elements were either simple geometric shapes or more complex clip art shapes, and the stimuli contained a homogeneous or heterogeneous collection of elements. Across the 35 training and 150 test sets, non-numerical cues, such as surface area, were randomly varied so that number was the only valid cue as to the ordinal position of each stimulus in the 4-item sequence (see Figure 6.3a).

After the monkeys learned each of the 35 training lists to a performance criterion, they were tested with 150 novel stimulus sets, each presented only for a single trial. These test

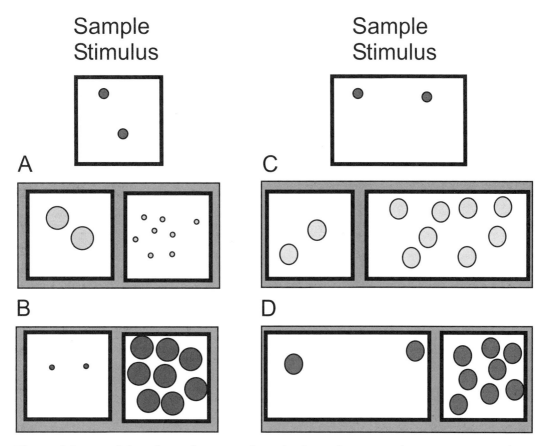

Figure 6.1. In a delayed match-to-sample task, three rhesus monkeys were required to match visual stimuli based on numerosity, independently of continuous dimensions such as surface area. Four example trial types are shown from two different phases of the experiment. All four trials contained a choice between a stimulus with two and eight elements in test. To control for surface area, trial types A and B were randomized so that on some trials (A) the smaller numerosity contained a larger surface area than the larger numerosity and on other trials (B) the larger numerosity contained a larger numerosity. Note that in no case did the surface area of the correct or incorrect choice match that of the sample. To control for density, trial types C and D were randomized so that on some trials density of the two and eight stimuli was equated (C) and on other trials the size of the stimulus background was reversed (D) so that background size could not be used as an indicator of the correct choice.

sessions provided no opportunity to memorize specific stimulus features; thus, above-chance performance would be evidence that the monkeys used a numerical rule. Figures 6.4a and 6.4b show that the monkeys' performance improved rapidly over the 35 training sets, and their performance was not impaired in the 5 test sessions that were composed of trial-unique stimulus sets. In addition, monkeys performed above chance on all 7 different stimulus classes. These data demonstrate that rhesus monkeys can discriminate the numerosities 1–4 without using non-numerical cues such as shape, color, or element size or cumulative element surface area.

Using a completely different experimental paradigm adapted from procedures used to study categorization in human infants, Hauser and colleagues (Hauser, Dehaene, Dehaene-Lambertz, & Patalano, 2002) tested tamarin monkeys in a habituation–dishabituation task where monkeys

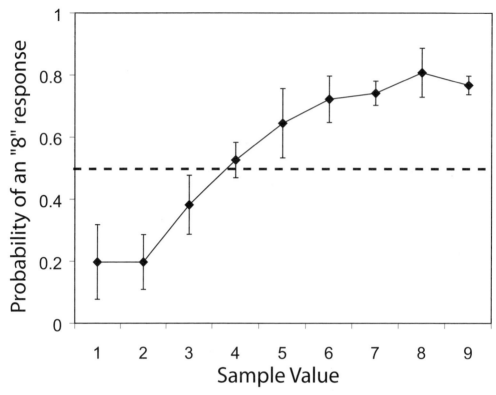

Figure 6.2. The probability with which an exemplar of the numerosity 8 is chosen rather than an exemplar of the numerosity 2, plotted as a function of the numerosity of the sample. Data reflect an average of 3 monkeys over approximately 100 unreinforced trials for each sample numerosity. Error bars indicate standard error of the mean.

were habituated to two or three tones and then tested with 2 or 3 spoken syllables, carefully controlling for the duration of the segments. The tamarin monkeys oriented significantly longer toward the speaker when it played the novel number compared to the familiar number of syllables, suggesting that the tamarins recognized the equivalence of 2 tones and 2 syllables.

A related question is whether animals appreciate the numerical equivalence between sets of auditory and visual stimuli. Church and Meck (1984) trained a group of rats to press a right-hand lever when presented with two sounds and a left-hand lever when presented with four sounds. The tones were then replaced with light flashes, and half of the rats were given the same contingency, whereas the other half of the rats were placed in a reversal condition that required them to make a left response when presented with 2 light flashes and a right response when presented with 4 light flashes (see Figure 6.5). The rats in the reversal condition took significantly longer to learn the new pairings compared to the group for which the number responses were unchanged. In a second experiment, Church and Meck (1984) provided even more dramatic evidence that rats represent number amodally. Rats were trained to make a right response to two tones or lights and a left response to four tones or lights. In unreinforced test sessions, the rats were then presented with 1 or 2 compound stimuli that contained 1 light flash and 1 tone presented simultaneously. The key finding was that rats classified two compound stimuli as a "four" stimulus, suggesting that they were summating the individual stimuli independent of stimulus modality. The Church and Meck experiments are one of the only attempts to address cross-modal number representation in animals, and more studies addressing this important issue are sorely needed.

A

Equal Size

Equal Surface Area

Random Size

Clip Art

Clip Art Mixed

Random Size & Shape

Random Size, Shape, & Color

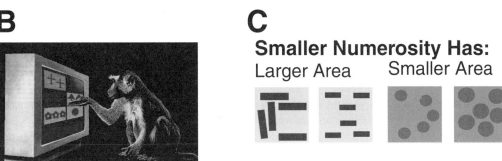

B

C
Smaller Numerosity Has:
Larger Area   Smaller Area

Figure 6.3. (a) Exemplars of the seven different types of stimulus sets used by Brannon and Terrace (1998). *Equal size*: elements were of same size and shape. *Equal area*: cumulative area of elements was equal. *Random size*: element size varied randomly across stimuli. *Clip art*: identical nongeometric elements selected from clip art software. *Clip art mixed*: clip art elements of variable shape. *Random size and shape*: elements within a stimulus were varied randomly in size and shape. *Random size, shape, and color*: same as previous with background and foreground colors varied between stimuli. (b) A drawing of a monkey responding on the touch screen. (c) Examples of stimulus sets used in the pairwise numerosity test. Reprinted from Brannon and Terrace, 1998.

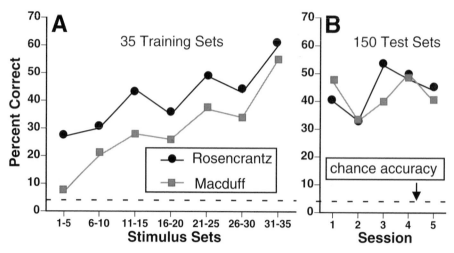

Figure 6.4. (a) Percent correct for 35 training sets. Each was presented for 60 trials and each data point reflects the average of 5 sessions (300 trials). (b) Percent correct for 150 trial unique test sets tested in 5 test sessions with 30 trials each. Chance accuracy is less than 4% in this task (.25 *.33 *.5). Reprinted from Brannon and Terrace, 1998.

ANIMAL ARITHMETIC

A handful of studies have examined whether animals can order, add, and subtract numerosities. Brannon and Terrace (1998) extended the ordinal experiment described in the previous section to determine whether the monkeys that were trained to respond in ascending order to the numerosities 1–4 appreciated the ordinal relations between the numerosities or instead represented the numerosities categorically. The same two monkeys were tested on their ability to order pairs of the numerosities 1–9 after the 1–4 training described earlier. The critical question was whether the monkeys would reliably order pairs of the novel values 5–9 in ascending order. To do so, they would need to be able to perceive the ordinal relations between novel values and infer that they should apply the ordinal rule learned with the values 1–4 to the novel values 5–9. The monkeys were presented with all the possible pairs of the numerosities 1–9, where the smaller number had a larger cumulative surface area than the larger number on half of the trials (see Figure 6.3c). To provide a pure test of ordinal numerical knowledge, the monkeys were not reinforced on any trial that contained a novel numerical value. Thus, only trials that contained two exemplars of the numerosities 1–4 were reinforced. The other 30 pairs were tested in the absence of positive or negative reinforcement. This was a powerful test of ordinal numerical knowledge because there was no laboratory-learned basis by which the monkeys could judge the ordinal relations between numerical values that were outside the training range. For example, if one learned only the beginning of a new alphabet, there would be no basis for ordering the latter part.

The monkeys' performance was extremely good for pairs composed of two familiar numerosities (e.g., 1 vs. 3 or 2 vs. 4) and pairs composed of 1 familiar and 1 novel value (e.g., 2 vs. 8 or 3 vs. 6). Most importantly, however, the monkeys performed above chance expectations on pairs composed of two novel values (e.g., 6 vs. 8). These results indicate that monkeys represent the ordinal relations between numerosities and do so spontaneously even when they could have instead formed arbitrary numerical categories and learned an arbitrary ordering of these nominal categories. The same pattern of results has since been obtained with a squirrel monkey and a baboon (Smith, Piel, & Candland, 2003).

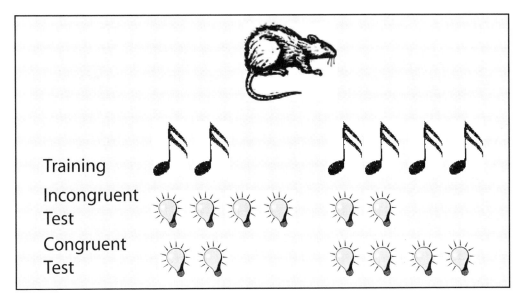

Figure 6.5. Rats were trained to make one response (e.g., right lever press) when presented with two tones and a second response (e.g., left lever press) when presented with four tones. Subsequently, rats were presented with two or four light flashes, and one group of rats was required to reverse the numerical rule (incongruent). The other group was required to use the same numerical rule (congruent).

In another approach, Washburn and Rumbaugh (1991) trained two rhesus monkeys to choose between two Arabic numerals on a touch-sensitive screen, with the choice resulting in the delivery of the corresponding number of food pellets. Both monkeys reliably chose the larger Arabic numeral and even did so when presented with novel combinations of Arabic numerals. Olthof, Iden, and Roberts (1997) used a similar paradigm and tested squirrel monkeys on problems in which they were required to choose between pairs or triplets of Arabic numerals. They found that the monkeys reliably chose the larger sum and that performance could neither be attributed to choosing the largest single value nor to avoiding the single smallest value.

A remarkable demonstration of addition comes from Boysen and Berntson's (1989) research with the chimpanzee Sheba. In previous research, Sheba had been trained to match numerosities with Arabic numerals. Subsequently, Sheba was led around a room to three hiding places, two of which contained 0, 1, 2, 3, or 4 oranges. Sheba was then allowed to choose one of the Arabic numerals 0–4, positioned in ascending order on a platform. Sheba chose the Arabic numeral that corresponded to the sum of the hidden oranges with above-chance accuracy on the very first session.

Sulkowski and Hauser (2000) asked whether rhesus monkeys can spontaneously subtract food quantities. They tested free-ranging rhesus monkeys, in which each monkey was tested for a single trial so that no learning could take place during the experiment. Monkeys viewed an occluded stage as experimenters subtracted 0 or 1 plum from collections of 1–3 plums. In 11 different experiments, Sulkowski and Hauser found that rhesus monkeys invariably chose the larger food quantity, even when this required choosing the quantity that was originally fewer in number. Although subjects could have represented a continuous quantity rather than number, these results suggest that monkeys can perform some type of subtraction. In summary, animals are not only capable of representing number, they are also adept at ordering, adding, and subtracting their numerical representations.

DO ANIMALS USE NUMBER AS A LAST-RESORT STRATEGY?

In 1988 Davis and Perusse published an influential target article in *Behavioral Brain Sciences,* arguing that although animals can be trained to make numerical discriminations, they do so only as a last-resort strategy when all other cues are eliminated and extensive training is provided. For example, if a problem were given to a rat that could be solved by attending to differences in number or surface area, the rat would encode surface area and not number. While few studies have directly addressed the relative salience of number versus other stimulus dimensions, a growing body of studies suggests that number may be a meaningful dimension for many animals.

Davis and Perusse's argument suggests that extensive laboratory training allows an animal to form an abstract numerical category such that they can appreciate the equivalence between three tadpoles and three jet planes. If this is the case, then the animal should not appreciate the inherent relationship between numerical categories; twoness and threeness should be as related to each other as cowness and rockness. However, the Brannon and Terrace (1998) study reviewed in the previous section suggests otherwise. Monkeys trained to order the numerosities 1–4 spontaneously ordered pairs of the values 5–9 without any training on the larger values. This suggests that the monkeys possessed an internal number line. A second piece of data from the same series of studies provides further evidence that monkeys represent the ordinal relations between numerosities. Brannon and Terrace originally attempted to train one of the two monkeys in their study to respond to the numerosities 1–4 in an arbitrary nonmonotonic order (Brannon and Terrace, 2000). Figure 6.6 shows that despite extended training on 13 different sets of stimuli, the monkey never learned to respond in the order 3-1-4-2. Subsequently when given new stimulus sets and required to respond in ascending order (1-2-3-4), the monkey's performance quickly accelerated. These data suggest that the monkey's inherent ordinal representation of the numerosities 1–4 prevented it from responding in an arbitrary nonmonotonic order. Together, these two findings suggest that number is a meaningful stimulus dimension for rhesus monkeys and do not support the idea that animals use number only as a last-resort strategy.

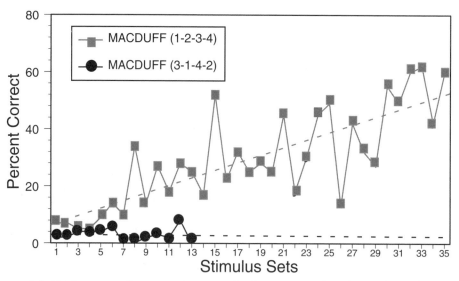

Figure 6.6. Performance for a monkey required to respond in the order 3-1-4-2 to visual arrays on a touch-sensitive screen (black circles) and subsequently required to respond to the same stimuli in ascending numerical order (gray squares). Reprinted from Brannon and Terrace, 2000.

Further evidence comes from Hauser and colleagues (Hauser, MacNeilage, & Ware, 1996; Hauser, Carey, & Hauser, 2000), who conducted a series of experiments with free-ranging rhesus macaques to ascertain what numerical skills rhesus monkeys possess spontaneously without laboratory training. In these studies, each animal is tested for a single trial and given no opportunity to learn. In one study, Hauser and colleagues tested rhesus monkeys in a modified version of Wynn's (1992b) famous experiments designed for human infants. Rhesus monkeys were shown two eggplants successively placed behind an opaque screen and then watched as the screen was raised to reveal one or wo eggplants. The monkeys looked longer at the impossible outcome of 1 (i.e., 1 + 1 = 1) compared to the possible outcome of 2 (i.e., 1 + 1 = 2), suggesting that the impossible outcome violated their expectations. In subsequent experiments Hauser and Carey (in press) showed that the rhesus monkeys were not basing their decisions on cumulative surface area.

Further evidence that number is an important variable for nonhuman animals comes from field studies that have investigated how animals might use number in their everyday lives. Lyon (2003) found that American coots (a species of bird) appear to base decisions about whether to develop an additional egg follicle on the number of their own eggs in the nest. This is particularly remarkable because the coots seem to discount the number of nonspecific parasitic eggs in the nest, suggesting that they can enumerate a subset of elements in a set. This study provides a rare window into how animals may actually use numerical abilities in the wild. In another field experiment, Wilson, Hauser, and Wrangham (2001) found that male chimpanzees only attack neighboring bands if the number of individuals in their party is sufficiently large to deal with the ensuing conflict. In that study, Wilson and colleagues played the pant–hoot vocalization of a single extra-group male to listening parties that varied in size. Only listening parties of three or more males cooperatively called and approached the loud-speaker.

In summary, although it has been argued that animals represent number as a last-resort strategy only when coaxed with extensive laboratory training, a growing body of evidence suggests that animals appreciate the ordinal relations between numerical values and spontaneously represent number without extensive laboratory training.

THE FORMAT OF ANIMAL NUMERICAL REPRESENTATIONS

Although number is a property of sets of discrete elements, number is represented nonverbally by animals, as precise integers, but instead as noisy mental magnitudes. This is illustrated nicely by a paradigm first designed by Mechner (1958) and later adapted by Platt and Johnson (1971). Rats were required to signal when they had completed N lever presses by poking their nose into a hole equipped with a photoelectric sensor. Figure 6.7a shows that the number of responses the rats made before head poking was roughly normally distributed around the required number. Thus, when required to make X presses, the animals were much more likely to make X − 1 or X + 1 presses than X − 4 or X + 4 presses. Furthermore, the standard deviation of the distribution of the obtained number of responses increased linearly with the required number of responses (see also Fetterman & MacEwen, 1989; Laties, 1972; Mechner, 1958; Rilling, 1967; Wilkie, Webster, & Leader, 1979). Such results suggest that rats do not represent number not as precise values but instead as mental magnitudes that are more likely to be confused with a neighboring quantity as the absolute magnitude increases.

It is not just rats that represent number as approximate magnitudes with variance that increases proportionally. Whalen, Gallistel, and Gelman (1999) tested human subjects in a modified version of the Platt and Johnson (1971) design. Adults were asked to make between 7 and 25 key presses as fast as they could without verbally counting. The results closely resembled the rat data obtained by Platt and Johnson three decades earlier and demonstrates scalar variance in number discrimination for both species. Scalar variance is defined as variance

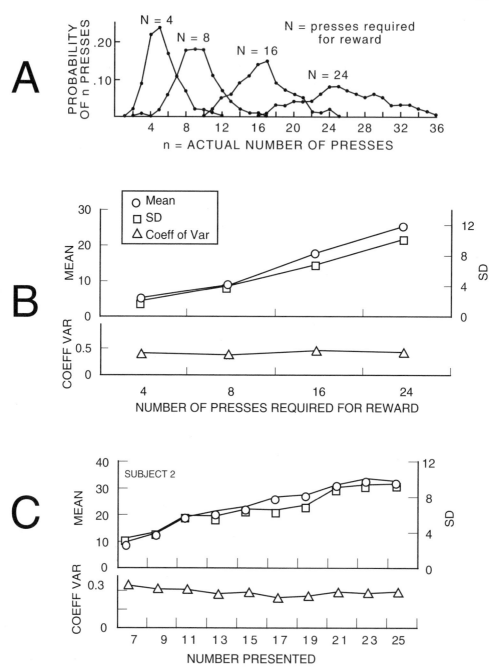

Figure 6.7. (A) The probability of signaling response completion as a function of the number of responses the rat made and the number that was required to obtain reward obtained by Platt and Johnson (1971). (B) The mean number of responses made (left axis, circles) and the standard deviation (right axis, squares) of the response distributions shown in A, and the coefficient of variation (CV), which is the ratio of the standard deviation to the mean, as a function of the number required. (C) The mean (left axis, circles), standard deviation (right axis, squares), and CV (lower panel) as a function of the number of button responses required, obtained by Whalen et al. (1999). The constant CV shown for rats in B and humans in C demonstrates that both species represent number with scalar variability. Reprinted from Whalen et al. (1999).

(standard deviation) that increases linearly with the mean value. Figures 6.7b and 6.7c show a linear increase in the standard deviation in the response distributions as a function of the mean number of responses required but no change in the coefficient of variation as a function of number for rats and humans respectively (see also Cordes, Gallistel, & Gelman, 2001). These tasks appear to have tapped a nonverbal system for representing number in adult humans that is quite similar to that of rats!

Gallistel, Gelman, and colleagues (Cordes, Gallistel, Gelman, & Whalen, 2001; Whalen, Gallistel, & Gelman, 1999) were not the first to show that adults represent number as mental magnitudes. In a classic study, Moyer and Landaeuer (1971) showed that when adults were required to choose the larger of two Arabic numerals, accuracy increased and latency to respond decreased with increasing numerical disparity. Furthermore, when distance was held constant, performance decreased with increasing numerical magnitude; this is referred to as the magnitude or size effect. In other words, both accuracy and latency were modulated by the ratio of the quantities that the numerals represented.

The numerical distance effect has been replicated in other languages (Dehaene, 1996; Tzeng & Wang, 1983), in other representational formats (e.g., dot patterns, Buckley & Gilman, 1974; double digits, Hinrichs, Yurko, & Hu, 1981), and with children as young as five years of age (e.g., Temple & Posner, 1995). This robust and highly replicable finding has been interpreted to mean that Arabic numerals are represented as analog magnitudes, much like line length, brightness, or weight. Figure 6.8a illustrates how numerosities, defined as collections of discrete entities, can be represented as continuous magnitudes, like the amount of water in a beaker.

Distance and magnitude effects have also been found in nonhuman animals (Beran, 2001; Tomonaga & Matsuzawa, 2000). For example, Brannon and Terrace (2002) tested rhesus monkeys and college students in the same experiment, in which both species were required to touch the smaller of two numerosities presented on a touch screen. The stimuli were constructed such that the smaller numerosity had a larger cumulative surface area on half of the trials and all 36 possible pairings of the numerosities 1–9 were presented. Although monkeys worked for banana pellets but humans worked for course credit, the tasks were otherwise identical. Figure 6.9 displays accuracy and latency to respond as a function of numerical disparity for each species and shows strikingly similar distance effects for the two species: both species were faster and more accurate as numerical disparity increased. Not shown here is the finding that when distance was held constant and size was increased, both species showed a tendency to decrease accuracy and increase reaction time. The similarity in the distance and size effects observed in monkeys and human adults provides strong support for the idea that animals and humans share a nonverbal system for representing number as mental magnitudes.

In another study from Hauser's group (Hauser, Tsao, Garcia, & Spelke, 2003), tamarin monkeys were tested in a familiarization–discrimination procedure in which they were familiarized with a given number of tones and then tested with the same number or a novel number of tones. The tamarins were said to discriminate the numerosities if they exhibited a significantly greater proportion of orienting to the speaker when the novel, compared to the familiar, number of tones was played. The tamarins spontaneously discriminated 4 versus 8, 4 versus 6, and 8 versus 12 tones but failed to discriminate 4 versus 5 and 8 versus 10. Thus, it was the ratio not the absolute values of the numerosities compared, that determined whether tamarin monkeys could discriminate them (they seem to require a 2:3 ratio). This suggests that Weber's law holds for spontaneous number discrimination in monkeys and that when monkeys make spontaneous number discriminations, they use a mechanism that is not strictly limited by set size.

Another important aspect of animal number representations is that number and time appear to be represented by a single currency. Meck and Church (1983) originally demonstrated

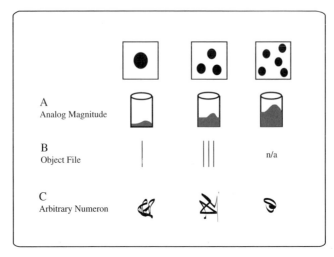

Figure 6.8. Format of number representations for the values 1, 3, and 5. (A) *Meck and Church mode-control* model; number is represented as the accrual of pulses from a pacemaker into an accumulator.(B) *Object file* model; each object is represented by an object file. There is no symbol that represents the set of objects. System is limited by the small number of available object-files. (C) *Arbitrary numeron* model; each number is represented by an abstract, arbitrary symbol. Reprinted from Brannon and Roitman, 2003.

this isomorphism between time and number, and the findings have since been replicated and extended by many laboratories (e.g., Church & Meck, 1984; Fetterman, 1993; Meck, Church, & Gibbon, 1985; Roberts, 1995; Roberts & Boisvert, 1998; Roberts, Coughlin, & Roberts, 2000; Roberts, Macuda, & Brodbeck, 1995; Roberts & Mitchell, 1994; Roberts, Roberts, & Kit, 2002; Santi & Hope, 2001). Meck and Church (1983) trained rats in a duration bisection procedure to make one response to a 2-s 2-cycle stimulus and another distinct response to an 8-s 8-cycle stimulus. Rats were then tested with duration held constant at 4-s and number varied or, alternatively, number held constant at 4 and duration varied. In both cases, the rats' behavior was modulated by the stimulus dimension that varied, showing that the rats had encoded both number and time when the two were confounded. In addition, when the probability of making a "long" or "many" response was plotted against stimulus duration or number, the psychophysical functions for time and number were virtually identical (see Roberts and Mitchell, 1994, for a replication with pigeons). Further, when methamphetamine was administered to the rats, the psychophysical curve that relates the probability of a "long" and "many" response to the actual times or counts with which the animal was presented was similarly shifted to the left, suggesting that methamphetamine functioned to speed up the clock so that it took less absolute time to produce a subjective stimulus of a given quantity or duration (Meck & Church, 1983).

Studies that evaluate working memory for time and number also suggest that a single mechanism is used to time and count. Spetch and Wilkie (1983) trained pigeons in a delayed-match-to-sample procedure to make one response after a short stimulus and a second response after a long stimulus. As the retention interval between the sample presentation and the choice was increased, the 2-s sample retention curve was unaffected, whereas the 8-s retention curve suffered substantially. Thus, as the retention interval increased, so too did the pigeons' bias to choose the small response. A parallel effect was found when pigeons discriminated small and large numbers of responses (Fetterman & MacEwen, 1989) or sequences of flashes (Roberts, Macuda, & Brodbeck, 1995), again suggesting a correspondence between time and number representation.

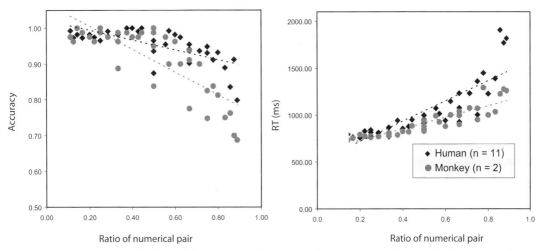

Figure 6.9. Accuracy (left) and latency (right) to the first response in a pairwise numerical comparison task as a function of numerical disparity. Monkeys (grey circles) and humans (black diamonds) were required to respond first to the stimulus with the fewer number of elements. Dotted lines reflect best-fit linear regressions.

The data reviewed above suggest that rats and pigeons use a single mechanism to time and count and that a single representational currency underlies both duration and number. A more controversial idea is that animals automatically engage in both counting and timing. A handful of studies have found that when both time and number are available as cues, animal behavior is controlled by time and not by number (Breukelaar & Dalrymple-Alford, 1998; Roberts, Coughlin, & Roberts, 2000). Thus, although there is considerable evidence for a profound similarity in the way that time and number are represented, it is unclear whether animals spontaneously count and time all stimuli. This may not be surprising, given the multitude of computations animals would need to make at each moment if they were tracking both dimensions on all environmental inputs at all times.

Are Animal Number Representations Always Mental Magnitudes?

Although there is definitive evidence that animals represent number as mental magnitudes, there is also suggestive evidence that animals share with humans a second system for representing small sets of objects. Evidence that infants use two distinct processes to represent small and large numbers of objects comes from a variety of paradigms, and some of these paradigms have been used to test rhesus monkeys and have revealed similar set-size limitations. In one set of studies, infants or monkeys watched as experimenters placed different numbers of food items in opaque containers. They were then allowed to approach the containers (Feingenson, Carey, & Hauser, 2002; Hauser, Carey, & Hauser, 2000). Infants successfully crawled to the bucket containing the larger number of graham crackers when the contrasts were 1 versus 2 or 2 versus 3, but failed to choose the larger quantity with any contrast that included quantities larger than 3, even when ratios were favorable (e.g., 2 versus 4). Similarly, rhesus monkeys tested in the same 2-container choice discrimination paradigm showed a set-size effect (Hauser, Carey, & Hauser, 2000). Monkeys succeeded with contrasts such as 1 versus 2, 2 versus 3, and even 3 versus 4, but failed with quantities larger than 4 (e.g., 5 versus 6 and 4 versus 8).

However, infants can also form mental magnitude representations of number. For example, 6-month-old infants have successfully discriminated values as large as 8 versus 16 in the visual-habituation paradigm (Xu & Spelke, 2000) and the head-turn procedure (Lipton & Spelke,

2003). Infants habituated to images that contain 8 dots look longer at new pictures with 16 dots than they do at new pictures with 8 dots, even when surface area, perimeter, and density are carefully controlled (Xu & Spelke, 2000; see also Brannon, 2002; Xu, 2003).

One possibility, then, is that infants and animals can form analogue magnitude representations of number, but that this system is not activated in some contexts and, instead, a distinct system is invoked that can only represent a few objects at a time. This second system has been termed the object file model (Feigenson, Carey, & Hauser, 2002; Feigenson, Carey, & Spelke, 2002; Leslie et al., 1998; Simon, 1997; Uller et al., 1999) and posits that infants represent number implicitly by representing each member of a set with a symbol (object file). Central to this model is the fact that no single symbol serves to represent the numerosity of the set instead, each to-be-enumerated item is represented by a single object file, and there is a limited supply of object files (see Figure 6.8b).

In summary, the data reviewed above demonstrate that animals represent number as noisy mental magnitudes and leave open the possibility that animals share a second system with human infants that functions to represent the numerosity of small sets as individual object files.

HOW ARE NONVERBAL REPRESENTATIONS OF NUMBER CONSTRUCTED?

The section above described the evidence that animals and humans represent number as mental magnitudes and that time and number are computed by a single mechanism. But how are numerical representations constructed, if not by verbal counting? Gelman and Gallistel (1978; Gallistel & Gelman, 1992, 2000) proposed that human children form numerical representations via a nonverbal counting process that follows the same principles as verbal counting. They provided a formal definition of counting that consists of three essential principles. (1) The one-to-one principle states that one, and only one, symbol can be applied to each to-be-counted element. Thus, we cannot apply the count word "three" to both the third and fourth element in an array. (2) The stable order principle stipulates that the symbols must be applied in a consistent order across counting episodes. We cannot count "1-2-3" today and "1-3-2" tomorrow. (3) The cardinal principle dictates that the last symbol applied serves to represent the numerosity of the set. Although the verbal counting system uses spoken words as symbols, Gelman and Gallistel's idea was that preverbal children could be using the same system but be applying arbitrary neuronal symbols, termed numerons, to each element instead of words. In the original formulation of Gelman and Gallistel's hypothesis, the numerons were arbitrary symbols and had no direct relationship with the numerosities they represented (see Figure 6.8c). The most important aspect of the idea, however, was that the counting principles were isomorphic in the verbal and nonverbal systems.

Since the numeron-list hypothesis, a handful of models have been proposed to explain how animals represent number in the absence of linguistic counting. Two models that achieve analogue number representations, rather than the arbitrary numerons originally proposed by Gelman and Gallistel (1978), are the Meck and Church mode-control and Dehaene and Changeux neural network models. The mode-control model (Meck & Church, 1983) was originally developed as an adaptation of an information-processing model of animal timing behavior (Gibbon & Church, 1984) to explain the correspondence between rats' discrimination of time and number. It was later adapted by Gallistel and Gelman (1992) and termed the accumulator model. Like the pure timing model, the mode-control model is composed of a pacemaker, an accumulator, a working memory buffer, reference memory, and a comparator (see Figure 6.10). The pacemaker produces pulses at a constant rate that can be gated into an accumulator. When a response by the organism is rewarded, the accumulator value is transferred from working memory to be stored in reference memory. A comparator process allows the organism to compare the current working memory content to the reference memory content.

Mode-Control Model

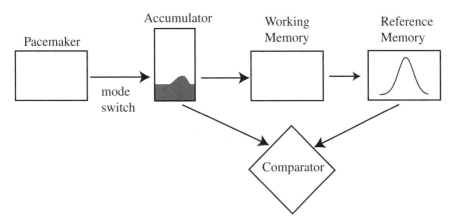

Figure 6.10. A diagram of the mode-control model, which consists of a pacemaker, switch, accumulator, working memory, reference memory, and a comparator.

The main advance of the mode-control model is that the switch that allows pulses to flow from the pacemaker to the accumulator can operate in one of three modes. Here, we focus on two of the modes: the run mode, which functions as a timer, and the event mode, which functions as a counter. In the run mode, the switch is closed for the whole trial; thus, the total pulses in the accumulator serves as a measure of duration. In contrast, in the event mode each stimulus results in the switch's closing for a fixed amount of time, regardless of stimulus duration; thus, the total pulses in the accumulator serve as a measure of the number of stimuli.

In this way, the mode-control model provides a unified theory of duration and number discrimination by positing that number and time are represented with a single currency. In addition, this model of number representation can be considered a form of nonverbal counting, as it obeys the three definitional criteria of counting put forth by Gelman and Gallistel (1978; see Broadbent, Rakitin, Church, & Meck, 1993; Meck, 1997). The one-to-one principle is met because each event results in a constant increment to the accumulator. The stable order principle, which requires that the order of assignment of numerons must be the same from one occasion to the next, is fulfilled because in no case can the accumulator operating in the event mode produce anything other than a fixed set of values whose order never varies (you must pass through the accumulator value of 7 to get to the accumulator value of 8). Finally, the cardinality principle is met because the value of the accumulator at the end of stimulus presentation represents the number of stimuli that were presented.

A second model of nonverbal number representation is the Dehaene and Changeux neural network model (Dehaene & Changeux, 1993), which posits that there are numerosity detectors that can represent the abstract number of objects independently of the size and configuration of stimuli. There are three layers to this model: an input "retina," a map of object locations, and an array of numerosity detectors. The map of object locations converts stimuli from the "retina" to a representation of each stimulus irrespective of object size (an echoic auditory memory also allows the system to enumerate sounds as well as objects). The location map sends its output to numerosity detectors, which consist of summation units and numerosity units. Each summation unit has a set threshold. When the total activity from the output of the location map (which is proportional to numerosity) exceeds the summation unit's threshold, it will be activated. These units differ from the event mode of the mode-control model in that they are only active when the number of events exceeds some level. Finally, the summation clusters project to numerosity clusters, which represent the numerosities 1 through 5. A given numerosity cluster will be activated if the corresponding summation cluster is active, but those representing higher values are not. Therefore, presentation of stimuli with the same numerosity, despite differences in size, location and modality, results in the activation of the same numerosity detectors.

Both the Meck and Church mode-control model and the Dehaene and Changeux neural network model result in analogue representations of number and predict that numerical discrimination should follow the Weber–Fechner law. However, the models differ in the process by which they achieve numerical representations. The Dehaene and Changeux neural network model predicts that number is perceived in parallel, whereas the mode-control model posits that numerical representations are achieved by a serial counting-like process. Very little empirical data address this important question in animals. Another distinction between the models is that the mode-control model uniquely predicts that number and time are represented by a single currency. The evidence in favor of this claim has already been reviewed.

In summary, important questions remain about the process by which animals form numerical representations and whether this process is universal across human and nonhuman species. Furthermore, the relationship between time and number should be studied in other species beyond rats and pigeons. Future research should investigate whether a serial counting-like process or a parallel process underlies nonverbal number representation.

NEURAL BASIS OF NUMBER REPRESENTATION

What areas of the brain are involved in representing number and making arithmetic calculations? Are homologous brain regions recruited by nonhuman animals as well as by humans when number is represented? The neural basis of numerical cognition has been extensively studied in adult humans using ERPs, fMRI, PET, and patient populations (for a review see Dehaene, 2000). Generally, this literature implicates parietal cortex in number processing (inferior or superior parietal lobule). However, the majority of these studies have employed tasks that require the recognition and manipulation of Arabic numerals and therefore engage symbolic numerical processing and not enumeration per se (but see Fink, Marshall, Gurd, Weiss, Zafiris, Shah, & Zilles, 2001; Sathian, Simon, Peterson, Patel, Hoffman, & Grafton, 1999).

In contrast, much less is known about the neural basis of number representation in animals. The first report of number-related neural activity was from the association cortex of the anesthetized cat (Thompson, Mayers, Robertson, & Patterson, 1970). The experimenters presented 10 auditory or visual stimuli to anesthetized cats and recorded neural activity. Five of the 500 tested neurons fired more to a particular position in the sequence of lights or tones (see Figure 6.11). These 5 number cells responded to the values 2, 5, 6, 6, and 7 in the series, regardless of stimulus modality or frequency (interstimulus intervals varied from 1 to 5 s). One broadly tuned number cell was found in an 8-day-old kitten. These results suggested that single cells are selective for particular numerical values and that tuning for number may increase over development. However, it took more than 30 years for the next demonstration of number-selective neurons. Two other research teams have now found evidence for number neurons in the monkey brain.

Sawamura, Shima, and Tanji (2002) found number-related activity in parietal cortex as monkeys performed a series of repetitive arm movements. Monkeys were trained to repeat a movement (pushing or turning a handle) for five trials, then switch to another movement for five trials, and so on. Neurons, located in the superior lobule of the parietal cortex, were modulated by the number of movements a monkey made. This number-modulated activity was observed during a nonmovement period in which the monkeys waited for a signal to execute the movement. Although firing rate increased during more than one period for many neurons,

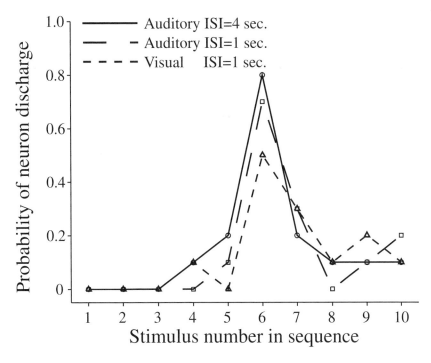

Figure 6.11. Neural basis of number representation. Number "6" neuron from cat association cortex. Action potentials were recorded as a sequence of 10 tones or lights with different interstimulus intervals (ISI) was presented to an anesthetized cat. Each sequence was repeated 10 times. The probability that the neuron discharged to a stimulus is plotted as a function of the stimulus's position in the sequence. This neuron was most active to the sixth stimulus in the sequence, regardless of modality or ISI. Reprinted from Thompson et al., 1970.

some neurons were selective just before a movement in one ordinal position of the sequence (see Figure 6.12). Neurons selective for each of the ordinal positions in the sequence were found across the population.

In an elegant set of studies, Nieder and colleagues (Nieder, Freedman, & Miller, 2002; Nieder & Miller, 2004) isolated cells in the prefrontal and parietal cortex of macaque monkeys that are associated with the number of elements in a visual display. In their original study (Nieder, Freedman, & Miller, 2002), they found that roughly 1/3 of prefrontal cells and only 5% of parietal cells were number selective. However, more recently, Nieder and Miller (2004) recorded from the fundus of the intraparietal sulcus and found that approximately 20% of cells were number selective, suggesting that their original sampling of pareital cortex was too anatomically superficial. In these experiments, monkeys were trained in a delayed same–different task in which a "same" answer was rewarded if two successively presented stimuli were equivalent in number. The numerosities 1–5 were tested with visual arrays that varied in element area, circumference, arrangement, density, and shape. Neural activity during the delay period (and the sample period) was maximal for one quantity and declined as distance from that quantity increased (see Figure 6.13). The majority of number selective cells preferred the numerosity 1, although cells were found that were selective for 2–5. Furthermore, Nieder and colleagues showed that neuronal selectivity was broader for larger numbers, suggesting a possible mechanism for the behavioral numerical distance and magnitude effects reviewed earlier.

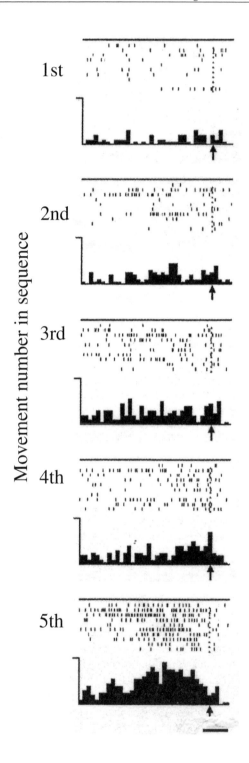

Figure 6.12. Number "5" neuron from monkey parietal cortex. Data are presented from 10 blocks of trials in which a monkey repeated an arm movement ("push") five times. Each of the panels depicts the trials from particular movement in the sequence. On the top half of each panel, each row represents one trial. The vertical tick marks indicate the time of each action potential relative to the time of the "go" signal to start the movement (arrows). On the bottom of each panel, the average activity from all trials was calculated in 50-ms time bins. Activity of this neuron was elevated before the fifth movement of the sequence, despite the fact that the movement itself did not differ from any others in the sequence. Reprinted from Sawamura, Shima, & Tanji, 2002.

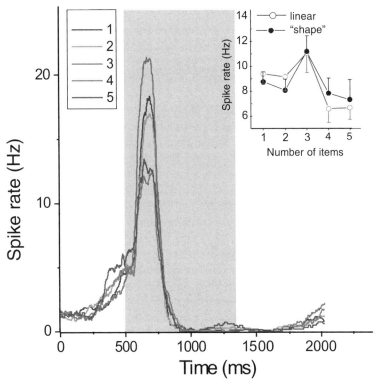

Figure 6.13. Spike density functions for a cell that was selective for visual displays with three elements. The colored lines illustrate the time course of neuronal activity for the five tested numerosities. Grey shadowing indicates the period for which the sample was present. Reprinted from Nieder, Freedman, & Miller, 2002. A color version of this figure can be viewed at www.psypress.com/campbell.

Nieder and Miller also found that number selective neurons were selective approximately earlier in parietal compared with prefrontal cortex suggesting that parital cortex may be the prime source of numerosity processing. More research is needed to elucidate the relationship between prefrontal and parietal cortex in number representation and to determine whether numerosity extracted from sequential and/or auditory events is re presented in the same way.

DRAWING CONCLUSIONS

Without question, human mathematical capacities exceed those of nonhuman animals. A rat will never calculate the time it would take a rocket to travel to the moon, the number of cartons it would take to hold 8,976 eggs, or the projected cost of a 4-year college education in the year 2085. However, the data reviewed above suggest that many animal species have a keen numerical sense. Animals represent number independently of continuous dimensions such as surface area, perimeter, and density, and there is suggestive evidence that they represent number independently of modality. Abstract numerical representations are used by animals in computations such as ordering, addition, and subtraction. Finally, numerical savvy appears to be a natural part of many animal species repertoire rather than an artificial laboratory skill.

This chapter has focused on the similarities between animal and human numerical sense. To summarize, both animals and humans show robust distance and magnitude effects when comparing numerosities, providing evidence that both species represent number as mental magnitudes. Paradoxically, although number is a property of sets of discrete elements, the format of nonverbal mental numbers is continuous, much like our representations of line length, weight, or time (Gallistel & Gelman, 2000). The nervous system, in essence, inverts the representational convention that allows us to use numbers to represent magnitudes, such as describing a person's height as 5 foot 2 inches, and instead uses magnitude to represent number (see Gallistel & Gelman, 2000). But what of the differences between humans and nonhuman animals?

While humans and nonhuman animals share a nonverbal number system, which serves to represent approximate values, humans later come to possess a verbal number system that can precisely represent numbers only one unit apart. Thus, while animals are limited to approximate numerical estimates, humans can enumerate the 7,962 jellybeans in a jar. Can animals learn something like verbal counting? Although a handful of animals have been taught the relationship between symbols and numerosities (Boysen & Berntson, 1989; Matsuzawa, 1985; Pepperberg, 1987, 1994; Xia, Siemann, & Delius, 2000; Xia, Emmerton, Siemann, & Delius, 2001), the data from these enterprises suggest that the training required is arduous, and that animals do not make the same kind of conceptual leaps and intelligent numerical inferences as do young children. For example, when Ai, a female chimpanzee, was trained to label sets of 1–9 objects, it took her approximately the same number of trials to learn each successive numerosity–symbol pairing (Matsuzawa, 1985). Ai first learned to match sets of 1 and 2 objects with the symbols "1" and "2." Subsequently, when collections of three objects and the Arabic numeral "3" were added to her training sessions, performance fell to chance levels for collections of two. Similarly, when collections of four were added, her performance fell to chance levels with collections of three. Ai seemed to learn 1 versus many, 1 and 2 versus many, 1, 2 and 3 versus many, etc., and never seemed to appreciate the successor principle. In striking contrast, at about 3.5 years of age, children typically make an induction that each symbol in the memorized count list refers to the previous numerosity plus one (Wynn, 1992a).

Another possible difference between humans and animals is that different conditions may be required to elicit analogue magnitude representations of number. As reviewed above, there is a great deal of evidence that human infants possess two distinct systems that serve to represent number and more limited evidence for the same distinction in animals. In some contexts monkeys and infants show similar set-size limitations (Feigenson, Carey, & Hauser, 2002; Hauser, Carey, & Hauser, 2000; Hauser & Carey, 2003). But in other situations, rhesus monkeys seem perfectly capable of applying rules learned with small numbers to larger values. For example, in the Brannon and Terrace (1998) study described earlier, monkeys easily transferred a numerical rule learned with the values 1–4 to pairs of the larger values 5–9; one might imagine that if two distinct processes were used for the two numerical ranges, then the animals would have been at chance on large values after training on small values. Similarly, rats in the Meck and Church paradigm (1983) and monkeys in the Jordan Brannon (2003) paradigm differentiated 2 versus 8 and showed a fine-tuned generalization gradient for intermediate values. Furthermore, rhesus monkeys tested by Hauser and colleagues in the modified Wynn paradigm tracked addition and subtraction events with small values such as 2 − 1 = 1 or 2 and 1 + 1 = 1 or 2 (Hauser, McNeilage, & Ware, 1996). They also succeeded at tracking addition and subtraction events with large values such as 4 + 4 = 4 or 8 (Flombaum, Junge, & Hauser, unpublished). In both studies, the rhesus monkeys looked longer at the impossible compared to the possible outcome, suggesting their ability to track number in this task is not limited to small values.

In conclusion, this chapter has surveyed a few key issues in the large and growing literature on animal numerical abilities. Although human mathematics far surpasses animal arithmetic, the studies described here show that animals have a rudimentary numerical sense that allows them to represent the approximate numerical value of discrete sets, appreciate correspondences between auditory and visual sets, and also order, add and subtract numerical representations. When adult humans are given tasks designed to bypass their verbal number system, they show a strikingly similar nonverbal numerical sense (Brannon & Terrace, 2002; Cordes et al., 2001; Whalen et al., 1999). A handful of studies have also implicated mental magnitude representations of number in human infants (e.g., Brannon, 2002; Lipton & Spelke, 2003; Xu, 2003; Xu & Spelke, 2000). Thus, studying the numerical mind of nonhuman animals is providing insight into the foundations of human mathematical capacities, and results of this endeavor are contributing to the important conclusion that precursors of human cognition are found throughout the animal kingdom.

REFERENCES

Beran, M. (2001). Summation and numerousness judgments of sequentially presented sets of items by chimpanzees (Pan troglodytes). Journal of Comparative Psychology, 115(2), 181–191.

Boesch, C. (1995). Innovation in wild chimpanzees (Pan troglodytes). International Journal of Primatology, 16(1), 1–16.

Boysen, S. T., & Berntson, G. G. (1989). Numerical competence in a chimpanzee (Pan troglodytes). Journal of Comparative Psychology, 103, 23–31.

Brannon, E. M. (2002). The development of ordinal numerical knowledge in infancy. Cognition, 83, 223–240.

Brannon, E. M., & Terrace, H. S. (1998). Ordering of the numerosities 1–9 by monkeys. Science, 282, 746–749.

Brannon, E. M., & Terrace, H. S. (2000). Representation of the numerosities 1–9 by rhesus monkeys (Macaca mulatta). Journal of Experimental Psychology: Animal Behavior Processes, 26, 31–49.

Brannon, E. M., & Terrace, H. S. (2002). The Evolution and ontogeny of ordinal numerical ability. In M. Bekoff, C. Allen, & G. M. Burghardt (Eds.), The cognitive animal. Cambridge, MA: MIT Press.

Breukelaar, J. W. C., & Dalrymple-Alford, J. C. (1998). Timing ability and numerical competence in rats. Journal of Experimental Psychology: Animal Behavior Processes, 24(1), 84–97.

Broadbent, H. A., Rakitin, B. C., Church, R. M., & Meck, W. H. (1993). Quantitative relationships between timing and counting. In S. Boysen & E. J. Capaldi (Eds.), Numerical skills in animals (pp. 171–187). Hillsdale, NJ: Erlbaum.

Buckley, P. B., & Gillman, C. B. (1974). Comparisons of digit and dot patterns. Journal of Experimental Psychology, 103, 1131–1136.

Church, R.M., & Meck, W.H. (1984). The numerical attribute of stimuli. In H. L. Roitblat, T. G. Bever, & H. S. Terrace (Eds.), Animal cognition (pp. 445–464). Hillsdale, NJ: Erlbaum.

Cordes, S., Gelman, R., Gallistel, C. R., & Whalen, J. (2001). Variability signatures distinguish verbal from nonverbal counting for both large and small numbers. Psychonomic Bulletin & Review, 8(4), 698–707.

Davis, H., & Perusse, R. (1988). Numerical competence: from backwater to mainstream of comparative psychology. Behavioral Brain Sciences, 11, 602–615.

Dehaene, S. (1996). The organization of brain activity in number comparison: Event-related potentials and the additive-factors methods. Journal of Cognitive Neuroscience, 8, 47–68.

Dehaene, S. (2000). Cerebral bases of number processing and calculation. In M. S. Gazzaniga (Ed.), The new cognitive neurosciences (2nd ed., pp. 987–998). Cambridge, MA: MIT Press.

Dehaene, S., & Changeux, J. (1993). Development of elementary numerical abilities: A neuronal model. Journal of Cognitive Neuroscience, 5(4), 390– 407.

Feigenson, L., Carey, S., & Hauser, M. (2002). The representations underlying infants' choice of more: Object files versus analog magnitudes. Psychological Science, 13(2), 150–156.

Feigenson, L., Carey, S., & Spelke, E. (2002). Infants' discrimination of number vs. continuous extent. Cognitive Psychology, 44(1), 33–66.

Fetterman, J. G. (1993). Numerosity discrimination: Both time and number matter. Journal of Experimental Psychology: Animal Behavior Processes, 19, 149–164.

Fetterman, G., & MacEwen, D. (1989). Short-term memory for responses: The "choose small" effect. Journal of the Experimental Analysis of Behavior, 52, 311–324.

Fink, G. R., Marshall, J. C., Gurd, J., Weiss, P. H., Zafiris, O., Shah, N. J., & Zilles, K. (2001). Deriving numerosity and shape from identical visual displays. Neuroimage, 13, 46–55.

Flombaum, J. I., Junge, J. A., & Hauser, M. D. Rhesus monkeys spontaneously compute addition operations over large numbers. Manuscript under review.

Gallistel, C. R., & Gelman, R. (1990). The what and how of counting. Cognition, 34, 197–199.

Gallistel, C. R., & Gelman, R. (1992). Preverbal and verbal counting and computation. Cognition, 44, 43–74.

Gallistel, R., & Gelman, R. (2000). Non-verbal numerical cognition: From reals to integers. Trends in Cognitive Sciences, 4(2), 59–65.

Gelman, R., & Gallistel, C. R. (1978). The child's concept of number. Cambridge, MA: Harvard University Press.

Gibbon, J., & Church, R. M. (1984). Sources of variability in an information processing theory of timing. In H .L. Roitblat, T. G. Bever, & H. S. Terrace (Eds.), Animal cognition (pp. 465–488). Hillsdale, NJ: Erlbaum.

Hauser, M., & Carey, S. (2003). Spontaneous representations of small numbers of objects by rhesus macaques: Examinations of content and format. Cognitive Psychology, 47(4), 367–401.

Hauser, M. D., Carey, S., & Hauser, L. B. (2000). Spontaneous number representation in semi-free-ranging rhesus monkeys. Proceedings of the Royal Society, London, 267, 829–833.

Hauser, M. D., MacNeilage, P., & Ware, M. (1996). Numerical representations in primates. Proceedings of the National Academy of Science, 93, 1514–1517.

Hauser, M. D., Dehaene, S., Dehaene-Lambertz, G., & Patalano, A. L. (2002). Spontaneous number discrimination of multi-format auditory stimuli in cotton-top tamarins (Saguinus oedipus). Cognition, 86(2), B23–B32.

Hauser, M., Tsao, F., Garcia, P., & Spelke, E. (2003). Evolutionary foundations of number: spontaneous *representation of numerical magnitudes by cotton-top tamarins. Proceedings of the Royal Society, London, B270: 1441–1446.*

Hinrichs, J. V., Yurko, D. S., & Hu, J. M. (1981). Two-digit number comparison: Use of place information. *Journal of Experimental Psychology: Human Perceptual Performance, 7,* 890–901.

Jordan, K. E., & Brannon, E. M. (2003). *Cardinal number representation in Rhesus monkeys.* Poster presented at the annual North Carolina Cognition Group Conference, Durham, NC.

Laties, V. (1972). The modification of drug effects on behavior by external discriminative stimuli. *Journal of Pharmacology and Experimental Therapeutics, 183,* 1–13.

Leslie, A., Xu, F., Tremoulet, P., & Scholl, B. (1998). Indexing and the object concept: Developing "what" and "where" systems. *Trends in Cognitive Sciences, 2,* 10–18.

Lipton, J. S., & Spelke, E. S. (2003). Origins of number sense: Large-number discrimination in human infants. *Psychological Science, 14*(5), 396–401.

Lyon, B. E. (2003). Egg recognition and counting reduce costs of avian conspecific brood parasitism. *Nature, 422,* 495–499.

Matsuzawa, T. (1985). Use of numbers by a chimpanzee. *Nature, 315,* 57–59.

Mechner, F. (1958). Probability relations within response sequences under ratio reinforcement. *Journal of the Experimental Analysis of Behavior, 1,* 109–122.

Meck, W. H. (1997). Application of a mode-control model of temporal integration to counting and timing behavior. In C. M. Bradshaw, E. Szabadi, et al. (Eds.), *Time and behavior: Psychological and neurobehavioral analyses. Advances in Psychology* (Vol. 120, pp. 133–184). Amsterdam: North-Holland.

Meck, W. H., & Church, R. M. (1983). A mode control model of counting and timing processes. *Journal of Experimental Psychology: Animal Behavior Processes, 9*(3), 320–334.

Meck, W. H., Church, R. M., & Gibbon, J. (1985). Temporal integration in duration and number discrimination. *Journal of Experimental Psychology: Animal Behavior Processes, 11,* 591–597.

Moyer, R. S., & Landaeur, T. K. (1967). Time required for judgments of numerical inequality. *Nature, 215,* 1519–1520.

Nieder, A., Freedman, D. J., & Miller, E. K. (2002) Representation of the quantity of visual items in the primate prefrontal cortex. *Science, 297,* 1708–1711.

Neider, A., & Miller, E. K. (2004). A parieto-frontal network of visual numerical information in the monkey. *Proceedings of the National Academy of Sciences, 1001*(19), 7457–7462.

Olthof, A., Iden, C. M., & Roberts, W. A. (1997). Judgments of ordinality and summation of number symbols by squirrel monkeys (*Saimiri sciureus*). *Journal of Experimental Psychology: Animal Behavior Processes, 23*(3), 325–339.

Pepperberg, I. M. (1987). Evidence for conceptual quantitative abilities in an African grey parrot: Labeling of cardinal sets. *Ethology, 75,* 37–61.

Pepperberg, I. M. (1994). Numerical competence in an African gray parrot (*Psittacus erithacus*). *Journal of Comparative Psychology, 108*(1), 36–44.

Platt, J. R., & Johnson, D. M. (1971). Localization of position within a homogeneous behavior chain: Effects of error contingencies. *Learning and Motivation, 2,* 386–414.

Rilling, M. (1967). Number of responses as a stimulus in fixed interval and fixed ratio schedules. *Journal of Comparative and Physiological Psychology, 63,* 60–65.

Roberts, W. A. (1995). Simultaneous numerical and temporal processing in the pigeon. *Current Directions in Psychological Science, 4,* 47–51.

Roberts, W. A., & Boisvert, M. J. (1998). Using the peak procedure to measure timing and counting processes in pigeons. *Journal of Experimental Psychology: Animal Behavior Processes, 24*(4), 416–430.

Roberts, W. A., Coughlin, R., & Roberts, S. (2000). Pigeons flexibly time or count on cue. *Psychological Science, 11,* 218–222.

Roberts, W. A., Macuda, T., & Brodbeck, D. R. (1995). Memory for number of light flashes in the pigeon. *Animal Learning & Behavior, 23*(2), 182–188.

Roberts, W. A., & Mitchell, S. (1994). Can a pigeon simulataneously process temporal and numerical information? *Journal of Experimental Psychology: Animal Behavior Processes, 20*(1), 66–78.

Roberts, W., Roberts, S., & Kit, K. A. (2002). Pigeons presented with sequences of false flashes use behavior to count but not to time. *Journal of Experimental Psychology: Animal Behavior Processes, 28*(2), 137–150.

Santi, A., & Hope, C. (2001). Errors in pigeons' memory for number of events. *Animal Learning & Behavior, 29*(3), 208–220.

Sawamura, H., Shima, K., & Tanji, J. (2002) Numerical representation for action in the parietal cortex of the monkey. *Nature, 415,* 918–922.

Sathian, K., Simon, T. J ., Peterson, S., Patel, G. A., Hoffman, J. M., & Grafton, S. T. (1999). Neural evidence linking visual object enumeration and attention. *Journal of Cognitive Neuroscience, 11,* 36–51.

Savage-Rumbaugh, S., Shanker, S. G., & Taylor, T. J. (1998). *Apes language, and the mind.*, Atlanta: Georgia State University Press.

Shields, W. E., Smith, J. D., & Washburn, D. A. (1997). Uncertain responses by humans and Rhesus monkeys (*Macaca mulatta*) in a psychophysical same-different task. *Journal of Experimental Psychology: General. 126*(2), 147–164.

Simon, T. J. (1997). Reconceptualizing the origins of number knowledge: A "non-numerical account." *Cognitive Development, 12,* 349–372.

Smith, B. R., Piel, A. K., & Candland, D. K. (2003). Numerity of a socially housed hamadryas baboon (*Papio hamadryas*) and a socially housed squirrel monkey (*Saimiri sciureus*). *Journal of Comparative Psychology, 117*(2), 217–225.

Spetch, M., & Wilkie, D. M. (1983). Subjective shortening: A model of pigeons' memory for event duration. *Journal of Experimental Psychology: Animal Behavior Processes, 9,* 14–30.

Sulkowski, G. M., & Hauser, M. D. (2000). Can rhesus monkeys spontaneously subtract? *Cognition, 79,* 239–262.

Temple, E., & Posner, M. (1998). Brain mechanisms of quantity are similar in 5-year-olds and adults. *Proceedings of the National Academy of Sciences, USA, 95,* 7836–7841.

Thompson, R. F., Mayers, K. S., Robertson, R. T., & Patterson, C. J. (1970). Number coding in association cortex of the cat. *Science, 168,* 271–273.

Tomasello, M., Call, J., & Hare, B. (2003). Chimpanzees understand psychological states—the question is which ones and to what extent. *Trends in Cognitive Sciences, 7*, 153–156.

Tomonaga, M., & Matsuzawa, T. (2000). Sequential responding to arabic numerals with wild cards by the chimpanzee (*Pan troglodytes*). *Animal Cognition, 3,* 1–11.

Tzeng, O. J. L., & Wang, W. (1983). The first to R's. *American Scientist, 71,* 238–243.

Uller, C., Carey, S., Huntley-Fenner, G., & Klatt, L. (1999). What representations might underlie infant numerical knowledge. *Cognitive Development, 14,* 1–36.

Van Schaik, C. P., Ancrenaz, M., Borgen, G., Galdikas, B., Knott, C. D., Singleton, I., Suzuki, A., Suci Utami, S., & Merrill, M. (2003). Orangutan cultures and the evolution of material culture. *Science, 3,* 299, 102–105.

Washburn, D., & Rumbaugh, D. M. (1991). Ordinal judgments of numerical symbols by macaques (*Macaca mulatta*). *Psychological Science, 2*(3), 190–193.

Whalen, J., Gelman, R., & Gallistel, C. R. (1999). Nonverbal counting in humans: The psychophysics of number representation, *Psychological Science, 10,* 130–137.

Whiten, A., Goodall, J., McGrew, W. C., Nishida, T., Reynolds, V., Sugiyama, Y., Tutin, C. E. G., Wrangham, R. W., & Boesch, C. (1999). Cultures in chimpanzees. *Nature, 399*(6737), 682–685.

Wilkie, D. M., Webster, J. B., & Leader, L. G. (1979). Unconfounding time and number discrimination in a Mechner counting schedule. *Bulletin of the Psychonomic Society, 13,* 390–392.

Wilson, M. L., Hauser, M. D., & Wrangham, R. W. (2001). Does participation in intergroup conflict depend on numerical assessment, range location, or rank for wild chimpanzees? *Animal Behaviour, 61*(6), 1203–1216.

Wright, A. A., Rivera, J. J., Hulse, S. H., Shyan, M., & Neiworth, J. J. (2000). Music perception and octave generalization in rhesus monkeys. *Journal of Experimental Psychology: General, 129*(3), 291–307.

Wynn, K. (1992a). Children's acquisition of the number words and the counting system. *Cognitive Psychology, 24*(2), 220–251.

Wynn, K. (1992b). Addition and subtraction by human infants. *Nature, 358,* 749–750.

Xia, L., Siemann, M., & Delius, J. D. (2000). Matching of numerical symbols with number of responses by pigeons. *Animal Cognition, 3*(1), 35–43.

Xia, L., Emmerton, J., Siemann, M., & Delius, J. D. (2001). Pigeons (*Columba livia*) learn to link numerosities with symbols. *Journal of Comparative Psychology, 115*(1), 83–91.

Xu, F. (2003). Numerosity discrimination in infants: Evidence for two systems of representations. *Cognition, 89*(1), B15–B25.

Xu, F., & Spelke, E. S. (2000). Large number discrimination in 6-month-old infants. *Cognition, 74,* B1–B11.

7

The Cognitive Foundations
of Mathematics
The Role of Conceptual Metaphor

Rafael Núñez
George Lakoff

In *The Tree of Knowledge*, biologists Humberto Maturana and Francisco Varela (1987) analyze the biological foundations of human cognition. A crucial component of their argument is a simple but profound aphorism: *Everything said is said by someone.* It follows from this that any concept, idea, belief, definition, drawing, poem, or piece of music has to be produced by a living human being, constrained by the peculiarities of his or her body and brain. The entailment is straightforward: without living human bodies with brains, there are no ideas—and that includes mathematical ideas. This chapter deals with the structure of mathematical ideas *themselves* and with how their *inferential organization* is provided by everyday human cognitive mechanisms such as conceptual metaphor.

THE COGNITIVE STUDY OF IDEAS AND
THEIR INFERENTIAL ORGANIZATION

The approach to mathematical cognition we take in this chapter is relatively new, and it differs in important ways from (but is complementary to) the ones taken by many of the authors in this volume. In order to avoid potential misunderstandings regarding the subject matter and goals of our piece, we believe that it is important to clarify these differences at the outset. The differences reside mainly on three fundamental aspects:

1. The level at which the subject matter, namely, mathematical cognition, is defined and studied
2. The scope of what is considered to be "mathematics"
3. The methods used to gather knowledge about the subject matter, mathematical cognition

Most chapters in this volume focus on performance, abilities, stereotypes, learning, belief systems, neurological or developmental disorders, and the effect of aging involved in some aspect of mathematical *behavior* (usually basic arithmetic tasks). For instance, some of the authors analyze the nature and locus of the most basic of brain functions and locations that give rise to extremely basic number-related behaviors like subitizing, numeration, counting, estimating, and so on. Others study the developmental dimensions involved in the learning of the number concept, others study the peculiarities of number processing, and others focus their efforts on studying mathematical abilities, problem-solving, and performance, investigating their psychological and biological underpinnings. What is common to these studies is the following:

a. Subject matter: Their primary concern is some aspect of the psychological, neurological, or educational reality involved in some mathematical behavior, performance, or competence of a *person*. The subject matter is defined at the level of an *individual* or at the level of an individual's nervous system. Mathematics per se is untouched. It is not the primary concern.

b. Scope: What is usually meant by "mathematics" is, in general, simple arithmetic, number processing, or numerical calculation. Occasionally, it also means basic geometry or basic algebraic thinking.

c. Method: The methods of investigation are mainly standard empirical methods used in behavioral studies in psychology, studies with neuropsychological syndromes, and computational models of numerical processing.

We, of course, celebrate this work and, building partially on their findings, move on to a radically different set of questions *about* mathematics. And here we mean the *inferential organization* of mathematics *itself*, not just performances or behaviors of individuals in some numerical domain. If mathematics does build on human ideas, how can we give a cognitive account of what *is* mathematics, with all the precision and complexities of its theorems, axioms, formal definitions, and proofs? What is the nature of what is taken to be truth (i.e., a theorem)? And, how do we get from numbers and baby arithmetic (proto-addition and subtraction up to three items) to higher forms of mathematics: full-blown arithmetic with rational and real numbers, set theory, logic, analytic geometry, trigonometry, exponentials and logarithms, calculus, complex analysis, transfinite numbers, abstract algebra, and so on?

We believe that these are questions for cognitive science—the scientific study of the mind, not for mathematics per se. We are asking, which cognitive mechanisms are used in structuring mathematical ideas? And more specifically, what cognitive mechanisms can characterize the inferential organization observed in mathematical ideas themselves? At this point we need to clarify the notion of *inferential organization*.

Consider the following two linguistic expressions: "Christmas is still *ahead* of us" and "That cold winter took place way *back* in the 60s." Literally, these expressions don't make any sense. "Christmas" is not something that can physically be in front of us in any measurable or observable way, and a "cold winter" is not something that can be physically behind us. Hundreds of thousands of these expressions, whose meaning is not literal but metaphorical, can be observed in human everyday language. A branch of cognitive science, cognitive linguistics (and, more specifically, cognitive semantics), has shown that these hundreds of thousands, metaphorical expressions can be modeled by a relatively small number of *conceptual metaphors* (Lakoff, 1993). A crucial component of what is modeled is, precisely, their *inferential organization*. In the previous example, although the expressions use completely different words (i.e., the former refers to a location *ahead* and the latter to a location *behind*), they are both linguistic manifestations of a single conceptual metaphor, namely, TIME EVENTS ARE THINGS IN UNIDIMENSIONAL SPACE,[1] which maps locations in front of ego with events in the future, co-

---

[1] Following a convention in cognitive linguistics, capitals here serve to denote the name of the conceptual mapping as such. Particular instances of these mappings, called metaphorical expressions (e.g., "she has a great future in front of her"), are not written with capitals.

locations with ego with events in the present, and locations behind ego with events in the past. This mapping preserves transitivity, such that if an object A in the source domain of space is further away than an object C, then the entailment "A is further away in front of ego than C" is preserved, via the mapping, in the target domain of Time: event A in time is further away in the future than event C (spatial construals of time are, of course, much more complex. For details see Lakoff, 1993; Lakoff & Johnson, 1999; Núñez, 1999. For experimental psychological studies based on priming paradigms see Boroditski, 2000; Gentner, 2001; Núñez, in preparation). For the purposes of this chapter, there are two very important aspects to keep in mind:

1. At this level of the cognitive analysis, what matters is not how *single individuals* learn how to use these metaphors, or how they use them under stressful situations, or how they may lose the ability to use them after a brain injury, and so on. What matters is to characterize (i.e., to model) across hundreds of linguistic expressions the structure of the inferences that can be drawn from them. For example, if "Christmas is ahead of us," we can infer that New Year's Eve (which takes place later in December) is not just ahead of us, but *further away in front of us*. Similarly, if "the cold winter took place way back in the 60s," we can infer that last winter is not only behind us but also *much closer to us*.

2. Truth is always relative to the inferential organization of the mappings involved in the underlying conceptual metaphor. For instance, "last summer" can be conceptualized as being *behind us* as long as we operate with the conceptual metaphor TIME EVENTS ARE THINGS IN UNIDIMENSIONAL SPACE mentioned above, which determines a specific bodily orientation respect to metaphorically conceived events in time. Núñez and Sweetser (2001; in preparation) have shown, based on lexical, metaphorical, and gestural empirical evidence, that the details of that mapping are not universal. In the Aymara culture of the Andes, for instance, "last summer" is conceptualized as being in front of ego, not behind ego (as it is conceptualized by speakers of many languages around the world, including English), and "from now on" not as a frontward motion but as backward motion. As we will see, truth in mathematics also depends on the details of the underlying conceptual metaphors.

In sum, this chapter analyzes mathematical cognition from the perspective of the cognitive components of the inferential organization of mathematics itself (focusing mainly on conceptual metaphor) and not with the behavior or performance of individual subjects doing some form of mathematics. We believe that the approach we present here is not inconsistent from standard approaches in mathematical cognition. We think, however, that it is different in what concerns its subject matter, scope, and methodology:

a. Subject matter: The primary concern of this approach is mathematics *itself*. The subject matter is defined at the level of the inferential organization of mathematical *ideas*. Behavior, performance, and competence of particular individuals are secondary.

b. Scope: Arithmetic (or numerical calculations) is not given any privileged status. The goal is to study mathematics in all its manifestations, most of which are not numerical at all (e.g., topology, set theory, and algebra).

c. Method: The methods of investigation used are mainly drawn from modeling in cognitive semantics. In particular, we will be using a technique we call *Mathematical Idea Analysis* (Lakoff & Núñez, 2000).

As we said earlier, the approach we present here is still relatively new, and in many ways it is still being explored. For those interested in studies involving behavior, performance, learning, brain injuries, and abilities in mathematical cognition, we believe that this approach should provide fruitful information for the elaboration of hypotheses that can be tested empirically.

THE COGNITIVE SCIENCE OF MATHEMATICS

In the last 15 years or so, the field of cognitive semantics has produced many interesting findings regarding the basic mechanisms of human thought as they are manifested through language. Important discoveries such as force dynamics schemas (Talmy, 1988, 2003), frames (Fillmore, 1982, 1985), prototypes of various kinds (Rosch, 1981, 1999), image schemas (Johnson, 1987; Lakoff, 1987), conceptual metaphor (Lakoff, 1993; Lakoff & Johnson, 1980/2003; Lakoff & Núñez, 1997; Núñez, 2000; Reddy, 1979; Sweetser, 1990), conceptual metonymy (Lakoff & Johnson, 1980), and conceptual blends (Fauconnier & Turner, 1998, 2002) have provided new, deep insights into the nature of human ideas. With this work in mind, the question we ask is: How are these basic mechanisms of thought (which manifest through language and gesture) used to characterize the inferential organization of mathematical ideas—ideas like exponentials, trigonometric functions, derivatives, and so on? We ask further how these mathematical ideas allow us to express in precise mathematical terms such ordinary ideas as proportion, difference, negation, change, reversal, recurrence, rotation, and even structure.

Moreover, we ask what the relation is between mathematical ideas and the symbolization of those ideas. Why do calculations mean what they do, and why do they "work?" In our book *Where Mathematics Comes From* (Lakoff & Núñez, 2000), we claim that the ensemble of those questions constitutes a new field of inquiry we call the Cognitive Science of Mathematics (see also Lakoff & Núñez, 1997). In the book, we provide an in-depth analysis of such questions and give preliminary answers to them. In addition, we outline the method of analysis we call Mathematical Idea Analysis. In short, The Cognitive Science of Mathematics asks foundational questions about the very nature of mathematics itself.

The present chapter can only give the barest suggestion of the answers to the questions we address in our book and a hint at how mathematical idea analysis works. Perhaps one of the most interesting findings in our research is that conceptual metaphors and conceptual blends are constitutive of the ideas of higher mathematics. In this essay we will limit our discussion to conceptual metaphor, since this particular cognitive mechanism has been studied in depth for at least 25 years and has gathered evidence from a wide range of sources: psychological experiments (Gibbs, 1994), historical semantic change (Sweetser, 1990), spontaneous gesture (McNeill, 1992; Núñez, 2004; Núñez & Sweetser, 2001), American Sign Language (Taub, 2001), child language development (C. Johnson, 1997), generalizations over polysemy (i.e., cases in which the same word has multiple systematically related meanings; Lakoff & Johnson, 1980/2003), generalizations over inference patterns (cases in which source and target domains have corresponding inference patterns; Lakoff, 1993), novel cases (new examples of conventional mappings, as in poetry, song, advertisements, and so on; Lakoff & Turner, 1989), discourse coherence (Narayanan, 1997), and cross-linguistic studies (Yu, 1998). For a thorough discussion of such evidence, see Lakoff and Johnson, 1999, Chapter 6).

In order to illustrate our arguments, we would like to consider a simple but deep example: *actual infinity*. As finite beings, we have no direct experience of infinity. However, via conceptual metaphor, we can extend our finite experiences metaphorically to create and conceptualize infinity as a *completed realized entity*, such as an infinite set, an infinite sequence, a point at infinity in projective geometry, an infinite sum, an infinite number, and even an infinite intersection of sets. Such cases of actual infinity are absolutely central to most of modern mathematics (for a brief historical analysis, see Maor, 1991). It is important to bear in mind during the discussion that follows that conceptual metaphors are precisely stateable and that they preserve inferences, which is what allows them to play a central role in mathematics.

THE BASIC METAPHOR OF INFINITY

Since the time of Aristotle, there have been two concepts of infinity, *potential* infinity and *actual* infinity. Suppose you start to count: 1, 2, 3, . . . and you imagine you go on indefinitely without stopping. That is an instance of potential infinity, infinity without an end. On the other hand, consider the set of *all* natural numbers. No one could ever enumerate all of them; the enumeration would go on without end. Yet we conceptualize a set containing *all of them*, even though the enumeration has never and could never produce them all. That is an instance of *actual infinity*—an infinite completed thing.

In *Where Mathematics Comes From,* we hypothesize that the idea of "actual infinity" in mathematics is metaphorical, that all the diverse ideas using actual infinity make use of the ultimate metaphorical *result* of a process without end. Literally, there is no such thing; if the process does not end, there can be no such "ultimate result." But the very human mechanism of metaphor allows us to conceptualize and construct the "result" of an infinite process—in terms of the only way we have for conceptualizing the result of a process—in terms of a process that *does* have an end.

We hypothesize that all cases of actual infinity—from infinite sets to points at infinity to limits of infinite series to infinite intersections to least upper bounds—are special cases of a single general conceptual metaphor in which processes that go on indefinitely (that is, without end) are conceptualized as having an end and an ultimate result. We call this metaphor the BASIC METAPHOR OF INFINITY, or the BMI for short (Lakoff & Núñez, 2000). (For details regarding how the BMI applies to Georg Cantor's transfinite cardinal numbers, see Núñez, in press.)

A conceptual metaphor is a cross-domain mapping (in the cognitive sense of "mapping") from one conceptual domain to another, where inferences from the source domain are mapped to the target. The source domain of the BMI is the domain of iterative processes with end, that is, what linguists call *perfective aspect* (Comrie, 1976). That is, the source domain consists of an ordinary iterative process with an indefinite (though finite) number of iterations with a completion and resultant state. The target domain of the BMI is the domain of processes without end, that is, processes having *imperfective aspect*. In itself, without the metaphorical mapping, the target domain characterizes *potential infinity*. The effect of the BMI is to add a metaphorical completion to the process that goes on and on indefinitely, so that it is seen as *having a final result*—an infinite *thing*. This metaphorical addition is indicated in boldface in the statement of the conceptual mapping given below.

The source and target domains are alike in certain essential ways:

- Both have an initial state.
- Both have an iterative process with an unspecified number of iterations.
- Both have a resultant state after each iteration.

In the metaphor, the initial state, the iterative process, and the result after each iteration are mapped onto the corresponding elements of the target domain. But the crucial effect of the metaphor is *to add to the target domain the completion of the process and its resulting state.* It is this last part of the metaphor that allows us to conceptualize the ongoing process in terms of a completed process and so to produce the concept of actual infinity. Table 7.1 shows the mapping of the BASIC METAPHOR OF INFINITY.

Notice that the source domain of the metaphor has something that does not correspond to anything in the *literal* target domain, namely, a final resultant state. The inferential organization of this conceptual mapping functions so as to impose a final resultant state on an unending process. The literal unending process is given on the right-hand side of the top three arrows. The metaphorically imposed final resultant state (which characterizes what is unique about actual infinity) is indicated in boldface on the right side of the fifth line of the mapping.

In addition, there is a crucial entailment that arises in the source domain and that is imposed by the metaphor on the target domain. In any completed process, the final resultant state is *unique*. The fact that it is the *final* state of the process means that:

Table 7.1
The Basic Metaphor of Infinity

Source Domain Completed Iterative Processes		Target Domain Iterative Processes That Go On and On
The Beginning State	$\rightarrow$	The Beginning State
State resulting from the initial stage of the process	$\rightarrow$	State resulting from the initial stage of the process
The process: from a given intermediate state, produce the next state	$\rightarrow$	The process: from a given intermediate state, produce the next state
The intermediate result after that iteration of the process	$\rightarrow$	The intermediate result after that iteration of the process
The Final Resultant State	$\rightarrow$	**"The Final Resultant State" (actual infinity)**
Entailment: the final resultant state is unique and follows every nonfinal state	$\rightarrow$	**Entailment: the final resultant state is unique and follows every nonfinal state**

- There is no earlier final state; that is, there is no distinct previous state within the process that follows the completion stage of the process yet precedes the final state of the process.
- Similarly, there is no later final state of the process; that is, there is no other state of the process that both results from the completion of the process and follows the final state of the process. Any such putative state would have to be "outside the process" as we conceptualize it.

Thus, the uniqueness of the final state of a complete process is a fact of human cognition, not a fact about some transcendental truth. That is, it follows from the way our brains and bodies allow us to conceptualize completed processes.

The BASIC METAPHOR OF INFINITY maps this uniqueness property for final resultant states of processes onto actual infinity. Actual infinity, as characterized by *any given application of the BMI*, is unique.

What results from the BMI is a metaphorical creation that does not occur literally, but it represents a process that goes on and on indefinitely and yet has a unique final resultant state, a state "at infinity." This metaphor allows us to conceptualize "potential" unending infinity, which has neither end nor result, in terms of a familiar kind of process that has a unique result. Via the BMI, infinity is converted from an open-ended process to a specific, unique entity with a precise inferential organization. (For details see Lakoff & Núñez, 2000, chapter 8.)

In *Where Mathematics Comes From,* we dedicate several chapters to showing that a wide range of mathematical concepts use actual infinity and that they can be precisely formulated using the BMI. The cases covered include infinite sets, points at infinity (in projective and inversive geometries), mathematical induction, infinite decimals, infinite sums, transfinite numbers, infinitesimal numbers, infinite intersections, least upper bounds, and limits of sequences of numbers. The general technique is to specify precisely what the parameters of the iterative process are. For example, in the case of the infinite set of natural numbers, we let the iterative process be to produce the next integer from a prior set of integers and form a new set containing the new integer and the integers in the prior set. At the metaphorical final resultant state, we conceptualize the set of *all* the natural numbers. Depending on the nature of the process involved (e.g., iterative sums and iterative nesting of sets) and on the way in which the elements of the process are parameterized, different instantiations of the BMI occur. It is important to mention that in many ways, the BMI plays a similar role to the various axioms of infinity in mathematics. The BMI and the axioms of infinity serve to "create" mathematical infinities. The main fundamental difference, however, is that the BMI is heavily constrained by findings in cognitive science (i.e., it has to be consistent with state-of-the-art knowledge about the peculiarities of the human brain, the properties of human language, and so on), whereas the axioms in mathematics don't have to meet the requirements of any of these empirical constraints. Axioms of infinity in mathematics are simply "made up" to assure the logical existence of mathematical infinities.

To get a sense of how conceptual metaphors work in mathematics, we will consider a relatively simple and well-known *apparent* paradox that allows us to see (a) the metaphorical structures that constitute the most fundamental of mathematical ideas and (b) the underlying inferential organization that make it appear as a paradox.[2] The example, which is taken from the domain of curves and functions in the Cartesian plane, has served as experimental material in research in mathematics education (Fischbein, Tirosh, and Hess, 1979) as well as in cognitive development (Núñez, 1993).

CURVES, FUNCTIONS, AND LIMITS: THE PROBLEM

There is a classical problem that involves the following mathematical construction, as given in Figure 7.1. Start at stage 1 with a semicircle of diameter 1, extending from 0 to 1 on the X-axis of the Cartesian Plane. The perimeter of the semicircle is of length $\pi/2$. The center will be at $x = 1/2$, and the semicircle is above the X-axis.

At stage 2, divide the diameter in half and form two semicircles extending from 0 to 1/2 and 1/2 to 1. The two centers will be at $x = 1/4$ and $x = 3/4$ (see Figure 7.2). The perimeter of each

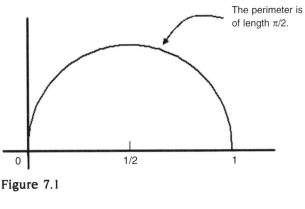

The perimeter is of length π/2.

Figure 7.1

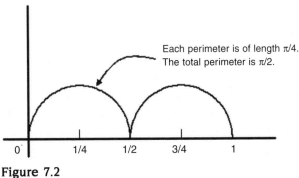

Each perimeter is of length π/4.
The total perimeter is π/2.

Figure 7.2

---

[2]Due to constraints of space, in what follows we will only give a general characterization of the underlying conceptual metaphors, without the details of the mappings involved.

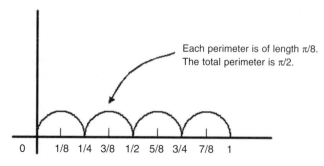

Each perimeter is of length π/8.
The total perimeter is π/2.

Figure 7.3

semicircle is $\pi/4$. The total length of both perimeters is $\pi/2$. The length of each diameter is $1/2$. The total length of both diameters is 1.

At stage 3, divide the diameters in half again to form two more semicircles. There will now be four semicircles (see Figure 7.3). The centers will be at $x = 1/8$, $x = 3/8$, $x = 5/8$, and $x = 7/8$. The perimeter of each semicircle will be $\pi/8$. The total length of all four perimeters is $\pi/2$. The length of each diameter is $1/4$. The total length of all four diameters is 1.

Continue this process without stopping. This is an infinite process without an end. At every stage n, there will be a bumpy curve made up of 2^{n-1} semicircles, whose total length is $\pi/2$, and where all the diameters taken together constitute a segment of length 1. As n gets larger, the bumpy curve gets closer and closer to the diameter line, with the area between the bumpy curve and the diameter line getting smaller and smaller. But the length of the bumpy curve remains $\pi/2$ at all stages, while the length of the diameter line remains 1 at all stages. As n approaches infinity, the area between the bumpy curve and the diameter line approaches zero, while the lengths of the curve and the line remain constant at $\pi/2$ and 1, respectively.

What happens at $n = \infty$?

LENGTHS, FUNCTIONS, AND SETS OF POINTS

At $n = \infty$, there is no area between the bumpy curve and the diameter line. They occupy the same place in space. Yet the bumpy curve is still of length $\pi/2$ and the diameter line is still of length 1. How is this possible? The bumpy curve and the diameter line appear to have become the same line, but with two different lengths! And as we know, a single line should have only a single length. Situations like this one provide perfect cases for the cognitive study of the inferential organization involved in mathematical conceptual systems.

A clearer statement of the problem will reveal why the apparent paradox arises. In the construction, there is an infinite sequence of curves approaching a limit. But sequences that have limits are sequences of *numbers*, as characterized by the BMI given above. How can one get from limits of sequences of *numbers* to limits of sequences of *curves?*

To do so, we will have to operate with a central metaphor developed in the late 19th century, in which *naturally continuous* curves and lines were reconceptualized in a fundamentally different way. Up to the work of Cauchy, Weierstrass, Dedekind, and others in the 19th century, continuity was predicated on holistic and dynamic entities such as "lines" or "planes" moving or extending over a background space. The work by Kepler and Euler, as well as the one by Newton and Leibniz, the inventors of calculus in the 17th century, built upon this notion of continuity. Euler, for instance, described (natural) continuity as "freely leading the hand." This conception of continuity, which is the same idea that students bring to math classes before they are exposed to calculus, changed dramatically via the introduction of new conceptual metaphors in which a space was conceived as constituted by sets of discrete elements called "points": SPACE IS A SET OF POINTS. Incidentally, motion in this metaphorical space completely disappeared. It was replaced by strict statements involving static existential and universal quantifiers operating on discrete sets of points (for details see Núñez & Lakoff, 1998; Núñez, Edwards, & Matos, 1999; Lakoff & Núñez, 2000). Given the inferential organization of this new metaphor SPACE IS A SET OF POINTS, we can pick an appropriate sequence of functions $f_1(x)$, $f_2(x)$, ..., and conceptualize the ith bumpy curve as a set of ordered pairs of real numbers $(x, f_i(x))$ in the unit square in the Cartesian plane. The first semicircle will be represented by the set of ordered pairs of real numbers $\{(x, f_1(x))\}$. Via this metaphor we are able to replace the sequence of geometric curves by a sequence of sets of ordered pairs of real numbers. In short, we have gone, via metaphor, from the geometry of natural space to a different mathematical domain consisting of sets and numbers.

Now that spaces, curves, and points have been replaced metaphorically by sets, ordered pairs, and numbers, can we use the characterization of limits of sequences of numbers, as given by the BMI. For each number x between 0 and 1, there will be a sequence of numbers y—$y_1, y_2, y_3, \ldots$—given by the values of y in the functions $f_1(x) = y_1$, $f_2(x) = y_2$, $f_3(x) = y_3$, ... Each of these sequences of y-values defined for the number x will have a limit as the ys get smaller and smaller—namely, zero. Thus, for each real number x between 0 and 1, there will be a sequence of ordered pairs (x, y_1), (x, y_2), (x, y_3), ... that converges to $(x, 0)$ (see Figure 7.4).

A subtle shift has occurred. We have replaced each bumpy curve by a bumpy curve set consisting of ordered pairs of numbers (x, y), with $y = f(x)$, where x ranges over all the real numbers between 0 and 1. But what converges to a limit is not this sequence of bumpy curve sets. Instead, we have an infinity of convergent sequences of y-values—one from each member of the sequence of bumpy curve sets—for each number x between 0 and 1. The limit of each such sequence is the pair $(x, 0)$. The set of all such limits is the set of ordered pairs of numbers $\{(x, 0)\}$, where x is a real number between 0 and 1. This set of ordered pairs of numbers corresponds, via the metaphors used, to the diameter line.

But this set is a *set of limits of sequences of ordered pairs* of numbers. What we wanted was the limit of a sequence of curves, that is, the *limit of a sequence of sets of ordered pairs* of numbers. Those are very different things conceptually.

To get what we want from what we have, we must operate with a new metaphor, which we will call the LIMIT-SET METAPHOR: THE LIMIT OF A SEQUENCE OF SETS IS THE SET OF THE LIMITS OF THE SEQUENCES. Only via such a metaphor can we get the diameter line *to be* the limit of the sequence of bumpy curve sets.

Two conceptual metaphors have provided the necessary inferential organization:

- CURVES (AND LINES) ARE SETS OF ORDERED PAIRS OF NUMBERS, AND
- THE LIMIT-SET METAPHOR

If we operate with these two conceptual metaphors, then the sequence of bumpy curves can be reconceptualized as a sequence of bumpy curve sets consisting of ordered pairs of numbers.

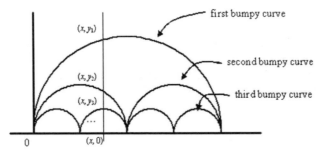

Figure 7.4

That sequence will have as its limit the set of ordered pairs $\{(x, 0)\}$, where x is between 0 and 1. This set has the *same* elements as the set of ordered pairs of numbers representing the diameter line under the metaphor CURVES (AND LINES) ARE SETS OF ORDERED PAIRS OF NUMBERS. Mathematically speaking, there is an axiom (i.e., the axiom of extensionality) that imposes the "truth" that a set is uniquely determined by its members. Via this artificially concocted axiom, the two sets become "identical." Cognitively speaking, however, the two sets are radically different. Here we can see that the LIMIT-SET METAPHOR is one of the sources of the apparent paradox.

WHAT IS THE LENGTH OF A SET?

In order to characterize the limit of a sequence of curves, we have had to metaphorically reconceptualize each curve as a set—a set of ordered pairs of numbers. The reason is that limits of sequences are technically defined only for numbers, not for geometric curves. But now a problem arises. What is "length" for such a set?

In physical space as we experience it every day, there are natural lengths, like the length of your arm or your foot. Hence, we have units of measurements like "one foot." But when curves are replaced by sets, we no longer have natural lengths. Sets, literally, have no lengths. To characterize the "length" of such a set, we will need a relation between the set and a number called its "length." In general, curves in the Cartesian Plane have all sorts of numerical properties—the area under the curve, the curvature at each point, the tangent at each point, and so on. Once geometric curves are replaced by sets, then all those properties of the curves will have to be replaced by relations between the sets and numbers.

The Length Function

The inferential organization of the length of a line segment $[a, b]$ along a number line is metaphorically provided by the absolute value of the difference between the numbers, namely, $|b - a|$. This is extended via the Pythagorean Theorem to any line segment oriented at any angle in the Cartesian Plane. Suppose its endpoints are (a_1, b_1), and (a_2, b_2). Its length is $\sqrt{(|a_2 - a_1|^2 + |b_2 - b_1|^2)}$.

What about the *length of a curve*? Choose a finite number of points along the curve (including the endpoints). Draw the sequence of straight lines connecting those points. Call it a *partition* of the curve. The length of the partition is the sum of the lengths of the straight lines in the partition (see Figure 7.5). Think of the length of the curve via the BMI appropriately

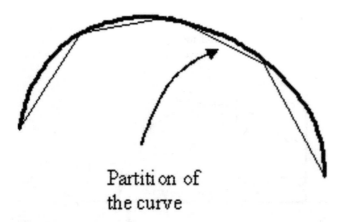

Partition of
the curve

Figure 7.5

parameterized as the *least upper bound of the set of the lengths of all partitions of the curve.* This gives us a *length function* for every curve.

Now think of the line segments as measuring sticks. As the measuring sticks get shorter and shorter, they measure the length of the curve more and more accurately. The length of the curve is *the limit of measurements as the length of the measuring sticks approaches zero.* Let us call this the CURVE LENGTH METAPHOR.

The Sources of the Apparent Paradox

The appearance of the paradox comes from two sources with mutually inconsistent inferential organization:

1. A set of expectations about naturally continuous curves.
2. The metaphors used to characterize curves in formal mathematics.

It should come as no surprise that our normal expectations are violated by the metaphors of formal mathematics.

Let us start with our normal expectations, that is, with the conceptual apparatus structured by the inferential organization of natural continuity.

- Length, curvature at each point, and the tangent at each point are inherent properties of a naturally continuous curve.
- Identical curves should have identical properties.
- Nearly identical curves should have nearly identical properties.
- If a sequence of curves converges to a limit curve, the sequence of properties of those curves should converge to the properties of the limit curve.

The reason we have these expectations is that we metaphorically conceptualize curves as *objects in space* and properties that are inherent to a curve as *parts of the curve.* For example, we naturally understand the curvature at a point in a curve as being *inherent to the curve.* If we think of a curve as being traced out by a point in motion (as did the brilliant mathematicians Kepler and Euler), we think of the direction of motion at each point (mathematicized as the tangent to the curve) as *inherent to the curve.* If we think of curves as objects and their inherent properties as parts of those objects, then as the curves get very close to each other, their properties should get correspondingly close. When the curves are so close that they cannot be distinguished, their properties should also be indistinguishably close.

The conceptual metaphors that characterize post-19th-century formal mathematics, when taken together, violate these expectations. Here are the relevant metaphors.

- FUNCTIONS ARE SETS OF ORDERED PAIRS OF REAL NUMBERS
- REAL NUMBERS ARE LIMITS OF SEQUENCES OF RATIONAL NUMBERS (uses the BMI)
- CURVES (AND LINES) ARE SETS OF POINTS
- POINTS IN THE (CARTESIAN) PLANE ARE ORDERED PAIRS OF NUMBERS
- THE LIMIT METAPHOR (uses the BMI for limits of sequences of numbers)
- THE LIMIT-SET METAPHOR (defines the limit of a sequence of curves as the set of point-by-point limits, as in Figure 7.4)
- PROPERTIES OF CURVES ARE FUNCTIONS
- SPATIAL DISTANCE (between points a and b on a line) IS NUMERICAL DIFFERENCE ($|b - a|$)
- THE CURVE LENGTH METAPHOR (uses the BMI)
- CLOSENESS (between two curves) IS A NUMBER (defined by a metric, which assigns numbers to pairs of functions)

It should be clear why such metaphors violate the expectations discussed above. Curves are not physical objects; they are sets. Inherent properties are not parts; they are functions from one entity to a distinct entity. When two "curves" (sets) are "close" (have a small number assigned by a metric), there is no reason to think that their "properties" (numbers assigned to them by functions) should also be "close."

Moreover, the LIMIT-SET METAPHOR that defines limits for curves says nothing about properties (like curvature, tangent, and length). From the perspective of the metaphors inherent in the formal mathematics, there is no reason to think that properties like curvature, tangent, and length *should* necessarily converge when the curves converge point by point.

Tangents and Length

Imagine measuring the length of a semicircle on one of the bumpy curves using measuring sticks that get shorter and shorter. If there were n semicircles on that bumpy curve, the measurements of each semicircle would approach $\pi/2n$ as a limit. The total length, n times $\pi/2n$, is always $\pi/2$.

As the measuring sticks get shorter, they change direction and eventually approach the orientations of tangents to the curve. The CURVE LENGTH METAPHOR thus provides a link between lengths of curves and orientations of tangents, which in turn are characterized by the first derivative of the function defining the curve.

Compare the semicircles with the diameter line. There the measuring sticks are always flat, with tangents at zero degrees. Correspondingly, the first derivative is zero at each point.

The Bumpy Curves in Function Space

A *function space* is defined by the metaphor that A FUNCTION IS A POINT IN A SPACE. The metaphor entails that there is a "distance" between the "points," that is, the functions. By itself, that metaphor does not tell us how "close" the "points" are to one another. For this, one needs a metric, a function from pairs of functions to numbers. The numbers are understood as metaphorically measuring the "distance" between the functions.

All sorts of metrics are possible, provided that they meet three conditions on distance d: $d(a, a) = 0$, $d(a, b) = d(b, a)$, and $d(a, b) + d(b, c) \geq d(a, c)$. In the field of *functional analysis*, metrics are defined so as to reflect properties of functions. To get an idea of how this works, imagine the bumpy curves and the diameter line as being points in a space. Imagine the metric over that space as being defined in the following way.

1. The distance between any two functions $f(x)$ and $g(x)$ is defined as the sum of
   a. the maximum difference in the values of the functions, plus
   b. the average difference in the values of the derivatives of the functions.

Formally, this is written:

$$d(f,g) = \sup_x |f(x) - g(x)| + \int_0^1 (|f'(x) - g'(x)|)dx$$

Via the metaphors CURVES ARE SETS OF POINTS and FUNCTIONS ARE ORDERED PAIRS OF REAL NUMBERS, let $g(x)$ be the diameter line and let $f(x)$ vary over the bumpy curves. As the bumpy curves get closer to the diameter line, the maximum distance (the first term of the sum) between each bumpy curve $f(x)$ and the diameter line $g(x)$ approaches zero. The second term of the sum does not, however, approach zero. It represents the average difference between the values of the tangents at each value (x). In the diameter line $g(x)$, the tangents are always zero, so $g'(x) = 0$ for all x. Since the tangents on each bumpy curve go through the same range of values, the average of the absolute values of the tangents will be the same for each bumpy curve. Thus, the second term will be a nonzero constant when $g(x)$ is the diameter line and $f(x)$ is any bumpy curve.

According to this new inferential organization, we obtain the following meaningful entailment:

- Curves that are close in the Cartesian Plane point-by-point, but *not* in their tangents, are not "close" in the function space defined by this metric.

In this function space, the metric given above takes into account more than the difference between the values of the functions. It also considers the crucial factor that keeps the length of the bumpy curves from converging to the length of diameter line, namely, the difference in the behavior of the tangents. In this metaphorical function space, the sequence of "bumpy curve" points do *not* get close to the diameter-line points as n approaches infinity.

In Figures 7.1–7.4, we represented the sequence of functions as curves—bumpy curves. This was a *metaphorical* representation of the functions, using the metaphors POINTS IN THE PLANE ARE ORDERED PAIRS OF NUMBERS AND FUNCTIONS ARE SETS OF ORDERED PAIRS OF NUMBERS, which are part of the inferential organization of the Cartesian Plane. This spatial representation of the function gave the illusion that, as n approached infinity, the bumpy curves "approached" (came indefinitely close to) the diameter line. But this metaphorical image leads one to ignore the derivatives (the tangents) of the functions, which are crucial to the question of length. In this sense, this particular metaphorical representation of these functions in the Cartesian Plane is degenerate: it leaves out crucial information. But in the function space defined by the metaphor FUNCTIONS ARE POINTS IN SPACE and metric above, this crucial information is included and it becomes clear that the bumpy curve functions do *not* come close to the diameter line function. There is not even the appearance of a paradox here. Under this metric, curves that are close *both* point-by-point *and* in their tangents will be represented by points that are close in this metaphorical function space.

CONCEPTUAL METAPHOR AND PARADOX

In the above discussion, we described the inferential organization involved in the conceptualization of the bumpy curves and the diameter lines as functions so that we could use the theory of function spaces to show that the bumpy curves do not really converge to the diameter lines. However, we do not have to bring functions into the discussion at all. Suppose we just look at the curves in geometric terms as curves. Then the appearance of a paradox remains, since the area under the bumpy curves does converge to zero and since the radii defining the heights of the bumpy curves also converge to zero. However, the length of the bumpy curves remains constant at $\pi/2$. The reason is that the curvatures of the semicircles, far from converging to zero, increase without bound. Curvature is a property of the curve. A sequence of curves can converge to another curve only if all its properties also converge. The appearance of paradox arises because we are not paying attention to the nonconvergent properties.

Most people tend to not pay attention to curvature and tangents in this case (Fischbein, Tirosh, Hess, 1979; Núñez, 1993). Moreover, most educated adults tend not to stop with the finite cases, but to move to the infinite case (via an inappropriate parameterization of the BMI, we hypothesize), which is where the "paradox" appears. But, as we said earlier, the BMI is a general conceptual metaphor, with an unlimited range of possible special cases. Which version you get depends on how you characterize and parameterize the special case. If you were to try to plug curvatures or tangents into the BMI for the bumpy curves, it wouldn't give you paradoxical inferences because the entailment of the BMI in such a case would not give you convergence. What is salient for most people in this example is not curvature or tangents but, rather, the constant lengths on the one hand and on the other, the distance between the curves (characterized by the radii) and the area under the bumpy curve—both of which converge to zero.

To get the appearance of a paradox, you have to operate with a version of the BMI highlighting the decreasing distance between the curves, while ignoring curvatures and tangents. The point here is that the general version of the BMI is cognitively real and can be applied in a way that is at odds with conventional mathematics. But there are other special cases of the BMI that are constitutive of conventional mathematics itself. The history of mathematics shows us that often these are precisely the cases developed in the field to deal with problems, paradoxes, and inconsistency. Depending on how the BMI is parameterized, one gets different results. From a cognitive perspective, there is nothing strange about this. The same general metaphor may be fleshed out in different ways for different purposes—in some cases defining an aspect of mathematics, in other cases contradicting conventional mathematics.

MATHEMATICAL IDEA ANALYSIS

It should now have become clear why conceptual metaphor is central to the analysis of the inferential organization of mathematical ideas. In modern geometry, for example, space is not a medium or a background in which one locates things. A space is a set and points are not *locations* but entities that are *members* of that set and therefore *constitute* that very space. A geometric figure, like a circle or a sphere, is not an entity located *in* space, but rather a set of the points that make up the space itself. Thus, for example, consider two spheres that touch at a point. According to the inferential organization of our ordinary conceptual system, the spheres are distinct entities, and touch at a point-location. But, in this metaphor, the spheres are two sets of points, *sharing* a point *in common*. A point that is constitutive of both spheres!

This is a simple example of how different metaphorical mathematical ideas can be from our ordinary conceptual system. This difference is often the cognitive reason as to why some mathematical entities and facts are so counterintuitive and difficult to learn. In the examples of the bumpy curve analyzed above, however, the mathematical concepts are metaphorically complex and the analysis is anything but obvious. A serious cognitive analysis of the inferential organization of metaphorical ideas is simply necessary if one is to understand the conceptual structure of mathematics itself.

In *Where Mathematics Comes From*, we take up even deeper cases of mathematical idea analysis, cases in which certain aspects (but not all) of the inferential organization of everyday ideas are reconceptualized in terms of mathematical ideas, which allows for a mathematicization of everyday concepts. A simple case is the concept of *difference*, which is metaphorically conceptualized in terms of *distance* between points in a space and mathematicized in terms of the arithmetical operation of subtraction—the subtraction of one number from another, in which the numbers metaphorically represent lengths of lines in space. This way of mathematicizing difference is ubiquitous not only in mathematics, but also in hundreds of disciplines applying mathematics to their subject matters, from descriptive and inferential statistics, to economics, biology, physics, psychology, and political science.

Another easy example is the concept of *change*, mathematicized in terms of derivatives. There is a general metaphor outside of mathematics that *change is motion in space from one location to another*. Qualities are represented conceptually as dimensions in space, degrees of qualities as distances along these dimensions, time as a spatial dimension, and change of a quality as movement from one point in that dimension to another. Instantaneous change is then conceived of as average change of location over an infinitesimally small interval.

In our book, we give much more complex examples. Exponentiation is shown to express the inferential organization of the concept of change in proportion to size. Trigonometric functions are shown to characterize recurrence, and so on. It is via this means that we explain why mathematics can work in the sciences. Scientists ultimately categorize the phenomena they experience by operating with the inferential organization of ordinary everyday concepts, like size, proportion, change, and recurrence. The inferential organization provided by the metaphor system of mathematics, as precisely formulated, allows us to mathematicize these concepts and perform calculations. Conceptual metaphors preserve inferences, and algorithmic calculations encode those inferences. Conceptual metaphors thus play a central role in permitting the calculation of predictions based on conceptual inferences.

CONCLUSION

Mathematics is a human enterprise. It uses the same conceptual mechanisms of thought as those used in other intellectual domains, which shows a remarkable optimal use of a human's limited and highly constrained biological resources. To understand the inferential organization that makes mathematics what it is, is to understand how the human mind uses everyday cognitive mechanisms in very special and sophisticated ways. Mathematics has very unique features. It is abstract (i.e., not directly perceivable through the senses), precise, consistent, stable, calculable, generalizable, and effective as a general tool for description, explanation, and prediction in a vast number of everyday activities. It is the inferential organization provided by conceptual metaphor, as used to constitute mathematics, that plays a fundamental role in making all this possible.

REFERENCES

Boroditski, L. (2001). Metaphoric structuring: Understanding time through spatial metaphors. *Cognition*, 75, 1–27.

Comrie, B. (1976). *Aspect: An introduction to the study of verbal aspect and related problems*. New York: Cambridge University Press.

Dauben, J. W. (1983). Georg Cantor and the origins of transfinite set theory. *Scientific American*, June, 122–154.

Dauben, J. (1979). *Georg Cantor: His mathematics and philosophy of the infinite*. Princeton, NJ: Princeton University Press.

Fauconnier, G., & Turner, M. (1998). Conceptual integration networks. *Cognitive Science*, 22(2), 133–187.

Fauconnier, G. & Turner, M. (2002). *The way we think: Conceptual blendings and the mind's hidden complexities*. New York: Basic Books.

Fillmore, C. (1982). Frame semantics. In Linguistic Society of Korea (Eds.), *Linguistics in the morning calm*. Seoul: Hanshin.

Fillmore, C. (1985). Frames and the semantics of understanding. *Quaderni di Semantica*, 6, 222–253.

Fischbein, E., Tirosh, D., & Hess, P. (1979). The intuition of infinity. *Educational Studies in Mathematics*, 10, 3–40.

Gentner, D. (2001). Spatial metaphors in temporal reasoning. In M. Gattis (ed.), *Spatial schemas and abstract thought*. Cambridge, MA: MIT Press.

Gibbs, R. (1994). *The poetics of mind: Figurative thought, language, and understanding*. New York: Cambridge University Press.

Johnson, C. (1997). Metaphor vs. conflation in the acquisition of polysemy: The case of SEE. In M. K. Hiraga, C. Sinha, & S. Wilcox (Eds.), *Cultural, typological and psychological issues in cognitive linguistics*. Amsterdam: John Benjamins.

Jahnke, H. N. (2001). Cantor's cardinal and ordinal infinities: An epistemological and didactic view. *Educational Studies in Mathematics*, 48, 175–197.

Johnson, M. (1987). *The body in the mind: The bodily basis of meaning, imagination, and reason*. Chicago: University of Chicago Press.

Lakoff, G. (1987). *Women, fire, and dangerous things: What categories reveal about the mind*. Chicago: University of Chicago Press.

Lakoff, G. (1993). The contemporary theory of metaphor. In A. Ortony (Ed.), *Metaphor and thought* (2nd ed.). New York: Cambridge University Press.

Lakoff, G., & Johnson, M. (1980/2003). *Metaphors we live by* (2nd ed.). Chicago: University of Chicago Press.

Lakoff, G., & Johnson, M. (1999). *Philosophy in the flesh*. New York: Basic Books.

Lakoff, G., & Núñez, R. (1997). The metaphorical structure of mathematics: Sketching out cognitive foundations for a mind-based mathematics. In L. English (Ed.), *Mathematical reasoning: Analogies, metaphors, and images*. Mahwah, NJ: Erlbaum.

Lakoff, G., & Núñez, R. (2000). *Where mathematics comes from: How the embodied mind brings mathematics into being*. New York: Basic Books.

Lakoff, G., & Turner, M. (1989). *More than cool reason: A field guide to poetic metaphor*. Chicago: University of Chicago Press.

Maturana, H., & Varela, F. (1987). *The tree of knowledge: The biological roots of human understanding*. Boston, MA: Shambhala.

Maor, E. (1991). *To infinity and beyond: A cultural history of the infinite*. Princeton, NJ: Princeton University Press.

McNeill, D. (1992). *Hand and mind: What gestures reveal about thought*. Chicago: Chicago University Press.

Narayanan, S. (1997). Embodiment in Language Understanding: Sensory-Motor Representations for Metaphoric Reasoning about Event Descriptions. Ph.D dissertation, Department of Computer Science, University of California at Berkeley.

Núñez, R. (1993). *En deçà du transfini: Aspects psychocognitifs sous-jacents au concept d'infini en mathématiques*. Fribourg, Switzerland: Éditions Universitaires.

Núñez, R. (1999). Could the future taste purple? Reclaiming mind, body, and cognition. In R. Núñez & W. J. Freeman (Eds.), *Reclaiming cognition: The primacy of action, intention, and emotion*. Thorverton, U.K.: Imprint Academic.

Núñez, R. (2000). Mathematical idea analysis: What embodied cognitive science can say about the human nature of mathematics. Opening plenary address in *Proceedings of the 24th International Conference for the Psychology of Mathematics Education, 1*, 3–22. Hiroshima, Japan.

Núñez, R. (2004). Do real numbers really move? The embodied cognitive foundations of mathematics. In F. Iida, R. Pfeifer, L. Steels, & Y. Kuniyoshi (Eds.), *Embodied artificial intelligence*. New York: Springer.

Núñez, R. (in press). Creating mathematical infinities: The beauty of transfinite cardinals. *Journal of Pragmatics*.

Núñez, R. (in preparation). Inferential statistics in the context of empirical cognitive linguistics. In M. Spivey, S. Coulson, M. González, & I. Mittelberg (Eds.), *Methods in cognitive linguistics*. Philadelphia, PA: John Benjamins.

Núñez, R., Edwards, L., & Matos, J. F. (1999). Embodied cognition as grounding for situated-ness and context in mathematics education. *Educational Studies in Mathematics, 39*(1–3), 45–65.

Núñez, R., & G. Lakoff (1998). What did Weierstrass really define? The cognitive structure of natural and ε–δ continuity. *Mathematical Cognition, 4* (2), 85–101.

Núñez, R. & Sweetser, E. (2001). *Spatial embodiment of temporal metaphors in Aymara*. Proceedings of the 7th International Cognitive Linguistics Conference, University of California, Santa Barbara, 249–250.

Núñez, R. & Sweetser, E. (in preparation). *In Aymara next week is behind you: Convergent evidence from language and gesture in the cross-linguistic comparison of metaphoric models*. Manuscript in preparation.

Reddy, M. (1979). The conduit metaphor. In A. Ortony (Ed.), *Metaphor and thought*. New York: Cambridge University Press.

Rosch, E. (1981). Prototype classification and logical classification: The two systems. In E. Scholnick (Ed.), *New trends in cognitive representation: Challenges to Piaget's theory*. Hillsdale, NJ: Erlbaum.

Rosch, E. (1999). Reclaiming concepts. In R. Núñez & W. J. Freeman (Eds.), *Reclaiming cognition: The primacy of action, intention, and emotion*. Thorverton, UK: Imprint Academic.

Sweetser, E. (1990). *From etymology to pragmatics: Metaphorical and cultural aspects of semantic structure*. New York: Cambridge University Press.

Talmy, L. (1988). Force dynamics in language and cognition. *Cognitive Science, 12*, 49–100.

Talmy, L. (2003). *Toward a cognitive semantics. Volume 1: Concept structuring systems*. Cambridge, MA: MIT Press.

Taub, S. (2001). *Language from the body: Iconicity and metaphor in American sign language*. Cambridge: Cambridge University Press.

Yu, N. (1998). *The contemporary theory of metaphor: A perspective from Chinese*. Amsterdam: John Benjamins.

Part 2

—

Learning and Development of Numerical Skills

—

8

The Young Numerical Mind
When Does It Count?

Sara Cordes
Rochel Gelman

Accounts of early counting differ in the degree of conceptual competence granted to the young child, as well as whether there are ontogenetic and/or phylogenetic continuities. Much of the debate is centered on whether various counting tasks license the conclusion that young learners understand the cardinal counting principle, that the last word in a count list represents the cardinal value of a collection.

Some theorists hold that a young child's initial count words have no numerical meaning for them. They first have to connect each of the first few count words to either a perceptual representation (Starkey & Cooper, 1995; Huttenlocher, Jordan, & Levin, 1994) or a nonverbal representation of the exact quantity for a given small N (Bloom, 2000; Wynn, 1990, 1992b). Others add that the language of count words grows out of the semantics of quantifiers in the language (Bloom 2000; Bloom & Wynn, 1997; Carey, 1998). Depending on the account, the requisite induction either co-occurs or sets the stage for learning the relationship between verbal counting and knowledge of addition and subtraction. Thus, it widely is assumed that learning the meaning of the counting procedure is developmentally prior to learning about addition and subtraction (but see Sophian, 1998). Gelman and Gallistel's (1978) account of a principled understanding of counting differs in this regard.

For Gelman and Gallistel, the counting principles always have been considered part and parcel of an implicit arithmetic structure, be it verbal or non-verbal. A meaningful verbal counting procedure is one that is consistent with the counting principles of: one–one (each item gets one and only one unique count tag), stable ordering (the count words are consistently used in a stable order), cardinality (the last word in the count represents the cardinality of the set), order irrelevance (the items may be counted in any order), and item–kind irrelevance (there are no restrictions on what counts as a countable entity). The execution of a competent plan of counting must be consistent with these principles for it to yield a cardinal value to which the operations of addition and subtraction can be applied. Thus, the counting principles do not stand alone. Successive count words represent ordered values because they are *subject to the axioms of arithmetic*. Below we argue that a domain-specific nonverbal counting and arithmetic structure provides very important domain-relevant clues for young children to use when learning the language and meaning of count words.

BACKGROUND

Much of the early work on numerical knowledge involves one or another counting task. Para-digms in which assessments of counting are combined with its role in arithmetic are much less prevalent. This is not surprising if we take into account the theoretical position of many labs. Given the assumption that young children do not understand their own counting, it hardly makes sense to ask them to relate counting to mathematical operations. For example, Piaget's (1952) theory is a set-theoretic one that grounds the understanding of cardinality in the operations of one–one correspondence and logical classification. For him, counting in pre-operational children is done by rote and without understanding. Bermejo (1996; Bermejo & Lago, 1990) adopts the Piagetian position that preschoolers cannot understand the cardinal principle on the basis of counting. This class of accounts rejects the view that preschoolers have any numerical abilities.[1] Theories in the empiricist tradition (e.g., Baroody & Wilkins, 1999; Mix, Levine, & Huttenlocher, 2002) share with developmentalists like Piaget the view that children must progress from the perceptual to the abstract—no matter what the conceptual domain. At first, children use only perceptual information to put together identical items for a count. Then they move to classifying together items of the same shape but of different color, then items that differ in kind but share color, and so on, until they can collect for a count widely heterogeneous "things." Understanding that a final count number, say 5, represents any set of 5 requires the use of an abstract classification structure. This criterion converges with Piaget's regarding the development of classification.

Mix et al. (2002) also place considerable emphasis on the role of language. McLeish (1991) shares their overall perspective. "The reason for animals' (and preverbal children's [authors' addition]) inability to separate numbers from the concrete situation is that they are unable to think in the abstract at all—and even if they could, they have no language capable of communi-cating, or absorbing, such abstract ideas as 'six,' or a 'herd'" (p. 7). Carey's (2001b) language-dependent account grants some role to a system for nonverbal counting and/or arithmetic. But for her, the verbal counting system reflects a conceptual change that is closely related to and emergent from the semantic/syntactic linguistic system of quantifiers (also see Spelke, 2000, for a related account).

We take up the differences in theoretical perspectives by considering two interrelated topics: (1) the evidence for early counting abilities and (2) the possibility that all humans, including preverbal infants and toddlers, possess an implicit understanding of the relationship between counting and the arithmetic principles.

MATTERS OF EVIDENCE

The Counting Tasks

One popular counting task, the "How Many?" one (HM), involves showing children N objects and asking "How many [objects]?" Task variables have included homogeneous vs. heterogeneous items, 2- vs. 3-dimensional pictures or objects, events or sounds, explicitness of instructions prior to the HM question, and so on. Across these conditions, the data converge. First, a majority of children succeed on at least some variant of the task. The older the child, the greater the probability of a correct count within and across conditions (Fuson, 1988). Second, the probability of the child repeating the last count word in response to an HM question is also a function of development. Third, the younger the child, the more likely it is she will be open to misinterpretations of what to count and of variables that influence the production of one–one and tag-generation errors. As such, younger children benefit from being told to count more slowly, touching and moving the items, and smaller set sizes (Gelman & Tucker, 1975). There is debate about the interpretation of these variables as well as scoring criteria. Some treat a child's emphasis of the last word in the count as positive evidence (Gelman & Gallistel, 1978). Others insist that even repetition of the last count word reflects nothing more than the child's imitation of a social rule of counting (Fuson, 1988). The difficulty of interpreting data from the seemingly straightforward HM task led us to work up alternative tasks.

Gelman, Meck, & Merkin (1986) designed a paradigm to test young children's flexibility with aspects of the counting procedure. In their study, 3-, 4-, and 5-year-olds watched a puppet count an array of objects and were told, "It is your job to tell [puppet] if it was OK to count the way he did or not." Children in this study were highly sensitive to violations of the one-one and cardinal principles, correcting the puppet when he double-counted, skipped an item, or repeated an incorrect cardinal value. In a different study—the "Doesn't Matter" task (Gelman & Gallistel, 1978; Gelman, Meck, & Merkin, 1986; Gelman & Meck, 1983, 1986)—preschoolers were asked to count a row of objects in an unconventional manner, by making an item in the middle be the "one" or the "two" in the count. Children quickly adopted successful strategies for complying, while honoring the counting principles. Challenges based on the order-irrelevance and item-irrelevance tasks appeared from various labs (Baroody & Wilkins, 1999; Briars & Siegler, 1984). However, Cowan, Dowker, Christakis, & Bailey's (1996) subsequent studies showed that 3- to 6-year-old children did well at working with novel counting examples if they did not have to be metacognitive. The authors concluded that question format is likely to influence whether children attend to underlying principles or various performance variables. This fits Gelman and Meck's (1986) report that youngsters benefit from instructions about the difference between a "silly" and "wrong" count sequence. But there must be more to the story.

Children younger than 3½ years almost always fail Wynn's "Give-N" task (1990, 1992b), which asks a child to give a puppet one to six small animals. Developmentally, youngsters can give one item before they give two items, and two before three animals. Wynn reports that once a child produces four items (at about 3½ years), she also does so with all larger set sizes in her count list. Until then a child engages in "grabbing." Wynn concludes that the shift reflects an understanding of the cardinal principle that "helps them to immediately acquire the meanings of all the number words [in their count list]" (Wynn, 1990, p. 186).

Although these results are robust, there is reason to question whether the "Give-N" task is a fair test of the acquisition of verbal counting. Brannon & Van de Walle (2001) observed different behavioral responses to the "Give-N," as opposed to the HM and "What's on the Card" (see below) tasks. Although children were quick to respond in the latter two tasks, they hesitated and verbalized much more confusion when participating in the "Give-N" task. Our lab made similar observations in a replication of the task. We conclude that the "Give-N" task is a very hard counting task, possibly for the following reasons.

In the "Give-N" task, the child has to create a set of objects, one by one, until she has created a set whose numerical value corresponds to one in memory. These conceptual requirements overlap to a considerable degree with variants of the number conservation task that have been paired with counting (e.g., Becker, 1989; Fuson, 1988; Gelman, 1982). Results of these task variations all agree that it is far from easy to get preschool children to use cardinal count values to construct and/or compare two sets. Becker (1989) reported that only some 3½-year-old children used the cardinal value resulting from counting each of two sets in correspondence to decide whether these were equal or not on the grounds of one-to-one correspondence. The convergence of ages in the "Give-N" and Becker tasks makes sense. Both involve using cardinal values in memory to generate or compare an equivalent value. The combined competence requirements exceed those of a beginning language user (Halford, in press).

No matter what the task, there is another consideration when beginning speakers are the subjects. Their language is very limited. The risk is nontrivial that whatever the instructions, they could be misinterpreted. To deal with this, we developed the "What's on the Card?" (WOC) task (Gelman, 1993). Subjects were three groups of children between the ages of 2½ and 3½ years, all within the age range who fail the "Give-N" task. The stimuli were a number of sets of cards, each with 1 through 7 stickers of given kind. As expected, the WOC question elicited a label response on the first card in a set, e.g., "a bee." The experimenter then said "that's right, that's a one-bee card" or "there's one bee," to communicate that the task was a number and not a labeling one. The subtle manipulation worked. Both 3-year-old groups performed at or above 80% for set sizes up to 6. The 2½-year-old group also performed better than predicted by Wynn's theory, especially when the score was based on all correct trials, including those with the minimal prompt of some pointing. Seventy percent of the youngest children counted and stated the cardinal value on set sizes up to 4.

Bullock & Gelman's (1977) instructions for their magic show avoided any talk about numbers. Still, their 2½-year-old subjects transferred an initial ordering relationship between 1 and 2 items to the novel displays with 3 and 4 items. Gelman (1993) analyzed the kinds of things that 2½-year-olds said following their encounter with the transfer displays. More than 60% of the 2½-year-olds either spontaneously counted the small sets or responded differentially to "How many..." and "Can you count..." questions, thus demonstrating the ability to relate knowledge of the cardinal principle to the ordering relation embedded in the count list. The counting observed here was in the name of explaining or thinking out loud about the relation between two pairs of ordered cardinal values. This could not occur if the children were not able to make arithmetic judgments to start. Nevertheless, even here the counting was variable. The same is true for the WOC task. This does not surprise us. A competent plan of action and its successful output involves much more than the use of the constraints of implicit knowledge of the counting principles and their representation of numerosity.

In addition to the issues considered above, there is one extremely demanding skill necessary for success on counting tasks, mastery of the count list. Once children identify the string of sounds that are relevant, they have to memorize a long list of words that lacks inherent structure. There is nothing about each of the sounds to indicate which one will follow. Children also need to cope with the information-processing demands involved in a successful output. For example, they have to coordinate the drawing of tags with points and separate counted from to-be-counted items. This is just the beginning of a discussion of the demands on performance (Gelman & Greeno, 1989; Canobi, Reeve, & Pattison, 2003). It should be clear why analyses of response variability should be the rule: even if children actively assimilate performance examples of counting to their nonverbal understanding, this process takes time and practice.

Arithmetic Tasks: A Window to Counting Competence

When knowledge of the effects of addition or subtraction is assessed with a magic show (in which items are surreptitiously added or removed from a set), many 2½-year-olds notice the change in the number of objects for small sets (Gelman, 1972). Sophian and Adams (1987) showed that even toddlers exhibit sensitivity to effects of arithmetic transformations on small sets. Hughes (1981) also found that 3-, 4-, and 5-year-old children were successful in solving simple addition and subtraction problems involving sets as large as 8. Zur and Gelman (2004) found similar results when they asked 3-, 4-, and 5-year-olds to make predictions about changes to a set. Each block of problems in their study started with a child counting a given number of items, e.g., donuts in a donut shop. Then she heard about the delivery or sale of N (1, 2, or 3) donuts. Next she predicted, without counting, how many items there were. Finally, she counted to check her prediction. Ninety percent of predictions were in the right direction, even for the youngest subjects, with a large proportion of responses differing from the correct value only by +/-1. The youngest children's responses (3:1–3:5 years) did not differ significantly from those of the older children, suggesting even the youngest subjects had some understanding of the cardinal principle.

In sum, when very young children count in the name of an arithmetic goal, data suggest that they do understand the verbal cardinal principle. We consider it premature to rule out the possibility that young children's learning of verbal counting benefits from a nonverbal counting and arithmetic.

NONVERBAL COUNTING DATA

Animals and Humans

A number of studies reveal that infants discriminate sets based upon the number of items in each set (e.g., Antell & Keating, 1983) and that they are even sensitive to set manipulations involving simple arithmetic (Wynn, 1992a). Numerical estimation data from rats, pigeons, monkeys, and humans of all ages yield similar data (Brannon, Wusthoff, Gallistel, & Gibbon, 2001; Mechner, 1958; Platt & Johnson, 1971; Rilling & McDiarmid, 1965), Pet dogs and dolphins can pick the larger of two sets (Kilian, Yaman, von Fersen, Gunturkun, 2003; West and Young, 2002), and even salamanders appear sensitive to the numerosity of stimuli (Uller, Jaeger, Guidry, & Martin, 2003). It is hard to continue to maintain that linguistic capacity is a condition for the representation of approximate quantities. The comparative data, in combination with those from adult psychophysical studies, open the door for our position that the nonverbal system serves as a foundation upon which the human verbal/symbolic numerical system is built.

Regardless of the species and task involved, a similar pattern of responses almost always is obtained. They obey Weber's law: that is, the "just noticeable difference" between two values is a constant proportion. More commonly, the ease (i.e., speed and accuracy) with which two numbers are discriminated is dependent upon the ratio of the two values (not their arithmetic difference, as one might suspect). This Weber characteristic is evidenced in the scalar variability found in the behavioral data, such that the variability of responses increases in proportion to the mean response. More precisely, the ratio of the standard deviation to the mean (coefficient of variation) is a constant value.

Scalar variability is not unique to the animal counting data. A constant Weber fraction has been measured in humans for a wide variety of perceived magnitudes, including weight, temperature, surface roughness, and duration (Stevens, 1970). Psychophysical research suggests that this is also the case with animals, as the extensive literature on animal timing reveals scalar variability to be a robust finding in the behavioral data. These cross-species and cross-modality consistencies suggest a similar mechanism of nonverbal representation for all quantities, both continuous and discrete (see Gallistel and Gelman, 2000; Walsh, 2003). Recently, direct tests of nonverbal counting abilities have revealed that humans share with animals this ability to represent approximate numerical values with scalar variability (Barth, Kanwisher, & Spelke, 2003; Cordes, Gelman, Gallistel, & Whalen, 2001; Whalen, Gallistel, and Gelman, 1999; with children, Huntley-Fenner, 2001; Whalen, Gelman, Cordes, & Gallistel, 2000).

These nonverbal counting results are not all that surprising. It is known that numerical discriminations in both animals and humans obey Weber's law, such that the speed and accuracy with which two sets are discriminated is negatively correlated with the absolute size of the sets and the numerical difference between the two sets. These numerical size and distance effects, respectively, have been demonstrated in animals, adult humans, and preschoolers (e.g., Dehaene & Akhavein, 1995; Huntley-Fenner & Cannon, 2000; Meck & Church, 1983). More interesting, however, is that the Weber characteristic of numerical discriminations holds even when the sets to be discriminated are replaced with Arabic numerals, suggesting that, at least in numerically fluent individuals (human or primate), the meanings of symbolic representations of numerosity are closely related to approximate nonverbal representations (Moyer & Landauer, 1967, 1973; Washburn, 1994).

Overall, we now know that humans and animals share a nonverbal counting ability to generate approximate representations of the Ns used in various tasks. For us, this implies that human infants similarly can approximate numerical representations that obey Weber's law.

Quantification in Infancy

A variety of habituation and preferential looking studies suggest infants are sensitive to displays of some numerosities (although see Mix, Huttenlocher, & Levin, 2002). For example, when habituated to a display of two objects, infants will then look longer to subsequent displays of three as opposed to two, and vice versa (Antell & Keating, 1983; Starkey & Cooper, 1980; Strauss & Curtis, 1981). Five-month-olds are sensitive to arithmetic transformations of small sets (Wynn, 1992) and changes in the number of grouped sets of moving dots (Wynn, Bloom, & Chiang, 2002).

The majority of work with infants has used visual arrays in which all items to be enumerated are presented simultaneously. A handful of studies have used sets of sequential events or sounds. For example, 6-month-olds discriminate between 2 and 3 jumps of a rabbit puppet (Wynn, 1996), and 4-day-old newborns' sucking rate habituates to a 2 (or 3) three-syllable utterance, they recover when they hear a 3 (or 2) syllable utterance, and vice versa (Bijeljac-Babic, Bertoncini, & Mehler, 1993). Infants preferred to look at a display with the same number of household objects as sounds they heard (Starkey, Spelke, & Gelman, 1983). Similarly, when a causal relationship was established between dropping objects and noises, 6-month-old infants expected a cross-modal match in numerosity (Kobayashi, Hiraki, & Hawegawa, 2002) (but see Mix, Levine, & Huttenlocher, 1997; Moore, Benenson, Reznick, Peterson, & Kagan, 1987[2]).

Preverbal numerosity discrimination is not limited to sets < 4. Xu and Spelke's (2000) 6-month-olds detected changes in the numerosity of visual arrays for large sets as long as the ratio of the numerosities was 2:1 (e.g., 16 from 8, and 32 from 16), but not when the ratio was as small as 3:2 (e.g., 16 from 12, or 32 from 24). A comparable result holds for sequentially presented sets (sounds; Lipton & Spelke, 2003).

Evidence from these studies and others lead us to favor the proposal of a nonverbal quantification system in humans. Many, but not all (Simon, 1997, 1999), concur. Still, there is debate about which kind of quantity-relevant representational system(s) best accounts for the data. Issues regarding discrete vs. continuous and numerical vs. non-numerical representations take center stage in the debate about the processes involved in infant quantification. Demonstrations of set-size discrimination limits around three or four items contribute heavily to differences between accounts. A key question is whether the quantification abilities of infants reflect the same nonverbal system revealed in the adult nonverbal counting tasks.

NONVERBAL QUANTIFICATION: HOW DO THEY DO IT?

The Accumulator Model

Originally proposed by Meck & Church (1983) to explain both the timing and counting data from nonverbal animals, the accumulator model has been adopted to explain nonverbal quantification abilities in the human domain as well (Gallistel & Gelman, 1992; 2000). According to this model, objective quantities (e.g., time, number, distance) are represented subjectively as continuous magnitudes in a mental accumulator. The mapping between continuous objective values (time, distance, intensity, amount, etc.) and continuous subjective values is a straightforward one—a small objective amount equates to a small subjective magnitude and a large amount equates to a large magnitude, such that there is a simple linear relationship between the two (but see Dehaene, Dupoux, & Mehler, 1990, for an alternative logarithmic account). But what about the case of number in which discrete objective values are mapped to continuous subjective magnitudes?

The case of number is a special one. The sole distinction between representations of discrete number and continuous values is found in the process by which mental magnitudes are mentally accumulated. While the accumulation process for continuous values is continuous (likened to running water from a hose into a bucket), nonverbal counting produces continuous magnitude representations via a discrete process. Each enumerated item increments the magnitude in the mental accumulator by an equal amount (equivalent to a cup of liquid being poured into the bucket for each enumerated item). Thus, whereas continuous and discrete objective values are represented by similar continuous mental magnitudes, the process by which these magnitudes are accumulated is distinct. The nonverbal counting process obeys the basic counting principles described earlier—each enumerated item is represented by one cup of activation (one-one) and each cup of activation increases the accumulated magnitude in memory, such that there is a discrete "next" (stable order), and the resulting magnitude represents the cardinality of the set (cardinality).

These mental magnitudes are not precise representations, however; that is, they are more appropriately described as probability density functions than as absolute values. Following the accumulation process, the resulting magnitude is transferred to memory, where it is subject to scalar noise—noise proportional to the magnitude of the representation. Thus, the scalar variability observed in the behavioral data is a reflection of the inherent scalar variability in the system.

The Mapping between Nonverbal and Written Number

The accumulator model provides a satisfying account of the ubiquitous data, indicating that magnitude discriminations obey Weber's law. If objective magnitudes are subjectively represented via a magnitude system with scalar variability, the ratio of two values directly reflects the extent to which two values (probability density functions) overlap; thus, as the ratio of two values approaches one, the amount of overlap in the two representations increases, making the values subjectively more similar. The fact that symbolic representations of numerosity obey Weber's law strongly suggests that at some point in the development of numerical fluency, a bidirectional map is achieved between the numerical words/symbols and magnitudes represented in the accumulator system. The question is when does this happen.

A number of recent studies with children have used a numerical Stroop-like task (in which numerical and physical size of the stimuli contrast with one another) to show the effect of schooling. Rubinsten, Henik, Berger, & Shahar-Shalev (2002) found that when children in the beginning of first grade chose the greater of two quantities, number did not interfere with their success. At the end of their school year, the children's quantity judgments were negatively influenced by the presence of irrelevant number dimensions. By the end of the same grade, there was interference.

An unpublished study by the authors and John Whalen in our UCLA lab[3] complements these kinds of results. Kindergarten through fifth-grade students and adults indicated which of two Arabic numerals (2–9) was larger, either numerically or physically. The stimuli differed in both physical and numerical size such that the numerically larger digit was either physically larger (congruent) or physically smaller (incongruent) than the other digit. Repeated measures analyses of variance of the median times[4] ($p < .05$, at least) revealed a reliable advantage of physical size, such that physical size of the display items interfered with judgments of numerical value for all age groups. Numerical size interfered with judgments of physical size for all age groups except for the youngest subjects (< 6½ years). Not only did the numerals fail to compromise the youngest children's response times when judging incongruent stimuli, they did not elicit a distance effect in the numerical condition. These two effects lead us to conclude that our youngest subjects' reading of numerals is very slow. Still, the process seems to be well on the way with about a year of schooling, which suggests to us that its beginnings should be placed earlier in development. Nöel, Rousselle, & Mussolin (chapter 11) provide relevant evidence in their extended treatment of the mapping between culturally defined symbols and nonverbal representations of numerosity practice.

Infant Accumulators

The animal and (noninfant) human nonverbal counting data are described well by an accumulator system. However, do magnitude representations of quantity explain the pattern of results obtained in the infant counting data? Clearly, some of the evidence for preverbal quantification can be accounted for by an accumulator-like system. Since the system is truly numerical by nature, there are no restrictions on what sorts of sets can be enumerated. Thus, data suggesting infants enumerate spatial displays as well as sequential events and match numerosities cross-modally are expected. In addition, there is no clear upper limit on the possible cardinal values this system can handle, so evidence of infant discrimination of sets as large as 32 from sets of 16 (and 16 from 8) also support claims of magnitude representation in these young subjects.

The Weber law characteristic of magnitude representations may be challenged, however, by some of the infant data. Infants successfully discriminate sets with ratios of 2:1, whereas they fail on tests of ratios of 3:2 in the "large number range" (16 vs. 12 or 32 vs. 24; Xu & Spelke, 2000). Under a magnitude-representation account, this result would suggest that the Weber fraction for a just-noticeable difference in number for infants this young was closer to .3 log units (2:1) than to .18 log units (3:2); thus, sets with logarithmic differences closer to .18 may simply be beyond the infants' discrimination capabilities. This account is questioned, however, by a variety of data revealing infants are able to successfully discriminate sets of 3 from 2 (e.g., Antell & Keating, 1983). These results suggest that the Weber fraction for numerosity discrimination may actually decrease in the small number range for infants.

The lack of a consistent Weber fraction for numerical discrimination in infants threatens theories positing magnitude representations as the sole basis for infant quantification results. The accumulator model incorporates scalar variability in order to account for the Weber characteristic of magnitude discrimination. The model does not make special allowances for violations of Weber's law. The infant data, however, suggest that numerical discrimination is subject to a Weber fraction of around .3 log units (2:1 ratio) but only for values *greater* than 3 or 4. For values under 4, discrimination abilities appear to be keener than predicted by this fraction. Why?

Perhaps the accumulator system is used only to represent values greater than 4. This cannot be the general case. Scalar variability characterizes the adult psychophysical function in both the small and large number ranges, without any signs of discontinuities below values of 3 or 4 (Balakrishnan & Ashby, 1992; Cordes, Gelman, Gallistel, & Whalen, 2001). In addition, animals are known to treat values above and below 4 in similar ways (Brannon & Terrace, 1998, 2000; Meck & Church, 1983).

Differences in data collection procedures for infants may contribute to their different response pattern. The majority of infant studies employ either preferential looking or habituation paradigms with amount of looking time as the crucial dependent variable. This implicit measure contrasts with the explicit responses obtained in both animal and adult human nonverbal counting tasks (i.e., lever/button presses or pecks). So, too, does the fact that most infant analyses are based on group data. Information regarding individual variability, patterns of responses, and developmental levels (necessary for arguments regarding underlying representations) are simply not available. Still, the apparent inconsistent Weber fraction for infants cannot be ignored as the results are fairly robust. Although the accumulator model accounts for most of the infant quantification data, the change in the Weber fraction for values fewer than four needs explanation. Many have proposed that the small number range is processed with object files/indexes.

Object Files

Kahneman, Treisman, & Gibbs (1992) introduced the notion of object files (or object indexes) to describe how humans track objects in their visual environment. Object files are often referred to as mental pointers with a record of some minimal information about the object being tracked, such as its location and shape. This information is used to identify objects, allowing one to determine if an object retrieved from behind an occluder is the same or different from the one originally placed behind the occluder (i.e., object permanence).

Although object files are discrete and can be counted, they are not numerical representations. They are merely mental pointers, and any estimate of the numerosity of the set of tracked objects must be performed via some other representational system (e.g., the accumulator system). A number of studies on multiple-object tracking by Pylyshyn and colleagues (1989; Trick & Pylyshyn, 1994; Scholl & Pylyshyn, 1999) have determined that there is also a limit on the number of objects one can simultaneously track. In adults, this limit is about 4 or 5, although with repeated practice, certain individuals have been able to track as many as 9 objects. Individuation experiments with infants suggests that this limit may also be subject to developmental changes, as work indicates that infants may only be able to track as many as 3 or 4 objects (Leslie, Xu, Tremoulet, & Scholl, 1998).

Object files have been implicated as an alternative representational system used for small set discrimination in both infants and adults (e.g., Leslie et al., 1998; Trick & Pylyshyn, 1994). Because object files are discrete and precise (noise free) by nature, they provide a viable explanation for the fact that studies have found that infants are able to discriminate 2 objects from 3 objects, but not 4 from 6, despite a similar ratio. The idea is that an accumulator system is used primarily for large number representations (wherever discrimination is ratio-dependent) and object files are used for small numbers (where discrimination has a set-size limit).

There have been claims that object-file representations "underlie most, if not all, of the infant successes in experiments that involve small sets of objects" (Carey, 2001a, p. 313). Although object files provide an account for much of the infant discrimination data for sets smaller than 4, they cannot possibly explain it all. Object files are constructs of the visual attention system, used for identification and mental tracking of discrete visual objects. By virtue of this definition, studies indicating infant discrimination of sounds or rabbit hops (e.g., Lipton & Spelke, 2003; Wynn, 1996) fail to be accounted for by object files, because events are not visual objects. Since these studies reveal successful discrimination of 3 events from 2 (Weber fraction of .18 log units), these data cannot be explained by an accumulator system of representation, either. Clearly, limitations on both of these models prevent a full explanation of the infant data. Further investigation into infant quantification abilities (preferably using repeated trials) as well as modifications to current theories or the introduction of novel ones are necessary for a greater understanding of the basis for numerical competence.

Continuous Extent Representations

There have been a number of developmental studies indicating that infants are able to differentiate sets based upon the quantity of continuous variables such as overall surface area, perimeter, or volume (independent of number). Recently, Feigensen, Carey, & Hauser (2002) placed different numbers of graham crackers of varying sizes into two different buckets in front of 10- and 12-month-old infants. Following the placement of the crackers, the infants were allowed to crawl to one of the buckets in order to retrieve the graham crackers. Results revealed that infants in their study crawled to the bucket containing the greater overall amount of crackers, even if that bucket contained the fewer (cardinal) number of crackers (interestingly, however, once either bucket contained more than four pieces of cracker, responding decreased to chance levels—suggesting object files also played a role in this task). Thus, it appears that infants also use a measure of continuous extent (i.e., amount of cracker) as a relevant dimension in set discrimination.

Because of results such as the ones reported above, most researchers involved in early quantification work agree that the data point to the existence of preverbal representations of both numerosity and continuous stimulus magnitudes. There are others, though, who offer an alternative, and decidedly different, explanation of the data. Mix et al. (2002) contest the proposition that infants are capable of evaluating sets based upon discrete numerosity. They insist that the successes found in counting experiments all are based upon representations of continuous stimulus properties. They argue that "development starts with only one principle of quantification in infancy based on amount of substance, which applies to both continuous quantity and sets of discrete objects" (p. 62). According to their account, "infants do not represent quantities numerically at all. Instead, the evidence points to the use of overall amount" (p. 81).

Principal support for their theory stems from failures to find evidence for infant sensitivity to numerosity once continuous stimulus variables are controlled. For example, in Clearfield & Mix (1999), 6- to 8-month-old infants were habituated to displays of either 2 or 3 objects. Following habituation, the infants saw two test displays: (1) displays with the same numerosity but different overall contour than the habituation displays (extent test) and (2) displays with a novel number of items (3 or 2) but with the same amount of overall contour (number test). Subjects looked significantly longer than during habituation at the extent test displays but did not behave as if they noticed a change in the number test displays, suggesting their task tapped into representations of continuous extent, not numerosity.

Although it is likely that some infant counting results are due to distinctions of continuous extent (and not number), it is unlikely that this is ubiquitously so. There are a number of studies that fail to be explained by infant quantification of continuous extent alone. Xu and Spelke (2000) varied continuous extent while maintaining number constant throughout the familiarization trials of their large number discrimination tasks. If the infants were only sensitive to changes in continuous extent, it would not be possible to habituate them to these stimuli. They did. In a study of ordinal relations by Brannon (2002), infants were habituated to sets of displays of increasing or decreasing numerosity (2-4-8 or 8-4-2) while controlling for overall surface area of the stimuli. When presented test displays of either ascending or descending numerosities (also with the same surface area), the 11-month-olds dishabituated to the novel ordering, suggesting they had attended to the numerical ordering of the habituation displays, not the extent. Most recently, Leslie, Glanville, & Lerner (2003) and Brannon & Gautier (2003) pitted continuous extent against number and found infants in their tasks responded significantly more to changes in number.

These projects, as well as studies of event number discrimination (e.g., puppet jumps, cross-modal matching, sound enumeration—Wynn, 1996; Starkey, Spelke, & Gelman, 1980; Lipton & Spelke, 2003) in which it is entirely unclear what would be defined as the continuous extent variable, imply that infants must also be sensitive to numerosity. For the reasons presented above, we can conclude that any representational model strictly confined to quantification of continuous magnitudes is limited and insufficient for explaining the data.

Infants and Quantities: What's the Story?

In sum, work on infant quantification suggests that preverbal infants are sensitive to changes in numerosity as well as to changes in continuous amounts (surface area, perimeter). Certain data sets revealing infant discrimination of continuous extent (Clearfield & Mix, 1994), of large numerosities (Xu & Spelke, 2000), and/or of the number of event sequences (Lipton & Spelke, 2003) can only be accounted for by an accumulator-like representational system. However, indications of a shift in the Weber fraction for values smaller than 3 also implicate object-files in some tasks involving small numerical values, provided the stimuli are discrete, visual objects. We propose that the infant successes in quantification tasks are due to an interaction of object file representations and approximate magnitude representations of both number and continuous variables. It is suggested that a number of task variables influence which mechanisms (object files or accumulator) and which relevant dimensions (number, surface area, etc.) present themselves in the data.

SOME CRITICAL POINTS

The persistence of the arguments from both the skill-first and language-dependency camps has taken the turn of listing the reasons why the accumulator model for animal counting cannot apply to the human case. The force with which they are presented is beginning to legitimize them, even though the arguments are faulty. We take up the statements to this effect one by one:

1. *The sequential nature of the nonverbal counting process makes enumeration of static sets impossible or at least more difficult than enumeration of sequential sets. "Seemingly, it would be difficult for infants to keep track of which items in a visual set had been 'accumulated' without physically partitioning the set, as we do in verbal counting" (Mix et al., 2002, p. 90). This comment is also relevant to the adult data, as new evidence suggests that the time required to discriminate large sets is solely a function of the ratio of the two sets, NOT their overall magnitude (Barth, Kanwisher, & Spelke, 2001).*[5]

The underlying accumulator system is not necessarily sequential by nature. The physical model of the accumulator is sequential in order to simplify understanding of the mathematical model. The true mathematical model of the system does not require each "cupful of activation" to be poured one after the other. It is quite possible to imagine that the cups are poured in all at once, or perhaps there is a limit to the number of cups poured at once (the same as the object file limit?). As Brannon points out, "It may be that two distinct processes yielded large approximate number representations; an iterative counting like procedure operating over sequentially presented arrays and a parallel mechanism operating over simultaneous arrays" (2003, p. 281).

The accumulator model is not strictly committed to an iterative nonverbal counting process and equally accounts for the enumeration of sequential and static sets. It should also be noted that the nonverbal counting routine is naturally implicit. It is not a conscious process—it occurs as one (whether in an infant, adult, or nonhuman animal) scans the display and does not require conscious partitions of counted items vs. to be counted items.

2. *The accumulator is only used for representations of number or duration, and not other continuous variables such as surface area or contour.*

The accumulator model goes hand in hand with the concept of mental magnitudes. These magnitudes are used to describe the subjective representation of all objective quantities that obey Weber's law. Although the accumulator model was originally proposed to account for the animal counting and timing data, more generally, it has been adopted to explain all subjective magnitude representations, including surface area, density, and length.

3. *Evidence of nonverbal arithmetic in infants (e.g., Wynn, 1992a) "cannot be explained without positing complicated maneuvers involving multiple accumulators" (Mix et al., 2002, p. 91).*

Central to the Gallistel & Gelman (1992) account of preverbal counting, subjective magnitudes are in the service of the arithmetic principles. Studies with both humans and animals reveal that magnitudes are subject to nonverbal computations (in animals—Boysen & Berntson, 1989; Brannon, Wusthoff, Gallistel, & Gibbon, 2001; Gibbon & Church, 1971; Leon & Gallistel, 1998; in adult humans—Barth, 2001; Cordes, Gallistel, Gelman & Latham, 2004; Zacks & Hasher, 2002; in infants—Aslin, Saffran, & Newport, 1999; for reviews, see Gallistel, 1990; Gallistel, Gelman, & Cordes, in press). While physical instantiations of how this works may be complicated, evidence suggests that arithmetic manipulations of accumulated magnitudes are regularly performed online.[6]

4. *"There is no direct evidence for the accumulator mechanism in infants and children"* (Mix *et al., 2002, p. 91*).

Nonverbal counting studies with young children have revealed the same scalar variability signature found in nonhuman animals (e.g., Huntley-Fenner, 2001; Huntley-Fenner & Cannon, 2000; Whalen, Gelman, Cordes, & Gallistel, 2000). There is also plenty of indirect evidence of magnitude representations of numerosity in infants as well as evidence of sensitivity to ordinal relations (Brannon, 2002).

5. *Limitations on the magnitude values in the accumulator are not mirrored in the generative verbal count list (Carey, 2001a). While the natural numbers proceed to infinity, the list of magnitude values represented is finite.*

This has been a criticism of the accumulator model, provided a linear mapping between objective and subjective magnitudes.[7] How do we deal with excessively large values without stressing the bounds of working memory? We propose an account similar to the "relative amount" case suggested by Mix et al.–the magnitude of the values in the accumulator is relative, not absolute. The magnitude of the representation of a given value varies as a function of the magnitude of the other values currently in working memory. For example, when dealing with numerical values of 1–50, the magnitude for 10 may look like this: _____. However, when working with values 1–100, the magnitude for 10 may only be: ____.[8] Magnitude sizes are determined by anchor values. This relative magnitude account allows for subjective representations of significantly large values without exceeding the capacities of working memory.

6. *Nonverbal representations are inherently different from the verbal ones, as are the two counting processes.*

Both routines strictly adhere to the basic how-to count principles, and both representational systems are ordered and embody a discrete process for generating new counts. Children may take time to learn the mapping between the two systems, but this is a function of the time it takes to memorize an ordered list, implicitly determine the parameters involved in the mapping between verbal and nonverbal magnitudes (see Cordes et al., 2001), and learn how to apply these nonverbal principles to the verbal domain. Noise in the nonverbal representation system also extends the acquisition process.

7. *Subitizing is a real phenomenon.*

Subitizing is reported as the rapid apprehension and identification of the numerosities of small sets (1–4) from a visual scene without counting. The literature on subitizing is closely related to that of object files (Trick & Pylyshyn, 1994). It could be said that subitizing is the rapid enumeration of open object files, without counting (verbal or nonverbal).

There is little clear evidence of subitizing in infants or young children. The evidence of this ability in adults is also questionable (Gallistel & Gelman, 1991). Mandler & Shebo (1982) found the observed subitizing data to be a function of recognizable canonical patterns (e.g., two points make a line; three, a triangle . . .). Balakrishnan & Ashby (1992) reanalyzed reaction time data from a variety of studies claiming to provide evidence of this ability in adults. Researchers who originally obtained the RT data had claimed the slope of the RT function in the small number range was significantly shallower than the slope of the RT function past that range (thus producing an "elbow" of discontinuity in the curve). The rigorous statistical tests run by Balakrishnan and Ashby failed to support this claim, and they concluded that subitizing was not, in fact, a true phenomenon. Whalen, West, & Cook (2003) also recently compared both response times and errors obtained when adult subjects were asked to count vs. estimate the numerosity of a set (size 1–16). Analyses revealed that what previously has been cited as evidence of subitizing (a shallow slope in the small number range) was well described as the result of nonverbal counting in a range where there is very little noise in the representation. Last, variability analyses revealed that there is no evidence of subitizing in the case of sequential stimuli (Cordes et al., 2001; Gelman & Cordes, 2001).

SUMMARY

Currently, the preschool counting data fail to provide conclusive evidence regarding competence of the early counter. While many studies point to a principles-before account, in which children have an inherent understanding of the basic counting principles, there are results from other studies that do not merit such strong conclusions. It is our position that even the data from these studies, in which children do not consistently act in accordance with the cardinality principle, support the existence of innate skeletal principles. Numerous factors, including strenuous task demands that tap into performance variables (as opposed to conceptual competence) and the expected trial-and-error associated with the acquisition of all skills, necessarily contribute to the observed variability in the data.

The available counting tasks are limited in their scope and breadth of assessment. There is a real need for new experimental paradigms to further investigate these issues and to provide more conclusive evidence. These tasks must be designed for use with children just beginning to count in order to look at the abilities of subjects younger than 3½ years old. As it is uncertain whether or not young children understand what the cardinal value of a count reveals, we favor investigations of early arithmetic competence, such as those demonstrated by Zur and Gelman (2004), as a means of determining counting competence.

The nonverbal counting data may also provide insight into the mind of young counters. Data from numerous studies support the existence of preverbal representational mechanisms for both number and continuous dimensions such as time, surface area, and contour. We propose that these representations are best described as accumulator magnitudes and object files, both of which appear to be available to the infant. Provided that object files are non-numerical by nature, we further suggest that it is the magnitude representations that are responsible for the young child's understanding of number and arithmetic. This nonverbal system provides the framework for the child to acquire a verbal count routine. The bidirectional mapping between this system and the linguistic one also allows the child to learn the meanings of the count words, one by one. Our account assumes both phylogenetic and ontogenetic continuities and is by far the most parsimonious description of early counting available.

Open questions remain regarding how young infants are able to discriminate between 2 and 3 events, as in Wynn (1996) and Kobayashi et al. (2002). In this case, the Weber fraction and the non-visual nature of the stimuli suggest that neither of the current models accounts for these results. Perhaps object files are less vision- and object-based than we think, and instead are simply a manner for individuating sensory stimuli (be they objects, sounds, events, etc.). Or maybe results of these experiments are somehow an artifact of a developmental shift in the Weber fraction (e.g., see Lipton & Spelke, 2003). The numerical nature of the object file representational system should also be examined more thoroughly. That is, if object files are the dominant representational system employed in small number tasks, it is unclear whether the basis for discrimination is truly numerical or solely object based (and non-numerical). For example, infants may look longer at displays of novel numerosities simply because an open object file no longer has an object to track, and vice versa. Further research should look into these issues. Clearly, data from repeated trials with individual infants are necessary in order to look at individual patterns of variability. In addition, investigations into the developmental trends will also help to shed light on these issues. Through these analyses, the validity of the current models can be assessed and we will gain insight into the nature of preverbal quantity representations and their relation to verbal ones.

ACKNOWLEDGMENT

This project was funded by an NSF predoctoral fellowship to Sara Cordes and NSF grants DFS-9209741 and SRB-97209741 to Rochel Gelman.

NOTES

1. Gelman and Gellistel (1978, Chapter 11) discuss the relation between the understanding of the cardinal count principle and the principle of one-to-one correspondence.
2. Both Mix et al. (1997) and Moore et al. (1987) claimed to replicate the paradigm used by Starkey et al. (1983) despite severe modifications to the experimental design. Despite these changes, both studies found that infants looked longer at the display with the nonequivalent numerosity—the opposite result of Starkey et al. Despite differing patterns of results, it is clear that all three studies revealed a preverbal attention to the numerosity of the displays and sounds.
3. These results were reported at meetings of the Psychonomics Society in 1999 and the Congress of the International Union of Psychological Science in Sweden in 2000.
4. Response times greater than 2200 ms, shorter than 150 ms, or for incorrect trials were excluded.
5. Barth et al.'s study need not rule out an iterative nonverbal counting process. The response times reported are long (in the neighborhood of 1450 ms). It is possible that these were a function of the decision criterion with the large sets. This may have overshadowed the relatively short time it took for subjects to enumerate (nonverbally count) the two sets. In addition, subjects may have used alternative strategies. For example, these results are consistent with subjects using dot density or overall amount of background area as relevant dimensions, as opposed to number. These alternatives and others need to be explored regarding the iterative or noniterative nature of nonverbal counts.
6. We note that Wynn's (1992a) results can also be accounted for by an object file system of representation.
7. The alternative mapping proposed—a logarithmic one (e.g., Dehaene, 1989)—does allow for unlimited representational capacities. Through a logarithmic mapping, larger values become subjectively closer together, thus preventing representations of arbitrarily large values from imposing arbitrarily large amounts of processing demands. However, when rats or pigeons respond to the difference between two temporal or numerical values (Time Left, Gibbon & Church, 1981; Number Left, Brannon, Wusthoff, Gallistel, & Gibbon, 2001), the data consistently support a linear mapping between objective and subjective quantities.
8. It could be argued that Meck, Church, & Gibbon's (1985) conclusion that the mental magnitude for one count takes about 200 ms contradicts these conclusions, because they indicate that magnitude values are absolute and consistent across individuals (at least within species). Balci & Gallistel (in preparation) show that the 200-ms results may be an artifact of the range of values tested, not an absolute measure of temporal and numerical magnitudes.

REFERENCES

Antell, S. E., & Keating, D. P. (1983). Perception of numerical invariance in neonates. *Child Development, 54,* 695–701.

Aslin, R., Saffran, J., & Newport, E. (1999). Statistical learning in linguistic and nonlinguistic domains. In B. MacWhinney (Ed.), *The emergence of language* (pp. 359–380). Mahwah, NJ: Erlbaum.

Balakrishnan, J. D., & Ashby, F. G. (1992). Subitizing: Magical numbers or mere superstition? *Psychological Research, 54,* 80–90.

Balci, F., & Gallistel, C. R. (2004). *It's all a matter of proportion.* Manuscript in preparation.

Baroody, A. J., & Wilkins, J. (1999). The development of informal counting, number, and arithmetic skills and concepts. In J. Copley (Ed.), *Mathematics in the early years* (pp. 48–65). National Council of Teachers in Mathematics.

Barth, H. (2001). *Numerical cognition in adults: Representation and manipulation of non-symbolic quantities.* Unpublished doctoral dissertation, MIT, Boston, MA.

Barth, H., Kanwisher, N., & Spelke, E. (2003). The construction of large number representations in adults. *Cognition, 86,* 201–221.

Becker, J. (1989). Preschooler's use of number words to denote one-to-one correspondence. *Child Development, 60,* 1147–1157.

Bermejo, V. (1996). Cardinality development and counting. *Developmental Psychology, 32*(2), 263–268.

Bermejo, V., & Lago, M. O. (1990). Developmental processes and stages in the acquisition of cardinality. *International Journal of Behavioral Development, 13*(2), 231–250.

Bijeljac-Babic, R., Bertoncini, J., & Mehler, J. (1991). How do four-day-old infants categorize multisyllabic utterances? *Developmental Psychology, 29,* 711–721.

Bloom, P. (2000). *How children learn the meanings of words.* Cambridge, MA: MIT Press.

Bloom, P., & Wynn, K. (1997). Linguistic cues in the acquisition of number words. *Journal of Child Language, 24,* 511–533.

Boysen, S., & Berntson, G. (1989). Numerical competence in a chimpanzee (*Pan Troglodytes*). *Journal of Comparative Psychology, 103,* 23–31.

Brannon, E. (2002). The development of ordinal numerical knowledge in infancy. *Cognition, 83,* 223–240.

Brannon, E. (2003). Number knows no bounds, *Trends in Cognitive Sciences, 7*(7), 279–281.

Brannon, E. M., & Gautier, T. (2003, April). *Continuous versus discrete representations of quantity in infancy.* Poster session presented at the biennial meeting of the Society for Research in Child Development, Tampa, Florida.

Brannon, E. M., & Terrace, H. (1998). Ordering of the numerosities 1–9 by monkeys. *Science, 282,* 746–749.

Brannon, E. M., & Terrace, H. (2000). Representation of the numerosities 1–9 by rhesus macaques (*Macaca mulatta*). *Journal of Experimental Psychology: Animal Behavior Processes, 26,* 31–49.

Brannon, E. M., & Van de Walle, G. A. (2001). The development of ordinal numerical competence in young children. *Cognitive Psychology, 43*(1), 53–81.

Brannon, E. M., Wusthoff, C. J., Gallistel, C. R., & Gibbon, J. (2001). Numerical subtraction in the pigeon: Evidence for a linear subjective number scale. *Psychological Science, 12*(3), 238–243.

Briars, D., & Siegler, R. S. (1984). A featural analysis of preschoolers' counting knowledge. *Developmental Psychology, 20*(4), 607–618.

Bullock, M., & Gelman, R., (1977). Numerical reasoning in young children: The ordering principle. *Child Development, 48,* 427–434.

Canobi, K. H., Reeve, R. A., & Pattison, P. E. (2003).

Young children's understanding of addition concepts. *Educational Psychology, 22*(5), 513–532.

Carey, S. (1998). Knowledge of number: Its evolution and ontogeny. *Science, 282*(5389), 641–642.

Carey, S. (2001a). On the possibility of discontinuities in conceptual development. In E. Dupoux (Ed.), *Language, brain, and cognitive development: Essays in honor of Jacques Mehler* (pp. 303–321). Cambridge, MA: MIT Press.

Carey, S. (2001b). Whorf versus continuity theorists: bringing data to bear on the debate. In M. Bowerman & S. C. Levinson (Eds.), *Language acquisition and conceptual development* (pp. 185–214). New York: Cambridge University Press.

Clearfield, M., & Mix, K. (1999). Number versus contour length in infants' discrimination of small visual sets. *Psychological Science, 10*(5), 408–411.

Cordes, S., Gallistel, C. R., Gelman, R., & Latham, P. (2004). *Nonverbal arithmetic in humans.* Manuscript submitted for publication.

Cordes, S., Gelman, R., Gallistel, C. R., & Whalen, J. (2001). Variability signatures distinguish verbal from nonverbal counting for both large and small numbers. *Psychonomic Bulletin and Review, 8*(4), 698–707.

Cowan, R., Docker, A., Chistakis, A., & Bailey, S. (1996). *Journal of Experimental Child Psychology, 62*(1), 84–101.

Dehaene, S. (1989). The psychophysics of numerical comparison: A reexamination of apparently incompatible data. *Perception & Psychophysics, 45*(6), 557–566.

Dehaene, S., & Akhavein, R. (1995). Attention, automaticity, and levels of representation in number processing. *Journal of Experimental Psychology: Learning, Memory, and Cognition, 21*(2), 314–326.

Dehaene, S., Dupoux, E., & Mehler, J. (1990). Is numerical comparison digital? Analogical and symbolic effects in two-digit number comparison. *Journal of Experimental Psychology: Human Perception & Performance, 16,* 626–641.

Feigenson, L., Carey, S., & Hauser, M. (2002). The representations underlying infants' choice of more: Object files versus analog magnitudes. *Psychological Science, 13*(2), 150–156.

Fuson, K. (1988). *Children's counting and concepts of number.* New York: Springer-Verlag.

Gallistel, C. R. (1990). *The organization of learning.* Cambridge, MA: MIT Press.

Gallistel, C. R., & Gelman, R. (1991). Subitizing: The preverbal counting process. In W. Kessen, A. Ortony, & F. Craik (Eds.), *Memories, thoughts, and emotions: Essays in honor of George Mandler* (pp. 65–81). Hillsdale, NJ: Erlbaum.

Gallistel, C. R., & Gelman, R. (1992). Preverbal and verbal counting and computation. *Cognition, 44,* 43–74.

Gallistel, C. R., & Gelman, R. (2000). Non-verbal numerical cognition: From reals to integers. *Trends in Cognitive Sciences, 4*(2), 59–65.

Gallistel, C. R., Gelman, R., & Cordes, S. (in press). The cultural and evolutionary history of the real numbers. In S. Levinson & P. Jaisson (Eds.), *Culture and Evolution.* Oxford: Oxford University Press.

Gelman, R. (1972). Logical capacity of very young children: Number invariance rules. *Child Development, 43,* 75–90.

Gelman, R. (1982). Accessing one-to-one correspondence: Still another paper about conservation. *British Journal of Psychology, 73,* 209–220.

Gelman, R. (1993). A rational-constructivist account of early learning about numbers and objects. In D. Medin (Ed.), *The psychology of learning and motivation. Advances in research and theory* (pp. 61–96).

Gelman, R., & Cordes, S. (2001). Counting in animals and humans. In E. Dupoux (Ed.), *Language, brain, and cognitive development: Essays in honor of Jacques Mehler* (pp. 279–303). Cambridge, MA: MIT Press.

Gelman, R., & Gallistel, C. R. (1978). *The child's understanding of number.* Cambridge, MA: Harvard University Press.

Gelman, R., & Greeno, J. G. (1989). On the nature of competence: Principles for understanding in a domain. In L. B. Resnick (Ed.), *Knowing and learning: Issues for a cognitive science of instruction* (pp. 125–186). Hillsdale, NJ: Erlbaum.

Gelman, R., & Meck, E. (1983). Preschooler's counting: Principles before skill. *Cognition, 13,* 343–359.

Gelman, R., & Meck, E. (1986). The notion of principle: The case of counting. In J. Hiebert (Ed.), *The relationship between procedural and conceptual competence* (pp. 29–57). Hillsdale, NJ: Erlbaum.

Gelman, R., Meck, E., & Merkin, S. (1986). Young children's numerical competence. *Cognitive Development, 1*(1), 1–29.

Gelman, R., & Tucker, M. (1975). Further investigations of the young child's conception of number. *Child Development, 46*(1), 167–175.

Gibbon, J., & Church, R. M. (1981). Time left: Linear versus logarithmic subjective time. *Journal of Experimental Analysis of Behavior, 7,* 87–107.

Halford, G. (in press). Cognitive development. In K. Holyoak & R. Morrison (Eds.), *Cambridge handbook of thinking and reasoning.* New York: Cambridge University Press.

Hughes, M. (1981). Can preschool children add and subtract? *Educational Psychology, 1*(3), 207–219.

Huntley-Fenner, G. (2001). Children's understanding of number is similar to adults' and rats': Numerical estimation by 5–7-year olds. *Cognition, 78*(3), B27–B40.

Huntley-Fenner, G., & Cannon, E. (2000). Preschoolers' magnitude comparisons are mediated by a preverbal analog mechanism. *Psychological Science, 11*(2), 147–152.

Huttenlocher, J., Jordan, N., & Levin, S. C. (1994). A mental model for early arithmetic. *Journal of Experimental Psychology: General, 123*(3), 284–296.

Kahneman, D., Treisman, A., & Gibbs, B. J. (1992). The reviewing of object-files: Object specific integration of information. *Cognitive Psychology, 24,* 174–219.

Kilian, A., Yaman, S., von Fersen, L., & Guentuerkuen O. (2003). A bottlenose dolphin discriminates visual stimuli differing in numerosity. *Learning & Behavior, 31*(2),133–142.

Kobayashi, T., Hiraki, K., & Hasegawa, T. (2002, May). *Intermodal numerical correspondences in 6-month old infants.* Paper presented at the International Conference on Infant Studies.

Leon, M., & Gallistel, C. R. (1998). Self-stimulating rats combine subjective reward magnitude and subjective reward rate multiplicatively. *Journal of Experimental Psychology: Animal Behavior Processes, 24*(3), 265–277.

Leslie, A. M., Glanville, M., & Lerner, S. (2003, April). *So, maybe infants do count after all.* Presented at the biennial meeting for the Society for Research in Child Development, Tampa, FL.

Leslie, A. M., Xu, F., Tremoulet, P., & Scholl, B. (1998). Indexing and the object concept: Developing "what" and "where" systems. *Trends in Cognitive Sciences, 2*, 10–18.

Lipton, J., & Spelke, E. (2003). Origins of number sense: Large number discrimination in human infants. *Psychological Science, 14*(5), 396–401.

Mandler, G., & Shebo, B. J. (1982). Subitizing: An analysis of its component processes. *Journal of Experimental Psychology: General, 111*(1), 1–22.

McCleish, J. (1991). *Number: The history of numbers and how they shape our lives*. New York: Fawcett Columbine.

Mechner, F. (1958). Probability relations within response sequences under ratio reinforcement. *Journal of Experimental Analysis of Behavior, 1*, 109–122.

Meck, W. H., & Church, R. M. (1983). A mode control model of counting and timing processes. *Journal of Experimental Psychology: Animal Behavior Processes, 9*, 320–334.

Meck, W. H., Church, R. M., & Gibbon, J. (1985). Temporal integration in duration and number discrimination. *Journal of Experimental Psychology: Animal Behavior Processes, 11*, 591–597.

Mix, K. S., Levine, S. C., & Huttenlocher, J. (1997). Numerical abstraction in infants: Another look. *Developmental Psychology, 33*(3), 423–428

Mix, K. S., Huttenlocher, J., & Levine, S. C. (2002). *Quantitative development in infancy and early childhood*. London: Oxford University Press.

Moore, D., Benenson, J., Reznick, J. S., Peterson, M., & Kagan, J. (1987). Effect of auditory numerical information on infants' looking behavior: Contradictory evidence. *Developmental Psychology, 23*, 665–670.

Moyer, R. S., & Landauer, T. K. (1967). Time required for judgments of numerical inequality. *Nature, 215*, 1519–1520.

Moyer, R. S., & Landauer, T. K. (1973). Determinants of reaction time for digit inequality judgments. *Bulletin of the Psychonomic Society, 1*, 167–168.

Piaget, J. (1952). *The child's conception of number*. London: Routledge & Kegan Paul.

Platt, J. R., & Johnson, D. M. (1971). Localization of position within a homogeneous behavior chain: Effects of error contingencies. *Learning and Motivation, 2*, 386–414.

Pylyshyn, Z. W. (1989). The role of location indexes in spatial perception: A sketch of the FINST spatial-index model. *Cognition, 32*, 65–97.

Rilling, M., & McDiarmid, C. (1965). Signal detection in fixed-ratio schedules. *Science, 148*, 526–527.

Rubinsten, O., Henik, A., Berger, A., & Shahar-Shalev, S. (2002). The development of internal representations of magnitude and their association with Arabic numerals. *Journal of Experimental Child Psychology, 81*, 74–92.

Scholl, B. J., & Pylyshyn, Z. W. (1999). Tracking multiple items through occlusion: Clues to visual objecthood. *Cognitive Psychology, 38*(2), 259–290.

Simon, T. (1997). Reconceptualizing the origins of number knowledge: A "non-numerical" account. *Cognitive Development, 12*(3), 349–372.

Simon, T. (1999). Numerical thinking in a brain without numbers? *Trends in Cognitive Science, 3*, 363–364.

Sophian, C. (1998). A developmental perspective in children's counting. In C. Donlan (Ed), *The develop-*

ment of mathematical skills. Studies in developmental psychology (pp. 27–46).

Sophian, C., & Adams, N. (1987). Infants' understanding of numerical transformations. *British Journal of Developmental Psychology, 5*(3), 257–264.

Spelke, E. (2000). Core knowledge. *American Psychologist, 55*(11), 1233–1243.

Starkey, P., & Cooper, R. G. (1980). Perception of numbers by human infants. *Science, 210*, 1033–1035.

Starkey, P., & Cooper, R. G. (1995). The development of subitizing in young children. *British Journal of Developmental Psychology, 13*(4), 399–420.

Starkey, P., Spelke, E. S., & Gelman, R. (1983). Detection of intermodal numerical correspondences by human infants. *Science, 222*(4620), 179–181.

Stevens, S. S. (1970). Neural events and the psychophysical law. *Science, 170*(3962), 1043–1050.

Strauss, M. S., & Curtis, L. E. (1981). Infant perception of numerosity. *Child Development, 52*, 1146–1152.

Trick, L., & Pylyshyn, Z. (1994). Why are small and large numbers enumerated differently? A limited capacity preattentive stage in vision. *Psychological Review, 101*, 80–102.

Uller, C., Jaeger, R., Guidry, G., & Martin, C. (2003). Salamanders (*Plethodon cinereus*) go for more: Rudiments of number in an amphibian. *Animal Cognition, 6*(2), 105–112.

Walsh, V. (2003). A theory of magnitude: common cortical metrics of time, space, and quantity. *Trends in cognitive science, 7*(11), 483–493.

Washburn, D. A. (1994). Stroop-like effects for monkeys and humans: Processing speed or strength of association? *Psychological Science, 5*(6), 375–379.

West, R. E., & Young, R. J. (2002). Do domestic dogs show any evidence of being able to count? *Animal Cognition, 5*(3), 183–186.

Whalen, J., Gallistel, C. R., & Gelman, R. (1999). Nonverbal counting in humans: The psychophysics of number representation. *Psychological Science, 10*(2), 130–137.

Whalen, J., Gelman, R., Cordes, S., & Gallistel, C. R. (2000). [Nonverbal counting in children]. Unpublished raw data.

Whalen, J., West, V., & Cook, B. (2003). *Don't count on subitizing: Evidence of non-verbal counting of small visual arrays*. Manuscript submitted for publication.

Wynn, K. (1990). Children's understanding of counting. *Cognition, 36*(2), 155–193.

Wynn, K. (1992a). Addition and subtraction by human infants. *Nature, 358*, 749–50.

Wynn, K. (1992b). Children's acquisition of the number words and the counting system. *Cognitive Psychology, 24*(2), 220–251.

Wynn, K. (1996). Infants' individuation and enumeration of actions. *Psychological Science, 7*(3), 164–169.

Wynn, K., Bloom, P., & Chiang, W. (2002). Enumeration of collective entities by 5-month-old infants. *Cognition, 83*(3), B55–B62.

Xu, F., & Spelke, E. (2000). Large number discrimination in 6-month-old infants. *Cognition, 74*, B1–B11.

Zacks, R., & Hasher, L. (2002). Frequency processing: A twenty-five year perspective. In P. Sedlmeier (Ed.), *Frequency Processing and Cognition* (pp. 21–36). London: Oxford University Press.

Zur, O., & Gelman, R. (2004). Young children can add and subtract by predicting and checking. *Early Childhood Research Quarterly, 19*, 121–137.

9

Development of Arithmetic Skills and Knowledge in Preschool Children

Jeffrey Bisanz
Jody L. Sherman
Carmen Rasmussen
Elaine Ho

Children and adults "do arithmetic" in a variety of contexts. They compute prices, keep track of scores in games, calculate statistics, generate answers for tests of mathematics in school, and solve a host of practical and sometimes theoretical problems. Understanding and skill in arithmetic are demonstrated in many ways. A person's proficiency might be judged by the accuracy of his or her answers, as in the case of achievement tests, but a much richer picture emerges when we examine *how* children and adults solve arithmetic problems. Sometimes they quickly remember arithmetic facts to generate answers, such as the value of 2^5, 9×8, or $3 + 4$. When answers are not immediately apparent, children and adults sometimes create very sophisticated problem-solving procedures. Implicit in these procedures is knowledge about the symbol system used to represent problems and about an array of concepts such as *cardinality* (the amount represented by a number), *ordinality* (relations of more and less among numbers), and the many principles that define what is or is not legitimate in a system of arithmetical operations. Documenting the knowledge and skills that support arithmetic performance provides insights not only into how children and adults do arithmetic but also into the organization, coordination, and development of human cognition.

In this chapter we focus on the development of arithmetic in children prior to formal instruction in school. Often arithmetic is considered narrowly to be a domain of knowledge that children acquire in school, but this view is quite misleading. The foundations of arithmetic emerge well before school begins, and preschool children often display striking knowledge of arithmetic facts, procedures, and concepts prior to entering school. Research on the early development of arithmetic in children is highly relevant to at least two broad areas of inquiry. One is the ontogeny of cognition, where questions concern the origins of knowledge, the development of cognitive processes and concepts, and the interaction of biological and cultural influences. The study of early arithmetic provides a valuable window on the development of cognitive development generally, as well as on a specific domain of knowledge, mathematics, that has been at the center of controversies over the origins of knowledge (e.g., Geary, 1995; Newcombe, 2002). Another area of inquiry is educational assessment and instruction. When instructional practices do not match the cognitive skills and inclinations children bring with them to school, learning can be hampered severely (e.g., Seo & Ginsburg, 2003). If instruction and early assessment are to be optimized for the benefit of children, they must be based on a thorough understanding of what children do and do not know about arithmetic prior to schooling (Ginsburg, Klein, & Starkey, 1998).

In restricting our view to children "prior to formal instruction in school," we recognize that this upper limit is vaguely defined. Certainly some children receive direct, intentional instruction in arithmetic prior to school from preschool teachers, relatives, or television. An argument to the contrary can be made, however, that some children fail to receive appropriate instruction until long after they have entered school. Nevertheless, age of school entry is fairly consistent around the world (4–7 years, roughly), and it is reasonable to assume that most children receive relatively little direct instruction in arithmetic prior to elementary school. Therefore, we focus primarily on children from infancy through approximately 5 years of age, where the latter might include children in transitional or early years of school (kindergarten or grade 1).

We begin by examining evidence for arithmetical capacity in infants. We then review the kinds of arithmetic achievements preschool children display as well as the methods researchers have used to probe the competence of preschool children. Next we explore *how* children do arithmetic, with a focus on what can be inferred about the processes and representational capacities children are likely to use as they solve arithmetic problems. Our tour of the arithmetical capacities in young children is, by necessity, brief and illustrative, and we omit a variety of research on individual differences, cultural factors, and early instruction that are not directly relevant to our immediate target. We refer readers to other texts for additional insights into the development of mathematical cognition in children (Baroody & Dowker, 2003; Bryant, 1995; Bryant & Nunes, 2002; Donlan, 1998; Geary, 1994; Ginsburg et al., 1998; Mix, Huttenlocher, & Levine, 2002b; Nunes & Bryant, 1996; Sternberg & Ben-Zeev, 1996).

ARITHMETIC IN INFANCY

Infants appear to have the capacity to discriminate between small sets of objects that differ in number, at least when set sizes are less than four (see reviews in Haith & Benson, 1998; Mix, Huttenlocher, & Levine, 2002a). For example, Starkey and Cooper (1980) found that 4-month-old infants could discriminate between sets of 2 and 3 but not between sets of 4 and 6. Because the relations between these sets are proportionally identical and because children were habituated to certain non-numerical cues, these results typically are interpreted as showing that quantity is the critical cue that infants use to discriminate sets. Similar results have been found in neonates (Antell & Keating, 1983) and 10- to 12-month-olds (Strauss & Curtis, 1981) with procedures designed to minimize the impact of potentially confounding stimulus variables, with moving stimuli (Van Loosbruk & Smitsman, 1990), and with events presented sequentially (Canfield & Smith, 1996). If infants are capable of preverbal and presymbolic quantification, then the question arises as to whether they might also have some nascent capacity for arithmetic operations on quantities. Evidence for any such capacity would be a stunning testament to the availability of domain-specific knowledge at or shortly after birth.

Initial Evidence and Conclusions

Results from a number of studies in the 1990s supported the view that infants are capable of arithmetic, at least with very small set sizes. The first demonstration came from Wynn (1992), who developed a method used in several subsequent studies. First, infants see a number of dolls on a stage (typically 1 or 2). A screen then covers this display, and then either a doll is added or removed from the stage. Because the screen is still in place, the infant can see the operation (addition or subtraction) but not the resulting set. With the screen in place, the experimenter can either (a) do nothing, thus leaving a set intact that is "possible" (i.e., arithmetically correct), or (b) surreptitiously remove or add a doll, thus creating an "impossible" (arithmetically incorrect) set. Finally, the screen is removed and the infants' visual behavior is recorded. If infants are capable of computing the correct answer, then presumably they would expect to see the arithmetically correct number of objects on the stage, and so they would look longer at an outcome that violated their expectations.

Wynn (1992) found that 4- and 5-month-old infants looked longer at impossible than possible outcomes across three problems: $1 + 1 = 2$ (possible) or 1 (impossible); $2 - 1 = 1$ or 2; $1 + 1 = 2$ or 3. Wynn noted that success on the first two problems might indicate only that infants are sensitive to the direction of the arithmetic transformation, but they may not be able to compute the exact answer. Success on the third problem shows, however, that infants are not merely sensitive to direction. Wynn concluded that "infants can compute the results of simple arithmetical operations" and that "the existence of these arithmetical abilities so early in infancy suggests that humans innately possess the capacity to perform simple arithmetical calculations, which may provide the foundations for the development of further arithmetical knowledge" (1992, p. 750).

Exploring the Evidence and Interpretations

Replications are especially important when striking claims are made. In several studies using Wynn's (1992) method or close variants (Cohen & Marks, 2002, Experiment 1; Feigenson, Carey, & Spelke, 2002, Experiment 6; Koechlin, Dehaene, & Mehler, 1997; Simon, Hespos, & Rochat, 1995; Uller, Carey, Huntley-Fenner, & Klatt, 1999), results have been found that are generally consistent with those of Wynn, although the expected effects depend at least to some extent on stimulus conditions (Koechlin et al., 1997; Uller et al., 1999). Wakeley, Rivera, and Langer (2000a), however, conducted three experiments with 5-month-olds and found no hint of the expected effects. Possible procedural differences between these experiments and Wynn's original study have been identified (Cohen & Marks, 2002; Wakeley, Rivera, & Langer, 2000b; Wynn, 2000) but have not yet been explored empirically. In their reviews of related research, Wakeley et al. (2000a, b) also pointed to a number of empirical inconsistencies across studies and concluded that "whatever arithmetic competence young infants may have must be fragile" (2000b, p. 1538). Aside from this issue, another concern has been raised based on data with older children (e.g., Wakeley et al., 2000a). If, as Wynn concluded, her data imply that 5-month-olds are capable of simple arithmetical calculations, then presumably older children should do as well or better on similar tasks. To the contrary, when Wynn's task has been adapted for use with 2.5-year-olds, these children have mixed success at best (Houdé, 1997; Vilette, 2002).

Even if the empirical effects found by Wynn (1992) were entirely replicable, the issue of how to interpret these effects remains. Wynn's conclusion about innate numerical and arithmetical abilities has been challenged on a number of grounds. One possibility is that the pattern of responses often observed in these studies may be due to a preference for familiar stimuli combined with a preference for displays with more objects (Cohen & Marks, 2002). Another possibility is that the physical transformation used in the procedure may lead to a violation of expectations based on infants' physical reasoning (Baillargeon, 1995) rather than on any particular numerical competency. For example, when an infant views the transformation $1 + 1$ followed by the impossible outcome 1, the disappearance of an object might be interpreted by the infant as abnormal because it violates expectations about physical reality (Haith & Benson,

1998). Simon et al. (1995) noted that numerical and physical identity must be inextricably confounded to some extent.

More generally, Simon (1997) proposed that what passes for numerical and arithmetical processing may in fact be due entirely to general-purpose, non-numerical processes such as the ability to individuate separate entities, to remember and compare entities, to encode information corresponding to individual entities, and to reason in simple ways about the existence and movement of physical entities. Simon suggested that infants, when faced with a problem such as 1 + 1 = 2 or 1, create an internal representation of the first object and then update that representation when the second object is presented. These internal representations could be abstract tokens or *object files* (Kahneman, Treisman, & Gibbs, 1992) that at first contain little or no information, but that later are enriched by subsequent attentional processes. When the screen is lowered and the outcome (possible or impossible) is viewed, the infant is able to map the internally represented set to the external display by using a one-to-one comparison process. When this comparison process produces a mismatch, as in the case of an impossible outcome, expectation is violated and visual attention is increased. Thus, what appears to be numerical processing may be due to basic attentional and memory processes that are recruited for particular situations.

The idea that non-numerical processes may account for what appears to be number-specific cognitive capacity has received empirical support recently (for an excellent review, see Mix et al., 2002a). Although infants appear to discriminate readily between small sets on the basis of number, the belief is growing that these "numerical" discriminations may be due to processes that are non-numerical. The problem is that in earlier studies number typically was confounded to some degree with one or more aspects of *continuous extent*, which includes variables such as total surface area, total length of contour, brightness, and spatial frequency. When continuous extent is carefully manipulated, infants tend to discriminate between sets based on continuous extent rather than number (Clearfield & Mix, 1999; Feigenson et al., 2002). Feigenson et al. (Experiment 7) found a similar effect for arithmetical transformations. For example, 6- and 7-month-old infants were presented with 1 + 1 = 2 or 1 using Wynn's (1992) procedure, but the outcomes varied in size (total area) as well as number so that these two dimensions were not confounded. Thus, infants in one condition would see one small object plus one small object followed by 2 large objects, an arithmetically possible outcome but covering an unexpectedly large area. In another condition infants would see one small object plus one small object followed by one large object, an arithmetically impossible outcome but covering an area equivalent to that of the two small objects combined. Infants looked longer at outcomes that were unexpected in terms of total area, not number. Thus, when number and continuous extent are unconfounded, infants appear to "solve" addition problems on the basis of continuous extent rather than number.

Although conclusions must be viewed as tentative at this point, the picture that is beginning to emerge is quite different from early claims about innate arithmetical abilities. Rather than supporting the conclusion that infants have mathematics-specific processes and representations that underlie small-number discriminations and arithmetic, the evidence seems to be consistent with the view that non-numerical capacities are recruited as infants perform these tasks. When presented with putatively numerical tasks, infants are able to use basic perceptual and attentional mechanisms to individuate a small number of objects (perhaps three or four) and to represent them internally as abstract tokens or object files. As attentional processes provide more and more details, each object file contains an increasing amount of information about its corresponding object, including information about continuous extent. This information is available in working memory for subsequent processing and computation, including, possibly, one-to-one comparisons or computations on continuous extent.

This sketch is obviously incomplete. For example, questions remain about how the proposed comparison processes work and how they are selected as well as how mathematical processes and representations develop in older children from these non-numerical origins. Also, the mechanisms activated by small quantities may differ from those used for large quantities (Lipton & Spelke, in press; Xu & Spelke, 2000). Although Wynn (1992) may be proved wrong in her claims about innate mathematical abilities, she may yet be proved right in a more general sense: the processes and representations used by infants on what appear to be numerical and arithmetical tasks may indeed provide the foundations for the development of further arithmetical knowledge, even if these processes and principles are, initially, entirely non-numerical.

PRESCHOOL CHILDREN'S PROFICIENCY IN ARITHMETIC

Whereas the capacity of infants for arithmetic is uncertain, older children clearly show some skill in solving arithmetic problems. Their success depends greatly, however, on problem characteristics and manner of presentation. We review young children's performance in two areas, their sensitivity to the directional effects of addition and subtraction and their ability to compute exact answers for addition and subtraction problems. We also describe some of the relevant studies in detail to illustrate the methods used to study arithmetic in preschool children.

Sensitivity to Arithmetic Operations

Older children and adults readily understand that adding items increases the quantity of a set and removing items has the opposite effect. This sensitivity to the directional effects of arithmetic operations presumably depends on an appreciation of ordinal relations among numbers. Three-year-olds show knowledge of ordinality when they compare sets differing in quantity, and this knowledge appears to be unrelated to counting skill (Huntley-Fenner & Cannon, 2000). Even 11-month-olds can distinguish between ascending and descending sequences of quantities (Brannon, 2002). The question, then, is whether young children can use their knowledge of ordinality to judge the directional effect of arithmetic transformations.

Brush (1978) presented 3- to 5-year-olds with two cylinders that were partially hidden behind a screen so that only the top portion of each cylinder was visible. An experimenter simultaneously placed many marbles into each cylinder such that, when asked, children correctly stated that both cylinders had an equal number of marbles. The screen prevented children from counting all the marbles. Children viewed the cylinders as having many marbles; the total number in each set was never counted or mentioned. After establishing equal sets for each new trial, the experimenter proceeded with a number of conditions, including simple addition (one marble added to one of the cylinders), simple subtraction (one marble removed from one of the cylinders), complex addition (two marbles added to one cylinder and one marble to the other), and complex subtraction (two marbles removed from one cylinder and one from the other). Children were asked which cylinder had more marbles. Accuracy was very high (above 96%) for all conditions except complex subtraction (65%). Unfortunately, possible age-related changes were not documented. In a second study, Brush used a similar procedure with 4- to 6-year-olds. Again, the majority (≥ 75%) of children were correct in judging which set contained more or fewer objects. Thus, children at these ages can show sensitivity to the directional effects of arithmetic (i.e., more and fewer) in situations that do not require exact computation. Sophian and Adams (1987), using a similar but simplified task, concluded that children from 14 to 28 months of age also showed sensitivity to the effects of insertions and deletions of objects on the magnitude of hidden sets. Performance was highly variable, however, especially at the lower age levels, and so conclusions about the earliest age of onset are only suggestive.

Vilette (2002) employed a different procedure to examine sensitivity to arithmetic operations in children from 2.5 to 4.5 years. Using a variant of Wynn's (1992) method, Vilette presented one addition and one subtraction problem, each with a possible and an impossible solution (2 + 1 = 3 or 2; 3 − 1 = 2 or 3). Children were asked whether the results of transformations were "normal" or "not normal." Responses were scored as correct when children identified both the possible and impossible solutions appropriately. Because the correct answer was larger than the augend for addition and smaller than the minuend for subtraction, accuracy can be taken as an indicator of sensitivity to the direction of these arithmetic transformations. Vilette observed that 4.5-year-olds answered at above-chance levels on addition and subtraction, 3.5-year-olds on addition only, and 2.5-year-olds on neither type of problem. These results were interpreted as indicating that sensitivity to the directional effect of addition develops before that of subtraction and that neither is present prior to 3 years of age.

The conclusion about these specific age-related limits may be misleading for two reasons, however. First, children were tested with only one problem of each type (i.e., one problem for each combination of addition/subtraction and possible/impossible). If children's performance is highly variable, sensitivity to arithmetic operations may have been underestimated. Second, Vilette's assumptions about chance levels of performance appear to have been questionable.[1] With a corrected level of chance, the 3.5-year-olds performed at above-chance levels on both addition and subtraction, and the 2.5-year-olds did so on addition.

Indeed, very young children have shown evidence of sensitivity to arithmetic operations in other tasks. Starkey (1992) developed a search box task to assess arithmetic skills in children aged 1.5 to 4 years. In this task, the child put objects into an opaque container. The experimenter either added or subtracted an object from the box in full view of the child. The child was then instructed to retrieve the objects one by one from the search box container. To prevent the child from feeling how many objects were left in the search box, a hidden trap door was installed so that each time the child reached in, only one object would be available to touch. If children recognized that adding objects to the original set increases the size of the set, presumably they would reach into the box more often than would be required by the original set. Subtraction would require fewer reaches. Children from 2 to 4 years of age showed this pattern on the great majority of problems, as did many 1.5-year-olds.

Thus, evidence from studies with three different methods converges on the conclusion that preschool children understand, in some sense, that addition increases set size and subtraction decreases set size. How young children represent and process numerical information in these tasks is not clear, but this sensitivity appears to emerge as early as 2 years of age and is well developed by approximately 4 years. At the early end of this age range, children show this sensitivity to arithmetic transformations well before they can count or use number words competently. Thus, preschool children have a capacity to represent and reason about ordinal relations based on arithmetic operations, which presumably is a prerequisite for computing exact answers to arithmetic problems.

Computing Exact Answers

Preschool children show some skill in exact addition and subtraction, but their levels of success vary greatly with age and depend on problem characteristics and how problems are presented. Evidence comes from research in which problems are presented with minimal or no verbal content. Consider, for example, the search box task described above (Starkey, 1992). Children were scored as computing an exact solution when the number of reaches corresponded

[1]Vilette (2002) appears to have assumed that chance level of performance was .50 (correct or incorrect). Because accuracy was based on two possible responses ("normal," "not normal") to two solutions (possible and impossible), however, four outcomes were possible. Only one of these outcomes ("normal" on possible, "not normal" on impossible) would result in scoring the child as correct. Thus, the chance of answering both problems correctly by guessing would be .25. When statistical analyses are conducted using this level of probability, the performance of 2.5-year-olds on addition (.64) and of 3.5-year-olds on subtraction (.45) was significantly greater than chance (α =.05).

exactly to the number of the set following the adding or subtracting operation. With problems ranging in size from small (e.g., 0 + 1 and 1 – 1) to large (e.g., 2 + 3 and 5 –1), accuracy improved with increasing age (from 49% for 2-year-olds to 62% for 4-year-olds) and tended to be higher on problems with smaller numbers. Even 1.5-year-olds performed with some accuracy on addition when the sum or minuend was less than 3. Huttenlocher, Jordan, and Levine (1994) examined computation in children from 2 years, 6 months to 3 years, 11 months using a somewhat different procedure. An experimenter placed the augend (represented with disks) on the table in front of a child and then covered the array. Then the experimenter added or subtracted disks from this array by sliding the disks under or out of the cover. The child was then prompted to represent how many disks were under the cover with his or her own disks. Accuracy rates are presented in Table 9.1. Clearly, preschool children can add and subtract to some extent, but their accuracy is strongly related to age and problem size and is very limited prior to three years of age.

Performance depends on problem format as well. Hughes (1981) tested 3- to 5-year-old children with arithmetic problems presented in a variety of verbal and nonverbal formats and with problems ranging from small (operands from 1 to 3) to large (operands from 5 to 8). Hughes (1981) found that small problems were solved with much greater accuracy than large problems. In both cases, nonverbal problems (similar to those used by Huttenlocher et al., 1994) were solved more accurately than the purely verbal problems (e.g., "what do x and y make?"), and hypothetical problems ("if there were x children in a store and y more walked in, how many would there be all together?") were intermediate in difficulty. Addition was easier than subtraction for large problems. Moreover, children from working-class neighborhoods lagged behind children from middle-class neighborhoods in performance by approximately 12 months.

In a similar study, Levine, Jordan, and Huttenlocher (1992) presented 4- to 6- year-olds with nonverbal (as in Huttenlocher et al., 1994) and verbal arithmetic problems. The verbal problems consisted of simple story problems ("Jon had x balls. He got y more. How many balls did he have altogether?") and number fact problems ("How much is x and y?"). Nonverbal problems were much easier than verbal problems for the 4-year-olds, but this difference was diminished for the 6-year-olds. Jordan, Huttenlocher, and Levine (1992) also found that nonverbal problems were easier than verbal problems for kindergarten children (aged 5 to 6 years) and that

Table 9.1
Percentage of Problems Solved Correctly as a Function of Age and Problem Size

Problem	2:6–2:8	2:9–2:11	Age Group 3:0–3:2	3:3–3:5	3:6–3:8	3:9–3:11	Mean
1 + 1	23	33	60	77	67	97	60
2 – 1	30	20	60	63	57	70	50
3 – 2	13	17	30	50	47	67	37
2 + 1	13	10	27	37	43	70	33
1 + 2	7	7	37	40	47	53	32
3 – 1	10	13	20	37	37	50	28
1 + 3	17	13	37	10	20	43	23
3 + 1	3	3	23	33	30	40	22
2 + 2	7	13	23	17	30	27	20
4 – 1	7	10	13	30	27	30	20
4 – 3	3	7	13	17	23	40	17
4 + 1	0	3	17	7	17	30	12
Mean	11	12	30	35	37	51	30

Note. From "A mental model for early arithmetic" by J. Huttenlocher, N. C. Jordan, and S. C. Levine, 1994, *Journal of Experimental Psychology: General, 123,* p. 291. Copyright 1994 by the American Psychological Association. Adapted with permission.

middle-income children outperformed low-income children on verbal problems but not on non-verbal problems.

How Preschool Children Solve Arithmetic Problems

Given that preschool children can solve arithmetic problems, albeit with limited success, the next important question is *how*? As is usually the case with questions about cognitive processes, the answer is not entirely straightforward. Siegler and Shrager (1984) presented two-term addition problems verbally to 4- and 5-year-old children and observed their solution procedures. Children typically solved the problems by using a variety of overt and covert procedures. When children used their fingers to externally represent the addends and then counted their fingers, they were coded as using the *counting fingers* procedure. Children who raised fingers to represent the addends but did not count their fingers were considered to use *finger recognition*. On other occasions, children used *counting* with no external representation. Each of these three procedures involved overt behaviors that could be coded relatively easily. In contrast, children solved some problems relatively quickly with no overt signs of counting. These covert solutions were presumed to involve retrieval of answers from memory. These four procedures, and others, have been identified in numerous studies with young children (Bisanz, Morrison, & Dunn, 1995; Geary, 1994; Jordan et al., 1992; Siegler & Jenkins, 1989; Siegler & Shrager, 1984), and some are used by adults even on simple, single-digit arithmetic problems (LeFevre, Sadesky, & Bisanz, 1996). Individual children typically use more than one procedure and select their procedures flexibly so that, for example, they are more likely to use overt procedures on difficult than on easy problems. Thus, children display a variety of procedures as they solve arithmetic problems, and they choose between these procedures, at least sometimes, as a function of problem difficulty.

The solution procedures described thus far form merely the tip of the iceberg. Preschool children, in contrast to their older counterparts, show the remarkable diversity and creativity in their solution processes that can often be expected in "immature" but capable learners (Bjorklund, 1997; Bransford & Heldmeyer, 1983). Examining the processes children use, the errors they make, and the changing patterns of procedure use provides insights into important aspects of how children represent and process information in the domain of mathematical thinking. We first describe research on how children use counting and retrieval to solve simple arithmetic problems, and how they might select particular solution procedures to solve particular problems. Next, we consider the types of representational processes that might be involved in solving arithmetic problems presented nonverbally. Finally, we discuss preschool children's knowledge of arithmetic concepts with reference to a particular concept, inversion.

Counting and Retrieval

Most of the solution procedures used by preschool children involve counting or retrieval. Siegler and Jenkins (1989), for example, identified eight procedures that 4- and 5-year-olds used to solve small addition problems (operands ≤ 5). Five of these procedures involved counting of some sort. The other three procedures were retrieval, guessing, and decomposition. The latter involves converting a problem with an answer not immediately known (e.g., 2 + 3) into a problem with a known answer plus an adjustment (e.g., 2 + 2 = 4 and 4 + 1 = 5). Neither guessing nor decomposition was used frequently by the children, however (see Table 9.2).

When preschool children count to solve arithmetic problems, they do so in a variety of ways (Siegler & Jenkins, 1989; for a detailed taxonomy, see Baroody, 1987). For instance, the *sum* or *count-all* procedure involves counting sets to correspond to each operand (e.g., 2 and 3 fingers for 2 + 3), and then counting all the enumerated fingers to determine the sum. With the *short-*

Table 9.2
Procedures Used by 4- and 5-Year-Old Children to Solve Addition Problems

Strategy	% Use	% Correct	Median RT (s)
Sum	34	89	10.8
Retrieval	22	89	5.0
Short-cut sum	17	85	13.2
Finger recognition	11	92	6.4
Min	9	86	9.0
Guess	2	20	9.9
Count-from-first	1	40	15.6
Unknown	4	71	–
Total/Mean	100	85	9.4

Note. From *How Children Discover New Strategies*, by R. S. Siegler and E. Jenkins, 1989, p. 60, Hillsdale, NJ: Erlbaum. Copyright 1989 by Lawrence Erlbaum Associates. Adapted with permission.

cut sum procedure, children count to the sum without first counting the two operands separately. Using the *count-from-first-addend* procedure, children count on from the augend, regardless of whether it is larger than the addend. The *min* procedure is defined by children's use of counting on from the larger of either the augend or addend. In this case, children would begin with the larger of the two operands (e.g., 3 in 2 + 3) and continue to count an amount that corresponds to the smaller (*min*imum) operand (i.e., "4, 5"). Of all these procedures, *min* involves the least amount of counting and, consequently, is likely to be more efficient than the other counting procedures, especially given that young children do not always count quickly or correctly (see Table 9.2). The variety of procedures children use is even greater than what we describe here, especially when children's use of fingers, other concrete objects, and mental representations are considered (Baroody, 1987).

Children's counting procedures change with practice, as illustrated in three microgenetic studies. Groen and Resnick (1977) taught preschool children with little knowledge of arithmetic to solve simple arithmetic problems (operands ≤ 5) by using the sum procedure with blocks. The blocks then were removed and children solved problems presented symbolically. After extended practice, 5 of the 10 children abandoned more laborious procedures for the more efficient min strategy without any further instruction. Siegler and Jenkins (1989) tested 4- and 5-year-olds on simple addition problems repeatedly over a 4-month period. Nearly all of these children (7 of 8) discovered and used the min procedure, and most were able to explicitly describe counting from the larger addend. Most of the children who eventually used min first discovered shortcut sum. The children who used min varied considerably, however, in the rate with which they discovered this procedure and the frequency with which it was used once it was discovered. Baroody (1987) followed the performance of 17 kindergarten children over nearly 9 months. Fifteen of these children eventually developed some sort of shortcut procedure, but by the end of the period only nine used shortcuts with any regularity and only five used min predominantly.

Completely documenting a detailed sequence of changes is difficult, and perhaps impossible, because children use many different counting-based procedures, they tend to use different procedures on different problems, and much of their practice is typically unobserved. Clearly, however, children's use of counting-based procedures is not static. Even without instruction, children invent arithmetically appropriate procedures that seem to reflect a "press towards cognitive efficiency" (Groen & Resnick, 1977, p. 651).

When young children count to solve arithmetic problems, they sometimes do so by using external referents, such as blocks or fingers. Methods for representing number externally vary across the world, and some cultures have developed ways to represent numbers up to 100 with various body parts and combinations of finger counting (Fuson & Kwon, 1992; Saxe, Dawson, Fall, & Howard, 1996). Children also represent quantities mentally, as, for example, when they solve 2 + 3 by counting on from 3 without first counting to 3 (e.g., "3, then 4, 5"). The ability to use counting in arithmetic is often interpreted as evidence that children (a) can represent quantities internally along an abstract number line that reflects ordinal relations among numbers and (b) can "move" along that number line as required by addition and subtraction, thus representing arithmetic transformations (Case & Okamoto, 1996). Given their ability to use counting in arithmetic, children presumably can map objects or fingers to the number line, and they can count up and down the number line to add or subtract numbers, within limits.

In contrast to counting, retrieval refers to the rapid process of solving an arithmetic problem by accessing an answer directly from memory, without any sort of mental computation or counting. Typically, lack of overt counting behaviors and short solution latencies are taken as indicators of retrieval use (Ashcraft, 1982, 1992; Siegler, 1988). Children's use of retrieval is sometimes studied by asking them to solve problems as quickly as possible and/or to refrain from using their fingers (Baroody, 1989).

When allowed to solve problems in any manner, the proportion of trials on which retrieval is used tends to increase with age. For example, Siegler and Jenkins (1989) found that 4- and 5-year-olds initially used retrieval on 22% of problems (operands $\leq$ 5), whereas adults in a study by LeFevre et al. (1996) used retrieval on more than 80% of problems (operands < 10). This sort of change might be due to any number of age-related variables, including schooling. Interestingly, the amount of schooling can have a strong effect on young children's accuracy on arithmetic, but its effect on use of procedures appears to be inconsistent (Bisanz et al., 1995; Naito & Miura, 2001).

Because retrieval is operationalized in terms of the absence of overt procedures as well as relatively quick solution latencies, the process of identifying retrieval and estimating its frequency may produce misleading results. In a study of Grade 3 children solving simple multiplication, Baroody (1999) found that what appeared to be retrieval may have been covert nonretrieval procedures and conceptually based shortcuts. The same caveat should apply to research with younger children. Children solve some problems very quickly, without evidence of covert procedures and, on occasion, with self-reports such as "It just popped into my head," so it may be reasonable to infer that they use retrieval on some occasions. Given the methodological problems in identifying retrieval unambiguously, however, researchers must be wary of overestimating the use of retrieval and of underestimating children's use of covert mathematical procedures.

Selection of Procedures

Given the variety of solution procedures available to preschool children, an important question is how children choose among these available procedures when solving arithmetic problems. Siegler and his colleagues (e.g., Shrager & Siegler, 1998; Siegler & Shipley, 1995; Siegler & Shrager, 1984) have developed computational models to represent this process. In these models, when an arithmetic problem is presented, a child first attempts to retrieve the answer from memory. If retrieval fails, he or she progresses to a more laborious back-up procedure (e.g., sum or min). The earlier forms of these models were developed primarily to gain insight into why children retrieve answers successfully on some trials but not on others.

In these models, children's knowledge about memorized arithmetic facts is represented in terms of associative strengths between specific problems and possible answers. For example, the problem 3 + 4 may be strongly associated with 7 and weakly associated with other possibilities, such as 2 and 6. The strengths of these associations are influenced by the experience of the child and by a learning mechanism that increments associative strengths as children are exposed to combinations of problems and answers. These exposures may accrue during the course of instruction or may be based on children's own attempts to solve problems (by counting, for example). Early in this learning process, the distribution of associative strengths across all possible answers is presumed to be relatively flat, thus representing a state of knowledge in which no problem–answer combinations are memorized. As children acquire experience, some associations (e.g., between 3 + 4 and 2) become relatively weak and others (e.g., 3 + 4 and 7) become strong. Still others (e.g., 3 + 4 and 6) might have intermediate values arising, for example, from occasional errors in counting. Eventually, the distribution of associative strengths becomes *peaked* in the sense that, for a given problem, one answer is associated much more strongly than all other possibilities.

Another assumption in these models is that the probability of retrieving a particular answer depends on the associative strength between the problem and that answer, relative to other answers. Answers with weaker associative strengths are less likely to be retrieved than answers with stronger associative strengths. Finally, a *confidence criterion* is established such that a retrieved answer is accepted only if its associative strength exceeds this criterion. Just how this confidence criterion is set is not clear, but it may be related to individual differences in how children approach problems (Siegler, 1988). Thus, according to this form of the model, children attempt to solve arithmetic problems first by retrieving an answer. The success of this operation depends on the distribution of associative strengths between the problem and various answers as well as on whether the answer initially retrieved has an associative strength that exceeds the confidence interval. If retrieval is successful, the child states an answer. If retrieval is unsuccessful, the child may attempt retrieval again or may use a back-up procedure, depending on system parameters that limit search.

The first version of this model (Siegler & Shrager, 1984) accounted for several observed characteristics in young children's arithmetic, including the increased use of retrieval as children gain experience, the tendency for children to use retrieval on "easier," more familiar problems, and counting on other problems. A second version (Siegler & Shipley, 1995) contained several improvements, including a mechanism that associated problems with individual solution procedures (e.g., sum) and adjusted the strengths of these associations according to the speed and accuracy with which these procedures solved problems. This version of the model thus gained the ability to select among back-up procedures, just as children must do. One glaring shortcoming, however, was the model's failure to mimic the ability of 4- and 5-year-old children to develop new counting-based procedures, such as shortcut sum and min, an ability well-documented in young children (e.g., Baroody, 1987; Groen & Resnick, 1977; Siegler & Jenkins, 1989).

To determine whether this shortcoming could be addressed within this computational framework, Shrager and Siegler (1998) developed another model known as Strategy Choice and Discovery Simulation (SCADS). One of the significant changes is that SCADS contains a "metacognitive" system with several characteristics. First, attentional resources are directed to insufficiently learned procedures to improve performance. As these procedures are strengthened, they require fewer attentional resources, and attention is again directed to less practiced procedures. Second, heuristics are employed that analyze the components of successful procedures for redundancies and efficiencies and then alter these procedures to increase efficiency. This latter capacity essentially generates new procedures from old, less efficient procedures. Third, *goal-sketch filters* prevent the use of newly generated procedures that fail to include both operands once and only once. Given $a + b$, for example, these filters would stifle the creation of any newly generated procedure that did not incorporate both a and b.

All three changes seem psychologically plausible: The first and second are entirely consistent with information-processing research and theory (cf. Kail & Bisanz, 1992), and the third represents the influence of very minimal conceptual knowledge about arithmetic on the part of young children. To determine whether the revised model is sufficient for producing arithmetic behavior similar to that of young children, Shrager and Siegler (1998) created a computer model based on their psychological theory. The model was given two procedures, retrieval and sum, and practice on a large number of single-digit arithmetic problems. Results were impressive. Like children, the model developed many new procedures. It selected counting-based procedures on more difficult problems and retrieval on more familiar problems, and both retrieval and accuracy increased with practice. Most strikingly, the model discovered first the shortcut sum and then the min procedures, the same sequence observed by Siegler and Jenkins (1989).

A simulation can never prove the validity of a theory, of course (Ashcraft, 1987). SCADS has been criticized for not reflecting some aspects of children's arithmetic, for using simplified assumptions, and for not incorporating children's conceptual knowledge (Baroody & Tiilikainen, 2003). Nevertheless, the plausibility of the processes in SCADS and its ability to mimic important aspects of children's behavior make it a compelling, if tentative, account of how children's problem-solving procedures develop.

Mental Models

To this point our discussion of how preschool children solve arithmetic problems has been focused on retrieval, counting-based procedures, and mechanisms for selecting and generating procedures. Speculation about how children *represent* arithmetic has been minimal. In SCADS, for example, knowledge about arithmetic facts is represented in terms of associations between operands and answers, but no explicit assumptions are made about how the quantities that correspond to those operands are represented and manipulated. These quantities could well be represented by quantity-specific symbols (e.g., "six") rather than anything similar to the object files of infancy. Indeed, retrieval is likely to be a process that operates to a large extent on verbal representations of number (Dehaene & Cohen, 1995; but see Whalen, McCloskey, Lindemann, & Bouton, 2002). The issue, then, is how young children, who may have the capacity to represent quantities with object files but who have little proficiency in naming numbers and in counting, represent and solve arithmetic problems.

Recall that young children have some success in solving very simple arithmetic problems that are presented nonverbally (Huttenlocher et al., 1994; Starkey, 1992). Huttenlocher et al. proposed that preschool children represent and solve these problems by using a *mental model* (Johnson-Laird, 1983). That is, children construct a mental representation of external objects and then modify this representation in a manner consistent with addition or subtraction. Consider, for instance, a problem such as 2 + 3 presented nonverbally using the procedures developed by Hughes (1981) and Huttenlocher et al. According to the mental models view, the child would generate internal tokens that map one-to-one with the objects of the augend, then would add three more tokens that correspond to the addend, and finally would generate an external set that matches the resulting internal set. These tokens are presumed to be symbolic representations that preserve some, but not necessarily all, the information available in the objects. The critical aspects of the constructed mental models are that they preserve quantitative information about the set and that they can be transformed in ways that correspond to addition and subtraction.

The capacity to use mental models in this fashion is presumed to be available to preschool children, perhaps even before children can count competently or represent numerical information verbally (Huttenlocher et al., 1994; Starkey, 1992). If so, young children might be expected to solve nonverbal problems more easily than verbal problems; a problem presented nonverbally could be mapped directly to an internal mental representation, whereas a problem presented verbally would have to be "translated" before being amenable to representation in a mental model. Evidence for the use of mental models in preschool children comes from findings that children as young as 2 years show some limited competency on nonverbal problems (Starkey, 1992), and that nonverbal problems are consistently easier than verbal problems for preschool children (Jordan et al., 1992; Levine at al., 1992).

Mental models should require working memory to store and manipulate tokens. Although working memory has been linked to mathematical performance in school-age children and adults (Gathercole & Pickering, 2000; Geary, Hoard, & Hamson, 1999; McLean & Hitch, 1999; Siegel & Ryan, 1989), far less research has been conducted on this relation in preschool children. One exception is a study by Klein and Bisanz (2000). Two-term addition and subtraction problems were presented to 4-year-olds using a nonverbal format. Children were fairly competent in solving the addition and subtraction problems with small sets (operands ≤ 5). If children used mental models and if success in using mental models is constrained by working-memory limitations, then performance should be closely linked to *representational set size* (RSS), the number of tokens that need to be stored in working memory to solve a given problem. For instance, when solving 2 + 1 the maximum number of tokens that must be held in working memory would be three (the sum), but for 2 – 1 the maximum number would be two. This model accounted well for differences in accuracy across problems and was clearly superior to an alternative model based on assumptions about attention and counting accuracy. Moreover, this same model also accounted for differences in problem difficulty for younger age groups tested by Huttenlocher et al. (1994; see Table 9.2). The fact that RSS is strongly related to performance supports the view that preschool children use mental models to solve nonverbal arithmetic problems.

Further support for this view was found in a study by Rasmussen and Bisanz (2004), who examined the relation between different problem formats (nonverbal and verbal) and different components of working memory (visual-spatial, phonological, central executive) in preschool and Grade 1 children. They replicated the findings of Levine et al. (1992) in that nonverbal problems were easier than verbal problems for preschool children and this difference was negligible for Grade 1 children. If children use mental models to solve nonverbal problems, then performance on these problems should correlate with performance on tasks measuring visual-spatial working memory, but not with other working-memory tasks. Rasmussen and Bisanz found that, of all the working-memory measures, visual-spatial working memory was the best predictor of performance on nonverbal problems for preschool children but not for older children. This finding is consistent with the view that preschoolers use mental models for arithmetic and this process requires visual-spatial working memory.

Early Concepts

When preschool children solve arithmetic problems, their performance can be interpreted not only in terms of solution procedures and internal representations, but also in terms of their conceptual knowledge about arithmetic. Assessing conceptual knowledge can be difficult (Bisanz & LeFevre, 1992). Consider, for example, a child who invents the *min* procedure for 2 + 3. Using min might be considered evidence for understanding commutativity, that is, the principle that $a + b = b + a$. Baroody (1987; Baroody & Gannon, 1984) has shown, however, that children who use min do not necessarily recognize that $a + b$ and $b + a$ yield the same answer (but see Cowan & Renton, 1996). Use of the min procedure implies that children accept the notion that they can vary the order in which operands are added, but it does not necessarily imply that they recognize the logical necessity of commutativity in addition. Thus, different types of evidence can reflect different types or levels of conceptual understanding (Bisanz & LeFevre, 1992; Canobi, Reeve, & Pattison, 1998).

Arithmetic is, in a sense, defined in terms of underlying principles that constrain operations and relations (Starkey & Gelman, 1982), including commutativity (Baroody, Wilkins, & Tiilikainen, 2003), inversion (Bisanz & LeFevre, 1990), equivalence (Alibali, 1999), and additive composition (Nunes & Bryant, 1996). Critical issues are whether and to what extent young children comprehend and use these concepts, the sequence in which concepts develop, and how these interact with procedures in development (Baroody, 2003; Bisanz & LeFevre, 1992; Rittle-

Johnson & Siegler, 1998). To illustrate the nature of research on children's understanding of arithmetic principles, we focus on inversion, that is, the principle that $a + b - b$ *must* equal a. Evidence for the use of inversion-based shortcuts to solve symbolic arithmetic problems has been found in school-aged children and adults (Bisanz & LeFevre, 1990; Siegler & Stern, 1998; Stern, 1992). Comprehension of inversion may be essential for understanding the additive composition of number (Bryant, Christie, & Rendu, 1999), and some have argued that reasoning arithmetically is impossible until the inverse relation between addition and subtraction is recognized (Inhelder & Piaget, 1958; Vilette, 2002).

Knowledge of inversion can be applied in either a qualitative or quantitative way (Bryant et al., 1999). *Qualitative* inversion involves recognizing that adding and subtracting the same things, not necessarily the same *number* of things, leaves the original amount unchanged. In contrast, a *quantitative* understanding of inversion implies consideration of the quantities being added and subtracted. Bryant et al. (1999) determined whether the inversion solutions used by young, school-aged children were qualitative or quantitative by presenting inversion and standard problems in a variety of conditions to children from 5 to 8 years of age. To illustrate, children were presented with a row of a blocks. Next b blocks were added to the row, then b or c blocks were taken away, and finally children were asked how many blocks were in the row. The middle portion of the array was covered throughout the manipulations to prevent counting. In these problems a, b, and c were sufficiently large so that young children would almost inevitably make errors if they tried to add and subtract sequentially. Solutions for inversion problems would be simplified if children were to recognize that adding and subtracting b must leave a unchanged. In a *concrete identical* (CI) condition, blocks were added and removed from the same side of the row. In the case of inversion problems, then, the very same blocks were added and subtracted. These problems might be solved on the basis of qualitative inversion, that is, by recognizing the same *thing* (or group of blocks) had been added and subtracted, without reference to the number of blocks in the transformations. In a *concrete nonidentical* (CN) condition, blocks were added to one side and then different blocks were removed from the other side of an array, therefore requiring children to attend to the number of blocks being added or removed. These two conditions are illustrated in Figure 9.1. Bryant and colleagues found that performance was much higher for inversion than for standard problems in both conditions, and they concluded that children from 5 to 8 years of age show evidence of quantitative inversion.

Whether children younger than 5 years show inversion has also received some attention. Starkey and Gelman (1982) reported that 3-year-olds were able to solve simple inversion problems, presented with small numbers of blocks, without using any overt counting strategies. Because the size of the operands was small and no standard problems were presented for comparison, the children may have been computing the answers covertly with addition and subtraction rather than using a shortcut based on inversion. Vilette (2002) also studied inversion in preschoolers by presenting a possible ($2 + 1 - 1 = 2$) and an impossible ($2 + 1 - 1 = 3$) inversion problem and asking children to judge whether the answer was "normal" or not. Most of the children in the oldest group (mean age 4.5 years) judged both problems correctly, whereas nearly all 2- and 3-year-olds were incorrect on one or both problems. Vilette concluded that 4- to 5-year-olds begin to understand the inverse relation between addition and subtraction, but younger children do not. This conclusion must be qualified for at least three reasons, however, because (a) children in the older group might have used a qualitative, rather than a truly quantitative, form of inversion, (b) no standard (i.e., noninversion) problems were administered and so older children may have covertly added and subtracted rather than using inversion (Klein & Bisanz, 2000), and (c) each child had very few opportunities to solve problems. Thus, the results provided by Starkey and Gelman and by Vilette are suggestive but not conclusive.

Inversion (5+2-2)   Standard (5+2-3)

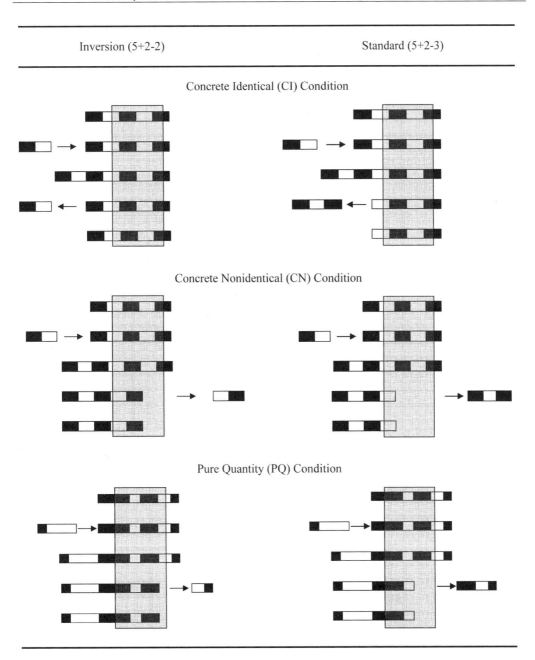

Figure 9.1. Conditions used to assess the use of inversion-based solution procedures. CI problems could be solved with solutions based on qualitative inversion, length cues, or quantitative inversion; CN problems could be solved with solutions based on length cues or quantitative inversion; and PQ problems could be solved with solutions based on quantitative inversion. Bryant et al., 1999 used the CI and CN conditions with larger numbers of blocks, Rasmussen et al. (2003) used all three conditions, and Sherman and Bisanz (2003) used the CI and PQ conditions. A partial, opaque cover over the array was used to prevent children from counting the array to obtain their answers.

Other evidence from three recent studies supports the view that use of inversion emerges early. Klein and Bisanz (2000) used a nonverbal procedure similar to that of Huttenlocher et al. (1994) to present three-term inversion and standard problems to 4-year-olds. These children generated a impressive range of creative solution procedures, both overt and covert. Of special interest were the covert solutions, where children showed no obvious strategy. When latencies on problems with covert solutions were compared, solutions were significantly faster for inversion than for standard problems, as would be expected if children were using a shortcut solution selectively on inversion problems. Moreover, on 30% of the inversion problems solved covertly, children reported spontaneously that counting was unnecessary because the second and third numbers (i.e., $+ b - b$) were the same.

Even more compelling evidence was provided by Rasmussen, Ho, and Bisanz (2003), who adapted the method used by Bryant et al. (1999) for use with 4- and 6-year-olds. Recall that Bryant et al. assumed that concrete identical (CI) problems could be solved with qualitative or quantitative inversion, whereas concrete nonidentical (CN) problems could be solved only with quantitative inversion. As is evident in Figure 9.1, however, children could have solved CN inversion problems correctly and without using inversion by noting that the length of the row is the same before and after transformations. Rasmussen et al. created a third condition, *pure quantity* (PQ), in which inversion problems could not be solved on the basis of either qualitative inversion or length cues (Figure 9.1). Both 4- and 6-year-olds solved inversion problems more accurately than standard problems, and their performance did not vary across the three conditions. The younger children were much less consistent across problems than the older children, however. Rasmussen et al. concluded that 4-year-olds are capable of creating and using an inversion-based shortcut in a fully quantitative manner, but that this capacity is not exercised consistently. Using a similar procedure, Sherman and Bisanz (2003) found that even 3-year-olds solve inversion problems more readily than standard problems and did so in a fully quantitative manner. Sherman and Bisanz also found that measures of counting, number naming, and cardinality correlated with each other but did *not* correlate with accuracy on inversion problems, indicating that individual differences in the use of inversion do not necessarily correspond with simple numerical skills.

The picture that emerges from this research is that 3- and 4-year-old children can construct a shortcut procedure consistent with a fully quantitative principle of inversion that enables them to solve inversion problems. This shortcut is not necessarily used regularly, a characteristic that may reflect a creative tendency to develop and try various procedures (Klein & Bisanz, 2000; Shrager & Siegler, 1998), or an incomplete conceptual understanding of inversion (Vilette, 2002). In either case, it is remarkable that children appear to generate and use inversion-based solutions well before the presumed onset of true reversibility, formal instruction and, in the case of 3-year-olds, reliable skill in counting.

Several issues remain to be addressed, however. First, the extent to which young children's performance is based on explicit and thorough understanding of inversion, as opposed to some implicit and incomplete version of the concept, remains to be determined. Just as children may commute a and b when solving simple addition problems without showing other evidence of understanding commutativity (Baroody & Gannon, 1984), young children's knowledge of inversion is likely to be immature (Bisanz & LeFevre, 1992). Moreover, even though 3- and 4-year-olds show some sensitivity to the principle of inversion, it is clear from other research that several more years will pass before children combine their developing knowledge about the relation between addition and subtraction with other concepts, such as part–whole relations, to understand arithmetic as an integrated system (Bryant, 1995; Bryant & Nunes, 2002; Piaget, 1952). Second, we do not yet know whether an appreciation for the principle of inversion is induced from quantitative experience or arises independently, perhaps based on a qualitative form that precedes significant enumeration skills. Rasmussen et al. (2003) speculated, for example, that quantitative inversion might evolve from a qualitative form that is based on social interactions involving giving and taking. Third, the process by which inversion-like solutions are generated remains a mystery.

Our discussion of research on inversion is intended to illustrate findings and issues that are common in studies of early conceptual development related to arithmetic. Young children sometimes show what appears to be precocious sensitivity to arithmetic concepts, and this knowledge clearly influences the kinds of solution procedures children generate. The precise extent and depth of this knowledge can be difficult to determine, however. Clearly, these conceptual advances need to be clearly defined and mapped to earlier and later acquisitions in the course of development.

CONCLUSIONS

The evidence from our review of arithmetic in preschool children is not sufficient to resolve questions about the ontogenetic origins of knowledge or optimizing early assessment and instruction, but a coherent, if speculative, story is beginning to emerge. Although infants may have little or no domain-specific knowledge about number or arithmetic, they are able to recruit general-purpose attentional and memory mechanisms to respond to situations that ostensibly involve number or arithmetic. One such mechanism, the use of object files to represent information about particular objects, may provide a basis for computations involving small numbers of objects. The similarity between the object files attributed to infants and the internal tokens used in mental models by older children is suggestive, and it is reasonable to suppose that the transition to mental models may reflect an emerging ability to create sets of object files and to transform these sets in ways analogous to addition and subtraction. The use of mental models enables young children to represent arithmetic problems and solve simple arithmetic problems without the use of verbal processes and symbols. During the preschool years children also begin to use external representations (e.g., fingers), word-based representations (e.g., "six") and verbal counting, and alternative internal representations (e.g., a number line) to represent numbers and relations, as well as to solve arithmetic problems. At the same time children develop rules and concepts, at least in a prototypic form, that inform and constrain their growing ability to manipulate numbers arithmetically. How the cognitive system coordinates the development of these various emerging resources is the key to advancing theoretical knowledge about the early development of mathematical cognition and to informing educational assessment and instruction.

For years the arithmetic knowledge of preschool children was assumed to be largely inconsequential for understanding cognitive development or irrelevant for educational concerns. Perhaps for these reasons research on young children has, until recently, been limited. We now are beginning to get a sense for the rich diversity of mathematical thinking in young children, and for the potential importance of understanding early arithmetic for developmental theory and educational practice. We also now have a reasonably well-developed empirical and theoretical base for advancing knowledge. Given the need for understanding the coordination of different aspects of development, we look forward to studies that include a range of tasks spanning procedural, conceptual, and factual knowledge of young children. Longitudinal and microgenetic studies that trace the course of change will provide insights into how different types of knowledge interact in development. Studies of the cultural conditions and demands that nurture, or interfere with, the development of mathematical knowledge will be essential for understanding the origins and consequences of early arithmetic knowledge.

REFERENCES

Alibali, M. W. (1999). How children change their minds: Strategy change can be gradual or abrupt. *Developmental Psychology, 35*, 127–145.

Antell, S. E., & Keating, D. P. (1983). Perception of numerical invariance in neonates. *Child Development, 54*, 695–701.

Ashcraft, M. H. (1982). The development of mental arithmetic: A chronometric approach. *Developmental Review, 2*, 213–236.

Ashcraft, M. H. (1987). Children's knowledge of simple arithmetic: A developmental model and simulation. In J. Bisanz, C. J. Brainerd, & R. Kail (Eds.), *Formal methods in developmental research* (pp. 302–338). New York: Springer-Verlag.

Ashcraft, M. H. (1992). Cognitive arithmetic: A review of data and theory. *Cognition, 44*, 75–106.

Baillargeon, R. (1995). Physical reasoning in infancy. In M. S. Gazzaniga (Ed.), *The cognitive neurosciences* (pp. 181–204). Cambridge, MA: MIT Press.

Baroody, A. J. (1987). The development of counting strategies for single-digit addition. *Journal for Research in Mathematics Education, 18*, 141–157.

Baroody, A. J. (1989). Kindergartners' mental addition with single-digit combinations. *Journal for Research in Mathematics Education, 20*, 159–172.

Baroody, A. J. (1999). The roles of estimation and the commutativity principle in the development of third graders' mental multiplication. *Journal of Experimental Child Psychology, 74*, 157–193.

Baroody, A. J. (2003). The development of adaptive expertise and flexibility: The integration of conceptual and procedural knowledge. In A. J. Baroody & A. Dowker (Eds.), *The development of arithmetic concepts and skills: Constructing adaptive expertise* (pp. 1–33). Mahwah, NJ: Erlbaum.

Baroody, A. J., & Dowker, A. (Eds.) (2003). *The development of arithmetic concepts and skills: Constructing adaptive expertise*. Mahwah, NJ: Erlbaum.

Baroody, A. J., & Gannon, K. E. (1984). The development of the commutativity principle and economical addition strategies. *Cognition and Instruction, 1*, 321–339.

Baroody, A. J., & Tiilikainen, S. H. (2003). Two perspectives on addition development. In A. J. Baroody & A. Dowker (Eds.), *The development of arithmetic concepts and skills: Constructing adaptive expertise* (pp. 75–125). Mahwah, NJ: Erlbaum.

Baroody, A. J., Wilkins, J. L., & Tiilikainen, S. H. (2003). The development of children's understanding of additive commutativity: From protoquantitative concept to general concept? In A. J. Baroody & A. Dowker (Eds.), *The development of arithmetic concepts and skills: Constructing adaptive expertise* (pp. 127–160). Mahwah, NJ: Erlbaum.

Bisanz, J., & LeFevre, J. (1990). Strategic and nonstrategic processing in the development of mathematical cognition. In D. F. Bjorklund (Ed.), *Children's strategies: Contemporary views of cognitive development* (pp. 213–244). Hillsdale, NJ: Erlbaum.

Bisanz, J., & LeFevre, J. (1992). Understanding elementary mathematics. In J. I. D. Campbell (Ed.), *The nature and origins of mathematical skills* (pp. 113–136). Amsterdam, North-Holland: Elsevier.

Bisanz, J., Morrison, F. J., & Dunn, M. (1995). Effects of age and schooling on the acquisition of elementary quantitative skills. *Developmental Psychology, 31*, 221–236.

Bjorklund, D. F. (1997). The role of immaturity in human development. *Psychological Bulletin, 122*, 153–169.

Brannon, E. M. (2002). The development of ordinal numerical knowledge in infancy. *Cognition, 83*, 223–240.

Bransford, J. D., & Heldmeyer, K. (1983). Learning from children learning. In J. Bisanz, G. L. Bisanz, & R. Kail (Eds.), *Learning in children* (pp. 171–190). New York: Spring-Verlag.

Brush, L. R. (1978). Preschool children's knowledge of addition and subtraction. *Journal for Research in Mathematics Education, 9*, 44–54.

Bryant, P. (1995). Children and arithmetic. *Journal of Child Psychology and Psychiatry, 36*, 3–32.

Bryant, P., Christie, C., & Rendu, A. (1999). Children's understanding of the relation between addition and subtraction: Inversion, identity, and decomposition. *Journal of Experimental Child Psychology, 74*, 194–212.

Bryant, P., & Nunes, T. (2002). Children's understanding of mathematics. In U. Goswami (Ed.), *Blackwell handbook of childhood cognitive development* (pp. 412–439). Malden, MA: Blackwell Publishers.

Canfield, R. L., & Smith, E. G. (1996). Number-based expectations and sequential enumeration by 5-month-old infants. *Developmental Psychology, 32*, 269–279.

Canobi, K. H., Reeve, R. A., & Pattison, P. E. (1998). The role of conceptual understanding in children's addition problem solving. *Developmental Psychology, 34*, 882–891.

Case, R., & Okamoto, Y. (with S. Griffin, A. McKeough, C. Bleiker, B. Henderson, & K. M. Stephenson). (1996). The role of central conceptual structures in the development of children's thought. *Monographs of the Society for Research in Child Development, 61*(1–2, Serial No. 246).

Clearfield, M. W., & Mix, K. S. (1999). Number versus contour length in infants' discrimination of small visual sets. *Psychological Science, 10*, 408–411.

Cohen, L. B., & Marks, K. S. (2002). How infants process addition and subtraction events. *Developmental Science, 5*, 186–212.

Cowan, R., & Renton, M. (1996). Do they know what they are doing? Children's use of economical addition strategies and knowledge of commutativity. *Educational Psychology, 16*, 407–420.

Dehaene, S., & Cohen, L. (1995). Towards an anatomical and functional model of number processing. *Mathematical Cognition, 1*, 83–120.

Donlan, C. (Ed.). (1998). *The development of mathematical skills*. Hove, UK: Psychology Press.

Feigenson, L., Carey, S., & Spelke, E. (2002). Infant's discrimination of number versus continuous extent. *Cognitive Psychology, 44*, 33–66.

Fuson, K. C., & Kwon, Y. (1992). Learning addition and subtraction: Effects of number word and other cultural tools. In J. Bideau, C. Meljac, & J. P. Fisher (Eds.), *Pathways to number* (pp. 351–374). Hillsdale, NJ: Erlbaum.

Gathercole, S. E., & Pickering, S. J. (2000). Working memory deficits in children with low achievements in the national curriculum at 7 years of age. *British Journal of Educational Psychology, 70*, 177–194.

Geary, D. C. (1994). *Children's mathematical development: Research and practical applications.* Washington, DC: American Psychological Association.

Geary, D. C. (1995). Reflections of evolution and culture in children's cognition: Implications for mathematical development and instruction. *American Psychologist, 50,* 24–37.

Geary, D. C., Hoard, M. K., & Hamson, C. O. (1999). Numerical and arithmetical cognition: Patterns of functions and deficits in children at risk for a mathematical disability. *Journal of Experimental Child Psychology, 74,* 213–239.

Ginsburg, H. P., Klein, A., & Starkey, P. (1998). The development of children's mathematical thinking: From research to practice. In W. Damon (Series Ed.), I. E. Siegel & K. A. Renninger (Vol. Eds.), *Handbook of child psychology: Vol. 4. Child psychology in practice* (5th ed., pp. 401–476). New York: Wiley.

Groen, G., & Resnick, L. B. (1977). Can preschool children invent addition algorithms? *Journal of Educational Psychology, 69,* 645–652.

Haith, M. M., & Benson, J. B. (1998). Infant cognition. In W. Damon (Series Ed.), D. Kuhn & R. S. Siegler (Vol. Eds.), *Handbook of child psychology: Vol. 2. Cognition, perception, and language* (5th ed., pp. 199–254). New York: Wiley.

Houdé, O. (1997). Numerical development: From the infant to the child. Wynn's (1992) paradigm in 2- and 3-year olds. *Cognitive Development, 12,* 373–391.

Hughes, M. (1981). Can preschool children add and subtract? *Educational Psychology, 1,* 207–219.

Huntley-Fenner, G., & Cannon, E. (2000). Preschoolers' magnitude comparisons are mediated by a preverbal analog mechanism. *Psychological Science, 11,* 147–152.

Huttenlocher, J., Jordan, N. C., & Levine, S. C. (1994). A mental model for early arithmetic. *Journal of Experimental Psychology: General, 123,* 284–296.

Inhelder, B., & Piaget, J. (1958). *The growth of logical thinking from childhood to adolescence.* New York: Basic Books.

Johnson-Laird, P. N. (1983). *Mental models.* Cambridge, MA: Harvard University Press.

Jordan, N. C., Huttenlocher, J., & Levine, S. C. (1992). Differential calculation abilities in young children from middle- and low-income families. *Developmental Psychology, 28,* 644–653.

Kahneman, D., Treisman, A., & Gibbs, B. J. (1992). The reviewing of object files: Object-specific integration of information. *Cognitive Psychology, 24,* 175–219.

Kail, R., & Bisanz, J. (1992). The information-processing perspective on cognitive development in childhood and adolescence. In R. J. Sternberg & C. A. Berg (Eds.), *Intellectual development* (pp. 229–260). New York: Cambridge University Press.

Klein, J. S., & Bisanz, J. (2000). Preschoolers doing arithmetic: The concepts are willing but the working memory is weak. *Canadian Journal of Experimental Psychology, 54,* 105–115.

Koechlin, E., Dehaene, S., & Mehler, J. (1997). Numerical transformations in five month old human infants. *Mathematical Cognition, 3,* 89–104.

LeFevre, J., Sadesky, G. S., & Bisanz, J. (1996). Selection of procedures in mental addition: Reassessing the problem size effect in adults. *Journal of Experimental Psychology: Learning, Memory, and Cognition, 22,* 216–230.

Levine, S. C., Jordan, N. C., & Huttenlocher, J. (1992). Development of calculation abilities in young children. *Journal of Experimental Child Psychology, 53,* 72–103.

Lipton, J. S., & Spelke, E. S. (in press). Origins of number sense: Large number discrimination in human infants. *Psychological Science.*

McLean, J. F., & Hitch, G. J. (1999). Working memory in children with specific learning disabilities. *Journal of Experimental Child Psychology, 74,* 240–260.

Mix, K. S., Huttenlocher, J., & Levine, S. C. (2002a). Multiple cues for quantification in infancy: Is number one of them? *Psychological Bulletin, 128,* 278–294.

Mix, K. S., Huttenlocher, J., & Levine, S. C. (2002b). *Quantitative development in infancy and early childhood.* New York: Oxford University Press.

Naito, M., & Miura, H. (2001). Japanese children's numerical competencies: Age- and schooling-related influences on the development of number concepts and addition skills. *Developmental Psychology, 37,* 217–230.

Newcombe, N. S. (2002). The nativist-empiricist controversy in the context of recent research on spatial and quantitative development. *Psychological Science, 13,* 395–401.

Nunes, T., & Bryant, P. (1996). *Children doing mathematics.* Cambridge, MA: Blackwell Publishers.

Piaget, J. (1952). *The origins of intelligence in children.* New York: International Universities Press.

Rasmussen, C., & Bisanz, J. (2003). *Representation and working memory in early arithmetic.* Manuscript submitted for publication.

Rasmussen, C., Ho, E., & Bisanz, J. (2004). Use of the mathematical principle of inversion in young children. *Journal of Experimental Child Psychology, 85,* 89–102.

Rittle-Johnson, B., & Siegler, R. S. (1998). The relation between conceptual and procedural knowledge in learning mathematics: A review. In C. Donlan (Ed.), *The development of mathematical skills* (pp. 75–110). Hove, UK: Psychology Press.

Saxe, G. B., Dawson, V., Fall, R., & Howard, S. (1996). Culture and children's mathematical thinking. In R. J. Sternberg & T. Ben-Zeev (Eds.), *The nature of mathematical thinking* (pp. 119–144). Mahwah, NJ: Erlbaum.

Seo, K., & Ginsburg, H. P. (2003). "You've got to carefully read the math sentence . . .": Classroom context and children's interpretations of the equals sign. In A. J. Baroody & A. Dowker (Eds.), *The development of arithmetic concepts and skills: Constructing adaptive expertise* (pp. 161–187). Mahwah, NJ: Erlbaum.

Sherman, J. L., & Bisanz, J. (2003, April). *Evidence for use of mathematical inversion in three-year-olds.* Poster presented at the biennial meeting of the Society for Research in Child Development, Tampa, FL.

Shrager J., & Siegler, R.S. (1998). SCADS: A model of children's strategy choices and strategy discoveries. *Psychological Science, 9,* 405–410.

Siegel, L. S., & Ryan, E. B. (1989). The development of working memory in normally achieving and subtypes of learning disabled children. *Child Development, 60,* 973–980.

Siegler, R. S. (1988). Strategy choice procedures and the development of multiplication skill. *Journal of Experimental Psychology: General, 117,* 258–275.

Siegler, R. S., & Jenkins, E. (1989). *How children discover new strategies.* Hillsdale, NJ: Erlbaum.

Siegler, R. S., & Shipley, C. (1995). Variation, selection, and cognitive change. In T. J. Simon & G. S. Halford (Eds.), *Developing cognitive competence: New approaches to process modeling* (pp. 31–76). Hillsdale, NJ: Erlbaum.

Siegler, R. S., & Robinson, M. (1982). The development of numerical understandings. In H. W. Reese & L. P. Lipsitt (Eds.), *Advances in child development and behavior* (pp. 241–312). New York: Academic Press.

Siegler, R. S., & Shrager, J. (1984). Strategy choices in addition and subtraction: How do children know what to do? In C. Sophian (Ed.), *Origins of cognitive skill* (pp. 229–294). Hillsdale, NJ: Erlbaum.

Siegler, R. S., & Stern, E. (1998). Conscious and unconscious strategy discoveries: A microgenetic analysis. *Journal of Experimental Psychology: General, 127,* 377–397.

Simon, T. J. (1997). Reconceptualizing the origins of number knowledge: A "non-numerical" account. *Cognitive Development, 12,* 349–372.

Simon, T. J., Hespos, S. J., & Rochat, P. (1995). Do infants understand simple arithmetic? A replication of Wynn (1992). *Cognitive Development, 10,* 253–269.

Sophian, C., & Adams, N. (1987). Infants' understanding of numerical transformations. *British Journal of Developmental Psychology, 5,* 257–264.

Starkey, P. (1992). The early developmental of numerical reasoning. *Cognition, 43,* 93–126.

Starkey, P., & Cooper, R. G. (1980). Perception of numbers by human infants. *Science, 210,* 1033–1035.

Starkey, P., & Gelman, R. (1982). The development of addition and subtraction abilities prior to formal schooling in arithmetic. In T. P. Carpenter, J. M. Moser, & T. A. Romberg (Eds.), *Addition and subtraction: A cognitive perspective* (pp. 99–116). Hillsdale, NJ: Erlbaum.

Stern, E. (1992). Spontaneous use of conceptual mathematical knowledge in elementary school children. *Contemporary Educational Psychology, 17,* 266–277.

Sternberg, R. J., & Ben-Zeev, T. (Eds.). (1996). *The nature of mathematical thinking.* Mahwah, NJ: Erlbaum.

Strauss, M. S., & Curtis, L. E. (1981). Infant perception of numerosity. *Child Development, 52,* 1146–1152.

Uller, C., Carey, S., Huntley-Fenner, G., & Klatt, L. (1999). What representations might underlie infant numerical knowledge? *Cognitive Development, 14,* 1–36.

Van Loosbroek, E., & Smitsman, A. W. (1990). Visual perception of numerosity in infancy. *Developmental Psychology, 26,* 911–922.

Vilette, B. (2002). Do young children grasp the inverse relationship between addition and subtraction? Evidence against early arithmetic. *Cognitive Development, 17,* 1365–1383.

Wakeley A., Rivera, S., & Langer, J. (2000a). Can young infants add and subtract? *Child Development, 71,* 1525–1534.

Wakeley, A., Rivera, S., & Langer, J. (2000b). Not proved: Reply to Wynn. *Child Development, 71,* 1537–1539.

Whalen, J., McCloskley, M., Lindemann, M., & Bouton, G. (2002). Representing arithmetic table facts in memory: Evidence from acquired impairments. *Cognitive Neuropsychology, 19,* 505–522.

Wynn, K. (1992). Addition and subtraction by human infants. *Nature, 358,* 749–750.

Wynn, K. (2000). Findings of addition and subtraction in infants are robust and consistent: Reply to Wakeley, Rivera, and Langer. *Child Development, 71,* 1535–1536.

Xu, F., & Spelke, E. S. (2000). Large number discrimination in 6-month-old infants. *Cognition, 74,* B1–B11.

10

Learning Mathematics in China and the United States
Cross-Cultural Insights into the Nature and Course of Preschool Mathematical Development

Kevin F. Miller
Melissa Kelly
Xiaobin Zhou

Compared to other educational topics, mathematics has an apparent universality that has made it a special focus of cross-national research on education and cognitive development. Unlike literacy, which is subserved by vastly different writing systems, the basic representational systems that underlie mathematics, from Arabic numerals to algebraic symbols, are in near-universal use throughout the world. Thus, it is not surprising that mathematics has been a major focus of large-scale studies that attempt to compare overall population levels of achievement (e.g., Beaton & Robitaille, 1999; Husén, 1967; Travers & Westbury, 1990).

These studies have revealed dramatic and consistent differences in children's mathematical competence in different societies. The most recent large-scale study, the Third International Math and Science Study (TIMSS) project (Peak, 1996, 1997) showed a typical pattern of results. Children were tested at two levels, grades 3 and 4 at the lower level and grades 7 and 8 for the upper level. At both grades, one significant regional generalization stands out. Students from all participating Asian countries (Singapore, South Korea, Japan, and the Hong Kong Special Administrative Region) showed the highest average performance. These differences are substantial. Peak (1997) reports that U.S. fourth graders at the 95th percentile did not perform significantly better than the average student in Singapore. These findings are not limited to the TIMSS and its predecessor studies. In a long series of studies comparing U.S. children with those in Taiwan, Japan, and the People's Republic of China, Stevenson (Stevenson & Lee, 1998) found equally large differences that increased with age and were focused on mathematics as opposed to science or literacy. For example, looking at average scores for schools, only one sample in Chicago at the fifth grade performed as well as the lowest-performing school in Beijing (Stevenson et al., 1990a).

The existence of such large differences in a fundamental aspect of cognitive development is a striking phenomenon but one whose meaning has struck different observers in different ways. Brown (1998) has decried what he terms the "tyranny of the international horse race," in which shortcomings in achievement are attributed to whatever defect in a school system a researcher decides is most striking. Any aspect of cognitive development is the confluence of a multitude of influences; mathematical development is no exception. It is unlikely that there is a single source for the documented mathematical superiority of East Asian children, but considering carefully the differences in how mathematics is acquired in China and the United States may nonetheless lead to important insights into the nature of mathematical competence and its development.

Children's learning is clearly the result of a complex set of vectors, including but not limited to: maturational factors, parental beliefs and activities, formal schooling processes, linguistic influences, differences in the content of what children learn, and children's own ideas, beliefs, and activities. Unraveling this complex skein is not a simple task, and it is unlikely that a single factor will account for effects of the magnitude found for mathematical development. Given the complexity of potential causes, it is easy for researchers to fall into the position of the mythical blind men who met an elephant and recognized it as different objects depending on which part they explored (Saxe, 1963), by identifying as the crucial variable some favored factor that differs between cultures.

This chapter will focus on identifying the nature of differences in mathematical competence that exist as children begin formal schooling. Schooling may well serve to exacerbate these differences (see Stevenson & Stigler, 1992, for a review of factors related to cross-national achievement differences in later years), but our concern here will be on describing the differences in mathematical competence that exist on the first day of first grade and considering the linguistic and social factors that may account for those differences. In some cases, it is possible to make more specific predictions than simply that East Asian students should outperform their North American peers. These cases provide much more convincing evidence for the causal role of particular factors. In other cases it is not possible to make such precise predictions. Nonetheless, identifying relevant factors that differ cross-culturally can be a step toward investigating the role such factors play within a society. Comparative research plays a vital role in delineating universal attributes of the course of cognitive development as well as finding sources of developmental variation that range beyond those encountered in any one language, culture, or society.

This chapter will focus on the knowledge that children bring to school, because many of the factors associated with differences in academic performance are present before children ever enter first grade. Once children enter school, many of these same factors—linguistic differences, beliefs about learning, parental educational practices—continue to affect learning. With school entry, however, a large set of additional factors are added to the mix. So the focus of this chapter is on what might account for the differences in performance that are found when children begin formal education.

SOURCES OF VARIATION IN MATHEMATICAL DEVELOPMENT

Language and Mathematical Content

It is useful to distinguish differences in the *content* of what children have to learn versus the *contexts* in which they learn it. The appeal of mathematics as a domain for cross-national comparisons lies in the relatively large amount of mathematical content that is universal in nature. Some of this is inherent in the abstract nature of some mathematical concepts; others—such as the universal use of Arabic numerals—reflect historical dispersion of ideas. The relatively large amount of universal content in mathematics makes it a promising domain for looking at the implications of those aspects that differ across languages. The representation of particular mathematical ideas in specific languages can vary in ways that may have consequences for mathematical development. Consider, for example, the term for "triangle" in Chinese and English. The Chinese term [三角形 : san jiao xing] can be literally translated as "three corner shape." The meaning of the English term "triangle" has a similar derivation (from Latin via Middle English), but one that is certainly obscure to most children when they first encounter it (Han & Ginsburg, 2001). If the linguistic representation of a concept is relatively transparent, it may be learned more readily and by younger children, and in turn it may be more likely to be taught by parents and preschool teachers.

Contexts of Learning

In addition to these differences in *content,* there are many ways in which early mathematics is acquired differs across cultures. Parental and societal beliefs about how children learn and what they should learn before entering school may affect the competence children bring to school. Parents may value some activities more than others and that, in turn, can affect the opportunities children have to learn in potentially significant ways.

There is not a simple way to disentangle the threads represented by these various factors because differences in the nature and difficulty of what children have to learn affect the organization and timing of efforts to help children learn. We will first discuss characteristics of the symbolic representation of mathematical ideas in Chinese and English, along with evidence that these differences affect the course of mathematical development. Then we will consider how differences in the nature and organization of social influences on mathematical development can affect children's early mathematical competence.

DIFFERENCES IN WHAT CHILDREN HAVE TO LEARN

Any symbol system created by human minds is organized in some way, and that organization has consequences for both its acquisition and its use. Mathematics is a particularly interesting domain for looking at effects of the organization of symbol systems because mathematical concepts are represented using a variety of different symbol systems, each of which is organized around certain rules. The base-ten system of Arabic numerals can be generated from a set of 10 unique symbols (0–9) and a positional system where successive places increase by powers of ten.

Number Names in Mathematics and Ordinary Language: Transparency of Base Ten Structure

Coexisting with Arabic numerals is another system for designating the value of those numbers in spoken language. Because spoken language has no "places," ordinary language number names form a "named value system" in which the multipliers that correspond to places are instead named. For example, the English name for "100" consists of two morphemes "one" (corresponding to the leading "1") and "hundred" (corresponding to the name of the third place to the left of the decimal point).

The difference between named value and place value systems is inherent in the fact that Arabic numerals are an exclusively written notation, while spoken numbers need to be express-ible in the stream of speech. But spoken number names differ from Arabic numerals in other ways, as well, that have potential consequences for the course of mathematical development in speakers of a particular language (e.g., Miller & Paredes, 1996).

Table 10.1 shows how cardinal number names are represented in Chinese and English. For purposes of comparison, it is useful to break the set of number names down into three ranges: (a) 1–10, (b) 11–19, and (c) 20–99.

Table 10.1

a) From one to ten

Arabic Numeral	1	2	3	4	5	6	7	8	9	10
English	one	two	three	four	five	six	seven	eight	nine	ten
Chinese (written)	一	二	三	四	五	六	七	八	九	十
Chinese (spoken)	yī	èr	sān	sì	wu	liù	qī	bā	jiu	shí

b) Eleven to twenty

Arabic Numeral	11	12	13	14	15	16	17	18	19	20
English	eleven	twelve	thirteen	fourteen	fifteen	sixteen	seventeen	eighteen	nineteen	twenty
Chinese (written)	十一	十二	十三	十四	十五	十六	十七	十八	十九	二十
Chinese (spoken)	shí yī	shí èr	shí sān	shí sì	shí wu	shí liù	shí qī	shí bā	shí jiu	èr shí

c) Twenty to ninety-nine

Language	Rule	Example
English	Decade name (twen,thir,for,fif,six,seven,eight,nine) + "-ty" + unit	thirty-seven
Chinese (written)	Decade unit (two,three,four,five,six,seven,eight,nine)+ten(shi2)+unit	三十七
Chinese (spoken)		sān shí qī

Number names from 1 to 10

In the range 1–10, both languages construct unique number names with no rule used to generate those names (the written Chinese characters for 1–3 are an exception, consisting of the corresponding numbers of horizontal strokes). There is no way to predict that "five" or "五: wu" comes after "four" or "四; si," respectively, in the English and Chinese systems. Thus, there is no rule that can be used to generate number names in any of these sequences in this portion of the list.

From 11 to 19

Above ten, the languages diverge in interesting ways. With one minor exception, Chinese maps directly onto the Hindu–Arabic number system used to write numerals in both countries. For example, a literal translation of "十七: shi qi" (17) into English results in "ten-seven." Chinese number names for numbers in the teens differ from those for other two-digit numbers only in applying a one-deletion rule (Hurford, 1975), in which the value for the tens unit (one) is usually not named (although it is acceptable to name 17 as "一十七: yi shi qi – one ten seven").
　　The formation of number names in English is much more complicated. English names for eleven and twelve bear only an historical relation to "one" and "two" (Menninger, 1969). The names for 13–19 can be derived from the corresponding number names for 3–9, but the derivation is somewhat complicated. Two of the seven numbers in this set modify the sound of the corresponding digit (three → thir, five → fif). More importantly, however, the English system reverses place value compared to the Hindu–Arabic and Chinese systems, following the

rule German uses for 2-digit number names less than 100. Thus, "13" is pronounced "thirteen" rather than "one-ty-three" or even "teen-thir."

From 20 to 99

Above twenty, English becomes much more regular in its formation of number names. Number names are consistently formed from a decade unit (e.g., "twen-") + "-ty" + a unit value in the range 1–9. Except for twenty, thirty, and fifty, the names of decades incorporate the corresponding unit name without modification. The only morphological difference between Chinese and English names for numbers in the range 20–99 is that Chinese is consistent in using unit values for decade names (instead of modifying them as English does in using "twen" for the two-tens decade and "thir" for the three-tens decade) and in using the unmodified name for ten to designate decades (instead of the special "-ty" that English uses). Chinese thus makes explicit the base ten structure of number names, which remains implicit in English.

The structure of number naming systems is well-characterized by Wittgenstein's (1958, p. 8) metaphorical description of language in general: "Our language can be seen as an ancient city: a maze of little streets and squares, of old and new houses, and of houses with additions from various periods; and this surrounded by a multitude of new boroughs with straight regular streets and uniform houses."

As with city streets, names for later numbers in the counting sequence can be generated from rules that are more consistent, straightforward, and transparent than those that generate names for smaller numbers. Although this holds true across a variety of languages (Miller & Paredes, 1995), Chinese and English differ in the length and complexity of the irregular portion of the system of names that must be learned. Possible effects of these differences on early mathematical development will be reviewed in the next section.

Psychological Effects of Number Naming Structure

Learning to Count in Chinese and English

A claim that language influences acquisition of mathematical competence is strengthened if the observed differences in development between speakers of different languages: (a) correspond in a sensible way to specific linguistic differences, (b) appear developmentally when children are acquiring concepts or skills related to those linguistic differences, and (c) are limited to those areas where languages differ. Specificity in identifying the *nature, timing,* and *limits* of cross-linguistic differences is particularly important in cross-cultural research, because cultures differ in a variety of ways (some of which will be reviewed in the second half of this paper) that could lead to global differences in the acquisition of mathematical competence.

Our review of differences in the morphology of cardinal number names in Chinese and English leads to clear predictions about the nature, timing, and limits of differences in counting acquisition that might be expected if the structure of number names is a key source of difficulty in acquisition. Differences should (a) favor Chinese-speaking children, (b) appear when children are learning the number names termed "teens" in English, and (c) be limited to the acquisition of number names and the base ten concept.

What aspects of counting should *not* be affected by differences between English and Chinese? Many aspects of counting are inherent in the underlying definition of enumeration and therefore should be universal across languages. Gelman and Gallistel (1978) described these as a set of counting principles, the first three of which correspond to an operational definition of counting systems, specifying that: (a) there be exactly one tag (such as a number name) per element when counting, (b) the tags be used in a consistent order, and (c) the last tag corresponds to the numerosity of the entire set.

A number of studies have confirmed that the nature, timing, and limits of differences in early counting by Chinese and American children conform to the predictions just described (Fuson & Kwon, 1991; Miller & Stigler, 1987; Miller, Smith, Zhu, & Zhang, 1995). Figure 10.1 shows results from a longitudinal study (Miller, Smith, & Zhang, 2004) in which children in China and the United States were followed in monthly sessions and administered a series of mathematical tasks for abstract counting. The children were asked to recite the number list. The slow and inconsistent progress of two-year-olds was nearly identical in both countries; learning to recite a list of ten items is difficult for young children, whether they be growing up in Beijing or in the U.S. Midwest. Importantly, it was *equally* difficult for children in both countries. Between 3 and 4 years, however, the course of acquisition began to diverge. U.S. children made steady but slow progress in learning the teens number names while Chinese children progressed much more rapidly. Four-year-olds in China made very rapid progress in generalizing number names up to 100 after they could count to approximately 40, while fewer U.S. children grasped the morphological patterns that would allow them to count to 100.

A finer analysis of the differences in early number name acquisition is presented in Figure 10.2, which shows a survival analysis of the first session data from this study, along with a group of five-year-olds included for comparison purposes. This graph shows the percent of children able to count to a given level, so downward deflections of the curve show areas of the number sequence where children had difficulty.

In both countries, less than 10% of this mixed-age group of children were unable to count to ten. Not surprisingly, these were primarily 2-year-olds, but, importantly, this did not differ between the two countries and there was nothing systematic about their stopping points. Counting from 10 to 20 was difficult for Chinese preschoolers, with only about three-quarters

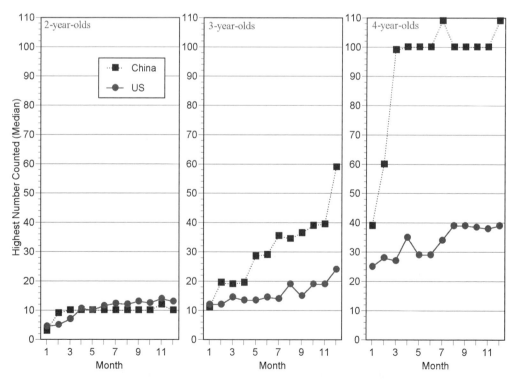

Figure 10.1. Preschoolers' mathematical development in China and the United States. Each panel shows a group of children who were followed for 1 year. Data shows median level of abstract counting performance at each session.

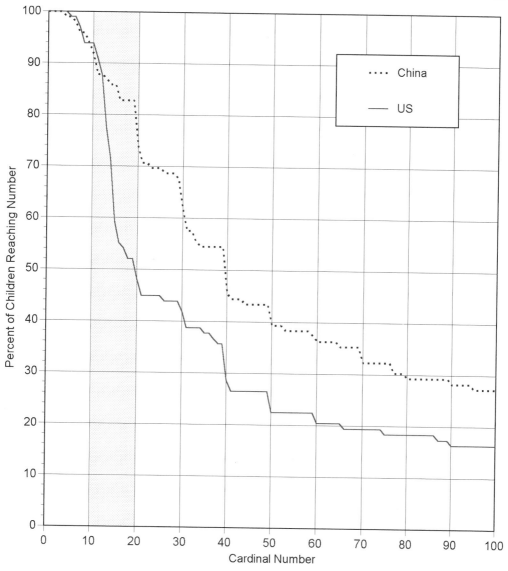

Figure 10.2. Survival plot of children's counting based on the first-session data. Figure shows percentage of a mixed-age group of children who were able to count to a given number. The second ("teens") decade is highlighted. This is the point in the number sequence where significant U.S.–Chinese differences appeared.

able to count to 20, but it was far more difficult for the U.S. children, with fewer than half still counting successfully at 20. After this point, children in both countries tended to stop or make mistakes at decade boundaries, such as counting "37, 38, 39, 20, ... " Survival analyses (McCullagh & Nelder, 1991) of these data confirm what is evident from inspection, that there are no significant differences between the percentage of Chinese and U.S. preschoolers who could count to ten, but that counting from 10 to 20 is significantly easier for Chinese children. Of the children who could count to 20, there was no significant difference in the percentage of American or Chinese preschoolers who could count to 100.

Thus, the nature and timing of differences in early counting between Chinese-speaking and English-speaking preschoolers correspond to predictions based on the morphology of number names. Evidence from object counting indicates that these differences are also limited to aspects of counting that involve number naming. Miller, Smith, Zhu, and Zhang (1995) looked at children's object counting and found that Chinese-speaking children were significantly more likely to report the conventional correct numerosity of a set, but that this was entirely due to a greater likelihood to correctly recite the sequence of names. Coordinating naming numbers and designating objects in counting is quite difficult for young preschoolers—37% of U.S. and 38% of Chinese preschoolers either pointed to an object and did not produce number name, or the reverse, but this did not differ between the two countries. Double-counting or skipping objects was even more common but, again, did not differ between the Chinese and U.S. preschoolers.

Base-Ten Concepts and Arabic Numerals

The structure of number names is associated with a specific, limited difference in the course of counting acquisition between English-speaking and Chinese-speaking children. One area where there may be conceptual consequences of these linguistic differences is in children's understanding of the base-ten principle that underlies the structure of Arabic numerals. This base-ten structure is a feature of a particular representational system rather than a fundamental mathematical fact, but it is a feature that is incorporated into many of the algorithms children learn for performing arithmetic and, thus, is a powerful concept in early mathematical development. Because English number names do not show a base-ten structure as consistently or as early as do Chinese number names, English-speaking children's conceptual understanding of this base-ten structure may be delayed compared to their Chinese-speaking peers. Miura and her colleagues (Miura, 1987; Miura, Okamato, Kim, Steere, & Fayol, 1993; Miura & Okamoto, 2003) have looked at the base ten understanding of two groups of first-grade children, speakers of East Asian languages whose number-naming systems incorporate a clear base-ten structure, usually based on Chinese, versus speakers of European languages that generally do not show a clear base ten structure in their number names. The primary task used has been asking children to represent the cardinal value associated with a given number name using sets of blocks representing units and tens. Children whose native language is Chinese, Korean, or Japanese are consistently more likely to represent numbers as sets of tens and ones as either a first or second choice than are children whose native language is English, French, or Swedish. Ho and Fuson (1998) compared the performance of Chinese-speaking preschool children in Hong Kong with English-speaking children in Britain and the United States and found that half of their Chinese-speaking five-year-olds (but none of their English-speaking children) who could count to at least 50 were able to take advantage of the base-ten structure of number names to quickly determine the answer to addition problems of the form "10 + n = ?," compared to other problems. Fuson and Kwon (1991) argued that the Chinese number naming structure facilitates the use of a tens-complement strategy for early addition. In this approach, when adding numbers whose sum is greater than 10 (e.g., "8 + 7"), the smaller addend is partitioned into the tens-complement of the first addend ("2") and the remainder ("5"); the answer is ten plus that remainder ("10 + 5"). In Chinese-structured number-naming systems, the answer corresponds to the result of the calculation (十五 shi wu − "10 5"); in English there is an additional step as the answer is converted into a different number name ("fifteen"). Fuson and Kwon reported that most Korean first graders they tested used this method before it was explicitly taught in school. Explicit instruction may be required for English-speaking children, but there is evidence that it can be quite successful even with children from at-risk populations. Fuson and her colleagues (Fuson, Smith, & Lo Cicero, 1997) report success with explicitly tutoring low-SES urban first graders about the base ten structure of numbers, with the result that their end-of-year arithmetic performance approximated that reported for East Asian children.

Towse and Saxton (1997; 1998) have argued that the effects of number terms are greatly influenced by task and instructional demands. In the context of Miura's task requiring children to represent cardinal numbers with blocks, they found that presenting English-speaking students with a "20" block increased the likelihood that they would use different units of blocks to construct numbers in the 20s and that minimal prompting was sufficient to induce English-speaking children to use multiple units. Towse and Saxton concluded that the difficulty English-speaking children have may be largely limited to difficulty understanding the irregular "teens" of English and may also in part be due to social factors of the type to be reviewed in the second section of this chapter.

Ordinal Numbers

Chinese forms ordinal numbers by adding an ordinal prefix (第: di) to the cardinal number name, in contrast to the more complex English ordinals (first, second, third, etc.) that often bear no clear relation to the corresponding cardinal number name. Because of this complexity, it is possible to study in older English-speaking children some of the counting acquisition processes previously described for preschoolers. Miller, Major, Shu, and Zhang (2000) reported differences between Chinese and U.S. children in the ability to count with ordinal numbers that far exceeded that found for cardinals (indeed, even at fourth grade, fewer than half of the U.S. sample could count correctly with ordinal numbers above "thirtieth"). Because it is not common to hear larger ordinal numbers, children used their understanding of number morphology to generate names. This resulted in three error patterns. The first involved overgeneralizing the "cardinal name + -th" transformation, producing names like "twenty-oneth." The second was a variant of the first, one that involved ordinalizing part of the number, producing numbers such as "twentieth-one." The final pattern involved treating "teenth" as an ordinalizing suffix, producing "twentyone-teenth." What is noteworthy here is that children did not ever misapply the ordinalizing rules to numbers in the teen, e.g., by producing names such as "third-teen." This is consistent with the view that English teen names do have a special status (Miller & Zhu, 1991; Towse & Saxton, 1998) that makes it difficult to access the base-ten status of those numbers.

Rational Numbers

The linguistic representation of fractions in Chinese differs from that used in English in three ways. Chinese names the fraction X/Y using the frame "Y 分之 X" (literally Y parts [attributive] X). This reverses the order used in English by naming the denominator before the numerator. The structural frame for naming fractions in Chinese also incorporates a common word that corresponds to "pieces" or "units" in a variety of settings, including the unit of money corresponding to a penny. English, by contrast, signals fraction names by using the ordinal term for the denominator and then making it plural (as in "three-ninths"), with the exception of "half" and "quarter." The difficulty English-speaking children have with ordinal names has been described, so the use of ordinal number names in generating the names for rational numbers may be a stumbling block for English speakers. Finally, the names for the components of a fraction may also be more transparent than those in English; the words for numerator and denominator correspond to "fraction child" (分子: fen zi), and "fraction mother" (分母: fen mu), respectively.

Miura, Okamoto, Vlahovic-Stetic, Kim, and Han (1999) compared U.S. and Croatian children (whose languages are similar in their names for fractions) with Korean children (Korean uses the Chinese structural frame for naming fractions) in their ability to match fractions with drawings showing a fractional part shaded in. Children in all countries performed poorly at the middle of grade 1, although the Korean children mastered the task by the start of grade 2, in contrast to the U.S. and Croatian children, who showed little improvement. Paik and Mix (2003) reported a similar study comparing U.S. and Korean children but found a smaller advantage for Koreans than Miura et al. had reported. In both countries, the most common mistake involved children picking a foil that showed the same number of parts as the sum of the numerator + denominator, with a number of parts corresponding to the numerator shaded in (i.e., for 3/5 they would pick a display that had 3 parts shaded and 5 parts unshaded, although it really corresponded to 3/8). In a second study, they presented U.S. children with fraction names reworded to emphasize the part–whole nature of rational numbers (e.g., "one of four parts" or "of four parts, one") and found significant improvement for first graders with this wording.

The concept of a fraction is a difficult one for a variety of reasons. Sophian, Garyantes, and Chang (1997) argued that the fact that dividing into *more* pieces or increasing the denominator means that one has *less* in each piece is counterintuitive. Gelman and Meck (1992) argued that preschoolers view all mathematical tasks as "opportunities to count," which is likely to lead one astray when it comes to thinking about rational numbers.

Simple, consistent, and transparent language may make concepts more accessible than they would otherwise be, but some concepts will certainly remain difficult for children to grasp. In our lab, we have been videotaping classes on rational number in China and the United States at grades 4 and 5. We have been struck by how much time U.S. teachers need to spend on teaching children the terms "numerator" and "denominator," often coming up with non-mathematical mnemonics such as "Notre Dame" to help children remember these terms. Chinese teachers do not face these difficulties, but rational number remains a difficult and somewhat counterintuitive concept, nonetheless.

Language and Arithmetic

Research comparing the mental arithmetic of adults educated in China with those educated in North America has shown consistent differences in speed and accuracy of calculation favoring those educated in Chinese school systems. In the most complete study, Campbell & Xue (2001) compared Canadian college students of Chinese or non-Asian origin with Chinese university students educated in Asia on both basic and multistep arithmetic. For simple arithmetic, the two Chinese-origin groups performed equally well and were superior to the non-Asian Canadians. For complex arithmetic, however, Chinese students educated in Asia outperformed both Canadian groups. The differences resulted from differences in the efficiency of retrieval and in the frequency with which subjects resorted to using procedural strategies. The differences between the two Canadian-educated groups are of particular interest, because both were educated in the same school system.

It is unlikely that there is a single source for these differences in calculation speed among adults. A first step in disentangling the factors that contribute to these adult differences is to look at their origin. Geary, Bow-Thomas, Liu, and Siegler (1996) reported that significant differences in calculation skill already exist when children enter first grade. They reported substantial differences in speed of arithmetic as well as in the sophistication of strategies used by U.S. and Chinese children starting at the end of the preschool period in kindergarten along with differences in digit span favoring Chinese speakers in the sophistication of arithmetic starting in kindergarten. Stigler, Lee, and Stevenson (1986) reported a similar digit-span advantage for Chinese speakers starting in kindergarten. They argued that, as with other cross-language differences in digit span, it can be explained by pronunciation rate (Chinese digits are all single syllables, and Chinese has a simpler syllable structure than English). Geary et al. argued that other differences were most likely the result of differences in opportunities to learn in school and at home, instructional methods, and parental emphasis—all issues that will be considered in the following section.

The research reviewed in this section shows that the linguistic representation of mathematical concepts in ordinary language can affect the ease of acquisition of these concepts. The coupling between concepts and ordinary language representations is, however, a loose and probabilistic one. As an analogy, consider a sidewalk that has a loose paving block. Most pedestrians will not trip over it, but it is likely that those who do trip in that area will stumble over this obstruction. The linguistic representation of mathematical concepts in particular languages can present stumbling blocks for children, but ones that can be overcome with instruction aimed at making clear what language obscures. Cross-linguistic research of the kind described here is useful in distinguishing the problems in mathematical development that reflect features of particular languages from those that stem from more general limitations of children's cognitive development.

DIFFERENCES IN THE CONTEXT OF LEARNING

In addition to the role of linguistic differences in the content of mathematics children learn, there are a variety of cultural factors that affect the contexts in which they learn it. These range from differences in the value placed on different activities, beliefs about how children learn and what they should learn when, and decisions about how to organize early mathematical learning. These factors interact with linguistic differences. As we will describe later, middle-class American parents put a great emphasis on teaching children the alphabet. This is a difficult task for preschoolers, but it is a key step toward literacy. Chinese parents teach their children some characters, but there is not a well-defined set of characters children are expected to know before starting first grade. Thus, parental values, children's interests, and the nature of what children need to learn can interact to produce differences in the informal education children receive before they begin formal education.

Parental Practices

Value Placed on Early Mathematics

Mothers of kindergartners in both China and the United States considered literacy skills the most important thing that they themselves learned in first grade (Kelly, 2002). However, when the same mothers were asked to rate how important the mastery of particular math and literacy skills before entry to first grade is for academic success, a different picture emerged. Mothers in China rated literacy and mathematical skills as equally important; U.S. mothers showed a clear bias toward rating the various literacy skills higher than the mathematical skills. Thus, some of the differences in math and reading ability that have been found when comparing young children in China and the United States may be due to the relative importance placed on reading and math skills by mothers in each country (Kelly, 2002).

One reason for the relative emphasis on mathematics in China may be the relatively high importance it plays in school (Stevenson & Lee, 1990). Reviewing research on differences in mathematics education among China, Japan, and the United States, Hatano (1990) argued that, in the same way that different countries emphasize different sports, school mathematics is a national intellectual pursuit in East Asian countries but not in the United States.

This is interesting in light of Cohen's (1982, pp. 3–4) work on numeracy in early American history, which includes this passage:

"We are a traveling and a calculating people," said Ohio booster James Hall in his book *Statistics of the West*, with evident satisfaction. "Arithmetic I presume comes by instinct among this guessing, reckoning, expecting and calculating people," said English traveler Thomas Hamilton, with evident distaste. Each man attached a different value to the idea, but both agreed that Americans in the 1830s had some sort of innate reckoning skill that set them apart from Europeans.

Taken together, these two evaluations suggest that cultural emphases on intellectual activities and accomplishments can change over time in the same way that preferred sports can. But it should not be surprising that the values of schools and the broader culture should also affect what parents try to teach their preschool children.

Indirect evidence for cohort changes in the importance of mathematics in the United States comes from work by Geary, Salthouse, Chen, & Fan (1996), who looked at college students and elderly adults in China and the United States. Geary and colleagues found that younger and older Americans showed comparable arithmetical abilities, although the Chinese population showed the decline with age that appeared on the other cognitive tasks included in the study. Although the evidence is indirect, it suggests that changes in computational skills within the lifetime of some living Americans are substantial enough to outweigh the cognitive decline that aging typically brings.

Belief and Ability

There is a fairly clear relationship between parental beliefs and child academic abilities. Kelly (2002) found that in two locations in China where mothers favored math skills over reading skills, children's reported math abilities were more advanced than in those in the United States or in other locations in China. In the United States, where mothers favored reading over math skills, children's reading abilities were more advanced. These differences correspond to results of studies of both preschoolers and older children. Blevins-Knabe and Musun-Miller (1996) found that the amount of time parents reported spending doing number-related activities with their preschoolers was a good predictor of their children's mathematical competence. Looking at mothers of first graders as well as older children in China, Japan, and the United States, Uttal, Lummis, and Stevenson (1988) found no differences in the reports of mothers of high-, average-, and low-achieving mathematics students in the amount of time spent studying or watching television by their children, but they did find that achievement was related to factors such as mothers' satisfaction with their child's performance and ratings of their child's mathematics abilities. Chao (2001) found that parenting style also has differential effects between cultures. She found that authoritative and authoritarian parenting styles can be associated with different school achievement patterns, depending on the child's culture. Higher school achievement is associated with authoritarian parenting in Chinese immigrant families and with authoritative parenting in European American families. Given this finding that general parenting practices such as discipline have culturally differentiated effects on academic achievement, it seems particularly important to examine practices that are directly related to academic achievement.

Interwoven with cultural differences in beliefs and academic achievement are cultural differences in parents' educational practices. Stevenson et al. (1990b) found that U.S. mothers and mothers in Taiwan reported similar levels of educational activities with their preschool children but that this changed dramatically with school entry. Mothers of first graders in Taiwan significantly increased their educational involvement as their children began first grade, but this did not occur with their sample in Minneapolis. Kelly (2002) also found that mothers of U.S. kindergartners reported doing more to prepare their children for first grade than did mothers in China. These preparations are the most likely link between parent belief and child academic ability in kindergartners, and there were cross-cultural differences in what mothers reported doing to prepare their children. The major difference in math preparation of U.S.

children and those in China was that mothers in the United States reported doing more to prepare their children for reading than for math, whereas mothers in China reported doing the same amount of preparation for math and reading. Thus, in reported behavior as well as in beliefs, U.S. mothers privilege early reading over mathematics competence.

In addition to beliefs about particular skills and the parental practices directed at those skills are beliefs about the factors that will account for later academic achievement. Stevenson, Stigler, and Lee (1998) found that mothers in Japan and Taiwan were more likely to believe that academic achievement is related to effort, whereas mothers in the United States were more likely to believe that academic ability is related to innate intellectual ability. This difference in beliefs may be one of the factors influencing differences in school involvement patterns, with mothers in China increasing involvement as their children begin school and mothers in the U.S. decreasing their involvement. A belief that effort is both a sign of intelligence and a key to success may lead to more involvement in directing effort during schooling. Alternatively, a belief that innate abilities are responsible for academic success may lead to involvement in providing early opportunities to develop skills but a lessening of involvement once schooling begins, with the assumption that the development of innate ability is not influenced by effort.

It also appears that cultural differences in parental expectations play a role in the observed cultural differences in mathematics achievement. Studies examining parental expectations for their child's schooling and profession in China and the United States show either higher expectations by U.S. parents or no difference (Stevenson et al., 1990b; Kelly, 2002). The critical difference in expectations seems to be specific to mathematics. Parents in China express less satisfaction with their child's performance, show more awareness of problems, and expect higher grades from their child than do mothers in the U.S. (Crystal & Stevenson, 1991; Stevenson et al., 1990b). U.S. mothers were found by Crystal and Stevenson to be less aware of problems their children were having in mathematics, but reported more problems related to basic calculation that did mothers in China. These findings suggest that added to mothers' increased involvement in schooling in China are higher expectations and greater and perhaps more detailed awareness of their child's performance.

One potential source of cross-national differences in parental expectations and knowledge of their child's academic performance is the communication between school and home. Kelly (2002) found that the majority of mothers in U.S. cities and Beijing believed they knew what abilities and skills the school would expect their child to have on entering first grade, but the source of that knowledge was different. A third of the mothers in Beijing had been informed by the school of what would be expected of their child in first grade. The U.S. mothers reported that their information came from the experience of an older child, a friend's child, or their own experience.

The picture that emerges from these surveys points to three important factors that have apparent consequences for the nature of early mathematical development.

1. U.S. parents tend to privilege reading over mathematics in preparing their children for school, compared to Chinese parents who show more balance between these two areas.
2. U.S. parents are more likely than Chinese parents to attribute success and failure to innate factors rather than to effort.
3. Finally, a relative lack of communication between home and school may make it difficult for U.S. parents to coordinate with schools any educational efforts they undertake. Stevenson and Stigler (1992) noted that parents of preschoolers in their Minneapolis sample devoted a relatively large amount of effort to teaching their children academic subjects before school started. When school started, that effort switched to nonacademic concerns (such as music lessons, athletics, etc.), at the same time that their East Asian parents were becoming heavily involved in helping their children with their schoolwork.

Because of the large immigrant population in the United States, it is possible to observe how some of these factors play out in Chinese American families. Huntsinger and her colleagues (Huntsinger, Jose, Larson, Balsink, & Shaligram, 2000) reported results of a 4-year longitudinal study comparing Chinese American and European American families, beginning in grade 1. Chinese American parents spent more time teaching, used more formal teaching methods, and expected their children to do much more homework, often assigning their own homework. Chinese American parents had higher expectations for their children, and their children performed better at school than the comparison group.

Surveys of parental attitudes and practices about mathematics yield a consistent picture showing a relative de-emphasis on the part of U.S. parents when compared with their Chinese counterparts. Exacerbating this difference may be the relative lack of communication with schools, which means that there is not a clear means of providing feedback about the importance of achievement in this area.

CONCLUSION

By the time children enter school, substantial differences in the mathematical competence of North American and East Asian children already exist. These differences reflect differences in the consistency and transparency of the linguistic representation of number as well as differences in parental beliefs and practices.

Language, culture, beliefs, and practices are interwoven influences affecting the course of early mathematical development. Not only are they often confounded with each other, but they also play off each other in ways that make simple causal conclusions nearly impossible to draw. For example, if something is difficult for children to understand, they are likely to resist efforts by their parents to learn or practice it. Busy parents are, in turn, likely to be guided in part by their children's predilections, unless achievement in a particular area is seen as so important as to override such preferences.

Despite the difficulty of isolating particular causes for cross-cultural variation in development, cross-cultural comparisons can play a critical role in understanding the nature of mathematical development. There are three main reasons that this is the case. First, some factors, such as linguistic representation in one's native language, differ only between cultures. Therefore, looking at a monolingual group would never permit one to understand which aspects of mathematics are affected by language. Second, the range of variation of values, beliefs, and achievement between cultures can greatly exceed that found within the confines of any national group. Finally, identification of those features of mathematical development that are universal can only be done on the basis of comparison between children growing up in different cultural settings.

The research summarized in this chapter focuses on the concepts and skills that children bring with them when they begin formal education. As such, it can be useful in identifying areas where instructional efforts can overcome the limitations presented by language and early experience. Although the base ten structure of number names is less obvious to children who speak English, for example, there are effective methods for teaching these concepts (e.g., Carpenter et al., 1999). The differences in mathematical understanding that children bring to school, while stark, need not imply that these initial differences should either persist or even widen. Rather, they should stand as a challenge and a call to action to find effective ways to help children build upon the skills and to overcome the limitations of what they bring with them as they enter school.

ACKNOWLEDGMENT

Preparation of this chapter was supported by NSF grant BCS 00-79973 to the first author.

REFERENCES

Beaton, A. E., & Robitaille, D. F. (1999). An overview of the Third International Mathematics and Science Study. In E. L. G. Kaiser & I. Huntley (Ed.), *International comparisons in mathematics education* (pp. 30–47). London: Falmer Press.

Blevins-Knabe, B., & Musun-Miller, L. (1996). Number use at home by children and their parents and its relationship to early mathematical performance. *Early Development & Parenting, 5*(1), 35–45.

Brown, M. (1998). The tyranny of the international horse race. In R. Slee, G. Weiner & S. Tomlinson (Eds.), *School effectiveness for whom? Challenges to the school effectiveness and school improvement movements* (pp. 33–47). London: Falmer Press.

Campbell, J. I. D., & Xue, Q. (2001). Cognitive arithmetic across cultures. *Journal of Experimental Psychology: General, 130*, 299–315.

Carpenter, T. P., Fennema, E., Fuson, K., Hiebert, J., Human, P., Murray, H. (1999). Learning basic number concepts and skills as problem solving. In E. Fennema & T. A. Romberg (Eds.), *Mathematics classrooms that promote understanding* (pp. 45–61).

Chao, R. K. (2001). Extending research on the consequences of parenting style for Chinese Americans and European Americans. *Child Development, 72*(6): 1832–1843.

Cohen, P. C. (1982). *A calculating people: The spread of numeracy in early America.* Chicago, IL: Chicago.

Crystal, D. S., & H. W. Stevenson (1991). Mothers' perceptions of children's problems with mathematics: A cross-national comparison. *Journal of Educational Psychology, 83*(3): 372–376.

Fuson, K. C., & Kwon, Y. (1991). Chinese-based regular and European irregular systems of number words: The disadvantages for English-speaking children. In K. Durkin & B. Shire (Eds.), *Language and mathematical education* (pp. 211–226). Milton Keynes: Open University Press.

Fuson, K. C., & Kwon, Y. (1992). Korean children's understanding of multidigit addition and subtraction. *Child Development, 63*(2), 491–506.

Fuson, K. C., Smith, S. T., & Lo Cicero, A. M. (1997). Supporting Latino first graders' ten-structured thinking in urban classrooms. *Journal for Research in Mathematics Education, 28*(6), 738–766.

Geary, D. C., Bow-Thomas, C. C., Liu, F., & Siegler, R. S. (1996). Development of arithmetical competencies in Chinese and American children: Influence of age, language, and schooling. *Child Development, 67,* 2022–2044.

Geary, D. C., Salthouse, T. A., Chen, G. P., & Fan, L. (1996). Are East Asian versus American differences in arithmetical ability a recent phenomenon? *Developmental Psychology, 32,* 254–262.

Gelman, R., & Gallistel, C. R. (1978). *The child's understanding of number.* Cambridge, MA: Harvard University Press.

Gelman, R., & Meck, B. (1992). Early principles aid initial but not later conceptions of number. In J. Bideaud, C. Meljac, & J.-P. Fisscher (Eds.), *Pathways to number: Children's developing numerical abilities* (pp. 171–189). Hillsdale, NJ: Erlbaum.

Han, Y., & Ginsburg, H. P. (2001). Chinese and English mathematics language: The relation between linguistic clarity and mathematics performance. *Mathematical Thinking & Learning, 3,* 201–220.

Hatano, G. (1990). Toward the cultural psychology of mathematical cognition. Comment on Stevenson, H. W., Lee, S.-Y. (1990). *Contexts of achievement. Monographs of the Society for Research in Child Development, 55* (1–2, Serial No. 221), 108–115.

Ho, C. S.-H., & Fuson, K. C. (1998). Children's knowledge of teen quantities as tens and ones: Comparisons of Chinese, British, and American kindergartners. *Journal of Educational Psychology, 90*(3), 1536–1544.

Huntsinger, C. S., Jose, P. E., Larson, S. L., Balsink, K. D., & Shaligram, C. (2000). Mathematics, vocabulary, and reading development in Chinese American and European American children over the primary school years. *Journal of Educational Psychology, 92*(4), 745–760.

Hurford, J. R. (1975). *The linguistic theory of numerals.* Cambridge, U.K.: Cambridge University Press.

Husén, T. (1967). *International study of achievement in mathematics.* New York: Wiley.

Husén, T. (1987). Policy impact of i.e.,A research. *Comparative Educational Review, 31*(1), 129–136.

Kelly, M.K. (2002). Getting ready for school: A cross-cultural comparison of parent and child beliefs about and preparations for entry into first grade in China and the United States. *Dissertation Abstracts International, 63*(11-B), 5550 (University Microfilms No. 3070347).

McCullagh, P., & Nelder, A. (1991). *Generalized linear models* (2nd ed.). New York: Chapman & Hall.

Miller, K. F., & Paredes, D. R. (1996). On the shoulders of giants: Cultural tools and mathematical development. In R. Sternberg & T. Ben-Zeev (Eds.), *The nature of mathematical thinking* (pp. 83–117). Hillsdale, NJ: Erlbaum.

Miller, K. F., Major, S. M., Shu, H., & Zhang, H. (2000). Ordinal knowledge: Number names and number concepts in Chinese and English. *Canadian Journal of Experimental Psychology, 54*(2), 129–140.

Miller, K. F., Smith, C. M., Zhu, J., & Zhang, H. (1995). Preschool origins of cross-national differences in mathematical competence: The role of number-naming systems.

Miller, K. F., Smith, C. M., & Zhang, H. (2004). *Language and number: A longitudinal study of learning to count in Chinese and English.* Unpublished manuscript, University of Illinois at Urbana-Champaign.

Miller, K. F., & Zhu, J. (1991). The trouble with teens: Accessing the structure of number names. *Journal of Memory & Language, 30*(1), 48–68.

Miller, M. F., & Stigler, J. (1987). Counting in Chinese: Cultural variation in basic cognitive skill. *Cognitive Development, 2,* 279–305.

Miura, I. T. (1987). Mathematics achievement as a function of language. *Journal of Educational Psychology, 79,* 79–82.

Miura, I. T., Okamoto, Y., Kim, C. C., Steere, M., & Fayol, M. (1993). First graders' cognitive representation of number and understanding of place value: Cross-national comparisons—France, Japan, Korea, Sweden, and the United States. *Journal of Educational Psychology, 85,* 24–30.

Miura, I. T., & Okamoto, Y. (2003). Language supports for mathematics understanding and performance. In A. J. Baroody & A. Dowker (Eds.), *The development of arithmetic concepts and skills: Constructing adaptive expertise. Studies in mathematical thinking and learning* (pp. 229–242).

Miura, I. T., Okamoto, Y., Vlahovi-Stetic, V., Kim, C. C., & Han, J. H. (1999). Language supports for children's understanding of numerical fractions: Cross-national comparisons. *Journal of Experimental Child Psychology, 74*, 356–365.

Mix, K. S., Levine, S. C., & Huttenlocher, J. (1999). Early fraction calculation ability. *Developmental Psychology, 35*(1), 164–174.

Paik, J. H., & Mix, K. S. (2003). U.S. and Korean children's comprehension of fraction names: A reexamination of cross-national differences. *Child Development, 74*(1), 144–154.

Peak, L. (1996). *Pursuing excellence: A study of U.S. eighth-grade mathematics and science achievement in international context.* Washington, DC: U.S. Government Printing Office.

Peak, L. (1997). *Pursuing excellence: A study of U.S. fourth-grade mathematics and science achievement in international context.* Washington, DC: U.S. Government Printing Office.

Saxe, J. G. (1963). *The blind men and the elephant.* New York: Whittlesey House.

Saxton, M., & Towse, J. N. (1998). Linguistic relativity: The case of place value in multi-digit numbers. *Journal of Experimental Child Psychology, 69*(1), 66–79.

Siegler, R. S., & Jenkins, E. A. (1989). *How children discover new strategies.* Hillsdale, NJ: Erlbaum.

Sophian, C., Garyantes, D., & Chang, C. (1997). When three is less than two: Early developments in children's understanding of fractional quantities. *Developmental Psychology, 33*(5), 731–744.

Stevenson, H. W., & Lee, S. (1998). An examination of American student achievement from an international perspective. In D. Ravitch (Ed.), *The state of student performance in American schools* (pp. 7–52). Washington, DC: Brookings.

Stevenson, H. W., Lee, S.-Y., Chen, C., Lummis, M., Stigler, J. W., Fan, L., & Ge, F. (1990a). Mathematics achievement of children in China and the United States. *Child Development, 61*(4), 1053–1066.

Stevenson, H. W., Lee, S.-Y.., Chen, C., Stigler, J. W., Hsu, C. C., & Kitamura, S. (1990b). Contexts of achievement: A study of American, Chinese, and Japanese children. *Monographs of the Society for Research in Child Development, 55* (Serial No. 221).

Stevenson, H. W., & Stigler, J. W. (1992). *The learning gap: Why our schools are failing and what we can learn from Japanese and Chinese education.* New York: Summit.

Stigler, J. W., Lee, S. Y., & Stevenson, H. W. (1986). Digit memory in Chinese and English: Evidence for a temporally limited store. *Cognition, 23*(1), 1–20.

Stigler, J. W., & Perry, M. (1988). Mathematics learning in Japanese, Chinese, and American classrooms. *New Directions for Child Development. No, 41*, 27–54.

Tobin, J. J., Wu, D. Y. H., & Davidson, D. (1989). *Preschool in three cultures.* New Haven: Yale.

Towse, J. N., & Saxton, M. (1997). Linguistic influences on children's number concepts: Methodological and theoretical considerations. *Journal of Experimental Child Psychology, 66*(3), 362–375.

Towse, J. N., & Saxton, M. (1998). Mathematics across national boundaries: Cultural and linguistic perspectives on numerical competence. In C. Donlan (Ed.), *The development of mathematical skills.* (pp 129–150) Hove, U.K.: Psychology Press.

Travers, K., J., & Weinzweig, A. I. (1999). The Second International Mathematics Study. In E. L. G. Kaiser & I. Huntley (Eds.), *International comparisons in mathematics education* (pp. 19–29). London: Falmer Press.

Uttal, D. H., Lummis, M., & Stevenson, H. W. (1988). Low and high mathematics achievement in Japanese, Chinese, and American elementary-school children. *Developmental Psychology, 24*(3): 335–342.

Wittengenstein, L. (1958). *Philosophical investigation* (3rd ed.). New York: Macmillan.

11

Magnitude Representation in Children
Its Development and Dysfunction

Marie-Pascale Noël
Laurence Rousselle
Christophe Mussolin

INTRODUCTION

The semantics of a given number is rich. For instance, the semantics of nine could include information such as "is larger than eight," "is close to ten," "is the square of three," "is an odd number," and "is the age of my elder son." Among these, the magnitude is extremely important. Miller and Gelman (1983) showed that when kindergartners and third graders are presented with triads of single digits and asked to select the two that are the more closely related to one another and the two that are the least, they base their judgments on magnitude information only. Later on, in sixth grade, magnitude is still the more used dimension, although other dimensions such as parity are used, also.

Magnitude of numbers refers to the cases in which numbers are used in a cardinal context, that is, when they denote the "manyness" of a set (e.g., five is the number of fingers I have on one hand; see Fuson, 1992). In reference to this cardinal concept, learning takes place along two directions. One of them is the distinction between the transformations that do or do not modify the cardinal of a set (e.g., spatial transformations, such as spreading or grouping the items, do not modify the cardinal, whereas addition or subtraction of items does). The other is the comparison between the cardinal of different sets (e.g., set A's cardinal could be smaller, larger, or equal to set B's). The child first learns these notions through his/her experience with sets of real objects. But later on, the child will learn to reason with symbols, such as words or Arabic numerals.

This chapter focuses on the magnitude comparison of numbers. The first part of the chapter will briefly present the effects that have been encountered in magnitude comparison tasks with adults as well as the models that have been proposed to account for these data. The second part of the chapter will review studies that have traced the development of these effects. The third part will aim at identifying the age at which number magnitude starts to be automatically activated in children. Finally, we will consider the hypothesis that developmental dyscalculia could be due to a basic dysfunction in representing number magnitude.

CLASSICAL EFFECTS REPORTED IN ADULT STUDIES AND EXPLANATORY MODELS

Adult studies of number magnitude comparison have identified several robust effects. First, response times (RTs) decrease monotonously as the numerical distance between the two numbers increases (e.g., 7–8 versus 7–2). This *distance effect* was observed first by Moyer and Landauer (1967) but has been replicated frequently since (e.g., Banks, Fujii, & Kayra-Stuart, 1976). Second, for equal numerical distance, RTs increase with the size of the numbers (e.g., –3 versus 7–8). This *size effect* has also been reported many times (e.g., Antell & Keating, 1983; Strauss & Curtis, 1981). Third, the *semantic congruity effect* (first observed by Banks, Fujii, & Kayra-Stuart, 1976) refers to the fact that large numbers are more quickly compared under the instructions to "choose the larger" as opposed to "choose the smaller," whereas small numbers are more quickly compared under the instructions to "choose the smaller." Finally, a *spatial congruency effect* has also been reported: subjects who respond "larger" with their right hand are faster than subjects who answer "larger" with their left hand (Dehaene, Dupoux, & Mehler, 1990).

Several models have been proposed to account for these effects, but, broadly speaking, two theoretical types of models can be distinguished: the symbolic and the analogue models of magnitude comparison.

Banks's Semantic Coding Model

The semantic coding model proposed by Banks and colleagues (Banks, Clark, & Lucy, 1975; Banks, Fujii, & Kayra-Stuart, 1976; Banks, 1977) belongs to the first type of models. It assumes that comparison is held on discrete codes and follows two processing steps: an encoding and a comparison stage. In the encoding stage, a very crude semantic description of the numbers is generated: each of them is independently coded as larger (L+) or smaller (S+) than a cutoff criterion. The value of the cutoff point would vary from trial to trial and present a skewed distribution that places its mean below the arithmetic midpoint of the digits used in the experiment. This is due to the compressive mapping of digits onto subjective magnitude. Consequently, smaller numbers are spaced farther apart on the subjective continuum than larger numbers, and the cutoff is more likely to fall between two small numbers than between two large ones. When considering a pair of numbers to compare, two possibilities can thus be encountered at this first stage: either the codes attributed to the two numbers are different (L+/S+) or they are identical (L+/L+ or S+/S+). In the latter case, more precise coding of the two numbers is needed to determine which of the two large digits is the larger one (e.g., L and L+) or which of the two small digits is the smaller one (e.g., S and S+).

When *discriminable* codes are finally obtained, the comparison stage can take place. At this stage, a correct response is computed by matching the instructional codes (e.g., "choose the larger") with the codes generated by the encoding stage. In the case of an L+/S+ pair, the response is easily computed. However, in the case of an L+/L pair, it is easier to provide a correct response under the instruction "choose the larger" than under the instruction "choose the smaller." Indeed, in the latter situation, a transformation of the initial labels is needed to match the instructions: the L+/L labels will have to be recoded into S/S+. The same reasoning can be held for S/S+ pairs under the instructions "choose the larger."

In this model, the distance effect is easily explained: digits that are farther apart are likely to be coded differently right away, whereas digits that are close are more likely to share the same primary coding and thus to need further semantic elaboration before comparison. The size effect comes about because the cutoff point is usually placed among the smaller numbers. Consequently, large digits are more likely to fall beyond the cutoff point and to share the same initial coding as the small digits. They will thus need further elaboration of the initial coding, which will slow down the encoding stage. Finally, the semantic congruity effect emerges because the codes of the digits depend on the overall size of the pair, and the comparison stage is faster when the codes of the digits match the form of the instructional codes. Otherwise, the initial labels have to be transformed to match the instructions, and this supplementary processing step slows down the response. However, this model cannot account for the spatial congruity effect.

Banks's semantic coding model thus postulates that the comparison takes place on discrete or categorical information, although an analogue representation of numbers is assumed in memory. On the contrary, analogue models assume that comparison takes place directly on this analogue medium.

Analogue Models

The assumption of a comparison process acting directly on analogue representations of number magnitude can be traced back to rather old papers, such as in Moyer and Landauer (1967) or Restle (1970). This type of model automatically accounts for the distance effect since numerically close numbers are also close on the analogue medium and thus more difficult to disambiguate than more distant numbers. Yet, two possible explanations have been proposed to account for the size effect: one in the context of the accumulator model and the other under the number line model.

The accumulator model was first proposed by Mech and Church (1983) and elaborated by Gallistel and Gelman (1992). According to this model, when faced with a collection of objects, the individual's accumulator fills up proportionally to the number of items to enumerate; for each counted entity, a fixed quantity of energy is delivered into the accumulator. The final state of the accumulator then represents the numerosity of the array. Yet, as the quantity of energy entering the accumulator may vary slightly from one trial to the next, the state of the accumulator for a given numerosity presents a variability that increases with the size of that numerosity. In other words, magnitude representation is approximate and the variability of the mental magnitude distribution for a given numerosity increases proportionally with the numerosity (i.e., scalar variability; see Cordes, Gelman, Gallistel, & Whalen, 2001, for recent data on this point). Such an assumption can account for the size effect, as the representations of the magnitude of two large numbers are noisier and more difficult to compare than those of two small numbers.

The other way to explain the size effect has been to assume that magnitude representations are quite precise but that the mapping on the analogue medium is not linear. According to Dehaene, for instance (Dehaene, Dupoux, & Mehler, 1990; Dehaene, 1992), the mental number line would be compressed in such a way that for equal numerical distance, the subjective distance between the corresponding mental representations would be smaller as the size of the numbers increases. This relationship would follow a logarithmic curve such as defined by the Weber–Fechner law (i.e., the subjective distance between two numbers would be a function of the difference between their logarithms). Such an assumption makes it possible to account for the size effect, as small numbers are farther apart on the number line than large numbers.

If the analogue models easily account for the distance and size effects, they are less suited to explain the semantic congruity effect. Yet, they are perfectly able to account for the spatial congruency effect: subjects who respond "larger" with their right hand are faster than subjects who answer "larger" with their left hand because the number line is spatially oriented with the small numbers being coded on the left and large numbers on the right. Congruency between the spatial orientation of the number line and the orientation of the answer key allows faster responses.

Yet, the origin of this effect is still a matter of debate. This spatial bias or SNARC effect (Spatial–Numerical Association Response Code) was first reported in a parity judgment task (saying if a number is odd or even; Dehaene, Bossini, & Giraux, 1993). But Dehaene et al. (1993) showed that this spatial orientation was inverted for Iranian subjects and might, thus, be related to cultural habits such as the direction of reading. Other authors have also shown that it can be manipulated by experimental instructions (Bächtold, Baumüller, & Brugger, 1998). Furthermore, one may wonder whether this SNARC effect is really linked to the magnitude information of numbers or simply to their ordinal characteristics. Indeed, a SNARC effect has also been obtained with non-numerical ordinal series such as the letters of the alphabet or the months of the year (see Gevers, Reynvoet, & Fias, 2003, for an in-depth discussion of this point, and see chapter 3 in this volume).

APPEARANCE AND MODULATION OF THESE EFFECTS THROUGHOUT CHILDHOOD

In this second section, we will trace the appearance of the effects reported in the comparison literature and describe their developmental modulation throughout childhood. The first part of the section will deal with perceptual comparison in infants and preschoolers, whereas the second part will cover symbolic comparison in school-aged children.

Perceptual Comparison in Infants and Preschoolers

The Facts

To test discrimination capacities in babies, much research has used the habituation or the preferential-looking paradigms. In both cases, the child is presented with a series of stimuli that share a common property (e.g., a series of pictures of animals differing in color, size, or spatial location, but always containing the same number of stimuli). After several presentations of this type, the child gets habituated to the stimuli and his looking time in response to the presentation of the display decreases. At this point, the experimenter introduces a novel stimulus (e.g., a picture of six animals) simultaneously or successively with an old one (e.g., another picture of three animals). If the child perceives the difference between the old and the new material, he will look longer or more preferentially at the new stimuli than at the old one (i.e., he will dishabituate). If this happens, the crucial question then is to determine the nature of the change between the novel and the old stimulus that was detected by the child.

Using this method, many experiments have provided evidence that babies, even neonates, are able to discriminate collections of varying numerosities. The first studies of this type tried mainly to identify the border at which the child could discriminate a collection of *n versus n+1* items. These studies found that although infants could detect a change in small collections (e.g., one versus two or two versus three), they would fail when the size of the set exceeded three or four elements (e.g., four versus five; Starkey & Cooper, 1980; Antell & Keating, 1983; Strauss & Curtis, 1981; van Loosbroek & Smistman, 1990).

The Interpretations

The Numerical Hypothesis

Two main hypotheses were first proposed to account for these observations. Several authors, such as Gallistel and Gelman (1992), Wynn (1998), and Dehaene, Dehane-Lambertz, and Cohen (1998), assumed that human infants are born with a specialized mental mechanism for processing numerosities. In their view, this mechanism is preverbal and is shared by certain animal species. For instance, the accumulator model proposed by Gallistel and Gelman (1992) can account for the limit of the precise number discrimination observed in infants, as it assumes an increasing imprecision of the magnitude representation as numerosities get bigger.

The General Non-Numerical Capacities Hypothesis

Others authors, however (Simon, 1997; Uller, Carey, Huntley-Fenner, & Klatt, 1999), have proposed that infants' behavior can be explained by cognitive capacities that are general and not specifically numerical. For instance, Simon (1997) proposed that infants use a mental token to represent each item to be enumerated. These tokens derive from a pre-attentive mechanism dedicated to the representation and tracking of individual objects within a visual scene called the "the object-files." According to this proposal, infants' numerical discrimination can be explained as follows: when infants see a collection, each entity is mentally represented by a mental token. These mental tokens can be stored in memory when the set disappears. The presentation of another set gives rise to the same process of mental token elaboration. These two sets of mental tokens are then compared by a process of one-to-one correspondence. The perception of a mismatch between models induces a reaction of surprise in babies. Such an explanation perfectly predicts the size effect observed in infant studies since the number of items that can be represented and stored in memory at once is supposed to be limited to three or four.

One way to oppose the numerical and object file models is to consider large numerosities. According to the numerical model, large numerosities could be discriminated, provided the distance between the two numerosities considered is great enough. On the contrary, the object file model assumes that large numerosities could not be discriminated at all. Recently, several studies have used large collections of items and have manipulated the ratio of their numerosities. Remember that according to the compressed number line model, for instance, the difference between the magnitude of two and four is subjectively bigger than the difference between the magnitude of eight and ten. This is because the subjective distance between two magnitudes is a function of the difference between the logarithm of each number. Number pairs which present the same difference between the logarithm of their constituting numbers also share the same ratio (e.g., the pairs two–four or five–ten enter in the ratio of 1/2 and $\log(4) - \log(2) = \log(10) - \log(5)$). Furthermore, the ratio combines the size and the distance effect given that it approaches one when the distance between two numerosities decreases (2/10, 2/8, 2/6 . . .) or when the size of the set increases (4/8, 8/12, 12/16 . . .).

Using large collections with a manipulation of the ratio, Xu and Spelke (2000) showed that 6-month-old infants could discriminate large visual arrays entering in a 1/2 ratio (8 vs. 16 elements) but not those entering in a 2/3 ratio (8 vs. 12).[1] Similarly, Lipton and Spelke (2003) reported that 6-month-old infants could discriminate sequences of sounds entering in a 1/2 ratio (e.g., 8 vs. 16 sounds) but not sequences entering in a 2/3 ratio (8 vs. 12). At 9 months of age, however, infants are able to discriminate sequences entering in a 2/3 ratio but not those in a 4/5 ratio, which suggests that the precision of numerical discrimination increases over the infancy period. In preschoolers, Huntley-Fenner and Cannon (2000) also reported a ratio effect with the performance of 3- to 5-year-old children being more accurate in magnitude comparison for a ratio of 1/2 than for a ratio of 2/3. These results are thus incompatible with the object file model but support the numerical models.

The Perceptual Hypothesis

A third interpretation has recently been proposed. According to Mix and colleagues (Mix, Huttenlocher, & Levine, 2002; Clearfield & Mix, 2001), infants discriminate and quantify sets by using perceptual non-numerical cues that naturally covary with number such as the volume, the area, and the length. According to them, infants are initially unable to represent discrete number properties independently of their correlated perceptual variables and instead represent discrete and continuous quantities in terms of overall amount. In this case, an analogue medium would probably serve to represent the amount since perceptual representations are inherently imprecise. This analogue representation of amount would explain why infants' quantitative performance is subject to Weber's law and would account for the size, the distance, and the ratio effects. Such a proposal is supported by recent data showing that when perceptual cues such as surface area or contour length are pitted against number, 6- to 7-month-old infants dishabituate to a change in the continuous variables but not to a change in number (Feigenson, Carey, & Spelke, 2002; Clearfield & Mix, 1999). Similar results were also obtained by Rousselle, Palmers, and Noël (2004) with 3-year-old children: they were able to select the larger of two collections of dots if number and surface area were confounded but performed randomly when surface area was equated in the two collections.

Concluding Remarks

Currently, there is a lack of strong empirical evidences to rule out the perceptual account. Indeed, as outlined by Mix et al. (2002), the main problem is the simultaneous control of all perceptual variables that naturally covary with number. However, even if we only consider the studies which took great care in the control of perceptual variables, a heterogeneous picture still emerges: children seem to be able to discriminate large collections entering in a 1/2 ratio (e.g., Xu & Spelke, 2000; Lipton & Spelke, 2003) but fail to do so for small collections such as one vs. two (e.g., Feigenson, Carey, & Spelke, 2002; Clearfield & Mix, 1999). Such an opposition has been clearly underlined by Xu (2003), who showed that 6-month-old infants succeeded in discriminating four from eight visual elements but failed to discriminate two from four elements. Faced with these surprising results, one may consider like Feigenson, Carey, and Spelke (2002) or Xu (2003) that children would have two available mechanisms: an analogue numerical magnitude process and an object file model. But several questions remain open under this hypothesis. For instance, one may wonder why the analogue magnitude process does not code numerosities when small collections are presented. One possibility would be to assume that the object file process is faster than the analogue process, meaning that the former would always be activated first except in cases in which it is overwhelmed (i.e., when faced with large collections). Second, if one assumes that the object file mechanism is used for small collections, it remains to be explained why infants are unable to discriminate them when continuous perceptive variables are controlled for. Feigenson, Carey, and Spelke (2002) propose that these object files may also code objects' properties such as their size so that computations on these object files could be establishing one-to-one correspondence but could also include comparison of overall continuous extent. However, even this modified view of the object files could not explain a child's failure to discriminate small sets controlled for perceptual variables, as the possibility of one-to-one correspondence still predicts discrimination capacities in such situations.

In summary, the issue of number magnitude representation in babies has yielded much information over the past decades. Many facts have been collected and several interesting models have been proposed. Yet future research will be needed to come up with a satisfactory explanation. A possible way to clarify this problem could be to use cross-modal or cross-format paradigms, such as those used by Barth, Kanwisher, and Spelke (2003) with adults. The presence of a similar ability to compare numerosities across formats (e.g., simultaneous and sequential sets) or modalities (e.g., visual and auditory stimulus sets) in young children would certainly constitute strong evidence in favor of the hypothesis of a real processing of numerosities. Attempts in this direction were made by Starkey, Spelke, and Gelman (1990) but not replicated by Moore, Benenson, Reznick, Peterson, and Kagan (1987) or by Mix, Levine, and Huttenlocher (1997).

Many of the problems raised in perceptual comparison of numerosities disappear, however, with symbolic comparison. In this case, the physical properties of the stimuli are completely unrelated to the numerical ones. This type of material has been used in studies with older children that will be reviewed in the following section.

SYMBOLIC COMPARISON IN SCHOOL-AGED CHILDREN

Basic Results

Two studies have tested children of different ages in symbolic number comparison tasks. Both aimed to trace the appearance of the classic effects as well as to describe and interpret their developmental changes.

The first of these studies was run by Sekuler and Mierkiewicz (1977). They tested kindergarten and first-, fourth-, and seventh-grade children as well as university students with pairs of single-digit Arabic numerals. They observed a global decrease in response time with increasing age. Moreover, a distance effect was observed in each group, the slope of which grew steeper in the younger groups.

These results were replicated by Duncan and McFarland (1980) who tested kindergarten and first-, third-, and fifth-grade children as well as university students with single-digit pairs. A distance effect was present in each group with a decreasing size as participants were older. These authors also considered the semantic congruity effect and observed it in each age group, with its size being greater in the younger groups.

Thus, effects of the numerical distance and of the semantic congruity in magnitude comparison tasks are already present from kindergarten with single-Arabic digits. However, the magnitude of these effects decreases across development. Duncan and McFarland (1980) tried to identify the processing stage at which these effects occur. They considered two possibilities: either these effects and their changes across development take place at the encoding stage or they occur at the comparison stage. If these effects are linked to the encoding stage, a manipulation of the quality of the stimuli might modify their size; if not, this manipulation would just add a constant to the response time. Based on this reasoning, they contrasted a magnitude comparison task of Arabic digits with or without a line grid being superimposed over the stimuli. The results were clear: while the distance effect was not affected by the manipulation, the semantic congruity effect was stronger in degraded than in nondegraded stimuli. These results thus suggest that the semantic congruity effect lies at the encoding level, whereas the distance effect comes from the comparison stage. As the size of both these effects decreases across development, Duncan and McFarland concluded that "both encoding and comparison improve with age" (p. 621).

Explanations for the Developmental Changes in Number Comparison

Given that comparison improves with age, one may wonder about the reasons underlying those changes. According to Sekuler et al. (1977), three types of modifications of magnitude representation could be evoked:

1. The average distance between analogue representations of the digits could be reduced in younger subjects because their analogue number line could be more compressed than in adults.
2. The discriminal dispersions around each mean representation could be larger in younger subjects.
3. Both explanations could be correct; that is, younger subjects' number magnitude representation could be both more compressed than the adults' and also present a higher dispersion.

These propositions actually correspond to different theoretical conceptions of the analogue magnitude representation of numbers: the first proposition is more compatible with the logarithmically compressed number line, whereas the second is more compatible with the scalar variability of the accumulator.

Siegler and Opfer (2003) contrasted the predictions of these two models in two estimation tasks. In the number-to-position task, participants were shown a one- to three-digit number and asked to estimate its position on a drawn number line, with the left end labeled "0" and the right end labeled "100" or "1000." In the position-to-number task, they were shown a position on a number line and asked to estimate the corresponding number. Second, fourth, and sixth graders, along with undergraduates, were presented with the two tasks. If their magnitude representation follows a logarithmic compression, as in the number line model, their mean estimates should increase logarithmically with numerical magnitude in the number-to-position task and exponentially with the number in the position-to-number task. The variability of these estimates should be constant across the number range. If, on the contrary, their magnitude representation is best modeled by the accumulator model, the mean estimates should increase linearly with the size of the number, and the variability of these estimates should increase with the size of the numbers on both tasks.

Results supported the logarithmic model in the 0–1000 number line in grades two and four. Yet, none of these above-mentioned models could account for the 0–100 number line in grades two and four nor for the 0–100 and 0–1000 number lines in grade six and in adults. Indeed, in the latter cases, mean estimates increased linearly while variability remained constant across numerosity. Siegler and Opfer referred to this profile as the linear-ruler model.

One could, however, wonder whether estimates on a physical number line are a perfect modelization of the magnitude representation on an internal number line. Indeed, the physical number line has attributes (such as the two ends marked, for instance) that allow the child to build specific strategies to deal with the task. For instance, the large numbers that are near the right end of the physical number line are consequently better estimated than smaller numbers that do not benefit from these external marks. The material used in the task thus induces biases that are not supposed to be present in the magnitude representation. Consequently, we fear that the use of such a paradigm may lead to erroneous conclusions.

In this sense, Huntley-Fenner's (2001) task might be considered the more appropriate. Collections of 5 to 11 black squares were flashed for 250 ms, and children (5–7 years old) were asked to estimate their cardinal and select the corresponding Arabic numeral between 1 and 20. Results are largely compatible with the accumulator model: the means of the estimates increased with the presented numerosity, and there was a scalar variability as the SD/mean estimate ratio was constant among the stimuli set. Moreover, the authors reported a slight developmental trend in which this SD/mean estimate ratio grew smaller in older children. This would suggest a growing precision of the magnitude representation with age. Based on these observations, one may speculate that this increasing precision due to a reduced dispersion around each mean magnitude representation might account for the decrease in the distance effect observed in magnitude comparison tasks.

Two Last Issues

Two other questions have been addressed in the literature. First, according to Dehaene, (1992) number magnitude representation is spatially oriented (see chapter 3 for a deep review of this topic). Accordingly, one may wonder whether this spatial orientation of the number line (SNARC effect) is precocious or appears late in development. Second, the magnitude representation is supposed to recruit the bilateral inferior parietal areas (Dehaene & Cohen, 1995). One could thus wonder whether the same brain areas are activated during magnitude processing in young children and in adults. The few studies that have addressed these two issues will be considered successively.

The question of the onset of a spatial bias in number magnitude processing in children is interesting because predictions in this matter differ according to the various interpretations that have been proposed to account for its observation in adults. At least three possibilities can be considered. First, one could suppose that the spatial orientation of the number line is an intrinsic property of number magnitude representation. In this case, the SNARC effect should be present simultaneously with the other effects, such as the distance and size effects. Second, one could argue that this spatial orientation is related to cultural habits such as the direction of reading. It should then appear only when children become used to that direction of reading. Third, this SNARC effect could be associated with the ordinal nature of numbers rather than with their cardinal meaning. Consequently, the SNARC effect should appear when children are familiar with the order of the numbers (i.e., when they are able to recite the number sequence). To our knowledge, only one study has addressed this issue. Berch, Foley, Hill, and Ryan's (1999) study asked children (grades two, three, four, six, and eight) to make an odd/even judgment on the 0–9 Arabic numerals. A significant SNARC effect appeared from grades three and up. However, the failure to obtain any SNARC effect in grade two was attributed to the high error rate and large RT variance in that age group. Further research will be needed, and, preferably, with simpler tasks as well as with tasks requiring a processing of number magnitude per se, to identify the time at which this spatial association of numbers appears.

The second question relates to the developmental changes in the brain regions supporting number magnitude representation and has only been addressed by one study. In this research project, Temple and Posner (1998) tested 5-year-old children in a magnitude comparison task of dots and Arabic-digit stimuli, using an event-related potentials paradigm. They observed a distance effect that appeared on the same locations of electrodes (in the bilateral parietal regions) as in adults and that was delayed by only 50 ms.

Concluding Remarks

In summary, studies on the development of Arabic number magnitude representation have put forward more similarities between a 5-year-old child and an adult than differences. Indeed, at this young age, children already show the distance and semantic congruity effects in magnitude comparison tasks with single-Arabic digits. The brain areas activated during this task appear to be remarkably similar to those of adults. The main developmental changes observed are quantitative rather than qualitative; over time, children's global RTs decrease, as does the size of the distance and semantic congruity effects. This is probably due to the general speed-up phenomenon that is observed across development in all speeded tasks (see Kail, 1993). Yet the reduction in the size of the distance effect probably also results from an increasing precision of the number magnitude representation. Even so, alongside these quantitative changes, it is possible that some qualitative changes may have gone unnoticed. For instance, it is possible that the spatial orientation of the number line could only develop later, around grade three, but more empirical evidence on that topic would be needed.

AUTOMATIC ACTIVATION OF NUMBER MAGNITUDE

Introduction

All the studies reported in the previous section used tasks that explicitly required the processing of number magnitude, and the obtained results have underlined the large commonalties between children and adults. Yet, adults have also been shown to process number magnitude in tasks for which this dimension is not relevant. For instance, when they are presented with pairs of digits and asked to judge if the two stimuli are physically identical or not, adults are slower to say "different" when the two numbers are numerically close than when they are numerically distant from one another (Dehaene & Akhavein, 1995). Similarly, if they are presented with a sequence of digits and asked to count the symbols (e.g., 3333, answer "four"), they are slower when the number of items differs from the identity of the items (555 vs. 333), and this interference is larger when the number of symbols is close to the identity of the digits (e.g., stronger in the case 444 than in the case 888; see Pavese & Umiltà, 1998). These interferences of the numerical dimension in these tasks, where it is irrelevant, argue for an automatic and unintentional activation of number magnitude. In this section, we will report on studies that have aimed to determine the age at which this automatic activation of number magnitude appears in children.

The Data

The first evidence in this domain comes from the study of Duncan and McFarland (1980). These authors presented pairs of single-digit Arabic numbers to participants of different ages (from kindergarten to university students) who had to decide whether the two symbols were physically identical or not. When different, the digits composing the pairs were numerically close (distance of 1, 2, or 3) or distant (i.e., distance of 6, 7, or 8). Both adults and children (even those from kindergarten) showed a distance effect. Thus, even kindergartners processed the digits up along the semantic stage in this simple physical judgment task.

Girelli, Lucangeli, and Butterworth (2000) drew a quite different conclusion. These authors used a Stroop paradigm: pairs of Arabic digits were presented in a numerical and in a physical comparison in which subjects had, respectively, to select the stimulus larger in magnitude or in physical size. In both tasks, congruency between the magnitude and the physical dimensions was manipulated: in congruent trials the digit that was physically bigger was also the numerically larger (e.g., 2-6); in incongruent pairs, the digit that was physically smaller was numerically larger (e.g., 2-6); and in neutral pairs, the digits were displayed with the same physical size (2-6). In these conditions, the presence of a (numerical) size-congruity effect in the physical comparison indicates that the irrelevant number magnitude information has been automatically processed. Further, pairs with a numerical distance of 1 or 5 were contrasted, as the presence of a distance effect in the physical judgment is another indicator of an automatic activation of number magnitude. Results indicated the presence of a size congruity and a distance effect in adults' physical judgment as well as in that of fifth-grade children. Third graders, however, only showed a size congruity effect, while none of these effects were significant in the first grade. The authors thus concluded that automatization is achieved gradually as younger children do not show any signs of an automatic activation of the magnitude information.

Recently, a very similar study was undertaken by Rubinsten and colleagues (2002). Five groups of students were tested (beginning of first grade, end of first grade, third grade, fifth grade, and university students), and three numerical distances between the single-Arabic digits of the pairs (1, 2, and 4) were considered. In the physical comparison task, the size congruity effect was absent in the beginning of the first grade but was significant by the end of that school year and later on.[2] Thus, by introducing this group of "end first graders," the authors were able to show much earlier signs of automatic activation of number magnitude than reported by Girelli et al. However, and contrary to Girelli et al., they failed to find any significant distance effect in the physical comparison (although it was present in the magnitude comparison condition).

In relation to these Stroop studies, two questions will be addressed. First, how can we account for the fact that the size congruity and distance effects sometimes dissociate in the physical tasks? Second, how can the failure to obtain any of these effects in certain age groups be interpreted?

Dissociations between Size-Congruity and Distance Effects

If both the size-congruity and the distance effects (observed in the physical task) are indicative of an automatic activation of number magnitude representation, then how is it possible to observe one of these effects without the other? Although intriguing, such a result profile is not rare. In Girelli et al.'s (2000) third graders and in all the groups in Rubinsten et al.'s study (2002), a significant size-congruity effect was observed without any distance effect. Tzelgov, Meyer, and Henik (1992) have proposed a possible interpretation of this dissociation. According to these authors, the distance and the size-congruity effects do not reflect the same process of number magnitude. In their view, the distance effect results from an algorithmic process that codes both numbers on the number line and enables their comparison, whereas the size-congruity effect reflects a different process. Indeed, as we accumulate experience of Arabic digit comparison, we store instances in which digits are judged as small or large quantities, and it is the retrieval from memory of those instances that is reflected by the size-congruity effect. In intentional conditions, that is, in number magnitude comparison tasks, the distance effect always appears and signs the use of the algorithmic process. However, in nonintentional conditions (e.g., in the physical comparison task), both mechanisms take place but, as memory retrieval is faster than the algorithmic process, only a size-congruity effect appears, even in adults.

Rubinsten et al. (2002) follow this reasoning to interpret their data. First, as the physical comparison task does not require an intentional access to number magnitude, the memory-based mechanism is dominant, which explains the absence of any significant distance effect in all the groups considered. Second, as the size-congruity effect (which is the signature of this memory-based mechanism) only appears when the child has accumulated enough experience with magnitude comparison of Arabic digits, it failed to appear in young and inexperienced beginners of first grade but was present in older groups.

Finally, Rubinsten et al. try to reinterpret the data obtained by Girelli et al. (2000). Remember that in this experiment, fifth graders and adults showed both a size-congruity and a distance effect. As magnitude information was not intentionally processed, the presence of this last effect is surprising under Tzelgov et al.'s interpretations. However, Rubinsten et al. noticed that in this experiment, numerical distance was totally confounded with the type of pairs in terms of "memory labels": stimuli with a small numerical distance of one were made of two numbers sharing the same labels (either two small or two large numbers), whereas the large-distance pairs were all made of one small and one large number. In these conditions, the algorithmic and the memory processes are impossible to disentangle: the distance effect might just reveal the autonomous activation of memory labels rather than of magnitude per se.

Although appealing, this interpretation does not seem able to account for two facts of Rubinsten et al.'s study. First, if the memory-based process dominates the nonintentional processing of magnitude, then in the physical task, same-label pairs should be processed faster than different-label pairs. Second, the size-congruity effect should be stronger in the different-label pairs than in the same-label pairs. The type of label of the pairs was not introduced as such in the study, but it was partially confounded with the numerical distance: pairs with a distance of 1 and 2 were all same-label pairs, whereas pairs with a distance of 4 were all different-label pairs. However, no distance effect emerged in the physical task, even between the distance 1–2 (same-label pairs) and 4 (different-label pairs). Furthermore, there is no mention of an interaction between size congruity and numerical distance.

A Relative-Speed Account

The second issue that needs to be addressed regards the interpretation of the null effect (i.e., the failure to measure any significant size-congruity or distance effect in certain age groups). Most of the time, the conclusion has simply been that number magnitude representation was not automatically activated in these young children who failed to show any of those significant effects. Alternatively, one may consider the possibility that this failure may be due to the large discrepancy between processing time for the physical and the magnitude dimensions: number magnitude could be activated in the physical comparison task, whereas a decision for the physical dimension could be reached before the magnitude information has had the time to interfere with the response. This possibility is mentioned briefly by Girelli et al. (2000) and by Rubinsten et al. (2002).

Recently, Schwarz and Ischebeck (2003) have proposed a relative speed account of the number-size interference in Stroop tasks. According to their model, decisions are not based on information conveyed in an all-or-none fashion but, rather, on noisy partial information that continuously accumulates until the decision is reached. As both the processing of the relevant and of the irrelevant dimensions is influenced by the distance (i.e., the physical and the numerical distance), decreasing the relevant distance or increasing the irrelevant distance should lengthen the period of time during which the irrelevant information has an opportunity to influence the processing of the relevant attribute. In other words, to favor the emergence of a numerical interference on the physical judgment, one should increase the difficulty of the physical comparison (i.e., presenting pairs of digits with close physical size) or increase the ease of the numerical comparison (i.e., presenting pairs of digits with large numerical distance).

In Girelli et al. (2000), the physical size distance was so important (24 points vs. 48 points) that in first grade, the physical judgment took about half the time required for the numerical judgment (in the neutral conditions, physical comparison took 1,188 ms, whereas numerical comparison took 2017 for a distance of 5 and 2,130 for a distance of 1). Later on, RTs decreased overall but much more significantly for the numerical task than for the physical task, which may account for the appearance of a number distance effect in the physical task for the older groups. For Rubinsten, the differences in physical size were much smaller (either 6 vs. 7 mm height or 7 vs. 9 mm height). The difference between the physical and the numerical judgments were thus smaller as well (mean difference of 257 over all the groups) and decreased with age (this difference was 128 ms greater in the beginning of first grade than by the end of first grade, but only 39 ms greater at the end of first grade compared with the third grade). These differences in ease of physical comparison may account for the more precocious observation of a size-congruity effect in Rubinsten et al.'s than in Girelli et al.'s studies.

Recently, Mussolin (2002) has tried to palliate this problem of processing time difference by balancing the speed of the physical and the numerical processing. A Stroop paradigm was used, but in contrast to the classic version of the task, the number pairs did not appear directly with a physical size difference but were first presented in a same intermediate physical size (e.g., 3-6). Only after a certain delay did their physical size differences emerge with one digit's physical size increasing and the other one's decreasing (e.g., 3-6). The delay before the appearance of the physical size difference was calculated for each participant and corresponded to his/her difference in processing speed between a physical comparison task on similar digits (e.g., 3-3) and a magnitude comparison of digits presented with the same physical size (e.g., 3-6). In this way, we could assume that the number magnitude information and the physical size information were reached simultaneously, which provides good conditions for the irrelevant number magnitude information to alter the physical comparison task.

The other aim of this study was to examine whether the age at which the numerical magnitude is automatically activated does or does not depend on the size of the numbers considered. Therefore, three numerical sizes of number pairs were used: pairs of single digits (e.g., 2–4), pairs of two-digit numbers smaller than 50 (e.g., 23–46), and pairs of two-digit numbers with at least one bigger than 50 (e.g., 34–68[3]). For each of them, the ratio was manipulated with half of the pairs having a ratio of 1/2 (e.g., 23–46) and the other having a ratio of 2/3 (e.g., 32–48).

Second, third, and fourth graders were presented with these number pairs and asked to select the one that was physically bigger. Besides the usual decrease in RTs with age, a highly significant size-congruity effect and an interaction between this effect and the ratio were observed. Congruent trials were processed faster than incongruent ones, but this was true for the ratio of 1/2 only. In other words, number magnitude interfered with the physical judgment when the two numbers of the pair were highly distant numerically, as predicted by Schwartz and Ischebeck's (2003) model. Another important finding was the failure to obtain any size effect, which means that this automatic activation of number magnitude was observed for both one- and two-digit numbers. Yet, analyses run separately in each group indicated that for second graders, only the single-digit and the small two-digit numbers gave rise to a size-congruity effect, which indicates that only those smaller numbers led to an automatic activation of their corresponding magnitude representation.

Summary

In conclusion, using a single-digit matching task, Duncan and McFarland (1980) reported a distance effect that suggested an automatic activation of number magnitude from as early as the age of 6 years. Converging evidence was also obtained in a Stroop paradigm by Rubinsten et al. (2002), who reported a size congruity effect from the end of first grade. The failure to observe similar results in Girelli et al. (2000) may be accounted for by the relative-speed model (Schwartz et al., 2003). Finally, the results of Mussolin (2002) indicate that second graders are able to automatically activate not only the magnitude of single-digit numbers but also that of two-digit numbers, provided the task at hand has been slowed down sufficiently to allow numerical information to interfere with it.

A BASIC DYSFUNCTION OF NUMBER MAGNITUDE REPRESENTATION IN DYSCALCULIC CHILDREN?

As we have underlined in the beginning of this chapter, magnitude is a key dimension to the semantic of numbers. The results reported in the two previous sections have shown that children starting elementary school show the same basic effects in Arabic number magnitude comparison as those observed in adults and that they automatically activate the magnitude of Arabic numerals, even when this dimension is not relevant for the task. About 6% of school-aged children have major difficulties in mathematics (Gross-Tsur, Manor, & Shalev, 1996). As number magnitude seems to be one of the roots of this learning, Butterworth (1999) has proposed that a dysfunction of that representation might well be one of the possible causes of mathematical disabilities. In support of this hypothesis, he reported the case of Charles, who had difficulty with mathematics for many years. At the age of 31, he still counted on his fingers to solve simple additions. A deep investigation of his number-processing capacities showed several abnormalities in his processing of number magnitude. Thus, when required to select the larger of two Arabic digits, he relied on counting, which led him to be four times slower than control subjects and to present a reverse distance effect (he was thus faster when digits were numerically close than when they were numerically distant). Finally, in a Stroop task such as reported in Girelli et al. (2000), he failed to show any distance effect in the physical comparison condition. This profile was interpreted by Butterworth as a basic dysfunction of Charles's number magnitude representation, which accounted for his mathematical difficulties.

Other pieces of evidence for this hypothesis can be found in the recent study of Isaacs, Edmonds, Lucas, and Gadian (2001). These authors compared teenagers who were born prematurely and who had normal versus weak calculation abilities with structural fMRI and observed more gray matter in the former group in the left intraparietal sulcus only. This result is of particular interest because this specific brain area is probably a major structure for supporting the representation of number magnitude. Indeed, it has been shown to be activated in Arabic magnitude comparison (Pesenti, Thioux, Seron, & De Volder, 2000) and to be sensitive to the numerical distance of numbers to be compared, independent of their presentation format (Arabic digits or words; Pinel, Dehaene, Rivière, & LeBihan (2001).

Neuropsychological data also provide converging evidence for a role of the parietal lobe in number magnitude representation and in dyscalculia. In acquired disorders, it is well known that a lesion of the parietal lobe of the dominant hemisphere may lead to acalculia, which often appears in association with finger agnosia, left–right disorientation, and dysgraphia (i.e., the Gerstmann syndrome). For instance, the patient MAR (Dehaene & Cohen, 1997), who suffered from an infarct of the parietal lobe of his dominant hemisphere, exhibited a Gerstmann syndrome and was mostly impaired in numerical tasks that required the manipulation of number magnitude.

The existence of the Gerstmann syndrome has inspired the study of Fayol, Barrouillet, and Marinthe (1998). These authors tested normal 5-year-old children's digital agnosia and found that these measures predicted arithmetic performance 1 year later. Following this research, Noël (2002) wondered whether these predictions concerned numerical performance in general or, more specifically, performance in tasks requiring the processing of number magnitude. Indeed, according to Dehaene's (1992) triple-code model, one could suppose that a parietal weakness would be associated with low performances in tasks based on the magnitude representation (e.g., number comparison or subitizing[4]) but might preserve number processing that could be realized without appealing to this representation (e.g., number transcoding or simple arithmetic). Digital agnosia was tested in first-grade children (at the beginning of the school year) and their numerical abilities one year later. The global results were not in favor of a specific relationship between digital agnosia and number magnitude processing. Yet children were doing quite well with the test of digital agnosia, and only two of them showed a real deficit at that level. One of them, Simon, had a very interesting profile. Although scoring very poorly on the digital agnosia test (Z score of –2.38), he did not exhibit a complete Gerstmann syndrome, as he scored normally on a left–right orientation test (Z score = 0.68). One year later, his numerical performance was tested. In a magnitude comparison of dot collections, he performed slowly (Z score of 1.71) and produced numerous errors (Z score = 2.59). He was also extremely slow (Z score of 2.78), although accurate (Z score of 0.02) when asked to select the bigger of two single-digit Arabic numbers. This slowness was not generalized, as his RTs were normal in a physical matching task of the same Arabic digits (Z = 0.47). Furthermore, he could only subitize two dots, which is very few (Z score = –2.00), and he made too many errors when asked to say how many fingers were raised (Z score = 2.36). However, his difficulties with numbers were not generalized: he scored above the mean for fast single-digit additions (Z=0.94) and number transcoding (Z score = 0.73). Finally, his deficits in numerical tasks were not accompanied by a reading disability as he scored above the mean for reading words (Z score = 1.18). The profile exhibited by Simon thus suggests that digital agnosia measured at entry level in elementary school may predict disabilities in learning mathematics 1 year later. Furthermore, these learning problems might specifically affect number magnitude processing, leaving intact more verbal numerical abilities (such as arithmetical facts and transcoding).

At this point, evidence supporting Butterworth's hypothesis of a basic number magnitude dysfunction in developmental dyscalculia is scarce and heterogeneous. Yet, these results are encouraging. It is hoped that further research will enable a deeper understanding of developmental dyscalculia in the case of otherwise normal children as well as in the case of genetic disorders (Ansari & Karmiloff-Smith, 2002).

GENERAL CONCLUSION

Magnitude is a key dimension of numbers' semantic. Its representation is usually evaluated through number comparison tasks. In such situations, children's performance is sensitive to the same variables as adults' (i.e., the size of the numbers and the distance between them). Furthermore, from the age of 6 or 7, the presentation of a one- or a two-digit number automatically activates its corresponding magnitude, even when irrelevant for the task. Given the importance of this dimension and its degree of development before any explicit mathematical instruction, we have considered Butterworth's hypothesis of a possible link between a dysfunction of the number magnitude representation and mathematics learning disabilities. Although strong evidence is currently not available, several pieces of information support the plausibility of this hypothesis. Much work remains to be done and several questions need to be addressed. First, what precisely is the dysfunction seen in the magnitude representation in dyscalculic children? Second, does this dysfunction correspond to structural or functional peculiarities of certain brain areas? Third, are all developmental dyscalculia linked to a dysfunction of the magnitude representation? Finally, in case of abnormalities in the magnitude representation, is all number processing impaired or is some preserved? We are confident that future research will provide answers to these questions.

ACKNOWLEDGMENT

The first two authors are supported by the National Research Fund of Belgium and by a concerted research action, ARC #01/06-267; the third author enjoys the support of an FSR (Special Research Fund) from the Catholic University of Louvain.

NOTES

1. However, inconsistent observations were reported by Feigenson and colleagues (2002) with 10- to 12-months- old infants failing to compare arrays that differed by a ratio of 1/2 (two vs. four, three vs. six).
2. The interference effect obtained at the end of the first grade was accompanied by a facilitation effect in the third grade and up.
3. All of the two-digit pairs were compatible; i.e., the comparison of the decade digits and of the unit digits led to the same result. Nuerk et al. (2001) have indeed underlined the impact of decade–unit compatibility on magnitude representation of two-digit Arabic numerals.
4. Subitizing refers to the fast and precise apprehension of small numerosities up to four or five.

REFERENCES

Ansari, D., & Karmiloff-Smith, A; (2002). Atypical trajectories of number development: A neuroconstructivist perspective. *Trends in Cognitive Science, 6*(12), 511–516.

Antell, S. E., & Keating, D P. (1983). Perception numerical invariance in neonates. *Child Development, 54,* 695–701.

Bächtold, D., Baumüller, M., & Brugger, P. (1998). Stimulus–response compatibility in the representational space. *Neuropsychologia, 36*(8), 731–735.

Banks, W. P. (1977). Encoding and processing of symbolic information in comparative judgments. In G. H. Bower (Ed.), *The psychology of learning and motivation* (Vol. 11, pp. 101–159). New York: Academic Press

Banks, W. P., Clark, H. H., & Lucy, P. (1975). The locus of the semantic congruity effect in comparative judgments. *Journal of Experimental Psychology: Human Perception and Performance, 1,* 35–47.

Banks, W. P., Fujii, M., & Kayra-Stuart, F. (1976). Semantic congruity effects in comparative judgments of magnitudes of digits. *Journal of Experimental Psychology: Human Perception and Performance, 2,* 435–447.

Barth, H., Knawisher, N., & Spelke, E. (2003). The construction of large number representations in adults. *Cognition, 86,* 201–221.

Berch, D. B., Foley, E. J., Hill, R. J., & McDonough Ryan, P. (1999). Extracting parity and magnitude from Arabic numerals: Developmental changes in number processing and mental representation. *Journal of Experimental Child Psychology, 74*, 286–308.

Butterworth, B. (1999). *The mathematical brain*. London: Macmillan.

Clearfield, M. W., & Mix, K. S. (1999). Number versus contour length in infants' discrimination of small visual sets. *Psychological Science, 10*, 408–411.

Clearfield, M. W., & Mix, K. S. (2001). Amount versus number: Infants' use of area and contour length to discriminate small sets. *Journal of Cognition and Development, 2*(3), 243–260.

Cordes, S., Gelman, R., Gallistel, C. R., & Whalen, J. (2001). Variability signatures distinguish verbal from nonverbal counting for both large and small numbers. *Psychonomic Bulletin & Review, 8*(4), 698–707.

Dehaene, S. (1992). Varieties of numerical abilities. *Cognition, 44*, 1–42.

Dehaene, S., & Akhavein, R. (1995). Attention, automaticity and levels of representation in number processing. *Journal of Experimental Psychology: Learning, Memory and Cognition, 21*, 314–326.

Dehaene, S., & Cohen, L. (1995). Towards an anatomical and functional model of number processing. *Mathematical Cognition, 1*, 83–120.

Dehaene, S., & Cohen, L. (1997). Cerebral pathways for calculation: double dissociation between rote verbal and quantitative knowledge of arithmetic. *Cortex, 33*, 219–250.

Dehaene, S., Bossini, S., & Giraux, P. (1993). The mental representation of parity and number magnitude. *Journal of Experimental Psychology: General, 122*, 371–396.

Dehaene, S., Dehaene-Lambertz, G., & Cohen, L. (1998). Abstract representations of numbers in the animal and human brain. *Trends In NeuroSciences, 21*(8), 355–361.

Dehaene, S., Dupoux, E., & Mehler, J. (1990). Is numerical comparison digital? Analogical and symbolic effects in two-digit number comparison. *Journal of Experimental Psychology: Human Perception and Performance, 16*, 626–641.

Duncan, E. M., & McFarland, C. E. (1980). Isolating the effects of symbolic distance and semantic congruity in comparative judgments: An additive-factors analysis. *Memory & Cognition, 8*(6), 612–622.

Fayol, M., Barrouillet, P., & Marinthe, C. (1998). Predicting arithmetical achievement from neuropsychological performance: A longitudinal study. *Cognition, 68*, B63–B70.

Feigenson, L., Carey, S., & Hauser, M (2002). The representation underlying infants' choice of more: Object files vs. analog magnitudes. *Psychological Science, 13*(2), 150–156.

Feigenson, L., Carey, S., & Spelke, E. (2002). Infants' discrimination of number vs. continuous extent. *Cognitive Psychology, 44*, 33–66.

Fuson, K. C. (1992). Relationships between counting and cardinality from age 2 to age 8. In J. Bideaud, C. Meljac, & J.-P. Fisher (Eds.), *Pathways to number. Children's developing numerical abilities* (pp. 127–149). Hillsdale, NJ: Erlbaum.

Gallistel, C. R., & Gelman, R. (1992). Preverbal and verbal counting and computation. *Cognition, 44*, 43–74.

Gevers, W., Reynvoet, B., & Fias, W. (2003). The mental representation of ordinal sequences is spatially organized. *Cognition, 87*, B87–B95.

Girelli, L., Lucangeli, D., & Butterworth, B. (2000). The

development of automaticity in accessing number magnitude. *Journal of Experimental Child Psychology, 76*, 104–122.

Gross-Tsur, V., Manor, O., & Shalev, R. S. (1996). Developmental dyscalculia: Prevalence and demographic features. *Developmental Medicine and Child Neurology, 38*, 25–33.

Huntley-Fenner, G. (2001). Children's understanding of number is similar to adults' and rats': Numerical estimation by 5–7-year-olds. *Cognition, 78*(1), B27–B40.

Huntley-Fenner, G., & Cannon, E. (2000). Preschoolers' magnitude comparisons are mediated by a preverbal analog mechanism. *Psychological Science, 11*(2), 147–152.

Isaacs, E. B., Edmonds, C. J., Lucas, A., & Gadian, D. G. (2001). Calculation difficulties in children of very low birthweight. A neural correlate. *Brain, 124*, 1701–1707.

Kail, R. (1993). Processing time decreases globally at an exponential rate during childhood and adolescence. *Journal of Experimental Child Psychology, 56*, 254–265.

Lipton, J. S., & Spelke, E. S. (2003). Origins of number sense: Large-number discrimination in human infants. *Psychological Science, 14*(5), 396–401.

Mech, W. H., & Church, R. M. (1983). A mode control model of counting and timing processes. *Journal of Experimental Psychology: Animal Behavior Processes, 9*, 320–334.

Miller, K., & Gelman, R. (1983). The child's representation of number: A multidimensional scaling analysis. *Child Development, 54*(6), 1470–1479.

Mix, K. S., Levine, S. C., & Huttenlocher, J. (1997). Numerical abstraction in infants: Another look. *Developmental Psychology, 33*, 423–428.

Mix, K. S., Huttenlocher, J., & Levine, S. C. (2002). Multiple cues for quantification in infancy: Is number one of them? *Psychological Bulletin, 128*(2), 278–294.

Moore, D., Benenson, J., Reznick, J. S., Peterson, M., & Kagan, J. (1987). Effect of auditory numerical information on infants' looking behavior: Contradictory evidence. *Developmental Psychology, 23*, 665–670.

Moyer, R. S., & Landauer, T. K. (1967). Time required for judgments of numerical inequality. *Nature, 215*, 1519–1520.

Mussolin, C. (2002). *L'automaticité de l'accès à la représentation numérique chez l'enfant*. Unpublished Master's thesis, Université Catholique de Louvain, Belgium.

Noël, M.-P. (2002). *Les signes du syndrome de Gerstmann: Une aide à la compréhension des bases neuro-anatomiques du calcul et de certaines dyscalculies développementales?* Presentation at the Troisièmes journées "troubles de l'apprentissage du langage oral et écrit." Marseille-Aix, 15–16 November.

Pavese, A., & Umiltà, C. (1998). Symbolic distance between numerosity and identity modulates Stroop interference. *Journal of Experimental Psychology, Human Perception & Performance, 24*, 1535–1545.

Pesenti, M., Thioux, M., Seron, X., & De Volder, A. (2000). Neuroanatomical substrates of Arabic number processing, numerical comparison and simple addition: A PET study. *Journal of Cognitive Neuroscience, 12*(3), 461–479.

Pinel, P., Dehaene, S., Rivière, D., & LeBihan, D. (2001).

Modulation of parietal activation by semantic distance in a number comparison task. *NeuroImage, 14,* 1013–1026.

Restle, F. (1970). Speed of adding and comparing numbers. *Journal of Experimental Psychology, 83,* 274–278.

Rousselle, L., Palmers, E., & Noël, M.-P. (2004). Magnitude comparison in preschoolers: What counts? Influence of perceptual variables. *Journal of Experimental Child Psychology, 87,* 57–84.

Rubinsten, O., Henik, A., Berger, A., & Shahar-Shalev, S. (2002). The development of internal representations of magnitude and their association with Arabic numerals. *Journal of Experimental Child Psychology, 81,* 74–92.

Schwarz, W., & Ischebeck, A. (2003). On the relative speed account of the number-size interference in comparative judgments of numerals. *Journal of Experimental Psychology: Human Perception and Performance, 29*(3), 507–522.

Sekuler, R., & Mierkiewicz, D. (1977). Children's judgments of numerical inequalities. *Child Development, 48,* 630–633.

Siegler, R. S., & Opfer, J. E. (2003). The development of numerical estimation: Evidence for multiple representations of numerical quantity. *Psychological Science, 14*(3), 237–243.

Simon, T. J. (1997). Reconceptualizing the origins of number knowledge: A "non-numerical" account. *Cognitive Development, 12,* 349–372.

Starkey, P., & Cooper, R. G. (1980). Perception of numbers by human infants. *Science, 210,* 1033–1035.

Starkey, P., Spelke, E. S., & Gelman, R. (1990). Numerical abstraction by human infants. *Cognition, 36,* 97–127.

Strauss, M. S., & Curtis, L. E. (1981). Infant perception of numerosity. *Child Development, 52,* 1146–1152.

Temple, E., & Posner, M. I. (1998). Brain mechanisms of quantity are similar in 5-year-old children and adults. *Proceedings of the National Academy of Science, 95,* 7836–7841.

Tzelgov, J., Meyer, J., & Henik, A. (1992). Automatic and intentional processing of numerical information. *Journal of Experimental Psychology: Learning, Memory and Cognition, 18*(1), 166–179.

Uller, C., Carey, S., Huntley-Fenner, G., & Klatt, L. (1999). What representations might underlie infant numerical knowledge? *Cognitive Development, 14,* 1–36.

van Loosbroek, E., & Smitsman, W. (1990). Visual perception of numerosity in infancy. *Developmental Psychology, 26*(6), 916–922.

Wynn, K. (1998). Psychological foundations of number: Numerical competence in human infants. *Trends in Cognitive Science, 2*(8), 296–303.

Xu, F., & Spelke, E. S. (2000). Large number discrimination in 6-month-old infants. *Cognition, 74,* B1–B11.

Xu, F. (2003). Numerosity discrimination in infants: Evidence for two systems of representations. *Cognition, 89,* B15–B25.

12

Development of Numerical Estimation
A Review

Robert S. Siegler
Julie L. Booth

Estimation is an important part of mathematical cognition, one that is pervasively present in the lives of both children and adults. Consider just a few everyday examples. How long will it take you to finish your chores? What will a large pizza cost us? How many people were at the game? About how much is 75 × 31? How fast can that Lamborghini go? Estimation may be used more often in everyday life than any other quantification process.

In addition to its pervasive use, estimation is also important because it is related to other specific aspects of mathematical ability, such as arithmetic skill, and also to general measures of mathematical ability, such as achievement test scores (Dowker, 2003). Whether estimation proficiency is causally related to other aspects of mathematical ability is unknown at present, but there are reasons to suspect that it might be. For example, experimental conditions aimed at improving number line estimation procedures have been found to result in improved conceptual understanding of decimal fractions as well (Rittle-Johnson, Siegler, & Alibali, 2001).

A third reason why estimation is important is that many types of estimation require going beyond rote application of procedures and applying mathematical knowledge in flexible ways. This type of adaptive problem solving is a fundamental goal of contemporary mathematics instruction.

Yet another basis of the importance of estimation is practical—most school-age children are surprisingly bad at it, and even many adults are far from good at it. This limited proficiency, together with the pervasiveness of estimation in everyday life, its correlation and possible causal connection to general mathematical ability, and its embodying the type of flexible problem solving that is viewed as crucial within modern mathematics education, has led the National Council of Teachers of Mathematics to assign a high priority to the goal of improving estimation skills within each revision of its Math Standards since 1980 (e.g., NCTM, 1980, 2000).

Despite the importance of estimation both in and out of school, far less is known about it than about other basic quantitative abilities, such as subitizing, counting, and adding (Dowker, 2003; Geary, 1994). One reason for the discrepancy is that estimation includes a varied set of processes rather than a single one. Some estimation tasks, for example, estimating the distance between two cities, time to finish a chore, or cost of a bag of groceries, require knowledge of measurement units such as miles, minutes, or dollars; other estimation tasks, for example, estimating the number of coins in a jar or answers to arithmetic problems, do not. Similarly, some uses of estimation, for example, estimating the cost of a pizza or speed of a Lamborghini, require prior knowledge of the entities whose properties are being estimated (i.e., pizzas, Lamborghinis); other uses, such as estimating the answers to arithmetic problems or number of coins in a jar, do not. This variability in the knowledge and processes required by different estimation tasks has hindered progress in understanding estimation. In particular, it has obscured which, if any, processes unite all types of estimation and which tasks most directly assess those common processes.

DEFINING ESTIMATION

The following definition seems a promising way of conceptualizing estimation: *Estimation is a process of translating between alternative quantitative representations, at least one of which is inexact.* The quantitative representations can be either numerical or non-numerical. *Numerical estimation* corresponds to the subset of estimation tasks in which one or both sides of the translation involve numbers. This category includes most of the prototypic forms of estimation. For example, computational estimation involves translating from one numerical representation (e.g., 75×29) to another (about 2,200). Numerosity estimation requires translating a non-numerical quantitative representation (e.g., a visual representation of the approximate volume and density of candies in a jar) into a number. Number line estimation either requires translating a number into a spatial position on a number line or translating a spatial position on a number line into a number. The other main category of estimation, *non-numerical estimation,* involves tasks in which neither quantitative representation is numerical. This category includes tasks used in psychophysical experiments that require translation between two non-numerical quantitative representations, for example, between brightness of a bulb and spatial position on a line.

Limitations of space, together with the vast and varied set of tasks that involve estimation, require us to focus this review on a subset of the estimation literature. One decision was to focus on numerical estimation; this decision reflected our interest in numerical operations and in placing numerical estimation in the context of algorithmic quantitative processes, such as counting and arithmetic. A second decision was to exclude from consideration tasks that require knowledge external to estimation, in particular, knowledge of measurement units (pounds, hours, miles) or real-world entities (population of Russia, number of people with AIDS). A third decision was to exclude studies of subitizing, because it appears to involve a different process than estimating larger sets of objects (Trick & Pylyshyn, 1994). Underlying all three decisions was the goal of focusing on processes common to a wide range of estimation tasks. These decisions led us to focus on three types of estimation that fit these criteria and about which a reasonable amount is known: computational, numerosity, and number line estimation.

A THEORETICAL FRAMEWORK FOR UNDERSTANDING THE DEVELOPMENT OF ESTIMATION

The diversity of estimation tasks has made it difficult to generate anything approaching a general model of numerical estimation. The main purpose of the present chapter is to examine whether overlapping waves theory might provide such a general model.

Overlapping waves theory is an attempt to account for cognitive change in a variety of domains; to date, it has been applied to development of arithmetic, reading, spelling, memory, problem solving, conceptual understanding, and a variety of other areas (Siegler, 1996). It is an evolutionary theory, both in the sense that change is viewed as occurring gradually, rather than in discontinuous stages, and in the sense that the model posits that cognitive change occurs through the processes of variation, selection, and inheritance, the same processes that produce biological evolution. The theoretical framework led us to focus on four main characteristics of cognition in this domain:

1. *Variability of strategies and representations*: People generally use a variety of strategies and representations to solve a given problem, rather than just a single one. The diverse strategies and representations coexist over prolonged periods of time, not just during brief transition periods.
2. *Strategy choice*: People choose strategies and representations adaptively. That is, they adjust their choices to problem and situational characteristics in ways that produce more accurate and rapid performance than could be produced by choosing randomly among them or by always using a single approach.
3. *Changes in strategy use*: Relevant experience leads to several types of strategic "inheritance" that improve future performance by maintaining the lessons of past processing. Among the most important processing experiences for producing cognitive change are generation of more advanced strategies and representations, increased use of the more advanced approaches from among the approaches that are known at a given time, increasingly precise fitting of approaches to problem and situational characteristics, and increasingly effective execution of each approach.
4. *Individual differences*: Because change in any one capability both reflects the status of other capabilities and contributes to changes in them, positive correlations should be present among individuals' proficiency in related capabilities.

In the remainder of this chapter, we utilize these characteristics as a framework for organizing the literatures on computational, numerosity, and number line estimation. For each area, we first examine developmental trends in the accuracy of estimates and then focus on variability in the strategies that children use, the adaptiveness of their choices among them, changes in their strategy use, and relations between individual differences in estimation strategies and estimation accuracy.

COMPUTATIONAL ESTIMATION

Computational estimation involves answering an arithmetic problem with the goal of approximating the correct magnitude rather than calculating the exact answer. Effective computational estimation requires several types of conceptual understanding: (a) that the goal of estimation is to produce an answer reasonably close in magnitude to the correct one, (b) that approximate numbers are useful for attaining this goal, (c) that estimation can involve multiple valid approaches and multiple reasonable answers, and (d) that context determines the adequacy of answers (LeFevre, Greenham, & Waheed, 1993; Sowder & Wheeler, 1989). Effective estimation also requires procedures for generating approximate numbers, for example, procedures for rounding the operands to simplify the calculation and for compensating for distortions introduced by rounding.

Development of Accurate Estimation

Development of computational estimation begins surprisingly late and proceeds surprisingly slowly. For example, when 5-year-olds are asked to estimate answers to single-digit addition problems that are slightly beyond their computational abilities, their most common approaches are either to state one of the addends or to state a number one greater than one of the addends (Baroody, 1989; Dowker, 2003). It is unclear whether such approaches even qualify as estimates, in the sense of constituting attempts to approximate the magnitude of the correct answer.

Lack of conceptual understanding of estimation seems to contribute to the use of these stereotyped approaches and to the slow development of computational estimation for years thereafter. LeFevre et al. (1993) found that the majority of the Canadian fourth graders in their sample did not even know what estimation was. When asked to define estimation, most said that it was "guessing" or indicated that they did not know. When asked to estimate the products of multi-digit multiplication problems, only 20% of fourth graders produced reasonable estimates (estimates that varied systematically with the product). Similarly, when U. S. third and fifth graders were asked to estimate the sums of two addends, more than 75% did not agree that two alternative estimates could both be acceptable (Sowder & Wheeler, 1989). In a study of British children, Dowker (1997) found that early elementary school children fairly often could perform exact computations in a numerical range but could not estimate answers in the same range. Children who could compute answers to problems with sums between 6 and 10 (mean age 6 years, 10 months) produced unreasonable estimates (answers off by more than 30%) on 40% of problems with sums in the same range. Similarly, children who were able to compute the correct answer on problems with sums of 11 to 32 (mean age 8.0) generated unreasonable estimates on 33% of problems in the same range, and children who could solve problems with sums less than 100 (mean age 8.5) also produced unreasonable estimates on 33% of problems.

Computational estimation does improve considerably, albeit gradually, after third or fourth grade. Adults and sixth graders are more accurate than fourth graders in estimating the sum of two 3-digit addends (Lemaire & Lecacheur, 2002), and sixth and eighth graders are more accurate than fourth graders in estimating the sums of long strings of addends (Smith, 1999). Similarly, adults are more accurate than eighth graders, who in turn are more accurate than sixth graders, in estimating the products of multi-digit multiplication problems (LeFevre et al., 1993). Improvements in speed of estimation of both addition and multiplication follow a similar course to improvements in accuracy over the same age range (LeFevre et al., 1993; Lemaire & Lecacheur, 2002).

The rate of improvement in computational estimation is sufficiently slow that some studies have not found any significant improvement with age. Schoen, Friesen, Jarrett, & Urbatsch (1981, Study 2) found no age improvements in estimates on addition and multiplication problems between fifth and sixth grade, and Booth and Siegler (in preparation) found that accuracy of estimates on multi-digit addition problems did not improve between second and fourth grades. The fact that these studies included relatively small age ranges and relatively brief time limits for generating answers may have constrained the range of estimation strategies, which may account for the lack of improvement. Nonetheless, the lack of significant change also appears to reflect slow development in this area.

Variability of Strategies and Representations

From early in the development of computational estimation, individual children use a variety of strategies. Evidence for such strategic variability comes both from observations of ongoing behavior and from immediately retrospective self-reports (LeFevre et al., 1993; Sowder & Wheeler, 1989). The strategies often are not mutually exclusive; for example, on a single problem, a child might first round one or both operands and then use compensation to reduce the distortion introduced by the rounding. Interestingly, the same computational estimation strategies appear to be used in all of the countries in which studies of computational estimation have been conducted: France (Lemaire, Lecacheur, & Farioli, 2000), Japan (Reys et al., 1991), Canada (LeFevre et al., 1993), Britain, (Dowker, 1997), and the United States (Reys, Rybolt, Bestgen, & Wyatt, 1982). The similarity is not attributable to children in the five countries being taught the same estimation strategies; indeed, all of the investigators noted that the children in their sample had received little or no formal instruction in estimation strategies. Rather, the children in each country seem to have generated the estimation strategies for themselves, in response to the nature of the decimal system and the working memory demands posed by computational estimation.

Computational estimation strategies can be classified at varying levels of generality. At a general level, children and adults have been found to use three families of strategies: reformulation, translation, and compensation (Reys et al., 1982; Reys et al., 1991; Sowder & Wheeler, 1989). *Reformulation* involves changing operands to more computationally convenient forms (e.g., by rounding both operands to the nearest 10). *Translation* involves changing the form of the equation to a more computationally convenient form, e.g, approximating the sum of a long list of numbers by estimating an average value, estimating the number of addends, and multiplying the two estimates. *Compensation* involves correcting for predictable distortions introduced by the estimation process, e.g., adding a percentage of an estimated sum after having rounded both addends downward.

It is also possible to classify computational estimation strategies at a more specific level (Dowker, Flood, Griffiths, Harriss, & Hook, 1996; LeFevre et al., 1993). The following is a list of the most common strategies for addition and multiplication:

1. *Rounding*: Converting one or both operands to the closest number ending in one or more zeroes (on 297 × 296, both multiplicands might be converted to 300).
2. *Truncating*: Changing to zero one or more digits at the right end of one or more operands (on 297 × 296, both multiplicands might be converted to 290).
3. *Prior compensation*: Rounding the second operand in the opposite direction of the first before performing any computation (on 297 × 296, 296 might be rounded to 290 rather than 300 to compensate for the effect of rounding 297 to 300).
4. *Postcompensation*: Correcting after a computation has been done for distortion introduced by earlier rounding or truncation (on 297 × 296, subtracting 2% from the product after multiplying 300 × 300).
5. *Decomposition*: Dividing numbers into simpler forms (on 282 × 153, multiplying 280 × 10 × 15).
6. *Translation*: Simplifying an equation, for example, by changing the operation (e.g., on 44 + 53 + 51 + 47, multiplying 50 × 4).
7. *Guessing.*

As might be expected, some of these strategies are used more often than others. Rounding is the most common approach (Lemaire et al., 2000; LeFevre et al., 1993; Reys et al., 1982, 1991); compensation tends to be the least frequently used. For example, in Lemaire et al.'s (2000) study of estimation of multi-digit sums, fifth graders used rounding on 64% of trials and compensation on 2%.

Consistent with the overlapping waves model, individuals often know and use a variety of computational estimation strategies. This is especially true among skillful estimators. For example, Dowker et al. (1996) examined the multiplication and division estimates of four groups of adults: mathematicians, accountants, psychology students, and English students. Their strategies were remarkably diverse; for example, the 176 participants used 27 different strategies for solving the single problem 4645 ÷ 18. Across the whole problem set, individuals in each of the four groups averaged more than 5 strategies apiece. In line with one of the most distinctive predictions of overlapping waves theory, strategic variability was evident within individual and problem. When the same problems were presented to participants a second time, mathematicians, for example, used a different strategy on 46% of problems and psychology students on 37%.

This strategic variability is present among children as well as adults. For example, when asked to estimate the sum of two 3-digit numbers, French fifth graders used four main strategies: rounding with decomposition, rounding without decomposition, compensation, and truncation (Lemaire et al., 2000). Almost all (95%) of the children used at least two of the strategies, 71% used at least three, and 38% used all four.

Strategy Choice

The overlapping waves model also predicts that children and adults will adapt their strategy choices to problem characteristics. Again, this is clearly the case.

One form that this adaptation takes is to use rounding more often on problems in which it introduces less distortion. For example, on multi-digit addition problems, the closer an addend is to a decade, and therefore the less distortion introduced by rounding, the more often fifth graders round (Lemaire & Lecacheur, 2002). Similarly, on multi-digit multiplication problems, sixth graders, eighth graders, and adults more often round both of the multiplicands when both have two or three digits but often only round the larger multiplicand when the smaller one is a single digit (LeFevre et al., 1993). This choice pattern minimizes distortion, because rounding single-digit multiplicands to the nearest 10 changes them by a greater percentage than rounding two or three digit multiplicands to the nearest 10.

Also consistent with the prediction that people choose estimation strategies in adaptive ways, the more strategies used by each of the adult participants in Dowker et al. (1996), the more accurate were their estimates. The relation held true within the four categories of participants as well as between them.

To account for such adaptive choices, LeFevre et al. (1993), proposed a model of computational estimation explicitly based on Siegler and Shrager's (1984) model of strategy choices in exact arithmetic. LeFevre et al. proposed that when presented with a computational estimation problem, people first attempt to retrieve the exact answer. If unsuccessful, the estimator then reformulates the problem (by rounding, decomposition, or some other strategy that changes operands to a more tractable form) and then attempts to either retrieve or calculate the answer to the reformulated problem. If this attempt is unsuccessful, the estimator further simplifies the operands and then again attempts to retrieve or calculate an answer. The reformulation efforts continue until an acceptable solution is reached. When reformulation is complete, the estimator may compensate for the error introduced by the reformulation, for example, by adding a correction term after rounding down both addends. Whether such compensation occurs, however, varies with the conceptual understanding, and perhaps the working memory capacity, of the estimator (LeFevre et al., 1993).

This model is consistent with several types of data. Both children and adults prefer to calculate the exact answer to a problem, often defying direct instructions not to do so (Levine, 1982; Ginsburg, Baroody, & Russell, 1982). The model is also consistent with the findings that individual children use multiple strategies, that they choose among them in adaptive ways, and that most children, even in middle school and high school, do not use compensation because they lack conceptual understanding of what constitutes reasonable compensation (Reys et al., 1982).

Changes in Strategy Use

The range and appropriateness of computational estimation strategies increase with age and mathematical experience. Adults use a considerably greater variety of multiplication strategies than do sixth or eighth graders (LeFevre et al., 1993). Similarly, mathematicians and accountants, who have unusually extensive numerical experience, use a greater variety of appropriate estimation strategies than do even the highly selected psychology and English students at

Oxford University (Dowker et al., 1996). The latter two groups used a greater variety of inappropriate estimation strategies than did the former two, which indicates that ability to generate appropriate variants is what distinguishes the mathematicians and accountants rather than greater variation per se.

A second type of change in strategy use involves the sophistication of the strategies that are used. Use of compensation, a strategy that requires a good conceptual understanding of estimation, shows especially substantial growth. In estimating the answers to multi-digit addition problems, far more ninth graders used postcompensation than did third or fifth graders (Lemaire et al., 2000; Sowder & Wheeler, 1989). Similarly, in multi-digit multiplication, adults used postcompensation strategies much more often than did sixth or eighth graders (LeFevre et al., 1993).

Also as predicted by the overlapping waves model, the adaptiveness of strategy choices seems to increase with age and experience. When presented a pair of three-digit addends and given the choice of either rounding both up or both down to the nearest decade, sixth graders and adults used the size of the units digits to choose their rounding strategy (Lemaire & Lecacheur, 2002). This approach makes sense, because rounding down introduces less distortion when the units digit is small and rounding up introduces less distortion when the units digit is large. In contrast, fourth graders' choices were not influenced by the magnitude of the units digit; instead, the largest influence on their rounding was the size of the hundreds and decades digits. The reason why the size of the hundreds and decades digits correlated with the direction of rounding was unclear, given that the rounding only involved the units digit.

The quality of strategy choices in multi-digit multiplication also appears to increase with age and mathematical experience. LeFevre et al. (1993) provided the example of strategy choices on 11×112. Among adults, 75% rounded the problem to 10×112, a computationally tractable approach that yields an answer within 9% of the correct answer. Although this approach would seem well within the capabilities of sixth graders (LeFevre et al., 1993), no sixth grader used it. Instead, most sixth graders rounded either to 10×100 or to 10×110.

Several factors have been hypothesized to cause these changes in strategy use and strategy choice. One is conceptual understanding of estimation. For example, LeFevre et al. (1993) hypothesized that accurate computational estimation requires understanding of the simplification principle (the understanding that mental arithmetic is easier with simple operands) and the proximity principle (the understanding that the goal of estimation is to obtain estimates close in magnitude to the correct answer). The self-reported strategy use of fourth graders, as well as of older children, indicated understanding of the principle of simplification; however, only the adults' explanations showed an understanding of the importance of generating an estimate close in magnitude to the correct answer. Sowder and Wheeler (1989) reached a similar conclusion for estimates of the answers to multi-digit addition problems, based on the reluctance of even ninth graders to accept that both of two alternative estimates could be acceptable and the infrequent use of compensation at all ages (third through ninth grade). The problem seemed to be that the children viewed estimation as a rigid algorithmic procedure that required following pre-set rules rather than as a flexible attempt to approximate the magnitude of an answer using whatever means made sense in the particular situation. The algorithmic emphasis is reflected in Sowder and Wheeler's (1989) observation that "some students in both grades five and seven objected to rounding 267 to 250 rather than 300, arguing, 'You're always taught to go up if it's past five,' or 'Seven is above five, so you have to go up, not down'" (p. 144).

On the other hand, Sowder and Wheeler also noted that by fifth grade, the large majority of children, when presented hypothetical estimation procedures in which rounding was or was not followed by compensation for the distortions introduced by rounding, recognized that rounding with compensation was superior. This finding suggests that some conceptual understanding of the importance of the proximity principle is present by fifth grade.

Sowder and Wheeler's finding that most fifth graders recognized the value of compensation but did not use it when generating computational estimates points to a second (nonexclusive) hypothesized source of age-related improvement in computational estimation: working memory capacity. Case and Sowder (1990) proposed that age-related increases in working memory allow children to maintain an increasing number of representations simultaneously. For example, the working memory growth allows older adolescents and adults, but not younger children, to remember the results of rounding, the operands, intermediate computations, and the need to compensate for the effects of rounding the operands. Case and Sowder found that children of a wide variety of ages succeeded at estimation tasks for which their working memory capacities appeared sufficient and not on tasks for which their memory capacities appeared insufficient.

A third hypothesized source of age-related improvement in computational estimation is improved computational skills. Given a problem such as 79×191, a child with good mental multiplication skills could solve 80×190, whereas one with limited skills might only be able to solve 80×200. Consistent with this analysis, proficiency at exact mental arithmetic correlates positively with estimation accuracy (LeFevre et al., 1993).

Individual Differences

Both children and adults show substantial individual differences in computational estimation (Dowker, 2003). Children's proficiency at computational estimation correlates positively, and often substantially, with IQ (Reys et al., 1982) and with a variety of measures of mathematical ability, including math SAT score (Paull, 1972), elementary school math achievement test score (Siegler & Booth, 2004), and arithmetic fluency score (Dowker, 1997, 2003; LeFevre et al., 1993).

Skill at arithmetic computation seems to be especially closely associated with computational estimation (Dowker, 2003). This is not surprising, given that computational estimation generally requires arithmetic computation of rounded numbers. As noted previously, estimators who are more proficient at computation can change operands to a smaller extent (rounding to the nearest 10 rather than the nearest 100) and still compute the answer.

Among adults, computational estimation skill seems to be uncorrelated with skill at other types of estimation (Dowker, 2003). This does not seem to be the case with children, however. For example, computational estimation proficiency has been found to correlate positively with number line and numerosity estimation among second, third, and fourth graders (Booth & Siegler, in preparation).

NUMEROSITY ESTIMATION

Numerosity estimation involves assigning a number to a set of discrete objects, such as pennies in a jar or people at a concert.

Development of Accurate Estimation

Accuracy of numerosity estimation increases over a prolonged age range. Adults estimate the number of discrete objects more accurately than sixth to eighth graders, who estimate more accurately than second to fifth graders (Siegel, Goldsmith, & Madson, 1982). Similar improvement is evident with two-dimensional (Luwel, Verschaffel, Onghema, & DeCorte, 2000; Verschaffel, DeCorte, Lamote, & Dherdt, 1998) and three-dimensional (Siegel et al., 1982) stimuli.

Variability of Strategies and Representations

The strategies used for numerosity estimation vary with the stimulus presentation format. When objects are presented in a regularly spaced grid of known proportions (e.g., 10 rows, each with 10 objects), children and adults use three strategies: addition, subtraction, and estimation (Verschaffel et al., 1998; Luwel et al., 2000, 2002). The addition strategy involves quantifying upward from zero. The subtraction strategy involves quantifying downward from the maximum number of objects in the grid. The estimation strategy is less well specified; it involves rapid approximation of the number of objects by a process other than counting, addition, or subtraction.

Though less is known about the strategies used when presentation formats are less constrained, a few general strategies have been identified. One strategy is anchoring, in which a known quantity is used to estimate an unknown one (e.g., I know that 600 beans fit in that jar, a bean is about one third of the size of a popped kernel of popcorn, so there must be about 200 kernels of popcorn in it) (Crites, 1992; Siegel et al., 1982). Another common strategy is decomposition (e.g., estimating the number of objects in a row or area and then multiplying by the estimated number of rows or areas of that size) (Crites, 1992; Siegel et al., 1982). Estimation in the sense of rapid approximation through processes other than counting, adding, or subtracting is also used with irregularly spaced objects.

Strategy Choice

As with choices in computational estimation, strategy choices in numerosity estimation are sensitive to problem characteristics. For regularly spaced objects presented in a grid of known proportions (i.e., a child knows that the objects are in a 10 × 10 grid), strategy choices are in large part determined by the relative numbers of filled and unfilled spaces. To illustrate this point, Verschaffel et al. (1998) presented adults, sixth graders, and second graders with 10 × 10 grids containing between 1 and 100 small squares; the participants had 20 seconds to indicate how many squares were present. A two-phase segmented linear regression analysis (Beem, 1995) was used to test the fit of accuracy and solution times to a model based on the hypothesis that addition would be used when relatively few squares were present, whereas subtraction would be used when many were. The implication was that solution times and error rates would show a curvilinear pattern, with greater speed and accuracy at both extremes of the 1–100 range than in the middle.

The two-phase regression model fit the data of adults and sixth graders fairly well, accounting for 56% of variance in adults' solution times on the 100 problems and 41% of variance in sixth graders' times. The model also fit the performance of second graders to some degree, accounting for 27% of the variance in their solution times. The fit was much better than that of the linear model that would be expected if participants only used the addition strategy. Verbal reports obtained after the estimation procedure provided converging evidence for the strategy assessments. Almost all participants indicated that they used the addition strategy when the number of filled squares was small and the subtraction strategy when the number of filled spaces was large.

Although the group-level analyses suggested that the model fit second graders' performance moderately well, analysis of individual children's performance suggested that their use of the approach was limited. Almost half of the second graders appeared to use the subtraction strategy only when almost all squares were filled. Most of the rest generated a flat or weak positive slope of solution times at the high end of the range rather than the negative slope that the two-phase model predicted. Verschaffel et al. suggested that these children were using a quick estimation approach when most squares were filled rather than the subtraction strategy that the model implied.

There also was some asymmetry in the range of problems on which the two strategies were chosen. The segmented regression analysis indicated that the break point between the ascending and descending solution times in Verschaffel et al.'s (1998) data was at 59, 63, and 56 for adults, sixth graders, and second graders, respectively. If choices were unbiased and speed of execution of the addition and subtraction strategies were equal, the expected break point would be 50. Verschaffel et al. suggested that the subtraction strategy required additional processing, which would be expected to result in a break point greater than 50. Whether the choices reflect execution of the subtraction strategy being more difficult, bias in favor of the addition approach above and beyond differences in execution difficulty, or some combination of the two is unknown.

More recently, Luwel, Beem, Onghena, & Verschaffel (2001) tested whether a three-phase model provided a better description of solution times and accuracy than the previously tested two-phase model. The logic was that when the matrix was neither nearly empty nor nearly full, participants might use a rapid estimation strategy that was not based on either addition or subtraction. Such a strategy would be expected to yield rapid times and high error rates, to be used more often when the filled matrix contained a larger number of objects and to be used with a wider range of matrix sizes at younger ages than at older ones.

To test these predictions, Luwel et al. (2001) presented second and sixth graders 7×7, 8×8, and 9×9 matrices; the time limit to generate estimates was 20 seconds. The three-phase model provided a better fit to most participants' solution times than did the two-phase model. The expected developmental trend was also present. The three-phase model better fit second graders' solution times for all three matrix sizes but better fit the solution times of sixth graders, who presumably could quantify more rapidly, only on the 9×9 matrix. On the two smaller matrices, the sixth graders apparently could execute the addition and subtraction strategies in the available time, so they did not need to use the less accurate estimation approach. Thus, the estimation strategy appeared to serve as a back-up approach for cases in which the combination of counting speed, matrix size, and number of filled squares precluded use of the addition or subtraction strategies.

For irregular arrangements of objects, little is known about how numerosity estimation strategies are chosen. Decomposition appears to be used less often with irregularly configured collections than with regularly configured ones, probably because the best means of decomposition is less obvious with irregular collections (Smith, 1999). In addition, when a reference point or anchor is provided, individuals often choose to compare the collection to the anchor and then to adjust the anchor value up or down to produce an estimate (Smith, 1999).

Changes in Strategy Use

Age-related improvements in the speed and accuracy of numerosity estimation stem in part from adoption of new, superior strategies. In estimating the number of dots in a regular grid with a known maximum number of dots, roughly half of second graders rarely, if ever, used the subtraction strategy, whereas almost all sixth graders used it (Verschaffel et al., 1998). Similarly, in estimating a regularly spaced collection of items when the maximum number was unknown, adults used the decomposition strategy more often than did sixth to eighth graders, who used it more often than did second to fifth graders (Siegel et al., 1982).

Choices among existing strategies also improve with age. Even those second graders who used the subtraction strategy tended to use it only on problems with very close to the maximum number of dots, that is, problems on which only small numbers of unfilled spaces needed to be subtracted (Verschaffel et al., 1998). Sixth graders and adults used the subtraction strategy on a considerably broader range of set sizes. Conversely, second graders used the relatively inaccurate estimation strategy on a broader range of problems than did sixth graders or adults (Luvel et al., 2001).

Finally, strategy execution improves with age. Sixth graders executed the subtraction strategy more rapidly than did second graders, allowing the older children to apply the strategy on problems on which second graders needed to use the relatively inaccurate estimation strategy because they could not execute the subtraction strategy in the available time (Luwel et al.,

2001). The older children also executed the subtraction strategy more accurately than did the younger ones.

Individual Differences

Individual differences in strategy use predict accuracy of numerosity estimation. The more adaptively adults and children switched between addition and subtraction strategies, the less their estimates deviated from the correct answer (Verschaffel et al., 1998).

Numerosity estimation proficiency is also related to other quantitative abilities. Adults' scores on Hitch's Numerical Abilities test and children's math achievement test scores are correlated with the accuracy of their numerosity estimation (Dowker, 2003). Second, third, and fourth graders' accuracy at numerosity estimation also correlates positively with their proficiency at computational and number line estimation (Booth & Siegler, in preparation).

NUMBER LINE ESTIMATION

Children's translation of numbers into positions on number lines provides particularly direct information about their representations of numerical magnitude. The mapping function between numbers and their magnitudes is embedded within all forms of numerical estimation; for example, if the function departs from linearity, it will distort the numbers used to label collections of objects. Studies of number line estimation demonstrate that such distortion due to nonlinear mappings between numbers and their magnitudes is more than a theoretical possibility.

Development of Accurate Estimation

Number line estimation improves steadily during the elementary school years, with accuracy at any given age being greater on smaller numerical scales. On 0–10 number lines, Pettito (1990) found that percent absolute error decreased from 14% late in first grade to 4% late in third grade. On 0–100 number lines, the same children's percent absolute error decreased from 19% late in first grade to 8% late in third grade. Siegler and Booth (2004) obtained similar findings on 0–100 scales (the only ones they studied): percent absolute error decreased from 24% to 10% between kindergarten and second grade. On 0–1,000 number lines, Siegler and Opfer (2003) found that percent absolute error improved from 21% in second grade to 14% in fourth grade, 7% in sixth grade, and 1% in adulthood.

These effects of numerical scale are present above and beyond the influence of the particular numbers being estimated. When the same children were asked to estimate the positions of an identical set of numbers on 0–100 and 0–1,000 scales, estimates were considerably more accurate on the 0–100 scale (Siegler & Opfer, 2003). Scale effects are particularly large when comparing estimates of integers and decimal fractions between 0 and 1. By third grade, children estimate integer magnitudes on a 0–100 scale very accurately (Pettito, 1990); in contrast, fifth graders' accuracy in estimating positions of decimal fractions on number lines is extremely inaccurate (Rittle-Johnson et al., 2001).

Variability of Strategies and Representations

As with other types of estimation, children and adults use multiple strategies in number line estimation. Early elementary school children most often use counting strategies. The three most common counting strategies are to always count upward from the smallest value, to sometimes do that and sometimes count downward from the largest value, and to use both of those strategies and also sometimes estimate a midpoint value and count upward or downward from there. About 80% of first, second, and third graders use such counting strategies (Newman & Berger, 1984; Petitto, 1990). An interesting feature of the counting strategies is that they involve imaginary breaks in what is physically a continuous, unbroken line; the counting is of entirely subjective units rather than discrete entities.

Older elementary school children (sixth graders) and adults appear to use a different type of strategy on 0–1,000 number lines, one based on proportional reasoning. They appear to subjectively divide the number line into quarters and to use the quartile labels (0, 250, 500, 750, and 1,000) as landmarks for estimating the locations of other numbers (Siegler & Opfer, 2003). This strategy was inferred from an analysis of the variability of estimates for each number that participants were asked to estimate. The reasoning was that if people use a landmark to estimate the locations of other numbers, the variability of estimates should increase with increasing distance between the number and the landmark. Thus, if people's smallest subjective landmarks on a 0–1,000 number line are 0 and 250, estimates for 240 should be less variable than estimates for 180, because 240 is closer to the nearest landmark. Distance from the closest quartile landmark on a 0–1,000 number line accounted for an average of 55% of the variance in the variability of estimates of sixth graders and adults on two number line tasks. This percent variance accounted for was much greater than the percentage that could be explained by alternative subjective landmark schemes that divided the number line into terciles, quintiles, or deciles, or by the accumulator model, which predicted that variability should increase linearly with numerical magnitude.

In addition to this variation in strategy use, variability is also present in the representations of numerical magnitude that children apply on number line tasks. One common approach is to employ a linear representation, in which representations of numerical magnitude increase linearly with the size of the number. Another common approach is to employ a logarithmic representation, in which representations of numerical magnitude increase logarithmically with numerical magnitude. When children use such a logarithmic representation, the spatial positions that they choose increase very quickly in the low range of numbers and then level off in the upper part of the range. For example, Siegler and Opfer (2003) found that on 0–1,000 number lines, second graders' estimates for very small numbers such as 2 and 5 were almost exactly correct, that their estimates for somewhat larger numbers such as 18, 25, 71, and 86 were much too high (the positions they marked corresponded to numbers between 300 and 500), and that their estimates for much larger numbers such as 780 and 810 were, again, relatively accurate.

Considerable evidence indicates that children use both of these representations. Early in children's learning of a given range of numbers, the fit of the logarithmic representation to children's pattern of estimates tends to be very high in absolute terms and much higher than the fit of the linear representation; later in learning, the two functions fit approximately equally well; and even later, the linear function fits much better. For example, in an experiment on kindergartners', first graders', and second graders' estimates on 0–100 number lines (Siegler & Booth, 2004, Experiment 2), kindergartners' median estimates were better fit by the logarithmic function than by the linear function (R^2 = .89 vs. .69), first graders' estimates were fit equally well by the two functions (R^2 = .94 and .92), and second graders' estimates were better fit by the linear function (R^2 = .97 vs. .85). Similarly, in an experiment on 0–1,000 number lines (Siegler & Opfer, 2003), second graders' estimates were fit better by the logarithmic function (R^2 = .95 vs. .63), fourth graders' estimates were fit equally well (nonsignificantly different) by the two functions (R^2 = .93 and .82), and sixth graders' estimates were fit better by the linear function (R^2 = 1.00 vs. .78).

This variability of representations was present within children as well as between them. For almost half of the second graders in Siegler and Opfer (2003), the best-fitting function for children's estimates was linear on the 0–100 line but logarithmic on the 0–1,000 line.

Strategy Choice

The factors that influence choices of strategies on number lines vary with the strategy being considered. For counting strategies, one major decision involves where to begin counting. Once children count from numbers other than 1, their choices of counting strategy are heavily influenced by the distance of the number being estimated from the nearest reference point that they use. By the end of first grade, roughly half of children count up from 1 when asked to estimate the positions of numbers near the low end of the scale and count down from the maximum value to estimate the positions of numbers near the high end (Newman & Berger, 1984; Pettito, 1990). By the end of third grade, most children use those approaches and about half also estimate a midpoint value and count from the midpoint when the number being estimated is near the middle.

Another dimension of strategy choice relevant to counting strategies concerns the unit of counting. For small scales (e.g., 1–23), second and third graders count by 1s; on larger scales (e.g., 0–100), they often count by 5s or 10s as well (Newman & Berger, 1984; Petitto, 1990).

As indicated above, the scale of numbers also influences choices of representations on number line tasks. For example, second graders often rely on the linear representation for numbers on the 0–100 scale, whereas they rely on the logarithmic representation for the 0–1,000 scale (Siegler & Opfer, 2003). This difference is not attributable to representations of the magnitudes of particular numbers; on a subset of numbers below 100 that were presented on both 0–100 and 0–1,000 scales, the same second graders generated logarithmic patterns of estimates on the 0–1,000 scale but linear ones on the 0–100 scale. Thus, the numerical scale seems to be a key determinant of young children's choice of numerical representation.

Changes in Strategy Use

The sources of improving accuracy of number line estimation are much like those in computational and numerosity estimation. One source is use of an increasing variety of strategies. Newman and Berger (1984) found that in estimating numbers on 1–23 number lines, third graders used more strategies than kindergartners or first graders and that the greater the number of strategies, the more accurate their estimates were. This relation between sophistication of strategy use and accuracy of estimation was present even when the effect of age was statistically controlled. The form of the relation also made sense. For large numbers, children who counted down from the high end of the range were more accurate than children who did not; for medium-size numbers, children who sometimes counted from the midpoint were more accurate than those who did not. The relation between use of the midpoint counting strategy and increased accuracy of estimates for medium-size numbers also has been found with 0–100 number lines (Petitto, 1990).

The improved use of counting strategies, in turn, seems to reflect development of both counting skills and conceptual understanding of numerical magnitude. First, consider the relation to counting skills. Counting by numbers other than one improves considerably in this age range, and skill at counting forward and backward from locations other than one correlates about $r = .50$ with accuracy of estimation (Newman & Berger, 1984). As with the relation between estimation accuracy and strategy use, the relation between counting skill and strategy use remained present even when age was partialed out. In addition, forward counting develops more rapidly than backward counting, which probably contributes to estimates of numbers at the low end of the 0–100 scale being more accurate than estimates of numbers at the middle and high ends in first grade and the early part of second grade (Petitto, 1990).

The relation between conceptual understanding and accuracy of number line estimation is not as well established, but Petitto (1990) provided some persuasive arguments for the likely existence of such a relation. She suggested that most first graders view numbers primarily as a sequence of entities with only ordinal relations to magnitude. Third graders, by contrast, were said to view numerical quantities on number lines primarily in terms of proportions; this allows children of this age, but not younger children, to estimate midpoints and to use these midpoints as landmarks for estimating numerical magnitudes. Third graders also are considerably more likely than younger children to consistently use rulers with equal intervals between numbers to measure lengths (rather than otherwise identical rulers with unequal intervals between numbers). This again reflects growing conceptual understanding of the need for proportionality between numerical magnitude and spatial extent (Petitto, 1990).

Petitto's proposal regarding how increasing conceptual understanding influences number line estimation strategies corresponds closely to Siegler and Opfer's (2003) proposal regarding how growing conceptual understanding influences representations of numerical magnitude. The ages at which the changes in representations and strategies are observed also correspond quite closely.

Individual Differences in Performance

Accuracy of number line estimation is linked to general mathematical ability. Significant and often substantial correlations between math achievement test scores and accuracy of number line estimation have been found among kindergartners, first graders, and second graders on 0–100 number lines (Booth & Siegler, in preparation; Siegler & Booth, 2004) and among second, third, and fourth graders on 0–1,000 number lines (Booth & Siegler, in preparation).

CONCLUSIONS

For all three types of estimation—computational, numerosity, and number line—the overlapping waves model provided an effective framework for understanding development. In each area, both children and adults use varied strategies. The number of strategies that people use increases with age and experience, as does the sophistication of the strategies that are used. Choices among strategies are adaptive for all three types of estimation, with both children and adults adjusting their strategies to the demands of problems. The degree of adaptiveness increases with the acquisition of new strategies; e.g., in both numerosity and number line estimation, children's speed and accuracy improves once their strategies make use of the maximum as well as the minimum value. The main sources of change that have been identified in domains other than estimation—introduction of new strategies, increased frequency of use of relatively advanced existing strategies, increasingly adaptive choices among strategies, and increasingly efficient execution of strategies—contribute to improved estimation as well. Finally, substantial individual differences in strategy use are present in all three types of estimation, and these individual differences correlate positively with proficiency in other types of estimation and with mathematical ability more generally. Thus, the overlapping waves model provides a useful structure for suggesting and organizing major phenomena in the three domains, for illuminating commonalities across the domains, and for placing the phenomena in a unified theoretical framework.

Several questions have been raised. Perhaps the most basic concerns why estimation skill develops so slowly. The late onset and exceptionally gradual rate of subsequent development cannot be attributed to children's not having any sense of quantitative magnitude; even infants in their first year discriminate fairly skillfully between non-numerical magnitudes, such as numbers of objects or sounds (Lipton & Spelke, 2003). Nor can the poor quality of mathematics instruction in the United States be blamed; development of estimation is also very slow in Japan, France, Britain, and Canada. Rather, the problem seems to stem from difficulties attaching numbers to magnitudes.

Several plausible sources of difficulty have been hypothesized in all three areas of estimation: limitations of conceptual understanding, of component skills such as counting and arithmetic, and of working memory. Consistent with these hypotheses, children and adults who estimate accurately also tend to have better conceptual understanding, better counting and arithmetic skills, and greater working memory capacity than do those who estimate less accurately. The relations are present even when age is partialed out. However, the direction of causation remains to be determined; although the usual hypothesis is that poor conceptual understanding of estimation results in poor estimation accuracy, it also seems likely that accuracy of estimation procedures contributes to development of conceptual understanding, by providing a data base from which understanding can be constructed (Rittle-Johnson et al., 2001).

Recent studies of number line estimation suggest an additional source of the slow and incomplete development of estimation skills: non-linear representations of numerical magnitudes. Many kindergartners and first graders represent numerical magnitudes in the range 0–100 as a logarithmically rather than a linearly increasing function. Similarly, many children in the grades between kindergarten and fourth grade utilize logarithmic representations with numerical magnitudes in the 0-1,000 range. The compression of most of the numerical range implied by a logarithmic representation may have a great deal to do with the slow pace of development of estimation. If representations of the magnitudes of different numbers are largely indistinguishable, children are unlikely to gain much of a sense of the types of numbers that are plausible answers to numerical problems or that typically accompany real world values (as illustrated by the constant confusion in newspaper and magazine articles of millions, billions, and trillions). This view suggests that helping young children develop linear representations of a wide range of numerical magnitudes may be a key step in allowing development of estimation to proceed more rapidly than it typically does. Given that ongoing research (Booth & Siegler, in preparation) has revealed positive and quite substantial correlations among elementary school age children's accuracy in number line, computational, and numerosity estimation, it also might be possible to improve estimation accuracy across multiple types of numerical estimation by providing a single, generalizable instructional experience. Whether this is possible remains an important question for future research.

REFERENCES

Baroody, A. J. (1989). Kindergartners' mental addition with single-digit combinations. *Journal for Research in Mathematics Education, 20,* 159–172.

Beem, A. L. (1995). A program for fitting two-phase segmented-curve models with an unknown change point, with an application to the analysis of strategy shifts in a cognitive task. *Behavior Research Methods, Instruments, & Computers, 27,* 392–399.

Booth, J. L., & Siegler, R. S. (in preparation). The relation between number line estimation and other types of estimation.

Case, R., & Sowder, J. T. (1990). The development of computational estimation: A neo-Piagetian analysis. *Cognition and Instruction, 7,* 79–104.

Crites, T. (1992). Skilled and less skilled estimators' strategies for estimating discrete quantities. *The Elementary School Journal, 92,* 601–619.

Dowker, A. (2003). Young children's estimates for addition: The zone of partial knowledge and understanding. In A. J. Baroody & A. Dowker (Eds.), *The development of arithmetic concepts and skills: Constructing adaptive expertise* (pp. 243–265). Mahwah, NJ: Erlbaum.

Dowker, A. (1997). Young children's addition estimates. *Mathematical Cognition, 3,* 141–154.

Dowker, A., Flood, A., Griffiths, H., Harriss, L., & Hook, L. (1996). Estimation strategies of four groups. *Mathematical Cognition, 2,* 113–135.

Geary, D. C. (1994). *Children's mathematical development: Research and practical implications.* Washington, DC: American Psychological Association.

Ginsburg, H. P., Baroody, A. J., & Russell, R. L. (1982). Children's estimation ability in addition and subtraction. *Focus on Learning in Mathematics, 4,* 31–46.

LeFevre, J., Greenham, S. L., & Waheed, N. (1993). The development of procedural and conceptual knowledge in computational estimation. *Cognition and Instruction, 11,* 95–132.

Lemaire, P., Lecacheur, M., & Farioli, F. (2000). Children's strategy use in computational estimation. *Canadian Journal of Experimental Psychology, 54,* 141–148.

Lemaire, P., & Lecacheur, M. (2002). Children's strategies in computational estimation. *Journal of Experimental Child Psychology, 82,* 281–304.

Levine, D. R. (1982). Strategy use and estimation ability of college students. *Journal for Research in Mathematics Education, 13,* 350–359.

Lipton, J. S., & Spelke, E. S. (2003). Origins of numer

sense: Large-number discrimination in human infants. *Psychological Science, 14,* 396–401.

Luwel, K., Verschaffel, L., Onghema, P., & DeCorte, E. (2000). Children's strategies for numerosity judgment in square grids of different sizes. *Psychologica Belgica, 40,* 183–209.

Luwel, K., Beem, A. L., Onghena, P., & Verschaffel, L. (2001). Using segmented linear regression models with unknown change points to analyze strategy shifts in cognitive tasks. *Behavior Research Methods, 33,* 470–478.

Luwel, K., Verschaffel, L., Onghema, P., & DeCorte, E. (2002). Strategic aspects of numerosity judgment: The effect of task characteristics. *Experimental Psychology, 49,* 1–13.

National Council of Teachers of Mathematics (1980). *An agenda for action: Recommendations for school mathematics of the 1980s.* Reston, VA: Author.

National Council of Teachers of Mathematics. (2000). *Principles and standards for school mathematics* [Online]. Available: http://standards.nctm.org/ document/index.htm

Newman, R. S., & Berger, C. F. (1984). Children's numerical estimation: Flexibility in the use of counting. *Journal of Educational Psychology, 76,* 55–64.

Paull, D. R. (1972). *The ability to estimate in mathematics.* Unpublished Doctoral Dissertation, Columbia University.

Petitto, A. L. (1990). Development of numberline and measurement concepts. *Cognition and Instruction, 7,* 55–78.

Pike, C. D., & Forrester, M. A. (1997). The influence of number sense on children's ability to estimate measures. *Educational Psychology, 17,* 483–500.

Reys, R. E., Rybolt, J. F., Bestgen, B. J., & Wyatt, J. W. (1982). Processes used by good computational estimators. *Journal for Research in Mathematics Education, 13,* 183–201.

Reys, R. E., Reys, B. J., Nohda, N., Ishida, J., Yoshikawa, S., & Shimizu, K. (1991). Computational estimation performance and strategies used by fifth- and eighth-grade Japanese students. *Journal for Research in Mathematics Education, 22,* 39–58.

Rittle-Johnson, B., Siegler, R. S., & Alibali, M. W. (2001). Developing conceptual understanding and procedural skill in mathematics: An iterative process. *Journal of Educational Psychology, 93,* 346–362.

Schoen, H. L., Friesen, C. D., Jarrett, J. A., & Urbatsch, T. D. (1981). Instruction in estimating solutions of whole number computations. *Journal for Research in Mathematics Education, 12,* 165–178.

Siegel, A. W., Goldsmith, L. T., & Madson, C. R. (1982). Skill in estimation problems of extent and numerosity. *Journal for Research in Mathematics Education, 13,* 211–232.

Siegler, R. S. (1996). *Emerging minds.* Upper New York: Oxford.

Siegler, R. S., & Booth, J. L. (2004). Development of numerical estimation in young children. *Child Development, 75,* 428–444.

Siegler, R. S., & Opfer, J. (2003). The development of numerical estimation: Evidence for multiple representations of numerical quantity. *Psychological Science, 14,* 237–243.

Siegler, R. S., & Shrager, J. (1984). Strategy choices in addition and subtraction: How do children know what to do? In C. Sophian (Ed.), *The origins of cognitive skills* (pp. 229–293), Hillsdale, NJ: Erlbaum.

Smith, H. D. (1999). Use of the anchoring and adjustment heuristic by children. *Current Psychology: Developmental, Learning, Personality, Social, 18,* 294–300.

Sowder, J., & Wheeler, M. (1989). The development of concepts and strategies used in computational estimation. *Journal for Research in Mathematics Education, 20,* 130–146.

Trick, L. M., & Pylyshyn, Z. W. (1994). Why are small and large numbers enumerated differently? A limited-capacity preattentive stage in vision. *Psychological Review, 101,* 80–102.

Verschaffel, L., DeCorte, E., Lamote, C., & Dherdt, N. (1998). The acquisition and use of an adaptive strategy for estimating numerosity. *European Journal of Psychology of Education, 13,* 347–370.

13

Understanding Ratio and Proportion as an Example of the Apprehending Zone and Conceptual-Phase Problem-Solving Models

Karen C. Fuson
Dor Abrahamson

Learning mathematics requires learning to use culturally specific mathematical language, formats, and methods (math tools). To use these math tools effectively in a problem situation, one must learn to identify the mathematical elements of that problem situation; i.e., one must learn to *mathematize*. In traditional approaches to mathematics learning, these aspects are often separated, with problem solving following learning about mathematical tools. We present in this chapter a model for learning mathematics with understanding that highlights the kinds of connections that can facilitate sense-making by the learner. We exemplify this model with a new approach to the learning of ratio and proportion. This approach addresses two major learning difficulties in this domain (e.g., Behr, Harel, Post, & Lesh, 1993; Harel & Confrey, 1994; Kaput & West, 1994; Lamon, 1999). First, students typically use additive rather than multiplicative solution methods (e.g., to solve 6:14 = ?:35, they find the difference between 6 and 14 and subtract it from 35 to find 27:35 rather than seek multiplicative relationships). Second, they have difficulty moving from easy problems that use the basic ratio (e.g., 3:7 = ?:14) to middle-difficulty nondivisible problems in which neither ratio is a multiple of the other (e.g., 6:14 = ?:35).

The two models of learning and teaching mathematics introduced here seek to enlarge our view of mathematical cognition by examining such cognition in process during teaching and learning. It is conceptually and methodologically difficult to capture such rich thick data, but our models are intended to serve as lenses to focus on certain central elements of such teaching and learning. We also introduce a new methodological tool for data organization and presentation, our *transcliptions*. These give the reader brief views of interactions in our classrooms via tables focused on the learning issues we identified in the domain of ratio and proportion.

The short length of this chapter prevents us from discussing the models, the ratio and proportion design, or the empirical results in any detail, but we provide references for more details in other papers.

THE APPREHENDING ZONE MODEL

Our *Apprehending Zone* (AZ) *Model* focuses attention on several aspects of teaching and learning. The first is relationships between the mathematical tools educational designers plan for students to use, how these tools are used in the classroom, and the conceptual schemes students develop (these are shown rising vertically in Figure 13.1). The design researcher's understandings of a conceptual domain become manifested in the *Design Space* as domain tools and activities that are designed (Figure 13.1, bottom) and then become part of students' understanding through their participation in the classroom interactions using the *Classroom Action Tools* (Figure 13.1, center), so that students come to share close-enough taken-as-shared mathematical interpretations of the domain tools in their own individual *Internalized Space* (Figure 13.1, top). A second aspect of the model is how students learn classroom-shared domain-specific body-based dynamic mathematical images (see Figure 13.1) through interacting with and communicating about the math tools. We combine Piagetian and Vygotskiian theoretical constructs in this model of how design research–based tools and materials are taught and learned in a constructivist social–cultural classroom. We intend both meanings of *apprehending* (holding and understanding) to highlight the crucial links between body-based perceptual actions (seeing, hearing, speaking, body sensing, and gesturing) and conceptual actions (a Piagetian perspective). The *Apprehending Zone* includes each student's *peri-personal space* (the space around a student within which the student can reach) and the *classroom communicative social space* within which students operate by externalizing–internalizing actions, words, inscriptions, and visual structures (a Vygotskiian perspective).

A third aspect of the model is how a teacher creates a classroom learning zone of focus, engagement, and participation by leading students' attention to critical mathematical elements and by continually helping students to make three kinds of crucial links. The first is conceptual links among the domain math formats (shown on the right center in Figure 13.1). The second is conceptual links among the real-world situations that can be recorded in and solved by the domain math formats (shown on the left center in Figure 13.1). The third is links across problem situations and math tools by *mathematizing* the problem situations and by *storyizing* the mathematical tools (shown in the arrows across the center of Figure 13.1). In making these links, and in understanding the situations and the math formats, the teacher and all student participants use body focusing, indicating acts, and gestures to lead their own attention and that of others in the class who may be watching or listening to them. Thus, the Apprehending Zone Model focuses on the time–space of problem-solving activity and cultural communicating.

The Apprehending Zone Model foregrounds the agency of student body and sensory perception in assimilating and linking mathematical formats, situational attributes, and relations among all of these. In our design research classrooms, teachers taught and students learned ratio and proportion by tacitly internalizing–externalizing dynamic visuo/body-sensed schematic images that systematically linked the word-problem situations with the spatial–numerical mathematical formats and solution methods (see Abrahamson, 2004a, for an analysis of the roles of gesturing in our classrooms). These visual and body-based images constructed and mediated the classroom *semiotic network* (Greeno, 1998) of ratio and proportion by linking the various row and column formats, by linking problem situation texts and the math tools through mathematizing and storyizing, and by linking students' developing interpretations of the domain tools with those of their peers and their teacher. The body-based structures of proportion

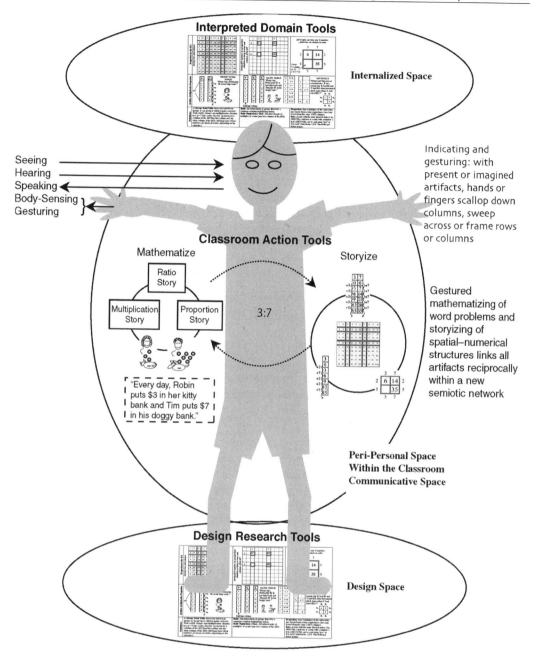

Figure 13.1. The body-based teaching–learning *Apprehending Zone Model*: The time–space of problem and cultural communicating.

became a classroom taken-as-shared artifact or *grammar of space–time* (Urton, 1997) linked to real-world proportional situations and to the various column forms of the *a:b* format. These attentional and gestural links became generative mathematical activity tools, or what Stetsenko (2002) calls "crystallized templates of action" (p. 129; see also Barsalou, 1999, p. 599, on *shared embodiment*). Examples of all three of these crucial kinds of linking during classroom discourse will be given after the ratio and proportion design is described.

THE CONCEPTUAL PHASE PROBLEM-SOLVING MODEL

Our *Conceptual Phase Problem-Solving Model* (see Figure 13.2) describes phases in the reciprocal meaning-making processes of *mathematizing* the problem situation (foregrounding the key mathematical aspects of the situation) and *storyizing* the math notations and methods (telling stories for each math tool). Mathematizing is shown as moving up in the model, and storyizing is shown as moving down. The vertical boxes show the different conceptual models solvers must form as they move from a real-world conception to a solution action sequence. Some of our designed classroom activities moved through all phases for a given problem, and others concentrated at particular spots (e.g., sharing different solution methods for the same problem). This model was developed for describing addition–subtraction word problem solving by students in kindergarten through grade 3 (Fuson, Hudson, & Ron, 1997; Ron, 1999). We modified it here to show in the left column the activities at each phase in which students and teachers need to engage in the classroom and individually when understanding ratio or solving a proportion problem. The fit of the model for these domains that span the elementary school years suggests that it is widely applicable, at least in numerical situations.

THE DESIGN FOR LEARNING ADDITIVE–MULTIPLICATIVE AND MULTIPLICATIVE SOLUTION METHODS FOR PROPORTION PROBLEMS

In our design we sought to introduce fifth graders to ratio and proportion by grounding it in multiplicative contexts that would enable students to avoid the usual additive solution errors. We also used middle-difficulty problem numbers in which the ratio pairs were not multiples of each other but were multiples of the smallest basic ratio (e.g., 3:7, such as 6 to 14 and 15 to 35), so that students would learn more general solution methods than the simple multiply/divide methods used with the easiest problem numbers involving only a basic ratio and a multiple of it (e.g., 3 to 7 and 15 to 35). We discuss at the end of the chapter how this approach can generalize to proportions involving fractions and decimals and to advanced solution methods such as finding unit rates and cross-multiplying. The math formats and situations linked in our design are shown in Figure 13.3 and will be explained in this section.

All approaches to teaching ratio and proportion need to help students use and understand ratio tables and some format for representing and solving proportions. Ratio tables are vertical or horizontal formats that record the results of repeated coordinated additions of a basic ratio pair of numbers. The middle cell of Figure 13.3 shows a ratio table for the ratio 3:7 in which the columns are made by repeatedly adding 3 to the left column and 7 to the right column. Any two rows from a ratio table are proportional because they are each multiples of the basic ratio (e.g., they are $3m_1$:$7m_1$ and $3m_2$:$7m_2$ and thus are multiples of each other). Ratio stories are situations that generate ratio tables. They involve two linked situations that begin at zero and in which the repeated addings are made together. Figure 13.3 gives one of our design ratio stories: "Every day Robin puts $3 in her kitty bank and Tim puts $7 in his doggy bank." Each ratio story involves an explicit or implicit linking column that coordinates the repeated adding actions in the two linked stories; in this story, the linking column numbers the days. The linking column enables one to find a given row by multiplying rather than by repeatedly building up within the ratio table to that row (e.g., on Day 5, Robin has 5 × $3 = $15 in her kitty bank and Tim has 5 × $7 = $35 in his doggy bank). If the rows are made by multiplying instead of by repeatedly adding, ratio tables can have rows omitted or reversed.

Each of the coordinated situations in a ratio story can be seen in isolation as a multiplication story made by repeatedly adding the same number. The Group Total Table shown in the left cell of the middle row in Figure 13.3 shows the multiplication story of Robin putting $3 in her

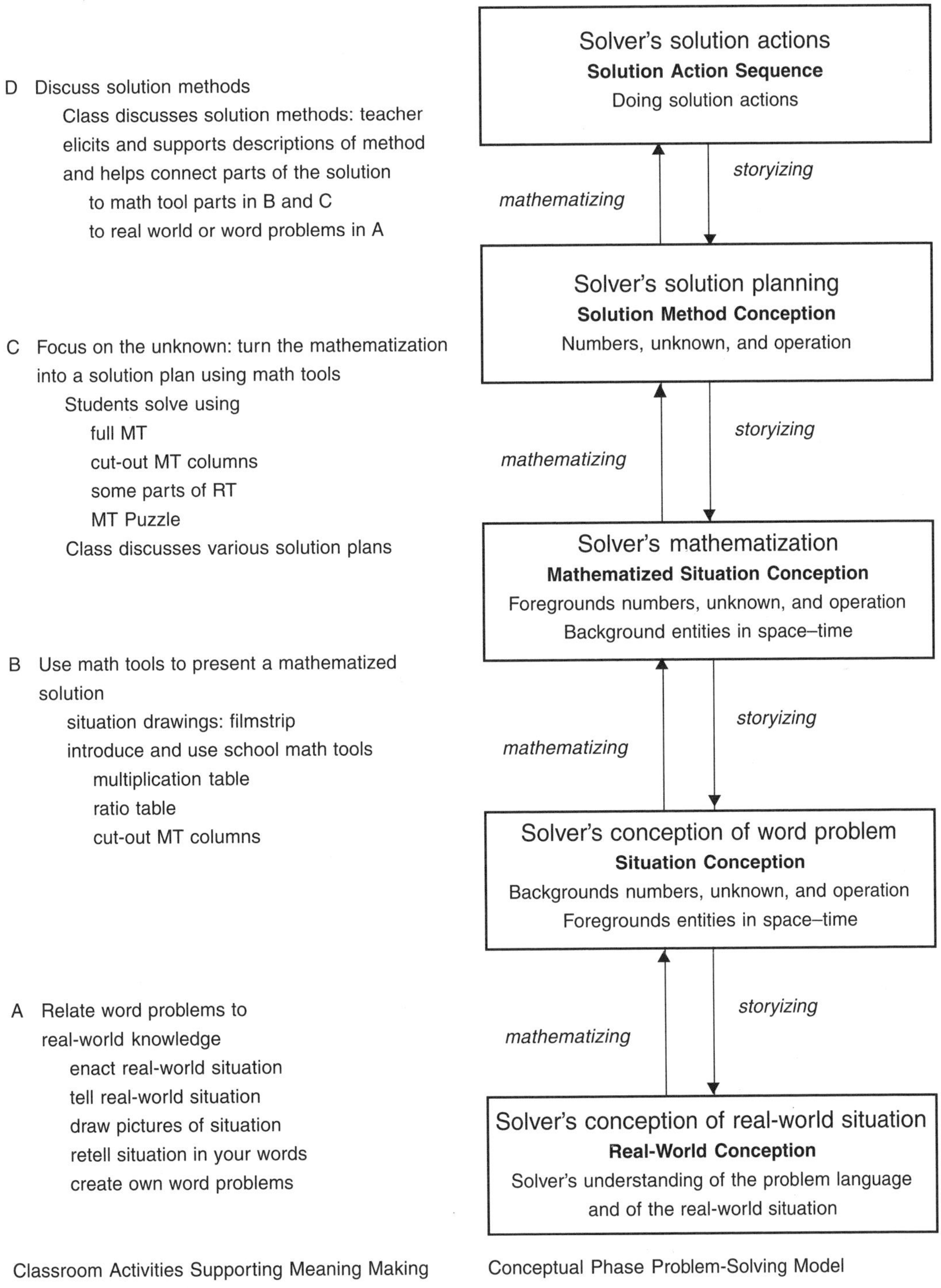

D   Discuss solution methods
      Class discusses solution methods: teacher
      elicits and supports descriptions of method
      and helps connect parts of the solution
         to math tool parts in B and C
         to real world or word problems in A

C   Focus on the unknown: turn the mathematization
      into a solution plan using math tools
      Students solve using
         full MT
         cut-out MT columns
         some parts of RT
         MT Puzzle
      Class discusses various solution plans

B   Use math tools to present a mathematized
      solution
         situation drawings: filmstrip
         introduce and use school math tools
            multiplication table
            ratio table
            cut-out MT columns

A   Relate word problems to
      real-world knowledge
         enact real-world situation
         tell real-world situation
         draw pictures of situation
         retell situation in your words
         create own word problems

Solver's solution actions
Solution Action Sequence
Doing solution actions

mathematizing / *storyizing*

Solver's solution planning
Solution Method Conception
Numbers, unknown, and operation

mathematizing / *storyizing*

Solver's mathematization
Mathematized Situation Conception
Foregrounds numbers, unknown, and operation
Background entities in space–time

mathematizing / *storyizing*

Solver's conception of word problem
Situation Conception
Backgrounds numbers, unknown, and operation
Foregrounds entities in space–time

mathematizing / *storyizing*

Solver's conception of real-world situation
Real-World Conception
Solver's understanding of the problem language
and of the real-world situation

Classroom Activities Supporting Meaning Making   Conceptual Phase Problem-Solving Model

Figure 13.2. The Conceptual Phase Problem-Solving Model in the classroom: mathematizing the situations and storyizing the math tools.

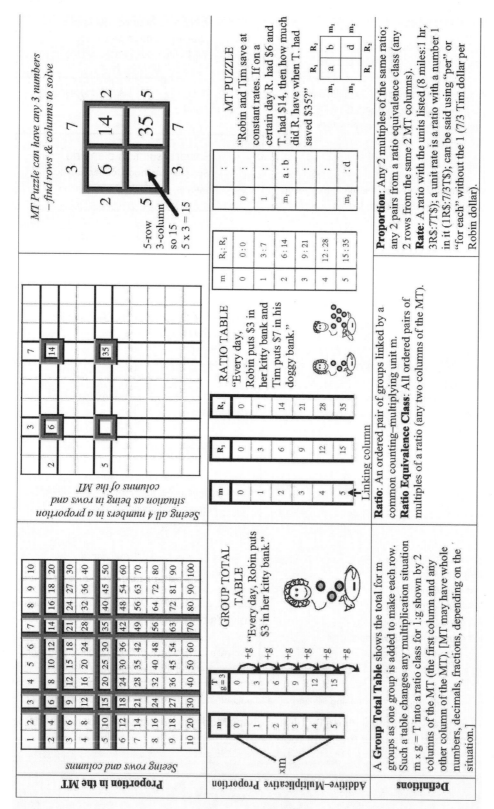

Figure 13.3. Mathematical tools for teaching and learning ratio and proportion.

kitty bank each day. Thus, we can begin students' introduction to ratio with multiplication stories involving repeatedly adding some amount. We call such a single column table (or its related two-column form with the ones column on the left) a Group Total Table to link such tables to students' early experience with multiplication as repeated groups (we would prefer to call these tables the same name as their stories but cannot call them multiplication tables because of confusion with the usual 9 × 9 or 10 × 10 table with that name). Use of these Group Total Tables allows students to explore different kinds of multiplication situations, see the Additive–Multiplicative repeated adding of the same amount in one column of the ratio table format, and relate this to making a particular group total by multiplication (multiplying the row number times the group number, as in "on Day 5, Robin has 5 × $3 = $15 in her kitty bank"). Connecting Additive–Multiplication and Multiplication meanings is an important basis for the continued growth of full understanding of all of the aspects of ratio and proportion (see Fuson and Abrahamson, 2004, for a fuller discussion of relationships to more advanced meanings of ratio and proportion and Fuson, Kalchman, Abrahamson, & Izsák, 2002, for discussion of such connections in multidigit multiplication, fractions, and linear functions).

The multiplication table (MT) is a cultural format widely used to display the products of numbers 1 through 10 (see the top left cell in Figure 13.3). Any ratio table using a basic ratio from these numbers can be made by pulling two columns from the multiplication table and putting them together (see the three and seven columns highlighted in the multiplication table). For students who understand the structure of the MT as columns made by repeatedly adding the same number (sometimes called "count-bys" as in "count by 3s"), making a ratio table from two MT columns can facilitate comprehension of the ratio table. For students who do not understand the structure of MT columns, linking multiplication stories to a single MT column and linking ratio stories to a ratio table as columns from an MT can facilitate comprehension of the repeated adding structure of the MT because of the repeated adding actions in the stories.

A proportion is made from any two rows of a ratio table. In the top row of Figure 13.3, one can see that a proportion also arises within an MT as the four corners of a rectangle made by the two columns that form the proportion's ratio table and the two rows containing the proportional pairs. One can solve a proportion with one unknown by thinking about which rows and which columns of the MT form that proportion. This is facilitated by writing the proportion as a mini-MT with one empty cell (see top right of Figure 13.3). Initially, only the three known values appear inside this mini-MT, and there are no values outside it. We call this format an MT puzzle (it was called a proportion quartet in early versions of the design). There are six solution paths for each MT Puzzle. You write the row and column numbers outside the MT Puzzle as you solve it. Working with an MT, you could simply copy these row and column numbers. Working without an MT, you need to determine which MT rows and columns make the MT Puzzle (i.e., find the common factors for both rows and both columns). You start with either the row or column in which you know two numbers. You then can move to the column or row perpendicular to what you just solved or to the other row or column in which you know two numbers. We found that all students from grades 5 through 7 could learn to solve MT Puzzles with, and then without, the support of an MT and that they loved to solve them. Given any proportion problem, one can set up an MT Puzzle (see the example in the right-most middle cell of Figure 13.3) and then solve it to find the unknown number in the proportion problem. It is helpful to label the rows and columns with situation labels to connect the MT Puzzle to the situation.

The usual format for setting up a proportion in the United States is the equivalent fraction format. This does not provide the conceptual links to multiplication given by the MT Puzzle format. It also introduces conceptual confusions between ratios and fractions. And because many students experience difficulties operating with fractions, it does not necessarily suggest helpful solution strategies. The MT Puzzle format used with the MT eliminates these problems.

These tools also can be used to examine and clarify differences and similarities between ratios and equivalent fractions. Fraction equivalents can be seen as two rows from the MT (see the chain of equivalents for 2/5 in the 2 row over the 5 row in the MT in Figure 13.3). Also an MT Puzzle can be used to find any of the four numbers unknown in a fraction equivalence. For example, the MT Puzzle in Figure 13.3 can be taken as the equivalent fractions 6/? = 14/35, and these numbers as vertical fractions can be seen in the MT in the 2s and 5s rows. For a more detailed analysis of these issues and related issues involving rates, see Fuson and Abrahamson (2004, where relationships between our perspective and those of others, especially Confrey, 1994, and Vergnaud, 1983, are discussed).

Our design for teaching ratio and proportion evolved through a series of design research studies (see Cobb, Confrey, diSessa, Lehrer, & Schauble, 2003, for a discussion of design research). Our design work in various domains has been directed by several core design principles. We continually seek to create teaching–learning materials that "start where children are and keep learning meaningful" (Fuson, De La Cruz, Smith, Lo Cicero, Hudson, Ron, & Steeby, 2000; Fuson, 1988). We use innovative approaches that are "intuitively convincing" (Abrahamson, 2000), but we continuously consider pragmatic constraints to ensure widespread usability of the design. We design to help students ground mathematical notations and methods in perception, intuition, and experience (Gelman & Williams, 1998; Wilensky, 1997; Freudenthal, 1981). We find or develop supports for core curricular concepts (Fuson, 1998, 2004) that align with and build on students' implicit models (Fischbein, Deri, Nello, & Marino, 1985) and their developing image-based understandings (Kieren, Pirie, & Gordon Calvert, 1999). Our design studies in ratio and proportion have included (a) two case studies, each with an individual high-achieving third-grade student, that explored an optical stretch–shrink model as grounding for proportional equivalence (Abrahamson, 2002a); (b) a constructionist study with 3 fourth-grade students who were asked to design and build a multiplication table that had no numerals (Abrahamson, 2002b); (c) one summer intervention study with fifth-grade low achievers who initiated creative transition links between the multiplication table, ratio table, and MT Puzzle, including a ratio table with empty rows between the given-values rows that they then collapsed into a MT Puzzle with those values (Abrahamson, 2002c); and (d) six classroom teaching experiments with four different teachers of grades 5 through 7 who taught successive iterations of the curricular unit evolving from our design research (Abrahamson, 2003; Abrahamson & Cigan, 2003; Abrahamson, 2004b; Abrahamson & Fuson, 2004). The classroom studies were a collaborative effort involving the teachers and district math resource staff.

Our most recent design is outlined in Table 13.1. The table details the three kinds of links described by the Apprehending Zone Model within and across the situations and the math formats (amplified in Table 13.1 as the "MT–RT numerical additive–multiplicative and multiplicative stream") and how these links were organized across days into streams of situational and math format numerical activities. Within the numerical stream, links were made between the multiplication table, ratio table, and MT Puzzle formats. Within the real-world situational stream, multiplication stories, ratio stories, and proportion stories were linked to each other. Continuing daily links were made between these two streams by mathematizing the stories (focusing on the mathematical elements to record them in the spatial–numerical math formats) and by storyizing the math formats (telling stories for each kind of format and usually working within a story context when using a math format).

Special materials for the unit included a large whole-class laminated multiplication table, individual multiplication tables from which students cut MT columns to form ratio tables, and filmstrips the students drew to show repeated adding situations (multiplication stories and ratio stories). Students also filled in scrambled multiplication tables in which the rows and columns of an MT were switched around and most of the products were missing. These were like big puzzles, and students used different strategies to solve them. These provided practice

Table 13.1
Mathematizing and Storyizing within the Designed Situational and Numerical Streams

Number of class periods (60 min)	Real-world situation stream	*mathematizing* →	← *storyizing*	MT–RT numerical additive-multiplication and multiplication stream
1				Find patterns in the MT using big class MT and small student MTs
4	Multiplication situations (stories) as a class built up by repeated adding of the same amount: Show actions of adding the same amount on filmstrip drawings.

Many different multiplication situations (Multiplication Stories)

Continual mixing in of non-multiplication situations

Writing multiplication and non-multiplication stories (continues into writing ratio and non-ratio stories) | | | Make group total tables from filmstrip drawings

Cut columns from MT and show group total table with 2 columns (1s column and group column)

Match group total tables to multiplication stories

Introduce and practice MT puzzles as coming from 2 rows and 2 columns of the MT

Identify group total and non-group total tables; match to stories

Introduce and practice scrambled multiplication tables |
| 5 to 8 | Linked multiplication stories (group total situations) are Ratio Stories

Proportion problems come from Ratio Stories

Writing proportion and nonproportion stories (continues all unit)

Gaining fluency solving a range of proportion problems and differentiating these from nonproportion problems | | | Ratio tables are made from a common linking column; show with 3 cut-out MT columns (leftmost is 1s column); students continue to use MT or RT to solve problems while gaining fluency with MT Puzzle solutions

Solve proportion problems with MT puzzles; rows and columns can be scrambled in any order

Gaining fluency with MT Puzzles, Scrambled MTs, and setting up and solving MT Puzzles from proportion problem situations |

Note: Relationships were continually established within and between elements in these two streams by *storyizing* the mathematical notations and *mathematizing* the situations through gestured discussions.

with multiplications and divisions and gave models for proportions in MT Puzzles that had smaller numbers in the second column or column.

LEARNING ISSUES IN USING MATH TOOLS IN THE CLASSROOM

Part of our ongoing design research was to identify learning issues that presented difficulties to students and then seek to minimize these in subsequent designs. This recursive process finally resulted in the eight learning issues given in Table 13.2. Of these, six (all but the first and the sixth issues) are learning issues for any teaching design in the domain of ratio and

Table 13.2

Learning Issues of the Ratio-and-Proportion Design Grouped by Type of Reasoning

Learning Issue	Definition
Theorems-in-Action	
Solving By Looking Up	Locating unknown values on a Multiplication Table or on a prefilled Ratio Table or MT Puzzle or selecting Multiplication Table cut-out columns. Students may only know how to find relevant parts of the tool to answer a question.
Additive–Multiplicative	
Zero Starting Point	Multiplication and ratio stories have a starting point at zero, from which the repeated addend is iterated (in some versions of the mathematical formats, this zero moment is omitted and the table begins with the ad-
dend	that will be repeatedly added).
Columns (or Rows) Are Repeated Addition Sequences	Attending to, parsing, constructing, and articulating multiplication stories or ratio stories as MT columns. Columns begin either at 0 or at the column number and then iterate the constant addend (the column number) without repeating or skipping rows.
Repeated Addends Versus Totals	Interpreting the sequence of values running down MT columns as running totals in multiplication stories or ratio stories and specifically distinguishing between these running totals and the constant addend (the column number).
Multiplicative	
Multiplicative Structure and Use of the Table Formats Multiplication Table, Ratio Table, and MT Puzzle	These grid-structured formats have rows and columns with uniform cell sizes, and each number is the product of the left row number and top column number. A 10-by-10 Multiplication Table can be modified by reordering (to make Scrambled Multiplication Tables or MT Puzzles) and by extending rows and columns.
Ratio Table	
Linking Column for the 2 Sequences	The number of iterations so far in the linked Ratio-Story columns can be represented in a separate left-most column, but it may be implicit rather than physically present (as in standard two-column ratio tables).
General	
Vocabulary	Using new and familiar terms for the formats (e.g., row, column), the situations that are grounded in these formats (e.g., miles an hour, growth unit, per), and the "pure" mathematics of the domain (e.g., multiple, common factor, rate, ratio, proportion).
Labeling ("Table Manners")	Labeling columns or rows with the kinds of quantities they represent in the story situation.

proportion. The first—Solving By Looking Up—would occur only in our design for the MT and MT cut-out columns, though it might be used for ratio tables in other designs. However, Solving By Looking Up was crucial in our approach because less-advanced students initially solved problems by finding relevant numbers on the MT (e.g., they found the three known proportion numbers as three corners of a rectangle in the MT and chose the fourth cell of the rectangle as the answer). Such uses of the MT enabled students of all levels to participate in problem solving from the beginning. The sixth learning issue—Linking Column for the 2 Sequences—also is much more explicit in our design than in most approaches. This explicit linking column supports mathematizing and storyizing, and it facilitates moving to multiplication methods because the multiplying number is written.

To exemplify the major learning issues, and to enable readers to see the design math tools in use in discussions in the classroom, we constructed Tables 13.3 through 13.7 to show one

Table 13.3

Understanding of and Difficulty with the Additive–Multiplicative Learning Issue "Columns/Rows Are Repeated-Addition Sequences"

Tools Used	Example from classroom data			
Understanding Multiplication Story Filmstrip Multiplication Table Ratio Table MT Cutout Columns	 <Day5 H1 53:12> **Fernando:** Ok, this comic is about the man and his beard. As you can see here, his beard started out as 3 inches right *here*,	 <53:17> and then each day it keeps growing.... [scallops his pointer down from top picture along penciled arc with the label "+3"] it keeps growing by 3...	<53:21> by 3 more inches every *day*. [note beard getting longer] **Ms W:** [to class] What are the columns you need to create a rate table for this situation?	 <53:43> [class responds that they need 2 columns, "1" and "3," that are labeled "Days" and "Inches." Students work with the MT and its column cutouts]
Difficulty Ratio Story Filmstrip Multiplication Table	 <Day3 T1 6:14> [Students are composing ratio-stories and preparing filmstrip columns that illustrate these stories. M'Buto's ratio story: "Bob was a race car driver so was M'Buto. One day Bob said I bet you in a race. M'Buto said we will race for 8 hours. Bob's car was 3 miles an hour and M'Buto's car was 5 miles an hour. Was Bob right?"	[D. asks if that's the same as saying that "Every hour, Bob's car goes 3 miles, etc.," and M. says it's the same. D. asks how many pictures there will be in the ratio-story filmstrip that M. is preparing, and M. says there will be 3: beginning, middle, and end. D. asks for more details, and M. looks up to the MT poster and says that there will be a picture after 1 hour.]	 <6:57> D: Oh, super, so '1, 2, 3, 4...,' — like that? M: Yeah. [thinks a moment— that's not what he had said—he had only promised *three* pictures, regardless of the hours or the miles in the story] No—wait a moment—[looks up at the MT, looks back at Dor] then I'll show it after 1 hour again.	 <7:15> D: Oh, so you're like a reporter, and you're taking a photograph every hour. M: Mm'hmm. D: Excellent.

display of understanding and one display of difficulty for each of the second through sixth learning issues. These tables used *transcliptions*, our method of data preparation that enabled the research team to see and communicate about the rich data in the raw videotapes of the classroom. These transcliptions were made by transcribing the videotapes and pasting in clips from the videotape to accompany the transcriptions. Tables 13.3 through 13.7 show typical examples of teaching and learning in action in the classroom. The limited space in this chapter does not permit discussion of these examples (see Abrahamson, 2004b, and Fuson & Abrahamson, 2004, for results of analyzing students' understanding of and difficulty with these learning issues).

These transcliption data made salient to us the centrality of gesturing and body-based communication within the classroom, and they contributed to the development of our Apprehending Zone Model (see also Alibali, Basso, Olseth, Syc, & Goldin-Meadow, 1999, concerning gesturing). In gesturing to mathematical objects within or displaced from their peri-personal space, students had opportunities to: (a) relate various math tools by *folding back* on the MT (i.e., use its familiar structure to make sense of a new format or situation; Kieren et al., 1999); (b) learn and practice verbalized mathematical terminology (e.g., row, column, common factor, multiple, product) supported by touching or gesturing; and (c) develop and practice the *body-based* imaging and action structures (or *haptic experience;* see Nemirovsky, Noble, Ramos-Oliveira, & DiMattia, 2003) necessary for problem solving and communicating in the absence of the math tools (e.g., draw an MT Puzzle in the air and point to cells of it). The results of the analysis of gesturing in student classroom learning are summarized in Abrahamson (2004a).

A BRIEF OVERVIEW OF LEARNING IN OUR CLASSROOMS

We briefly summarize here some of the learning results from the two classes (n = 19 and 20) that were videotaped and studied most intensely (see Abrahamson, 2004b, and Fuson & Abrahamson, 2004, for details). These both were extremely heterogeneous classrooms of fifth grade students, with 20% African American students, 20% Latino students, 38% of students on free lunch, and learning-disabled and English-language learners in both classrooms. Many students had had Everyday Mathematics (Bell et al., 1998) since kindergarten, so they were used to discussing their thinking in class. Both teachers were excellent teachers and led math discussions well. The transcliption data in Tables 13.3 through 13.7 are from one of these classrooms.

On the pretest, most of the students in both classrooms approached ratio-and-proportion word problems using *additive reasoning*, the typical error made even by older students. In independent work-alones given at the beginning of each class to track student learning or on the posttest, all students used *additive–multiplicative* or *multiplicative reasoning* successfully to solve at least some middle-difficulty nondivisible proportion problems in which neither ratio is a multiple of the other. The low-achieving students depended longer into the interventions on the MT as a support for their participation in classroom problem solving and discussion (e.g., they found the three numbers from a problem in the MT and then traced down and across to find the fourth number), but eventually all students successfully made ratio tables and/or MT Puzzles to solve some problems.

Throughout the unit, students showed variability in the ways in which they made ratio tables and MT Puzzles to solve problems. This variability suggested that they were assimilating the formats to their own ways of understanding. Examples of such variability are shown in Figure 13.4.

On the critical three posttest items that involved medium difficulty problems in which the proportions were not multiples of each other (e.g., see Figure 13.5), the middle half of the students (20 of 39) rose from 0% correct on the pretest to 100% correct on the posttest. In the

(*Text continued on page 230*)

Table 13.4

Understanding of and Difficulty with the Additive–Multiplicative Learning Issue "Repeated Addends Versus Totals"

Tools Used	Example from classroom data		
Understanding Multiplication Story Multiplication Table MT Cutout Columns	 <Day5 H1 01:04 – 9:20> **Ms W**: [reads] "Big Bird collects snails. Every day, he adds 4 snails into his terrarium. How many snails does Big Bird have after 1 day?" [Students use their MT and cutout columns to model the situation then discuss the situation, labels, and vocabulary]	 <09:21> **Ms W**: How many snails does Big Bird collect on the second day? **Class**: 8…. 4…. **Odelia**: 4 more, because you said *on the second day how many did he collect*, and he collects 4 each day …so on the second day he would have 4 more, which would equal 8 in total. **Ms W**: Right.	 <10:33> **Dor**: I'm just confused— Odelia told us that every day he collected 4, but I see here that opposite the 2 there's an 8, so, how does that work out? **Ms W**: Odelia?	 <10:41> **O**: She asked how many snails he collected on the 2nd day, and he collects 4 snails every day, so on the second day he would have collected 4 *more*, and not 8—he would have collected 8 in total.
Difficulty Multiplication Story Multiplication Table	 <Day4 H1 4:35> **Violet:** Duffy Duck was going one day to Porky Pig's house,	 <4:41> **Violet:** and, uhhm, [turns around to look at the MT poster; turns back] one hour… in one hour he walked 3 miles […] So the first mile… the first hour…hmnn… Duffy Duck walked 3 miles…	 <4:57> **Violet:** In the second hour [turns around to look at the MT poster; turns back] Duffy Duck walked 6 miles, in the third hour Duffy Duck walked 9 miles…	 <5:09> **Ms. W**: That would be a total of 18 miles. [scallops down from 3 to 6, waits for V.'s response, then scallops to 9, 12, etc.] **Violet:** In the first hour he walked 3 miles, in the second hour he walked 3 *more miles…*

Table 13.5

Understanding of and Difficulty with the Additive–Multiplicative Learning Issue
"Multiplicative Structure and Use of the Table Formats"

Tools Used	Example from classroom data			
Understanding Ratio Story Ratio Table	**<Day3 H1 36:18>** [Ms W projects the next problem on the overhead screen: "Mario and Fatima save their money on a regular basis. Fill in the numbers that are missing in this table." The format is a labeled ratio table with missing values.]	**<36:52>** **Saul:** You see what times 4 equ... gives you... [points from '4' to '28' and '36'] This would give you the first week,	**<36:57>** **Saul:** ...and then you keep on going [drives pencil in the air, down along column while looking away from table and up at Ms. W.]	**<36:58>** **Saul:** 'What times 4 <u>equals</u> 36,' 'What times 4 equals 28.'

Difficulty
Multiplication Table
MT Puzzle
	<Day6 T2 29:19>
	
	[Margarita has completed an unknown-value MT Puzzle with '9' (should be 45). Also, she has written the factors 3 in the 2nd row rather than above and below the left column. She is copying from the MT that is on her desk directly into the MT Puzzle on her worksheet. Dor asks her to explain her solution.]
	Margarita: 9... 9 times 3 is 27, so you put the 3 here [to left and right of the bottom row] and you put the 7 here [top row] **Dor:** You know what, let's do this one together. Erase the 9 and we'll work together. [Following, D. and M. move between the MT and M's writing of numbers into the MT Puzzle]
	
	Grid:
	`3`
	`7 │ 21 │ 35 │ 7`
	`3 │ 27 │  9 │ 3`
	`3`
		<30:20>
		Grid:
		`3`
		`7 │ 21 │ 35 │ 7`
		`    27`
		`3`
		
		Dor: Ok, so you found that 7 is a common multiple of 21 and 35. Ok, so what column is 21 in? **M:** The 7... oh, no, in the 3. **D:** So put a 3 here [on top]...and immediately put a 3 across [below] because it's in the same column.
			<30:26>
			Grid:
			`3   5`
			`7 │ 21 │ 35 │ 7`
			`    27`
			`3   5`
			
			Dor: Good. 35—what column is it in? **M:** 5 [makes '5' w/ LH five fingers splayed]. **D:** ok, so put a 5... and immediately put a '5' across. [M. writes in the 5's] Alright!
				<30:33>
				Grid:
				`3   5`
				`7 │ 21 │ 35 │ 7`
				`9 │ 27 │    │ 9`
				`3   5`
				
				D: 27, what... see, 3 times what? It has to be... **M:** 9. **D:** Right, and immediately put it across. **D:** You see, so now you have an empty cell here. Kind of '9*5 is 'what'? **M:** 9*9? **D:** Look, you wrote it: 5... **M:** Ahh, 45 [writes 45].

Table 13.6

Understanding of and Difficulty with the Ratio-Table Learning Issue "Zero Starting Point"

Tools Used	Example from classroom data		
Understanding Ratio Story Filmstrip			
	<Day3_H1_3:33> **Moses:** [LD student. Reads his ratio story towards creating a filmstrip] "One day Bart at work for AJ Car Store. He makes $5 an hour. Lisa makes $3 an hour…"	<later:_23:17> **Moses:** I put zero so it will be at zero dollars. They didn't make money yet. And the next day,	<23:20> Bart's going to have 5, uhhhm 5 [jerks LH forward] dollars and [twists paper clockwise]	<23:21> Lisa's going to have <u>3</u> [quick anticlockwise t dollars.
Difficulty Ratio Story Filmstrip Multiplication Table			
	<Day 7_H1_25:12zoom in> [Ms W. discusses with students Kay's filmstrip ratio-story. The story is about a hair-growing competition between girls and boys. Form day to day, beards and hair grow longer, each by some constant increment. Numerals 1 – 4 show order of Ms W.'s gesturing, as she explains how to insert arcs with the constant addend marked in them. Note, at the top of Kay's poster is the "zero moment," before the hair-growing competition had even started.]	<25:26> **Ms W**: [pointing above the boys column] Because in fact, these two points—on our chart—what would these two points be? [Ms W. compares picture columns to MT columns; prompts students to see this.]	<25:31> [Students look back at th MT] **Kay**: [returns gaze Ms W] 1? **Ms W**: 1? Do we start at **K**: Zero. **Ms W**: Zero. And in son ways, this space represen zero. [points again above picture columns in poste

Table 13.7

Understanding of and Difficulty with the Ratio-Table Learning Issue "Linking Column for the 2 Sequences"

Tools Used	Example from classroom data			
Understanding and Difficulty Ratio Story Ratio Table Multiplication Table				
	<Day4_H1 41:08>	<41:37>	<42:15>	<44:28>
	[Students are discussing the following problem: "A pair of lizards—Creepy and Crawley—walk down the side of the Sears Tower. When Creepy has walked 18 floors down, Crawley walks 42 floors down. What could their walking rates be?" That is, students are asked to reduce 18:42 to a smaller ratio] **Ms W**: In some unit of time, Creepy walked 18 and Crawley walked 42. How are we going to find out how many time-units this all happened at?	**Alice**: I know the way: you can look on the chart and you can go to 18 and 42, and since they're across from each other... you could go up and see what column they're in; and 42's in 7, and 18's in the 3 column... [...] Crawley's rate would be 7 and Creepy's rate would be 3.	**Dor**: So, tell me, Alice, how did you know to go to *this* 18 and *this* 42? ['18' and '42' each appear twice on the MT] **Alice**: I just tried it—I used 'guess and check' [...] I looked at *this* 18 and it didn't have a 42, so I looked at *this* one and it had a 42. **Ms W**: How did you know they had to be next to each other? **Alice**: I donno. **Ms W**: You're not sure, but you knew that they had to be next to each other? **Alice**: Yeah. **Ms W**: Ok, just like in our table...	**Ms W**: Can anybody support or explain why the 18 and 42 have to be in the same row? **Odelia**: Because it's in the same amount of time, so that this [points to 1-column] will be the 'time,' sort of, so that's how you could tell [gestures across the 6-row, beginning from '6' in the 1-column and towards the right, covering 18 and stopping at 42] **Ms W**: They have to be next to each other because they represent the same period of time. **Odelia**: Yeah.

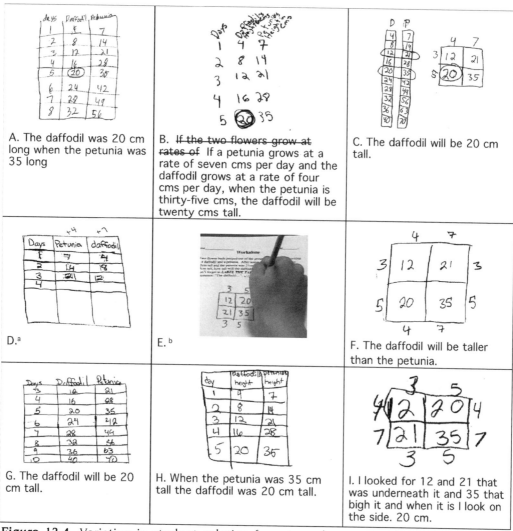

Figure 13.4. Variation in student solution formats and accompanying verbatim written responses in solving individually the Day 5 in-classroom word problem, "Two flower buds peeped out of the ground on the same morning—a daffodil and a petunia. After some days, the daffodil was 12 cm tall and the petunia was 21 cm tall. When the petunia is 35 cm, how tall will the daffodil be?" Students' work suggests a classroom bootstrapping—each student at their personal pace and along their personal path—the familiar structure and function of the multiplication table that was available for their use in developing an understanding of additive–multiplicative properties of situated ratio and proportion. Although the MT-Puzzle format was taught after the ratio table (RT) in the design, students using the MT-Puzzle do not necessarily evidence deeper understanding (e.g., compare B., an RT solution and full explanation, to I., an MT Puzzle copied out of an MT).

[a]This student's incomplete table was included to demonstrate students' flexibility in column order in the RT format (e.g., compare to Item A.) as well as in the PQ format (e.g., compare Items C. and F.). On the posttest (1 week later), she correctly solved all three *critical* items (items with proportional ratios that are related by a non-integer multiple).

[b]Picture E. has been included to demonstrate both our access to work-in-the-making, and specifically to show that such access informed us of students' strategies: this student apparently consulted the MT rather than factoring the PQ.

top fourth of the students, eight rose from 33% to 100% correct, and two were at ceiling on the pretest (but moved from pictorial to numerical solution methods). Of the lowest nine students, five rose from 0% to 53% correct, and four did not solve any of these nondivisible problems completely correctly. Thus, overall, the percent correct on the posttest was 84%.

The errors of the lowest-achieving students showed that they were at various points of mastery ranging from correct setting up of problems in an MT Puzzle with some multiplication or division error to still using a pictorial strategy. Typical pre- and posttest responses for the successful low achievers are shown in Figure 13.5. Each set up a different MT Puzzle, which interviews and observations in class indicated that they could explain. The lowest-achieving students could have benefited from more time on the unit.

Some high-achieving students did use multiplicative strategies on the pretest; these were elaborate concrete pictorial–numerical solutions involving units. All of these students began to use MT Puzzles during the unit and related in interviews or in whole-class discussions their initial solution methods to this more general method.

Much of the class became able to extend the MT Puzzle to three columns to solve complex proportion problems that involved a total, such as: "Monica and Lin are putting together a pony puzzle. Each kid is working at a steady pace. At a certain moment Monica has put in 24 pieces and Lin has put in 32. When they have put in 63 pieces *together* how many pieces has each put in?"

Teachers were very positive about the ratio-and-proportion unit. They said that they felt that their less advanced students had understood multiplication more deeply, that all students had learned a great deal about ratio and proportion, and that their more advanced students had connected multiplication, division, proportions, and fractions. Their students expressed liking the MT-Puzzle solution method because most trusted and were familiar with the MT and

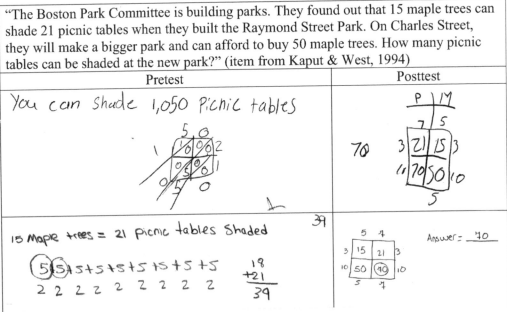

Figure 13.5: Typical pre- and posttest responses from low-achieving students. One student initially misapplied a multiplication strategy (using the lattice technique), and the other miscoordinated the proportion addends–factors. Later, both successfully used the MT-Puzzle format, each setting up a different MT Puzzle. Interviews and observations in class indicated that they could explain their use of the MT Puzzle to solve such problems.

because the format helped them organize the given information during problem solving. The ideas in the unit were presented at a district workshop to thirty fifth-grade teachers. These teachers found the approach accessible and appealing. Thus, the approach seems to fit within the learning zone of a wide range of fifth-grade students, and it appears to move all of them along their own learning paths to using additive–multiplicative and multiplicative solution methods for ratio and proportion.

EXTENDING THE MULTIPLICATION TABLE APPROACH BEYOND WHOLE NUMBER RATIO MULTIPLES

The MT-Puzzle approach transfers to all cases of proportional, fraction, and measure equivalencies and to other topics that use proportions. We did three types of mini-extensions with different classes: these were on percentage, similarity geometry, and coordinate graphing. Following a three-day mini-unit on percentage, one class progressed from 26% to 76% correct on percentage items. Following a two-day mini-unit on finding sides of similar figures, one class progressed from 5% to 78% correct on the nondivisible item. This unit was introduced through the *eye trick* (Abrahamson, 2002a), an optical illusion in which two proportionally equivalent pictures look identical when you hold them up, shutting one eye, with the smaller picture nearer your eye, followed by measuring and tabulating lengths in the pictures. For coordinate graphing, students aligned sets of proportionally equivalent (i.e., similar) rectangles from the eye-trick activity so that their corners were together and used the line made by the diagonally opposite corners to introduce graphs into the coordinate system (Abrahamson, 2002c).

Students can also move from our approach to using unit ratio and cross-multiplication strategies. Unit ratios can be seen as a row in the ratio table in which one number is 1. For the Robin and Tim story in Figure 13.1, these unit ratio rows would be 3/7:1 and 1:7/3. Some of the high-achieving fifth-grade students came to understand fraction unit rates (e.g., 3/7) that they had been using before the intervention as such unit ratio rows above the 3:7 row. A general unit ratio solution method involves moving up the ratio table (by dividing) to find the unit ratio row and then down a mostly empty ratio table (by multiplying) to find the row containing the unknown.

Cross-multiplication can be developed by factoring within the MT Puzzle and observing that the same four factors are in both diagonals. Therefore, the products of the two diagonals are identical, i.e., *top-left x bottom-right = top-right x bottom-left}*. One can then pursue cases in which different cells are the unknown to see that this factor structure allows you to find any unknown by multiplying the two known numbers in a diagonal and dividing by the number in the diagonal with the unknown, e.g., *top-left = (top-right x bottom-left)/bottom-right*. Such cross-multiplication was successfully pursued in a multisession individual tutorial with a low achiever in one of the classrooms. The unit ratio strategy, based within the ratio table, and the cross-multiplication strategy, based within the MT Puzzle, are general enough to be used with any numbers (whole numbers, fractions, or decimals) or with algebraic expressions. If one solves the same problem in all three ways (unit ratio, cross-multiplication, and MT Puzzle), one can see the relationships among the multiplication–division expressions involved in each strategy. Thus, all of these solution methods can come to be understood as different ways of seeing and solving a proportion. However grounding the unit ratio and the cross-multiplication strategies in MT Puzzles may help to avoid the rote learning of these strategies that is often decried in the literature.

CONCLUSION

Our studies indicate that fifth-grade students are ready to learn ratio and proportion. Their comfort with addition and growing facility with multiplication enabled them to understand

and relate the additive–multiplicative multiplication story situations created by repeated addition, the filmstrip drawings of these situations, and vertical ratio tables, all within the supportive context of the multiplication table. Students then moved on to solve proportion problems multiplicatively by thinking of MT Puzzles as two rows of two columns from the multiplication table or as two rows of a ratio table. The continual focus on ratio pairs as rows in vertical multiplication columns almost completely eliminated the typical inappropriate additive reasoning of subtracting within a ratio pair. The MT Puzzle enabled students to set up and solve middle-difficulty nondivisible proportion problems such as 6:14 = ?:35).

The Apprehending Zone Model and the Conceptual Phase Problem-Solving Model identify key learning processes that support sense-making in the classroom. They go beyond static or even dynamic models of mathematical cognition to address desirable features of the teaching–learning setting in action. They also focus on crucial attributes of designed teaching/learning experiences and thus support analyses that can result in recursive improvements in such designs. Our new transcliption method of video data organization and presentation enable a research team and readers to experience classroom teaching and learning data in a richer way than is usual. As these models and methods are applied to other domains, we are hopeful that richer and deeper understandings of mathematical cognition will emerge.

ACKNOWLEDGMENTS

We wish to thank the teachers who participated in our design-research studies: Christian Cigan, Noreen Winningham, Suzanne Farrand, and Soundarya Radhakrishnan. Their expertise, dedication, and insight were invaluable. We also thank Barbara Hiller, Randee Blair, and Priscilla Smith for support from the district in organizing teacher workshops and supporting our teachers to attend collaborative planning sessions throughout the research and for participating in these stimulating planning sessions. We thank Mindy Kalchman for classroom and conceptual help with the first summer intervention study and Peggy Tinzmann for ideas and questions when writing the most recent unit for teachers. Above all, we salute the many students who participated in our project: their eagerness to help was a blessing, their patience with our own confusions admirable, and their natural joy of life and of learning a prime motivator. They proved that students of all backgrounds can learn ratio and proportion concepts and methods. Thanks to Gabrielle Klausner for help with the figures. The research described in this chapter was supported in part by the National Science Foundation under Grant No. REC-9806020. The opinions expressed in this paper are those of the authors and do not necessarily reflect the views of NSF.

This chapter and all of the research were full collaborations, except that the transcliptions and gesture work were done by Dor Abrahamson.

REFERENCES[1]

Abrahamson, D. (2000). *The effect of peer-argumentation on cognitive development: The case of acquiring the concept of fractions.* Unpublished Master's thesis, Tel Aviv University, Israel.

Abrahamson, D. (2002a). When "the same" is the same as different differences: Aliya reconciles her perceptual judgment of proportional equivalence with her additive computation skills. In D. Mewborn, P. Sztajn, E. White, H. Wiegel, R. Bryant, and K. Nooney (Eds.), *Proceedings of the Twenty Fourth Annual Meeting of the North American Chapter of the International Group for the Psychology of Mathematics Education*, Athens, GA, October 26–29, 2002: Vol. 4 (pp. 1658–1661).

Columbus, OH: Eric Clearinghouse for Science, Mathematics, and Environmental Education.

Abrahamson, D. (2002b). *The multiplication table as an 'object to think with': A constructionist project with a phenomenological twist.* Unpublished manuscript, Northwestern University, Evanston, IL.

Abrahamson, D. (2002c). *Optical illusions and computation formats: Supporting Chandra's learning path to advanced ratio and proportion word problems.* Unpublished manuscript, Northwestern University, Evanston, IL.

Abrahamson, D. (2003). Text talk, body talk, table talk: A design of ratio and proportion as classroom parallel

---

[1]For more extensive references, please see individual papers.

events. *Proceedings of the 27th annual meeting of the International Group for the Psychology of Mathematics Education*, Honolulu, Hawaii, 2003. Columbus, OH: Eric Clearinghouse for Science, Mathematics, and Environmental Education.

Abrahamson, D. (2004a). *Handing down mathematics: The roles of gesturing in the teaching and learning of ratio and proportion*. Manuscript in preparation.

Abrahamson, D. (2004b). *Keeping meaning in proportion: The multiplication table as a case of pedagogical bridging tools*. Unpublished doctoral dissertation, Northwestern University, Evanston, IL.

Abrahamson, D., & Cigan, C. (2003). A design for ratio and proportion. *Mathematics Teaching in the Middle School, 8*(9), 493–501. Reston, VA: National Council of Teachers of Mathematics.

Abrahamson, D. & Fuson, K. (2004). *The multiplication table as the grounding for understanding ratio and proportion: Moving from additive–multiplicative Ratio Table to multiplicative MT Puzzle solutions*. Manuscript in preparation.

Alibali, M. W., Bassok, M., Olseth, K. L., Syc, S. E., & Goldin-Meadow, S. (1999). Illuminating mental representations through speech and gesture. *Psychological Sciences, 10*, 327–333.

Barsalou, L. W. (1999). Perceptual symbol systems. *Behavioral and Brain Sciences, 22*, 577–660.

Behr, M. J., Harel, G., Post, T., & Lesh, R. (1993). Rational number, ratio, and proportion. In D. A. Grouws (Ed.), *Handbook of research on mathematics teaching and learning* (pp. 296–333). New York: Macmillan.

Bell, M., Bretzlauf, J., Dillard, A., Hartfield, R., Isaacs, A., McBride, J., Pitvorec, K., Saeker, P., Balfanz, R., Carroll, W., & Sconniers, S. (2002). *Everyday mathematics*. Chicago, IL: Everyday Learning Corporation.

Cobb, P., Confrey, J., diSessa, A., Lehrer, R., & Schauble, L. (2003). Design experiments in educational research. *Educational Researcher, 32*(1), 9–13.

Confrey, J. (1994). Splitting, similarity, and rate of change: A new approach to multiplication and exponential functions. In G. Harel & J. M. Confrey (Eds.) *The development of multiplicative reasoning in the learning of mathematics* (pp. 291–330). Albany: State University of New York.

Fischbein, E., Deri, M., Nello, M. S., & Marino, M. S. (1985). The role of implicit models in solving verbal problems in multiplication and division. *Journal for Research in Mathematics Education, 16*(1), 3–17.

Freudenthal, H. (1981). Major problems of mathematics education. *Educational Studies in Mathematics, 12*, 133–150.

Fuson, K. (1988). Summary comments: Meaning in middle grade number concepts. In J. Hiebert & M. Behr (Eds.), *Number concepts and operations in the middle grades* (pp. 260–264). Reston, VA: National Council of Teachers of Mathematics.

Fuson, K. C. (1998). Pedagogical, mathematical, and real-world conceptual-support nets: A model for building children's mathematical domain knowledge. *Mathematical Cognition, 4*, 147–186.

Fuson, K. C. (2004). Pre-K to Grade 2 goals and standards: Achieving mastery for all. In D. H. Clements, J. Sarama, & A.-M. DiBiase (Eds.). *Engaging young children in mathematics: Standards for early childhood mathematics education* (pp. 105–148). Mahwah, NJ: Erlbaum.

Fuson, K. C., & Abrahamson, D. (2004). *A representational–situational perspective on the mathematics of proportion: A domain analysis towards designing, teaching, and initial learning of the domain with understanding*. Manuscript in preparation.

Fuson, K. C., De La Cruz, Y., Smith, S. B., Lo Cicero, A., Hudson, K., Ron, P., & Steeby, R. S. (2000). Blending the best of the twentieth century to achieve a mathematics equity pedagogy in the twenty-first century. In M. J. Burke (Ed.), *Learning mathematics for a new century* (pp. 197–212). Reston, VA: National Council of Teachers of Mathematics.

Fuson, K. C., Hudson, K., & Ron, P. (1997). *Phases of classroom mathematical problem-solving activity: The PCMPA framework for supporting algebraic thinking in primary school classrooms*. Unpublished manuscript, Northwestern University, Evanston, IL.

Fuson, K. C., Kalchman, M., Abrahamson, D., & Izsák, A. (2002, April). *Bridging the addition–multiplication learning gap: Teaching studies in four multiplicative domains*. Symposium conducted at the annual meeting of the American Educational Research Association, New Orleans, LA.

Gelman, R., & Williams, E. (1998). Enabling constraints for cognitive development and learning: Domain specificity and epigenesis. In D. Kuhn & R. Siegler (Eds.). *Cognition, perception and language. Vol. 2. Handbook of Child Psychology* (5th ed., pp. 575–630). New York: John Wiley and Sons.

Greeno, J. G. (1998). The situativity of knowing, learning, and research. *American Psychologist, 53*(1), 5–26.

Harel, G. & Confrey, J. (Eds.) (1994). *The development of multiplicative reasoning in the learning of mathematics*. Albany, NY: SUNY.

Kaput, J., & West, M. M. (1994). Missing-value proportional reasoning problems: Factors affecting informal reasoning patterns. In G. Harel & J. Confrey (Eds.), *The development of multiplicative reasoning in the learning of mathematics* (pp. 237–287). Albany, NY: SUNY.

Kieren, T. E., Pirie, S. E. B., & Gordon Calvert, L. (1999). Growing minds, growing mathematical understanding: Mathematical understanding, abstraction and interaction. In L. Burton (Ed.), *Learning mathematics, from hierarchies to networks* (pp. 209–231). London: Falmer Press.

Lamon, S. J. (1999). *Teaching fractions and ratios for understanding: Essential content knowledge and instructional strategies for teachers*. Mahwah, NJ: Erlbaum.

Nemirovsky, R., Noble, T., Ramos-Oliveira, D., & DiMattia, C. (2003). *The symbolic body*. Paper presented at the annual meeting of the American Educational Research Association, Chicago, IL, April 21–25, 2003.

Ron, P (1999). Spanish/English language issues in the math classroom. In L. Ortiz-Franco, N. G. Hernendez, & Y. De La Cruz (Eds.), *Changing the faces of mathematics: Perspectives on Latinos* (pp. 23–34). Reston, Virginia: National Council of Teachers of Mathematics.

Stetsenko, A. (2002). Commentary: Sociocultural activity as a unit of analysis: How Vygotsky and Piaget converge in empirical research on collaborative cognition. In D. J. Bearison & B. Dorval (Ed.), *Collaborative cognition: Children negotiating ways of knowing* (pp. 123–135). Westport, CT: Ablex Publishing.

Urton, G. (1997). *The social life of numbers: A Quechua ontology of numbers and philosophy of arithmetic.* University of Texas Press.

Vergnaud, G. (1983). Multiplicative structures. In R. Lesh & M. Landau (Eds.), *Acquisition of mathematical concepts and processes* (pp. 127–174). New York: Academic Press.

Wilensky, U. (1997). What is normal anyway? Therapy for epistemological anxiety. In R. Noss (Ed.), Computational environments in mathematics education [Special issue]. *Educational Studies in Mathematics, 33*(2), 171–202.

14

Stereotypes and
Math Performance

Talia Ben-Zeev
Seth Duncan
Chad Forbes

In 1994, Mattel created a Barbie™ doll, which said: "Math is hard!," highlighting gender stereotypes about math ability in American society. Disconcertingly, Barbie's frustration with math reflects a social reality in which males outperform females on standardized achievement tests such as the SAT-M and the GRE-Q (e.g., Brown & Josephs, 1999), young girls are less likely to participate in math-related activities (Eccles & Jacobs, 1987), female adolescents pursue fewer high-level math courses (Geary, 1996), and mathematically gifted males are about twice as likely as their mathematically gifted female counterparts to attain a bachelor's degree in mathematics and to gain employment in math-related fields (Benbow, Lubinski, Shea, & Eftekhari-Sanjani, 2000). Why do females who are at the vanguard of their group in mathematics show poorer performance and less success than high-achieving males? To address this question, we examine biological and environmental theories of gender differences in math ability and attempt to demonstrate how the social contextual can largely explain these and other group differences (e.g., Steele, 1997).

BIOLOGY VERSUS SOCIALIZATION AND
THE PROBLEM OF UNDERPERFORMANCE

Most of the more strictly biological explanations of gender differences in mathematics have been based on the finding that the largest differences in performance among males and females are found in gifted populations. Benbow and Stanley (1980, 1983) have shown that in a sample of young mathematically gifted adolescents, boys outperformed girls by about half a standard deviation on a SAT-M test and were overrepresented by a ratio of 13:1 in the group that scored above 700. These data, according to Benbow and Stanely, revealed a biological difference of "superior male mathematical ability" (1980, p 1264; Benbow, 1988). This reasoning is based on the following "logic": because this sample of gifted males and females had taken the same math classes and thus shared the same environmental influences, the differences must be biological. This argument is severely flawed. Research has shown that not all individuals experience the same environment in identical ways, especially when individuals are stigmatized in a given domain (Steele, 1997).

Moreover, the case for biological differences in mathematics ability is weak, at best. For example, gender differences in spatial mathematical performance have been diminishing over time (Halpern, 1992). Thus, even though biology may be implicated in gender differences in spatial ability, a larger part of the variance can be attributed to environmental differences. Bussey and Bandura (1999) raise the important point that evolution has created biological structures that enable a range of possible outcomes rather than create a fixed type of gender differentiation (for a similar argument, see Geary, 1996).

Both Bussey and Bandura (1999) and Geary (1996) noted that children's preferred activities may influence their spatial-mathematical ability. In particular, as compared to girls, boys tend to choose, and to be reinforced for, engaging in activities that are spatially complex (e.g., playing outside). In cultures in which boys and girls engage in similar spatially-oriented activities, however, there are no spatial-mathematical differences to be found (Fausto-Sterling, 1992). Aside from activities, there may be other social influences, such as parental expectations that may affect the development of mathematical skills. Eccles, Jacobs, and Harold (1990), for example, have shown that parents' beliefs about their daughters' vs. sons' math abilities were related subsequently to their children's math self-efficacy, identification, and performance.

The biological theories of gender differences in mathematics, in particular, fall short of explaining a robust finding: women who are highly successful in mathematics show *underperformance* in the mathematics domain (Steele, 1997). Underperformance refers to a phenomenon in which a group of individuals performs more poorly in a given domain relative to equally skilled peers. For example, females who score high on math and science aptitude tests tend to underperform on technical and physical science courses as compared to males who have demonstrated the same level of skill (Ramist, Lewis, & McCamley-Jenkins, 1994, as cited in Steele, 1997). Another way of stating this phenomenon is that ability tests tend to overpredict the achievement of successful female math students. Clearly then, underperformance has to do with causes that are different from skill levels (Steele, 1997).

STEREOTYPE THREAT: A FRAMEWORK FOR INVESTIGATING CAUSES OF FEMALES' UNDERPERFORMANCE

A useful framework for investigating the causes of females' underperformance in the math domain can be found in recent work on *stereotype threat*—a situational phenomenon that occurs when high-achieving individuals, who are targets of stereotypes alleging intellectual inferiority, are reminded of the possibility of confirming these stereotypes (e.g., Aronson, Lustina, Good, Keough, Steele, & Brown, 1999; Aronson, Quinn, & Spencer, 1998; Spencer, Steele, & Quinn, 1999; Steele & Aronson, 1995; Steele, 1997).

Spencer et al. (1999) (Experiment 1) showed that successful female college students performed significantly worse than males on a standardized math test when the stereotype about their math ability was made salient (participants were told that males had performed better than females on this test in the past) but that females performed just as well as males when the stereotype was removed by changing the wording used for describing performance on the math test (participants were told that males and females had performed equally well on this test in the past). Thus, a gender difference was eliminated simply because of the wording used to frame a test-taking situation, one in which stereotypes were said to be irrelevant to performance.

Stereotype threat effects have been shown in a variety of other stigmatized groups, such as in African Americans (e.g., Steele & Aronson, 1995), Latinos (e.g., Aronson & Salinas, 1997), and students of low socioeconomic status (SES) (Croizet & Claire, 1998), among others. Given the nature of this handbook, we will focus primarily on women in mathematics, but we advise that readers who wish to examine the broad-ranging effects of stereotype threat consult Steele, Aronson, and Spencer (2002).

Not all threats, as in the aforementioned Spencer et al.'s (1999) studies, need be explicit to produce performance deficits. Stereotype threat can be triggered in subtle ways, such as by the gender composition of the individuals in the environment. Inzlicht and Ben-Zeev (2000) found that females' math performance on portions of a GRE-Q test was hurt significantly when females were asked to take this math test in a mixed- vs. same-sex setting (Cohen's ds =.73 and .80, for Experiment 1 and Experiment 2, respectively). Furthermore, females' deficits were proportional to the number of males in their environment.

Often, reminding individuals of negative stereotypes about their group works to hinder these individuals' performance. Research has also shown the reverse effect: priming individuals with positive stereotypes can help to facilitate performance (for a review of hindering and facilitating effects, see Wheeler & Petty, 2001). A particularly compelling example of how the social context may hinder or facilitate intellectual performance via stereotype priming comes from the work of Shih, Pittinsky, and Ambady (1999). In this experiment, Asian female college students were randomly assigned to one of two conditions: being primed with their ethnicity or with their gender by completing pretest questionnaires. Both groups were then asked to solve a difficult math test. A control group of Asian American females was asked to take the same math test without answering any demographic questions first. The data showed that females who were primed with their Asian identity achieved higher scores on the math test than did controls. In contrast, females who were primed with their gender performed more poorly than controls. These results are dramatic, given that a subtle priming of one aspect of self was sufficient for either facilitating or hindering performance in similarly skilled individuals. This finding is a good illustration of how social identity may be relevant to understanding stereotype threat effects (Steele et al., 2002).

The facilitating effects of positive stereotypes in mathematics can also be seen in a trend for males, across multiple studies, to increase their performance when they are reminded of the female inferiority stereotype. The first researchers to identify this trend have been Spencer et al. (1999). They reported that although in individual threat studies alleging female inferiority in math, males do not show a significant improvement in threat vs. nonthreat conditions statistically; there is a consistent trend across diverse studies for males to perform better under female threat conditions. That is, if males were truly unaffected by female threat, we would expect that across studies, males under threat would be hovering around the same performance levels as males under no threat, sometimes showing slightly lower or higher performance levels. However, across most studies, males under female threat tend to show consistently higher performance levels than those under no threat, which suggests an "enhancement effect." Spencer et al. conjectured that this enhancement might be due to two reasons: (a) males show their "true" math performance under female threat conditions because male and female problem solving usually occurs in mixed-sex settings, such as classrooms. Thus, it is possible that a nonthreat situation may negatively affect males' performance; or (b) males show their "true" math performance in the no-threat condition, whereas threat provides men with a "boost" because they are reminded of the male superiority stereotype in mathematics. Future research may be able to differentiate between these hypotheses. However, whichever one is supported, the reality remains that there is a trend for males to enhance their performance under threat conditions over multiple studies (Inzlicht, 2001).

Males can also show situational performance deficits under threat to their own math identity. In Aronson et al.'s (1999) study, European American males were given a difficult math test. Half of the males were told that the aim of the study was to assess their math ability, whereas the other half was told that the goal was to understand the Asian superiority effect in mathematics, that is, to investigate why Asians tend to outperform European Americans on math tests. Males in the latter group, stereotype threat condition, showed performance deficits compared to their peers. This study showed that stereotypes could hurt the performance of a group that has the potential to assimilate to a negative stereotype, even if that group is not generally disadvantaged in society (Inzlicht, 2001).

What mechanisms are responsible for producing stereotype threat effects? What resides in the black box that mediates the relationship between stereotype priming and underperformance? One possibility, as suggested by ideomotor activity (e.g., Bargh & Ferguson, 2000), is that stereotype priming results in direct and automatic assimilation to stereotype related behavior. In the next section, we discuss how stereotype activation may play a role in stereotype-threat effects and the resulting implications for women in mathematics.

Stereotype Activation

The activation of stereotypes may affect encoding of information, perception of self and others, and intellectual and physical performance on implicit and automatic levels (Bargh & Ferguson, 2000; Lepore & Brown, 1997; Kawakami, Dovidio, Moll, Hermsen, & Russin, 2000). Our focus will be on the latter part, on how automatic activation of stereotypes affects problem solving in a relevant domain. For example, Bargh, Chaiken, Raymond, and Hymes (1996) (Experiment 2) showed that priming college students with the concept ELDERLY caused students to walk more slowly than controls, presumably because of the activation of an association such as SLOW. In the case of women in math, the priming of FEMALE, MATH, or both gender and domain, may often lead to activation of existing associations that juxtapose inferiority and math. Activating these associations, in turn, might lead to decreased cognitive performance.

The strength of stereotype activation (links between FEMALE and BAD in MATH) depends, in part, on people's ideologies, motivations, and personal beliefs (Wittenbrink, Judd, & Park, 2001; Devine, 1989; Kawakami, Dion, & Dovidio, 1998; Devine, Plant, Amodio, & Jones, 2002; Lepore & Brown, 1997; Blair, 2002; Kawakami, Young, & Dovidio, 2002; Devine, 2001). Kawakami et al. (1998) found that people who scored higher on prejudice measures also showed a greater degree of implicit stereotype activation. The link to women's performance on math tests seems very important, but at the present moment, it is impossible to come to any strong conclusions. Based on the Kawakami et al. study, it is reasonable to conjecture that high-math-identified women who would score lower on explicit measures of math inferiority would also show lower implicit activation of math inferiority stereotypes. However, it may also be possible that women who identify highly with mathematics find themselves in many more situations in which stereotypes about math get activated than do their low-math-identified peers. The frequency of activation may then cause high-math-identified females to have higher levels of stereotype activation, but this hypothesis, as well, requires empirical demonstration. The link between stereotype activation and behavioral assimilation may also depend on the nature of the priming, task, and individual differences involved.

Stereotype activation seems to be an integral part of stereotype threat. Steele and Aronson (1995) had African American and European American students take a verbal test, which was introduced as either diagnostic (threat) or nondiagnostic (no threat) of intelligence. Participants were asked to complete measures of stereotype activation before taking the test. The stereotype activation measure was composed of 80 word fragments, 11 of which could be completed with words associated with African American stereotypes, among others (e.g., _ _ C E [RACE], B R _ _ _ _ _ [BROTHER], or W E L _ _ _ _ [WELFARE]). Results showed that African American students under threat resolved more word fragments with stereotype-related words, showing higher stereotype activation levels.

Stereotype activation sets the foundation for understanding stereotype threat, but it cannot explain this phenomenon in its entirety. Steele et al. (2002) have argued that in stereotype-removed conditions (males and females have performed equally on this math test in the past), there is stereotype activation due to reminding people of the stereotypes. However, making the stereotype seem irrelevant helps to negate the threat effects by a mechanism that is other than activation.

What Factors May Underlie Stereotype Threat Effects on Math Performance?

Historically, the first wave of stereotype threat work focused on showing stereotype threat effects empirically. Current work is primarily devoted to examining potential mediators of stereotype threat (Steele, Spencer, & Aronson, 2002). In this section, we will discuss evidence for several mediational variables that could help shed light on underperformance.

Ideomotor Activity

Ideomotor activity, first proposed by William Carpenter (1874) and William James (1890), assumes a strong automatic connection between perception of an action and the execution of that action. More recently, Bargh and colleagues (e.g., Bargh, Chaiken, Raymond, & Hymes, 1996; Bargh & Ferguson, 2000) have provided evidence for ideomotor activity in social-psychological domains. In a particularly dramatic demonstration, which was alluded to previously, Bargh, Chen, and Burrows (1996) imbedded elderly-related words (e.g., wrinkled) in a scrambled-word puzzle that was administered to one sample while another sample of participants received a word-puzzle without elderly-related words. While leaving the experimental room, the amount of time it took each participant to walk down a corridor to the elevator was measured unbeknownst to the participants. In support of an ideomotor mechanism, participants who had been primed with elderly-related words walked significantly slower than the control participants. In a similar study, Dijksterhuis et al. (2000) found that a group of participants primed with elderly-related words were less able to recall, later on, objects that were present in the testing room than nonprimed participants. Ideomotor effects also appear to be very specific to the activated stereotype. For example, Dijksterhuis and Van Knippenberg (1998) found that pariticpants primed with professor and soccer hooligan attributes showed increased and decreased performance, respectively, on questions from the game Trivial Pursuit. Furthermore, individuals primed with secretary attributes answered the questions more quickly than professor- or nonprimed participants.

In support of an ideomotor activity account of stereotype threat, Wheeler and Petty (2001) noted that studies using explicit (e.g., Keller, 2002) and implicit cues (e.g., Inzlicht & Ben-Zeev, 2000) may simply increase stereotype accessibility and behavioral assimilation without need to resort to more complex psychological explanations, such as the fear of confirming a negative stereotype about one's group (Steele, 1997). For example, Keller et al. (2002) told females in a threat condition that males typically outperform females on a math test. As expected, females in the threat condition produced lower scores on the test than females in the no-threat condition. According to Petty and Wheeler (2001), such results can be explained by behavioral assimilation to the stereotype activated in the threat condition. Because an ideomotor mechanism does not require conscious activation of a stereotype, it may also explain the results of studies using more subtle stereotype cues, such as a female minority status in a math test environment.

Ideomotor activity is an attractive mediator of stereotype threat because of its parsimony. There are two key problems, however, to consider. First, stereotyped individuals do not always underperform when the stereotype is explicitly activated, as would be predicted by an ideomotor account. Stereotype threat manipulations often attempt to remove the stereotype's applicability by telling participants that a test is race or gender fair. For example, Spencer et al. (1999, Experiment 3) found that females who were told that a test showed no gender differences performed better on a math test than females in a condition in which no mention of stereotypes was made. This and similar studies demonstrate that there must be an additional component to stereotype threat mediation because stereotype activation is the same in threat and threat-removed conditions, yet these conditions produce differential effects on performance

A second problem with ideomotor theory is that it fails to account for the consistent finding that only the vanguard, or high identifiers, are at risk for stereotype threat. To be threatened by a stereotype, an individual must identify with the stereotyped domain (see Steele, 1997). Whereas ideomotor theory predicts that anyone will mimic an activated negative stereotype, research indicates that only high achievers are susceptible to stereotype threat (Aronson et al., 1999). It is important to conduct future studies that examine whether high- vs. low- math-identified women have different levels of stereotype activation under threat conditions (see section on stereotype activation above).

Performance Expectancy

Women tend to have lower expectancies about their math performance than do men (Crandall, 1969; Dweck & Bush, 1976; Eccles, Jacobs, & Harold, 1990; Meece et al., 1982). Under conditions of threat, women may become particularly vulnerable to lowered expectations and thus become less motivated to perform (e.g., Stangor, Carr, & Kiang, 1998). Furthermore, expectancies and motivation are intimately linked to effort (Bandura, 1977, 1986), such that a decrease in expectancies would be associated with a resultant decrease in effort. When stereotype threat is removed, however (e.g., telling females that a task is non-diagnostic of math ability), an expectancy hypothesis would predict that performance is unaffected.

Performance expectancy studies have produced inconsistent results. Stangor, Carr, and Kiang (1998, Experiment 1) gave females a verbal task and provided positive or neutral pseudofeedback about their performance, regardless of participants' actual performance. Participants were then told that they would be administered a test of spatial ability. In the stereotype threat condition, participants were told that men performed better on the task, and in the no-threat condition participants were told that the test produced no gender differences. Before taking the test, participants were asked how well they expected to do on it. As predicted, stereotype-threatened females reported lower performance expectancy than nonthreatened females. Furthermore, the effect of stereotype threat moderated the effect of initial confidence on performance expectancy. Positive feedback on the verbal test did not affect performance expectancy in the stereotype-threatened group but did increase expectations in the non-threatened group. Although stereotype threat decreased performance expectancy in this study, performance on the spatial task was not measured and mediation could not be assessed.

Sekaquaptewa and Thompson (2003) measured the mediating effect of performance expectancy in women taking a math test. In this study, males and females were given a math test in the presence of other participants. The researchers used two types of stereotype threat manipulations. In the first condition, participants were told that the test was a traditional math task or that it was a nontraditional gender-fair math test. In the second condition, participants were either the only male or female in a group or were in a same-sex group. Before the math task, participants rated how well they expected to perform. Both stereotype threat manipulations affected performance in females, with females in the traditional math and female minority conditions performing more poorly. Performance expectancy, however, mediated only the effect of minority status on performance.

A similar study failed to find a relationship between stereotype threat and performance expectancy. Spencer et al. (1999, Experiment 3) assessed the mediational role of performance expectancy in stereotype-threatened females while solving math problems from the GMAT. In the low-stereotype-threat condition, participants were told that males and females typically performed equally well on the test, while no mention of gender differences was mentioned in the control group. Just prior to administering the task, the participants were asked a series of questions related to self-efficacy (e.g., "I am concerned about whether I have enough mathematical ability to do well on the test"). In contrast to the results of Stangor, Carr, & Kiang (1998), the stereotype threat manipulation had no effect on reported self-efficacy.

Another collection of mixed results has been found in studies of stereotype threat and athletic performance. Stone et al. (1999) told European American and African American athletes that a miniature golf task reliably measured either "athletic intelligence" or "natural athletic ability." The stereotype threat manipulation affected performance, with European American participants performing worse in the "natural athletic ability" condition and African American participants performing worse in the "athletic intelligence" condition. Before the golf task, participants were asked to predict how many strokes would be required to complete the course. Consistent with the findings of Spencer et al. (1999), these initial performance expectancies were unaffected by stereotype threat. However, in a follow-up study participants were asked how many strokes would be required to putt the ball before each hole. After the first hole, performance expectancy was associated with both the threat manipulation and performance, although it is unclear if stereotype threat or poor performance affected these expectations.

What can be learned from the disparate findings of performance expectancy mediation investigations? In most studies that asked participants how well they expected to do on a given task, there is evidence that stereotype threat elicited decreased performance expectancy (i.e., Sekaquaptewa & Thompson, 2003; Stangor, Carr, & Kiang, 1998; Stone et al., 1999). Stereotype threat manipulations did not affect performance expectancy when no threat groups were told that a test was gender neutral and threat groups were told nothing about a test's gender fairness (i.e., Sekaquaptewa & Thompson, 2003; Spencer et al., 1999). It is possible then, that performance expectancy decreases only when there is a stereotype-related cue, such as minority status or explicit mention of differential gender performance. It is also important to note that Sekaquaptewa & Thompson (2003) found that performance expectancy only partially mediated the effect of threat on performance. If performance expectancy does actually cause stereotype-threatened females to have impaired performance, it is likely to occur in conjunction with other mediators.

Evaluation Apprehension

One tenet of stereotype threat theory is that at-risk individuals fear confirming a negative stereotype. It has been proposed that fear of negative evaluation may interfere with concentration in females taking math tasks (Spencer et al., 1999, Experiment 3). To test this hypothesis, Spencer et al. (1999, Experiment 3) asked females to rate their evaluation apprehension (e.g., "If I do poorly on this test, others may question my ability") after a stereotype threat manipulation. Interestingly, they found that high evaluation apprehension was associated with good performance. However, evaluation apprehension was not affected by the stereotype threat manipulation and is therefore unlikely to mediate stereotype threat effects.

Self-Handicapping

Several investigations of stereotype threat mediation have assessed the role of self-handicapping. According to self-handicapping theory, individuals actively arrange circumstances that enable them to make an external attribution of failure in order to preserve a sense of competence (Jones & Berglas, 1978). To maintain the image of competency, individuals use external sources of underachievement (e.g., not getting enough sleep) as a rationale for poor performance.

Studies investigating the relationship between self-handicapping and stereotype threat have been inconsistent. In the study by Stone et al. (1998), described in detail above, participants in the threat condition did not self-report greater self-handicapping compared to controls. In another study, however, Stone (2002, Experiment 2), did find that high-athletic-identified European American participants practiced less than Hispanic participants.

Similar inconsistency has been found in studies of stereotype threat and intellectual performance. In a study of stereotype threat and socioeconomic status by Croizet and Claire (1998), low-SES participants were told that a verbal test measured either intellectual ability (threat group) or attention (no-threat group). The threat group did not report greater self-handicapping (i.e., poorer sleep, more worrying, more stress, etc.) than participants in the no-threat group. Although not tested in a mediational analysis, Steele and Aronson (1995) found that African Americans anticipating a test of intellectual ability reported less sleep and more difficulty concentrating than African Americans who were told the test would be nondiagnostic.

Keller (2002) is the only study, to our knowledge, that has found positive results for self-handicapping using a mediational analysis. Females were told that males typically performed better on a math test (threat) or were told nothing (no-threat). As predicted, there was a statistically significant relationship between threat manipulation and performance. Furthermore, the use of self-handicapping as a covariate reduced the relationship between threat and performance to insignificance, as expected.

Stereotype Suppression

Once someone becomes aware that his behavior may confirm a negative stereotype about his group, he may attempt to suppress the stereotype and related distress (Steele, Spencer, & Quinn, 2003). The stereotype suppression may then have an ironic effect, actually keeping the thought activated. According to this account, ironic activation interferes with concentration and, consequently, with performance. Spencer and colleagues (as cited in Steele et al., 2002) tested this hypothesis in a series of experiments. In one study, women and men took a difficult math test under either cognitive-load or no-load cognitions. Women in the cognitive-load condition performed worse and showed greater stereotype activation than the other three groups. Spencer and colleagues argued that the data show stereotype suppression's ironic effect. Flustered by the cognitive load, females presumably attempted to suppress the stereotype. A second study found that the increased cognitive load did not impair performance when the participants were told the test was not gender biased.

It is unclear, however, if the increase in stereotype activation arose from thought suppression or simply because the test was more difficult, thereby increasing the risk of confirming a negative stereotype or by increasing physiological arousal or both. Furthermore, removing the applicability of the stereotype does not necessarily indicate a decrease in thought suppression.

In a third study, a group of female participants who were told to think of a valued identity when stereotype-related thoughts arose performed as well as men, and it outperformed female control groups. Presumably, this technique increased the successfulness of stereotype suppression.

Anxiety and Physiological Arousal

Anxiety and its biological correlate, physiological arousal, are implicated directly or indirectly in most of the suggested mediators of stereotype threat but has not been examined sufficiently (e.g., Steele & Aronson, 1995). Recently, Osborne (2001) found correlational evidence to support the idea that gender differences in mathematics performance were related to self-reported anxiety levels. Unfortunately, however, Osborne noted that the study failed to determine whether stereotype threat was present during test administration (there was no empirical manipulation of threat), which leaves open the possibility that factors other than stereotype threat may have been causally linked to arousal.

Spencer et al. (1999) showed that although participants' degree of nervousness and anxiety was related to both performance and threat, it did not significantly reduce the direct relationship between threat and test performance. This analysis does not, however, rule out the possibility of anxiety as a mediator, because self-reports of anxiety are problematic. First, as is the case with any form of introspection, verbal reports of anxiety may not be reliable between individuals. Identical responses on a Likert scale may index different levels of subjective anxiety for different people. Second, self-reports of anxiety are complicated by poor interceptive acuity. The correlations between self-reports of anxiety and physiological markers of anxiety tend to be low. Heart palpitations, respiration, and heart rate show low correlations (rs between .15 and 4) with verbal reports of anxiety and distress (Ehlers & Breuer, 1996; Wilhelm & Roth, 1998). Physiological measures of arousal may account for significant portions of mediation between stereotype threat and performance, despite inconclusive results using self-reported anxiety.

Other data support the idea that arousal may mediate stereotype threat. Consider, for example, a study on the effects of stereotype threat on blood pressure (Blascovich, Spencer, Quinn, & Steele, 2001). African American participants taking a test under stereotype threat showed a more elevated blood pressure level that rose faster and remained higher relative to the blood pressure of European American participants or African American participants in the nonthreat control group.

The theoretical foundation for the importance of arousal lies in the Yerkes-Dodson (1908) law, which demonstrates that performance is optimal at intermediate levels of arousal and decreases when arousal is either low or high. Ben-Zeev, Fein, and Inzlicht (2003) have proposed that stereotype threat may interfere with performance, in part, by triggering physiological arousal that exceeds an optimal performance level.

To provide experimental evidence for the arousal hypothesis, Ben-Zeev et al. employed indirect methods based on classical social-psychological theories. In Experiment 1 they used a social facilitation paradigm (Zajonc, 1965). Specifically, they placed high-math-identified women under stereotype-threat and no-threat conditions. Women in both conditions were led to believe that they would be asked to take a difficult math test. In the interim, half of the women were asked to perform a familiar and easy task: writing their name. The other half, in contrast, were asked to perform a less familiar and more difficult task: writing their name backward. This paradigm has been employed successfully in previous social facilitation research (e.g., Schmidt, Gilovitch, Goore, & Joseph, 1986). The prediction was as follows: if arousal is implicated in stereotype threat, then females in the threat condition will do *better* on the easy task but *worse* on the difficult task in comparison to females in the no-threat condition. This prediction was supported by the study's results.

Experiment 2 was designed to provide further evidence by using a misattribution paradigm, which has been used in the past to examine the role of arousal as a potential mediator variable without the need to resort to either self-report or use invasive procedures (e.g., Olson, 1988; Savitsky, Medvec, Charlton, & Gilovich, 1998; Zanna, & Cooper, 1974, 1976). The hypothesis was as follows: if stereotype threat increases arousal that impedes problem solving, then giving women an opportunity to misattribute their arousal to a benign external source might attenuate these performance deficits.

Specifically, female participants divided into threat and no-threat conditions (the manipulation of threat was an implicit one—gender composition) and were then told that one of the goals of the study was to examine the effects of subliminal noise on test performance. The test of choice, they were informed, was a difficult mathematics one. The alleged source of the subliminal noise was a large machine that was introduced as the subliminal noise generator. The control group was told that the subliminal noise generator would have no discernible physical effects, whereas those in the misattribution condition were told that the subliminal noise generator had been shown to elicit several side effects, such as an increase in nervousness, among other symptoms. The findings supported the arousal prediction: performance deficits in the stereotype threat condition were mitigated when women were given an opportunity to misattribute their arousal to the subliminal noise generator or to an external source. In sum,

Experiments 1 and 2 converge on the hypothesis that arousal plays an important mediating role in stereotype-threat effects.

Via which cognitive mechanisms might arousal affect performance negatively? Work done by Ashcraft and colleagues (for a review, see chapter 18, this volume) suggests that individuals who are high in math anxiety may experience difficulties in working memory processing when asked to carry out arithmetic procedures such as carrying, borrowing, keeping track, and applying rules because some of their working memory capacity becomes devoted to task-irrelevant processing such as worrying.

Arousal itself might be mediated by cognitive appraisals of threat vs. challenge (Folkman & Lazarus, 1986; Lazarus & Folman, 1984; Tomaka et al., 1993, 1997). The cognitive appraisal of a situation as posing a threat (potential loss is perceived to exceed coping resources) has been associated with an increase in pituitary-adrenal-corticol arousal, which stimulates the release of the glucocorticoid cortisol (Dienstbier, 1989; Tomaka et al., 1993, 1997). When a situation is appraised as a challenging one, on the other hand (coping resources are perceived to exceed potential loss), the hypothalamus, acting through the sympathetic nervous system, tends to stimulate adrenaline release from the medulla (Dienstbier, 1989; Lupien & McEwen, 1997).

Furthermore, threat vs. challenge arousal is associated differentially with cognitive and behavioral changes. For example, Ursin, Baade, and Levine (1978) have shown that Norweigian Army paratroopers who exhibited increased adrenaline levels were also more successful at jumps from airplanes than were paratroopers who exhibited increased cortisol levels. Similar patterns of intellectual and behavioral deficits following an increase in cortisol vs. optimal behavior associated with increases in adrenaline have been shown in a variety of human and animal studies (for an excellent review, see Dienstbier, 1989).

The importance of this work to stereotype-threat work in general, and to understanding women's underperformance in math in particular, is that cognitive assessments of perceived coping resources (e.g., math skills) to perceived loss (e.g., failure and all its consequences), may be malleable, depending on contextual cues such as stereotype primes (see Ben-Zeev et al., in press). It would be useful to examine how situational beliefs about intellectual resources to perform well in a stereotyped domain affect performance under stereotype threat to help women to perceive the same situation (taking a difficult math test) as challenging rather than as threatening.

Helping Females to Achieve Their Potential: Reflections on Combating Stereotype Threat

The reality of stereotype threat is highly disconcerting. Students who are high achieving, at the vanguard of their groups, show underperformance as a result of stereotype priming. Females in mathematics may fall short of their potential when they are reminded of stereotypes alleging their inferiority in the math domain either explicitly or implicitly, despite these women's true abilities.

Can we help high-achieving students to develop coping skills for combating the detrimental effects of stereotype threat? The first wave of proposed interventions, most notably "Wise schooling," has been based on changing the nature of a student's environment, by helping students to overcome suspicion and to develop trust or by changing diversity in a student's community (e.g., Steele, 1997).

Wise Schooling

Steele's (1997) concept of "Wise schooling" was designed to focus on the needs of stigmatized individuals by increasing their confidence and self-esteem and by decreasing their belief about being representatives of stereotypes. Steele proposed that to achieve these goals, for both domain-identified and domain-unidentified students, it is important to foster a solid teacher–student relationship. In this relationship it is understood that students' abilities are not in question, that students are challenged in a way that helps them to actualize their potential without becoming overwhelmed, and that intelligence is malleable as opposed to being fixed (Dweck, 1986; Steele, 1997). The Wise schooling approach emphasizes the values of diversity and role models.

Steele (1997) found some empirical support for this intervention in a freshman-year program conducted at the University of Michigan. In this study, ethnic minorities along with European Americans were randomly assigned to either a program that implemented Wise strategies, a remedial minority program, a combination of each, or a control. In the Wise schooling program, participants were told that the program was designed to maximize their potential and that the university already had high expectations for them. Students were also encouraged to voluntarily attend a "challenge workshop" and weekly discussion groups, in which students shared their personal experiences with each other. In the remedial minority program, minority participants received much individual attention but in a more traditional format that lacked the aforementioned characteristics. The findings showed that African American students who were enrolled in the Wise schooling program attained a significantly higher GPA than students in all other programs. Furthermore, African American students who were enrolled in the Wise schooling program had essentially the same GPA as European American participants who were enrolled in that program. Steele (1997) concluded that by implementing Wise schooling techniques, minority students were able to transcend the fear of being perceived as representative of negative stereotypes, whereas the remedial minority program only seemed to perpetuate the minority students' pre-existing fears.

Changing Fixed to Malleable Notions of Intelligence

A component of Wise schooling—educating students about the malleability of intelligence—has been given some further corroboration as one of the strategies for combating stereotype threat. Dweck and colleagues (Dweck & Legget, 1988; Dweck, 1999) have found that students' implicit theories about intelligence affect their problem-solving performance. Students who believe that intelligence is somewhat malleable and affected by effort ("incremental" theorists) often approach difficult tasks with a "mastery-oriented" style that helps them to achieve successful outcomes. Students who believe that intelligence is more of a fixed, genetic quality ("entity" theorists), on the other hand, are more vulnerable to feeling "helpless" in trying to solve difficult tasks, which in turns leads these students to disengage from tasks and to underperform, even in domains in which they have shown success (Dweck, 1999).

Importantly, Dweck found that these implicit beliefs about intelligence can be changed when students are exposed to different models of intelligence. For example, college students who had performed poorly on a test were more apt to express interest in taking a tutorial to improve their score after hearing a lecture on the incremental theory of intelligence, in contrast to those who had attended a lecture on an entity theory of intelligence (Hong et al., 1998 in Dweck 1999). Aronson (1998) and Aronson and Fried (1998) found that exposing students to an incremental view of intelligence helped to mitigate the impact of stereotype threat on college students' performance but not on their perceived prejudice. These findings are encouraging because they imply that by simply exposing students to the notion of the malleability of intelligence, students can begin to cope with the harmful effects of stereotype threat.

Additional Interventions

As research on mediation of stereotype threat progresses, the ways to combat it become even more conceivable. Recent data offer a variety of potential tactics to reverse threat effects, such as by redefining the context with which a test is taken to be less threatening explicitly (Croizet & Claire, 1998; Steele & Aronson, 1995), having a stigmatized individual engage in self-affirmative thoughts prior to taking a test (Croizet & Despres, 2003), or priming women who are taking a difficult math exam with stories of women who have succeeded in male-dominated fields (McIntyre, Paulson, & Lord, 2003). The self-affirmation manipulation is especially promising, given recent work by Fein (e.g., Fein, 1999; Fein & Maron, 1998; Specer, Fein, & Lomore, 2001), which had shown that self-affirmation can buffer the self against perceptions of failure.

Although most of the research to date has focused on explicit methods to counteract stereotype threat, we may be able to utilize implicit training tactics and methods as well. As was discussed in an earlier section, there appears to be a component of stereotype threat that involves the automatic activation of stereotypes and its negative effects on performance (Shih et al., 1999; Steele & Aronson, 1995). There is evidence to suggest that stereotype-negation training can be successful in training individuals to negate stereotypes that are associated with a given category and to ultimately decrease stereotype activation after stereotype priming (Kawakami et al., 2000). It is conceivable to reason that we could train individuals to lower the automatic activation of stereotypes, which may prove useful in helping students to immunize against the effects of stereotype threat.

Another future stereotype-threat intervention may involve the use of biofeedback, mindful meditation, and other relaxation techniques to help counteract the negative effects of threat arousal. Because an examination of the factors that may lead to threat effects points to arousal as a potentially important mechanism, teaching stigmatized individuals who are motivated to excel to relax under conditions of threat may be a promising direction for future research.

SUMMARY AND CONCLUSION

The phenomenon of stereotype threat is disconcerting. Individuals in the same classroom, who are exposed to the same teacher and instructional materials, do not necessarily experience the learning environment in the same way (Steele, 1997). It is important to understand that stereotypes may affect cognition via arousal and other mechanisms; thereby hindering students from realizing their potential. This argumentation also carries assessment implications. If test scores are depressed because of stereotype-threat effects, then test scores are not a valid proxy for ability.

It may be counterintuitive that individuals who are excelling in their fields would be the ones most susceptible to the effects of stereotypes. These students have "made it" despite stereotypes about their groups, so what makes these students vulnerable? The answer is one of identification. The more a student identifies with achieving success in a domain, the more a possible "failure," such as achieving a low test score or performing well below one's peers, could hurt. For a stereotyped individual, a personal failure also incurs the risk of affirming a negative stereotype about the person's group (Steele, 1997).

By better understanding what mechanisms may mediate stereotype threat, such as a heightened level of physiological arousal combined with stereotype suppression, we can begin to combat this effect. For example, it is possible that arousal-reduction techniques combined with self-affirmation (including challenge appraisals) may help to alleviate the detrimental effects of stereotype threat.

In sum, as more evidence is accumulated to show how powerful stereotype-threat effects can be, it becomes crucial to examine how different mediators combine to produce these effects and what individual differences may be implicated. We hope that future research will bring us even closer to understanding stereotype threat and ways to combat it—to turn situations in which students are threatened into situations in which they are challenged to perform to their full potential.

REFERENCES

Aronson, J., & Salinas, M. F. (1997). *Stereotype threat, attributional ambiguity, and Latino underperformance.* Unpublished manuscript, University of Texas.

Aronson, J., Fried, C. B., & Good, C. (2002). Reducing the effects of stereotype threat on African American college students by shaping theories of intelligence. *Journal of Experimental Social Psychology, 38,* 113–125.

Aronson, J., Lustina, M. J., Good, C., Keough, K., Steele, C. M., & Brown, J. When white men can't do math: Necessary and sufficient factors in stereotype threat. *Journal of Experimental Social Psychology, 35,* 29–46.

Aronson, J., Quinn, D. M., & Spencer, S. J. (1998). Stereotype threat and the academic underperformance of minorities and women. In J. K. Swim & C. Stangor (Eds.), *Prejudice: The target's perspective* (pp. 83–103). San Diego, CA: Academic Press.

Bandura, A. (1977). Self-efficacy: Toward a unifying theory of behavioral change. *Psychological Review, 84,* 191–215.

Bandura, A. (1986). The explanatory and predictive scope of self-efficacy theory. *Journal of Social and Clinical Psychology, 4,* 359–373.

Bargh, J .A., & Chaiken, S., Raymond, P., & Hymes, C. (1986). The automatic evaluation effect: Unconditional automatic attitude activation with a pronunciation task. *Journal of Experimental Social Psychology, 31,* 104–128.

Bargh, J. A., Chen, M., & Burrows, L. (1996). Automaticity of social behavior: Direct effects of trait construct and stereotype activation on action. *Journal of Personality and Social Psychology, 71,* 230–244.

Bargh, J. A., & Ferguson, M. J. (2000). Beyond behaviorism: The social-cognitive psychology of automatic human behavior. *Psychological Bulletin, 126,* 925–945.

Benbow, C. P., & Stanley, J. C. (1980). Sex differences in mathematical ability: fact or artifact? *Science, 210,* 1262–1264.

Benbow, C. P., & Stanley, J. C. (1983). Sex differences in mathematical reasoning ability: more facts. *Science, 222,* 1029–1031.

Benbow, C. P. (1988). Sex differences in mathematical-reasoning ability in intellectually talented preadolescents: Their nature, effects, and possible causes. *Behavioral Brain Sciences, 11,* 169–232.

Benbow, C. P., Lubinski, D., Shea, D. L., & Eftekhari-Sanjani, H. (2000). Sex differences in mathematical reasoning ability at age 13: Their status 20 years later. *Psychological Science, 11,* 474–479.

Ben-Zeev, T., Carrasquillo C. M, Ching, A., Kliengklom, T. J., McDonald, K. L., Newhall, D. C., Patton, G. E., Stewart, T. D., Stoddard, T., Inzlicht, M., & Fein, S. (in press). "Math is hard!" (Barbie, 1994): Responses of threat vs. challenge mediated arousal to stereotypes alleging intellectual inferiority. In A. M. Gallagher & J. C. Kaufman (Eds.), *Gender differences in mathematics.* Cambridge, MA: Cambridge University Press.

Ben-Zeev, T., Fein S., & Inzlicht M. (in press). Arousal and stereotype threat. *Journal of Experiment of Social Psychology.*

Blair, I. V. (2002). The malleability of automatic stereotypes and prejudice. *Personality and Social Psychology Review, 6,* 242–261.

Blascovich, J., Spencer, S. J., Quinn, D., & Steele, C. (2001). African Americans and high blood pressure: The role of stereotype threat. *Psychological Science, 12,* 225–229.

Brown, R. P., & Josephs, R. A. (1999). Stereotype relevance and gender differences in math performance. *Journal of Personality and Social Psychology, 76,* 246–257.

Burrows, L., Bargh, J. A., & Chen, M. (1996) Automaticity of social behavior: Direct effects of trait construct and stereotype activation on action. *Journal of Personality & Social Psychology, 71,* 230–244.

Bussey, K., & Bandura, A. (1999). Social cognitive theory of gender development and differentiation. *Psychological Review, 106,* 676–713.

Carpenter, W. B. (1874). *Principles of mental physiology with their applications to the training and discipline of the mind, and the study of its morbid conditions.* New York: Appleton.

Crandall, V. C. (1969). Sex differences in expectancy of intellectual and academic reinforcement. In C. P. Smith (Ed.), *Achievement related behavior in children* (pp. 11–45). New York: Russell Sage Foundation.

Croizet, J. C., & Claire, T. (1998). Extending the concept of stereotype threat to social class: The intellectual underperformance of students from low socioeconomic backgrounds. *Personality and Social Psychology Bulletin, 24,* 588–594.

Croizet, J. C., & Despres, G. (2003, February). *How does stereotype threat undermine performance?* Presented at the Society for Personality and Social Psychology's Annual Meeting, Los Angeles.

Devine, P. G. (1989). Stereotypes and prejudice: Their automatic and controlled components. *Journal of Personality and Social Psychology, 56,* 5–18.

Devine, P. G. (2001). Implicit prejudice and stereotyping: How automatic are they? *Journal of Personality and Social Psychology, 81,* 757–759.

Devine, P. G., Plant, E. A., Amodio, D. M., & Harmon-Jones, E. (2002). The regulation of explicit and implicit race bias: The role of motivations to respond without prejudice. *Journal of Personality and Social Psychology, 82,* 835–848.

Dienstbier, R. A. (1989). Arousal and physiological toughness: Implications for mental and physical health. *Psychological Review, 96,* 84–100.

Dijksterhuis, A., Aarts, H., Bargh, J. A., & Van Knippenberg, A. (2000). On the relation between associative strength and automatic behavior. *Journal of Experimental Social Psychology, 36,* 531–544.

Dijksterhuis, A., & Van Knippenberg, A. (2000). Behavioral indecision: Effects of self-focus on automatic behavior. *Social Cognition, 18,* 55–74.

Dweck, C. S. (1986). Motivational processes affecting learning. *American Psychologist, 41,* 1040–1048.

Dweck, C. S. (1999). *Self-theories: Their role in motivation, personality and development.* Philadelphia: Psychology Press.

Dweck, C. S., & Bush, E. S. (1976). Sex differences in learned helplessness: I. Differential debilitation with peer and adult evaluators. *Developmental Psychology, 12,* 147–156.

Dweck, C. S., & Leggett, E. L. (1988). A social-cognitive approach to motivation and personality. *Psychological Review, 95,* 256–273.

Eccles, J. S., & Jacobs, J. E. (1987). In M. R. Walsh (Ed.), *The Psychology of Women* (question 10, pp. 333–354). New Haven, CT: Yale University Press.

Eccles, J. S., Jacobs, J. E., & Harold, R. D. (1990). Gender role stereotypes, expectancy effects, and parents' socialization of gender differences. *Journal of Social Issues, 46*, 183–201.

Ehlers, A., & Breuer, P. (1996). How good are patients with panic disorder at perceiving their heartbeats? *Biological Psychology, 42*, 165–182.

Fausto-Sterling, A. (1992). *Myths of Gender: Biological Theories about Women and Men* (2nd ed.). New York: Basic Books.

Fein, S. & Maron, B. A. (1998, August). *Self-affirmation and athletic and academic performance under pressure*. Presented at the 1998 Conference of the American Psychological Association, San Francisco.

Fein, S., & Spencer, S. J. (1997). Prejudice as self-image maintenance: Affirming the self through negative evaluations of others. *Journal of Personality and Social Psychology, 73*, 31–44.

Folkman, S., & Lazarus, R. (1986). Stress process and depressive symptomatology. *Journal of Abnormal Psychology, 95*, 107–113.

Geary, D. C. (1996). Sexual selection and sex differences in mathematical abilities. *Behavioral and Brain Sciences, 19*, 229–284.

Halpern, D. (1992). *Sex Differences in Cognitive Abilities* (2nd ed.). Hillsdale, NJ: Erlbaum.

Inzlicht, M., & Ben-Zeev, T. (2000). A threatening intellectual environment: Why females are susceptible to experiencing problem-solving Deficits in the presence of males. *Psychological Science, 11*, 365–371.

Inzlicht, M. (2001). *Threatening intellectual environments: When and why females perform worse in the presence of males*. Unpublished doctoral dissertation, Brown University, Providence, RI.

James, W. (1950). *The principles of psychology*. New York: Holt. (Original work published 1890)

Jones, E. E., & Berglas, S. (1978). Control of attributions about the self through self-handicapping strategies: The appeal of alcohol and the role of underachievement. *Personality and Social Psychology Bulletin, 4*, 200–206.

Jones, E. E., & Pittman, T. S. (1982). Toward a general theory of strategic self-presentation. In J. Suls (Ed.), *Psychological Perspectives on the Self* (Vol 1, pp. 231–262). Hillsdale, NJ: Erlbaum.

Kawakami, K., Dion, K. L., & Dovidio, J. F. (1998). Racial prejudice and stereotype activation. *Personality and Social Psychology Bulletin, 24*, 407–416.

Kawakami, K., Dovidio, J. F., Moll, J., Hermsen, S., & Russin, A. (2000). Just say no (to stereotyping): Effects of training in the negation of stereotypic associations on stereotype activation. *Journal of Personality and Social Psychology, 78*, 871–888.

Kawakami, K., Young, H., & Dovidio, J. F. (2002). Automatic stereotyping: Category, trait, and behavioral activations. *Personality and Social Psychology Bulletin, 28*, 3–15.

Keller, J. (2002). Blatant stereotype threat and women's math performance: Self-handicapping as a strategic means to cope with negative performance expectations. *Sex Roles, 47*, 193–198.

Lazarus, R. S., & Folkman, S. (1984). *Stress, appraisal and coping*. New York: Springer Publishing.

Lepore, L., & Brown, R. (1997). Category and stereotype activation: Is prejudice inevitable? *Journal of Personality and Social Psychology, 72*, 275–287.

Leyens, J. P., Desert, M., Croizet, J. C., & Darcis, C. (2000). Stereotype threat: are lower status and history of stigmatization preconditions of stereotype threat? *Personality and Social Psychology Bulletin, 26*, 1189–1199.

Lupien, S. J., & McEwen, B. S., (1997). The acute effects of corticosteroids on cognition: Integration of animal and human model studies. *Brain Research Reviews, 24*, 1–27.

Meece, J. L., Parsons, J. E., Kaczala, C. M., & Goff, S. B. (1982). Sex differences in math achievement: Toward a model of academic choice. *Psychological Bulletin, 91*, 324–348.

McGuire, W. J., McGuire, C. V., & Winton, W. (1979). Effects of household sex composition on the salience of one's gender in the spontaneous self-concept. *Journal of Experimental Social Psychology, 15*, 77–90.

McIntyre, R. B., Paulson, R. M., & Lord, C. G. (2003). Alleviating women's mathematics stereotype threat through salience of group achievements. *Journal of Experimental Social Psychology, 39*, 83–90.

National Science Foundation. (1996). *Women, minorities, and persons with disabilities in science and engineering: 1996* (NSF Publication No. 96-311). Arlington, VA: National Science Foundation.

O'Brien, L. T., & Crandall, C. S. (2003). Stereotype threat and arousal: Effects on women's math performance. *Personality and Social Psychology Bulletin, 29*, 790–801.

Olson, J. M. (1988). Misattribution, prepatory information, and speech anxiety. *Journal of Personality and Social Psychology, 54*, 758–767.

Osborne, J. W. (2001). Testing stereotype threat: Does anxiety explain race and sex differences in achievement? *Contemporary Educational Psychology, 26*, 291–310.

Quinn, D. M., & Spencer, S. J. (2001). The interference of stereotype threat with women's generation of mathematical problem-solving strategies. *Journal of Social Issues, 57*, 55–71.

Savitsky, K., Medvec, V. H., Charlton, A. E., & Gilovich, T. (1998). "What, me worry?": Arousal, misattribution, and the effect of temporal distance on confidence. *Personality and Social Psychology Bulletin, 24*, 529–536.

Schacter, S., & Singer, J. E. (1962). Cognitive, social, and physiological determinants of emotional state. *Psychological Review, 69*, 379–399.

Schmidt, B. H., Gilovich, T., Goore, N., & Joseph, L. (1986). Mere presence and social facilitation: One more time. *Journal of Experimental Social Psychology, 22*, 242–248.

Sekaquaptewa, D., & Thompson, M. (2003). Solo status, stereotype threat, and performance expectancies: Their effects on women's performance. *Journal of Experimental Social Psychology, 39*, 68–74.

Shih, M., Pittinsky, T. L., & Ambady, N. (1999). Stereotype susceptibility: Identity salience and shifts in quantitative performance. *Psychological Science, 10*, 80–83.

Spencer, S. J., Steele, C. M., & Quinn, D. (1999). Stereotype threat and women's math performance. *Journal of Experimental Social Psychology, 35*, 4–28.

Spencer, S. J., Fein, S., & Lomore, C. D. (2001). Maintaining one's self-image vis-à-vis others: The role of self-affirmation in the social evaluation of the self. *Motivation and Emotion, 25*, 41–64.

Stangor, C., Carr, C., & Kiang, L. (1998). Activating stereotypes undermines task performance expectations. *Journal of Personality and Social Psychology, 75*, 1191–1197.

Steele, C. M., & Aronson, J. (1995). Stereotype threat and the intellectual test performance of African Americans. *Journal of Personality and Social Psychology, 69,* 797–811.

Steele, C. M. (1997). A threat in the air. How stereotypes shape intellectual identity and performance. *American Psychologist, 52,* 613–629.

Steele, C. M. (1998). The psychology of self-affirmation: Sustaining the integrity of the self. In L. Berkowitz (Ed.), *Advances in experimental social psychology, Vol. 21: Social psychological studies of the self: Perspectives and programs* (pp. 261–302). San Diego, CA: Academic Press.

Steele, C. M. (1997). A threat in the air: How stereotypes shape intellectual identity and performance. *American Psychologist, 52,* 613–629.

Steele, C. M., Spencer, S. J., & Aronson, J. (2002). Contending with group image: The psychology of stereotype and social identity threat. In M. P. Zanna (Ed.), *Advances in experimental social psychology* (Vol. 34, pp. 379–440). San Diego, CA: Academic Press.

Steele, C. M., & Aronson, J. (1995). Stereotype threat and the intellectual test performance of African Americans. *Journal of Personality and Social Psychology, 69,* 797–811.

Steele, C. M., Spencer, S. J., & Lynch, M. (1993). Self-image resilience and dissonance: The role of affirmational resources. *Journal of Personality and Social Psychology, 64,* 885–896.

Stone, J. (2002). Battling doubt by avoiding practice: The effect of stereotype threat on self-handicapping in white athletes. *Personality and Social Psychology Bulletin, 28,* 1667–1678.

Stone, J., Lynch, C. I., Sjomeling, M., & Darley, J. M. (1999). Stereotype threat effects on black and white athletic performance. *Journal of Personality and Social Psychology, 77,* 1213–1227.

Tomaka, J., Blascovich, J., Kelsey, R. M., & Leitten, C. L. (1993). Subjective, physiological, and behavioral effects of threat and challenge appraisal. *Journal of Personality and Social Psychology, 65,* 248–260.

Tomaka, J., Blascovich, J., Kibler, J., & Ernst, J. M. (1997). Cognitive and physiological antecedents of threat and challenge appraisal. *Journal of Personality and Social Psychology, 73,* 63–72.

Ursin, H., Baade, E., & Levine, S. (Eds.) (1978). *Psychobiology of stress: A study of coping men.* New York: Academic Press.

Wheeler, S. C., & Petty, R. E. (2001). The effects of stereotype activation on behavior: A review of possible mechanisms. *Psychological Bulletin, 127,* 797–826.

Wilhelm, F. H., & Roth, W. T. (1998). Taking the laboratory to the skies: Ambulatory assessment of self-report, autonomic, and respiratory responses in flying phobia. *Psychophysiology, 35,* 596–606.

Wittenbrink, B., Judd, C. M., & Park, B. (2001). Spontaneous prejudice in context: Variability in automatically activated attitudes. *Journal of Personality and Social Psychology, 81,* 815–827.

Wittenbrink, B., Judd, C.M., & Park, B. (1997). Evidence for racial prejudice at the implicit level and its relationship with questionnaire measures. *Journal of Personality and Social Psychology, 72,* 262–274.

Yerkes, R. M., & Dodson, J. D. (1908). The relationship of strength of stimulus to rapidity of habit-formation. *Journal of Comparative Neurology of Psychology, 18,* 459–482.

Zajonc, R. B. (1965). Social facilitation. *Science, 149,* 269–274.

Zanna, M. P., & Cooper, J. (1974). Dissonance and the pill: An attribution approach to studying the arousal properties of dissonance. *Journal of Personality and Social Psychology, 29,* 703–709.

Zanna, M. P., & Cooper, J. (1976). Dissonance and the attribution process. In J. Harvey, W. Ickes, & R. Kidd (Eds.), *New direction in attribution research.* Mahwah, NJ: Erlbaum.

—

Part 3

Learning and Performance Disabilities in Math and Number Processing

—

15

Learning Disabilities in Arithmetic and Mathematics
Theoretical and Empirical Perspectives

David C. Geary
Mary K. Hoard

The breadth and complexity of the field of mathematics make the identification and study of the cognitive phenotypes that define learning disabilities in mathematics (MD) a formidable endeavor. A learning disability can result from deficits in the ability to represent or process information in one or all of the many mathematical domains (e.g., geometry) or in one or a set of individual competencies within each domain. The goal is further complicated by the task of distinguishing poor achievement due to inadequate instruction from poor achievement due to an actual cognitive disability (Geary, Brown, & Samaranayake, 1991). One approach that can be used to circumvent this assessment confound is to apply the theories and methods used to study mathematical competencies in normal children to the study of children with MD (Bull & Johnston, 1997; Garnett & Fleischner, 1983; Geary & Brown, 1991; Geary, Widaman, Little, & Cormier, 1987; Jordan, Levine, & Huttenlocher, 1995; Jordan, Hanich, & Kaplan, 2003a; Jordan & Montani, 1997; Ostad, 1997, 1998a; Russell & Ginsburg, 1984; Svenson & Broquist, 1975). When this approach is combined with studies of dyscalculia, that is, numerical and arithmetical deficits following overt brain injury (Shalev, Manor, & Gross-Tsur, 1993; Temple, 1991), and brain-imaging studies of mathematical processing (Dehaene, Spelke, Pinel, Stanescu, & Tsivkin, 1999), a picture of the cognitive and brain systems that can contribute to MD begins to emerge.

The combination of theoretical and empirical approaches has been primarily applied to the study of numerical and arithmetical competencies and is therefore only a first step to a complete understanding of the cognitive and brain systems that support mathematical competency and any associated learning disabilities. It is, nonetheless, a start. We overview what this research strategy has revealed about children with MD in the second section and discuss diagnostic, prevalence, and etiological issues in the first section. In the third section, we present a general organizational framework for approaching the study of MD in any mathematical domain and use this framework and an earlier taxonomy of MD subtypes (Geary, 1993) to better understand the cognitive deficits described in the second section.

BACKGROUND CHARACTERISTICS OF CHILDREN WITH MD

Diagnosis

Unfortunately, measures that are specifically designed to diagnose MD are not available; thus, most researchers and practitioners rely on standardized achievement tests, often in combination with IQ scores. A score lower than the 25th or 30th percentile on a mathematics achievement test combined with a low-average or higher IQ score are common criteria for diagnosing MD (Geary, Hamson, & Hoard, 2000; Gross-Tsur, Manor, & Shalev, 1996). However, a lower-than-expected (based on IQ) mathematics achievement score does not, in and of itself, indicate the presence of MD. Many children who score poorly on achievement tests one academic year score average or better in subsequent years. These children do not appear to have any of the underlying memory or cognitive deficits described in the next section, and thus a diagnosis of MD may not be appropriate (Geary, 1990; Geary et al., 1991; Geary et al., 2000). Many children who have lower than expected achievement scores across successive academic years, in contrast, often have some form of memory or cognitive deficit, and thus a diagnosis of MD is often warranted. Many of these children do show year-to-year improvements in achievement scores and on some math cognition measures, but they do not catch up to their normal peers and show more persistent deficits in some areas, such as fact retrieval (Hanich, Jordan, Kaplan, & Dick, 2001; Jordan et al., 2003a).

It should be noted that the cutoff of the 30th percentile on a mathematics achievement test does not fit with the estimation, described below, that between 5% and 8% of children have some form of MD. The discrepancy results from the nature of standardized achievement tests and the often rather specific memory or cognitive deficits of children with MD. Standardized achievement tests sample a broad range of arithmetical and mathematical topics, whereas children with MD often have severe deficits in some of these areas and average or better competencies in others. The result of averaging across items that assess different competencies is a level of performance (e.g., at the 20th percentile) that overestimates the competencies in some areas and underestimates them in others.

In addition to the development of diagnostic instruments, another issue that needs to be explored is whether treatment resistance can be used as one diagnostic criterion for MD. As described later, many children with MD have difficulties retrieving basic arithmetic facts from long-term memory, and these difficulties often persist despite intensive instruction on basic facts (Howell, Sidorenko, & Jurica, 1987). Although the instructional research is preliminary, it does suggest that a retrieval deficit resistant to instructional intervention might be a useful diagnostic indicator of arithmetical forms of MD.

Prevalence and Etiology

Experimental measures that are more sensitive to MD than are standard achievement tests have been administered to samples of more than 300 children from well-defined populations (e.g., all fourth graders in an urban school district) in the United States (Badian, 1983), Europe (Kosc, 1974; Ostad, 1998b), and Israel (Gross-Tsur et al., 1996; Shalev et al., 2001). These measures have largely assessed number and arithmetic competencies and were constructed based on neuropsychological deficits associated with dyscalculia (see Geary & Hoard, 2001; Shalev et al., 1993). Performance that deviates from age-related norms and is similar to that associated with dyscalculia has been used in these studies as an indication of MD, and suggests that 5% to 8% of school-age children exhibit some form of MD. Many of these children have comorbid disorders, including reading disabilities (RD), spelling disability, attention deficit hyperactivity disorder (ADHD), or some combination of these disorders.

Very little is currently known about the etiology of MD, although preliminary twin and familial studies suggest genetic and environmental contributions (Light & DeFries, 1995; Shalev et al., 2001). For instance, Shalev and her colleagues studied familial patterns of MD, specifically learning disabilities in number and arithmetic. The results showed that family members (e.g., parents and siblings) of children with MD are 10 times more likely to be diagnosed with MD than are members of the general population, suggesting a heritable risk for the development of MD. It is possible that this risk is only expressed under certain environmental conditions, but these are not yet understood.

COGNITIVE PHENOTYPE OF CHILDREN WITH MD

In the respective sections below, we provide a brief overview of theoretical models of normal development in the number, counting, and arithmetic domains, along with patterns that have been found with the comparison of children with MD to their normal peers. Unless otherwise noted, MD refers to children with low achievement scores—relative to IQ in many of the studies—in mathematics. When studies have only focused on children with low mathematics achievement scores but average or better reading achievement scores, they will be referred to as children with MD only. If the study assessed children with low achievement in mathematics and reading, they will be identified as children with MD/RD.

Number Representation

The comprehension and production of number require an understanding of and the ability to access representations of the associated magnitudes (Gallistel & Gelman, 1992). In addition, children must learn to process verbal (e.g., "three hundred forty two") and Arabic representations (e.g., "342") of numbers and to translate numerals from one representation to another (e.g., "three hundred forty two" to "342"; Dehaene, 1992; Seron & Fayol, 1994). It appears that young children with MD and MD/RD have a normal, or only a slightly delayed, understanding of small quantities and can associate these with corresponding Arabic and number–word representations (Geary et al., 2000; Gross-Tsur et al., 1996; Temple & Sherwood, 2002).

One area in which number representation has not been studied in children with MD involves their ability to form a spatially based mental number line and then use this line to make estimates of numerical magnitude. Jordan and her colleagues (Hanich et al., 2001; Jordan et al., 2003a) found that children with MD only and MD/RD were not as skilled as other children, including RD children, at estimating whether the answer to problems such as 9 + 8 is closer to 20 or 30. As noted by Jordan et al., it is not clear how these children were making these estimates, although use of some form of spatially based mental number line is one possibility (Dehaene et al., 1999). Implications are discussed in a later section.

Counting

Normal Development

Children's understanding of the principles that constrain counting behavior appears to emerge from a combination of inherent constraints and counting experience (Briars & Siegler, 1984; Geary, 1995; Gelman & Gallistel, 1978). Early inherent constraints can be represented by Gelman and Gallistel's five implicit principles. These principles are one–one correspondence (one and only one word tag, e.g., "one," "two," is assigned to each counted object), stable order (the order of the word tags must be invariant across counted sets), cardinality (the value of the final word tag represents the quantity of items in the counted set), abstraction (objects of any kind can be collected together and counted), and order irrelevance (items within a given set can be tagged in any sequence). The principles of one–one correspondence, stable order, and cardinality define the "how to count" rules, which, in turn, provide the skeletal structure for children's emerging knowledge of counting (Gelman & Meck, 1983).

In addition to inherent constraints, children make inductions about the basic characteristics of counting by observing standard counting behavior and associated outcomes (Briars & Siegler, 1984; Fuson, 1988). These inductions appear to elaborate and add to Gelman and Gallistel's counting rules (1978). One result is a belief that certain unessential features of counting are essential. These unessential features include standard direction (counting must start at one of the endpoints of a set of objects); and adjacency. The latter is the incorrect belief that items must be counted consecutively and from one contiguous item to the next, that is, "jumping around" during the act of counting results in an incorrect count. By five years of age, many children know most of the essential features of counting described by Gelman and Gallistel but also believe that adjacency and start at an end are also essential features of counting. The latter beliefs indicate that young children's understanding of counting is rather rigid and immature and influenced by the observation of standard counting procedures.

Children with MD

Using the procedures developed by Gelman and Meck (1983) and Briars and Siegler (1984), Geary, Bow-Thomas, and Yao (1992) compared the counting knowledge of first-grade children with MD/RD with that of their normal peers. The procedure involved asking the children to watch a puppet count a set of objects. The puppet sometimes counted correctly and sometimes violated one of Gelman and Gallistel's (1978) counting principles or Briars and Siegler's unessential features of counting. The child's task was to determine if the puppet's count was "OK" or "not OK and wrong." In this way, the puppet performed the procedural aspect of counting (i.e., pointing at and tagging items), leaving the child's responses to be based on her or his understanding of counting principles.

The results revealed that children with MD/RD identified correct counts as well as violations of most of the principles identified by Gelman and Gallistel (1978). They also understood that counting from right to left was just as appropriate as the standard left-to-right counting (Geary et al., 1992). As the same time, many children with MD/RD did not understand Gelman and Gallistel's (1978) order-irrelevance principle and believed that adjacency is an essential feature of counting. There were also group differences on trials in which either the first or the last item was counted twice. Children with MD/RD correctly identified these counts as errors when the last item was double-counted, suggesting that they understood the one–one correspondence principle. Double counts were often labeled as correct when the first item was counted, suggesting that many children with MD/RD had difficulties holding information in working memory—in this case noting that the first item was double-counted—while monitoring the act of counting (see also Hitch & McAuley, 1991).

In a more recent study, children with IQ scores in the 80–120 range were administered a series of cognitive and achievement tests in first and second grade (Geary, Hoard, & Hampson, 1999; Geary et al., 2000). Children with low-average or better IQ scores and poor achievement scores in reading and/or math in both grades were considered learning disabled (LD). Among other findings, the results were consistent with those of Geary et al. (1992); that is, children with MD/RD and MD only differed from the children with RD only and normal children on adjacency trials in first and second grade and on double-counting trials (the first item) in first grade. The pattern suggests that even in second grade, many children with MD/RD and MD only do not understand all counting principles and in first grade may have difficulty holding an error notation in working memory while monitoring a short counting sequence (see also

Hoard, Geary, & Hampson, 1999). Children with RD only performed as well as the normal children.

In summary, many children with MD, independent of reading achievement levels or IQ, have a poor conceptual understanding of some aspects of counting. These children understand most of the inherent counting rules identified by Gelman and Gallistel (1978), but consistently err on tasks that assess order-irrelevance or adjacency from Briars and Siegler's (1984) perspective. The poor counting knowledge of these children appears to contribute to their delayed competencies in the use of counting to solve arithmetic problems and may result in poor skill at detecting and thus correcting counting errors (Ohlsson & Rees, 1991).

Arithmetic

Normal Development

The most thoroughly studied developmental and schooling-based improvement in arithmetical competency is change in the distribution of procedures, or strategies, children use during problem solving (Ashcraft, 1982; Carpenter & Moser, 1984; Geary, 1994; Siegler, 1996). During the early learning of how to solve simple addition problems, for instance, children typically count both addends (e.g., 5 + 3). These counting procedures are sometimes executed with the aid of fingers (finger-counting strategy) and sometimes without them (verbal counting strategy; Siegler & Shrager, 1984). The two most commonly used counting procedures, whether children use their fingers or not, are termed min or sum (Fuson, 1982; Groen & Parkman, 1972). The min procedure typically involves stating the larger valued addend and then counting a number of times equal to the value of the smaller addend, such as counting 5, 6, 7, 8 to solve 5 + 3. Sum involves counting both addends starting from 1. Max involves stating the small values addend and counting a number of times equal to the value of the larger added. The development of procedural competencies is related, in part, to improvements in children's conceptual understanding of counting and is reflected in a gradual shift from frequent use of sum counting to min counting (Geary et al., 1992; Siegler, 1987).

The use of counting procedures appears to result in the development of memory representations of basic facts (Siegler & Shrager, 1984; but see Temple & Sherwood, 2002). Once formed, these long-term memory representations support the use of memory-based problem-solving, specifically direct retrieval of arithmetic facts and decomposition. With direct retrieval, children state an answer that is associated in long-term memory with the presented problem, such as stating "eight" when asked to solve 5 + 3. Decomposition involves reconstructing the answer based on the retrieval of a partial sum. For instance, the problem 6 + 7 might be solved by retrieving the answer to 6 + 6 (i.e., 12) and then adding 1 to this partial sum. The use of retrieval-based processes is moderated by a confidence criterion that represents an internal standard against which the child gauges confidence in the correctness of the retrieved answer. Children with a rigorous criterion only state answers that they are certain are correct, whereas children with a lenient criterion state any retrieved answer, correct or not (Siegler, 1988).

Figure15.1 shows the common developmental and schooling-based changes in the strategy mix. As the mix matures, children solve problems more quickly because they use more efficient memory-based strategies and because, with practice, it takes less time to execute each strategy (Delaney, Reder, Staszewski, & Ritter, 1998; Geary, Bow-Thomas, Fan, & Siegler, 1996; Lemaire & Siegler, 1995). The transition to memory-based processes results in the quick solution of individual problems and reductions in the working memory demands associated with solving these problems. The eventual automatic retrieval of basic facts and the accompanying reduction in working memory demands, in turn, facilitate the solving of more complex problems (Geary & Widaman, 1992; Geary, Liu, Chen, Saults, & Hoard, 1999).

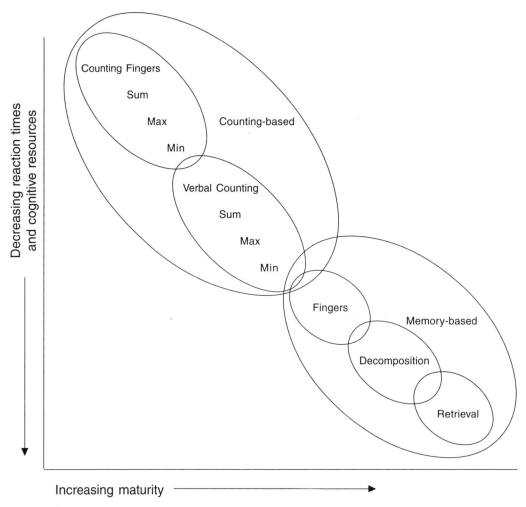

Figure 15.1. With development and schooling, children shift from the use of counting-based to memory-based processes to solve simple arithmetic problems.

Children with MD

When they solve simple arithmetic problems (4 + 3) and simple word problems, children with MD/RD and MD only use the same types of strategies (e.g., verbal counting) as normal children but differ in the strategy mix and in the pattern of developmental change in this mix (Geary, 1990; Hanich et al., 2001; Jordan et al., 2003a; Jordan, Hanich, & Kaplan, 2003b). In comparison to their normal peers, children with MD often (a) rely on developmentally immature strategies, such as finger counting, (b) frequently commit counting errors, (c) use immature counting procedures [they often use sum counting rather than min counting], and (d) have difficulties retrieving basic facts from long-term memory. These differences have been found in the United States (Geary & Brown, 1991; Hanich et al., 2001; Jordan & Montani, 1997), in several European nations (Barrouillet, Fayol, & Lathuliere, 1997; Ostad, 1997, 1998a, 1998b, 2000; Svenson, & Broquist, 1975), and in Israel (Gross-Tsur et al., 1996).

As an example, Geary et al. (1999, 2000) and Jordan et al. (2003a; Jordan & Montani, 1997) found consistent differences in the strategy mix across groups of MD/RD, MD only, RD only, and normal children. In first through third grade, children with MD only and children with MD/RD committed more counting errors and used the developmentally immature counting-all procedure more frequently than did the children in these other groups. The children in the RD only and normal groups showed a shift, across grades, from heavy reliance on finger counting to verbal counting and retrieval (see Figure 15.1). The children in the MD/RD and MD only groups, in contrast, did not show this shift but instead relied heavily on finger counting, even in third grade (Jordan et al., 2003a). These patterns replicated previous studies of children with MD/RD and demonstrated that many of the same deficits, although to a lesser degree, are evident for children with MD only (Geary et al., 2000; Ostad, 1998a). There were, however, a few differences comparing MD only and MD/RD children: MD only children made fewer counting procedure errors (Geary et al. 2000) and were more accurate at solving simple word problems, presumably because of better reading comprehension (Jordan et al., 2003a).

The most consistent finding in this literature is that children with MD/RD and MD only differ from their normal peers in the ability to use retrieval-based processes to solve simple arithmetic and simple word problems (Barrouillet et al., 1997; Garnett & Fleischner, 1983; Geary, 1990, 1993; Hanich et al., 2001; Jordan et al., 2003a; Jordan & Montani, 1997; Ostad, 1997, 2000; Temple & Sherwood, 2002). Unlike the use of counting strategies, it appears that the ability to retrieve basic facts does not substantively improve across the elementary-school years for many children with MD/RD and MD only. When these children do retrieve arithmetic facts from long-term memory, they commit many more errors and sometimes show error and reaction time (RT) patterns that differ from those found with younger, normal children (Barrouillet et al., 1997; Fayol, Barrouillet, and Marinthe, 1998; Geary, 1990; Geary & Brown, 1991; Räsänen & Ahonen, 1995). Moreover, these patterns are sometimes found to be similar to the patterns evident with children who have suffered from an early (before age 8 years) lesion to the left hemisphere or associated subcortical regions (Ashcraft, Yamashita, & Aram, 1992). The overall pattern suggests that the memory-retrieval deficits of children with MD/RD or MD only reflect a cognitive disability and not, for instance, a lack of exposure to arithmetic problems, poor motivation, a low confidence criterion, or low IQ.

There are at least two potential sources of these retrieval difficulties: a deficit in the ability to represent phonetic/semantic information in long-term memory (Geary, 1993) or a deficit in the ability to inhibit irrelevant associations from entering working memory during problem solving (Barrouillet et al., 1997). The latter form of retrieval deficit was first discovered by Barrouillet et al. (1997), based on the memory model of Conway and Engle (1994), and was recently confirmed in our laboratory (Geary et al., 2000; see also Koontz & Berch, 1996). In the Geary et al. study, one of the arithmetic tasks required children to only use retrieval—the children were instructed not to use counting strategies—to solve simple addition problems (see also Jordan & Montani, 1997). Children with MD/RD, MD only, as well as children with RD, committed more retrieval errors than did their normal peers, even after controlling for IQ. The most common error was a counting-string associate of one of the addends. For instance, common retrieval errors for the problem 6 + 2 were 7 and 3, the numbers following 6 and 2, respectively, in the counting sequence. Hanich et al. (2001) found a similar pattern, although the proportion of retrieval errors that were counting-string associates was lower than that found by Geary et al. (2000). A third potential source of the retrieval deficit is a disruption in the development or functioning of a more modularized—independent of phonetic/semantic memory and working memory—cognitive system for the representation and retrieval of arithmetical knowledge, including arithmetic facts (Butterworth, 1999; Temple & Sherwood, 2002).

Finally, research results on more complex forms of arithmetic are beginning to emerge (Fuchs & Fuchs, 2002; Jordan & Hanich, 2000), and appear to support the separation of MD only and MD/RD groups. In comparison to MD only children, children with MD/RD show more pervasive deficits as problem complexity increases from simple operations to complex, multistep story problems, although children in both groups demonstrate performance below normal peers.

FRAMEWORK FOR MD RESEARCH

As noted earlier, the complexity of the field of mathematics results in a very large number of potential sources of MD. In Figure 15.2 we present a conceptual scheme for focusing future MD research and for better understanding the number, counting, and arithmetic deficits we just described. As noted in the figure, competencies in any given area of mathematics will depend on a conceptual understanding of the domain and procedural knowledge that supports actual problem solving (Geary, 1994). Base-10 arithmetic is one example whereby instruction focuses on teaching the conceptual foundation (i.e., the repeating number system based on sequences of 10) and related procedural skills, such as trading from the tens column to the units column while solving complex arithmetic problems (e.g., 243 – 129; Fuson & Kwon, 1992). Conceptual and procedural competencies, in turn, are supported by an array of cognitive systems, as shown in the bottom sections of Figure 15.2.

The central executive controls the attentional and inhibitory processes needed to use procedures during problem solving, and much of the information supporting conceptual and procedural competencies is likely to be represented in the language or visuospatial systems (Baddeley, 1986), although a distinct modular system for arithmetic has also been proposed (Butterworth, 1999; Temple & Sherwood, 2002). Geary (1995), in fact, proposed an evolved system for processing simple quantities, but this is more circumscribed than the system proposed by Butterworth and Temple and Sherwood, and would not include arithmetic facts.

In any case, Engle (2002) has argued and empirically demonstrated (Conway & Engle, 1994) that Baddeley's central executive is synonymous with the working memory components of attentional and inhibitory control, and thus working memory and central executive will be used interchangeably. The language systems are important for certain forms of information representation, as in articulating number words during the act of counting. These same systems may support the formation of associations between arithmetic problems and answers generated by counting, and thus a poor ability to represent information in these systems would, in theory, result in a fact retrieval deficit (Geary, 1993), although Temple and Sherwood (2002)

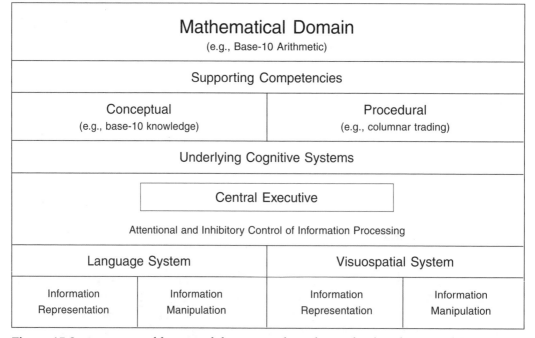

Figure 15.2. A conceptual framework for approaching the study of mathematical disabilities.

argued that the retrieval deficits are specific to the arithmetic module. The visuospatial system appears to be involved in representing some forms of conceptual knowledge, such as number magnitudes (Dehaene & Cohen, 1991), and for representing and manipulating mathematical information that is cast in a spatial form, as in a mental number line (Zorzi, Priftis, & Umiltá, 2002). On the basis of this framework, MD would be manifest—be evident while solving mathematics problems—as a deficit in conceptual or procedural competencies that define the mathematical domain. These conceptual or procedural deficits, in theory, could be due to underlying deficits in (1) the central executive or (2) the information representation or manipulation (i.e., changing the way the information is represented) systems of the language or visuo-spatial domains.

The organizational framework shown in Figure 15.2 can also be used to understand MD in the number, counting, and arithmetic domains we described earlier. What we do understand in these domains is outlined in Table 15.1 as a preliminary taxonomy of three subtypes of MD, specifically, procedural, semantic memory, and visuospatial. The taxonomy was developed based on an earlier review of the cognitive deficits of children with MD and related dyscalculia and behavioral genetic literatures (Geary, 1993). Eventually, the taxonomy will need to be expanded to include all of the features shown in Figure 15.2 and for additional mathematical domains (e.g., algebra). The goal here is to try to understand the above described performance and cognitive patterns of children with MD/RD and MD only in terms of the procedural, semantic memory, and spatial subtypes in Table 15.1, and in terms of the systems shown in Figure 15.2. For ease of presentation, children with MD will refer to both MD only and MD/RD children, unless specific differences were found.

Organization of Cognitive Deficits

Procedural Deficits

As described earlier, a common procedural deficit of children with MD involves use of developmentally immature strategies, such as sum counting and finger counting, and miscounting when using these procedures to solve simple arithmetic problems. Potential sources of these procedural deficits include: (a) a poor conceptual understanding of counting concepts (Geary et al., 1992, 2000) or, (b) poor working memory/central executive resources (Hitch & McAuley, 1991). Geary et al. (1992) found that children with MD who had a delayed understanding of counting concepts rarely used the min counting procedure. They seemed to believe that counting always had to start from 1 and thus relied on sum counting. Our current work indicates a strong relation between accuracy of procedural execution and performance on a measure of working memory/central executive functioning (Byrd-Craven, Hoard, & Geary, 2002; Geary, Hoard, Byrd-Craven, & DeSoto, 2004) and confirms the relation between conceptual knowledge and procedural competency.

Semantic Memory Deficits

If a general deficit in the ability to retrieve information from long-term memory contributes to arithmetic fact retrieval deficits of children with MD, then these children should also show deficits on measures that assess skill at accessing other types of semantic information, such as words, from long-term memory (Geary, 1993). In fact, Geary argued that the comorbidity of MD and RD is related, in part, to difficulties in accessing both words and arithmetic facts from semantic memory, although the data on this are mixed (e.g., Jordan et al., 2003a). In terms of the organizing framework shown in Figure 15.2, the deficit would reside in the systems that support information representation in the language system. It seems that some MD children with fact-retrieval deficits do have a language-representation deficit (Geary et al., 2000), but others may not (Jordan et al., 2003a).

Table 15.1

Subtypes of Learning Disabilities in Mathematics

	Cognitive and performance features	Neuropsychological features	Genetic features	Developmental features	Relation to RD
Procedural	• Relatively frequent use of developmentally immature procedures (i.e., the use of procedures that are more commonly used by younger, normal children) • Frequent errors in the execution of procedures • Poor understanding of the concepts underlying procedural use • Difficulties sequencing the multiple steps in complex procedures	Unclear, although some data suggest an association with left hemispheric dysfunction and in some cases (especially for feature 4 above? a prefrontal dysfunction	Unclear	Appears, in many cases, to represent a developmental delay (i.e., performance is similar to that of younger, normal children, and often	Unclear
Semantic Memory	• Difficulties retrieving mathematical facts, such as answers to simple arithmetic problems • When facts are retrieved, there is a high error rate • For arithmetic, retrieval errors are often associates of numbers in the problems (e.g., retrieving 4 to $2 + 3 = ?$; 4 is the counting-string associate that follows 2, 3) • RTs for correct retrieval are often unsystematic	• Appears to be associated with left-hemispheric dysfunction, possibly the posterior regions for one form of retrieval deficit and the prefrontal regions for another • Possible subcortical involvement, such as the basal ganglia	Appears to to be a heritable deficit	Appears to represent a developmental difference (i.e., cognitive and performance features differ from that of younger, normal children, and do not change substantively across age or grade)	Appears to occur with phonetic forms of RD
Visuospatial	• Difficulties in spatially representing numerical and other forms of mathematical information and relationships • Frequent misinterpretation of misunderstanding of spatially represented information	Appears to be associated with right hemispheric dysfunction, in particular, posterior regions of the right hemisphere, although the parietal cortex of the left hemisphere may be implicated as well	Unclear, although the cognitive and performance features are common with certain genetic disorders (e.g. Turner's syndrome)	Unclear	Does not appear to be related

As we described earlier, Barrouillet et al. (1997) argued that the retrieval deficit may result from response competition during the retrieval process (Conway & Engle, 1994; Engle, 2002; Koontz & Berch, 1996). As an example, presentation of the problem 4 × 5 not only prompts retrieval of 20, but it also prompts retrieval of related, but irrelevant to this problem, numbers, such as 9 (4 + 5) and 25 (5 × 5; Campbell, 1995). There is now strong evidence that individuals with poor working memory/central executive resources have difficulties inhibiting these irrelevant associations (Engle, Conway, Tuholski, & Shisler, 1995). For these individuals, poor information retrieval is more strongly related to the central executive than to the language system per se. There is evidence that some children with MD do not inhibit irrelevant associations during fact retrieval (Geary et al., 2000), but evidence to date is not conclusive (Hanich et al., 2001). We are currently conducting studies that should help to clarify whether response competition, semantic retrieval, or some combination of these potential forms of cognitive deficit are the primary source or sources of the difficulties children with MD have with retrieving arithmetic facts. As noted, an alternative view is that the retrieval deficits are specific to an arithmetic module (Temple & Sherwood, 2002).

Spatial Deficits

As noted in Table 15.1, spatial deficits have been associated with misalignment of numbers when setting up arithmetic problems (e.g., writing 45 × 68 out horizontally) and in interpreting the positional, base-10 meaning of the numbers (Geary, 1993; Russell & Ginsburg, 1984). There are many other areas of mathematics that are dependent on spatial abilities (e.g., many subareas of geometry), including some basic competencies in the areas of number representation and comparison. We suggested earlier that children with MD might have difficulties spatially representing number magnitude, but this hypothesis has not yet been tested. Using the framework shown in Figure 15.2, difficulties might, in theory, reside in the ability to represent number information in a spatial form or in the ability to easily change spatial representations.

Dehaene and Cohen (1997), for instance, argued that magnitude representations of numbers are based on a spatial representation, specifically, a logarithmic number line. One way to represent this number line is in terms of an exponential increase in the distance between consecutive pairs of numbers, as contrasted with the equal distances between numbers in the formal Arabic system. The formal and learned relations are shown as the first number line in Figure 15.3, and the logarithmic number line is below this. In a cross-sectional study of second, fourth, and sixth graders as well as college students, Siegler and Opfer (2003) showed that children's estimates of where numbers fit on a number line ranging from 1 to 100 or 1 to 1,000 fit either the formal or logarithmic model but tended to shift toward the formal model

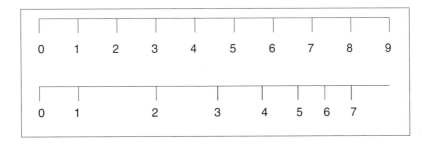

Figure 15.3. The top section shows spatial-based number representations that conform to the formal and school-taught Arabic system. The bottom section shows the spatial-based logarithmic form of number representation that is common before schooling.

in higher grades. The shift reflects a change in the representational format in the spatial domain. The results support Dehaene and Cohen's model and suggest that magnitude representations can be spatially based.

These results are in keeping with the distinction in Figure 15.2 between information representation and the ability to change the form of this representation. The results also suggest two potential spatial-based forms of MD, as they might affect magnitude representation. The first would, in theory, manifest as a nonlogarithmic form of spatial-based number representations. If children with MD show the normal—before schooling—logarithmic representations, then the second potential deficit would manifest as difficulties in changing the representational form to match the formal Arabic system. We are currently conducting pilot research to explore the likelihood of these two forms of spatial-based MD.

CONCLUSION

Over the past decade, a reasonable understanding of the number, counting, and arithmetical competencies and deficits of children with MD has emerged (Geary et al., 2000; Hanich et al., 2001; Ostad, 2000). Most of these children appear to have near-normal number-processing skills, at least for the processing of simple numbers (e.g., 3, 6), but their representational and processing skills for larger numbers (e.g., 345) remains largely unexplored, as does their ability to form spatial number lines. Whatever future studies might reveal in these areas, it is clear that children with MD have persistent deficits in some areas of arithmetic and counting knowledge. Many of these children have an immature understanding of certain counting principles. They often use problem-solving procedures in arithmetic that are more commonly used by younger, academically-normal children, and frequently commit procedural errors. For some of these children, procedural skills, at least as related to simple arithmetic, improve over the course of the elementary-school years and thus the early deficit may not be due to a permanent cognitive disability. At the same time, many children with MD also have difficulties retrieving basic arithmetic facts from long-term memory, a deficit that often does not improve for many of these children.

On the bases of the framework shown in Figure 15.2, these developmental delays and deficits can be understood as being related to a combination of disrupted functions of the central executive, including attentional control and poor inhibition of irrelevant associations, or difficulties with information representation and manipulation in the language system. In theory, MD can also result from compromised visuospatial systems, although these potential forms of MD are not well understood. Some insights have also been gained regarding the potential neural mechanisms contributing to these procedural and retrieval characteristics of children with MD (see Geary & Hoard, 2001), although definitive conclusions must await brain-imaging studies of these children.

Despite important advances during the past decade, much remains to be accomplished. In comparison to simple arithmetic, relatively little research has been conducted on ability of children with MD to solve more complex arithmetic problems (but see Russell & Ginsburg, 1984), and even less has been conducted in other mathematical domains. Even in the area of simple arithmetic, the cognitive and neural mechanisms that contribute to the problem-solving characteristics of children with MD are not fully understood. Other areas in need of attention include the development of diagnostic instruments for MD; cognitive and behavioral genetic research on the comorbidity of MD and other forms of LD and ADHD; and, of course, the development of remedial techniques. If progress over the past decade is any indication, then we should see significant advances in many of these areas in the years to come.

REFERENCES

Ashcraft, M. H. (1982). The development of mental arithmetic: A chronometric approach. *Developmental Review, 2,* 213–236.

Ashcraft, M. H., Yamashita, T. S., & Aram, D. M. (1992). Mathematics performance in left and right brain-lesioned children. *Brain and Cognition, 19,* 208–252.

Baddeley, A. D. (1986). *Working memory.* Oxford: Oxford University Press.

Badian, N. A. (1983). Dyscalculia and nonverbal disorders of learning. In H. R. Myklebust (Ed.), *Progress in learning disabilities* (Vol. 5, pp. 235–264). New York: Stratton.

Barrouillet, P., Fayol, M., & Lathulière, E. (1997). Selecting between competitors in multiplication tasks: An explanation of the errors produced by adolescents with learning disabilities. *International Journal of Behavioral Development, 21,* 253–275.

Briars, D., & Siegler, R. S. (1984). A featural analysis of preschoolers' counting knowledge. *Developmental Psychology, 20,* 607–618.

Bull, R., & Johnston, R. S. (1997). Children's arithmetical difficulties: Contributions from processing speed, item identification, and short-term memory. *Journal of Experimental Child Psychology, 65,* 1–24.

Butterworth, B. (1999). *The mathematical brain.* London: Macmillan.

Byrd-Craven, J., Hoard, M. K., & Geary, D. C. (2002). *Counting span, counting knowledge, and procedural competencies in children with mathematical disabilities.* Presented at the annual meeting of the Psychonomic Society, Kansas City, MO.

Carpenter, T. P., & Moser, J. M. (1984). The acquisition of addition and subtraction concepts in grades one through three. *Journal for Research in Mathematics Education, 15,* 179–202.

Campbell, J. I. D. (1995). Mechanisms of simple addition and multiplication: A modified network-interference theory and simulation. *Mathematical Cognition, 1,* 121–164.

Conway, A. R. A., & Engle, R. W. (1994). Working memory and retrieval: A resource-dependent inhibition model. *Journal of Experimental Psychology: General, 123,* 354–373.

Dehaene, S., & Cohen, L. (1991). Two mental calculation systems: A case study of severe acalculia with preserved approximation. *Neuropsychologia, 29,* 1045–1074.

Dehaene, S. (1992). Varieties of numerical abilities. *Cognition, 44,* 1–42.

Dehaene, S., & Cohen, L. (1997). Cerebral pathways for calculation: Double dissociation between rote verbal and quantitative knowledge of arithmetic. *Cortex, 33,* 219–250.

Dehaene, S., Spelke, E., Pinel, P., Stanescu, R., & Tsivkin, S. (1999). Sources of mathematical thinking: Behavioral and brain-imaging evidence. *Science, 284,* 970–974.

Delaney, P. F., Reder, L. M., Staszewski, J. J., & Ritter, F. E. (1998). The strategy-specific nature of improvement: The power law applies by strategy within task. *Psychological Science, 9,* 1–7.

Engle, R. W. (2002). Working memory capacity as executive attention. *Current Directions in Psychological Science, 11,* 19–23.

Engle, R. W., Conway, A. R. A., Tuholski, S. W., & Shisler, R. J. (1995). A resource account of inhibition. *Psychological Science, 6,* 122–125.

Fuchs, L. S., & Fuchs, D. (2002). Mathematical problem-solving profiles of students with mathematics disabilities with and without comorbid reading disabilities. *Journal of Learning Disabilities, 35,* 573–573.

Fuson, K. C. (1982). An analysis of the counting-on solution procedure in addition. In T. P. Carpenter, J. M. Moser, & T. A. Romberg (Eds.), *Addition and subtraction: A cognitive perspective* (pp. 67–81). Hillsdale, NJ: Erlbaum.

Fuson, K. C. (1988). *Children's counting and concepts of number.* New York: Springer-Verlag.

Fuson, K. C., & Kwon, Y. (1992a). Korean children's understanding of multidigit addition and subtraction. *Child Development, 63,* 491–506.

Gallistel, C. R., & Gelman, R. (1992). Preverbal and verbal counting and computation. *Cognition, 44,* 43–74.

Garnett, K., & Fleischner, J. E. (1983). Automatization and basic fact performance of normal and learning disabled children. *Learning Disabilities Quarterly, 6,* 223–230.

Geary, D. C. (1990). A componential analysis of an early learning deficit in mathematics. *Journal of Experimental Child Psychology, 49,* 363–383.

Geary, D. C. (1993). Mathematical disabilities: Cognitive, neuropsychological, and genetic components. *Psychological Bulletin, 114,* 345–362.

Geary, D. C. (1994). *Children's mathematical development: Research and practical applications.* Washington, DC: American Psychological Association.

Geary, D. C. (1995). Reflections of evolution and culture in children's cognition: Implications for mathematical development and instruction. *American Psychologist, 50,* 24–37.

Geary, D. C., & Brown, S. C. (1991). Cognitive addition: Strategy choice and speed-of-processing differences in gifted, normal, and mathematically disabled children. *Developmental Psychology, 27,* 398–406.

Geary, D. C., Brown, S. C., & Samaranayake, V. A. (1991). Cognitive addition: A short longitudinal study of strategy choice and speed of processing differences in normal and mathematically disabled children. *Developmental Psychology, 27,* 787–797.

Geary, D. C., Bow-Thomas, C. C., Fan, L., & Siegler, R. S. (1996). Development of arithmetical competencies in Chinese and American children: Influence of age, language, and schooling. *Child Development, 67,* 2022–2044.

Geary, D. C., Bow-Thomas, C. C., & Yao, Y. (1992). Counting knowledge and skill in cognitive addition: A comparison of normal and mathematically disabled children. *Journal of Experimental Child Psychology, 54,* 372–391.

Geary, D. C., Hamson, C. O., & Hoard, M. K. (2000). Numerical and arithmetical cognition: A longitudinal study of process and concept deficits in children with learning disability. *Journal of Experimental Child Psychology, 77,* 236–263.

Geary, D. C., & Hoard, M. K. (2001). Numerical and arithmetical deficits in learning disabled children:

Relation to dyscalculia and dyslexia. *Aphasiology, 15,* 635-647.

Geary, D. C., Hoard, M. K., Byrd-Craven, J., & DeSoto, M. C. (2004). Strategy choices in simple and complex addition: Contributions of working memory and counting knowledge for children with mathematical disability. *Journal of Experimental Child Psychology, 88,* 121-151.

Geary, D. C., Hoard, M. K., & Hamson, C. O. (1999). Numerical and arithmetical cognition: Pattern of functions and deficits in children at-risk for a mathematical disability. *Journal of Experimental Child Psychology, 74,* 213-239.

Geary, D. C., Liu, F., Chen, G.-P., Saults, S. J., & Hoard, M. K. (1999). Contributions of computational fluency to cross-national differences in arithmetical reasoning abilities. *Journal of Educational Psychology, 91,* 716-719.

Geary, D. C., Widaman, K. F., Little, T. D., & Cormier, P. (1987). Cognitive addition: Comparison of learning disabled and academically normal elementary school children. *Cognitive Development, 2,* 149-169.

Geary, D. C., & Widaman, K. F. (1992). Numerical cognition: On the convergence of componential and psychometric models. *Intelligence, 16,* 47-80.

Gelman, R., & Gallistel, C. R. (1978). *The child's understanding of number.* Cambridge, MA: Harvard University Press.

Gelman, R., & Meck, E. (1983). Preschooler's counting: Principles before skill. *Cognition, 13,* 343-359.

Gernsbacher, M. A. (1993). Less skilled readers have less efficient suppression mechanisms. *Psychological Science, 4,* 294-298.

Groen, G. J., & Parkman, J. M. (1972). A chronometric analysis of simple addition. *Psychological Review, 79,* 329-343.

Gross-Tsur, V., Manor, O., & Shalev, R. S. (1996). Developmental dyscalculia: Prevalence and demographic features. *Developmental Medicine and Child Neurology, 38,* 25-33.

Hanich, L. B., Jordan, N. C., Kaplan, D., & Dick, J. (2001). Performance across different areas of mathematical cognition in children with learning difficulties. *Journal of Educational Psychology, 93,* 615-626.

Hitch, G. J., & McAuley, E. (1991). Working memory in children with specific arithmetical learning difficulties. *British Journal of Psychology, 82,* 375-386.

Hoard, M. K., Geary, D. C., & Hamson, C. O. (1999). Numerical and arithmetical cognition: Performance of low- and average-IQ children. *Mathematical Cognition, 5,* 65-91.

Howell, R., Sidorenko, E., & Jurica, J. (1987). The effects of computer use on the acquisition of multiplication facts by a student with learning disabilities. *Journal of Learning Disabilities, 20,* 336-341.

Jordan, N. C., & Hanich, L. B. (2002). Mathematical thinking in second-grade children with different forms of LD. *Journal of Learning Disabilities, 33,* 567-578.

Jordan, N. C., Hanich, L. B., & Kaplan, D. (2003a). A longitudinal study of mathematical competencies in children with specific mathematics difficulties versus children with co-morbid mathematics and reading difficulties. *Child Development, 74,* 834-850.

Jordan, N. C., Hanich, L. B., & Kaplan, D. (2003b). Arithmetic fact mastery in young children: A longitudinal investigation. *Journal of Experimental Child Psychology, 85,* 103-119.

Jordan, N. C., Levine, S. C., & Huttenlocher, J. (1995). Calculation abilities in young children with different patterns of cognitive functioning. *Journal of Learning Disabilities, 28,* 53-64.

Jordan, N. C., & Montani, T. O. (1997). Cognitive arithmetic and problem solving: A comparison of children with specific and general mathematics difficulties. *Journal of Learning Disabilities, 30,* 624-634.

Koontz, K. L., & Berch, D. B. (1996). Identifying simple numerical stimuli: Processing inefficiencies exhibited by arithmetic learning disabled children. *Mathematical Cognition, 2,* 1-23.

Kosc, L. (1974). Developmental dyscalculia. *Journal of Learning Disabilities, 7,* 164-177.

Lemaire, P., & Siegler, R. S. (1995). Four aspects of strategic change: Contributions to children's learning of multiplication. *Journal of Experimental Psychology: General, 124,* 83-97.

Light, J. G., & Defries, J. L. (1995). Comorbidity of reading and mathematics disabilities: Genetic and environmental etiologies. *Journal of Learning Disabilities, 28,* 96-106.

Ohlsson, S., & Rees, E. (1991). The function of conceptual understanding in the learning of arithmetic procedures. *Cognition and Instruction, 8,* 103-179.

Ostad, S. A. (1997). Developmental differences in addition strategies: A comparison of mathematically disabled and mathematically normal children. *British Journal of Educational Psychology, 67,* 345-357.

Ostad, S. A. (1998a). Developmental differences in solving simple arithmetic word problems and simple number-fact problems: A comparison of mathematically normal and mathematically disabled children. *Mathematical Cognition, 4,* 1-19.

Ostad, S. A. (1998b). Comorbidity between mathematics and spelling difficulties. *Log Phon Vovol, 23,* 145-154.

Ostad, S. A. (2000). Cognitive subtraction in a developmental perspective: Accuracy, speed-of-processing and strategy-use differences in normal and mathematically disabled children. *Focus on Learning Problems in Mathematics, 22,* 18-31.

Rasanen, P., & Ahonen, T. (1995). Arithmetic disabilities with and without reading difficulties: A comparison of arithmetic errors. *Developmental Neuropsychology, 11,* 275-295.

Russell, R. L., & Ginsburg, H. P. (1984). Cognitive analysis of children's mathematical difficulties. *Cognition and Instruction, 1,* 217-244.

Seron, X., & Fayol, M. (1994). Number transcoding in children: A functional analysis. *British Journal of Developmental Psychology, 12,* 281-300.

Shalev, R. S., Manor, O., & Gross-Tsur, V. (1993). The acquisition of arithmetic in normal children: Assessment by a cognitive model of dyscalculia. *Developmental Medicine and Child Neurology, 35,* 593-601.

Shalev, R. S., Manor, O., Kerem, B., Ayali, M., Badichi, N., Friedlander, Y., & Gross-Tsur, V. (2001). Developmental dyscalculia is a familial learning disability. *Journal of Learning Disabilities, 34,* 59-65.

Siegler, R. S. (1987). The perils of averaging data over strategies: An example from children's addition. *Journal of Experimental Psychology: General, 116,* 250-264.

Siegler, R. S. (1988). Individual differences in strategy choices: Good students, not-so-good students, and perfectionists. *Child Development, 59,* 833-851.

Siegler, R. S. (1996). *Emerging minds: The process of change in children's thinking.* New York: Oxford University Press.

Siegler, R. S., & Opfer, J. (2003). The development of numerical estimation: Evidence for multiple representations of numerical quantity. *Psychological Science, 14,* 237–243.

Siegler, R. S., & Shrager, J. (1984). Strategy choice in addition and subtraction: How do children know what to do? In C. Sophian (Ed.), *Origins of cognitive skills* (pp. 229–293). Hillsdale, NJ: Erlbaum.

Stadler, M. A., Geary, D. C., & Hogan, M. E. (2001). Negative priming from activation of counting and addition knowledge. *Psychological Research, 65,* 24–27.

Svenson, O., & Broquist, S. (1975). Strategies for solving simple addition problems: A comparison of normal and subnormal children. *Scandinavian Journal of Psychology, 16,* 143–151.

Temple, C. M. (1991). Procedural dyscalculia and number fact dyscalculia: Double dissociation in developmental dyscalculia. *Cognitive Neuropsychology, 8,* 155–176.

Temple, C. M., & Sherwood, S. (2002). Representation and retrieval of arithmetical facts: Developmental difficulties. *Quarterly Review of Experimental Psychology, 55A,* 733–752.

Zorzi, M., Priftis, K., & Umiltá, C. (2002). Neglect disrupts the mental number line. *Nature, 417,* 138.

16

Math Performance in Girls with Turner or Fragile X Syndrome

Michèle M. M. Mazzocco
Michael McCloskey

Knowledge of mathematical cognition may be enhanced not only by studies of mathematical *ability* in normal individuals, but also by research on math *disabilities* (MD). In this chapter we review research on MD in two genetic disorders that have cognitive phenotypes associated with poor math achievement: Turner syndrome and fragile X syndrome. We begin with a brief overview of Turner and fragile X syndromes, and then turn to research on math abilities and disabilities in persons with these syndromes. The research is in early stages, but holds promise for shedding light on the cognitive dysfunctions that may give rise to math disabilities, and on the biological basis of mathematical ability.

TURNER AND FRAGILE X SYNDROMES

Turner Syndrome

Turner syndrome is a sporadic chromosome abnormality that occurs in approximately 1:2000 to 1:5000 live female births (Rieser & Underwood, 1989). It results from complete or partial absence of one of two X chromosomes normally present in a female. A typical human karyotype consists of 46 chromosomes; in females, both sex chromosomes are X chromosomes, so a typical female has a 46XX karyotype. Approximately 60% of Turner syndrome cases result from total loss of an X chromosome, leaving 45 intact chromosomes, or 45X (Lippe, 1991). As a group, girls who have a 45X/46XX mosaic karyotype (some cells with 45X, others with the typical female 46XX composition) exhibit a less severe phenotype than girls with classic 45X (Temple & Carney, 1993). Alternative karyotypes include partial versus total X chromosome deletion, wherein impairment severity appears influenced by the region deleted (Ross, Roeltgen, Kushner, Wei, & Zinn, 2000). Physical characteristics of Turner syndrome include webbing of the neck (see Figure 16. 1), lack of pubertal maturation, and short stature (Palmer & Reichmann, 1976; Park, Bailey, & Cowell, 1983). However, many girls with Turner syndrome lack observable physical features (Figure 16.2).

Figure 16.1. Child with observable features of Turner syndrome.

Figure 16.2. Child without observable features of Turner syndrome (aside from short stature).

In addition to different karyotypes, random X–inactivation may influence phenotypic variation in Turner syndrome. Because of random X–inactivation—a process that occurs in typically developing females—one of the two X chromosomes present in females is inactivated (Lyon, 1991). Thus, females typically have two populations of cells, one in which the paternal X chromosome is active while the maternal X chromosome is inactive, and one with the reverse pattern. Some genes on the "inactivated" X chromosome escape inactivation and are expressed (Goodfellow, Pym, Mohandas, & Shapiro, 1984; Schneider-Gadicke, Beer-Romero, Brown, Nussbaum, & Page, 1989); these genes may be expressed among girls with partial deletion karyotypes. If only one X chromosome is present in a cell, the process of X inactivation is not initiated; thus in the case of classic 45X, no X inactivation occurs. Another proposed influence on the Turner syndrome phenotype is whether the single or intact X chromosome is of paternal or maternal origin. Skuse and colleagues (Skuse, James, Bishop, et al., 1997) suggest such an effect, although others have not found evidence to support these claims (Mathur et al., 1991; Ross, Roeltgen, Kushner, et al., 2000).

Fragile X Syndrome

In 1943, Martin and Bell (Martin & Bell, 1943) described a pedigree depicting familial mental retardation syndrome. The disorder was known as *Martin-Bell Syndrome* until 1969, when Lubs (1969) reported a characteristic fragile site on the X chromosome of affected family members. By the time it was labeled *fragile X syndrome*, this disorder was recognized as the leading known familial cause of mental retardation.

Fragile X syndrome occurs in approximately 1:1000 to 1:6000 births (Crawford et al., 1999; Sherman, 1991; Turner, Webb, Wake, & Robinson, 1996). The syndrome has a variable physical phenotype, discussed elsewhere in more detail (Hagerman, 2002). Facial features such as a long face and protruding ears are among the hallmark features of the physical phenotype (see Figure 16.3) but are absent in many children with fragile X (see Figure 16.4).

In the vast majority of cases, fragile X syndrome is caused by a mutation of a single gene on the X chromosome; this gene—referred to as the fragile X mental retardation (fmr1) gene—was identified in 1991 (Verkerk et al., 1991). The fmr1 gene is a triplet repeat gene (Oostra & Halley, 1995; Verkerk et al., 1991); in its mutation state, the gene is unstable, replicates, and

Figure 16.3. Child with observable facial features of fragile X syndrome.

Figure 16.4. Child without observable facial features of fragile X syndrome.

thus expands through subsequent generations. Both normal and mutated states of the fmr1 gene contain up to 54 repeated sequences of three DNA base pairs (i.e., trinucleotide repeats), specifically cytosine-guanine-guanine (CGG repeats; Fu et al., 1991). When an expansion exceeds ~200 repeats, it is a *full mutation*. Hypermethylation and transcriptional silencing effectively shut down the gene, ultimately leading to reduction in fragile X mental retardation protein (fmrp) and to clinical manifestations of the syndrome (Hansen, Gartler, Scott, Chen, & Laird, 1992; Pai et al., 1994; Pieretti et al., 1991).

In addition to the normal and full mutation states of the fmr1 gene, intermediate CGG repeat expansions (i.e., ~55 to 200 repeats) are categorized as *premutations*. There is much controversy regarding whether the premutation is associated with a cognitive phenotype, because study findings are inconsistent (e.g., Franke et al., 1999; Mazzocco & Holden, 1996; Mazzocco, Pennington, & Hagerman, 1993; Myers, Mazzocco, Maddalena, & Reiss, 2001), and data in support of premutation effects suggest a phenotype that differs from the full mutation phenotype (e.g., Hagerman et al., 2001; Tassone et al., 2000). Therefore, work on the premutation is not reviewed in this chapter.

As is typical with X-linked disorders, fragile X syndrome affects males more severely than females; approximately 50% of females with fragile X have mental retardation (Rousseau et al., 1994) versus nearly 100% of males (Bailey, Hatton, & Skinner, 1998). Females without mental retardation may have borderline to average levels of intellectual ability. The cognitive phenotypic variation seen in females is due at least in part to random X inactivation: the percentage of *active* chromosomes that have the mutation can vary, so "activation ratio" (AR) values range from nearly 0 (all active chromosomes have the mutation) to 1 (all active chromosomes are normal). Activation ratio (Abrams et al., 1994; Reiss, Freund, Baumgardner, Abrams, & Denckla, 1995) and fmrp levels (Bailey, Hatton, Tassone, Skinner, & Taylor, 2001; Loesch et al., 2002) correlate with severity of syndrome manifestation.

In our studies of math cognition, we are interested in the primary, biological correlates of math performance versus deficits secondary to mental retardation. To decrease the likelihood of identifying secondary effects, we include only females without mental retardation as participants in our studies. Most of the research reviewed in this chapter also primarily concerns females with fragile X without mental retardation.

MATH DISABILITY IN TURNER AND FRAGILE X SYNDROMES

Turner and fragile X syndromes lead to substantially different cognitive phenotypes. A primary difference is in overall intellectual development. Females with Turner syndrome have minimal reduction in full-scale IQ scores (FSIQ), with mean scores typically in the average range (Elliott, Watkins, Messa, Lippe, & Chugani, 1996; Mazzocco, 1998; Rovet, 1993; Temple & Carney, 1993). Despite this minimal effect on FSIQ, the discrepancy between verbal and performance IQ scores is remarkable and consistent. On average, the verbal score is 8 to 24 points higher than the performance score (Balottin et al., 1998; LaHood & Bacon, 1985; Pennington et al., 1985; Rovet, & Ireland, 1994; Skuse et al., 1997; Tamm, Menon, & Reiss, 2003), as observed among girls with either 45X or mosaic karyotypes (Ross & Zinn, 1999). In contrast, females with fragile X typically do not show significant verbal/performance IQ discrepancies (Bennetto, Taylor, Pennington, Porter, & Hagerman, 2001; Brainard, Schreiner, & Hagerman, 1991) but have below-average FSIQ scores. Even when samples are limited to participants whose FSIQ scores are above the mental retardation range (e.g., FSIQ > 69), the mean FSIQ score for groups of females with fragile X syndrome is typically close to 85 (Abrams et al., 1994; Bennetto et al., 2001; Kwon et al., 2001; Loesch et al., 2002; Mazzocco, Hagerman, Cronister, & Pennington, 1992).

Despite these differences, general descriptions of the Turner and fragile X cognitive phenotypes are similar. For both groups, descriptions often include reference to poor math achievement. Our work suggests that poor math achievement is evident in both syndromes as early as age 5 years (Mazzocco, 2001). However, it is unclear what aspects of math, or of cognitive performance more broadly defined, underlie these apparent math deficiencies, because most studies have been based on standardized achievement tests and the arithmetic subtest of Wechsler IQ tests.

Questions

In exploring math deficits in girls with Turner or fragile X syndrome, we consider several questions in the context of each syndrome:

Do girls with the syndrome show higher-than-normal rates of MD?
What specific components of mathematical ability are affected?
Are the observed math disabilities transient, or do they persist across development?
Does the syndrome affect general cognitive functions implicated in math performance (e.g., working memory), and, if so, what are the consequences for understanding the math disabilities?

Incidence and Persistence of Math Disability

To determine whether Turner or fragile X syndrome is associated with higher-than-normal rates of MD, it is necessary to establish a priori criteria for MD and prevalence figures in the general population. There is no consensus definition in the field, but researchers often define MD on the basis of standard score criteria (e.g., a standard score < 90 on a math achievement test; see Geary & Hoard, this volume). Despite a lack of consensus in how we define MD, most researchers report a prevalence of 5 to 8% in school-age children (Badian, 1983; Shalev, Auerbach, Manor, & Gross-Tsur, 2000).

Poor math achievement in a single school year may result from factors other than a biologically based MD, such as poor instruction, interruption in instruction during absences or illness, or changes in curriculum that occur when moving to a new school. Therefore, poor math achievement over 2 or more school years is a stronger indicator of MD.

Math-Specific and General Cognitive Functions Affected

If (as we will argue) girls with Turner or fragile X syndrome show higher-than-normal rates of MD, it is important to ask what underlying cognitive deficits are responsible for the disabilities. Impaired math performance may result from disruption to any one or more of a wide range of math-specific or more general cognitive skills. Examples of math-specific skills are counting, cardinality, arithmetic fact retrieval, and calculation procedure skills; these may be differentially spared or deficient in persons with different MD subtypes.

Deficits affecting math-specific skills may be limited to these skills or may reflect more general cognitive dysfunctions. For example, deficient arithmetic fact retrieval may stem from an impairment limited to the domain of arithmetic facts or may reflect a broader cognitive deficit. Thus, researchers have hypothesized that general long-term memory deficits may lead to co-occurring math and reading disabilities by affecting learning and retrieval of arithmetic facts, words, and letter-phoneme associations (Geary, Hamson, & Hoard, 2000). Deficient phonological processing has also been suggested as an underlying cause of co-occurring reading and math disability (Geary, Hamson, & Hoard, 2000; Hanich, Jordan, Kaplan, & Dick, 2001; Russell & Ginsburg, 1984). Similarly, working memory deficits could affect math performance in a variety of ways, and executive function deficits might lead to impairments in executing math procedures, by interfering with planning, attention, or inhibitory functions (see chapter 15).

In some cases, MD appears related to weak visuo-spatial cognition. Visuo-spatial difficulties may interfere with the ability to understand or work with basic spatial properties such as length and width, more complex spatial concepts such as *isosceles triangle*, and the spatially based concept of place value. Spatial deficits may also impair arithmetic performance, for example, by causing difficulty in maintaining the appropriate alignment of digits in carrying out multidigit calculations.

Given these considerations, it is obviously important to consider not only math performance but also more general cognitive functions when probing the underlying causes of math disabilities.

MATH PERFORMANCE IN GIRLS WITH TURNER SYNDROME

Incidence and Nature of Math Disabilities in Turner Syndrome

Appendix 16.A lists the available studies concerning math difficulties in girls with Turner syndrome. The first major study to specifically address math was reported by Rovet (1993). In her comparison of girls with or without Turner syndrome, group differences on the Wide Range Achievement Test (WRAT) were evident on both reading and arithmetic subtests. Reading scores differed to a lesser extent; the group of girls with Turner syndrome had average reading scores versus high-average to above-average scores for the comparison group. Differences were more apparent for the arithmetic subtest, in which girls with Turner syndrome had a mean percentile score of 23.8 versus 45.7 for the comparison group. Girls with Turner syndrome scored more poorly than the comparison group on all subtests of the KeyMath portion, although statistically significant differences emerged on only five of the nine subtests, including conceptual (numeration subtest, numerical reasoning, geometry) and computational (addition, subtraction) subtests.

Using WRAT scores in the bottom 25th percentile as criteria for learning disability (LD), 55% of girls with Turner syndrome and 7% of the control group met LD criteria. None of the girls with Turner syndrome met criteria for reading disability alone; 35% had both reading and math disability, and 20% had only MD. These results clearly implicate Turner syndrome as a risk factor for MD, although math deficiencies were not limited to any specific aspect(s) of math cognition.

In a follow-up study, Rovet, Szekely, and Hockenberry (1994) examined performance on individual items from the WRAT Arithmetic subtest, which is a timed test. Some items primarily require arithmetic fact retrieval, whereas others involve procedural knowledge. Girls with Turner syndrome attempted fewer problems than girls in the comparison group for both types of items (fact retrieval, procedural knowledge) and for all four arithmetic operations (addition, subtraction, multiplication, division). The percentage of attempted items solved correctly was lower for girls with Turner syndrome, among both fact retrieval and procedural knowledge-based items. No significant group difference was observed in the relative frequency of specific error types.

Rovet and colleagues (1994) carried out a more in-depth analysis with a subset of participants who received the KeyMath. Girls with Turner syndrome performed significantly more poorly on conceptual tasks (numeration, fractions), operations (addition, subtraction, multiplication, and division), and applications (mental computations, numerical reasoning). However, only on the Geometry subtest the group with Turner syndrome did *not* show significant impairment. (This finding is opposite that which we later found among kindergartners with Turner syndrome, who scored more poorly than controls on the Geometry subtest of the KeyMath–Revised but not on the remaining subtests administered; Mazzocco, 2001). Rovet et al. further reported that girls in the Turner and comparison groups attempted comparable percentages of fact retrieval problems, with comparable accuracy for all operations except division. Girls with Turner syndrome were less accurate on division but correctly solved 92% of the items they attempted (vs. 100% for girls in the comparison group). Procedural knowledge was less accurate among girls with Turner syndrome than for girls in the comparison group (~55% vs. 75%, respectively). Girls with Turner syndrome made more errors completing or correctly carrying out component steps during calculations. These findings are partially consistent with later findings implicating multiple sources of calculation errors and slowed math fact retrieval, despite intact number-processing skills, in girls with Turner syndrome (Temple & Marriott, 1998).

Rovet and colleagues conclude that the Turner syndrome phenotype is broad rather than specific and that arithmetic deficits in girls with Turner syndrome result from more than an underlying spatial deficit, because of the lack of deficits noted on the KeyMath Geometry subtest. However, the girls with Turner syndrome were below grade level on this subtest. Moreover, the Geometry test is not necessarily the most spatially relevant. For example, the Measurement subtest involves ranking items along various dimensions and estimating the number of units covered by an obstacle. Despite a lack of consistent evidence for the source of their difficulty in math, this study further supports the notion that girls with Turner syndrome are at risk for MD.

In a later study, we carried out a post hoc error analysis of items from the Woodcock Johnson–Revised Math Calculations subtest (Mazzocco, 1998). Girls with Turner syndrome were compared to a normal peer group and to a sibling comparison group. Math scores were significantly lower than reading scores for the girls with Turner syndrome, even among girls under 10 years of age. Reading–math differences were minimal for the two comparison groups. We examined the number of girls per group who made the following types of errors: operation errors (e.g., adding instead of subtracting), table errors (associated but incorrect responses, such as $5 \times 5 = 20$), other fact errors (such as being off by "one"), procedural errors, and alignment errors. Consistent with error analyses conducted by Rovet, there were no significant differences in the distribution of errors across types between girls with versus without Turner syndrome.

Most recently, we reported that poor math achievement is apparent in Turner syndrome as early as kindergarten. Using a conservative criterion for MD—scoring below 86 on the Test of Early Math Ability–Second Edition (TEMA-2)—we reported a four-fold increase in the prevalence of MD in kindergartners with Turner syndrome (43%) versus age- and FSIQ-matched kindergartner girls without Turner syndrome (10%). Item analyses failed to reveal any specific items or types of items more likely to be missed specifically by girls with Turner syndrome (Mazzocco, 2001).

Taken together, these studies demonstrate a higher-than-normal incidence of MD in Turner syndrome. The studies do not, however, provide evidence that any specific aspect(s) of math ability are selectively affected. One possibility is that the effects of the syndrome on math skills are nonspecific, or variable across individuals; an alternative possibility is that the studies conducted to date have not succeeded in pinpointing the specific processes that are affected. The use of standardized tests in the aforementioned studies may be insufficient for identifying distinct cognitive and mathematical processes.

Persistence of Math Disabilities in Turner Syndrome

The available evidence suggests that math deficiencies are seen in girls with Turner syndrome from kindergarten through high school. Rovet reported cross-sectional evidence for an increase in MD prevalence with age. In our longitudinal studies, we have thus far seen 23 girls with Turner syndrome for two or more assessments between kindergarten and fourth grade. During each visit, we administer the TEMA-2 (Ginsburg & Baroody, 1990). Of these 23 girls, 20 received a TEMA-2 score < 90 during at least one visit, and 17 of the 20 scored < 90 on all subsequent visits. This is a significantly higher frequency of MD (17/23, or 74%) than the frequency of "persistent MD" reported for a normative sample in a prospective study, which was 10.5% (Mazzocco & Myers, 2003). However, the percentage of children who continue to have MD, if they ever meet MD criteria in primary school, is comparable across girls with Turner syndrome (17/20, or 85%) and children in a normative sample (63%). Thus, the risk for MD in Turner syndrome appears to be a risk for persistent math LD. Our ongoing studies will help determine whether girls with Turner syndrome are more likely to manifest a later-emerging MD (after grade 4) than their peers.

Math-Related Cognitive Functions in Turner Syndrome

Reading

Although many children with MD also have reading disability (RD; for a review, see chapter 15, this volume), RD occurs in girls with Turner syndrome at a rate comparable to that in the general population. In fact, reading skills are typically at least intact, if not above average, in girls with Turner syndrome (Elliott et al., 1996; Mazzocco, 2001; Rovet, 1993; Temple, Carney, & Mullarkey, 1996). Vocabulary skills and verbal reasoning are generally well above average (Bender, Linden, & Robinson, 1993; LaHood & Bacon, 1985; Temple & Carney, 1995; Temple, 2002), as are decoding skills measured by nonword reading (Elliott et al., 1996; Mazzocco, 2001) and perception of speech sounds (Pennington et al., 1985). Spelling achievement is also grade appropriate (Rovet, 1993). In the few cases in which language difficulties are reported in girls with Turner syndrome, the difficulties appear secondary to hearing loss resulting from the physical phenotype.

The exceptions to this generalization are rapid automatized naming (RAN) and oral fluency performance (Temple, 2002). RAN performance is predictive of reading achievement in the general population, as is phonological decoding skill (Davis et al., 2001; Vellutino, Scanlon, & Spearing, 1995). On RAN subtests, girls with Turner syndrome are slower than age- and grade-level-matched controls (Mazzocco, 2001) but have intact decoding skills. Thus, slower RAN is the only reading-related task with significant effects, but in light of overall reading achievement levels, it does not appear to suggest reading deficiency in this population. Temple proposes that reduced oral fluency stems from impairment in executive functions (2002).

Short-Term Memory

Reports of short-term memory difficulties in Turner syndrome are mixed. Digit span scores are lower than other verbal IQ subtest scores (e.g., McCauley et al., 1987; Rovet, 1993) and comparable to those of children with nonverbal learning disabilities (Williams, Richman, & Yarbrough, 1991). However, sentence memory performance is intact (Williams et al., 1991; Mazzocco, 2001). Both verbal and visual short-term memory tasks appear difficult for girls with Turner syndrome, and both difficulties appear to be mitigated by estrogen treatment (Ross, Roeltgen, Feuillan, Kushner, & Cutler, 1998, 2000).

Executive Function

Temple et al. (1996) administered a variety of executive function tasks to girls with or without Turner syndrome. The tasks included word fluency tests with phonological constraints (e.g., name as many words as possible that begin with s, within a time limit) or semantic constraints (e.g., name as many animals as possible); the Wisconsin Card Sorting Task (WCST; Heaton, 1981); the Tower of London task (Shallice, 1982); the Stroop test (Stroop, 1935); and an adaptation of the self-ordered pointing task with either abstract or concrete drawings. (This last task involved pointing to each of six items, one per page; all items appear on each page, yet their spatial locations differ on each page.) No group differences were noted on the WCST, a test traditionally used to measure perseverative response patterns and the inability to shift response sets; this result is consistent with earlier reports (Pennington et al., 1985). There were also no differences on the Tower of London, a task requiring planning for efficient sequential responses toward a goal state. However, girls with Turner syndrome performed more poorly than girls in the comparison group on the word fluency tests, which require an organized search of the lexicon and monitoring of words already named. Also, girls with Turner syndrome were slower during the nonexecutive naming trials of the Stroop (i.e., naming the color of Xs and reading aloud color words printed in black) and showed a significantly stronger Stroop effect on the executive function trial (i.e., naming the ink color of color words printed in colors inconsistent with their meaning, such as the word *red* printed in green ink). The latter result reflects difficulty *inhibiting* a prepotent response set. (This finding may appear to contradict the absence of impairment on the WCST, but Stroop interference is probably more difficult to inhibit than the response set established in the WCST.) On the self-ordered pointing task, girls with Turner syndrome performed as well as the comparison group on the concrete-pictures subtest but were significantly more impaired on the abstract-pictures subtest. Considered together, these findings are consistent with earlier studies of selective executive dysfunction in girls with Turner syndrome and suggest difficulty inhibiting strongly prepotent responses and a lack of organization in rapid retrieval of information but intact skills in planning ahead to execute a strategy and intact ability to shift response set.

These findings parallel our recent study of working memory, using the Contingency Naming Test (CNT; Anderson, Anderson, Northam, & Taylor, 2000; Taylor, Albo, Phebus, Sachs, & Bierl, 1987). Our study included 8- and 9-year-old girls with Turner syndrome (n = 20) and girls in an age- and FSIQ-matched comparison group (n = 90). The CNT requires naming stimuli that vary in shape and color. Each stimulus includes a circle, square, or triangle that contains a smaller shape. Each outer shape is one of three colors. Naming of colors only, or outer shapes only, is all that is required during the two warm-up trials. During the two experimental test trials, participants name each stimulus on the basis of a one- or two-attribute contingency rule. The one-attribute rule requires naming the color if the inner and outer shapes match and naming the shape if the inner and outer shapes do *not* match. The two-attribute contingency builds upon the latter rule by adding that, if a backward arrow appears over a stimulus, the rule is to be reversed (i.e., name the color instead of the shape if the inner and outer shapes do *not* match, and name the shape instead of the color if the inner and outer shapes *do* match). Dependent measures include the number of practice trials needed to master a rule, response time to name all stimuli on the test trials, and the number of self-corrections or errors made during the test trial. In our study, girls with Turner syndrome were significantly slower than their peers when simply naming colors or shapes during timed warm-up test trials (60 versus 51 seconds, respectively; Kirk, Kover, & Mazzocco, 2004; Kirk, Mazzocco, & Kover, submitted). They did not take significantly longer to complete the two contingency trials. Whereas slowing down from the warm-up to the experimental trials helped the comparison group participants perform accurately, the girls with Turner syndrome made significantly more errors than their peers on the two-attribute contingency rule (mean = 14.8 vs. 4.9), despite taking as much time as their peers to complete the task and despite needing more practice trials to master the rule (3.5 vs. 2.1 trials). These findings point to an inefficiency with online processing, or working memory, demands. However, the difficulty cannot be attributed only to poor inhibitory skills, because there were no group differences in the number of self-corrections made.

Functional neuroimaging results also implicate weak executive function skills in girls with Turner syndrome. Tamm, Menon, & Reiss (2003) administered a computerized "Go/NoGo" task to girls with or without Turner syndrome. The task required attention to letters and response inhibition when an X appeared. Girls with Turner syndrome performed as well as girls in the comparison group, perhaps because of the relatively limited demands of the task. Whereas both groups of girls showed the expected activation in frontal regions, girls with Turner syndrome showed more bilateral activation than controls, specifically in the dorsal and superior frontal regions. These results implicate executive function difficulties in Turner syndrome. Similar conclusions were drawn by Molko and colleagues (Molko, Cachia, Rivière, Mangin, Bruandet, Le Bihan, Cohen, & Dehaene, 2003). These authors found evidence of abnormal parietal activation in girls with Turner syndrome during calculation tasks that were also relatively more difficult for children in a control group (e.g., tasks with large numbers). No group differences emerged on other quantitative tasks; for these tasks there were no differences in activation during number versus letter tasks. Thus, the authors emphasized how abnormalities in parietal functioning may be related to attention or working memory demands rather than to arithmetic skills per se.

Visuospatial Skills

A limited but growing literature on spatial deficits in Turner syndrome suggests difficulties in visual perception (Alexander, Ehrhardt, & Money, 1966; Temple & Carney, 1995) and visual construction tasks (Alexander et al., 1966; Temple & Carney, 1995; Waber, 1979). However, efforts to establish the specific nature of the deficits have thus far been inconclusive (e.g., Buchanan, Pavlovic, & Rovet, 1998).

In our ongoing longitudinal study, we sought to examine visual and spatial skills further and their association with math performance (Lesniak-Karpiak & Mazzocco, 2004). First, we administered the Developmental Test of Visual Perception–Second Edition (DTVP-2; Hammill, Pearson, & Voress, 1993) motor-reduced subtests. These subtests assess several aspects of visuo-spatial cognition, including judgment of spatial orientation (Position in Space), figure/ground distinctions and shape recognition in embedded designs (Figure/Ground), form detection from degraded designs (Visual Closure), and shape constancy across figures of different sizes and orientations (Form Constancy). The participants in this study include third graders with Turner syndrome. From a related ongoing longitudinal study (Mazzocco & Myers, 2002, 2003), we have normative data from more than 100 girls with no known disorder. As seen in Table 16.1, girls with Turner syndrome performed more poorly than the comparison group on

Table 16.1

Performance on the DTVP-2 Standard and Memory Subtests

Variable	Turner	Group Fragile X	Comparison
Number of Participants	19	9	107
Mean age (SD) in years	9.08 (.89)ₐ	9.26 (1.39)	8.60 (.31)
Age range in years	7.55–11.04	7.30–12.08	7.9–9.19
DTVP-2 Mean (SD) scaled scores			
Position in Space	7.90 (3.09) [a]	6.25 (3.77) [a]	10.62 (2.52)
Figure Ground	9.90 (2.87)	10.11 (2.64)	10.81 (2.52)
Visual Closure	7.84 (4.09) [a]	6.38 (5.40) [a]	11.33 (3.95)
Form Constancy	10.63 (2.14)	9.63 (3.42) [a]	11.91 (3.01)
FG-Memory % (#) passed (Grid-like)	94.7 (18)	44.4 (4) [ab]	97.3 (101)
FG-memory locations recalled/10	3.16 (1.68) [a]	3.88 (3.23)	5.94 (2.70)
FG-memory locations recalled–range	0 to 6	0 to 9	0–9

Note. [a]Performance level is significantly different from comparison group. [b]Performance levels are significantly different between Turner and fragile X groups.

the Position in Space and Visual Closure subtests but not on the Figure/Ground or Form Constancy subtests. Thus at least basic form perception skills are intact, in view of age-appropriate performance on the latter pair of subtests.

In addition to the four DTVP-2 subtests, we administered an experimental measure of incidental visual short-term memory. The Figure/Ground subtest involves selecting, from a fixed array of 10 shapes, two to five shapes embedded in a target illustration. For each trial, the same array of 10 shapes is presented in identical fashion, in 2 horizontal rows of 5 shapes each, in a rectangular box. Following administration of this subtest, we presented each girl with an empty rectangle box identical to that used in the subtest and with the 10 individually cut-out shapes. The girls were instructed to place each shape in the box, in the exact location in which it had appeared during the subtest.

Two measures were obtained from this task. First, the child received a pass-fail score for creating a "grid-like" array of shapes placed in two rows within the rectangle. Any violation of this 'two-row' response was coded as a failure (see Figure 16.5). This measure assessed the child's appreciation of the global pattern of the shape array. The second measure was the number of shapes placed in the correct grid location, with a possible score of 0 to 10. For children who produced non-gridlike arrays, shapes were assigned to the closest grid location, provided that at least half of the shape fell within that location.

Our results indicate important group differences on this supplemental task, despite the fact that both groups of girls performed well within the average range on the standardized Figure/Ground subtest itself. Most girls in both groups created a gridlike array when responding, Yet, girls with Turner syndrome placed significantly fewer shapes in the correct locations relative to the comparison group. Since the Figure/Ground standardized subtest scores were age appropriate for both groups, poor visual discrimination skills are unlikely to underlie this finding. The fewer "locations recalled" by girls with Turner syndrome may reflect poor visual memory versus poor visual perception. This is consistent with findings from Buchanan's study (1998), wherein location and shape identification tasks failed to show a dissociation in skills among girls with Turner syndrome. When separate visual-interference and verbal-interference tasks were introduced to impose a response time delay on their task, Buchanan demonstrated impaired performance among girls with Turner syndrome, but only when the delay resulted from a visual-memory interference task. The authors concluded that visual working memory—versus visual, spatial, or memory skills per se—may be a hallmark deficit in girls with Turner syndrome. Their conclusion is consistent with earlier results (e.g., LaHood & Bacon, 1985), and our findings provide additional support for this contention.

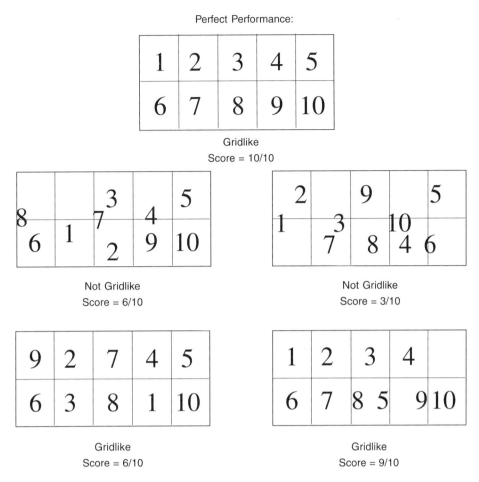

Figure 16.5. Examples of performance on the DTVP-2 incidental memory task. Examples of non-gridlike arrays are from girls with fragile X syndrome. Examples of gridlike arrays with location errors are from girls with Turner syndrome.

Processing Speed

Several findings pointing to cognitive deficiencies in girls with Turner syndrome take the form of slowed performance. For example, girls with Turner syndrome completed fewer problems than controls on timed math tasks (Rovet & Ireland, 1994), produced fewer words on timed word fluency tests (Temple et al., 1996), and were slower than controls on rapid automatized naming tests (Mazzocco, 2001). These findings raise the possibility that girls with Turner syndrome suffer from a general slowing of cognitive processing and that this slowing underlies some of the observed deficits on cognitive tasks, including math tasks.

Correlations between Math Performance and Math-Related Cognitive Function Measures

In one of our studies (Mazzocco, 1998), we examined whether math achievement scores were correlated with performance on a Go/NoGo continuous performance task (the Test of Variables of Attention, or TOVA; Greenberg, 1990) a task of two-dimensional spatial orientation (the Judgment of Line Orientation, or JLO; Benton, Hamsher, Varney, & Spreen, 1983), and the three factor scores of the Wechsler intelligence scales. These factors include Verbal Comprehension, Perceptual/Organizational Reasoning, and the "Third Factor" which assesses speeded accuracy aspects of attention and short-term memory. Only the JLO and Wechsler Third factor scores were correlated with math performance in girls with Turner syndrome (.57 and .56, respectively). In a separate study of kindergartners with Turner syndrome, visual spatial scores and reading scores *not* correlated with math scores (Mazzocco, 2001), despite consistent correlations between these scores and math achievement in a normative comparison sample from kindergarten to third grade (Mazzocco & Myers, 2003). Thus, it remains very much an open question how and to what extent the deficits in "math-related" cognitive functions seen in girls with Turner syndrome are related to their math disabilities.

MATH PERFORMANCE IN GIRLS WITH FRAGILE X SYNDROME

Incidence and Nature of Math Disabilities in Fragile X Syndrome

Appendix 16.B lists the available studies concerning math difficulties in girls with fragile X syndrome. Several of the studies reveal selectively poor performance on the Wechsler Arithmetic subtest (Bennetto et al., 2001; Brainard et al., 1991; Grigsby, Kemper, & Hagerman, 1987; Kemper, Hagerman, Ahmad, & Mariner, 1986; Miezejeski et al., 1986) and on measures of math achievement (Bennetto et al., 2001; Mazzocco et al., 1993; Mazzocco, 2001; Miezejeski et al., 1986). Of the few studies directed specifically at math performance in girls with fragile X syndrome, only our initial preliminary study (Mazzocco, 2001) directly examined several subtests of math performance. That study was limited to 9 kindergarten girls with fragile X; these girls performed significantly more poorly than controls on the TEMA-2 and on two of the three age-appropriate subtests of the KeyMath that were administered (numeration and geometry, but not measurement). Five of the 9 girls (56%) scored below the 10th percentile on the TEMA-2, a rate more than double the frequency of such low scores in the FSIQ-matched comparison group (20%). Although there were no specific TEMA-2 items that girls with fragile X were more likely to fail, the small sample size may have diminished the statistical power to detect such effects.

In an earlier study with older girls, we carried out a post hoc error analysis of items from the Woodcock Johnson–Revised Math Calculations subtest (Mazzocco, 1998). Girls with fragile X syndrome were compared to a normal peer group and to a sibling comparison group. Math scores were significantly lower than reading scores for girls with fragile X syndrome, and this pattern was evident even when analyses were limited to participants under 10 years of age. Math–reading differences were minimal for both comparison groups. There were no significant differences between girls with fragile X syndrome and either of the comparison groups in the distribution of errors across error types.

Rivera and colleagues (Rivera, Menon, White, Glaser, & Reiss, 2002) examined the performance of girls with fragile X syndrome on two- and three-operand addition tasks, such as 2 + 3 = ?, versus 2 + 3 + 4 = ?; all operands were one-digit numbers. Girls with fragile X performed significantly more poorly on the three-operand problems but not on the two-operand problems. Rivera found that FSIQ was correlated with accuracy on the three-operand task for the group with fragile X, but not in the comparison group. This may relate to the wider range in FSIQ scores in the fragile X group (52 to 108) versus the comparison group (99 to 142) and the significant difference in FSIQ across the two groups (means = 84 and 123, respectively). It may be that FSIQ correlates with this math task only up to a certain level, with threshold effects depending on the complexity of the arithmetic computation; and that single-digit addition skills would not vary much among persons with IQ scores above ~100. This illustrates the importance of selecting an appropriate comparison group when attempting to delineate reasons for poor math achievement. Not surprisingly, the 3-operand task was significantly more difficult than the two-operand task for girls with fragile X, but not for the comparison group.

Although research on fragile X is even more limited than current studies of Turner syndrome, the findings consistently indicate that fragile X syndrome is a risk factor for MD; the risk for poor math achievement is evident across studies that utilize a wide range of math measures (WRAT, KeyMath, TEMA-2, Peabody Individual Achievement Test, and Kaufman Assessment Battery for Children) during early childhood, adolescence, and adulthood.

Persistence of Math Disabilities in Fragile X Syndrome

As summarized above, cross sectional studies of females with fragile X indicate poor math achievement from kindergarten through adulthood, but it has not yet been demonstrated how these difficulties change over time in the same individuals. In our longitudinal studies, we have seen 18 girls with fragile X for one to five annual assessments between kindergarten and fourth grade. Girls for this study are recruited if both a telephone screen and report review fail to implicate mental retardation. However, some of the girls with fragile X who do participate in our research, and who do not have mental retardation by age 4 or 5, may score in the mentally retarded range at a later point during the elementary school years. (Children with fragile X often show IQ declines over time as they fall farther behind their peers cognitively; see, Brun et al., 1995; Fisch et al., 1999). Of the 18 girls we have seen, 14 have received a math standard score < 90 during at least one of their annual visits. If we omit the four girls whose FSIQ scores later fell below 70 (the cutoff for mentally retarded range), 10 of the remaining 14 girls have a TEMA-2 score < 90, and all of those with subsequent assessments continue to score in the bottom 25th percentile. This is a significantly higher incidence of MD (10/14, or 71%) than in the general population (5–8%). However, it is important to note that we have found the frequency of MD to be higher (20%) in a comparison group matched in FSIQ to the fragile X group than in a sample representative of the general population (Mazzocco & Myers, 2003).

The frequency of continued or persistent MD (100% to date) is also higher than the frequency reported in the general population (63%; Mazzocco & Myers, 2003). If this finding is replicated, it will reflect an important difference between girls with fragile X and children without fragile X: whereas poor math achievement in one year does not necessarily indicate future poor math achievement in the general population, among girls with fragile X poor math achievement at one time point is a stronger indicator of future math performance. This has important implications for immediate and sustained interventions for young girls with fragile X syndrome.

Math-Related Cognitive Functions in Fragile X Syndrome

Reading

The math difficulties reported in fragile X appear in the absence of comorbid reading disability. Although many children with fragile X do have reading difficulties, these difficulties are less apparent in females with fragile X who do not have mental retardation. Relative to their own cognitive profile, decoding skills are a strength even among boys with fragile X who have mental retardation (Hodapp et al., 1992). Vocabulary and general verbal comprehension skills are typically age appropriate in girls (Mazzocco, 2001) and women (Brainard et al., 1991; Mazzocco, Pennington, & Hagerman, 1993, 1994; Sobesky, Pennington, Porter, Hull, & Hagerman, 1994) with fragile X. Language abnormalities, when present, generally reflect qualitative aspects of speech, such as phrase repetition (Lesniak-Karpiak, Mazzocco, & Ross, 2003), or occur at the discourse level (Simon et al., 2001). Underlying anxiety, and social anxiety in particular

(Lesniak-Karpiak et al., 2003; Sobesky et al., 1994), is a hypothesized source of discourse abnormalities in fragile X, whereas comprehension difficulties have been theoretically linked to weak executive function skills, particularly those involving cognitive set-shifting (Simon, 2001). Regardless of the source of these qualitative language difficulties, basic reading and decoding skills are relatively intact in females with fragile X.

Memory

Females with fragile X perform as well as females in a comparison group on both immediate and delayed story memory tasks (Jäkälä et al., 1997; Bennetto et al., 2001). They learn as many words from a list learning task as controls, and recall as many words from learning tasks after a delay (Jäkälä et al., 1997). However, memory span differences do appear on Wechsler Digit Span *backwards* but not on Digit Span forward (Jäkälä et al., 1997), which may underlie the overall Digit Span scaled score differences reported for this population (e.g., Bennetto et al., 2001) and may further explain why there are reports of poor performance on Digit Span but age-appropriate performance on Sentence Memory (Mazzocco, 2001).

Executive Function

Bennetto and colleagues (2001) propose that executive function deficits underlie the cognitive phenotype seen in women with fragile X. They base this hypothesis on their study of women with FSIQ scores > 70. All women completed a test battery including measures of verbal and nonverbal memory, two executive function tasks—the Wisconsin Card Sorting Task (WCST) and the Contingency Naming Test (CNT)—and the Woodcock Johnson–Revised spatial relations subtest. Scores from the two executive function tasks were combined into a composite score. Women with fragile X had poorer performance on executive function, poor short- and long-term figural memory, weaker performance on the spatial relations test, and stronger performance on verbal short- and long-term-memory tests. However, when statistically controlling for effects of FSIQ, the only difference to remain statistically significant was in executive function performance. This result is consistent with findings that women with fragile X are more prone to interference effects on Stroop tasks (Tamm et al., 2003), and with the impairment in backwards digit span (which implicates executive function). However, the results do not make clear what aspects of executive function are deficient, and whether the deficiencies contribute to difficulties in math performance.

One route to delineating executive function domains is to examine multiple performance variables from a single test that involves several aspects of executive function. The Contingency Naming Test (CNT; Taylor et al., 1986; Andersen et al., 2000) is such a test. In our study of CNT performance (mentioned earlier with regard to performance by girls with Turner syndrome), we included 8- and 9-year-old girls with fragile X syndrome (n = 11) and girls in an FSIQ-matched comparison group (n = 12). The girls with fragile X syndrome took significantly longer than their peers to name colors and shapes during timed warm-up test trials (65 versus 53 seconds, respectively; Kirk, Mazzocco, & Kover, 2004). They did not take significantly longer to complete either of the two contingency trials and did not make significantly more self-corrections, but they nevertheless demonstrated more difficulty on these tasks. Whereas girls with Turner syndrome showed significantly more difficulty on the *two*-attribute contingency rule, girls with fragile X had significant difficulty on the *one*-attribute contingency rule. They required more practice trials to learn the one-attribute rule (group means = 3 vs. 1.5, respectively); and made more errors on the one-attribute trial (group means = 7.6 vs. 1.4, respectively) relative to girls in their comparison group. There were no group differences in performance on the two-attribute contingency rule, most likely because the comparison group was limited to the 12 girls (from 109 in our normative study) whose FSIQ scores matched those of the fragile

X group, and these girls also did not perform well on this task. Three of the girls with fragile X failed to complete the two-attribute task (versus one girl in the comparison group). These findings demonstrate the importance of including an IQ-matched group in efforts to delineate cognitive skills in phenotype studies; more importantly, our findings suggest that girls with fragile X may have inefficient working memory skills not accounted for by low FSIQ and relatively low thresholds for working memory demands.

Visuo-Spatial Skills

Several studies have reported evidence of visuo-spatial deficits in girls with fragile X syndrome. In one study we administered the Developmental Test of Visual Perception—Second Edition (DTVP-2) to nine third graders with fragile X syndrome (Lesniak-Karpiak & Mazzocco, 2004). Among the four motor-reduced subtests described earlier in our review of math-related skills in Turner syndrome—Position in Space, Figure/Ground, Visual Closure, and Form Constancy—girls with fragile X syndrome performed more poorly than the comparison group on all of the subtests except for Figure/Ground (see Table 16.1). On the experimental measure of incidental visual short-term memory described earlier, girls with fragile X were more likely to miss the overall configuration of the shape array, failing to use a gridlike format when arranging the shapes. However, girls with fragile X syndrome were not dramatically impaired in recalling the locations of the individual shapes; they performed at least as well as the girls with Turner syndrome (who did much better in producing gridlike arrays) and only marginally worse than the children in the comparison group. If these findings persist with a larger sample size, it will be important to probe the basis for the dissociation between fragile X and Turner syndrome phenotypes. Such a study is underway.

Cornish and her colleagues (Cornish, Munir, & Cross, 1998) also sought to characterize the spatial deficits in females with fragile X. They administered a battery of tests to girls with fragile X, mental-age-matched controls, and chronological-age-matched controls. Their test battery included a visual perception task (face recognition), visuo-constructional tasks (e.g., Wechsler Block Design, object assembly, and draw-a-person), gestalt closure, visual motor performance with a grooved pegboard, and a spatial memory task that involved recalling the location of a nameable, concrete stimulus. The only tasks on which significant group differences emerged were the three visuo-construction tasks (block design, object assembly, and draw-a-person). Poor performance on block design has also been reported in earlier studies (e.g., Grigsby, Kemper, Hagerman, & Myers, 1990). It is unlikely that motor demands of the construction tasks underlie these difficulties, in view of the lack of group differences on grooved pegboard performance. In contrast to our DTVP-2 memory findings (which suggest impaired processing of overall spatial configurations, or gestalts), the girls in Cornish's study did not differ from the control groups on their Gestalt Closure performance, although their accuracy score was lower. A possible explanation for this apparent discrepancy is that the Gestalt Closure task used by Cornish involved recognizing degraded pictures of common objects, whereas our task involved observing and remembering the overall configuration of a shape array. In our study of DTVP-2 performance, we found weaker performance on the "Visual Closure" subtest, which is comparable to the gestalt closure task.

Correlations between Math Performance and Math-Related Cognitive Function Measures

We examined correlations between math achievement levels and measures of various math-related cognitive functions in school-age girls with fragile X syndrome. We found, surprisingly, that the Wechsler Verbal Comprehension factor score was strongly correlated with math achievement scores, as was the Third Factor score. Also correlated was performance on a Go/

NoGo task (the TOVA), although this association was somewhat weaker and was significant only for the omissions score, which is used to measure attention skills. The association with errors of commission (used to measure impulsivity) did not reach statistical significance. Scores on the Judgment of Line orientation task (which were significantly correlated with math achievement among girls with Turner syndrome) were not associated with math achievement, nor was there any correlation between math and a complex figure-drawing task (Mazzocco, 1998). In a later study, neither verbal nor spatial scores were correlated with math scores during primary-school-age years (Mazzocco, 2001), despite apparent correlations between these scores and math achievement in a normative comparison sample (Mazzocco & Myers, 2003). However, this result was based on a small sample size and will need to be reassessed when additional girls are seen during primary-school-age years.

These findings suggest that executive function deficiencies may well play a role in the math disabilities of girls with fragile X syndrome. The results also make clear the need for further study of the relations between math performance and visuo-spatial, memory, and language skills in the fragile X phenotype.

Functional Neuroimaging Studies

Grigsby and colleagues were the first to report a study of brain activation during arithmetic task performance by women with fragile X syndrome (Grigsby et al., 1999). Using single photon emission computed tomography (SPECT), they examined activity during mental calculation of two 2- or 3-digit numbers. Although "grossly abnormal" SPECT images were reported for women with fragile X, the researchers found no uniform pattern of activation. Degree of abnormality was not associated with FSIQ. However, 3 of the 4 participants with fragile X showed reduced activation in dorsolateral prefrontal cortex, and activation in the remaining areas was variable across the 4 subjects.

When Rivera and colleagues (2002) carried out functional imaging of participants with or without fragile X, they observed group differences in *amount* of activation but not in *areas* of activation. Whereas persons in the control group showed an increase in prefrontal and parietal activation from the two-operand to three-operand mental arithmetic tasks, females with fragile X did not show this increase. The findings suggest a "shutting down" when task demands increase beyond a threshold that, for females with fragile X, is lower than in controls. Tamm and colleagues (2002) report similar findings during a Stroop interference task, during which women with fragile X did not exhibit the parietal activation seen in the control group, and also had reduced activation in the left orbitofrontal gyrus. These findings parallel our observation that females with fragile X completed the one-attribute contingency rule of the CNT, albeit with more difficulty than their FSIQ-matched controls, and that the lack of differences during the two-attribute contingency rule appeared to result from this more difficult task not being successfully completed by many participants in either group.

CONTRIBUTIONS OF THE STUDY OF COGNITIVE PHENOTYPES

Studies of Turner and fragile X syndrome—and of any known genetic disorder—support the notion that mathematics ability is influenced by biology. This conclusion does not negate the roles of environmental influences (Kameenui & Griffin, 1989) or the interaction of the two, nor does it imply that a known disorder will manifest itself equivalently in all persons with the disorder. Commonalities in children with a relatively homogeneous background can serve as models of MD subtypes, but studies of cognitive phenotypes can also inform us about the variability that is seen in math cognition skills, within and beyond groups with a known disorder.

Cognitive Phenotypes as Models of Learning Disability

Understanding the cognitive phenotype of fragile X or Turner syndrome can inform us about different pathways leading to poor math achievement. This knowledge can be further enhanced by careful assessment of fragile X *versus* Turner syndrome. For example, we described a dissociation in incidental visual memory performance of the DTVP-2, wherein girls with Turner syndrome recalled the gestalt of a visual array, but erred on positioning shapes within that array, whereas girls with fragile X had close to the opposite pattern of performance. Girls with Turner syndrome had difficulty on the CNT when working memory demands involved a two-attribute contingency rule; in girls with fragile X, the one-attribute rule was sufficient to significantly tax working memory demands. In our post hoc analysis of Woodcock-Johnson Math Calculations performance, most girls with Turner or fragile X syndrome made errors; but a higher percentage of girls with Turner syndrome made operation errors (57%) or alignment errors (48%) relative to girls with fragile X syndrome (19% and 14%, respectively; Mazzocco, 1998). Thus, comparing across syndromes may elucidate specifics of a cognitive phenotype.

Cognitive Phenotypes as Models of Associated Behaviors

Comparisons across studies can also illustrate different relationships among behaviors or mental processes, such as the interaction of math cognition and anxiety. Chapter 18 in this volume presents a review of math anxiety, as differentiated from more general anxiety (Ashcraft). Anxiety is a characteristic of the fragile X phenotype (Sobesky et al., 1994), although not specifically linked to math. Although girls with Turner syndrome are reported to have more social difficulties, anxiety per se does not appear to be heightened in this population (McCauley, Feuillan, Kushner, & Ross, 2001). We examined psychophysiological arousal in girls with Turner or fragile X syndrome during computerized tests of mental arithmetic (adding three one-digit numbers) and divided attention (magnitude judgments made during simultaneous monitoring for the occurrence of "0"s on a computer screen; Keysor, Mazzocco, McLeod, & Hoehn-Saric, 2002). During tasks and baseline periods, psychophysiological measures of arousal were obtained as indices of anxiety. Girls with fragile X showed effects only at baseline, with significantly higher levels of arousal relative to girls in their age- and FSIQ-matched comparison group. Although their accuracy on mental arithmetic was significantly lower than that of the controls, there were no differences on any psychophysiologic measures obtained during mental arithmetic. There were no group differences on the divided attention task in either accuracy or arousal. Girls with Turner syndrome did not differ from controls in performance accuracy on either task, nor were there any differences in arousal levels at baseline. However, girls with Turner syndrome showed significantly higher arousal than their age- and FSIQ-matched comparison group on both the arithmetic and the divided-attention tasks. Correlations between performance accuracy and arousal differed across groups. Among girls in the control group, heightened arousal was associated with a greater number of correct responses and higher accuracy on the mental arithmetic task. Among girls with Turner syndrome, heightened arousal was associated with fewer problems attempted on the mental arithmetic task. No significant correlations were found for the group with fragile X. These associations illustrate how cognitive phenotypes that might initially appear similar may have important differences and that such differences offer alternative models of brain-behavior relationships underlying cognitive processes.

Variability within Phenotypes and in the General Population

Even when a general phenotype description is strongly associated with a specific disorder, rarely does a phenotype description represent all members of the population in question.

Broad features such as mental retardation may be characteristic of most or all children with a syndrome, but even in such cases there will be phenotypic variation. For example, although most girls with Turner syndrome have poor math achievement in primary school, not all girls in this group are deficient in math. The variability is biologically determined, in part, as a function of different karyotypes, X inactivation patterns, and possible parent-of-origin effects. In fragile X, effects vary with X inactivation and fmrp levels. In cases where biological/cognitive correlates are robust, such as seen with karyotype variability (Ross, Roeltgen, Kushner et al., 2000) or fmrp levels (Bailey et al., 2001; Bennetto et al., 2001), these associations still do not lead to perfect correlations because of additional sources of variation from other genes and environmental influences.

Such interactions in persons with known disorders can inform us of sources of variation in the general population. For example, all humans have fmrp, and studies of reduction of fmrp in fragile X have led to the discovery of its role in learning and memory (Lombroso, 2003) through its effects on formation and development of neuronal dendritic spines (Irwin, Galvez, & Greenough, 2000). Studies of Turner syndrome can contribute to investigations of how sex hormones influence math cognition and performance (Ross et al., 1998; Ross, Roeltgen, Feuillan et al., 2000; Ross et al, 2003; Ross & Zinn, 1999). Regardless of the sources of performance variation, it is important to acknowledge that the group effects described in this report represent group differences relative to the general population, but they are not descriptions of all individuals within a population.

FUTURE DIRECTIONS

In this chapter, we reviewed evidence for MD in two known disorders, and we illustrated how studies of cognitive phenotypes are valuable for studying MD and its subtypes. A critical point clearly stands out in this review. Whereas studies of Turner and fragile X syndromes have unequivocally established that both syndromes are associated with math disability, much less progress has been made toward identifying the cognitive dysfunctions underlying these phenotypes. Most previous studies have involved tasks that, while adequate for assessing whether a math disability is present, are not well suited for differentiating the various cognitive processes required for successful math performance. Future research should focus on selectively probing each of these component processes, in order to determine which processes are intact and which are impaired in Turner and fragile X syndromes. Thus, we are suggesting a shift toward research that is more theory based—because a cognitive theory provides the basis for identifying the relevant processes—and focuses not on behaviors per se (e.g., performance on a particular standardized math test) but, rather, on underlying cognitive processes.

ACKNOWLEDGMENTS

This work was supported by NIH grant RO1-034061, National Institutes of Child Health and Human Development. The authors wish to thank Project Manager Gwen F. Myers for her dedicated role in our ongoing research. The authors also thank the children who participated in this research, their parents, and their teachers.

Appendix 16.A
Summary of Studies Related to Math in Females with Turner Syndrome

Study	Turner group N:	Karyotype	Age range	IQ data reported	Measures used*	Comparison group
Alexander, Ehrhardt, et al. (1966)	18	Not reported (NR)	10–24 years	Range: 74–130 Group mean = 101	• Benton Visual Retention Test • Bender Visual Motor Gestalt • Draw-A-Person Test	None
Balottin, Isola, et al. (1998)	5	45, XO (n = 3) 46, X (n = 2)	12–22 years	Range: 57–97 Group mean = 77.6 SD=16.5	• WISC-R, WAIS • individual interviews	None
Buchanan, Pavlovic, et al. (1998)	9	45, X (n = 3) mosaicism (n = 2) isochromosome for the long arm (n = 2)	12–18 years	(Only Verbal IQ reported) Group mean = 100.3	"visuo-spatial processing tasks" comparing recall of location and/or form of visual stimuli; and comparison of immediate vs. delayed visual memory	Age-, SES-, and verbal IQ-matched female controls
Elliott, Watkins, et al. (1996)	6	45, X (n = 3) 46, X, i[X]q (n = 1) 45,X/46, X, r(X) (n = 1) 45,X/4 6, XX (n = 1)	11–15 years	Range: 70–126 Group mean = 99.0 SD = 14.7	• WISC-R • Raven's Progressive Matrices • Judgment of Line Orientation (JLO) • Benton Visual Form discrimination • Beery Visual-Motor Integration (VMI) • Keymath-R	Age-matched controls with a normal MRI and PET
Keysor, Mazzocco, et al. (2002)	11	Not reported	12–20 years	Range: 65–126 Group mean = 96.5, SD = 18.0	• Mental arithmetic task • Divided attention task • Risk-taking task	Age-matched control females
Mazzocco (1998)	9	Not reported	5–16 years	Range: 72–135 Group mean = 95, SD = 13.5	• WISC-R • WJ-R (four subtests) • TOVA • JLO • ROCF	• Peer Controls • Sibling Controls • Girls with fragile X

(Continued)

Appendix 16.A
Continued

Study	Turner group N:	Karyotype	Age range	IQ data reported	Measures used*	Comparison group
McCauley, Kay, et al. (1987)	17	45X (n = 10) 45X/46XX (n = 2) partial deletion (n = 5)	9–17 years	VIQ: mean = 95.4, SD=10.6 PIQ: mean = 91.4 SD=10.3	• WISC-R • VMI • Embedded Figures Test	Short-stature female patients
Pennington, Heaton, et al. (1985)	10	45X	Mean: 23.10	Range: 81–106 Group mean: 96.70, SD: 7.35	• WAIS • Peabody Individual Achievement Test • Thurstone Word Fluency • WCST-Seashore Tonal Memory • Story and Figure Memory • Dynamometer-Grooved Pegboard-Static Steadiness tests	• Normal females (n = 20) • Female patients with right hemisphere lesions (n = 12) • Female patients with left hemisphere lesions (n = 10) • Female patients with diffuse hemisphere lesions (n = 10)
Ross, Roeltgen, et al. (1998)	47 (23 on placebo, 24 on estrogen)	45X	5–12 years	VIQ group mean ~ 102 PIQ group mean ~ 94	• WISC-R • Motor function • Lafayette pegboard • VMI MFFT • Test of Facial Recognition	Verbal IQ-matched control girls
Ross, Roeltgen, Kushner, et al. (2000)	34	Partial deletion	7–46 years	VIQ > 80	• WISC-R, WAIS-R • WRAT • Word list recall	N/A

Study	n	Karyotype	Age	IQ/Score	Measures	Comparison
Ross, Roeltgen, Feuillan, et al. (2000)	83 children 51 adults	45X 46XX partial deletion	7–55 years	Not reported	• WISC-R, WAIS-R • WRAT • word recall list • Denman story recall • Rey complex figure • LO–motor-free visual perception • Money street map • facial recognition • Warrington faces • Gestalt closure • VMI • tests of variables of attention • MFFT	N/A
Rovet (1993)	67	45, X (n = 24) structural rearrangement (n = 9) mosaic (n = 17) unknown (n = 23)	6–16 years	Group mean Score: 90.2 Group SD: 15.3	• WISC-R • VMI • WRAT-R • WJRM-R • Keymath	Age-matched controls
Rovet, Szekely, et al. (1994)	Study 1: 45 Study 2: 10	45X (55%) structural rearrangement (20%) mosaicism (25%) unknown (5%)	• Study 1: 7.4–16.8 years • Study 2: 8.8–15.2 years	Group mean: 94.5, SD: 16.8	Study 1: • WISC-R • WRAT-R Study 2: • WISC-R • WRAT-R • Keymath-R	Age-matched controls
Skuse, James, et al. (1997)	88	45Xm-(n = 80) 45Xp- (n = 8)	6–25 years	Group mean $45X^m$: 96.2 SD = 15.9 mean, $45x,^p$: 106.4 SD = 45, X^p: 14.4	• WISC-III-UK • WAIS-R • Same-Opposite World subtest from the Test of Everyday Attention for Children • Tower of Hanoi task	"Normal female comparisons"

(Continued)

Appendix 16.A
Continued

Study	Turner group N:	Karyotype	Age range	IQ data reported	Measures used*	Comparison group
Temple & Carney (1995)	15	• 45, XO (n = 7) • mixed genotypes (isochromes of X [n = 1], mosaicism[n = 6] and partial deletion of X [n = 1])	8;9 - 12;2 years	Range: 78–117 Group Mean Score: 95 Group SD: NR	• Street task • Benton's Line Orientation task • Mental Relation task • Block Design • Object Assembly • Cornish Jigsaw • Draw-a-man • Draw-a-bicycle	Age-matched controls
Temple, Carney & Mullarkey (1996)	16	• 45, XO (50% of N) • mosaic patterns, partial deletions, translocations (50% of N)	• 45, XO: 8:9– 12;2 years • mixed genotypes: 9;2–11;8	Range: NR Group Mean Score, 45 XO: 90 Group Mean Score, mixed genotypes: 96 Group SD: NR	• WCST • Stroop test • Tower of London task • Self-ordered Pointing task	Age-matched controls
Temple & Marriott, (1998)	11	45X (n = 5) mosaic (n = 6)	8;11–12;1	Range = 80–115 Group mean = 90.2	Nonstandardized number processing and calculation tasks	Age-matched controls
Williams, Richman, et al. (1991)	13	• 45X (n = 9) • deletion (n = 1) • mosaicism (n = 3)	7–14 years (M= 115.3 months)	Not administered	• Digit Span • Sentence Repetition Test • Rey Auditory Verbal Learning Test • Continuous Performance Test-2	Children with nonverbal learning disability diagnosis

*Not a complete list of measures. Only measures relevant to the discussion are listed.
**NR = not reported

Appendix 16.B

Summary of Studies Related to Math in Females with Fragile-X Syndrome

Study	Fragile-X sample	Gender	Age range	IQ	Measures used*	Comparison group
Abrams, Reiss, et al. (1994)	31	Female	4–27 years	Range: 38–116 Group Mean: 82S D: NR	• Stanford-Binet Intelligence Scale or WISC-R • Revised Behavior Problem Checklist (includes Attention Problems)	None
Bennetto, Taylor, et al. (2001)	32	Female	18–45 years	Range: NR** Group Mean, Full mutation: 82.7 Group SD, Full mutation: 9.2	• WAIS-R • WCST • CNT • WJ-R: Spatial relations • Wechsler Memory Scale-R Figural memory I and II • Wechsler Memory Scale-R Logical Memory I and II	• women who grew up with a fragile X family member • age- and IQ-matched controls
Brainard, Schreiner, & Hagerman (1991)	74	Female	Not reported	Range: NR Group Mean: 99.65 SD: NR	WAIS-R	N/A
Cornish, Munir, & Cross (1998)	17	Female	7–14 years	Not administered	Verbal Mental Age Face Recognition Block Design Object Assembly Triangles Draw-A-Person Gestalt Closure Annett pegboard Visual Recognition	• 15 mental-age-matched control children • 14 chronological-age-matched control children

(Continued)

Appendix 16.B
Continued

Study	Fragile-X sample	Gender	Age range	IQ	Measures used*	Comparison group
Cronister, Schreiner et al. (1991)	105	Female	5–63 years	Range: NR Group mean "normally functioning" group: 104 Group mean, "impaired group": 72	• physical assessment • historical assessment • WISC-R, or WAIS-R or K-ABC	• normally functioning women, mothers of developmentally delayed children with Fragile X • impaired functioning, fragile-X negative women with an FSIQ< 85
Grigsby, Froelich et al. (1990)	8	Female	22–46 years	Not administered	• arithmetic test • Behavioral Dyscontrol Scale • motor learning task, adapted from Seitz • mental calculation task	• 4 women negative for fragile X, ages of 21 to 40 years, • 2 women with the fragile X premutation
Jäkälä, Hänninen et al. (1997)	20 total female • 10 full mutation • 10 premutation	Male and Female	• fM female: 34.2 ± 15.8 • pM female: 48.3 ± 15.0	VIQ: 71.8 ± 17.6; P IQ 73.0 ± 15.8	• Mini-Mental Status exam • Vineland • WAIS-R • Logical Memory Test • Russell's adaptation of the Visual Reproduction Test • Buschke Selective Reminding	None
Keysor, Mazzocco et al. (2001)	13	Female	13–22 years	Range: 59–125 Group mean: 88.5, SD=17.4	• Mental arithmetic task • Divided attention task • Risk-taking task	Age-matched control females Females with Turner syndrome
Kwon, Menon, et al. (2001)	10	Female	10–23 years	Group mean: 84	1-back and 2-back visuo-spatial working memory tasks	Age-matched controls
Loesch, Huggins, et al. (2002)	263	Male and Female	5–75 years	For Females: Range: NR Group mean: 93.1, SD: 20.0	FSIQ	"normal" relatives of the subjects with fragile X

Study	N	Sex	Age	Score	Measures	Controls
Mazzocco (1998)	26	Female	5–16 years	Range: 66–116 Group mean: 85.8, SD: 14.3	• WISC-R • WJ-R (four subtests) • TOVA • JLO • ROCF	Peer Controls Sibling Controls
Mazzocco, Hagerman, & Pennington (1992)	10	Female	18–48 years	Range: 76–109 Group mean: 85.7	• CNT • Tower of Hanoi	Mothers of developmentally delayed children known not to have fragile X
Mazzocco, Pennington, & Hagerman (1993)	57 total	Female	Expressing: mean age: 31.2, SD: 6.7 Obligate Carrier: mean age: 34.5, SD: 5.9	Group Mean Score, Expressing: 90.8; SD = 14.8 Group Mean, Obligate Carrier: 100.6, SD = 11.3	• WAIS-R • PIAT-R (Peabody Individual Achievement Test–Revised) • Nonword reading • Verbal (story) short-term memory • Woodcock Johnson Spatial Relations • Tonal memory • Figure short-term memory • Verbal delayed story memory • Nonverbal figural delayed memory • CNT (Contingency Naming Test) • WCST • Visual Verbal Test	60 women not carrying the fragile X mutation, but from families with one or more persons affected by fragile X
Rivera, Menon, et al. (2002)	16	Female	10.12–22.73 years	Range: 52–108 Group Mean: 83.6	• WISC-III • WAIS-III	16 female unaffected controls
Sobesky, Pennington, et al. (1994)	21	Female	18–45 years	Group mean 85.00 SD = 11.3	• WAIS-R • Wechsler Logical Memory Test • Woodcock Johnson Spatial Relations Test • Tonal Memory Test • Wechsler Memory Scale Revised • Wechsler Visual Reproduction I and II tests-CNT·WCST·V-VT	Control women with or without a family member with fragile X syndrome
Tamm, Menon, et al. (2002)	14	Female	Not reported	Group mean = 84.43, SD= 15.8	• Wechsler IQ test • CBCL-counting Stroop task	Age-matched healthy controls

*Not a complete list of measures. Only measures relevant to the discussion are listed.

**NR = not reported

REFERENCES

Abrams, M. T., Reiss, A. L., Freund, L. S., Baumgardner, T. L., Chase, G. A., & Denckla, M. B. (1994). Molecular-neurobehavioral associations in females with the fragile X full mutation. *American Journal of Medical Genetics, 51*, 317–327.

Alexander, D., Ehrhardt, A. A., & Money, J. (1966). Defective figure drawing, geometric and human, in Turner's syndrome. *Journal of Nervous and Mental Disorders, 152*, 161–167.

Anderson, P., Anderson, V., Northam, E., & Taylor, H. G. (2000). Standardization of the Contingency Naming Test (CNT) for school aged children: A measure of reactive flexibility. *Clinical Neuropsychological Assessment, 1*, 247–273.

Badian, N. A. (1983). *Dyscalculia and nonverbal disorders of learning.* New York: Stratton.

Bailey, D. B., Jr., Hatton, D. D., & Skinner, M. (1998). Early developmental trajectories of males with fragile X syndrome. *American Journal of Mental Retardation, 1*(103), 29–39.

Bailey, D. B., Jr., Hatton, D. D., Tassone, F., Skinner, M., & Taylor, A. K. (2001). Variability in FMRP and early development in males with fragile X syndrome. *American Journal of Mental Retardation, 106*(1), 16–27.

Balottin, U., Isola, V., Larizza, D., Piccinelli, P., Rossi, G., & Curto, F. L. (1998). Cognitive functions in Turner's syndrome. *Minerva Pediatrica, 50*(10), 419–425.

Bender, B. G., Linden, M. G., & Robinson, A. (1993). Neuropsychological impairments in 42 adolescents with sex chromosome abnormalities. *American Journal of Medical Genetics (Neuropsychiatric Genetics), 48*, 169–173.

Bennetto, L., Taylor, A. K., Pennington, B. F., Porter, D., & Hagerman, R. J. (2001). Profile of cognitive functioning in women with the Fragile X mutation. *Neuropsychology, 15*(2), 290–299.

Benton, A. L., Hamsher, K., Varney, N., & Spreen, O. (1983). Judgment of line orientation. In *Contributions to neuropsychological assessment* (pp. 44–54). New York: Oxford University Press.

Brainard, S. S., Schreiner, R. A., & Hagerman, R. J. (1991). Cognitive profiles of the carrier fragile X woman. *American Journal of Medical Genetics, 38*, 505–508.

Brun, C., Obiols, J. E., Cheema, A., O'Connor, R., Riddle, J., Di Maria, M., Writght-Talamante, C., & Hagerman, R. (1995). Longitudinal IQ changes in fragile X females. *Developmental Brain Dysfunction, 8*, 230–241.

Buchanan, L., Pavlovic, J., & Rovet, J. (1998). A reexamination of the visuospatial deficit in Turner syndrome: Contributions of working memory. *Developmental Neuropsychology, 14*, 341–367.

Cornish, K. M., Munir, F., & Cross, G. (1998). The nature of the spatial deficit in young females with fragile-X syndrome: a neuropsychological and molecular perspective. *Neuropsychologia, 11*(36), 1239–1246.

Crawford, D. C., Meadows, K. L., Newman, J. L., Taft, L. F., Pettay, D. L., Gold, L. B., Hersey, S. J., Hinkle, E. F., Stanfield, M. L., Holmgreen, P., Yeargin-Allsopp, M., Boyle, C., & Sherman, S. L. (1999). Prevalence and phenotype consequence of FRAXA and FRAXE alleles in a large, ethnically diverse, special education-needs population. *American Journal of Human Genetics, 2*(64), 495–507.

Davis, C. J., Gayan, J., Knopik, V. S., Smith, S. D., Cardon, L. R., Pennington, B. F., Olson, R. K., & DeFries, J. C. (2001). Etiology of reading difficulties and rapid naming: The Colorado twin study of reading disability. *Behavior Genetics, 31*(6), 625–635.

Elliott, T. K., Watkins, J. M., Messa, C., Lippe, B., & Chugani, H. (1996). Positron emission tomography and neuropsychological correlates in children with Turner's syndrome. *Developmental Neuropsychology, 12*(3), 365–386.

Fisch, G. S., Carpenter, N., Holden, J. J., Howard-Peebles, P. N., Maddalena, A., Borghgraef, M., Steyaert, J., & Fryns, J. P. (1999). Longitudinal changes in cognitive and adaptive behavior in fragile X females: A prospective multicenter analysis. *American Journal of Medical Genetics, 4*(83), 308–312.

Franke, P., Leboyer, M., Hardt, J., Sohne, E., Weiffenbach, O., Biancalana, V., Cornillet-Lefebre, P., Delobel, B., Froster, U., Schwab, S. G., Poustka, F., Hautzinger, M., & Maier, W. (1999). Neuropsychological profiles of FMR-1 premutation and full-mutation carrier females. *Psychiatry Research, 87*, 223–231.

Fu, Y. H., Kuhl, D. P., Pizzuti, A., Pieretti, M., Sutcliffe, J. S., Richards, S., Verkerk, A. J., Holden, J. J., Fenwick, R. G., Warren, S. T., Oostra, B. A., Nelson, D. L., & Caskey, C. T. (1991). Variation of the CGG repeat at the fragile X site results in genetic instability: Resolution of the Sherman paradox. *Cell, 67*, 1047–1058.

Geary, D. C., Hamson, C. O., & Hoard, M. K. (2000). Numerical and arithmetical cognition: A longitudinal study of process and concept deficits in children with learning disability. *Journal of Experimental Child Psychology, 77*(3), 236–263.

Ginsburg, H., & Baroody, A. (1990). *Test of Early Mathematics Ability* (PRO-ED, 2nd ed.). Austin, TX.

Goodfellow, P. N., Pym, B., Mohandas, T., & Shapiro, L. J. (1984). The cell surface antigen locus, MIC2X, escapes X-inactivation. *American Journal of Human Genetics, 36*, 777–782.

Greenberg, L. (1990). *Test of variables of attention 5.01.* St. Paul, MN: Attention Technology, Inc.

Grigsby, J., Froelich, J. W., Brautigam, A., Sandberg, E. J., Busenbark, D., Hagerman, R. J. (1999). Brain activation during motor learning and mental arithmetic among women with fragile X syndrome. *Journal of the International Neuropsychological Society, 5*, 153.

Grigsby, J., Kemper, M., & Hagerman, R. (1987). Developmental Gerstmann syndrome without aphasia in the fragile X syndrome. *Neuropsychologia, 25*, 881–891.

Grigsby, J. P., Kemper, M. B., Hagerman, R. J., & Myers, C. S. (1990). Neuropsychological dysfunction among affected heterozygous fragile X females. *American Journal of Medical Genetics, 35*, 28–35.

Hagerman, R. J. (2002). Physical and behavioral phenotype. In R. J. Hagerman & P. J. Hagerman (Eds.), *Fragile X syndrome: Diagnosis, treatment, and research* (3rd ed., pp. 3–109). Baltimore, MD: Johns Hopkins University Press.

Hagerman, R. J., Leehey, M., Heinrichs, W., Tassone, F., Wilson, R., Hills, J., Grigsby, J., Gage, B., & Hagerman, P. J. (2001). Intention tremor, Parkinsonism, and generalized brain atrophy in male carriers of fragile X. *Neurology, 57*(1), 127–130.

Hammill, D., Pearson, N., & Voress, J. (1993). *Developmental test of visual perception* (2nd ed.). Austin, TX: PRO-ED.

Hanich, L. B., Jordan, N. C., Kaplan, D., & Dick, J. (2001). Performance across different areas of mathematical cognition in children with learning disabilities. *Journal of Educational Psychology, 93*, 615–626.

Hansen, R. S., Gartler, S. M., Scott, C. R., Chen, S. H., & Laird, C. D. (1992). Methylation analysis of CGG sites in the CpG island of the human FMR1 gene. *Human Molecular Genetics, 1*, 571–578.

Heaton, R. K. (1981). *Wisconsin card sorting test manual.* Odessa, FL: Psychological Corporation.

Hodapp, R. M., Leckman, J. F., Dykens, E. M., Sparrow, S. S., Zelinsky, D. G., & Ort, S. I. (1992). K-ABC profiles in children with fragile X syndrome, Down syndrome, and nonspecific mental retardation. *American Journal of Mental Retardation, 97*, 39–46.

Irwin, S. A., Galvez, R., & Greenough, W. T. (2000). Dendritic spine structural anomalies in fragile-X mental retardation syndrome. *Cerebral Cortex, 10*(10), 1038–1044.

Jäkälä P., Hänninen, T., Ryynanen, M., Laakso, M., Partanen, K., Mannermaa, A., & Soininen, H. (1997). Fragile-X: neuropsychological test performance, CGG triplet repeat lengths, and hippocampal volumes. *Journal of Clinical Investigation, 100*, 331–338.

Kameenui, E. J., & Griffin, C. C. (1989). The national crisis in verbal problem solving in mathematics: A proposal for examining the role of basal mathematics programs. *The Elementary School Journal, 89*, 575–593.

Kemper, M. B., Hagerman, R. J., Ahmad, R. S., & Mariner, R. (1986). Cognitive profiles and the spectrum of clinical manifestations in heterozygous fragile (X) females. *American Journal of Medical Genetics, 23*, 139–156.

Keysor, C. S., Mazzocco, M. M. M., McLeod, D. R., & Hoehn-Saric, R. (2002). Physiological arousal in females with fragile X or Turner syndrome. *Developmental Psychobiology, 41*(2), 133–146.

Kirk, J. W., Kover, S. T., & Mazzocco, M. M. M. (2004). Executive functioning in girls with Turner or fragile X syndrome. In *International Neuropsychological Society 32nd Annual Meeting* (pp. 135). Baltimore.

Kwon, H., Menon, V., Eliez, S., Warsofsky, I. S., White, C. D., Dyer-Friedman, J., Taylor, A. K., Glover, G. H., & Reiss, A. L. (2001). Functional neuroanatomy of visuospatial working memory in fragile X syndrome: Relation to behavioral and molecular measures. *American Journal of Psychiatry, 158*(7), 1040–1051.

LaHood, B. J., & Bacon, G. E. (1985). Cognitive abilities of adolescent Turner's syndrome patients. *Journal of Adolescent Health Care, 6*, 358–364.

Lesniak-Karpiak, K., Mazzocco, M. M., & Ross, J. L. (2003). Behavioral assessment of social anxiety in females with Turner or fragile X syndrome. *Journal of Autism and Developmental Disorders, 33*(1), 55–67.

Lesniak-Karpiak, K. Mazzocco, M. M. M. (2004). Examination of visual spatial skills in girls with Turner or fragile X syndrome. In *International Neuropsychological Society 32nd Annual Meeting* (pp. 135). Baltimore.

Lippe, B. (1991). Turner syndrome. *Endocrinology and Metabolism Clinics in North America, 20*(1), 121–152.

Loesch, D. Z., Huggins, R. M., Bui, Q. M., Epstein, J. L.,

Taylor, A. K., & Hagerman, R. J. (2002). Effect of the deficits of fragile X mental retardation protein on cognitive status of fragile X males and females assessed by robust pedigree analysis. *Journal of Developmental and Behavioral Pediatrics, 23*(6), 416–423.

Lombroso, P. J. (2003). Genetics of childhood disorders: XLVIII: Learning and memory, part 1: Fragile X syndrome update. *Journal of the American Academy of Child and Adolescent Psychiatry, 42*, 372–375.

Lubs, H. A. (1969). A marker X-chromosome. *American Journal of Human Genetics, 21*, 231–244.

Lyon, M. F. (1991). The quest for the X-inactivation centre. *Trends in Genetics, 7*, 69–70.

Martin, J. P., & Bell, J. (1943). A pedigree of mental defect showing sex linkage. *Journal of Neurology and Psychiatry, 6*, 154–157.

Mathur, A., Stekol, L., Schatz, D., MacLaren, N. K., Scott, M. L., & Lippe, B. (1991). The parental origin of the single X chromosome in Turner syndrome: Lack of correlation with parental age or clinical phenotype. *American Journal of Human Genetics, 48*, 682–686.

Mazzocco, M. M. M. (1998). A process approach to describing mathematics difficulties in girls with Turner syndrome. *Pediatrics, Supplement 3*(102), 492–496.

Mazzocco, M. M. M., Hagerman, R. J., Cronister, S. A., & Pennington, B. F. (1992). Specific frontal lobe deficits among women with the fragile X gene. *Journal of the American Academy of Child and Adolescent Psychiatry, 31*, 1141–1148.

Mazzocco, M. M. M., & Holden, J. J. (1996). Neuropsychological profiles of three sisters homozygous for the fragile X premutation. *American Journal of Medical Genetics, 2*(64), 323–328.

Mazzocco, M. M. M., & Myers, G. F. (2002). Maximizing efficiency of enrollment for school-based educational research. *Journal of Applied Social Psychology, 32*, 1577–1587.

Mazzocco, M. M. M., Pennington, B. F., & Hagerman, R. J. (1993). The neurocognitive phenotype of female carriers of fragile X: Additional evidence for specificity. *Journal of Developmental and Behavioral Pediatrics, 14*, 328–335.

Mazzocco, M. M. M., Pennington, B. F., & Hagerman, R. J. (1994). Social cognition skills among females with fragile X. *Journal of Autism and Developmental Disorders, 24*, 473–485.

Mazzocco, M. M. M. (2001). Math learning disability and MD subtypes: Evidence from studies of Turner syndrome, fragile X syndrome, and neurofibromatosis type 1. *Journal of Learning Disabilities, 34*(6), 520–533.

Mazzocco, M. M. M., & Myers, G. F. (2003). Complexities in identifying and defining mathematics learning disability in the primary school age years. *Annals of Dyslexia, 53*.

McCauley, E., Feuillan, P., Kushner, H., & Ross, J.L. (2001). Psychosocial development in adolescents with Turner syndrome. *Journal of Developmental and Behavioral Pediatrics, 22*(6), 360–365.

McCauley, E., Kay, T., Ito, J., & Treder, R. (1987). The Turner syndrome: Cognitive deficits, affective discrimination, and behavior problems. *Child Development, 58*, 464–473.

Molko, N., Cachia, A., Rivière, D., Mangin, J., Bruandet, M., Le Bihan, D., Cohen, L., & Dehaene, S. (2003). Functional and structural alterations of the intraparietal sulcus in a developmental dyscalculia of genetic origin. *Neuron, 40*, 847–858.

Miezejeski, C. M., Jenkins, E. C., Hill, A. L., Wisniewski, K., French, J. H., & Brown, W. T. (1986). A profile of cognitive deficit in females from fragile X families. *Neuropsychologia, 24*, 405–409.

Myers, G. F., Mazzocco, M. M. M., Maddalena, A., & Reiss, A. L. (2001). No widespread psychological effect of the fragile X premutation in childhood: Evidence from a preliminary controlled study. *Journal of Developmental and Behavioral Pediatrics, 22*(6), 353–359.

Oostra, B. A., & Halley, D. J. (1995). Complex behavior of simple repeats: The fragile X syndrome. *Pediatrics Research, 38*(5), 629–637.

Pai, J. T., Tsai, S. F., Horng, C. J., Chiu, P. C., Cheng, M. Y., Hsiao, K. J., & Wuu, K. D. (1994). Absence of FMR-1 gene expression can be detected with RNA extracted from dried blood specimens. *Human Genetics, 93*, 488–493.

Palmer, C. G., & Reichmann, A. (1976). Chromosomal and clinical findings in 110 females with Turner syndrome. *Human Genetics, 35*, 35–49.

Park, E., Bailey, J. D., & Cowell, C. A. (1983). Growth and maturation of patients with Turner's syndrome. *Pediatrics Research, 17*, 1–7.

Pennington, B. F., Heaton, R. K., Karzmar, P., Pendleton, M. G., Lehman, R., & Schucard, D. W. (1985). The neuropsychological phenotype in Turner syndrome. *Cortex, 21*, 391–404.

Pieretti, M., Zhang, F. P., Fu, Y. H., Warren, S. T., Oostra, B. A., Caskey, C. T., & Nelson, D. L. (1991). Absence of expression of the FMR-1 gene in fragile X syndrome. *Cell, 66*, 817–822.

Reiss, A. L., Freund, L. F., Baumgardner, T. L., Abrams, M. T., & Denckla, M. B. (1995). Contribution of the FMR1 gene mutation to human intellectual dysfunction. *Nature Genetics, 11*, 331–334.

Rieser, P. A., & Underwood, L. E. (1989). *Turner syndrome: A guide for families.*

Rivera, S. M., Menon, V., White, C. D., Glaser, B., & Reiss, A. L. (2002). Functional brain activation during arithmetic processing in females with fragile X syndrome is related to FMR1 protein expression. *Human Brain Mapping, 16*(4), 206–218.

Ross, J. L., Roeltgen, D., Feuillan, P., Kushner, H., & Cutler, G. B., Jr. (1998). Effects of estrogen on nonverbal processing speed and motor function in girls with Turner's syndrome. *Journal of Clinical Endocrinology and Metabolism, 83*(9), 3198–3204.

Ross, J. L., Roeltgen, D., Feuillan, P., Kushner, H., & Cutler, G. B., Jr. (2000). Use of estrogen in young girls with Turner syndrome: Effects on memory. *Neurology, 54*(1), 164–170.

Ross, J. L., Roeltgen, D., Kushner, H., Wei, F., & Zinn, A. R. (2000). The Turner syndrome-associated neurocognitive phenotype maps to distal Xp. *American Journal of Human Genetics, 67*(3), 672–681.

Ross, J. L., Roeltgen, D., Stefanatos, G. A., Feuillan, P., Kushner, H., Bondy, C., & Cutler, G. B., Jr. (2003). Androgen-responsive aspects of cognition in girls with Turner syndrome. *Journal of Clinical Endocrinology and Metabolism, 88*(1), 292–296.

Ross, J. L., & Zinn, A. (1999). Turner syndrome: Possible hormonal and genetic influences on the neurocognitive profile. In Tager-Flusberg (Ed.), *Neurodevelopmental Disorders* (pp. 251–268). Cambridge, MA: MIT Press.

Rousseau, F., Heitz, D., Tarleton, J., MacPherson, J., Malmgren, H., Dahl, N., Barnicoat, A., Mathew, C., Mornet, E., Tejada, I., Maddalena, A., Spiegel, R., Schinzel, A., Marcos, J. A. G., Schwartz, C., & Mandel, J. L. (1994). A multicenter study on genotype-phenotype correlations in the fragile X syndrome, using direct diagnosis with probe StB12.3: the first 2,253 cases. *American Journal of Human Genetics, 55*, 225–237.

Rovet, J., & Ireland, L. (1994). Behavioral phenotype in children with Turner syndrome. *Journal of Pediatric Psychology, 19*(6), 779–790.

Rovet, J., Szekely, C., & Hockenberry, M. N. (1994). Specific arithmetic calculation deficits in children with turner syndrome. *Journal of Clinical and Experimental Neuropsychology, 16*, 820–839.

Rovet, J. F. (1993). The psychoeducational characteristics of children with Turner syndrome. *Journal of Learning Disabilities, 26*, 333–341.

Russell, R. L., & Ginsburg, H. P. (1984). Cognitive analysis of children's mathematics difficulties. *Cognition and Instruction, 1*, 217–244.

Schneider-Gadicke, A., Beer-Romero, P., Brown, L. G., Nussbaum, R., & Page, D. C. (1989). ZFX has a gene structure similar to ZFY, the putative human sex determinant, and escapes X inactivation. *Cell, 57*(7), 1247–1258.

Shalev, R. S., Auerbach, J., Manor, O., & Gross-Tsur, V. (2000). Developmental dyscalculia: prevalence and prognosis. *European Child and Adolescent Psychiatry, 9 Supplement 2*, 1158–1164.

Shallice, T. (1982). Specific impairment in planning. *Philosophical transactions of the royal society of London, Series B*(298), 199–209.

Sherman, S. L. (1991). Genetic epidemiology of the fragile X syndrome with special reference to genetic counseling. *Progress in Clinical Biology Research, 368*, 79–99.

Simon, J. A., Keenan, J. M., Pennington, B. F., Taylor, A. K., & Hagerman, R. J. (2001). Discourse processing in women with fragile X syndrome: Evidence for a deficit establishing coherence. *Cognitive Neuropsychology, 18*(1), 1–18.

Skuse, D. H., James, R. S., Bishop, D. V., Coppin, B., Dalton, P., Aamodt-Leeper, G., Bacarese-Hamilton, M., Creswell, C., McGurk, R., & Jacobs, P. A. (1997). Evidence from Turner's syndrome of an imprinted X-linked locus affecting cognitive function. *Nature, 387*(6634), 705–708.

Sobesky, W. E., Pennington, B. F., Porter, D., Hull, C. E., & Hagerman, R. J. (1994). Emotional and neurocognitive deficits in fragile X. *American Journal of Medical Genetics, 51*, 378–385.

Stroop, J. R. (1935). Studies of interference in serial verbal reactions. *Journal of Experimental Psychology, 18*, 643–662.

Tamm, L., Menon, V., & Reiss, A. L. (2003). Abnormal prefrontal cortex function during response Inhibition in Turner Syndrome: Functional magnetic resonance imaging evidence. *Biological Psychiatry, 53*(2), 107–111.

Tassone, F., Hagerman, R. J., Taylor, A. K., Gane, L. W., Godfrey, T. E., & Hagerman, P. J. (2000). Elevated levels of FMR1 mRNA in carrier males: A new mechanism of involvement in the fragile-X syndrome. *American Journal of Human Genetics, 66*(1), 6–15.

Taylor, H. G., Albo, V., Phebus, C., Sachs, B., & Bierl, P.

(1987). Postirradiation treatment outcome with acute lymphoblastic leukemia: Clarification of risks. *Journal of Pediatric Psychology, 12*, 395–411.

Temple, C. M. (2002). Oral fluency and narrative production in children with Turner's syndrome. *Neuropsychologia, 40*(8), 1419–1427.

Temple, C. M., & Carney, R. A. (1993). Intellectual functioning of children with Turner syndrome: A comparison of behavioural phenotypes. *Developmental Medicine and Child Neurology, 35*(8), 691–698.

Temple, C. M., & Carney, R. A. (1995). Patterns of spatial functioning in Turner's syndrome. *Cortex, 31*, 109–118.

Temple, C. M., Carney, R. A., & Mullarkey, S. (1996). Frontal lobe function and executive skills in children with Turner's syndrome. *Developmental Neuropsychology, 12*(3), 343–363.

Temple, C.M., Marriott, A.J. (1998). Arithmetical ability and disability in Turner's syndrome: A cognitive neuropsychological analysis. *Developmental Neuropsychology, 14*(1), 47–67.

Turner, G., Webb, T., Wake, S., & Robinson, H. (1996). Prevalence of the fragile X syndrome. *American Journal of Medical Genetics, 64*(1), 196–197.

Vellutino, F. R., Scanlon, D. M., & Spearing, D. (1995). Semantic and phonological coding in poor and normal readers. *Journal of Experimental Child Psychology, 59*(1), 76–123.

Verkerk, A. J., Pieretti, M., Sutcliffe, J. S., Fu, Y. H., Kuhl, D. P., Pizzuti, A., Reiner, O., Richards, S., Victoria, M. F., Fuping Zhang, M. F. V., Eussen, B. E., van Ommen, G. J. B., Blonden, L. A. J., Riggins, G. J., Chastain, J. L., Kunst, C. B., Galjaard, H., Caskey, C. T., Nelson, D. L., Oostra, B. A., & Warren, S. T. (1991). Identification of a gene (FMR-1) containing a CGG repeat coincident with a breakpoint cluster region exhibiting length variation in fragile X syndrome. *Cell, 65*, 905–914.

Waber, D. P. (1979). Neuropsychological aspects of Turner's syndrome. *Developmental Medicine and Child Neurology, 21*, 58–70.

Williams, J., Richman, L., & Yarbrough, D. (1991). A comparison of memory and attention in Turner syndrome and learning disability. *Journal of Pediatric Psychology, 16*, 585–593.

17

Number Processing in Neurodevelopmental Disorders
Spina Bifida Myelomeningocele

Marcia A. Barnes
Brenda Smith-Chant
Susan H. Landry

Understanding how children learn to read and why some children have difficulty with reading has benefited from multi-disciplinary research in cognitive development, learning disabilities, and neurobiological factors. This integrated knowledge base has led to substantial changes in public policy that have affected both the assessment of reading and teaching practices (Fletcher et al., 2002). Understanding how children come to learn mathematics and why some find mathematics difficult may require a similar sustained research effort that builds knowledge across several domains of inquiry (Geary, 1993; Lyon, Fletcher & Barnes, 2003). The research presented in this chapter concerns math disabilities in children and adults with spina bifida myelomeningocele (SBM), a congenital disorder affecting the development of spine and brain.

Individuals with brain lesions have often been used to investigate the cognitive and neural architecture of various cognitive and academic skills such as math. These types of studies have been used to both investigate and develop theories of mathematical cognition (Dehaene, 1992; McCloskey, 1992). Such studies of acquired dyscalculia are also used to determine whether the selective disruption of a specific mathematical skill is related to a particular type of brain damage. More recently, cognitive neuroscience studies have used functional brain imaging to study mathematical cognition both in individuals with acquired brain lesions and in normal adults (Cohen, Dehaene, Cochon, Lehericy, & Naccache, 2000; Dehaene, Spelke, Pinel, Stanescu, & Tsivkin, 1999; Gruber, Indefry, & Kleinschmidt, 2001). These lesion and imaging studies have largely focused on adult math performance. While these investigations have been helpful in determining how math is organized in a mature cognitive system, they are less well suited to address issues specific to the developing cognitive and neural systems for math. Studies of how math is acquired in typically- and atypically-developing populations are needed to address such issues.

Much less research on math difficulties has been conducted in children with either acquired brain injuries (but see Ashcraft, Yamashita, & Aram, 1992) or neurodevelopmental disorders. There are a number of neurodevelopmental disorders associated with problems in math cognition, such as spina bifida, fragile X syndrome, and Turner syndrome (Mazzocco, 1998, 2001; Rovet, Szekely, & Hockenberry, 1994; Wills, 1993). Children with these disorders are of interest to the study of math disability for several reasons.

First, many of these disorders can be identified at or before birth. The ability to identify a population at risk of math disability very early in development provides a powerful tool for the longitudinal investigation of developmental precursors of math disability (Mazzocco, 2001). Neurodevelopmental conditions are also useful for studying life span issues in math disability such as whether the disability persists into adulthood and, if so, what the functional consequences of the disability might be. Furthermore, longitudinal investigations in these populations could allow for the study of interactions between environmental and neurobiological factors that affect the growth of math skills (Lyon et al., 2003). This latter research strategy has proven to be important for understanding the development of cognitive and academic skills in other groups of biologically "at risk" children (e.g., low-birth-weight children; Landry, Smith, Swank, & Loncar, 2000).

Second, the skill dissociations that often occur under conditions of brain disorder are useful for testing learning disability models. In many math disability models, for example, the presence or absence of a comorbid reading disability is related to the type of math disability that arises (Geary, 1993; Rourke, 1993). In math-disabled children with no neurological disorder, reading and math deficits typically co-occur (Alacron, DeFries, Light, & Pennington, 1997) and specific math disabilities, that is math disability without reading disability, are relatively less common (Lewis, Hitch, & Walker, 1994). In contrast, some neurodevelopmental disorders such as SBM and Turner syndrome are associated with fairly high rates of specific math disability (Fletcher et al., in press; Mazzocco, 2001; see chapter 16, this volume). These sorts of disorders, then, provide models within which to study different types of math disabilities and the core cognitive processes associated with those disabilities.

Third, to the extent that the neuropathology of a neurodevelopmental disorder is known, it provides a model within which to test brain-behavior hypotheses about the development of math. Such information cannot always be gathered from studies of acquired lesions in adulthood because different brain systems might be involved in the initial learning of math skills in contrast to those involved in skilled performance (Rourke & Conway, 1997). Such differences in brain activation during reading have been found for novice versus expert readers (Simos et al., 2001). SBM is a condition in which math is acquired by a disordered brain. Conditions in which a skill develops or fails to develop in the presence of brain abnormalities are of particular interest to issues of neural plasticity. When regions of the brain implicated in math cognition are damaged early in development, one can ask whether there is some reorganization of brain systems involved in math processing and also whether there are costs associated with this reorganization. This chapter describes recent research on math disability in individuals with SBM in relation to the three issues discussed above.

WHAT IS SPINA BIFIDA?

SBM is the most common severely disabling birth defect in North America and occurs in 0.5–0.7 per 1,000 live births. It arises from a complex pattern of gene/environment interactions, which produce a neural tube defect that is associated at birth with distinctive physical, neural, and cognitive phenotypes. The *physical phenotype* of SBM, with its spinal cord defect and orthopedic sequelae, is what is most commonly associated with this developmental disorder. The spinal dysraphism produces impairment of lower and upper extremity coordination, often with significant paraplegia and limited ambulation. Less well known and less well studied is the *neural phenotype* of SBM that involves significant disruption of brain development. The failure of neuroembryogenesis is associated with anomalies in the regional development of the brain, especially the corpus callosum, midbrain and tectum, and cerebellum. Additional injury to the brain is produced because of hydrocephalus, which arises from a blockage of cerebral spinal fluid flow due to a malformed cerebellum and hindbrain. Hydrocephalus necessitates shunt treatment in 80–90% of cases of SBM (Reigel & Rotenstein, 1994), and it disrupts not only the development of white matter tracts and myelination but also cortical neuronal development, particularly in posterior brain regions (del Bigio, 1993).

The *cognitive phenotype* of SBM involves a modal profile of preserved and impaired cognitive and academic skills. As a group, children with SBM are stronger in language and weaker in perceptual and motor skills (Barnes, 2002; Barnes & Dennis, 1998; Dennis et al., 1981; Fletcher et al. 1992). However, within visual-spatial perception, some skills such as object-based visual perception are better preserved than others such as action-based visual perception (Dennis et al., 2002). In the language domain many basic language skills such as vocabulary and syntax are intact, but inferential and discourse-level skills are not (Barnes & Dennis, 1998; Barnes, Faulkner, Wilkinson, & Dennis, 2004). In terms of academic competencies, math is impaired relative to word-recognition skills, and writing problems are common (Fletcher et al., 1995; Barnes et al., 2002). Aspects of this cognitive phenotype are associated with the diverse brain compromises in SBM. For example, children with SBM who have a thin posterior (parieto-occipital) cortex relative to their own anterior cortex, have problems in nonverbal cognition and visual-spatial function (Dennis et al., 1981; Fletcher et al., 1996). The combination of relatively strong verbal and reading decoding abilities, deficits in visual-spatial function, and known problems with math make SBM an interesting disorder in which to test current models of math disabilities.

A LIFE SPAN APPROACH TO THE STUDY OF MATH DISABILITY: PREVALENCE AND PATTERNS OF MATH DIFFICULTIES IN PRESCHOOLERS, ADULTS, AND SCHOOL-AGE CHILDREN WITH SBM

SBM has long been associated with math difficulty, based on studies of standardized achievement scores on tests of written or mental computation (Friedrich, Lovejoy, Shaffer, Shurtleff, & Beilke, 1991; Halliwell, Carr, & Pearson, 1980; Wills, Holmbeck, Dillon, & McLone, 1990). New findings from a program project on spina bifida with our colleagues Jack Fletcher at the University of Texas–Houston and Maureen Dennis at the Toronto Hospital for Sick Children provide important epidemiological information on learning difficulties in children with SBM. In a sample of over 300 children with SBM, only 2% had problems in word decoding alone, 20% had problems in both reading and math, and 21% had problems in math but not reading. We used a cut point of low achievement at the 25th percentile on the Letter–Word Identification and Calculations tests from the Woodcock-Johnson Revised Tests of Achievement (Woodcock & Johnson, 1989). This cut point has been used in several recent large studies of learning disabilities and has been shown to be a reliable marker of learning difficulties in children without general mental deficiency (see Fletcher et al., 2002; Stuebing et al., 2002). Even among children with SBM who were not math disabled, reading was typically better developed than math. Of interest was the finding that over a fifth of the sample had specific math disability, that is, math disability without comorbid reading disability (Fletcher et al., in press). Available figures for math disability in the general population are largely based on European studies that use more stringent cut points than those used in North America. In any event, these studies suggest a prevalence rate for math disabilities of about 6 percent in the general school-age population (Fleishner, 1994; Kosc, 1974; Shalev, Auerbach, Manor, & Gross-Tsur, 2000), and a population rate of specific math disability between 1–2% (Lewis et al., 1994).

The pattern of math deficits associated with SBM is observed across the lifespan. The rates of math disability in young adults with SBM are very similar to the prevalence of math disabilities observed in school-aged samples. In a group of 31 adults with SBM, over a third were disabled on tests of calculation and functional numeracy involving skills needed in grocery shopping, telling time, banking, following recipes, and so forth (Dennis & Barnes, 2002). In contrast, only one individual had a reading disability (Barnes, Dennis, & Hetherington, 2004). Of importance were the findings that math skills, but not reading skills, were related to functional independence and occupational status in adults with SBM. Lower scores on functional math skills were associated with unemployed status and overall lower quality of life (Hetherington, Dennis, Barnes, Drake, & Gentili, in press). These findings are consistent with human resource studies showing that numeracy skills predict employment status and productivity in the general population as well as, and sometimes better than, literacy (Rivera-Batiz, 1992).

As part of the program project on SBM, we have been prospectively following a birth cohort of children with SBM and their typically developing controls from southern Ontario and two cities in Texas. At 36 months of age, the children's early quantitative skills were assessed using both standardized and experimental math measures. The standardized measures were the Quantitative subtest from the Stanford-Binet Intelligence Scale–Fourth Edition (Thorndike, Hagen, & Sattler, 1986) and the Test of Early Math Ability–II or TEMA-II (Ginsburg & Baroody, 1990). In the Ontario sample, 41% and 74% of the 3-year-olds with SBM scored below the 25th percentile on the Quantitative subtest and the TEMA-II, respectively, compared to 13% and 39% of controls. The pattern of deficits in math for the SBM group relative to controls replicates the pattern observed in school-age children and adult math performance. However, the large number of children falling below the 25th percentile on these measures may reflect a problem in the ability of standardized tests to reliably capture skills that are beginning to emerge at the time of assessment, particularly when assessing children who are at the youngest age of the standardization sample (Mazzocco, 2001).

The preschool, school-age, and adult studies reported above are cross-sectional, and different math tasks were used across studies. Yet, the results support the notion that there may be considerable consistency in math difficulties from early childhood to adulthood among individuals with SBM. However, longitudinal data are needed to test how the development of early informal number skills is related to the acquisition of math skills at school age and how school-age math deficits and their remediation are related to functional outcomes in young adults. These relations are of particular importance given that we found learning disabilities in math have significant implications for employment and quality of life in adulthood.

Math Disability and SBM: Testing the Validity of Math Disability Subtypes

The presence or absence of a comorbid reading disability is central to several models of math disability, as reading disability plus math disability is associated with different cognitive markers than math disability alone (Morrison & Siegel, 1991; Rourke, 1993). Children with comorbid reading and math disability are characterized by deficits in verbal and visual working memory (Siegel & Ryan, 1989) and phonological processing (Swanson & Sachse-Lee, 2001). In contrast, specific math disability has been associated with difficulties in visual memory, visual-spatial working memory (McLean & Hitch, 1999; Siegel & Ryan, 1989), and visual-spatial function (Ackerman & Dykman, 1995; Rourke & Finlayson, 1978; Share, Moffit, & Silva, 1988). Within the domain of mathematical processing itself, recent studies show that the pattern of impairment on specific math skills is also related to the presence of a reading disability (Jordan, Hanich, & Kaplan, 2003). Children with math disability, regardless of their reading status, have difficulty with numerical estimation and rapid retrieval of number facts. Those with both reading and math disabilities have particular difficulty in areas of math assumed to be mediated by language, such as word problems and verbal counting (Hanich, Jordan, Kaplan, & Dick, 2001).

Models of math disability specify subtypes that are characterized by deficits in different core cognitive and neuropsychological processes and that are related in different ways to reading. For example, Geary (1993) proposed that deficits in math computation may arise from: (a) problems in learning, representing, and retrieving math facts from semantic memory, a subtype related to reading disability through a common proposed deficit in verbal working memory and phonological processing; (b) difficulties in the acquisition and use of developmentally-mature problem-solving strategies or procedures to perform mental or written calculations, a subtype in which the relation to reading is not specified; and (c) difficulties in the spatial representation and manipulation of number information, a less common subtype that is thought to characterize those individuals who have specific math impairment, with no reading disability.

As a disorder, SBM provides a particularly interesting test of this model of math disability. First, many children with SBM have specific math disabilities as well as visual-spatial dysfunction, which means that this group provides a strong test of the visual-spatial subtype. Second, a smaller number of children with SBM have comorbid reading and math disability in addition to visual-spatial dysfunction. These characteristics make this group a test case for a math disability involving deficits in both visual-spatial and phonological skills.

Subtyping models are based on the notion that deficits in different core cognitive skills result in different types of math disabilities. Another class of models is based on neurodevelopmental hypotheses about relations between the development of brain and behavior (Butterworth, 1999). Such models have implications for both typical and atypical development of math skills. For example, Butterworth (1999) has proposed that because fingers are represented in parietal lobes and young children use fingers to count, number also comes to be represented in the parietal lobe. These ideas arise from observations in the neuropsychological literature of links between calculation, finger function, and parietal lobe, in both acquired and developmental disorders of math (e.g., Kinsbourne & Warrington, 1963; Rourke & Strang, 1978; Verney, 1984), as well as from observations of the ways in which children develop counting systems. Young children across cultures use their fingers to count and when they begin to do simple arithmetic, they use fingers to calculate. Thus, using fingers to count and calculate is thought to result in instantiation of number concepts in parietal lobes (Butterworth, 1999). Little research has been conducted on the relationship between the development of finger abilities and math skills. Fayol and his colleagues have shown that perceptuo-tactile abilities of 5-year-old children predict their performance on a variety of math tasks in kindergarten, and on arithmetic word problem solving at the end of first grade (Fayol, Barrouillet, & Marinthe, 1998).

Why is the relation between fingers and math ability relevant with respect to SBM? The brain anomalies associated with SBM affect finger function, motor planning, and fine motor speed (Fletcher et al., 1995; Hetherington & Dennis, 1999), which are related to relatively greater thinning of posterior than anterior cerebral cortex (Fletcher et al., 1996). Thus, SBM is a condition in which fine motor deficits are common and related to damage to the parietal lobes. If normal development of counting and basic arithmetic is based on proficiency in using fingers to count, then children with fine motor deficits ought to have difficulty in acquiring counting and calculation skills. Because parietal lobes are implicated in both fine motor and visual-spatial function, SBM provides one research strategy for studying the relative contributions of these abilities to math.

We discuss three approaches to understanding the nature of math disability in SBM. One is the investigation of the nature of math processing itself using methods adopted from cognitive developmental studies of math cognition and math disability (Geary, 2003; Geary, Hamson, & Hoard, 2000; Jordan & Hanich, 2000). Another is an investigation of the relations between performance on various math tasks and particular neuropsychological skills such as visual-spatial and fine motor function. The third is a study of the emergence of early math skills in the preschool years to identify developmental precursors and predictors of early numeracy. We discuss these three research strategies below.

Experimental Studies of Computational Skills in Children with SBM and in Typically Developing Controls

We were interested to see whether the known visual-spatial deficits associated with SBM might also be related to their math disability. Although this putative connection between visual-spatial skill and math has been discussed in the SBM literature for some time (Wills, 1993), the relation had not been explicitly tested. Based on the math disability model proposed by Geary (1993), we expected that children with SBM who were good word decoders would not differ from controls in processes related to math fact retrieval (a skill associated with reading ability) but that children with comorbid reading and math disability would have deficits in this area. We also expected that computational errors made by children with SBM would reflect problems in visual-spatial processing, regardless of reading status.

We tested these hypotheses using a 20-problem multidigit written subtraction task (vanLehn, 1982) in which errors were coded as reflecting problems related to the three math disability subtypes. Three types of errors were coded:

1. Math fact retrieval errors reflecting an error on single-digit subtraction within the multi-digit problem even when borrowing procedures might have been accomplished correctly. This type of math difficulty is presumed to characterize children with reading disability.
2. Errors reflecting the misapplication of arithmetic procedures, which could take several forms including always subtracting the smaller from the larger number and problems in borrowing across multiple zeros. These types of difficulties are not thought to be related to reading ability.
3. Errors due to problems in visual-spatial processing or manipulation of numbers such as misreading or miswriting numbers, neglecting one side of the problem, misalignment of numbers in columns, and so forth (Hartje, 1987). These types of math difficulties are thought to be unrelated to reading ability. Examples of error types can be found in Table 17.1.

We compared 60 good readers with SBM to 60 age- and grade-matched controls and a smaller group of 24 poor readers with SBM to age-matched controls. The children ranged in age from 8 to 16 years, with an average age of close to 12 years. As predicted, children with SBM who had comorbid reading and math difficulties made more math fact-retrieval errors as well as more procedural and visual-spatial errors. Also, consistent with our prediction, good readers with SBM and controls made very few math fact-retrieval errors. However, in contrast to predictions, the SBM group did not make more visual-spatial errors. Rather, this group differed from controls only in the rate of procedural errors (Khemani & Barnes, 2004; Fletcher et al., in press; see similar results in Barnes et al., 2002). Visual-spatial deficits are found in both good and poor readers with SBM, suggesting that these results are not simply due to group differences in visual-spatial function. The results are not particular to multidigit subtraction but have also been found for multidigit addition, multiplication, and division (Barnes, Pengelly, Dennis, Falkner, & Wilkinson, 1998).

Although error analyses are informative for investigating cognitive processes, they may not be as sensitive as other measures for inferring underlying cognitive deficits. Errors reflect processes on only a subset of trials. In contrast, measures such as reaction time and strategy use can tap cognitive processing on all trials. Although the error analyses revealed no deficit in math fact retrieval for good readers with SBM, a more stringent test of the hypothesis that their math fact retrieval is intact requires knowledge not only of math fact retrieval accuracy,

Table 17.1
Examples of Errors for Written Subtraction

Math fact error:

$$\begin{array}{r} {}^{5}\llap{\raise1ex\hbox{$/$}}562 \\ -\ 3 \\ \hline 558 \end{array}$$

Procedural errors:

$$\begin{array}{r} 311 \\ -214 \\ \hline 103 \end{array} \qquad \begin{array}{r} 742 \\ -136 \\ \hline 616 \end{array} \qquad \begin{array}{r} 9007 \\ -6880 \\ \hline 3127 \end{array}$$

Smaller from larger   No decrement with   Problems borrowing
borrow   across zero

Visual-spatial / Visual monitoring errors:

$$\begin{array}{r} 647 \\ -45 \\ \hline 682 \end{array} \qquad \begin{array}{r} 10012 \\ -214 \\ \hline 788 \end{array}$$

Add instead of subtract   Error due to crowding
for part of problem

Notes.
[1]In theory, the ability to distinguish between math fact errors and errors due to miswriting or misreading numbers (coded as visual errors) would appear difficult. In practice, math fact errors typically differ from the correct answer by "1," suggesting retrieval of a closely associated but incorrect math fact: in this example, 11 – 3 = 8 instead of 12 – 3 = 9. Errors due to misreading or miswriting numbers were very rare. Examples would be: (a) writing a "6" when the answer is "9" or (b) writing "48" as the answer to 79 – 28, with the assumption that 79 was misread as 76.
[2]The distinction between certain visual and procedural errors is related to the context in which the error occurs. The first example of a visual error above was coded as such because the child added instead of subtracted the middle column in only one problem. Had the child consistently added the middle column of each subtraction problem the error would be procedural.

but also of retrieval speed and use of computational strategies. Recent studies of children with specific math disability and no neurological disorder have shown that math fact retrieval in good readers may not be entirely intact (Hanich, et al., 2001; Jordan et al., 2003). To more closely investigate math fact-retrieval processes, we employed a cognitive addition task commonly used in cognitive and developmental studies of math cognition (e.g., Ashcraft, 1992; Siegler, 1988).

The same 60 good readers with SBM, and their controls, completed a task in which single-digit addition problems were presented on a computer screen (e.g., 4 + 3 = ?). The child had to say the answer as quickly, but as accurately as possible. On a per-trial basis, computational strategies were observed by the experimenter and verified by asking the child to say how he or she got the answer. Strategy use was coded in sequence from most- to least-developmentally mature as follows: (a) direct retrieval: the child just knew the answer for 3 + 4 was 7; (b) counting up or on: the child counted up from the highest number: 4, 5, 6, 7; (c) counting all or sum: the child counted: 1, 2, 3, 4, 5, 6, 7. Finger counting and verbal counting were also recorded.

Based on the subtyping model, good readers with SBM were expected to show intact math fact retrieval relative to controls in terms of accuracy, speed, and developmentally appropriate use of strategies. However, we predicted that good readers with SBM would be slower than controls on trials in which they used a finger-counting strategy due to poor fine motor skills or because counting strategies have been related to visual-spatial skill (Geary, 1993). Therefore, mean reaction times for retrieval and each strategy type were calculated separately.

Consistent with the prediction that math fact retrieval should be intact in good readers, the SBM group was as accurate as controls in solving the single-digit arithmetic problems (85% and 86% accuracy, respectively), and both groups showed high consistency between their reported use of strategies and examiner-observed strategies. Although both groups solved most problems using direct retrieval, the SBM group used retrieval on fewer trials and counting up on more trials than controls (Direct Retrieval: 71% vs. 81%; Counting Up: 23% vs. 11%). In terms of reaction time measures, the SBM group was slower than controls on both the counting up trials and memory retrieval trials (Barnes & Wilkinson, 2002; Fletcher et al., in press; Khemani & Barnes, in press). These results are not simply related to general speed of processing deficits in SBM, as good readers with SBM are not slow at reading words (Barnes, Faulkner, & Dennis, 2001). Slower reaction times for the SBM group appear attributable to a specific difficulty with solving simple arithmetic problems.

These results are *not* consistent with models of math disability in which math fact retrieval would be expected to be intact in good readers. They add to a growing body of literature suggesting that difficulties in mastering math facts, including fluency of fact retrieval, may constitute a core or defining deficit in math disabilities regardless of reading status (Jordan et al., 2003). We suggest that slow math fact retrieval may lead to processing bottlenecks, reducing cognitive resources needed for learning and applying more complex arithmetic procedures (Goldman, Pellegrino, & Mertz, 1988). In other words, slow and effortful retrieval processes in simple calculation could lead to problems in learning and applying procedural knowledge in multidigit arithmetic. Our ongoing longitudinal study may provide information about whether efficiency in basic arithmetic computations is a foundation skill upon which more complex math concepts and procedures are based.

Correlation Studies of Visual-Spatial and Fine Motor Abilities and Math

A commonly used approach in the math disability literature has been to look at relations between math performance and measures of cognitive skills of interest, such as working memory (e.g., Wilson & Swanson, 2001). The error analysis reported earlier failed to find differences in rates of visual-spatial errors for good readers with SBM and controls. Here we used a correlation approach to examine the association between visual-spatial abilities, fine-motor skill, and performance on a calculation test, being careful to use a relatively motor-free test of visual-spatial ability (Spatial Relations from the Woodcock Johnson–Revised Tests of Cognitive Ability; Woodcock & Johnson, 1989) and a relatively visual-spatial-free test of fine motor ability (Purdue Pegboard).

Multiple-regression analysis was used to predict written subtraction accuracy from the visual-spatial and fine motor measures. The resulting model was able to account for 28% of the variance on written subtraction. However, only the contribution of fine motor skills was significant. The results of the multiple regression are consistent with those from the error analysis; visual-spatial skills appear unrelated to multidigit calculation. Rather, the ability to calculate was associated with fine motor skill. We will return to the issue of fine motor skills and the relation to math performance when we discuss math studies in preschoolers with SBM.

Are Visual-Spatial Skills Related to Other Aspects of Math in SBM?

Other areas of math including estimation, geometry, and word problems are associated with visual-spatial skill in normal adults (Dehaene et al., 1999; Geary, 1996). These areas of math might be particularly disrupted in individuals with SBM and also related to their visual-spatial deficits. Using a traditional multi-domain diagnostic math test, the Keymath Test–Revised

(Connolly, 1991; Barnes et al., 2002) found that school-age children with SBM were more impaired on Keymath Geometry, Estimation, and Word Problems relative to their performance on tests of Keymath written Operations. Furthermore, visual-spatial skills were related to performance on the geometry and estimation tasks for both SBM and control groups. Children with SBM do have particular difficulties with aspects of math known to be associated with visual-spatial ability.

The school-age studies of math in children with SBM are informative for several reasons. We proposed that good readers with SBM provide a test case for a visual-spatial subtype of disability in math calculation because these children have visual-spatial deficits related to their congenital brain abnormalities as well as a very high rate of math disability. Neither the investigations of calculation errors nor the regression study provided support for this subtype. Deficits in multidigit calculation and visual-spatial skill clearly co-occur but appear not to be related in our studies. This information adds to a growing evidence base that questions those aspects of math disability models that relate underlying visual-spatial deficits to problems in calculation (Cirino, Morris, & Morris, 2002; Mazzocco, 2001; Rovet et al., 1994). However, this is not to say that visual-spatial abilities are entirely unrelated to calculation skills. The nature of the relation between math and visual-spatial ability may depend on a number of factors, including which math skills are considered, the type of visual-spatial processing involved (e.g., visual-spatial working memory vs. other aspects of spatial processing), and when in the development of a particular math skill the relationship is measured. For example, strategy choice in acquiring computational skills may be related to spatial ability (Geary & Burlingham-Dubree, 1989), and solving nonverbal problems involving addition and subtraction is related to visual-spatial working memory in preschoolers (see chapter 9 of this volume).

These studies of math in children with SBM are informative for models of math disability in another way, in that in combination with what is known about calculation deficits in children with math disability and no neurological disorder, they provide evidence that a limited number of cognitive mechanisms may underlie problems in calculation. Children with SBM and comorbid reading and math disability have pervasive problems in many math processes, including accuracy and fluency of math fact retrieval as well as knowledge of math procedures. These findings are consistent with those from cognitive studies of comorbid reading and math disability in children without neurological disorder (Geary, 2003; Hanich et al., 2001; Jordan and Hanich, 2000; Jordan et al., 2003). Good readers with SBM are accurate but slow at math fact retrieval, and they have problems with computational procedures in both mental and written arithmetic. These findings are similar to those observed in children with specific math disability and no neurological disorder (Jordan et al., 2003). Such consistency across different groups of math-disabled children, some with frank brain injury and others without, provides constraints on learning disability models and converging evidence for core deficits in math disability subtypes.

It is likely that the math disabilities in SBM have their origin in early childhood. These math difficulties might best be understood by studying the developmental precursors of the deficits in math and by identifying the factors that influence growth in math skills during infancy and the preschool years. In the next section, we discuss the cognitive skills that are related to emerging numeracy in three-year-olds with SBM.

EARLY NUMERACY SKILLS OF CHILDREN WITH SBM AND CONTROLS

We used the Ontario cohort of young children with SBM and their controls at 3 years of age to explore emerging numeracy skills and their relation to developing cognitive and motor competencies. Prior to the 36-month assessment, these groups had been followed at several time points from 6 months of age. At their 3-year visit, the children were assessed using standardized and experimental tests of language, visual-spatial and fine motor skill, social and behavioral development, attention and problem solving, and early number and quantitative skills. In this section we discuss relations between three math measures and visual-spatial and fine motor function to follow on the themes of the school-age studies.

The three math tests were:

1. The Quantitative subtest from the Stanford-Binet-IV, which largely measures matching on the basis of number at 36 months.
2. The TEMA-II, which measures object counting and finger counting (e.g., "show me two fingers") as well as quantitative vocabulary at this age. The TEMA-II was treated as an experimental test, in that individual items within trials were scored, which provided a larger range of outcomes at 36 months.
3. A derived score from the Mental Scale of the Bayley Scales of Infant Development–2nd Edition (Bayley, 1993), consisting of four items measuring counting concepts (the number series, or knowledge of counting number series to 3; one-to-one correspondence, or knowledge that items are counted once and only once; stable order, or the knowledge that the order of the counting series is invariable; and cardinality, or the knowledge that the final number reached in a count represents the quantity).

The measure of visual-spatial function was Pattern Analysis from the Stanford-Binet-IV, which, at 36 months, involves placing shapes into a puzzle board and putting simple shapes together. The fine motor measure was the Visual-Motor Integration test (Beery, 1989), which, for 3-year-olds, involves using a pencil to copy lines and circles. Unlike the tasks used in the studies of school-age children, the visual-spatial test at 36 months has a motor component and the fine motor test has a visual-spatial component. However, the analyses consider the unique variance in math scores predicted by each task.

Based on the assumption that math disabilities at school age arise from deficits in core cognitive skills affected by the early brain insult associated with SBM, we expected to find relations between early number skills and these core cognitive skills at 36 months. We predicted that fine motor skill might be related to counting (Butterworth, 1999), as measured by the items tapping conceptual knowledge of counting principles from the Bayley Mental Scale and as measured by the TEMA-II that requires the child to demonstrate the ability to count. Based on the school-age findings, we did not make predictions about visual-spatial contributions to performance on the math measures.

To provide an analogue to the good-reader SBM group in the studies of school-age children, we considered relations between math and cognitive skills only for those children with SBM and their controls scoring at or above the 25th percentile on the Stanford-Binet Vocabulary subtest. Because the samples were relatively small and because there is every reason to expect that the purported relations between math and core cognitive skills should apply to both typical and atypical development, we combined the SBM and control groups for analysis.

A multiple regression analysis was used to look at the unique association of visual-spatial and fine motor abilities in predicting performance on the three math measures. We found that the test of fine motor skill predicted significant and unique variance on both the Counting Concepts measure from the Bayley Mental Scale and on the experimental measure from the TEMA-II. Visual-spatial abilities did not contribute to the prediction of scores on these two math tasks. In contrast, the test of visual-spatial ability predicted significant and unique variance on the Quantitative subtest from the Stanford-Binet-IV, but fine motor ability did not predict significant variance on this task. These findings suggest that visual-spatial skills are related to math tasks involving visual-perceptual abilities such as matching by quantity, whereas fine motor abilities are related to counting, independent of visual-spatial ability (Ladd et al., 2002). This pattern is consistent with what we observed in school-age children. The data we have presented are correlational. We cannot infer that finger use is important for the *acquisition* of counting and basic computational abilities, nor can we infer that visual-spatial skills are related to the *development* of other aspects of math ability. Our longitudinal data from infancy to 36 months in conjunction with ongoing model-driven assessments of mathematical processing and visual-spatial and fine motor skills as these children turn 5 may provide such information.

BRAIN-BEHAVIOR RELATIONSHIPS IN MATH AND NEURODEVELOPMENTAL DISORDERS

In the previous section, SBM was considered to be of interest to the study of mathematical cognition and math learning disability because it is associated with a cognitive phenotype of preserved and deficient cognitive skills implicated in models of math disability. This cognitive phenotype can also be studied in relation to the neural phenotype of SBM to investigate brain-behavior relations in skill development. SBM might also be used to understand possible cerebral reorganization of cognitive and academic functions in these children and whether there are costs in terms of lags in skill development or deficits in skill mastery or skill fluency (Dennis, 1988) as a result of this reorganization. Almost nothing is known about cerebral reorganization in any population of children with either congenital or acquired brain insults (Broman & Fletcher, 1999).

Quantitative segmentations of anatomical magnetic resonance images in children with SBM have been correlated with scores on standardized tests of cognitive and motor functions (Fletcher et al., 1992, 1996). These studies have shown that the distribution of gray matter, white matter, and cerebral spinal fluid (CSF) is different in children with SBM and their age peers. The posterior regions of brain have reduced volumes of gray and white matter and increased CSF volume. In contrast, anterior regions of brain are more similar to those of age-match controls. Fine motor skills are strongly and consistently correlated with these posterior brain measurements, and weaker, but still significant, relations between scores on visual perception tests and posterior brain volume have been found. These findings are of considerable interest in light of the previous discussion of putative relations between visual-spatial and fine motor function and math skills.

Whether and how visual-spatial processing and fine motor function are related to the development of math skills in both typical and atypical development, is currently unknown. The study of children with damage to areas of brain involved in visual-spatial processing and fine motor function may be particularly informative in testing some of these relations. We are currently looking at correlations between brain volume in regions of interest in children with SBM and visual-spatial, fine motor, and math function, which may provide some clues about the relation between cognitive and neural phenotypes for math in these children. However, correlation cannot establish whether certain brain mechanisms actually mediate cognitive, motor, and academic functions. One fruitful avenue for research may be the use of functional brain-imaging methods to study specific cognitive processes such as math fact retrieval (Whalen, McCloskey, Lesser, & Gordon, 1997) in children with and without math difficulties. Such methods have been used to provide information about patterns of brain activation and developmental changes in activation in both nondisabled and reading-disabled children (Simos et al., 2001). These methods may also be informative for studies of potential reorganization of brain circuits in response to early brain insults, which is of interest to the study of plasticity and vulnerability in the development of mathematical cognition.

CONCLUSIONS

We described recent findings from an ongoing study of mathematical cognition in children with the neurodevelopmental disorder spina bifida myelomeningocele that is associated with difficulties in math, spatial cognition, and fine motor skill. Findings are summarized in Table

Table 17.2
Math Disability in Children with and without SBM

	SBM	No SBM
Prevalence		
Total MD (MD + RD & MD Only)	40%[1]	6–7% [2]
Specific MD (MD only)	20–25%[1]	1–2%[3]
MD + RD		
Math Fact Retrieval	Deficit [1, 4]	Deficit[5, 6, 7]
Procedural Skills: Addition Strategies,		
Multidigit Arithmetic Algorithms	Deficit [1, 4]	Deficit[6,7]
Specific MD		
Math Fact Retrieval	Accurate but slow[1,4, 8]	Accurate but slow [5, 6]
Procedural Skills: Addition Strategies,		
Multidigit Arithmetic Algorithms	Deficit [1,4, 8, 9]	Deficit [6, 10]

Note. RD = Reading Disability, MD = Math Disability
[1] Fletcher et al., in press
[2] Fleishner, 1994; Kosc, 1974; Shalev et al., 2000
[3] Lewis et al., 1994
[4] Barnes et al., 2004
[5] Hanich et al., 2001
[6] Jordan et al., 2003
[7] Geary et al., 2000
[8] Barnes & Wilkinson, 2002; Khemani & Barnes, 2004
[9] Barnes et al., 2002
[10] Geary, 2003

17.2. Math difficulties in this group are common at school age, measurable very early in development, and persist into adulthood, with implications for employment and functional independence. SBM was used as a test case for cognitive deficit models of math disability in which visual-spatial problems are presumed to underlie calculation disorders in children with specific math disability. We found no evidence to support this aspect of the math disability model. However, the studies of school-age children and preschoolers did provide support for the notion that different domains of mathematical function may rely on different core cognitive processes (Geary, 1994; LeFevre, 2000). Investigation of developmental and individual differences in math will need to consider measurement of various math domains as well as the possibility that growth in these domains may be associated with different cognitive skills and trajectories of development. Our ongoing longitudinal investigations of children with SBM, and their typically developing controls from infancy into the preschool and school-age years, will be informative for addressing some of these issues.

ACKNOWLEDGMENT

This research was supported by project grants to M. Barnes from the Ontario Mental Health Foundation and to M. Barnes and S. Landry from the Canadian Institutes of Health Research, and by NICHD Grant HD35946. We thank Margaret Wilkinson, Stephanie Lane, Amy Boudousquie, Laura Lomax-Bream, Michelle Ladd, and Kim Copeland for their assistance with this research, the children and their parents who participated in these studies, and the children, teachers, and staff of the Hamilton-Wentworth Catholic School Board for their participation.

REFERENCES

Ackerman, P. T., & Dykman, R. A. (1995). Reading-disabled students with and without comorbid arithmetic disability. *Developmental Neuropsychology, 11*, 351–371.

Alarcon, M., DeFries, J. C., Light, J. G., & Pennington, B. F. (1997). A twin study of mathematics disability. *Journal of Learning Disabilities, 30*, 617–623.

Ashcraft, M. (1992). Cognitive arithmetic: A review of data and theory. *Cognition, 44*, 75–106.

Ashcraft, M. H., Yamashita, T. S., & Aram, D. M., (1992). Mathematics performance in left and right brain-lesioned children and adolescents. *Brain and Cognition, 19*, 208–252.

Barnes, M. A. (2002). The decoding-comprehension dissociation in the reading of children with hydrocephalus: Reply to Yamada. *Brain and Language, 80*, 260–263.

Barnes, M. A., & Dennis, M. (1998). Discourse after early-onset hydrocephalus: Core deficits in children of average intelligence. *Brain and Language, 61*, 309–334.

Barnes, M. A, Dennis, M., & Hetherington, R. (2004). Reading and Writing Skills in Young Adults with Spina Bifida and Hydrocephalus. *Journal of the International Neuropsychological Society, 10*, 680–688.

Barnes, M. A., Faulkner, H., & Dennis, M. (2001). Poor reading comprehension despite fast word decoding in children with hydrocephalus. *Brain and Language, 76*, 35–44.

Barnes, M. A., Faulkner, H., Wilkinson, M., & Dennis, M. (2004). Meaning construction and integration in children with hydrocephalus. *Brain and Language, 89*, 47–56.

Barnes, M. A., Wilkinson, M., Boudousquie, A., Khemani, E., Dennis, M., & Fletcher, J. M. (2004). *Arithmetic processing in children with spina bifida: Calculation accuracy, strategy use, and fact retrieval fluency.* Manuscript submitted for review.

Barnes, M. A., Pengelly, S., Dennis, M., Faulkner, H., & Wilkinson, M. (1998). *Math processing in good readers with hydrocephalus.* Abstracts, Meeting of the Canadian Society for Brain and Behavior and Cognitive Sciences, Ottawa, Ontario.

Barnes, M.A., Pengelly, S., Dennis, M., Wilkinson, M., Rogers, T., & Faulkner, H. (2002). Mathematics skills in good readers with hydrocephalus. *Journal of the International Neuropsychological Society, 8*, 72–82.

Barnes, M. A., & Wilkinson, M. (2002). Math fact retrieval in good readers with spina bifida: Speed and strategy choice. *Journal of the International Neuropsychological Society, 8*, 316.

Bayley, N. (1993). *Bayley Scales of Infant Development–2nd Edition.* San Antonio TX: The Psychological Corporation.

Beery, K. (1989). *The Beery-Buktenica Test of Visual-Motor Integration–3rd Edition.* Cleveland, OH: Modern Curriculum Press.

Broman, S. H., & Fletcher, J. M. (Eds.). *The changing nervous systems: Neurobehavioral consequences of early brain disorders.* New York: Oxford University Press, 1999

Butterworth, B. (1999). *What counts: How every brain is hardwired for math.* New York: Simon and Schuster.

Cirino, P.T., Morris, M. K., & Morris, R. D. (2002). Neuropsychological concomitants of calculation skills in college students referred for learning difficulties. *Developmental Neuropsychology, 21*, 201–218.

Cohen, L., Dehaene, S., Cochon, F., Lehericy, S., & Naccache, L. (2000). Language and calculation within the parietal lobe. A combined cognitive, anatomical and fMRI study. *Neuropsychologia, 38*, 1426–1440

Connolly, A. J. (1991). *Canadian Edition of KeyMath-Revised.* Toronto, Ontario: Psycan.

Dehaene, S. (1992). Varieties of numerical abilities. *Cognition, 44*, 1–42.

Dehaene, S., Spelke, E., Pinel, P., Stanescu, R., & Tsivkin, S. (1999). Sources of mathematical thinking: Behavioral and brain-imaging evidence. *Science, 284*, 970–974.

del Bigio, M. (1993). Neuropathological changes caused by hydrocephalus. *Acta Neuropathologica, 18*, 573–585.

Dennis, M. (1988). Language and the young damaged brain. In T. Boll & B.K. Bryant (Eds.), *Clinical neuropsychology and brain function: Research, measurement, and practice: Volume 7. The master lecture series* (pp. 89–123). Washington, DC: American Psychological Corporation.

Dennis, M., & Barnes, M. A. (2002). Math and numeracy in young adults with spina bifida and hydrocephalus. *Developmental Neuropsychology, 21*, 141–156.

Dennis, M., Fitz, C. R., Netley, C. T., Sugar, J., Harwood-Nash, D. C .F., Hendrick, E. B., Hoffman, H. J., & Humphreys, R. P. (1981). The intelligence of hydrocephalic children. *Archives of Neurology, 38*, 607–615.

Dennis, M., Fletcher, J.M., Rogers, S., Hetherington, R., & Francis, D. (2002). Object-based and action-based visual perception in children with spina bifida and hydrocephalus. *Journal of the International Neuropsychological Society, 8*, 95–106.

Fayol, M., Barrouillet, P., Marinthe, C. (1998). Predicting arithmetical achievement from neuro-psychological performance: A longitudinal study. *Cognition, 68*, 63–70.

Fleishner, J. E. (1994). Diagnosis and assessment of mathematics disabilities. In G.R. Lyon (Ed.), *Frames of reference for the assessments of learning disabilities: New views on measurement issues* (pp. 441–458). Baltimore, MD: Brooks.

Fletcher, J. M., Bohan, T. P., Brandt, M. E., Brookshire, B. L., Beaver, S. R., Francis, D. J., Davidson, K. C., Thompson, N. M., & Miner, M. E. (1992). Cerebral white matter and cognition in hydrocephalic children. *Archives of Neurology, 49*, 818–824.

Fletcher, J. M., Bohan, T. P., Brandt, M. E., Kramer, L. A., Brookshire, B. L., Thorstad, K., Davidson, K. C., Francis, D. L., McCauley, S. R., & Baumgartner, J. E. (1996). Morphometric evaluation of the hydrocephalic brain: Relationships with cognitive development. *Child's Nervous System, 12*, 192–199.

Fletcher, J. M., Brookshire, B. L., Bohan, T. P., Brandt, M. E., & Davidson, K. C. (1995). Early hydrocephalus. In B. P. Rourke (Ed.), *Syndrome of nonverbal learning disabilities: Neurodevelopmental manifestations* (pp. 206–238). New York: Guilford.

Fletcher, J. M., Dennis, M., Northrup, H., Barnes, M.

A., Hannay, H. J., Landry, S. H., Copeland, K., Blaser, S. E., Kramer, L. A., Brandt, M. E., & Francis, D. J.(in press). Spina bifida: Genes, brain, and development. In Glidden, L. M. (Ed.), *Handbook of research on mental retardation* (Vol. 28). San Diego: Academic Press.

Fletcher, J. M., Lyon, G. R., Barnes, M. A., Stuebing, K. K., Francis, D. J., Olson, R. K., Shaywitz, S. E., & Shaywitz, B. A. (2002). Classification of learning disabilities: An evidence-based evaluation. In R. Bradley, L. Danielson, & D. Hallahan (Eds.), *Identification of learning disabilities: Research in practice* (pp. 185–250). Mahwah, NJ: Erlbaum.

Friedrich, W. N., Lovejoy, M.C., Shaffer, J., Shurtleff, D B., & Beilke, R. L. (1991). Cognitive abilities and achievement status of children with myelomeningocele: A contemporary sample. *Journal of Pediatric Psychology,16*(4), 423–428.

Geary, D. C. (1993). Mathematical disabilities: Cognitive, neuropsychological, and genetic components. *Psychological Bulletin, 114,* 345–362.

Geary, D. C. (1994). *Children's mathematical development.* Washington, DC: American Psychological Association.

Geary, D. C. (1996). Sexual selection and sex differences in mathematical abilities. *Behavioral and Brain Sciences, 19,* 229–284.

Geary, D. C. (2003). Learning disabilities in arithmetic: Problem-solving differences and cognitive deficits. In H. L. Swanson, K. R. Harris, & S. Graham (Eds.), *Handbook of learning disabilities* (pp. 199–212). New York: Guilford.

Geary, D. C., & Burlingham-Dubree, M. (1989). External validity of the strategy choice model for addition. *Journal of Experimental Child Psychology, 47,* 175–192.

Geary, D. C., Hamson, C. O., & Hoard, M. K. (2000). Numerical and arithmetical cognition: A longitudinal study of process and concept deficits in children with learning disability. *Journal of Experimental Child Psychology, 77,* 236–263.

Ginsburg, H. P., & Baroody, A. J. (1990). *Test of Early Mathematics Ability (TEMA-2).* Pro-Ed Inc.

Goldman, S. R., Pellegrino, J. W., & Mertz, D. L. (1988). Extended practice of basic addition facts: Strategy changes in learning-disabled students. *Cognition and Instruction, 5,* 223–265.

Gruber, O., Indefrey, P., & Kleinschimdt, A. (2001). Dissociating neural correlates of cognitive components in mental calculation. *Cerebral Cortex, 11,* 350–359

Halliwell, M. D., Carr, J. G., & Pearson, A. M. (1980). The intellectual and educational functioning of children with neural tube defects. *Zeitschrift fur Kinderchirurgie, 31,* 375–381.

Hanich, L., Jordan, N., Kaplan, D., & Dick, J. (2001). Performance across different areas of mathematical cognition in children with learning difficulties. *Journal of Educational Psychology, 93,* 615–626.

Hartje, W. (1987). The effect of spatial disorders on arthimetical skills. In G. Deloche & X. Seron (Eds.), *Mathematical disabilities: A cognitive neuropsychological perspective* (pp. 121–135). Hillsdale, NJ: Erlbaum.

Hetherington, R., & Dennis, M. (1999). Motor function profile in children with early onset hydrocephalus. *Developmental Neuropsychology, 15,* 25–51.

Hetherington, R., Dennis, M., Barnes, M. A., Drake, J., & Gentilli, F. (in press). Functional outcomes in young adults with spina bifida and hydrocephalus. *Child's Nervous System.*

Jordan, N. C., & Hanich, L. (2000). Mathematical thinking in second-grade children with different forms of LD. *Journal of Learning Disabilities, 33,* 567–578.

Jordan, N. C., Hanich, L. B., & Kaplan, D. (2003). A longitudinal study of mathematical competence in children with specific math difficulties versus children with comorbid mathematics and reading difficulties. *Child Development, 74,* 834–850.

Khemani, E., & Barnes, M. A. (in press). Basic computational math skills and math fluency in children with spina bifida. *Journal of the International Neuropsychological Society* (Abstract).

Kinsbourne, M., & Warrington, E. K. (1963). The developmental Gerstmann syndrome. *Archives of Neurology, 8,* 490–501.

Kosc, L. (1974). Developmental dyscalculia. *Journal of Learning Disabilities, 7,* 46–59.

Ladd, M., Lane, S., Smith-Chant, B., Wilkinson, M., Landry, S., & Barnes, MA. (2002). The development of number skills in preschoolers and school-age children with Spina Bifida. *International Society for the Study of Behavioral Development,* ISSBD Abstracts CD ROM

Landry, S. H., Smith, K. E., Swank, P. R., & Loncar, C. L. (2000): Early maternal and child influences on children's later independent cognitive and social functioning. *Child Development, 71*(2), 358–375.

LeFevre, J. (2000). Research on the development of academic skills: Introduction to the special issue on early literacy and early numeracy. *Canadian Journal of Experimental Psychology, 54,* 57–60.

Lewis, C., Hitch, G. J., & Walker, P. (1994). The prevalence of specific arithmetic difficulties and specific reading difficulties in 9- to 10-year-old boys and girls. *Journal of Child Psychology Psychiatry, 35,* 283–292.

Lyon, G. R., Fletcher, J. M., & Barnes, M. A. (2003). Learning disabilities. In E. J. Marsh & R. A. Barkley (Eds.), *Child psychopathology* (2nd ed., pp. 520–586). New York: Guilford.

Mazzocco, M. M. (1998). A process approach to describing mathematics difficulties in girls with Turner syndrome. *Pediatrics, 2*(3), 492–496.

Mazzocco, M. M. (2001). Math learning disability and math LD subtypes: Evidence from studies of Turner syndrome, fragile X syndrome, and neurofibromatosis type 1. *Journal of Learning Disabilities, 34,* 520–533.

McLean, J. F., & Hitch, G. J. (1999). Working memory impairments in children with specific arithmetic learning difficulties. *Journal of Experimental Child Psychology, 74,* 240–260.

McCloskey, M. (1992). Cognitive mechanisms in numerical processing: Evidence from acquired dyscalculia. *Cognition, 44,* 107–157.

Morrison, S. R., & Siegel, L. S. (1991). Learning desabilities: A critical review of definitional and assessment issues. In J. E. Obrzut & G. W. Hynd (Eds.), *Neuropsychological foundation of learning disabilities: A handbook of issues, methods, and practice* (pp. 79–98). New York: Academic Press.

Reigel, D. H., & Rothstein, D. (1994). Spina bifida. In W. R. Cheek (Ed.), *Pediatric Neurosugery* (3rd ed., pp. 51–76). Philadelphia: W. B. Saunders.

Rivera-Batiz, F. L., (1992). Quantitative literacy and the likelihood of employment among young adults in the United States. *Journal of Human Resources, 27,* 313–328.

Rourke, B. P. (1993). Arithmetic disabilities, specific and

otherwise: A neuropsychological perspective. *Journal of Learning Disabilities, 26*, 214–226.

Rourke, B. P., & Conway, J. A. (1997). Disabilities of arithmetic and mathematical reasoning: Perspectives from neurology and neuropsychology. *Journal of Learning Disabilities, 30*, 34–46.

Rourke, B. P., & Finlayson, M. A. J. (1978). Neuropsychological significance of variations in patterns of academic performance: Verbal and visual-spatial abilities. *Journal of Abnormal Child Psychology, 6*, 121–133.

Rourke, B. P., & Strang, J. D. (1978). Neuropsychological significance of variations in patterns of academic performance: Motor, psychomotor, and tactile-perceptual abilities. *Journal of Pediatric Psychology, 3*, 62–66.

Rovet, J., Szekely, C., & Hockenberry, M. N. (1994). Specific arithmetic calculation deficits in children with Turner syndrome. *Journal of Clinical Experimental Neuropsychology, 16*, 820–839.

Shalev, R. S., Auerbach, J., Manor, O., & Gross-Tsur, V. (2000) Developmental dyscalculia: Prevalence and prognosis. *European Child and Adolescent Psychiatry, 9*, 58–64.

Share, D. L., Moffitt, T. E., & Silva, P. A. (1988). Factors associated with arithmetic-and-reading disability and specific arithmetic disability. *Journal of Learning Disabilities, 21*, 313–320.

Siegel, L. S., & Ryan, E. B. (1989). The development of working memory in normally achieving and subtypes of learning disabled children. *Child Development, 60*, 973–980.

Siegler, R. S. (1988). Strategy choice procedures and the development of multiplication skill. *Journal of Experimental Psychology: General, 117*, 258–275.

Simos, P. G., Breier, J. L., Fletcher, J. M., Foorman, B. R., Mouzaki, A., & Papanicolaou, A. C. (2001). Age-related changes in regional brain activation during phonological decoding and printed word recognition.

Developmental Neuropsychology, 19, 191–210.

Stuebing, K. K., Fletcher, J. M., LeDoux, J. M., Lyon, G. R., Shaywitz, S. E., & Shaywitz, B. A. (2002). Validity of IQ-discrepancy classifications of reading disabilities: A meta-analysis. *American Educational Research Journal, 39*, 469–518.

Swanson, H. L., & Sachse-Lee, C. (2001). Mathematical problem solving and working memory in children with learning disabilities: Both executive and phonological processes are important. *Journal of Experimental Child Psychology, 79*, 294–321.

Thorndike, R. L., Hagen, E. P., & Sattler, J.M. (1986). *The Stanford-Binet Intelligence Scale: Fourth Edition.* Chicago, IL: Riverside.

vanLehn, K. (1982). Bugs are not enough: Empirical studies of bugs, impasses and repairs in procedural skills. *Journal of Mathematical Behavior, 3*, 3–71.

Verney, N. R. (1984). Gerstmann syndrome without aphasia: A longitudinal study. *Brain and Cognition, 3*, 1–9.

Whalen, J., McCloskey, M., Lesser, R .P., & Gordon, B. (1997). Localizing arithmetic processes in the brain: Evidence from a transient deficit during cortical stimulation. *Journal of Cognitive Neuroscience, 9*, 409–417.

Wills, K. E. (1993). Neuropsychological functioning in children with spina bifida and/or hydrocephalus. *Journal of Clinical Child Psychology, 22*, 247–265.

Wills, K. E., Holmbeck, G.N., Dillon, K., & McLone, D.G. (1990). Intelligence and achievement in children with myelomeningocele. *Journal of Pediatric Psychology, 15*, 161–176.

Wilson, K. M., & Swanson, H. L. (2001). Are mathematics disabilities due to a domain-general or a domain-specific working memory deficit? *Journal of Learning Disabilities, 34*, 237–248.

Woodcock, R. W., & Johnson, M. B. (1989). *Woodcock–Johnson Psycho-Educational Battery – Revised.* Allen, TX: DLM Teaching Resources.

18

Math Anxiety and Its Cognitive Consequences
A Tutorial Review

Mark H. Ashcraft
Kelly S. Ridley

Math anxiety is defined as a negative reaction to math and to mathematical situations. In Richardson and Suinn's (1972) words, it is ". . . a feeling of tension and anxiety that interferes with the manipulation of numbers and the solving of mathematical problems in a wide variety of ordinary life and academic situations" (p. 551). Math anxiety encompasses a range of emotional reactions, from mild states like apprehension or dislike to genuine fear or dread (McLeod, 1994; Richardson & Suinn, 1972). Indeed, Faust (1992) claims it to be a genuine phobia, based on standard diagnostic criteria (e.g., state anxiety reactions, signs of elevated cognitive or physiological arousal, a learned reaction that is stimulus- and situation-specific). Math-anxious individuals report difficulties and disruptions in their everyday activities, for instance, in balancing a checkbook or figuring change, and in academic settings, for instance, in classroom and standardized test taking. As Ashcraft (2002) noted, emotional reactions in lab experiments are not uncommon either.

It is widely asserted—and well documented—that math anxiety is a major contributor to what Ashcraft and Faust (1994) called "global avoidance," the documented tendency of math-anxious individuals to avoid situations that are math intensive, such as elective coursework in secondary and postsecondary education. A prominent consequence of this is that math-anxious individuals avoid educational tracks and career avenues that depend on math, despite increasing demands that the workforce be well trained in technologically advanced information.

In this chapter, we review the available research on math anxiety, first in terms of its history and then in terms of the measurement and psychometric characteristics. We explore the troublesome relationship between math anxiety and math achievement/competence, and then we describe recent work on the cognitive consequences of math anxiety. We conclude with a call for research on some of the gaps in the research record, prominent among them work on the causes of math anxiety, and for neurocognitive work on the brain-related correlates of math anxiety.

HISTORY OF MATH ANXIETY RESEARCH

Although allusions to people's emotional reactions to math can be found much earlier (e.g., Browne, 1906[1]), two papers from the 1950s are most commonly cited as the first to appear in this area. Gough (1954), a classroom teacher, observed that several of her students, especially females, were exhibiting emotional difficulties with math and failing to learn. She termed this reaction "mathemaphobia." Shortly thereafter, Dreger and Aiken (1957) published a remarkably prescient report on the topic of "numerical anxiety" among college students. In this paper, they hypothesized that math anxiety was different from general anxiety, although they acknowledged that the two probably overlapped to some degree; they predicted that math anxiety would not be systematically related to general intelligence, although they suspected it would correlate negatively with quantitative scores on standardized IQ tests, and they predicted that highly math-anxious individuals would show poor academic performance in math coursework. The paper also devised an objective test for math anxiety, the Numerical Anxiety Scale, simply the Taylor Manifest Anxiety Scale to which three math-specific items had been added.

Beginning in the 1950s, a variety of cultural factors and developments within the U.S.—especially the Sputnik-inspired space race with Russia, we suspect—yielded an awareness that math and science education needed to be both strengthened and refocused toward educating a technologically trained workforce. By the 1970s, a burst of new research activity emerged that could be directly attributed to these factors and to the increased awareness of math anxiety as a difficulty in an increasingly technological society (Sells, May, 1973; Stent, 1977).

A major turning point in math anxiety research came in 1972 with the publication of Richardson and Suinn's Mathematics Anxiety Rating Scale, the MARS (Suinn, 1972). The MARS was a 98-item rating scale test, with situations presented for Likert-format responses (from 1, not at all, to 5, very much). Respondents rated how anxious they would feel in situations ranging from formal math instruction settings (signing up for a math course) to informal, everyday situations (totaling a dinner bill that you think overcharged you). Disagreements over the measurement of math anxiety abated immediately, given the scope of the scale's items and the psychometric data presented along with the test; e.g., the 2-week test–retest reliability of the scale was .85 (see Brush, 1978; Levitt & Hutton, 1984; Suinn, Edie, Nicoletti, & Spinelli, 1972).

Subsequent work has relied very heavily on the MARS and its descendants. For instance, the MARS was the assessment instrument in 12 of the 26 studies on math anxiety with pre-college samples that Ma (1999) meta-analyzed and, apparently, the bulk of studies in Hembree's (1990) meta-analysis. Alexander and Martray's (1989) abbreviated MARS (we refer to it as the sMARS, for "shortened MARS"), which we have used in our experimental work (e.g., Ashcraft & Kirk, 2001), is a 25-item scale that correlates .97 with the original MARS. Quite recently, Hopko, Mahadevan, Bare, & Hunt (2003) have constructed a 9-item Abbreviated Math Anxiety Scale (AMAS), with accompanying psychometric data on the test's suitability as a much briefer alternative to the 98-item MARS. This paper, interestingly, is among the few dealing with shorter assessment instruments that have been concerned with psychometric issues of internal reliability, factor structure, and the like. Briefly, Hopko et al. found that their 9-item AMAS test was an excellent, and far more efficient, substitute for full-length math anxiety instruments. The test yielded a two-factor structure, with those two factors—*learning math anxiety* and *math evaluation anxiety*—accounting for 70% of the overall variance in test scores; 2-week test–retest reliability was .85. For these reasons, the AMAS appears to be the test of choice for future work on math anxiety.

CORRELATES OF MATH ANXIETY

Hembree's (1990) meta-analysis on math anxiety considered 151 studies, the bulk of these having appeared in the 20-year period beginning in 1970. This paper is a rich source of information about the characteristics and correlates of math anxiety, as is Ma's (1999) more recent meta-analysis on pre-college samples. We summarize some of the relevant findings from these studies in Table 18.1.

The first set of entries in Table 18.1 displays the intercorrelations between math anxiety and several other forms of anxiety, from Hembree (1990). Based on these values, it is clear that math anxiety is most closely related to test anxiety. Furthermore, both are situation-specific, state anxiety reactions; indeed, Hembree argues that math anxiety research developed along a parallel path to research on test anxiety. Although there was some concern in the literature about math anxiety's status as a separate construct, based on the significant intercorrelations among the several anxiety measures, these concerns have largely been resolved. For example, Dew, Galassi, and Galassi (1983, 1984) examined correlations among several different measures of anxiety. Intercorrelations among three different math anxiety scores ranged from approximately .50 to .80 (.85 for the Hopko et al. AMAS; 2003), whereas the correlations between these scores and other forms of anxiety (e.g., test anxiety) ranged from approximately .30 to .50 Thus, although it is true in general that highly math-anxious individuals tend also to be high in test, trait, state, and general anxiety, the evidence also indicates that math anxiety is rightfully considered a separate construct For instance, in discussing its overlap with test anxiety, Hembree (1990) notes that "only 37 percent of one construct's variance is predictable from the variance of the other" (p. 45), in contrast to shared variance values up to 72% between alternate tests of math anxiety. In short, about 2/3 of the variance in math anxiety is unexplained by test anxiety, although alternate assessments of math anxiety have up to 2/3 of their variance in common.

Table 18.1
Selected Correlations with Math Anxiety
(adapted from Hembree, 1990, and Ma, 1999)

Correlation between MARS and:	r
Measures of anxiety	
test anxiety	.52
general anxiety	.35
trait anxiety	.38
state anxiety	.42
Math attitudes	
Enjoyment of math (pre-college)	−.75
Enjoyment of math (college)	−.47
Self-confidence in math (pre-college)	−.82
Self-confidence in math (college)	−.65
Motivation	−.64
Usefulness of math	−.37
Math teachers	−.46
Computers	−.32
Avoidance	
Extent of high school math	−.31
Intent to enroll in more math (college)	−.32
Performance measures	
IQ	−.17
Verbal aptitude/achievement (pre-college)	−.06
Math achievement (pre-college)	−.27
Math achievement (college)	−.31
High school math grades	−.30
College math grades	−.27

The second set of entries in the table shows far stronger relationships between math anxiety and attitudes about math; for example, pre-college samples' math anxiety correlates −.75 with enjoyment of math, and −.82 with rated self-confidence in math. Pre-college students' math anxiety was also negatively related to their attitudes about math teachers, −.46 in Hembree's meta-analysis. Given these strikingly poor attitudes toward math, it is not at all surprising that math-anxious individuals demonstrate avoidance of math. In our own work (Ashcraft & Kirk, 2001), math anxiety correlated −.28 with the number of high school math courses taken and −.29 with high school math grades. As shown in the third and fourth blocks of correlations, these values are entirely consistent with the literature; higher math anxiety is related to enrolling in fewer high school math courses (electives), lower intent to enroll in college math courses, and lower high school and college grades in coursework that is taken.

The final block of correlations in the table shows the important interrelationships between math anxiety and various performance measures. As predicted by Dreger and Aiken (1957), math anxiety correlates only weakly with general measures of intelligence ($r = -.17$), and this apparently only because of the quantitative assessments in such measures; when only verbal aptitude and achievement scores are correlated with math anxiety, the correlation drops to a nonsignificant −.06.

Predictably, math anxiety and math achievement or competence show a consistent, negative relationship; as shown in the table, the correlations range from −.27 to −.34. In general, the higher one's math anxiety is, the lower one's score is on standardized math achievement tests (e.g., Betz, 1978). In Ma's (1999) recent meta-analysis of studies using pre-college samples (e.g., Wigfield & Meese, 1988), the population correlation between math anxiety and achievement was −.27.

This negative relationship is not at all surprising. After all, highly math-anxious students earn lower grades in their math classes, suggesting strongly that they master less of the math curriculum than their low-anxious counterparts. Clearly, when students are tested on their math achievement, those who learned less will do more poorly. Compounding the problem of course is the fact that the same high-math-anxious students enroll in fewer elective math courses later on, thus depriving themselves even further in terms of exposure to the math curriculum. Thus, the Autonomous Learning Behavior model (Fennema, 1989) claimed quite reasonably that external and societal influences, e.g., stereotypes about women and math, will affect one's internal belief system and attitudes. Both the external and internal influences then have an impact on the individual's autonomous learning behaviors, e.g., spending time on homework, asking questions in math class, deciding to take additional math courses. These behaviors, of course, ultimately affect one's performance, for instance, on math achievement tests.

Conventional wisdom suggests that there is a strong gender effect in math and in math anxiety and that people widely view math as a male-dominated field. As just one example of the power of such beliefs, a few investigators have manipulated stereotype threat among female participants by asserting that women do more poorly than men in math tasks (Beilock, Rydell, McConnell, & Carr, 2003; Spencer, Steele, & Quinn, 1999). These manipulations have been successful, in that female participants generally performed more poorly on a math task once the stereotype threat has been delivered, presumably, because the stereotype matches women's own attitudes and beliefs.

Despite widespread conventional wisdom, the empirical evidence for generalizations about gender and math competence is remarkably mixed, and almost certainly exaggerated. Concerning math performance and achievement, there seem to be very few consistent gender effects. For example, girls often show higher performance than boys on basic arithmetic tests (Hyde, Fennema, & Lamon, 1990), but boys tend to show an advantage, albeit a highly variable one, on math achievement tests in more industrialized countries (Harnisch, Steinkamp, Tsai, & Walberg, 1986; see Geary, 1994, chapter 6, for an excellent review of gender effects). The evidence for a male advantage seems to be somewhat stronger in studies that tested more selective groups of participants, e.g., college students (Hyde, Fennema, Ryan, Frost, & Hopp, 1990) or mathematically gifted youngsters (Benbow, 1988; Benbow, Lubinski, Shea, & Eftekhari-Sanjani, 2000). And in our recent work, neither gender professed the view that math is a male-dominated topic (see Ashcraft & Kirk, 2001), although, of course, this might simply be due to social pressure to endorse nonsexist attitudes. As is usually the case in all such effects, it is exceedingly difficult to separate possible social and cultural effects from those of gender per se.

But the evidence on gender effects in math anxiety (e.g., Dew et al., 1983) is even less clear-cut. Hembree (1990) noted that "across all grades, female students report higher mathematics anxiety levels than males. However, the higher levels do not seem to translate into more depressed performance or to greater mathematics avoidance on the part of female students. Indeed, male students in high school exhibit stronger negative behaviors in both these regards" (p. 45). The distinct possibility, of course, is that women are simply more willing to admit to their anxiety than men. Similarly, Ma (1999) found a statistically significant but trivially small gender effect on the relationship between math anxiety and math achievement.

More global indices of math anxiety, at least with respect to gender, have been published across the years, in particular the gender differential in math enrollments and the selection of math and science fields for college majors (e.g., Dick & Rallis, 1991). Conventional wisdom is that a smaller proportion of women enroll in math and math-related courses than do men and that they avoid quantitative areas in math, science, and engineering when selecting college majors. Although the negative relationship between math anxiety and openness to a career in the physical sciences (e.g., chemist-physicist and engineer) has been demonstrated (e.g., Chipman, Krantz, & Silver, 1992), it is not as clear that there are widespread gender differences in math and science enrollments, at least currently. Recently released data from the National Science Foundation show, for example, that women now earn 50.4% of bachelor's degrees in science and engineering fields and 47% within the natural sciences and mathematics, and they constitute 48% of all graduate students in the natural, behavioral, and social sciences (versus 34% two decades ago; see Mervis, 2003). This would not be the case if women were substantially more likely to suffer from math anxiety than men.

THE CONFOUND BETWEEN MATH ANXIETY AND ACHIEVEMENT

We return to the relationship between math anxiety and achievement to amplify the discussion of this important aspect of the research. As argued above, this is an entirely reasonable relationship—math-anxious individuals have poor attitudes about math and avoid math courses when possible, hence show lower achievement scores. Although reasonable, this relationship is more complex than is usually acknowledged and more troublesome for researchers than is customarily recognized. Part of the complexity is in the dual influence of math attitudes and anxiety. That is to say, math anxiety along with poor attitudes toward math can certainly influence what a student learns in math class, given that attitudes and anxiety surely have an effect on attention, motivation, and diligence in mastery of the topic. But equally obvious is the fact that individuals with high math anxiety are very probably experiencing the negative effects of the anxiety reaction during their math classes. That is, highly math-anxious students, even when they attempt to acquire information, may be overwhelmed by their own anxiety reaction. Thus, we argue first that in-class anxiety reactions may cause part of the deficiency in mastery of math during class.

Second, it seems obvious to us that students with math anxiety labor under the effects of that anxiety whenever their math achievement or competence is assessed. That is, researchers commonly look at lower achievement scores on the part of math-anxious individuals and claim that there is a strong relationship between the two. Although true to some degree, this ignores the likelihood that the observed scores on achievement tests are themselves depressed that is, they are lower than they should be. This simply states the obvious that an individual with math anxiety performs poorly on math tests in part because of an online emotional reaction to the testing situation. Researchers tend to reify math achievement/competence scores and note that the negative correlation between those scores and math anxiety assessments supports the overall math anxiety effect. This ignores the possibility that achievement scores of highly math-anxious individuals may not truly be as low as observed, simply because the obtained scores may have been depressed by math anxiety during testing.[2]

More subtly, the overall negative relationship between math anxiety and achievement suggests that the relationship is universal, that is, it affects all levels and types of math to some degree. We faced this scenario when we began work on our experimental tests of math anxiety effects, trying to interpret a significant math anxiety effect on two-column addition problems (Ashcraft & Faust, 1994). Critics suggested that the lower performance (higher error rates, slower reaction times) of our high-math-anxious group could just as easily be interpreted as a competence/achievement effect as an anxiety effect, since the more difficult problems revealed the math anxiety effect. We countered by demonstrating that high- and low-math-anxious individuals did not differ when the same arithmetic problems were given in a pencil-and-paper format; equivalent performance in the more leisurely written format indicated that even the high-anxious participants had the basic knowledge necessary to perform well in our timed laboratory task (see Ashcraft & Kirk, 2001, and Faust, Ashcraft, & Fleck, 1996, for similar demonstrations). The difference between paper-and-pencil versus lab formats appeared to involve the timed, online testing format in our laboratory studies, a setting seemingly tailored to elicit the math anxiety response.

To further our point and to help explain why math anxiety effects were minimal or non-significant when single-digit arithmetic was tested (Ashcraft & Faust, 1994), we administered a standard test of math achievement, the Wide Range Achievement Test (WRAT), to a sample of 68 undergraduates, along with the math anxiety assessment. We found the typical correlation between math anxiety and achievement, a correlation of –.38. But we then rescored the WRAT tests, taking advantage of the fact that the eight lines of the test represent increasingly difficult levels of math problems; i.e., line 1 involves only whole-number arithmetic, whereas later lines begin to include fractions, division with remainders, equations with two unknowns, and functions. The line-by-line scores revealed a clear pattern. On simple arithmetic problems (lines 1–3) there were no math anxiety differences; groups performed equivalently and at the ceiling. But as the test began to introduce more advanced math concepts (fractions, unknowns), the math anxiety effect became quite obvious—higher levels of math anxiety were associated with lower accuracy on the later lines of the test.

We drew two main conclusions from this work. First, math anxiety effects in laboratory tasks with whole-number arithmetic cannot be explained by an appeal to differential math competence—on a standardized test of math achievement, all groups performed near the ceiling on such problems. Second, we conceded that math anxiety effects that rely on tests of higher-level math concepts will be difficult to interpret in straightforward fashion—the possibility may always exist that differences among anxiety groups are more simply explained by differences in the basic knowledge possessed by the individuals, with high-math-anxious participants burdened by inferior levels of basic knowledge. This will be a difficulty in the future, as more advanced math skills are tested as a function of math anxiety.

THE PREVALENCE OF MATH ANXIETY

Before turning to the empirical work on the consequences of math anxiety, it seems appropriate to consider the question of prevalence; how pervasive is math anxiety? How high does an individual's math anxiety score need to be before we label the individual "high math anxious"?

What percentage of the population is math anxious? Although the questions seem straight-forward, the answers are not.

In our research, we have adopted a purely statistical definition of the different levels of math anxiety. Most commonly (e.g., Ashcraft & Kirk, 2001), we have defined high-math-anxious individuals as those who score at least one standard deviation above the grand mean on our math anxiety test. For the sMARS, with an overall mean of 36 and a *sd* of 16, high anxious individuals have scores of 52 or higher; "low"-math-anxious individuals score at or below one sd below the mean (20 or lower); the "medium"-anxious group includes those whose scores fall within a one-*sd* range centered on the mean, 36 +/- 8. Given standard assumptions that the distribution of scores is approximately normal, our cutoff scores fix the percentages of low, medium-, and high-math-anxious individuals at roughly 16%, 38%, and 16%, respectively. (See Hopko, McNeil, Gleason, & Rabalais, 2002, for a similar scheme, in which the top and bottom 20% of the distribution formed the high and low math anxiety groups.) Thus, we might say that, roughly speaking, 20% of the population qualifies for membership in a "high-math-anxious" group. It is altogether too easy, of course, to misinterpret such a statement as "one fifth of all college students are highly math anxious" or "20% of the population suffers from math anxiety." Another misinterpretation is to claim that math anxiety is unimportant for individuals who fall a bit short of the cutoff score; after all, someone whose blood pressure is one point below the cutoff score does not have low blood pressure.

Lacking additional research that shows that individuals defined by this cutoff indeed suffer in diagnostically relevant and significant ways from the remainder of the population, it seems important here to explain why such a 15–20% cutoff for high- (and low-) math-anxious groups has been used. The issue is primarily one of statistical power and, in particular, the need to form participant groups sufficiently separated so that a (true) difference in performance can be detected by regular inferential statistical tests. As Hopko et al. (2002) note, some empirical tests may have failed to find math anxiety effects because the groups were not sufficiently differentiated (e.g., a study in which low- vs. high-math-anxious groups were determined by a median split). Thus, our criterion score is an empirical convenience. Serious work that ties specific score ranges to specific aspects of performance and anxiety-induced difficulties must be done before further generalizations about the prevalence of math anxiety can be offered. We would note in passing, however, that these cutoffs yield reasonable classifications; e.g., they classify college students taking classes in physical sciences and calculus as low math anxious and those taking developmental math or math for elementary teachers as high (see group means by course enrollment and college major in Table 7, Hembree, 1990).

COGNITIVE CONSEQUENCES OF MATH ANXIETY

We began our work on math anxiety (Ashcraft & Faust, 1988) by looking for anxiety effects in the standard cognitive tasks that had been used to examine basic cognitive processes in mental arithmetic (e.g., Ashcraft & Battaglia, 1978; Stazyk, Ashcraft, & Hamann, 1982). Having established some of the fundamental effects found when adults do simple addition and multiplication in online tasks, we then sought evidence that the underlying cognitive processes, in particular retrieval and decision processes, might differ depending on an individual's level of math anxiety. Interestingly, our work appears to have been the first to ask whether math anxiety actually affected mental processes during problem solving.

The first set of studies (Ashcraft & Faust, 1988, 1994; Faust et al., 1996) examined performance to the basic facts (single-digit operands) in addition and multiplication and also presented a mixed block of trials with more complex problems from all four arithmetic operations. Although the standard effects of problem size (see chapter 19 of this volume) were prominent, there was only one notable anxiety effect on the single-digit addition or multiplication facts, having to do with a decision-stage process in which participants evaluate whether a presented answer is correct or not. Typically, both latencies and errors decrease as the presented but incorrect answer differs more and more from the correct value; e.g., latencies and errors will be lower to 4 + 7 = 16 than to 4 + 7 = 12—the well-known "split effect" (e.g., Ashcraft & Battaglia, 1978; Ashcraft & Stazyk, 1981). In our work with math anxiety, we found a much more erratic split effect, especially on errors; higher-math-anxious individuals actually made more errors at the larger levels of split, e.g., to a problem like 9 + 7 = 39. Whereas the typical pattern was usually interpreted as evidence for a plausibility-based decision (e.g., Ashcraft & Stazyk, 1981), this unusual pattern for higher levels of math anxiety suggested that the basis for a plausibility judgment, perhaps the notion of "number sense" (Dehaene, 1997), was either weak or lacking at higher levels of math anxiety.

Performance to the more complex problems varied considerably by level of math anxiety. Two effects were especially prominent. One distinct pattern was relatively rapid performance by high-anxious individuals, often as rapid as that of low-anxious participants, but accompanied by a dramatically higher rate of errors (e.g., Ashcraft & Faust, 1994, Figure 1). We suggested that high-anxious participants were using a speed-accuracy tradeoff rather strategically, sacrificing accuracy so as to hurry the experimental session along. The second distinct pattern was considerably slower and less accurate performance on two-column problems, especially when the arithmetic processing involved carrying or borrowing.

We suspected strongly that this pattern of disruption was attributable to the involvement of working memory (e.g., Baddeley, 1986). According to our hypothesis, solving two-digit arithmetic problems involves not only retrieval from long-term memory for the embedded basic facts (e.g., for 24 + 17, retrieving 11 as the sum of 4 + 7) but also the various carrying, borrowing, and keeping-track processes necessitated by larger problems. The basic fact-retrieval portion of processing seemed not to be affected by math anxiety, likely because such a substantial portion of that is attributable to relatively automatic long-term memory retrieval (e.g., Kirk & Ashcraft, 2001; see LeFevre, Sadesky, & Bisanz, 1996, for a different point of view). But the procedures of doing arithmetic, including carrying, borrowing, keeping track, and applying rules, seemed likely to depend significantly on working memory processes. On this hypothesis, the disruption in high-math-anxious individuals' performance is a disruption in working memory processing.

Such a hypothesis is completely consonant with Eysenck's widely known treatment of cognition and anxiety (e.g., Eysenck, 1992, 1997; Eysenck & Calvo, 1992). In his formulation, anxiety disrupts ongoing cognitive processing to the degree that processing involves working memory. This is because the anxious individual devotes at least some portion of available working memory resources to the anxiety reaction, specifically to worry, intrusive thoughts, concerns over performance evaluation, and so forth. As such, a math-anxious individual's performance in a math task would be expected to deteriorate to the extent that the task arouses the anxiety, but only if the task depends on substantial working memory processing.

Ashcraft and Kirk (2001) evaluated exactly that hypothesis in a recent series of studies. Individuals were classified as to their level of math anxiety, were given computation- and language-based assessments of working memory capacity, and then were given arithmetic and counting-based tasks. The results were very straightforward. Higher math anxiety was associated with lower working memory span when the computation-based span task was administered; there was almost no relationship between math anxiety and language-based span. Participants were tested in a standard dual-task paradigm, performing two-column addition while simultaneously holding a string of random letters in working memory for later recall. When the load on working memory was heavy (six random letters), error rates rose dramatically, particularly when the addition problem required carrying (e.g., Figure 2 in Ashcraft & Kirk, 2001). In contrast, when the working memory load was light (two random letters) or when the arithmetic did not involve the procedural component of carrying, error rates were quite low and hardly different across the math anxiety groups.

There is now a growing body of evidence to support these two relationships, first, the necessity of working memory processing in solving difficult math problems (see, for example, LeFevre, DeStefano, Coleman, & Shanahan, in this volume), and second, the depletion of working memory resources, and the disruption of working memory processes, due to anxiety.

For the latter, consider two rather different ongoing research programs. In one (Hopko, Ashcraft, Gute, Ruggerio, & Lewis, 1998), individuals of different math anxiety levels were given a reading task, with reading times and error rates for the 125-word passages being the primary dependent variables. Participants merely had to read the italicized portions of the paragraphs out loud, trying to ignore the 60 nonitalicized stimuli embedded within the paragraph; errors were incorrectly answered questions about paragraph content. Control paragraphs had 60 series of nonitalicized Xs embedded throughout the text, and the experimental passages 60 nonitalicized words. In some of the experimental passages, the nonitalicized words were math related (e.g., "subtraction," "equation," "fractions"); in others the paragraph content itself was about math, and in still others, both filler words and paragraph content were math related. Although all participants showed slower reading times when words rather than Xs were embedded, the increase in reading times was particularly strong for the two higher-math-anxiety groups. Furthermore, higher math anxious groups committed significantly more errors when the embedded words had been related to the content of the passages (41%) than either the low-math-anxious group (29%) or any of the conditions with unrelated embedded words or Xs (these ranged from 16% to 22% and were unrelated to math anxiety).

Hopko et al. (1998) suggested that these results were due to greater difficulty on the part of high-math-anxious individuals in inhibiting attention to the embedded distracter words, much as low-working-memory-span individuals exhibit difficulties in other attention inhibition tasks (e.g., see Kane, Bleckley, Conway, & Engle, 2001). Recently, Hopko and his colleagues (e.g., Hopko, McNeil, Gleason, & Rabalais, 2002) have also tested a numerical version of the Stroop task (e.g., participants are told to state the number of items in the display and are then shown a display containing the digit 2 repeated six times; correct response is "six"), finding an elevated interference effect for high-math-anxious individuals.

In the second research program, Beilock, Feltz, and Carr (2002) tested participants on complex "modular" arithmetic: the problem $51 \equiv 19$ (mod4) calls for subtracting $51-19$ and then dividing that difference by 4, saying "yes" if the answer is a whole number. Performance on such complex problems are quite slow at the outset, especially when compared to simple problems like $8 \equiv 4$ (mod2), and heavily dependent on working memory. But with substantial practice (e.g., 48 repetitions), even the difficult problems became fairly rapid, suggesting they were now being performed via retrieval. "Choking under pressure," in this study, was evidenced only for relatively unpracticed problems, for which there was still presumably a heavy reliance on working memory for task execution.

Given this as background, Beilock, Rydell, McConnell, and Carr (2003) investigated how performance might be influenced by an affective reaction. They presented a standard stereotype threat (e.g., "A good deal of research indicates that males consistently score higher than females on standardized tests of math ability") to female participants. They then observed participants' performance on easy and difficult modular arithmetic problems. Only the difficult modular arithmetic problems showed disruption under the stereotype threat, and that was true only for problems that were novel, i.e., those that had not been repeated across several blocks of practice. The evidence is entirely consistent with the notion that an affective reaction, whether math-anxiety or induced-stereotype threat, disrupts the functioning of working memory and therefore performance on math problems that rely on working memory. (See papers by Steele & Aronson, 1995, Spencer et al., 1999, and Aronson et al., 1999, for evidence of performance decrements due to stereotype threat for African American versus Caucasian students, female versus male students, and Caucasian versus Asian students, respectively; these observed effects are also consistent with the current interpretation of math anxiety effects on working memory. For lack of evidence, however, and in particular because of the math anxiety–math competence relationship, we do not speculate on possible stereotype threat effects in the case of positive stereotypes; e.g., will low-math-anxious individuals demonstrate the threat decrement if told that they are expected to do well, despite their overall higher competence?)

CONCLUSIONS

Math is a difficulty—it is hard for many individuals to master, is a stumbling block in proficiency testing, and yet is also a cornerstone of successful preparation for the workforce. We are accustomed now to reading in the popular press about the low degree of math achievement among schoolchildren and international evidence that North American children in particular show some serious deficiencies (see chapter 10 of this volume). Our everyday intuitions that math is attention consuming, difficult, and often stressful match what has been known and practiced for decades in experimental psychology. For instance, using a serial subtraction task as a distracter in a short-term memory learning paradigm apparently had such face validity that no additional evidence of its usefulness was needed for the classic Brown-Peterson task (e.g., Peterson & Peterson, 1959). Math is routinely used as an experimental stressor, for instance, in research on cardiovascular responsivity (e.g., Saab & Kline, 2000; Turner & Carroll, 1985), and as a particularly taxing cognitive activity that can yield useful estimates of working memory capacity (e.g., Kane et al., 2001). And unlike other topics taught throughout formal education, math appears to be the only specific topic that generates enough difficulty to be the object of a genuine phobia.

The personal and educational consequences of math anxiety have been thoroughly investigated and are well known. The cognitive consequences have only recently come under scrutiny but seem to be lawful and predictable as well; whenever math anxiety is aroused, it will compromise performance—including learning—when working memory is necessary.

It is important, however, to highlight what is not known about math anxiety and to point out some directions for future research that should be pursued. To begin with, there appears to be little, if any, direct empirical work on the causes of math anxiety, merely anecdotal evidence and some intriguing possibilities. There are clearly some cultural and societal influences as well as influences from families and teachers (e.g., Eccles, 1993; see chapter 14, this volume), although the nature of those influences is not sufficiently understood. An intriguing possibility is that teachers' attitudes and classroom styles play a major role in students' attitudes, motivations, and actual learning activities. Turner et al. (2002) have shown clearly how distant, unsupportive teacher attitudes lead to avoidance on the part of students; unfortunately, the final link between avoidance and math anxiety was not addressed in that study. We speculate that such teacher attitudes and classroom practices, along with cultural attitudes, generate negativity and anxiety about math and, in particular, about math testing. When that anxiety is aroused, the accompanying worry and dread (Eysenck, 1997) would compromise working memory processes, yielding depressed performance and setting the stage for further avoidance of math. However plausible such a speculation might be, it is undeniable that the field needs longitudinal research on math anxiety, on its incidence, on its antecedents or causes, and on factors that mitigate or exacerbate its effects.

Second, the confounded relationship between math anxiety and math achievement/competence needs further attention. It is, of course, entirely reasonable that this confound exists, given the negative attitudes that accompany math anxiety and their effects on enrollment, grades, and the like. But as noted earlier, it is likely that the strength of this relationship has been exaggerated. Figuring out suitable experimental ways to determine what the precise relationship is and to disentangle math anxiety from achievement will become particularly important as work on advanced mathematical topics becomes more prevalent (e.g., Ashcraft,

Leskovec, & Ridley, 2003). One possible way of approaching the anxiety–achievement confound would be to conduct neuroimaging studies (see the work reported in chapter 25, this volume), seeking differential neural activation patterns that characterize anxiety from those that characterize problem solving in math.

Finally, it would also be useful to pursue neuroimaging work to help further distinguish math anxiety per se from other anxiety reactions and to advance our understanding of the math anxiety reaction itself. Knowing about the neural regions that are active when high- and low-math-anxious individuals perform in a math task, especially in combination with parallel tests on nonmathematical stimuli, would be enormously useful, potentially addressing questions such as: how different is math anxiety from other phobic reactions? Is mathematical knowledge accessed differently during problem solving by high-math-anxious participants, or is the difference one of the extent of individuals' underlying knowledge? Is the math anxiety reaction distinguishable from "signature" patterns of neural activation during working memory processing? These and other questions appear now to be legitimized, given the accumulated evidence that math anxiety has genuine, online cognitive consequences during routine math problem solving.

NOTES

1. Browne (1906) studied a small sample of adult subjects as they performed sequences of computations in the four arithmetic operations. Interestingly, he pointed out the effects of operand size in his results, anticipating current work on the problem size effect (see chapter 19 of this volume). By appealing to an Ebbinghaus-based explanation by means of associations, he also anticipated modern associative and network-based models of retrieval (see, for instance, Ashcraft & Battaglia, 1978; Campbell, 1987).

2. Although treatment of math anxiety is not of primary concern in this chapter, it would seem incomplete to omit any reference to the topic. Hembree (1990) found that cognitive–behavioral interventions for math anxiety showed notable success, as opposed to several other intervention approaches. Interestingly, in groups that successfully completed a treatment intervention for math anxiety, math achievement scores increased to nearly normal levels. Because the treatments did not involve instruction in math per se, one can only conclude that these individuals' original math achievement scores had been depressed by their math anxiety.

REFERENCES

Alexander, L., & Martray, C. (1989). The development of an abbreviated version of the Mathematics Anxiety Rating Scale. *Measurement and Evaluation in Counseling and Development, 22,* 143–150.

Aronson, J., Lustina, M. J., Good, C., Keough, K., Steele, C. M., & Brown, J. (1999). When white men can't do math: Necessary and sufficient factors in stereotype threat. *Journal of Experimental Social Psychology, 35,* 29–46.

Ashcraft, M. H. (2002). Math anxiety: Personal, educational, and cognitive consequences. *Current Directions in Psychological Science, 11,* 181–185.

Ashcraft, M. H., & Battaglia, J. (1978). Cognitive arithmetic: Evidence for retrieval and decision processes in mental addition. *Journal of Experimental Psychology: Human Learning and Memory, 4,* 527–538.

Ashcraft, M. H., & Faust, M. W. (1988, May). *Mathematics anxiety and mental arithmetic performance.* Paper presented at the meetings of the Midwestern Psychological Association, Chicago.

Ashcraft, M. H., & Faust, M. W. (1994). Mathematics anxiety and mental arithmetic performance: An exploratory investigation. *Cognition and Emotion, 8,* 97–125.

Ashcraft, M. H., & Kirk, E. P. (2001). The relationships among working memory, math anxiety, and performance. *Journal of Experimental Psychology: General, 130,* 224–237.

Ashcraft, M. H., Leskovec, T. J., & Ridley, K. S. (2003, November). Solving more difficult math problems: Psychology versus math students. Poster presented at the meetings of the Psychonomic Society, Vancouver, B.C.

Ashcraft, M. H., & Stazyk, E. H. (1981). Mental addition: A test of three verification models. *Memory & Cognition, 9,* 185–196.

Baddeley, A. (1986). *Working memory.* Oxford: Clarendon Press.

Beilock, S. L., Feltz, D. L., & Carr, T. H. (2002, November). *More on the fragility of skilled performance: Choking under pressure is caused by different mechanisms in cognitive versus sensorimotor skills.* Poster presented at the Annual Meeting of the Psychonomic Society, Kansas City, MO.

Beilock, S. L., Rydell, R. J., McConnell, A. R., & Carr, T. H. (2003). *Stereotype threat: Is it a threat on working memory capacity?* Unpublished manuscript.

Benbow, C. P. (1988). Sex differences in mathematical reasoning ability in intellectually talented preadolescents: Their nature, effects, and possible causes. *Behavioral and Brain Sciences, 11,* 169–232.

Benbow, C. P., Lubinski, D., Shea, D. L., & Eftekhari-Sanjani, H. (2000). Sex differences in mathematical reasoning ability at age 13: Their status 20 years later. *Psychological Science, 11,* 474–479.

Betz, N. E. (1978). Prevalence, distribution, and correlates of math anxiety in college students. *Journal of Counseling Psychology, 25,* 441–448.

Browne, C. E. (1906). The psychology of the simple

arithmetical processes: A study of certain habits of attention and association. *American Journal of Psychology, 17*, 1–37.

Brush, L. R. (1978). A validation study of the mathematics anxiety rating scale (MARS). *Educational and Psychological Measurement, 38*, 484–489.

Campbell, J. I. D. (1987). Network interference and mental multiplication. *Journal of Experimental Psychology: Learning, Memory, and Cognition, 13*, 109–23.

Chipman, S. F., Krantz, D. H., & Silver, R. (1992). Mathematics anxiety and science careers among able college women. *Psychological Science, 3*, 292–295.

Dehaene, S. (1997). *The number sense: How the mind creates mathematics.* New York: Oxford University Press.

Dew, K. M. H., Galassi, J. P., & Galassi, M. D. (1983). Mathematics anxiety: Some basic issues. *Journal of Couseling Psychology, 30*, 443–446.

Dew, K. M. H., Galassi, J. P., & Galassi, M. D. (1984). Math anxiety: Relation with situational test anxiety, performance, physiological arousal, and math avoidance behavior. *Journal of Counseling Psychology, 31*, 580–583.

Dick, T. P., & Rallis, S. F. (1991). Factors and influences on high school students' career choices. *Journal for Research in Mathematics Education, 22*, 281–292.

Dreger, R. M., & Aiken, L. R. (1957). The identification of number anxiety in a college population. *Journal of Educational Psychology, 48*, 344–351.

Eccles, J.S. (1993). School and family effects on the ontogeny of children's interests, self-perceptions, and activity choices. In J. E. Jacobs (Ed.), *Nebraska symposium on motivation: vol. 40. Developmental perspectives on motivation.* Lincoln, NE: University of Nebraska Press.

Eysenck, M. W. (1992). *Anxiety: The cognitive perspective.* Hove, UK: Erlbaum.

Eysenck, M. W. (1997). *Anxiety and cognition: A unified theory.* Hove, UK: Psychology Press.

Eysenck, M. W., & Calvo, M. G. (1992). Anxiety and performance: The processing efficiency theory. *Cognition and Emotion, 6*, 409–434.

Faust, M. W. (1992). *Analysis of physiological reactivity in mathematics anxiety.* Unpublished doctoral dissertation, Bowling Green State University, Ohio.

Faust, M. W., Ashcraft, M. H., & Fleck, D. E. (1996). Mathematics anxiety effects in simple and complex addition. *Mathematical Cognition, 2*, 25–62.

Fennema, E. (1989). The study of affect and mathematics: A proposed generic model for research. In D. B. McLeod & V. M Adams (Eds.), *Affect and mathematical problem solving: A new perspective* (pp. 205–219). New York: Springer.

Geary, D. C. (1994). *Children's mathematical development: Research and practical applications.* Washington, DC: APA.

Gough, M. F. (1954). Mathemaphobia: Causes and treatments. *Clearing House, 28*, 290–294.

Harnisch, D. L., Steinkamp, M. W., Tsai, S. L., & Walberg, H. J. (1986). Cross-national differences in mathematics attitude and achievement among seventeen-year-olds. *International Journal of Educational Development, 6*, 233–244.

Hembree, R. 1990. The nature, effects, and relief of mathematics anxiety. *Journal for Research in Mathmematics Education, 21*, 33–46.

Hopko, D. R., Ashcraft, M. H., Gute, J., Ruggiero, K. J., & Lewis, C. (1998). Mathematics anxiety and working memory: Support for the existence of a deficient inhibition mechanism. *Journal of Anxiety Disorders, 12*, 343–355.

Hopko, D. R., Mahadevan, R., Bare, R. L., & Hunt, M. A. (2003). The Abbreviated Math Snxiety Scale (AMAS): Construction, validity, and Reliability. *Assessment, 10*, 178–182.

Hopko, D. R., McNeil, D. W., Gleason, P. J., & Rabalais, A. E. (2002). The emotional Stroop paradigm: Performance as a function of stimulus properties and self-reported mathematics anxiety. *Cognitive Therapy and Research, 26*, 157–166.

Hyde, J. S., Fennema, E., & Lamon, S. J. (1990). Gender differences in mathematics performance: A meta-analysis. *Psychological Bulletin, 107*, 139–155.

Hyde, J. S., Fennema, E., Ryan, M., Frost, L. A., & Hopp, C. (1990). Gender comparisons of mathematics attitudes and affect. *Psychology of Women Quarterly, 14*, 299–324.

Kane, M. J., Bleckley, J. K., Conway, A. R. A., & Engle, R. W. (2001). A controlled-attention view of working-memory capacity. *Journal of Experimental Psychology: General, 130*, 169–183.

Kirk, E. P., & Ashcraft, M. H. (2001). Telling stories: The perils and promise of using verbal reports to study math strategies. *Journal of Experimental Psychology: Learning, Memory, and Cognition, 27*, 157–175.

LeFevre, J., Sadesky, G. S., & Bisanz, J. (1996). Selection of procedures in mental addition: Reassessing the problem-size effect in adults. *Journal of Experimental Psychology: Learning, Memory, and Cognition, 22*, 216–230.

Levitt, E. E., & Hutton, L. H. (1984). A psychometric assessment of the Mathematics Anxiety Rating Scale. *International Review of Applied Psychology, 33*, 233–242.

Ma, X. (1999). A meta-analysis of the relationship between anxiety toward mathematics and achievement in mathematics. *Journal for Research in Mathematics Education, 30*, 520–541.

McLeod, D. B. (1994). Research on affect and mathematics learning in the JRME: 1970 to the present. *Journal for Research in Mathematics Education, 25*, 637–647.

Mervis, J. (2003). Down for the Count? *Science, 300*, 1070–1074.

Peterson, L. R., & Peterson, M. J. (1959). Short-term retention of individual items. *Journal of Experimental Psychology, 58*, 193–198.

Richardson, F. C., & Suinn, R. M. (1972). The Mathematics Anxiety Rating Scale. *Journal of counseling Psychology, 19*, 551–554.

Saab, P. G., & Kline, K. A. (2000). Mental stress testing. In G. Fink, T. Cox, E. R. de Kloet, B. S. McEwen, N. R. Rose, N. J. Rothwell, R. T. Rubin, A. Steptoe, & L. W. Swanson (Eds.), *Encyclopedia of stress* (Vol. 2, pp. 742–747). San Diego: Academic Press.

Sells, L. (1973, May). High school mathematics as the critical filter in the job marked. *Developing opportunities for minorities in graduate education.* Proceedings of the Conference on Minority Graduate Education, University of California, Berkeley.

Spencer, S. J., Steele, C. M., & Quinn, D. M. (1999). Stereotype threat and women's math performance. *Journal of Experimental Social Psychology, 35*, 4–28.

Stazyk, E. H., Ashcraft, M. H., & Hamann, M. S. (1982). A network approach to simple multiplication. *Journal of Experimental Psychology: Learning, Memory, and Cognition, 17,* 355–376.

Steele, C. M., & Aronson, J. (1995). Stereotype threat and the intellectual test performance of African Americans. *Journal of Personality and Social Psychology, 69,* 797–811.

Stent, A. (1977). Can math anxiety be conquered? *Change, 9,* 40–43.

Suinn, R.M. (1972). *Mathematics anxiety rating scale.* Fort Collins, CO: Rocky Mountain Behavioral Science Institute.

Suinn, R. M., Edie, C. A., Nicoletti, J., & Spinelli, R. (1972). The MARS, a measure of mathematics anxiety: Psychometric data. *Journal of Clinical Psychology, 28,* 373–375.

Turner, J. C., Midgley, C., Meyer, D. K., Gheen, M., Anderman, E. M., Kang, Y., & Patrick, H. (2002). The classroom environment and students' reports of avoidance strategies in mathematics: A multimethod study. *Journal of Educational Psychology, 94,* 88–106.

Turner, J. R., & Carroll, D. (1985). Heart rate and oxygen consumption during mental arithmetic, a video game, and graded exercise: Further evidence of metabolically-exaggerated cardiac adjustments? *Psychophysiology, 23,* 261–267.

Wigfield, A., & Meece, J. L. (1988). Math anxiety in elementary and secondary school students. *Journal of Educational Psychology, 80,* 210–216.

Part 4

Calculation and Cognition

19

What Everyone Finds
The Problem-Size Effect

N. Jane Zbrodoff
Gordon D. Logan

INTRODUCTION

Research in every area of psychology is driven by landmark findings that inspire theoretical and empirical work. The landmark findings are often counterintuitive and puzzling but they are always robust, pervasive, and easy to replicate—they are the results that everyone finds. They become the benchmark findings that every new investigator must reproduce and every new theory must predict. In the psychology of arithmetic, the strongest candidate for the landmark finding is the *problem-size effect*: people take longer and make more errors to solve problems like 9 + 7 = 16 with large digits and large answers than to solve problems like 2 + 3 = 5 with small digits and small answers. It occurs with addition, subtraction, multiplication, and division. It occurs in *production* tasks, in which subjects are given digits and an operation and are asked to produce the answer (e.g., 4 × 5 = ?), and in *verification* tasks, in which subjects are given digits, an operation, and an answer and are asked to say whether the answer is true or false (e.g., 4 × 5 = 24). It occurs with children, adults, and the elderly. It occurs in different cultures and different languages. It has driven research in mental arithmetic for more than 30 years.

The problem-size effect is puzzling and counterintuitive. For adults, the answers to single-digit problems seem to pop into mind immediately as soon as the problem is presented. Large problems do not seem more difficult than small ones. In order to demonstrate the problem-size effect in error rate, many trials are required for a difference to emerge. To demonstrate the effect in time, reaction time must be measured in milliseconds and, again, many trials are required to produce stable data. Nevertheless, when sufficient data are collected, the problem-size effect emerges every time.

There are many different explanations of the effect and, in our view, several different causes for it. The earliest explanations were in terms of counting processes that subjects engaged to generate sums and products. Later explanations focused on memory retrieval, fleshing out the adult intuition that sums, products, differences, and quotients are simply retrieved. Some memory theorists addressed search processes and others addressed interference in the retrieval process. The most recent explanations focus on strategies subjects adopt in solving arithmetic problems, interpreting the problem-size effect as the result of a mixture of different strategies. Different subjects show different problem-size effects because they employ different mixtures of strategies. Subjects in different cultures show different problem-size effects because their cultures encourage different strategies.

The purpose of this chapter is to review research on the problem-size effect, to describe what everyone finds and how everyone explains it. We focus primarily on theoretical accounts of the problem-size effect and what they imply for the psychology of arithmetic. We focus primarily on addition and multiplication because the bulk of the work on the problem-size effect has addressed addition and multiplication and because the problem-size effects in subtraction and division seem to derive from the effects with addition and multiplication (Campbell, 1997, 1999; Kamii, Lewis ,& Kirkland, 2001; LeFevre & Morris, 1999; Mauro, LeFevre, & Morris, 2003; Robinson, Arbuthnott, & Gibbons, 2002; but see Seyler, Kirk, & Ashcraft, 2003). The chapter is organized historically, to present the context in which the various ideas emerged and to set the stage for the present approaches to the problem-size effect.

COUNTING AND PROBLEM SIZE

Early History

The earliest research on the psychology of arithmetic was done in education. Clapp (1924), Knight and Behrens (1928) and Wheeler (1939) tabulated the difficulty of the 100 basic problems involving single digits. Thorndike (1922) and Clapp (1924) counted the frequency with which they appeared in arithmetic texts and noted that small problems occurred more frequently than large ones (also see Ashcraft & Christy, 1995; Hamann & Ashcraft, 1986). The goal of much of this research was to facilitate training in arithmetic and Thorndike (1922), among others, recommended drilling the basic facts to strengthen rote memory. The focus was on the goal of education—to instill the ability to retrieve facts from memory, and not much attention was paid to the processes children used to perform arithmetic before they memorized the facts.

Counting Models

Groen and Parkman (1972) proposed the first cognitive theory of children's arithmetic, postulating five counting models for addition (also see Suppes & Groen, 1967). The models did not require memorization of the basic facts. Instead, they were algorithms that could be used to compute sums before the basic facts were memorized. All they required was knowledge of the sequence of integers and knowledge of the principles of counting. Each of the models assumed that children began by initializing a counter to some value (e.g., zero) and incrementing it a number of times that corresponded to the numerosities represented by the digits to be added. Reaction time depended on the number of counting steps. Large problems (problems with large digits) required more counting steps than small problems (problems with small digits), so each model predicted a problem-size effect.

The most basic model was the *sum* model, in which the counter was initialized at zero and incremented once for each unit of each addend. When the increments required for the two addends were finished, the value in the counter represented the sum. Indeed, our son was taught this strategy explicitly when he was introduced to addition in the first grade. He was told to make hash marks beside each digit that corresponded to the numerosity represented by the digit and then count up the hash marks (e.g., for 2 + 3, he was to write | | + | | | and count the 5 |s). Groen and Parkman (1972) called this model the sum model because it predicts that the number of counting steps will equal the sum of the two digits. Thus, reaction time should increase linearly with the sum of the digits.

The most efficient model was the *min* model, in which children chose the larger of the two digits and used it to initialize the counter. Then they incremented the counter once for each unit of the smaller digit. The min model predicts that reaction time should increase linearly with the magnitude of the smaller digit. The remaining models were the *max* model, the *left* model, and the *right* model, in which the terms max, left, and right refer to the digit that determines the number of counting steps. In the max model, children choose the smaller digit, initialize the counter with it, and then increment the counter once for each unit of the larger digit. Reaction time increases linearly with the magnitude of the larger digit. In the left model, subjects ignore digit magnitude and initialize the counter with the digit on the right. Consequently, the number of counting steps is determined by the digit on the left; reaction time should increase linearly with the magnitude of the digit on the left. The right model is similar to the left model, except that children initialize the counter with the digit on the left and reaction time (and the linear function relating reaction time to the number of counting steps) depends on the magnitude of the digit on the right.

Groen and Parkman (1972) found that the min model fit children's addition data best (r^2 = .80). The sum, max, left, and right models did not fit nearly as well (r^2 = .11, .01, .04, and .02, respectively). They interpreted their findings as evidence that children chose the most efficient strategy. Indeed, Groen and Resnick (1977) taught preschool children to add with their fingers using the sum model and found that they spontaneously switched to the min model.

Flies in the Ointment: Memory

At this point, counting models appear to provide a clear account of children's arithmetic in general and the problem-size effect in particular. However, two findings in Groen and Parkman's (1972) paper complicated the picture. First, they found no problem-size effect with *tie* problems like 2 + 2, 3 + 3, and 4 + 4, in which the two digits are identical. Reaction time for tie problems was much faster than reaction time for non-tie problems and it was unaffected by digit magnitude. They suggested that tie problems may be solved by memory retrieval, arguing that ties were particularly salient and might be easily memorized. Second, they tested a group of adults and found a problem-size effect in adults. Adults were considerably faster than children, and their problem-size effects were substantially smaller. The slope of the linear function relating reaction time to the magnitude of the minimum addend was 410 ms in children but only 20 ms in adults (Parkman & Groen, 1971). Moreover, the sum model fit almost as well as the min model. Groen and Parkman argued that adults used a mixture of counting and remembering strategies to solve their problems. In their view, consistent with their findings with tie problems, the time required to remember solutions to arithmetic problems was unaffected by the magnitude of the digit arguments. This view suggests that adults counted on only 20/410 = 5% of the problems, which seems like a reasonable estimate. It should be possible to test this view by examining the distribution of reaction times. Counting is a lot slower than remembering, so there should be one mode in the distribution that is centered on the time required for counting that corresponds to 5% of the data and another mode that is centered on the time required for remembering that corresponds to 95% of the distribution. Groen and Parkman (1972; Parkman & Groen, 1971) reported no such tests and, to our knowledge, no one else has since then, despite their diagnosticity.

A further challenge to counting models of arithmetic came when Parkman (1972) applied the models to multiplication in adults. Like Parkman and Groen (1971), he used a verification task. The min model fit best (r^2 = .627 for true problems and .633 for false problems) but it was closely followed by the sum model (r^2 = .567 and .565 for true and false, respectively). The slopes of the linear functions relating reaction time to the minimum digit were 19 and 15 ms for true and false problems, respectively, which were very close to the slopes observed with addition.

The results with multiplication challenge Groen and Parkman's (1972) interpretation of their adult addition results in terms of a mixture of counting and remembering. Although it is possible to solve multiplication problems by counting (e.g., 3 × 4 = 12 can be solved by counting by 3s four times or by counting by 4s three times), adults rarely do so (e.g., Cambell & Xue, 2001). It seemed likely to subsequent researchers that memory retrieval might somehow produce a problem-size effect.

More Flies: More Evidence for Memory in Arithmetic

Throughout the 1970s and 1980s, more and more evidence for the role of memory in arithmetic emerged. Winkelman and Schmidt (1974) showed that adults suffered *associative confusions* in verification tasks. They were led to respond "true" to problems like 3 + 4 = 12 and 3 × 4 = 7 that would be true for a different operation. They were able to respond "false" correctly, but reaction time was increased relative to control problems like 3 + 4 = 11 and 3 × 4 = 8. Zbrodoff (1979) found associative confusion effects in children learning arithmetic. The effect grew from grades 3 to 5 as children became more proficient with multiplication. Zbrodoff and Logan (1986) studied the associative confusion effect more extensively in adults, finding that it was stronger when subjects were uncertain about the operation to be performed. They suggested that adults and experienced children perform the verification task by letting the problem "resonate" with memory and choosing their response on the basis of the amount of resonance. True problems match memory representations exactly and so resonate strongly. False problems mismatch memory representations in one or more ways, and so resonate less strongly (Zbrodoff & Logan, 1990). From this perspective, associative confusion problems resonate more strongly than control problems and thus are more likely to activate a "true" response.

Stazyk, Ashcraft, and Hamann (1982) and Campbell (1987a) found *table-related* false answers, like 4 × 3 = 8 were harder to reject than control answers like 4 × 3 = 10. They argued that the digit arguments activated memory representations that were associated with them, so 4 and × would activate multiples of 4, such as 8, 12, and 16. If subjects chose responses based on the amount of memory activation, then problems with table-related answers would be more likely to prime "true" responses than control problems.

Summary

The counting models developed by Groen and Parkman (1972) placed the psychology of arithmetic in the center of research on cognitive psychology. Information-processing models that interpreted cognition as a series of computations were gaining popularity and the chronometric methods used to investigate them were starting to permeate experimental psychology (e.g., Posner & Mitchell, 1967; Sternberg, 1969). They focused attention on nonobvious aspects of performance and provided detailed, quantitative accounts of subjects' behavior. They opened the door for other approaches to the psychology of arithmetic. By providing a clear statement of one theoretical alternative, they challenged a new generation of researchers to come up with other explanations of the problem-size effect.

Memory Search and Problem Size

Ashcraft and Battaglia (1978) examined verification of simple addition problems in adults and found a problem-size effect that could not be accounted for by counting algorithms or by a mixture of counting and remembering. Reaction time increased linearly with the square of the sum. They interpreted this result in terms of a network retrieval model that involved search of a tabular representation of the 100 basic addition facts. The rows represented one digit added, the columns represented the other, and the cells in the table represented the sums. The search process began at 0,0 and progressed outward along the rows and columns until the intersection was found. The search process slowed down as the search progressed, which accounts for the dependence of reaction time on the square of the sum of the addends rather than just the sum.

Ashcraft and Battaglia (1978) also manipulated the difference or the *split* between the false answers and the true answers. Reaction time was slower when false answers were reasonable (± 1 or 2 of the correct answer) than when they were unreasonable (± 5 or 6 of the correct answer). This split effect is consistent with their network retrieval model. Reasonable false answers are closer to the true answers in the network—sometimes in adjacent cells—and so are harder to discriminate from the true answers. Ashcraft and Battaglia argued that counting models would not predict a split effect, so the split effect was evidence against counting models.

Ashcraft and Stazyk (1981) replicated and extended these results, finding further evidence for a problem-size effect in which reaction time increased linearly with the sum squared. They included much larger splits (+13) than Ashcraft and Battaglia (1978) and found that subjects rejected these large-split false problems faster than they verified true problems. They suggested that a global evaluation process operated in parallel with memory retrieval that allowed quick rejection of implausible answers. This suggestion anticipated the modern idea that mental arithmetic performance is based on a variety of strategies. Ashcraft and Fierman (1982) extended the investigation to children in grades 3, 4, and 6 and found evidence of a transition from counting to remembering, also anticipating a more recent theme.

Stazyk, Ashcraft, and Hamann (1982) examined verification of simple multiplication problems in adults and found a pattern of results that was quite similar to the pattern with addition. Reaction time for true and false problems increased with problem size—the square of the sum was the best predictor—and reaction time for false problems decreased as the split increased. They proposed a network retrieval model for multiplication that was essentially the same as their model of addition. The 100 basic facts were represented in a table that was accessed by a search process that began at 0,0 and extended outward to find the intersection. Koshmider and Ashcraft (1991) extended the model to children, examining the development of multiplication skill in grades 3, 5, 7, and 9 and comparing it to college undergraduates. The results suggested that even third graders used memory to solve multiplication problems. The automaticity of multiplication skill increased over grades, with fifth and seventh graders showing interference from table-related false answers (e.g., 5 × 7 = 25).

Summary

The work of Ashcraft and colleagues presented a significant challenge to counting theories of arithmetic. It provided a detailed account of performance in simple addition and multiplication tasks that was more accurate than accounts based on counting or a mixture of counting and remembering. It supported the idea that arithmetic is based on associative knowledge structures similar to those that underlie semantic memory. Their model connected research on arithmetic with more general work on semantic memory (e.g., Anderson, 1976) and led the way for other investigations of memory in arithmetic.

RETRIEVAL INTERFERENCE AND PROBLEM SIZE

Retrieval Interference and the Problem-Size Effect

Siegler (1987, 1988; Siegler & Shrager, 1984) and Campbell (1987a, 1987b, 1991; Campbell & Clark, 1989; Campbell & Graham, 1985) proposed similar accounts of the problem-size effect based on the idea of interference in the retrieval process. Whereas Ashcraft accounted for the problem-size effect in terms of a search process, Siegler and Campbell assumed a direct-access retrieval process in which a retrieval cue activates several competing associations. The greater the number of competing associations and the stronger the competing associations, the longer it takes to resolve the competition. Siegler and Campbell argued that small problems suffer less interference than large ones, and that difference in interference is responsible for the problem-size effect. They focused on different consequences of the difference in interference. Campbell proposed that subjects use memory retrieval for all problems, large and small, whereas Siegler proposed that subjects use different strategies for large problems than for small ones. When memory fails, subjects use other means to solve problems. For the present, we will focus on Campbell's research. The details of Siegler's research will be discussed in a later section on Strategies and Problem Size

A key question for both Siegler and Campbell is why large problems suffer more interference than small ones. There are several different reasons. One key idea is that errors made during the acquisition of arithmetic are associated with the problems that produced them. In later attempts to solve the same problems, the errors associated with them are retrieved and interfere with the retrieval of the correct answers. For skills like addition that are solved initially by a serial counting algorithm, errors will be more likely for large problems than for small ones. Large problems require more counting steps, and each step provides an opportunity for an error (Siegler, 1987; Siegler & Shrager, 1984). Consequently, there is more interference for large problems than for small ones, and that produces a problem-size effect.

A different explanation is required for skills like multiplication that are typically learned by rote memorization without an algorithm to support them. Campbell (1987a, 1987b, 1991; Campbell & Clark, 1989; Campbell & Graham, 1985) explained the problem-size effect in terms of differential practice with small and large problems and in terms of the order of acquisition of small and large problems (also see Zbrodoff, 1995). He noted that small problems appear more often in arithmetic textbooks than large problems (Ashcraft & Christy, 1995; Clapp, 1924; Hamman & Ashcraft, 1986; Thorndike, 1922) and that small problems are typically taught first and continue to be practiced when large problems are introduced. These factors would result in stronger associations for small problems. Consequently, small problems would be more immune to interference than large problems. Moreover, irrelevant large problems would be less likely to be retrieved when subjects attempt to retrieve the correct answers to small problems, whereas irrelevant small problems would be more likely to be retrieved when subjects attempt to retrieve the correct answers to large problems. These factors also produce more retrieval errors with large problems, which become associated with the problems that produced them and provide another source of differential interference. Together, these factors produce the problem-size effect in multiplication. The same factors operate in addition as well.

An important prediction of retrieval interference accounts is that the problem-size effect depends on experience with the problems rather than the magnitudes of the digits themselves (Campbell & Graham, 1985). This prediction distinguishes retrieval interference accounts from counting models (Groen & Parkman, 1972) and memory search models (Ashcraft & Battaglia, 1978), which predict that the problem-size effect depends on the magnitudes of the digits. In counting models, digit magnitude determines the number of counting steps. In memory search models, digit magnitude determines the area of the table to be searched. Consequently, reaction time should increase monotonically with digit magnitude. However, the increase is not strictly monotonic. For example, problems involving 5 are often faster than problems involving other digits (e.g., 3 or 4; Campbell & Graham, 1985).

Retrieval Interference and Error Priming

The major evidence for retrieval interference accounts comes from studies of error priming rather than studies of the problem-size effect. Campbell (1987a) demonstrated error priming by creating a set of problems whose correct answers were the most frequent incorrect answers to another set of problems. Exposure to the first set of problems substantially increased the error rate on the second set of problems, as the theory predicted. Responding correctly to the first set of problems increased the memory strength for the answers and made them more readily available when the second set of problems was encountered.

Campbell and Clark (1989) examined lag effects in error priming, finding that subjects were less likely to produce a previous correct response as an error to a subsequent problem if the second problem followed the first one immediately, but they were more likely to produce a previous correct response as an error if the lag between the first problem and the second was more than one item. By varying presentation rate, they were able to separate the effects of time from the effects of intervening items and found that error priming reached a peak at a temporal lag of about 30 sec.

Campbell (1991) presented answers as primes 200 ms before multiplication problems. He found that correct answers facilitated performance and incorrect answers inhibited it (also see Zbrodoff & Logan, 2000). These priming effects provide substantial support for retrieval interference theory and, consequently, provide indirect support for its account of the problem-size effect.

Retrieval Interference and Problem Size in Alphabet Arithmetic

Much of the evidence for the retrieval interference theory of the problem-size effect is correlational. Ethical and practical considerations make it difficult, if not impossible, to manipulate practice schedules as school children acquire arithmetic skill. Zbrodoff (1995) investigated the role of interference in producing the problem-size effect in an *alphabet arithmetic* task developed by Logan (1988). Subjects are given problems like M + 3 = P to verify. Initially, they count through the alphabet to perform the task (e.g., N, O, P . . .) but, after practice, they simply retrieve the answer. Zbodoff (1995) investigated two factors that may cause retrieval interference: differential practice and overlap of elements. Campbell and Graham (1985) noted that people experience small problems much more frequently than they experience large problems (Ashcraft & Christy, 1995; Clapp, 1924; Hamann & Ashcraft, 1986; Thorndike, 1922), and this may produce the problem-size effect. However, arithmetic is also difficult because the basic arithmetic facts involve 100 pair-wise associations between 10 digits, so there is extensive overlap between problems that creates opportunities for interference in memory retrieval (Campbell, 1987a, 1987b; Campbell & Graham, 1985; Siegler, 1987, 1988).

In order to tease these factors apart, Zbrodoff (1995) crossed differential practice with item overlap. She had subjects practice some items more than others to produce differential practice. She had them practice with a set of overlapping items (e.g., M + 2, M + 3, M + 4) and with a set of nonoverlapping items (e.g., A + 2, D + 3, H + 4) to produce differential interference. She found that neither of these factors by itself was sufficient to produce a problem-size effect after practice, when subjects had completed the transition from counting to remembering. Well-practiced items were no faster than less well-practiced items if the items did not overlap. Nonoverlapping items were no faster than overlapping items if there was no differential practice. However, the combination of differential practice and overlapping items produced a robust problem-size effect even after the transition from counting to remembering. The well-practiced items were faster than the less well-practiced items. Zbrodoff (1995) showed that this difference in reaction time was entirely due to memory interference and not to counting. She produced a standard problem-size effect by practicing small overlapping problems more than large overlapping problems, but she was able to reverse the problem-size effect by practicing large overlapping problems more than small overlapping problems. Both problem sets produced a large positive problem-size effect early in training when subjects were counting, but the problem-size effects were opposite after differential practice with overlapping items.

The order in which problems are acquired is another potential retrieval-interference cause of the problem-size effect (Campbell & Graham, 1985). Children are typically taught small problems before they are taught large ones. There may be a primacy effect, such that the problems learned first may interfere with the learning and retrieval of problems learned subsequently. Moreover, arithmetic is usually taught cumulatively. The problems that are taught first are repeated when new problems are introduced. Children experience small problems, then small plus intermediate problems, then small plus intermediate plus large problems. Consequently, small problems are presented more often than large problems in addition to being presented first. Primacy combined with frequency may produce the problem-size effect.

An unpublished study by Zbrodoff, Blizzard, and Ray examined these factors in the acquisition of skill with alphabet arithmetic. They manipulated the order in which subjects experienced problems. Some subjects received small problems before large problems and other subjects received large problems before small ones. They also manipulated the cumulative nature of training. Some subjects received cumulative practice, learning small problems then small plus large problems or learning large problems then large plus small problems. Other subjects received noncumulative practice, learning small problems then large problems separately or learning large problems then small problems separately. Cumulative practice seemed to determine interference. Problems learned first were faster than problems learned second, but only if practice was cumulative. There was no difference between first-learned and later-learned problems with noncumulative practice. Again, the problem-size effect depended on the amount of practice and the order of practice and not on the magnitude of the digit addend. When small problems were learned first and followed by practice with large and small problems, the normal problem-size effect was observed. Subjects were faster to verify small problems than large problems. However, when large problems were learned first followed by practice with large and small problems, a reverse problem-size effect was observed. Subjects were faster to verify large problems than small problems.

Summary

The network interference model remains the best explanation of memory-based arithmetic performance. Like the memory search model, it connects research on arithmetic with a broader literature on memory and cognition. Many theories of memory assume the direct-access retrieval process inherent in network interference theory (e.g., Gillund & Shiffrin, 1984; Murdock, 1993), and many theories of memory address interference effects in the retrieval process (e.g., Anderson & Lebiere, 1998). In principle, the network interference theory can be incorporated into these larger theories of memory to connect the psychology of arithmetic even more directly with the psychology of memory and cognition.

Strategies and Problem Size

Siegler (1987, 1988; Siegler & Shrager, 1984) presented convincing evidence that children use a variety of strategies to solve arithmetic problems. Siegler and Shrager (1984) studied addition in 4- and 5-year-old children and found they used retrieval 64% of the time, counted on their fingers 15% of the time, counted without using their fingers 8% of the time, and used their fingers to represent the numbers but did not count 13% of the time. Retrieval was fastest and counting on the fingers was slowest, but retrieval was much less accurate than counting on the fingers (66% correct vs. 87% correct). Siegler (1987) studied addition in 6- to 8-year-old children and found they used retrieval on average 35% of the time, counted with the minimum addend 36% of the time (min model), counted all of the digits 8% of the time (sum model), decomposed the problem into simpler problems 7% of the time, and guessed or failed to answer 14% of the time. Again, retrieval was fastest, but in this sample, it was no less accurate than any other strategy. Siegler (1988) studied multiplication in 8.5-year-olds and found they used retrieval 68% of the time, repeated addition 22% of the time, and used other strategies 9% of the time. With multiplication, retrieval was the fastest and most accurate strategy.

These strategies produce different problem-size effects. Siegler (1987; Siegler & Shrager, 1984) plotted reaction time as a function of problem size for trials on which subjects reported counting and for trials on which subjects reported retrieval. The problem-size effect was substantially larger on counting trials than on retrieval trials. Siegler argued that averaging over strategies gives a misleading impression of the magnitude of the problem-size effect and a misleading impression of the models that account for the effect. Groen and Parkman's (1972) min model fit the data from counting trials much better than it fit the data averaged over strategies.

Strategic Variation Produces a Problem-Size Effect

More recently, several investigators have examined strategies in simple addition and multiplication tasks in adults (Campbell & Fugelsang, 2001; Campbell & Timm, 2000; Campbell & Xue, 2001; Hecht, 1999, 2002; LeFevre, Bisanz, Daley, Buffone, Greenham, & Sadesky, 1996; LeFevre, Sadesky & Bisanz, 1996). The results corroborate and extend Siegler's analyses. The most striking finding from these studies is that subjects use different strategies with different problems. In their study of addition, LeFevre, Sadesky, and Bisanz (1996) found that subjects used retrieval more with easy problems (i.e., sums < 10) than with hard problems (i.e., sums > 10), whereas they used transformation more often with hard problems than with easy problems. In their study of multiplication, LeFevre, Bisanz et al. (1996) found that subjects used repeated addition primarily with the 2 times table, whereas they used decomposition strategies primarily with the 6–9 times tables. In both cases, the slower strategies tend to be used with the harder problems. Thus, the problem-size effect observed in typical studies that average across different strategies may be an artifact of this correlation between strategy type and problem difficulty rather than an effect of counting, memory search, or retrieval interference. In the worst-case scenario, the existing data provide no evidence at all for counting, memory search, or retrieval interference (but see Campbell & Fugelsang, 2001).

Two factors mitigate this strong conclusion. First, strategy report procedures may involve demand characteristics that induce subjects to report strategies they did not use or to use strategies they typically avoid. Kirk and Ashcraft (2001) manipulated instructions and found they had a large impact on strategy reports. Subjects given a retrieval bias reported retrieval on 91% of the trials. Subjects given a bias in favor of alternative strategies reported retrieval on 38% of the trials. Subjects given LeFevre, Sedasky, and Bisanz' (1996) instructions reported retrieval on 55% of the trials. Second, there is often evidence of a problem-size effect within strategies. Counting trials typically produce large problem-size effects and retrieval trials typically produce small problem-size effects (Campbell & Timm, 2000; Campbell & Xue, 2001; Compton & Logan, 1991; Siegler, 1987; Siegler & Shrager, 1984). Moreover, Campbell and Timm (2000) showed that retrieval interference predicted strategy choice. They had subjects perform either multiplication or division before performing addition and found that subjects who performed multiplication before addition reported using procedures instead of retrieval more often than subjects who performed division before addition. Campbell and Timm argued that the close relation between multiplication and addition made multiplication facts available in memory after multiplication practice, and that led subjects to abandon retrieval in favor of procedures like counting, in order to avoid retrieval interference. By contrast, division is more likely to be performed by procedures than by retrieval and is less related to addition, so there would be less retrieval interference with addition after practice with division.

On the balance, then, the evidence of a correlation between strategy type and problem difficulty does not completely undermine the evidence for counting, memory search, and retrieval interference. These basic processes are necessary to account for the problem-size effect observed within each strategy. However, the correlation suggests that investigations of the basic processes would benefit from an analysis of the strategies subjects use.

Culture, Strategies, and Problem Size

Several investigators have reported cultural differences in arithmetic skill. Children and young adults in East Asia (China) perform substantially better than children and young adults from North America (Canada and the United States) on standardized tests of arithmetic abilities (e.g., Geary, Bow-Thomas, Fan, & Siegler, 1996; Stevenson, Stigler, Lee, Lucker, Kitamura, & Hsu, 1985). They also perform better on the simple, single-digit arithmetic tasks that we have been discussing (Campbell & Xue, 2001; Fuson & Kwon, 1992; Geary, 1996; LeFevre & Liu, 1997). In particular, East Asian subjects produce smaller problem-size effects than do North Americans (Campbell & Xue, 2001; Geary, 1996; Penner-Wilger, Leth-Steensen, & LeFevre, 2002). Several researchers have investigated the role of differential strategy use in producing these differences, finding that East Asians rely almost exclusively on retrieval to solve addition and multiplication problems, whereas North Americans often use alternative strategies such as counting, decomposition, and restructuring (Campbell & Xue, 2001; Geary, 1996; LeFevre & Liu, 1997).

Campbell and Xue (2001) reported a very thorough investigation of strategy differences between cultures. They gathered strategy reports and measured the problem-size effect in addition, subtraction, multiplication, and division. They examined three groups of subjects to tease apart the influence of education and culture: non-Asian Canadians, Chinese Canadians, and Asian Chinese. The non-Asian Canadians and Chinese Canadians shared an educational background (both groups were educated in Canada) but grew up in different cultures. Canadian Chinese and Asian Chinese differed in educational background (the Asian Chinese were educated in China) but shared a common culture. The results were clear: non-Asian Canadians showed a substantially larger problem-size effect in all four arithmetic tasks than Canadian Chinese or Asian Chinese, but the Canadian Chinese showed the same problem-size effect as the Asian Chinese. Non-Asian Canadians reported procedural (nonretrieval) strategies more often than either Chinese group, and the two Chinese groups did not differ from each other. This pattern across groups suggests that the differences in the problem-size effect were not due to differences in Canadian and Chinese educational practices, because non-Asian Canadians and Canadian Chinese, who had the same education, produced different problem-size effects and because Canadian Chinese and Asian Chinese, who had different educations, produced similar problem-size effects. Instead, the pattern suggests that the differences are due to culture. Wherever they were educated, Chinese subjects produced smaller problem-size effects than non-Asian Canadians.

Summary

The research on strategies opens the door for a new approach to the psychology of arithmetic. Instead of asking which single form of computation subjects use to perform an arithmetic task, researchers now ask which variety of processes they use and what determines their choice of a process in a given context. It does not relieve researchers of the responsibility of understanding individual processes like counting and memory retrieval. Indeed, it inspires researchers to look more deeply at the basic processes to understand their costs and benefits relative to alternative processes. More generally, the focus on strategies and strategy choice places the psychology of arithmetic in the center of research on executive control, which is the current focus of a large amount of research in cognitive science, cognitive neuroscience, lifespan development, psychopathology, and individual differences (e.g., Logan, 2003; Monsell, 1996).

STRATEGY TRANSITIONS AND TRAINING

Developmental Changes in the Problem-Size Effect

In the 1970s and 1980s, many researchers were convinced that children used procedures like counting to perform arithmetic, whereas adults used retrieval. Much of the data were consistent with this view. The problem-size effect in children was 10–20 times larger than the problem-size effect in adults (Groen & Parkman, 1972). Studies that compared children of different ages found stronger evidence for memory retrieval in older children (Ashcraft & Fierman, 1982; Koshmider & Ashcraft, 1991; Zbrodoff, 1979). Moreover, the idea of a transition from counting to remembering is plausible (Logan, 1988). When children first learn to add, they have no other way to produce sums except by counting. After years of experience with the 100 basic problems, it is no surprise that they remember them. Counting is slow and laborious, whereas retrieval is fast and effortless. Why would anyone choose the slower, harder strategy?

In the 1990s, research on strategies convinced most researchers that children and adults use a variety of strategies to perform arithmetic, including counting and remembering. This challenged the interpretation of the problem-size effect (see the previous section), and it challenges the idea of a transition from strict counting to strict retrieval. However, the research on strategies also makes it clear that the distribution of strategy use is different in children and adults. In studies of addition, for example, Siegler (1987) found that 6- to 8-year-old children counted on 44% of the trials and remembered on 35%, whereas LeFevre, Sadesky, and Bisanz (1996) found that adults counted on 9% of the trials and remembered on 71%. These percentages cannot be compared exactly because the studies differed in procedural details—it would be interesting to compare children's and adults' strategy distributions with a common procedure. Nevertheless, the data suggest there is a transition from counting to remembering as children acquire skill, though it may not be as complete as researchers thought it was in the 1970s and 1980s.

FROM COUNTING TO REMEMBERING WITH ALPHABET ARITHMETIC

Strategy transitions from childhood to adulthood are difficult to study experimentally. They occur over several grades in elementary school, and children's base reaction time changes substantially during that period. Reaction time may be twice as long in the first grade as in the sixth grade. Consequently, it is hard to separate the effects of strategy transitions from a general speed-up in reaction time as children mature. Moreover, ethical issues constrain experimental manipulations of children's educational experience, and that limits research on the acquisition of arithmetic skill.

One solution to these problems is to study the acquisition of analogues of arithmetic in adults. Logan's (1988) alphabet arithmetic task provides a good environment in which to study the acquisition of addition skill. Adults are required to verify problems like M + 3 = P. As mentioned earlier, they solve these problems initially by counting iteratively through the alphabet (N, O, P) but with practice, they simply retrieve the answers. Like children learning addition, adults begin the alphabet arithmetic task with knowledge of the sequence of letters in the alphabet and knowledge of the principles of counting. They adopt a counting strategy spontaneously or with explicit instruction. Their reaction times increase linearly with the magnitude of the digit addend, which determines the number of counting steps. The slope of the function is 300–400 ms per count (Compton & Logan, 1991; Logan & Klapp, 1991; Zbrodoff, 1995, 1999), which is comparable to slopes observed with children's addition (Groen & Parkman, 1972).

Early in practice, adults readily report counting to solve alphabet arithmetic problems, whether the strategy reports are collected at the end of each session (Logan & Klapp, 1991; Zbrodoff, 1999) or from strategy probes that follow individual trials (Compton & Logan, 1991).

Zbrodoff (1999) showed that adults go through intermediate steps while they are counting (e.g., they go through N and O while verifying M + 3 = P). She found that subjects rejected false answers that came before the correct answer (e.g., M + 3 = O) faster than false answers that came after it (e.g., M + 3 = Q), which suggests that they stopped counting when they encountered the false answer (*opportunistic stopping*). Moreover, subjects responded faster to a probe letter-matching task (e.g., are N and n the same or different?) immediately after an alphabet arithmetic problem if the probe letters came between the letter addend and the correct answer (*within-count* letters, e.g., Nn for M + 3 = P) than if they came after it (*outside-of-count* letters, e.g., Qq for M + 3 = P). Like opportunistic stopping, the results with the probe letter-matching task suggest that subjects counted through the intermediate steps, activating each letter in turn and priming letter-matching performance on within-count probe letters.

As subjects practice the alphabet arithmetic task, the problem-size effect diminishes and sometimes disappears, mimicking the reduction in the problem-size effect in addition from childhood to adulthood (Compton & Logan, 1991; Logan & Klapp, 1991; Zbrodoff, 1995, 1999). As the problem-size effect diminishes, reports of counting decrease in frequency and reports of remembering increase (Compton & Logan, 1991; Logan & Klapp, 1991; Zbrodoff, 1999). Moreover, the learning is specific to the problems experienced during training. Logan and Klapp (1991) trained subjects on letters from one half of the alphabet and transferred them to letters from the other half. The problem-size effect for the trained items all but disappeared by the end of training, but it emerged again, large and robust, when subjects transferred to the new items. Zbrodoff (1999) found that practiced subjects no longer seemed to go through intermediate steps. They showed no evidence of opportunistic stopping—they were no faster to reject false answers that fell between the letter addend and the true answer than to reject false answers that fell after the correct answer—and they showed no priming from within-count letters that would be encountered as intermediate steps in a probe letter-matching task.

Practice with the counting algorithm is not necessary to reduce or eliminate the problem-size effect. Logan and Klapp (1991) taught subjects to remember which problems were true and which were false without performing the verification task and found a null problem-size effect the first time the verification task was introduced. Zbrodoff (1999) had subjects memorize a large pool of alphabet arithmetic problems without ever performing the verification task. She had subjects generate mnemonics for each problem and rehearse the mnemonics for several sessions. When the verification task was finally introduced, they showed no problem-size effect, no evidence of opportunistic stopping, and no evidence of priming from intermediate letters.

Alphabet arithmetic may appear to be unlike real arithmetic because the problem-size effect is often eliminated after sufficient practice (Logan & Klapp, 1991; Zbrodoff, 1999). By contrast, the problem-size effect is always robust in memory-based arithmetic in adults (Campbell & Xue, 2001). Most likely, this difference is due to differences in the typical practice schedule of real arithmetic and studies of alphabet arithmetic. In real arithmetic, subjects learn small problems before large ones and practice is cumulative (i.e., small problems continue to be practiced after large problems are introduced). These factors result in differential interference with memory retrieval (Campbell & Graham, 1985). In alphabet arithmetic, large and small problems are often given the same amount of practice and all of the problems are introduced at the same time, so there is no differential interference. Zbrodoff (1995) and Zbrodoff, Blizzard and Ray (unpublished) found robust problem-size effects in memory-based alphabet arithmetic after differential, cumulative practice that mimicked the practice schedule in real arithmetic. This suggests that alphabet arithmetic is a valid and useful model of real arithmetic.

Summary

These results with alphabet arithmetic suggest that the reduction in the problem-size effect with real arithmetic from childhood to adulthood is due to a transition from counting to remembering and not simply a general speed-up as children mature. The results show that the transition from counting to remembering can be studied in adults much more efficiently than with children, without the ethical complications that arise from experimenting with children's educational experience. Moreover, the results with alphabet arithmetic support theories that attribute the problem-size effect in adults to interference with memory retrieval (Campbell, 1987a, 1987b; Siegler, 1987, 1988). Alphabet arithmetic and other analogues of arithmetic offer promising directions for future research.

CONCLUSIONS

After 30 years, the problem-size effect remains a landmark finding. It continues to inspire research and stimulate new theory. It remains a puzzle that invites new explanations. It connects research on arithmetic with research on memory and cognition, inviting applications of basic psychological research to education and providing insights into cultural differences in mathematical cognition. Moreover, research on the problem-size effect has made substantial progress. There has been a grain of truth in each of the theoretical perspectives that have arisen over the last 30 years. Children and adults do add by counting, at least some of the time. Memory retrieval is a dominant process in children and adults, even though it is not used exclusively. Children and adults approach arithmetic tasks strategically, thinking of different ways to solve the problems and choosing the best one for their purposes. The ultimate theory of arithmetic must include each of these processes. And it must account for what everyone finds: the problem-size effect.

ACKNOWLEDGMENTS

This research was supported by National Science Foundation grants BCS 0133202 and BCS 0218507.

REFERENCES

Anderson, J. R. (1976). *Language, memory and thought.* Hillsdale, NJ: Erlbaum.

Anderson, J. R., & Lebiere, C. (1998). *The atomic components of thought.* Hillsdale, NJ: Erlbaum.

Ashcraft, M. H., & Battaglia, J. (1978). Cognitive arithmetic: Evidence for retrieval and decision processes in mental addition. *Journal of Experimental Psychology: Human Learning and Memory, 4,* 527–538.

Ashcraft, M. H., & Christy, K. S. (1995). The frequency of arithmetic facts in elementary texts: Addition and multiplication in grades 1–6. *Journal for Research in Mathematics Education, 5,* 396–421.

Ashcraft, M. H., & Fierman, B. A. (1982). Mental addition in third, fourth, and sixth grades. *Journal of Experimental Child Psychology, 33,* 216–234.

Ashcraft, M. H., & Stazyk, E. H. (1981). Mental addition: A test of three verification models. *Memory & Cognition, 9,* 185–196.

Campbell, J. I. D. (1987a). Network interference and mental multiplication. *Journal of Experimental Psychology: Learning, Memory and Cognition, 13,* 109–123.

Campbell, J. I. D. (1987b). Production, verification, and priming of multiplication facts. *Memory & Cognition, 15,* 349–364.

Campbell, J. I. D. (1991). Conditions of error priming in number-fact retrieval. *Memory & Cognition, 19,* 197–209.

Campbell, J. I. D. (1997). On the relation between skilled performance of simple division and multiplication. *Journal of Experimental Psychology: Learning, Memory and Cognition, 23,* 1140–1159.

Campbell, J. I. D. (1999). Division by multiplication. *Memory & Cognition, 27,* 791–802.

Campbell, J. I. D., & Clark, J. M. (1989). Time course of error-priming in number-fact retrieval: Evidence for inhibitory and excitatory mechanisms. *Journal of Experimental Psychology: Learning, Memory and Cognition, 15,* 920–929.

Campbell, J. I. D., & Fugelsang, J. (2001). Strategy choice for arithmetic verification: Effects of numerical surface form. *Cognition, 80,* B21–B30.

Campbell, J. I. D., & Graham, D. J. (1985). Mental multiplication skill: Structure, process and acquisition. *Canadian Journal of Psychology, 39,* 338–366.

Campbell, J. I. D., & Timm, J. C. (2000). Adults' strategy choices for simple addition: Effects of retrieval interference. *Psychonomic Bulletin & Review, 7,* 692–699.

Campbell, J. I. D., & Xue, Q. (2001). Cognitive arithmetic across cultures. *Journal of Experimental Psychology: General, 130,* 299–315.

Clapp, F. L. (1924). The number combinations: Their relative difficulty and the frequency of their appearance in textbooks. *University of Wisconsin Bureau of Education Research, Bulletin No. 2.*

Compton, B. J., & Logan, G. D. (1991). The transition from algorithm to retrieval in memory based theories of automaticity. *Memory & Cognition, 19,* 151–158.

Fuson, K. C., & Kwon, Y. (1992). Korean children's single-digit addition and subtraction: Numbers structured by ten. *Journal for Research in Mathematics Education, 23,* 148–165.

Geary, D. C. (1996). The problem-size effect in mental addition: Developmental and cross-national trends. *Mathematical Cognition, 2,* 63–93.

Geary, D. C., Bow-Thomas, C. C., Fan, L., & Siegler, R. S. (1996). Development of arithmetical competencies in Chinese and American children: Influences of age, language, and schooling. *Child Development, 67,* 2022–2044.

Gillund, G., & Shiffrin, R. M. (1984). A retrieval model for both recognition and recall. *Psychological Review, 91,* 1–67.

Groen, G. J., & Parkman, J. M. (1972). A chronometric analysis of simple addition. *Psychological Review, 79,* 329–343.

Groen, G. J., & Resnick, L. B. (1977). Can preschool children invent addition algorithms? *Journal of Educational Psychology, 69,* 645–652.

Hamann, M. S., & Ashcraft, M. H. (1986). Textbook presentations of the basic addition facts. *Cognition and Instruction, 3,* 173–192.

Hecht, S. A. (1999). Individual solution processes while solving addition and multiplication math facts in adults. *Memory & Cognition, 27,* 1097–1107.

Hecht, S. A. (2002). Counting on working memory in simple arithmetic when counting is used for problem solving. *Memory & Cognition, 30,* 447–455.

Kamii, C., Lewis, B. A., & Kirkland, L. D. (2001). Fluency in subtraction compared with addition. *Journal of Mathematical Behavior, 20,* 33–42.

Knight, F. B., & Behrens, M. (1928). *The learning of the 100 addition combinations and the 100 subtraction combinations.* New York: Longmans.

Koshmider, J. W., & Ashcraft, M. H. (1991). The development of children's multiplication skills. *Journal of Experimental Child Psychology, 51,* 53–89.

LeFevre, J.-A., Bisanz, J., Daley, K. E., Buffone, L., Greenham, S. L., & Sadesky, G. S. (1996). Multiple routes to solution of single-digit multiplication problems. *Journal of Experimental Psychology: General, 125,* 284–306.

LeFevre, J.-A., & Liu, J. (1997). The role of experience in numerical skill: Multiplication performance in adults from China and Canada. *Mathematical Cognition, 3,* 31–62.

LeFevre, J.-A., & Morris, J. (1999). More on the relation between division and multiplication in simple arithmetic: Evidence for mediation of division solutions via multiplication. *Memory & Cognition, 27,* 803–812.

LeFevre, J.-A., Sadesky, G. S., & Bisanz, J. (1996). Selection of procedures in mental addition: Reassessing the problem-size effect in adults. *Journal of Experimental Psychology: Learning, Memory and Cognition, 22,* 216–230.

Logan, G. D. (1988). Toward an instance theory of automatization. *Psychological Review, 95,* 492–527.

Logan, G. D. (2003). Executive control of thought and action: In search of the wild homunculus. *Current Directions in Psychological Science, 12,* 45–48.

Logan, G. D., & Klapp, S. T. (1991). Automatizing alphabet arithmetic: I. Is extended practice necessary to produce automaticity? *Journal of Experimental Psychology: Learning, Memory and Cognition, 17,* 179–195.

Mauro, D. G., LeFevre, J. A., & Morris, J. (2003). Effect of problem format on division and multiplication performance: Division facts are mediated via multiplication-based representations. *Journal of Experimental Psychology: Learning, Memory and Cognition, 29,* 163–170.

Monsell, S. (1996). Control of mental processes. In V. Bruce (Ed.), *Unsolved mysteries of the mind: Tutorial essays in cognition* (pp. 93–148). Hove, UK: Erlbaum.

Murdock, B. B. (1993). TODAM2: A model for the storage and retrieval of item, order, and serial-order information. *Psychological Review, 100,* 183–203.

Parkman, J. M. (1972). Temporal aspects of simple multiplication and comparison. *Journal of Experimental Psychology, 95,* 437–444.

Parkman, J. M., & Groen, G. J. (1971). Temporal aspects of simple addition and comparison. *Journal of Experimental Psychology, 89,* 335–342.

Penner-Wilger, M., Leth-Steensen, C., & LeFevre, J.-A. (2002). Decomposing the problem-size effect: A comparison of response time distributions across cultures. *Memory & Cognition, 30,* 1160–1167.

Posner, M. I., & Mitchell, R. F. (1967). Chronometric analysis of classification. *Psychological Review, 74,* 392–409.

Robinson, K. M., Arbuthnott, K. D., & Gibbons, K. A. (2002). Adults' representations of division facts: A consequence of learning history? *Canadian Journal of Experimental Psychology, 56,* 302–309.

Seyler, D. J., Kirk, E. P., & Ashcraft, M. H. (2003). Elementary subtraction. *Journal of Experimental Psychology: Learning, Memory and Cognition, 29,* 1339–1352.

Siegler, R. S. (1987). The perils of averaging data over strategies: An example from children's addition. *Journal of Experimental Psychology: General, 116,* 250–264.

Siegler, R. S. (1988). Strategy choice procedures and the development of multiplication skill. *Journal of Experimental Psychology: General, 117,* 258–275.

Siegler, R. S., & Shrager, J. (1984). A model of strategy choice. In C. Sophian (Ed.), *Origins of cognitive skills* (pp. 229–293). Hillsdale, NJ: Erlbaum.

Stazyk, E. H., Ashcraft, M. H., & Hamann, M. S. (1982). A network approach to mental multiplication. *Journal of Experimental Psychology: Learning, Memory and Cognition, 8,* 320–335.

Sternberg, S. (1969). The discovery of processing stages: Extensions of Donders' method. In W. G. Koster (Ed.), *Attention and Performance II.* Amsterdam: North Holland.

Stevenson, H. W., Stigler, J. W., Lee, S.-Y., Lucker, G. W., Kitamura, S., & Hsu, C. C. (1985). Cognitive performance and academic achievement of Japanese, Chinese, and American children. *Child Development, 56,* 718–734.

Suppes, P., & Groen, G. J. (1967). Some counting models for first grade performance on simple addition facts. In J. M. Scandura (Ed.), *Research in mathematics education.* Washington, DC: National Council of Teachers of Mathematics.

Thorndike, E. L. (1922). *The psychology of arithmetic.* New York: Macmillan.

Wheeler, L. (1939). A comparative study of the difficulty of the 100 addition problems. *Journal of Genetic Psychology, 54,* 295–312.

Winkelman, J. H., & Schmidt, J. (1974). Associative confusions in mental arithmetic. *Journal of Experimental Psychology, 102,* 734–736.

Zbrodoff, N. J. (1979). *Development of counting and remembering as strategies for performing simple arithmetic.* Master's thesis, University of Toronto.

Zbrodoff, N. J. (1995). Why is 9 + 7 harder than 2 + 3? Strength and interference as explanations of the problem-size effect. *Memory & Cognition, 23,* 689–700.

Zbrodoff, N. J. (1999). Effects of counting in alphabet arithmetic: Opportunistic stopping and priming of intermediate steps. *Journal of Experimental Psychology: Learning, Memory and Cognition, 25,* 299–317.

Zbrodoff, N. J., Blizzard, J. S., & Ray, V. L. *Why is 9+ 7 harder than 2+3? Order and interference as explanations of the problem-size effect.* Unpublished manuscript.

Zbrodoff, N. J., & Logan, G. D. (1986). On the autonomy of mental processes: A case study of arithmetic. *Journal of Experimental Psychology: General, 115,* 118–130.

Zbrodoff, N. J., & Logan, G. D. (1990). On the relation between production and verification tasks in the psychology of simple arithmetic. *Journal of Experimental Psychology: Learning, Memory and Cognition, 16,* 83–97.

Zbrodoff, N. J., & Logan, G. D. (2000). When it hurts to be misled: Stroop-type interference in a simple arithmetic production task. *Memory & Cognition, 28,* 1–7.

$$\boxed{20}$$

Architectures for Arithmetic

Jamie I. D. Campbell
Lynette J. Epp

This chapter presents a review of research on the nature of the cognitive architecture that supports basic arithmetic memory, that is, memory for elementary number facts such as 4 + 6 and 6 × 3. Over the last 15 years, an extensive literature has accumulated that addresses the organization of the processes that subserves this fundamental intellectual skill. To begin, it is worthwhile to briefly define what a "cognitive architecture" is. To specify the cognitive architecture for a particular domain, one identifies the processing stages or modules believed to be involved and how they interact or communicate. For example, we can decompose the process of answering a simple arithmetic problem such as 3 + 4 = ? into a sequence of processing stages:

1. Convert the stimulus into the appropriate internal codes.
2. Retrieve or calculate the answer.
3. Produce the answer.

This decomposition implies an architecture comprised of cognitive subsystems for encoding, calculation, and answer production. We also need to specify how the subsystems communicate in order to make inferences about the behavior that the cognitive architecture predicts. There are a variety of ways to conceptualize this communication (see Shallice, 1988), but perhaps the most basic question is whether the stages are independent and additive or integrated and interactive. If two stages are additive, this implies that each completes its operations independently. For example, in simple arithmetic, if problem encoding and calculation stages are additive, this implies that once encoding is complete, calculation processes proceed in the same way independently of the conditions of encoding. In contrast, if encoding and calculation are interactive, then the conditions of encoding could directly affect how calculation proceeds.

The issue of interactive versus additive encoding-retrieval mechanisms is important—deciding it will influence the methods and theoretical directions of both cognitive and neuropsychological research in number processing (McCloskey & Macaruso, 1995). Furthermore, whether one can assume additive or interactive processes between modular systems has immediate implications for the interpretation of dissociations of number processing skills observed with brain injury (e.g., Whetstone, 1998). To pursue this issue, we will begin by introducing three approaches to the architecture for arithmetic that assume different positions on the underlying cognitive architecture. We will then review evidence concerning whether encoding and calculation processes are additive or interactive. To foreshadow our main conclusion, we argue that the balance of evidence favors the view that arithmetic encoding and calculation stages are interactive rather than strictly additive stages.[1]

ARCHITECTURES FOR NUMERICAL COGNITION

Abstract Code Model

Figure 20.1 depicts the model of number processing proposed by Michael McCloskey and his colleagues (e.g., McCloskey, 1992; McCloskey & Macaruso, 1994, 1995; Sokol, McCloskey, Cohen, & Aliminosa, 1991). The abstract code model identifies three types of cognitive systems in numerical processing: comprehension, calculation, and response production systems. Central to this model is the assertion that these subsystems communicate through the common use of a single, abstract, semantic quantity code. The comprehension system functions to encode different numerical input (e.g., Arabic digits or written or spoken number words) into the abstract code, which becomes the input upon which the calculation and production systems operate. The calculation system includes memory for basic number facts and rules (e.g., 5 + 7 = 12, 5 × 7 = 35, 0 × N = 0, 0 + N = N) and is also implicated in carrying out more complex arithmetic procedures (e.g., multidigit addition or multiplication). Arithmetic facts, as well as the numerical output of the calculation system, are in abstract code format. The production subsystem reverses the procedure of the comprehension system by converting the abstract output from the comprehension and calculation systems into Arabic, written, or spoken verbal number form as required.

The assumption of a unitary, abstract code as the basis for numerical calculation has implications for the independence of the processes involved. Because stimuli are recoded into the abstract code before calculation processes occur, input format necessarily has no impact upon calculation. Consequently, according to this model, calculation processes should exhibit no differences as a result of the original format of the numerical input. The abstract code model, therefore, implies that numerical encoding and calculation processes are independent and strictly additive in nature.

Triple Code Model

An alternative architecture for number processing was proposed by Dehaene (1992; Dehaene & Cohen, 1995). The *triple code model* is depicted in Figure 20.2. This theory posits that there are three codes upon which numerical processing is based: an analogue magnitude representation,

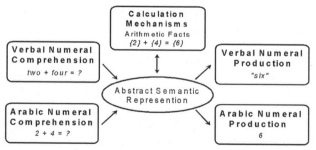

Figure 20.1. McCloskey's (1992) abstract code mode (adapted from Cohen & Dehaene, 1995, p. 132).

a visual-Arabic number form, and an auditory-verbal code system. In contrast with the abstract code model, it is assumed that the three codes can directly activate one another without the intervention of an abstract, amodal code. Like the abstract code model, however, each component is assumed to contribute to different number processing tasks. The analogue-magnitude code supports approximate calculation and estimation and number size comparisons and possibly has a role in subitizing. Digital input and output and multi-digit operations are mediated by the Arabic form. The auditory-verbal code mediates written and spoken input and output and provides the representational basis for simple addition and multiplication facts. The triple-code model thus assumes language-based representations in memory for number facts, as opposed to the language-independent processes assumed by the abstract code model. There is a variety of evidence that supports the assumption that memory for number facts involves linguistic codes (Campbell, 1994, 1997, 1998; Cohen, Dehaene, Chochon, Lehericy, & Naccache, 2000; Dehaene, Spelke, Pinal, Stanescu & Tsivkin, 1999; Spelke & Tsivkin, 2001; but see Brysbaert, Fias, & Noël, 1998; Noël & Fias, 1999; Whalen, McCloskey, Lindemann, & Bouton, 2002).[2]

Despite the absence of a central abstract code, Dehaene and Cohen's triple code model nonetheless predicts additive, not interactive, encoding/retrieval processes. In the triple code model, once input is transformed into the appropriate code, processing occurs in the same manner regardless of input format. Thus, any format-based differences in performance for a given numerical operation (e.g., magnitude judgment, numeral reading, number fact retrieval) should be attributable to differences in the efficiency of transcoding from the stimulus code to the type of internal code required for that operation (Dehaene, 1996; Dehaene & Akhavein, 1995; Dehaene, Bossini, & Giraux, 1993). Thus, as in the abstract code model, encoding and calculation processes in the triple code model are strictly additive.

Encoding-Complex Hypothesis

Campbell and Clark (1988, 1992; see also Campbell 1992, 1994; Clark & Campbell, 1991) pointed out that basic phenomena of number processing are not addressed by such simple, additive architectures. The view of an "encoding complex" is suggested by experimental evidence that resolution of interference among competing numerical responses and operations is fundamental to skilled numerical cognition. Numerals are strongly associated with a variety of numerical functions (e.g., number reading or transcoding, number comparison, estimation, and arithmetic facts); consequently, numerals automatically activate a rich network of associations that, in the context of a given task, includes both relevant and irrelevant information. Successful performance requires overcoming interference from this irrelevant information. For example, when skilled adults perform simple addition and multiplication under instructions for speed, the errors they produce reveal a plethora of influences. Errors usually involve

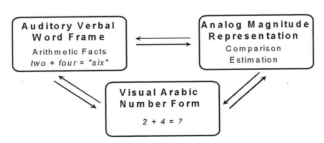

Figure 20.2. Dehaene & Cohen's (1995) triple code model (adapted from Cohen & Dehaene, 1995, p. 132).

associative or semantic neighbors in the same (3 × 6 = 21) or a related operation (3 × 6 = 9). Errors frequently involve intrusions by one of the problem operands (e.g., 2 + 9 = 9) or by an answer retrieved on a preceding trial. Furthermore, errors are most likely when such factors combine their influences on a specific trial. Factors that increase errors also tend to increase time for a correct response, which implies that resolution of interference is a pervasive factor in performance. Moreover, the influence of these factors can vary greatly depending upon surface format (e.g., Arabic digits vs. written number words; Campbell, 1994; Campbell & Clark, 1992; Campbell, Kanz, & Xue, 1999).

In the encoding-complex view, the importance of these phenomena is that they potentially demonstrate that the modular systems that subserve number processing often communicate interactively rather than additively. As in the triple code model, the encoding-complex view is that number processing involves task-specific activation of information in one or more representational codes (e.g., visual, visuo-spatial, verbal, motoric). The encoding-complex view assumes additionally, however, that communication between representational systems often involves interactive rather than strictly additive processes. Interactive processes are products of task-specific practice, which creates excitatory and inhibitory connections within and between systems to optimize resistance to interference (i.e., maximize activation of relevant information and minimize activation of irrelevant information). The development of such integrated encoding-retrieval procedures is a basic mechanism of acquisition of skilled number processing. Hence, the concept of *skilled processing* is at the heart of the encoding complex hypothesis.

Number Format and Simple Arithmetic

Researchers have extensively investigated the effects of surface form on arithmetic in order to analyze the relationship between encoding and calculation processes. Basically, if encoding and calculation are independent and additive, then calculation processes should not be affected by format. Before we examine this research, however, we need to distinguish situations in which effects of format on calculation are not diagnostic of the theoretically different positions outlined above. Zhang and Norman (1995) described how different numeration systems can entail unique representational properties that directly affect the ways in which numerical tasks are performed. If numerical notations vary in terms of the information they provide as external representations, then they will also vary in their effectiveness as memory aids, the information and structure that can be directly perceived, and operations that can be performed. In these ways notational systems can structure cognitive behavior and change the nature of a task. For example, Noël and Seron (1997) examined verification of simple addition and subtraction involving Arabic numerals and Roman numerals. They demonstrated that people can exploit the structure of Roman notation to solve simple true–false arithmetic verification equations. Specifically, relative to written word answers, people were faster when a Roman numeral answer matched the problem operands (e.g., VII = 5 + 2, IV = 5 – 1) than when they did not match (VII = 3 + 4, IV = 6 – 2). Thus, the specific componential structure of Roman numerals affords unique strategies for this arithmetic task. In contrast, the relation between quantity and the surface form of single Arabic digits or individual verbal number words is largely arbitrary. Consequently, as we discuss next, research investigating the relation between encoding and calculation has focused on how arithmetic performance varies depending on whether operands appear as written words or Arabic numerals.

Format Typicality and Arithmetic

Numerous experimental studies of simple addition and multiplication have compared performance with problem operands presented as Arabic digits to performance with operands as written number words. A wide range of languages has been examined, including French,

Dutch, English, German, Chinese, and Filipino (Bernardo, 2001; Blankenberger & Vorberg, 1997; Campbell, 1992; 1994; Campbell et al., 1999; Campbell, Parker, & Doetzel, 2004; Noël, Fias, & Brysbaert, 1997). These researchers developed elaborate theoretical arguments concerning format effects (see following sections), but in this section we want to highlight the most obvious and consistent result: performance of simple arithmetic with written number words (seven × six) is much more difficult than with Arabic problems (7 × 6). Results vary across specific experimental situations, but arithmetic with written words is as much as 30% slower and 30% more error prone compared to Arabic problems (Campbell, 1994). Thus, arithmetic for the less typical written word format is substantially impaired relative to the typical Arabic format.

The critical question, of course, is whether these large word-format costs arise in calculation or do they arise at another stage of processing. One possibility is that it simply takes longer to encode written number words than Arabic numerals (McCloskey, Macaruso, & Whetstone, 1992; Noël et al., 1997). Furthermore, longer encoding times for written problems could reduce the time allotted to calculation processes if people try to respond under a self-imposed deadline. Reduced calculation time for words relative to digits would naturally lead to the higher error rate observed with written word problems.

Although this is plausible, there are good reasons to reject a simple encoding account. Noël et al. (1997) compared word and digit multiplication to word and digit performance on a number-comparison task. The comparison task potentially estimated differences in encoding times for word and digit problems. For the comparison task, participants viewed two dot patterns for two seconds, and then either a pair of Arabic digits or a pair of number words appeared. Participants indicated with a button press whether or not the two digits or the two words corresponded to the numerosities represented by the dots. If word format response time (RT) costs arise during encoding, then these costs ought to be about the same in the multiplication and comparison tasks. Instead, Noël et al. also observed a large Format × Task RT interaction: Overall, the RT cost for words relative to digits was about 2.5 times larger in the multiplication task (≈ 335 ms) than the comparison task (≈ 140 ms). Thus, the majority (perhaps 200 ms) of the word-format cost in multiplication was not accounted for by encoding as measured by the number-comparison task.

Similarly, Campbell et al. (2004) compared simple addition, multiplication, and parity comparison tasks on pairs of Arabic digits or pairs of English number words. For the arithmetic tasks, participants stated the answer aloud as quickly as possible. For the parity task, participants saw two numerals separated by a horizontal line (e.g., 7 | 9) and indicated whether the two numbers had the same parity (i.e., odd–even status) by stating "yes" or "no." There was a large Format × Task RT interaction that reflected much larger word-format costs for addition (264 ms) and multiplication (241 ms) than comparison (123 ms). Campbell et al. (1999) compared Chinese-English bilinguals' performance with Arabic and Mandarin numerals (which function like number words) and found that word format costs for addition and multiplication (114 ms) were large compared to word format costs in the time to choose the larger or smaller of two Arabic or two Mandarin digits (43 ms).

Thus, word format costs to add or multiply two single digit numbers are much larger than can be accounted for by format-specific differences in the time required to identify or compare semantic properties of those two numbers. This makes it very unlikely that word format costs can be attributed simply to encoding differences. Another possibility is that word format costs arise during the production of the response, possibly because written number words activate phonological output codes that interfere with producing a spoken answer (Noël et al., 1997). Campbell and Fugelsang (2001) demonstrated, however, that large word format costs on RT and errors are observed using an addition verification task (4 + 8 = 11, true or false). In this task, participants responded with a button press rather than a spoken answer; consequently, word format costs cannot be attributed to interference with verbal production processes. In the following sections we review other types of experiments investigating format effects in arithmetic.

Working Memory

Blankenberger and Vorberg (1997) concluded that different surface forms may or may not access a common number-fact representation, depending upon the involvement of working memory: if solving a problem requires holding one or both operands in working memory (e.g., in phonological format), this will force conversion to the common working memory code, regardless of surface format. In contrast, if a problem is solved by direct retrieval and does not depend upon holding numerical operands in working memory, then the retrieval processes engaged may be format specific. To test this, participants produced answers to simple addition and multiplication problems (operands 2 to 6) presented in three different formats (Arabic digits, German number words, dice patterns). Participants either were shown both operands (visual display condition) or one operand was presented and other was held in working memory (memory display condition). In the memory condition, addition was faster than multiplication, but multiplication was faster in the visual condition. This difference was due entirely to multiplication number-word problems in the visual condition; specifically, multiplication was faster than addition with simultaneously displayed word pairs but was slower than addition in all other conditions. Blankenberger and Vorberg suggested that multiplication performance may be especially susceptible to phonological interference when the two operands appear simultaneously in word format.

Transfer of Practice

Rickard and Bourne (1996) examined transfer of practice in simple multiplication and division. They predicted that if number-fact representations are format specific, then the benefits of practicing specific problems (e.g., 6 × 7) should not transfer across formats (six × seven); however, if the storage of number facts is format independent then identical transfer should be observed within and across formats. Participants were tested on simple multiplication and division problems that were extensively practiced in either Arabic or verbal word format and then tested in both formats. RT analyses indicated strong format-specific transfer in both formats and also strong format-independent transfer. Reduction in the problem-size effect was primarily associated with format-independent transfer, but there was also some evidence for a format-specific component in this reduction. The authors suggested that extensive practice in a given format could lead to direct, format-specific associations, although the strong format-independent transfer suggested a primarily amodal representation.

Sciama, Semenza, and Butterworth (1999) conducted transfer experiments to investigate format and simple addition. In the first experiment, participants studied sets of simple addition problems presented in either Arabic or number-word format and then were tested with problems that were presented in the same format (matched), different format (mismatched), or were unstudied (new). Regardless of format, both match and mismatch conditions showed an RT advantage relative to new problems, but only words showed an advantage for match relative to mismatch; Arabic performance at test was equivalent for the format match and mismatch study conditions. A second experiment that examined addition transfer with Arabic and dot patterns for numbers produced comparable results: at test, Arabic problems appeared to benefit equally from matched and mismatched format at study, but addition of dot patterns was faster at test when format matched study than when it mismatched. Based on this asymmetry, the authors concluded that format-specific arithmetic representations mediated atypical forms (i.e., written words or dot patterns); but this leaves unexplained why Arabic problems at test benefited equally from matched (Arabic study) and mismatched (atypical at study) forms. A potential factor in the asymmetrical transfer for Arabic and the atypical formats is floor effects: matched Arabic problems at test were only 45 ms faster than new Arabic problems; in contrast, matched word problems in Experiment 1 were 96 ms faster than new word problems and matched dot problems were 106 ms faster than new dot problems. The much larger matched-format transfer effects for atypical, relative to Arabic format, would make the atypical conditions more sensitive to format-specific transfer.

There is also neuropsychological evidence for a format-specific component in transfer of practice with arithmetic. Whetstone (1998) studied the multiplication skills of patient MC, who had a left parietal lesion. MC was able to comprehend, transcode, and produce numbers and complete simple addition and subtraction problems, but his multiplication skill was severely impaired. MC was tested on simple multiplication problems from 2 × 2 to 9 × 9, presented in three formats (Arabic, verbal number, and written number form) and answered in verbal form. From these problems, the 18 problems with the worst overall performance were chosen for a retraining task in which MC received extensive practice on a given problem presented only in one format, followed by test sessions in which every problem was presented in each of the three formats. Whetstone reasoned that if storage of multiplication problems was format specific, an advantage for test problems whose format matched the study phase format for that problem would be found, with no transfer of practice effects to nonmatching problems. Indeed, problems in which the practice format matched the test format were faster than non-matching problems.

Problem Difficulty

Another type of evidence that format affects calculation concerns the *problem-size effect*, which is the common finding that the difficulty of simple arithmetic problems tends to increase with the numerical size of the operands. Small-number problems have stronger memory representations because they are encountered more frequently and may be less susceptible to retrieval interference (see chapter 19, this volume, and Campbell & Xue, 2001 for a detailed discussion of the PSE). Several studies have demonstrated that the problem-size effect in addition and multiplication is larger with problems in written verbal format (e.g., three + eight) than in digit format (3 + 8; Campbell, 1994, 1999; Campbell & Clark, 1992; Noël et al., 1997). For example, Campbell (1994) contrasted performance on "small" addition problems (both operands ≤ 5) to performance on "large" addition problems (at least one operand > 5) and found that the RT problem-size effect was much larger with English number words (+192 ms) than Arabic digits (+108 ms). Similar effects exist for other languages, for which the problem-size effect for simple addition or multiplication is smaller with Arabic digits than with number words written in French, Dutch, English, or Chinese (Campbell et al., 1999; Noël et al., 1997).

Given that the problem-size effect arises during calculation, the Format × Size interaction suggests that format affects the efficiency of calculation, with greater word format costs for more difficult problems. According to the encoding complex view, this occurs because word problems produce less efficient activation of relevant semantic information (e.g., weaker contribution of magnitude information with word problems) and stronger activation of irrelevant processes (e.g., stronger reading-based interference with word problems). Retrieval processes for larger problems, which often entail very weak problem–answer associations, are especially disrupted by the inefficient and unfamiliar encoding complex activated by word problems (Campbell, 1994; Campbell et al., 2004).

In contrast, Noël et al. (1997; see also McCloskey et al., 1992) argued that the Format × Size interaction in multiplication arises during operand encoding and demonstrated a comparable Format × Size effect when participants simply matched operands to dot patterns. In turn,

Campbell (1999) argued that if the Format × Size effect occurred during encoding, then an 800 ms preview of one of the two operands ought to cut the magnitude of the interaction in half. Participants received simple addition problems with operands presented as Arabic digits (e.g., 2 + 3, 8 + 6) or as English number words (two + three, eight + six). Operands either were displayed simultaneously or sequentially, with the left operand appearing 800 ms before the right operand. In the simultaneous condition, both operands would contribute to format-related differences in encoding, whereas in the sequential condition, encoding differences would arise only in connection with the second operand. The results showed that the Format × Size interaction did not differ between the sequential and simultaneous conditions, although the experiment had ample power to detect such an effect.

Campbell and Fugelsang (2001) tested adults on simple addition problems in a true/false verification task with equations in digit format (3 + 4 = 8) or written English format (three + four = eight). They found that the Format × Size effect (i.e., greater word-format RT costs for large than for small problems) was almost twice as large for true as for false equations. Error rates presented a similar pattern. As encoding and response requirements were the same for true and false equations, the triple interaction cannot be attributed to effects arising at these stages. Instead, surface format apparently affected the efficiency of retrieval or calculation processes differently for true and false equations. Campbell and Fugelsang proposed that performance on true verification trials is a more sensitive measure of the efficiency of arithmetic processes than is performance on false trials. For example, the problem-size effect was substantially larger for true (+ 368 ms) than for false equations (+ 281 ms). This would occur because arithmetic processing is less likely to need to run to completion for false equations, especially those involving relatively large-magnitude discrepancies (e.g., more than ±2 from correct), because such discrepancies can be detected while retrieval or calculation is in progress. In contrast, the difference in difficulty between small and large problems is more fully expressed on true trials. Consequently, the problem-size effect on true trials is more sensitive to manipulations that affect the efficiency of retrieval. Thus, the fact that the Format × Size effect was larger for true than for false equations suggests that the word format reduced the efficiency of arithmetic-retrieval processes.

Campbell et al. (2004) sought additional evidence that word-format costs tend to increase with problem difficulty. In two experiments with university students they demonstrated a parity effect for simple addition, whereby difficulty increased with the number of odd operands (i.e., even + even < even + odd < odd + odd). Furthermore, this parity effect was greater with word compared to Arabic format. There was no Format × Parity effect for simple multiplication, which rules out encoding as the source of the interaction for addition. Thus, like the Format × Size interaction, the Format × Parity interaction suggests that word format costs increase with factors associated with increased problem difficulty. This reinforces the hypothesis that format directly affects calculation.

Finally, Campbell et al. (1999) tested adult Chinese-English bilinguals on simple addition (2 + 2 to 9 + 9) and multiplication (2 × 2 to 9 × 9). Problem operands appeared as Arabic or as Mandarin numerals, which rarely appear in Chinese contexts involving calculation. Participants were cued prior to each trial to respond in Chinese or in English. The problem-size effect was larger when problems appeared in the unusual Mandarin format compared to Arabic format. Furthermore, there was a robust Format × Language interaction. Specifically, mean arithmetic RT to respond in Chinese was 84 ms faster with Arabic (985 ms) than with Mandarin stimuli (1069 ms), whereas mean RT for English responses was 121 ms faster with Arabic (1099 ms) than with Mandarin (1220 ms). Campbell et al. argued that the form of this interaction largely reflected participants' task-specific experience with each Format × Language combination. More generally, the Format × Language interaction is incompatible with the assumption that arithmetic performance in the different input–output combinations was mediated by a single, abstract retrieval stage.

Strategy Choice

Campbell and Fugelsang (2001) provided another type of evidence that format can affect the efficiency of arithmetic retrieval processes. Recall that, in their experiment, adults solved simple addition problems in a true/false verification task with equations in digit format (3 + 4 = 8) or written English format (three + four = eight). After each trial, participants also reported their solution strategy (direct retrieval or a procedural strategy such as counting or transformation [e.g., 6 + 7 = ? 6 + 6 = 12 + 1 = 13]. Campbell and Fugelsang replicated the standard Format × Size RT interaction, with greater word-format costs for large than for small problems. Crucially, reported use of procedures was much greater with word (41%) than digit stimuli (26%), and the increase in procedure use with words relative to digits was greater for numerically larger problems. As procedural strategies were about 500 ms slower on average compared to retrieval, the disproportionate use of procedures for large word-format problems contributed to the Format × Size interaction on RTs.

Campbell et al. (2004) extended this finding to the arithmetic production task (7 + 8 = ?) by demonstrating that Canadian university students were 50% more likely to report procedural strategies (e.g., counting, transformation) for simple addition with written English operands compared to Arabic digits. The results of Campbell and Fugelsang (2001) and Campbell et al. (2004) demonstrate that cognitive arithmetic can be directly affected by surface form, because the unfamiliar word-problem format greatly increased reported use of procedural strategies. According to Siegler and Shipley's (1995) Adaptive Strategy Choice Model (ASCM), selection of an arithmetic strategy depends on its relative efficiency (i.e., speed and probability of success). Consequently, manipulations that reduce retrieval efficiency promote a switch to procedures (Campbell & Timm, 2000). For example, one way that the word format interferes with performance is by promoting operand-intrusion errors (e.g., 8 × 4 = "twenty four," 2 + 8 = "eight"), in which one of the operands appears in the error. Operand intrusions are much more likely with word than digit stimuli, particularly for numerically larger problems (Campbell, 1994; Campbell et al., 1999; LeFevre, Lei, Smith-Chant, & Mullins, 2001; Noël et al., 1997). This word-specific interference reduces the efficiency of retrieval relative to digit problems, which could promote a switch from retrieval to procedures according to the ASCM model. Furthermore, because simple arithmetic problems are rarely seen in written-word format, the visual familiarity of word problems is low relative to the familiarity of digit-format problems. Consequently, the low familiarity of word problems could result in less retrieval and more use of procedures (Schunn, Reder, Nhouyvanisvong, Richards, & Stroffolino, 1997).

Types of Arithmetic Errors

The errors people make performing simple arithmetic have been an important source of evidence about the underlying cognitive processes. To investigate whether different input–output formats for calculation are mediated by a common number-fact representation, Sokol et al. (1991) carefully analyzed the multiplication deficit of a brain-injured patient, PS, who suffered left-hemisphere cerebral vascular damage. Multiplication problems from 0 × 0 to 9 × 9 were tested in combinations of three formats (Arabic numbers, written number words, and dots), resulting in nine stimulus-format by response-format combinations. They found no differences in error rates over the three formats for either stimulus or response format (stimulus: 12.4% Arabic, 13.0% Verbal, 13.0% Dots; response: 12.8% Arabic, 13.8% Verbal, 11.7% Dots). PS made several different types of errors, including operand errors (in which the given answer was the correct answer to a problem sharing one of the multiplicands with the given problem), table-related errors (in which the given answer was a correct answer for any single-digit multiplication question that did not share an operand with the given problem), and omission errors (in which no answer was given). Sokol et al. found that the proportions of each type of error were constant across changes in the stimulus or response format. They concluded that the results from patient PS support the assumption that arithmetic facts are stored in a format independent code.

Nonetheless, there is ample evidence that format has large effects on the specific errors that people produce (see Campbell, 1994, 1999; Campbell et al., 1999; Campbell et al., 2004; LeFevre & Liu, 1997; Noël et al., 1997). As noted previously, intrusion errors, in which one of the operands appears in the error (e.g., 2 + 9 = "nine" or 9 × 6 = "thirty six") are much more common and account for a higher percentage of errors with word stimuli than digit stimuli. Words may have a stronger capacity to activate numeral reading processes that interfere with answer retrieval (Campbell, 1997, 1998, 1999; but see Noël et al., 1997). In contrast, operation errors (e.g., 2 + 4 = "eight" or 2 × 4 = "six") are more common with Arabic than word stimuli (Campbell, 1994; Campbell et al., 1999; Campbell et al., 2004), suggesting that Arabic stimuli produce relatively stronger activation of arithmetic associations. Similarly, most errors involve answers that would be correct if one of the operands were changed by ±1 ("near" errors), but the word format produces a higher percentage of "far" errors relative to digit stimuli (Campbell, 1994; Campbell et al., 1999). Thus, arithmetic errors with word stimuli appear to be less constrained by semantic distance, suggesting that numerical-magnitude information is utilized less efficiently with word than Arabic stimuli.

Campbell (1994, 1997, 1998) argued that, relative to Arabic stimuli, word stimuli more-strongly activate numeral-reading processes that interfere with retrieval. This is supported by the higher rate of intrusion errors with words than digits. Campbell also pointed out that intrusion errors usually preserve arithmetically relevant information. For example, intrusion errors are as likely to be semantically related (e.g., be an answer in the correct times table; 3 × 7 = 27) as are non-intrusions (Campbell, 1994, 1997; Campbell et al., 1999). This would be expected if reading-based interference occurs during retrieval rather than only at production.

LeFevre et al. (2001) tested Chinese and English speakers who provided answers to visual Arabic and auditory multiplication problems in their native language. Because arithmetic often is practiced in silent auditory rehearsal, we would expect performance on auditory problems to be good. Indeed, LeFevre et al. found only subtle differences in RT. Overall, English speakers made more errors than Chinese speakers, but with Arabic format the Chinese speakers produced more operand intrusions than the English. LeFevre et al. suggest that this occurred because the Chinese emphasize verbal rote memory drills during acquisition; conse-quently, their number memory is especially susceptible to phonological interference from the operands.

Finally, Campbell (1994) demonstrated that another major influence on arithmetic errors, namely *inter-trial error priming*, is format specific. Error priming is the phenomenon that errors (e.g., 4 × 8 = 24) frequently match the correct answer to a problem solved earlier in the experimental session (see Campbell, 1999, and Campbell & Arbuthnott, 1996, for reviews of error priming research). Campbell (1994) tested adults on simple addition and multiplication under speed pressure to obtain a relatively high rate of errors. Arabic (4 + 8) and word format (six + three) alternated across trials. For both addition and multiplication, analysis of error priming showed that errors made on Arabic problems were primed by previous Arabic prob-lems but not by word problems, and vice versa. Format-specific inter-trial error priming strongly suggests that Arabic and word problems activated distinct processes for calculation.

Neuropsychological Dissociations

Although Sokol et al. (1991) found no evidence that the multiplication errors of patient PS depended on format, other researchers have found evidence for format-specific multiplication. Kashiwagi, Kashiwagi, and Hasegawa (1987) studied Japanese aphasics with impaired perfor-mance for simple multiplication. Despite extensive practice, the patients could not relearn multiplication with verbal presentation and responses. They did, however, learn to generate the multiplication facts given visual presentation combined with written responses. Such findings support the theory that the representations underlying multiplication facts can involve multiple codes that are differentially involved as a function of surface form. Similarly, Deloche and Willmes (2000) examined format effects on the multiplication verification performance of several patients. Stimuli were presented in either spoken number form or visual Arabic form using all the problems from 2 × 2 to 9 × 9 in both true and false equations. Based on the pattern of spared and intact multiplication facts as a function of format, the authors concluded that spoken verbal and Arabic stimuli involved distinct multiplication processes.

Such dissociation is not restricted only to simple multiplication. Cipolotti, Warrington, and Butterworth (1995) examined patient BAL, who suffered from aphasic hemiplegic hemianopia. In arithmetic tasks, BAL could successfully solve simple addition and subtraction problems with written input/spoken output and Arabic input/Arabic output conditions, but was slower and more error prone with Arabic input/spoken output. Thus, BAL's arithmetic impairment depended on a specific input/output combination. The authors concluded that surface form had a profound effect on BAL's processing of numbers and calculation, which they took as evidence for separate processing routes for the two number formats.

McNeil and Warrington (1994) investigated HAR, a 73-year-old male with right homoynmous hemianopia that seemed to affect his reading skills and verbal output skills but left his writing and comprehension of numbers intact. In a series of studies, HAR performed single-digit addition, subtraction, and multiplication problems that combined two formats of input (verbal spoken and visual Arabic) with the same two forms of output. HAR could accurately solve all types of problems with spoken input but was impaired in producing answers to Arabic problems involving addition and multiplication, although subtraction was intact. The authors interpreted these results as evidence for a "modality-specific, operation specific deficit" (p. 720).

Similarity of Calculation across Formats

Our review identified a variety of types of evidence for the conclusion that retrieval processes for simple arithmetic depend to some extent on surface format. In other words, much of the research favors the assumption that encoding and retrieval processes are interactive rather than strictly additive. This suggests that surface formats acquire task-specific associative links to the specific codes that mediate performance. How do we explain cases, however, in which the evidence seems to favor format-independent arithmetic?

One argument for format-independent arithmetic is the similarity of performance when arithmetic problems are presented in different stimulus formats and modalities (e.g., Sokol et al., 1991; McCloskey et al., 1992). Indeed, performance on Arabic digit and word problems typically are highly correlated (Campbell & Clark, 1992). One reason for this is that people may sometimes translate different stimulus codes to a single preferred code so that calculations are performed predominantly via one specific code, regardless of surface form (Blankenberger & Vorberg, 1999; Noël & Seron, 1993). Another possibility is that associative structures for arithmetic involving different codes all develop under common learning constraints, which produces similarities in performance across codes. Thus, it is not surprising that arithmetic performance across formats has substantial similarities.

The issue of skill may be relevant to some failures to find format-specific retrieval processes in acalculic subjects (e.g., Sokol et al., 1991). Brain-injured patients do not typically present the fluent performance characteristic of skilled retrieval. Brain-injured patients often cannot be tested with the speed-oriented paradigms common to cognitive psychology, either because patients have multiple impairments that restrict the kinds of tests that are possible or because even though the patient can complete a task with nearly perfect accuracy, the former skilled fluency of performance on that task is not preserved. According to the encoding-complex hypothesis, the interactive encoding-retrieval processes that give rise to format-specific effects often are an emergent characteristic of extensive practice and skill. If we assume that such skill entails a distributed system of interactive excitatory and inhibitory mechanisms, then the integrated system of interactive processes (cf. Dehaene & Cohen, 1997, p. 246), which *is* the skill, may be especially susceptible to damage. Consequently, even finely localized damage might destroy critical components of the complex interconnections acquired during skill acquisition and disrupt format-specific processing. The spared remnants may be configured to complete specific tasks by exploiting available associative and semantic structures and available transcoding paths; however, such a process would tend to emphasize the modular components of the system and provide little evidence for the interactivity of encoding and retrieval mechanisms that seems to characterize normal, skilled performance.

CONCLUSIONS

Our review demonstrated that many types of experimental and neuropsychological evidence indicate that retrieval processes for arithmetic vary with surface form and, hence, that encoding and retrieval processes for calculation are interactive rather than strictly additive. These phenomena challenge both the abstract code model (e.g., McCloskey, 1992; McCloskey & Macaruso, 1995) and the triple code model (Deheane & Cohen, 1995). Both models assume transcoding mechanisms that convert one format of representation into a different format, and that the transcoded information constitutes a new stimulus in the relevant system. Consequently, processing within that system should be the same regardless of the form in which it received the input. The theoretical advantage of positing such simple, non-interactive transcoding mechanisms is that they permit straightforward predictions about effects of manipulating surface form and about expected patterns of performance dissociations with brain injury. Indeed, without such assumptions, interpretation of dissociation data may be greatly complicated (Clark & Campbell, 1991; Plaut, 1995). Given the potential importance of interactive encoding-retrieval processes, can the abstract code and triple code models be reconciled with the data?

The abstract code model could be modified to allow input–output routes that bypass the hypothetical abstract code (Cipolotti & Butterworth, 1995). This would allow encoding processes for different numeral surface forms to interact directly with calculation mechanisms. A different modification would be to assume that processing of the abstract code itself can vary with format. This would allow format-specific effects to penetrate to calculation processes and produce interactive effects between encoding and calculation mechanisms. Although seemingly reasonable, such modifications fundamentally undermine the model, because the hypothetical abstract code no longer imposes constraints on how encoding, retrieval, and production processes can communicate. As this is the basic function of the abstract code assumption such modifications defeat the theoretical utility of the model. At this juncture, the onus is on proponents of the abstract code concept to identify phenomena that clearly require the assumption of a unitary, abstract quantity code.

In contrast, it is straightforward, in principle, for the triple code model to accommodate evidence for encoding-retrieval interactions. The theory inherently assumes format-specific links between encoding and number-fact retrieval processes but assumes that these links are additive. By allowing interactive effects to propagate between the three representational codes, the triple code theory becomes compatible with this assumption of the encoding-complex view and can accommodate format-specific calculation processes. This framework of interactive processing components within the architecture for arithmetic allows for the influence of numerical format not just on encoding stages but throughout all stages of numerical processing. Future theoretical and empirical work needs to focus on detailed modeling of the interactive processes that characterize the human cognitive architecture for number processing and arithmetic.

ACKNOWLEDGMENT

This research was supported by a grant from the Natural Sciences and Engineering Research Council of Canada.

NOTES

1. This chapter primarily concerns the relation between arithmetic encoding and calculation processes. For information in this volume about the memory processes that underlie arithmetic, see the chapters 5, 9, 19, and 21. See also Ashcraft (1992, 1995) and Campbell (1995) for reviews of research on memory processes for elementary arithmetic.
2. Evidence that linguistic codes contribute to number fact memory does not imply that arithmetic facts are always or exclusively stored in a linguistic format. For example, the possibility of a visual code for number facts is suggested by the results of Kashiwagi, Kashiwagi, and Hasegawa (1987), who successfully retrained patients on simple multiplication with Arabic-written input–output, although these patients could not relearn the multiplication facts with verbal input–output (see also McNeil & Warrington, 1994). Additionally, retrieval of arithmetic facts appears to involve magnitude processing that provides an approximate range for the correct answer (Campbell, 1995; Dehaene & Cohen, 1991). Thus, although there is substantial evidence that linguistic codes have a role to play, they probably are neither necessary nor exclusive codes for number fact memory.

REFERENCES

Ashcraft, M. H. (1995). Cognitive psychology and simple arithmetic: A review and summary of new directions. *Mathematical Cognition, 1*, 3–34.

Ashcraft, M. H. (1992). Cognitive arithmetic: A review of data and theory. *Cognition, 44*, 75–106.

Bernardo, A. B. I. (2001). Asymmetric activation of number codes in bilinguals: Further evidence for the encoding-complex model of number processing. *Memory & Cognition, 29*, 968–976.

Blankenberger, S., & Vorberg, D. (1997). The single-format assumption in arithmetic fact retrieval. *Journal of Experimental Psychology: Learning, Memory, and Cognition, 23*, 721–738.

Brysbaert, M., Fias, W., & Noël, M.-P. (1998). The Whorfian hypothesis and numerical cognition: Is "twenty-four" processed in the same way as "four-and-twenty"? *Cognition, 66*, 51–77.

Campbell, J. I. D. (1999). The surface form × problem-size interaction in cognitive arithmetic: Evidence against an encoding locus. *Cognition, 70*, 25–33.

Campbell, J. I. D. (1998). Notational and linguistic influences in cognitive arithmetic: Comment on Noël, Fias, & Brysbaert (1997). *Cognition, 67*, 353–564.

Campbell, J. I. D. (1997). Reading-based interference in cognitive arithmetic. *Canadian Journal of Experimental Psychology, 51*, 74–81.

Campbell, J. I. D. (1995). Mechanisms of simple addition and multiplication: A modified network-interference theory and simulation. *Mathematical Cognition, 1*, 121–164.

Campbell, J. I. D. (1994). Architectures for numerical cognition. *Cognition, 53*, 1–44.

Campbell, J. I. D. (1992). In defense of the encoding-complex approach: Reply to McCloskey, Macaruso & Whetstone. In J. I. D. Campbell (Ed.), *The nature and origins of mathematical skills* (pp. 539–556). Amsterdam: Elsevier Science.

Campbell, J. I. D., & Arbuthnott, K. D. (1996). Inhibitory processes in sequential retrieval: Evidence from variable-lag repetition priming. *Brain and Cognition, 30*, 59–80.

Campbell, J. I. D., & Clark, J. M. (1992). Numerical cognition: An encoding-complex perspective. In J. I. D. Campbell (Ed.), *The nature and origins of mathematical skills* (pp. 457–491). Amsterdam: Elsevier Science.

Campbell, J. I. D., & Clark, J. M. (1988). An encoding-complex view of cognitive number processing: Comment on McCloskey, Sokol, & Goodman (1986). *Journal of Experimental Psychology: General, 117*, 204–214.

Campbell, J. I. D., & Fugelsang, J. (2001). Strategy choice for arithmetic verification: Effects of numerical surface form. *Cognition, 80*, B21–B30.

Campbell, J. I. D., Kanz, C. L., & Xue, Q. (1999). Number processing in Chinese-English bilinguals. *Mathematical Cognition, 5*, 1–39.

Campbell, J. I. D., Parker, H. R., & Doetzel, N. L. (2004). Interactive effects of numerical surface form and operand parity in cognitive arithmetic. *Journal of Experimental Psychology: Learning, Memory, and Cognition, 30*, 51–64.

Campbell, J. I. D., & Timm, J. C. (2000). Adults' strategy choices for simple addition: Effects of retrieval interference. *Psychonomic Bulletin & Review, 7*, 692–699.

Campbell, J. I. D., & Xue, Q. (2001). Cognitive arithmetic across cultures. *Journal of Experimental Psychology: General, 130*, 299–315.

Cipolotti, L., & Butterworth, B. (1995). Toward a multiroute model of number processing: Impaired number processing with preserved calculation skills. *Journal of Experimental Psychology: General, 124*, 375–390.

Cipolotti, L., Warrington, E. K., & Butterworth, B. (1995). Selective impairment in manipulating Arabic numerals. *Cortex, 31*, 73–86.

Clark, J. M., & Campbell, J. I. D. (1991). Integrated versus modular theories of number skills and acalculia. *Brain and Cognition, 17*, 204–239.

Cohen, L., Dehaene, S., Chochon, F., Lehericy, S., & Naccache, L. (2000). Language and calculation within the parietal lobe: A combined cognitive, anatomical, and fMRI study. *Neuropsychologia, 38*, 1426–1440.

Dehaene, S. (1996). The organization of brain activations in number comparison: Event-related potentials and the additive-factors method. *Journal of Cognitive Neuroscience, 8*, 47–68.

Dehaene, S. (1992). Varieties of numerical abilities. *Cognition, 44,* 1–42.

Dehaene, S., & Akhavein, R. (1995). Attention, automaticity, and levels of representation in number processing. *Journal of Experimental Psychology: Learning, Memory and Cognition, 21,* 314–326.

Dehaene, S., Bossini, S., & Giraux, P. (1993). The mental representation of parity and number magnitude. *Journal of Experimental Psychology: General, 122,* 371–396.

Dehaene, S., & Cohen, L. (1997). Cerebral pathways for calculation: Double dissociation between rote verbal and quantitative knowledge of arithmetic. *Cortex, 33,* 219–250.

Dehaene, S., & Cohen, L. (1995). Toward an anatomical and functional model of number processing. *Mathematical Cognition, 1,* 83–120.

Dehaene, S., & Cohen, L. (1991). Two mental calculation systems: A case study of severe acalculia with preserved approximation. *Neuropsychologia, 29,* 1045–1074.

Dehaene, S., Spelke, E., Pinal, P., Stanescu, R., & Tsivkin, S. (1999). Sources of mathematical thinking: Behavioral and brain-imaging evidence. *Science, 284,* 970–974.

Deloche G., & Willmes K. (2000). Cognitive neuropsychological models of adult calculation and number processing: The role of the surface format of numbers. *European Child and Adolescent Psychiatry, 9* (Suppl. 2), 27–40.

Kashiwagi, A., Kashiwagi, T., & Hasegawa, T. (1987). Improvement of deficits in mnemonic rhyme for multiplication in Japanese aphasics. *Neuropsychologia, 25,* 443–447.

LeFevre, J., Lei, Q., Smith-Chant, B. L., & Mullins, D. B. (2001). Multiplication by eye and by ear for Chinese-speaking and English-speaking adults. *Canadian Journal of Experimental Psychology, 55,* 285–295.

LeFevre, J., & Liu, J. (1997). The role of experience in numerical skill: Multiplication performance in adults from China and Canada. *Mathematical Cognition, 3,* 31–62.

McCloskey, M. (1992). Cognitive mechanisms in numerical processing: Evidence from acquired discalculia. *Cognition, 44,* 107–157.

McCloskey, M., & Macaruso, P. (1995). Representing and using numerical information. *American Psychologist, 50,* 351–363.

McCloskey, M., & Macaruso, P. (1994). Architecture of cognitive numerical processing mechanisms: Contrasting perspectives on theory development and evaluation. *Cahiers de Psychologie Cognitive/Current Psychology of Cognition, 13,* 275–295.

McCloskey, M., Macaruso, P., & Whetstone, T. (1992). The functional architecture of numerical processing mechanisms: Defending the modular model. In J. I. D. Campbell (Ed.), *The nature and origins of mathematical skills* (pp. 493–537). Amsterdam: Elsevier.

McNeil, J. E., & Warrington, E. K. (1994). A dissociation between addition and subtraction with written calculation. *Neuropsychologia, 32,* 717–728.

Noël, M.-P., & Fias, W. (1999). Bilingualism and numeric cognition. *Psychologica-Belgica, 38,* 231–250.

Noël, M.-P., Fias, W., & Brysbaert, M. (1997). About the influence of the presentation format on arithmetical-fact retrieval processes. *Cognition, 63,* 335–374.

Noël, M.-P., & Seron, X. (1997). On the existence of intermediate representations in numerical processing. *Journal of Experimental Psychology: Learning, Memory, and Cognition, 23,* 697–720.

Noël, M.-P., & Seron, X. (1993). Arabic number reading deficit: A single case study or when 236 is read (2306) and judged superior to 1258. *Cognitive Neuropsychology, 10,* 317–339.

Plaut, D. C. (1995). Double dissociation without modularity: Evidence from connectionist neuropsychology. *Journal of Clinical and Experimental Neuropsychology, 17,* 291–321.

Rickard, T. C., & Bourne, L. E., Jr. (1996). Some tests of an identical elements model of basic arithmetic skills. *Journal of Experimental Psychology: Learning, Memory, and Cognition, 22,* 1281–1295.

Schunn, C. D., Reder, L. M., Nhouyvanisvong, A., Richards, D. R., & Stroffolino, P. J. (1997). To calculate or not to calculate: A source activation confusion model of problem familiarity's role in strategy selection. *Journal of Experimental Psychology: Learning, Memory, and Cognition, 23,* 3–29.

Sciama, S., Semenza, C., & Butterworth, B. (1999). Repetition priming in simple addition depends on surface form and typicality. *Memory & Cognition, 27,* 116–127.

Shallice, T. (1988). *From neuropsychology to mental structure.* Cambridge, UK: Cambridge University Press.

Siegler, R. S., & Shipley, C. (1995). Variation, selection, and cognitive change. In G. Halford & T. Simon (Eds.), *Developing cognitive competence: New approaches to process modelling* (pp. 31–76). Hillsdale, NJ: Erlbaum.

Sokol, S. M., McCloskey, M., Cohen, N. J., & Aliminosa, D. (1991). Cognitive representations and processes in arithmetic: Inferences from the performance of brain-damaged subjects. *Journal of Experimental Psychology: Learning, Memory, and Cognition, 17,* 355–376.

Spelke, E. S., & Tsivkin, S. (2001). Language and number: A bilingual training study. *Cognition, 78,* 45–88.

Whalen, J., McCloskey, M., Lindemann, M., & Bouton, G. (2002). Representing arithmetic table facts in memory: Evidence from acquired impairments. *Cognitive Neuropsychology, 19,* 505–522.

Whetstone, T. (1998). The representation of arithmetic facts in memory: Results from retraining a brain-damaged patient. *Brain and Cognition, 36,* 290–309.

Zhang, J., & Norman, D. A. (1995). A representational analysis of numeration systems. *Cognition, 57,* 271–295.

21

Mathematical Cognition and Working Memory

Jo-Anne LeFevre
Diana DeStefano
Benjamin Coleman
Tina Shanahan

INTRODUCTION

Mathematical cognition involves a variety of complex mental activities such as identification of relevant quantities, encoding or transcribing those quantities into an internal representation, mental comparisons, and calculations. Working memory encompasses "those mechanisms or processes that are involved in the control, regulation, and active maintenance of task-relevant information in the service of complex cognition" (Miyake & Shah, 1999, p. 450). Thus, it seems likely that mathematical cognition will involve working memory. In accord with this view, researchers have periodically emphasized the importance of working memory for understanding mathematical processing (Ashcraft, 1992, 1995; Ashcraft & Kirk, 2001; Hayes, 1973; Heathcote, 1994; Hitch, 1978). Despite the longevity and unanimity of the conclusion that mathematics and working memory should be closely connected, however, research on the role of working memory in mathematical cognition is sparse (Ashcraft, 1995; DeStefano & LeFevre, 2004) and none of the existing theories of mathematical cognition include an explicit role for working memory. This chapter is divided into three sections. First, we provide a brief overview of working memory and discuss models, methodologies, and tasks, using examples from the literature on mathematical cognition and working memory. Second, we review recent empirical research on mathematical cognition and working memory, focusing on four areas of particular interest. Third, we discuss directions for future research.

WORKING MEMORY FRAMEWORK

We assumed that working memory has the following characteristics. First, working memory and short-term memory are distinct constructs (Kintsch, Healy, Hegarty, Pennington, & Salthouse, 1999; Miyake, Friedman, Rettinger, Shah, & Hegarty, 2001). Short-term memory involves storage of information (e.g., remembering a phone number or a short grocery list), whereas working memory involves both storage and processing and is central to effortful mental activity (Kail & Hall, 2001; Miyake & Shah, 1999). Second, executive or central control of the processes and structures that constitute complex cognition is crucial to the construct. Third, the working memory system is limited in the amount of processing or storage, extent of interaction, or degree of control that it can accomplish in a given situation. Fourth, working memory includes both general aspects (such as attentional control functions that apply across cognitive tasks) and domain-specific aspects (such as processes that apply only to mathematical tasks; Miyake, 2001). Individuals may bring a domain-general working memory capacity to any task and, thus, in the early stages of acquisition of a complex skill (either for children or for novice adults), a large domain-general working memory may allow an individual to acquire new knowledge and domain-specific procedures more easily than someone with a smaller working memory (Conway & Engle, 1994; Engle, Cantor, & Carullo, 1992; Engle, Carullo, & Collins, 1991; Engle, Tuholski, Laughlin, & Conway, 1999; Hambrick & Engle, 2002; Turner & Engle, 1989). However, after mastery of the skill, measures of working memory will reflect both domain-general capacity and the domain-specific capacity related to expertise (Cocchini, Logie, Della Sala, MacPherson, & Baddeley, 2002; Daneman & Carpenter, 1980, 1983; Just & Carpenter, 1992). Individuals who are skilled at a particular cognitive task such as math or reading will have developed accessible representations of the information required for that task (i.e., number facts) as well as efficient procedures (such as counting). In accord with the model of long-term working memory developed by Ericsson and colleagues (Ericsson & Delaney, 1999; Ericsson & Kintsch, 1995), practice in a domain leads to the development of domain-specific, long-term retrieval structures that interact very efficiently with conscious working memory processes. Thus, the relative influence of domain-specific versus domain-general working memory capacity may depend on developmental level, expertise, and the particular task that is being performed. As discussed in the remainder of this chapter, both domain-specific and domain-general aspects of working memory need to be considered for understanding the role of working memory in mathematical cognition.

Methodologies

To simplify the discussion of particular experiments, we provide an overview of the main methodologies that have been used in research on mathematical cognition and working memory. Both experimental and correlational methods have been used to study working memory and mathematics. As in other areas of cognitive research, the methodologies that have been used in any particular research are linked to specific theories. For example, dual-task methodologies are closely linked to Baddeley's multiple-component model (e.g., Baddeley & Hitch, 1974), whereas correlational research on individual differences in working memory is more closely linked to unitary resource or attentional frameworks (e.g., Engle et al., 1999). Most of the methods, however, share an emphasis on individuals performing more than one task at the same time.

Experimental Methods

Baddeley's multi-component model of working memory includes two slave or storage systems, the phonological loop and the visual-spatial sketchpad, that are specialized for verbal and visual-spatial information, respectively (Baddeley, 1986; Baddeley & Hitch, 1974; Baddeley & Logie, 1999). A third component of the model, termed the central executive, is assumed to have a variety of functions related to controlling, scheduling, and managing working memory processes (Baddeley, 1986, 1996). Recently, Baddeley has proposed a fourth component of the model, the episodic buffer (Baddeley, 2002; Baddeley & Wilson, 2002). The episodic buffer is a storage system that integrates information from the phonological loop and the visual-spatial sketchpad. There has, as yet, been no empirical investigation of this component of the model as it relates to mathematical cognition. Although there are other multi-component models of working memory (e.g., Barnard, 1999; Kieras, Meyer, Mueller, & Seymour, 1999), Baddeley's version is the one most often used to frame research in mathematical cognition.

According to the multi-component model, activity in one slave system (e.g., the phonological loop) is independent of the other (e.g., the visual-spatial sketchpad). Hence, dual-task or memory-load approaches have typically been used to study the codes used to store and process information. In dual-task and memory-load approaches, participants perform a criterion task (e.g., reading or arithmetic) while either processing or storing some other information. In the *concurrent dual-task approach*, primary and secondary tasks are done simultaneously. Load tasks are chosen to represent different components of the working memory model, for instance, random letter, number, or interval generation is used to tax the central executive (DeRammelaere, Stuyven, & Vandierendonck, 1999, 2001); verbal tasks, such as articulating "the, the, the" are chosen to tap the phonological loop (DeRammelaere et al., 1999); and visual or spatial tasks are chosen to tax the visual-spatial sketchpad, such as tapping in a fixed pattern (Seitz & Schumann-Hengsteler, 2002). In the *memory-load version* of the dual-task method, the participant is given some items to remember (such as the letters "b d g h p"), next solves an arithmetic problem such as 42 – 8, and then reproduces the letters (Ashcraft & Kirk, 2001; Seyler, Ashcraft, & Kirk, 2003; Trbovich & LeFevre, 2003). In the concurrent and memory-load methods, performance when the primary and load tasks are combined (e.g., arithmetic + memory load) is compared to performance when the tasks are done alone. The underlying assumption is that changes in performance in the combined-task conditions provide evidence for the involvement of working memory in processing. The dual-task approach has been used in the literature on math and working memory to explore the working memory demands of simple arithmetic (e.g., DeRammelaere et al., 1999; Hecht, 2002; Seyler et al., 2003) and of multi-digit arithmetic (e.g., Fürst & Hitch, 2000; Seitz & Schumann-Hengsteler, 2000, 2002). Dual-task methods have also been used to test the hypothesis that the phonological loop and the visual-spatial sketchpad are both involved in mathematical processing (Heathcote, 1994; Logie, Gilhooly, & Wynn, 1994; Trbovich & LeFevre, 2003).

Correlational Methods

Another common methodology in the working memory literature is the use of correlational techniques to evaluate relations between criterion tasks (e.g., math) and measures of working memory. An underlying assumption of these methods is that variations in working memory capacity are general and relevant to a wide variety of cognitive tasks (Cowan, 1999; Engle et al., 1999; Kane, Bleckley, Conway, & Engle, 2001; Turner & Engle, 1989). According to a single-capacity or domain-general view of working memory, variations in working memory across individuals reflect the capacity of the central executive. Processes that have been attributed to the central executive include inhibition of irrelevant information, task switching, information updating, goal management, and strategic retrieval from long-term memory (Baddeley, 1996; Bull & Scerif, 2001; Engle et al., 1999; Miyake, Friedman, Emerson, Witzki, Howerter, & Wager, 2000; Oberauer, Süb, Schulze, Wilhelm, & Wittman, 2000).

Memory span measures are frequently used to index the central executive capacity of individuals. In a *short-term* memory task, such as forward digit span, participants are required to listen to a string of digits and then reproduce them in order. In a *working memory* version, participants remember the digits while performing some other task that requires processing. For example, backward digit span (i.e., in which participants reproduce the string of digits in the reverse order) is used as a working memory task because it indexes the concurrent storage and processing of information. According to Miyake et al. (2000), working memory span is closely related to the updating function of the central executive. Bull and Scerif (2001) studied the relation between central executive processing and mathematics performance among third-grade children. In addition to a counting span measure (described later), they assessed domain-general working memory using three other tasks. Task switching ability was measured with the Wisconsin Card Sorting Task (WCST), in which participants match items based on changing criteria (e.g., after 10 trials of matching on color, items have to be matched on shape). The amount of time it takes for the participant to adapt to the new criterion indexes the ability to switch tasks or strategies (cf. Miyake et al., 2000). The ability to inhibit irrelevant information was tested using two versions of the Stroop task, the traditional color-word version and a number version. People who are better at inhibiting irrelevant information show less interference from incongruent stimuli (e.g., were less likely to respond "three" when the stimulus was "222" and the task was to report the identity of digits in the string). Bull and Scerif found that counting span, task switching, and the number-Stroop task all predicted unique variance in the math ability of third graders. A fourth measure, dual-task performance, did not correlate with math ability. Thus, a variety of measures are available to researchers interested in the role of domain-general working memory in mathematical performance.

Working memory span is also used to index domain-specific aspects of working memory performance. The reading span task, developed by Daneman and Carpenter (1980, 1983), has provided the standard methodological framework for measuring individual differences in working memory (Daneman & Merikle, 1996). In the reading span task, participants read or listen to a series of sentences and remember the last word in each sentence. After all of the sentences have been presented, they recall the final words. Daneman and Carpenter viewed this reading span task as indexing the tradeoff between storage and processing. The span measure was correlated with performance on a variety of reading tasks across a very broad range of studies (Daneman & Merikle, 1996). Daneman and Carpenter assumed that reading span assessed functional capacity for working memory relative to reading and language performance because the processing task was language based.

A measure of working memory span called operation span replaces the sentence processing in the reading span task with an arithmetical equation (e.g., $[4 \times 2] - 5 = 7$; true or false?; Hitch, Towse, & Hutton, 2001; LeFevre, 2003; Salthouse & Babcock, 1989; Turner & Engle, 1989). The individual evaluates the truth of the mathematical statement and then remembers the last number in each equation. Counting span is a variant developed for children in which participants are shown a set of items (e.g., colored circles), are required to count a subset of them (e.g., the blue circles), and to remember the number counted. A series of such displays is shown and the counting span is the longest sequence for which participants can remember all the counts (Case, Kurland, & Goldberg, 1982). Despite the availability of operation and counting span measures for indexing individual differences in working memory, until recently, few researchers have used them for studying individual differences in math performance (Hitch et al., 2001; Leather & Henry, 1994; LeFevre, 2003).

In another correlational approach, researchers measure participants' performance on a large number of tasks and then use confirmatory factor analysis (CFA) to test hypotheses about the relations among the tasks (Miyake et al., 2000; 2001; Oberauer et al., 2000). For example, Miyake et al. (2001) explored the question of whether short-term memory and working memory performance are functionally distinct in the visual-spatial domain. Miyake et al. measured participants' performance on memory tasks that required visual and/or spatial memory. In contrast to the findings for verbal tasks where short-term and working-memory tasks are functionally distinct (Kail & Hall, 2001), the CFA indicated that short-term and working memory measures were indistinguishable when the memory content was visual or spatial. CFA shows promise for testing other questions about working memory, such as whether the functions proposed for the central executive are empirically separable (Baddeley, 1996).

Summary

Both experimental and correlational methods have been used to study working memory processes. All share an underlying assumption that working memory demands are tapped in complex situations that require the coordination of multiple processes. Thus, working memory measures may require participants to (a) perform more than one task simultaneously (as in dual-task or memory-load paradigms), (b) switch between tasks or processes (as in the Wisconsin Card Sorting Task or random number generation), (c) update incoming information (as in working memory span tasks), or (d) inhibit information that is irrelevant to the main task (as in Stroop tasks). The tasks vary in content; researchers who favor a domain-general view of working memory are more likely to choose measures in which performance is assumed to be independent of specific knowledge or skills (e.g., Wisconsin Card Sorting, backwards digit span), whereas researchers who favor a domain-specific view choose task variants that use knowledge or processes that are specific to the criterion task (e.g., operation span, number-Stroop).

The Role of Working Memory in Mathematical Cognition

To explore the relation between mathematical cognition and working memory, we conducted a broad survey of the literature. We found that working memory was often invoked as an explanation for effects or proposed as a source of variance in mathematical cognition. Empirical investigations of the link between the two constructs were less common, however (see DeStefano & LeFevre, 2004, for a review of research on working memory and mental arithmetic). We found that four issues or topics provided a reasonably comprehensive overview of the important issues and trends in the literature and, thus, used these to organize our discussion.

PROBLEM COMPLEXITY AND WORKING MEMORY

Problem complexity is the central variable in research on mathematical cognition (Ashcraft, 1992, 1995). There are at least three ways to operationalize problem complexity: (a) operand magnitude (e.g., 1 + 1 vs. 9 + 9); (b) number of digits in the operands (i.e., 2 + 3 vs. 25 + 67); and (c) the presence or absence of carry operations (e.g., 23 + 41 vs. 29 + 46). We propose that all of these variations in complexity can be linked to working memory demands by considering the number of steps required to solve the problems (DeStefano & LeFevre, in press). Thus, problems that can be retrieved directly from memory require the fewest steps (even if they have a large number of digits, such as 100 + 100). Problems that involve more digits (e.g., 23 + 4 vs. 23 + 14) require more steps than those that require fewer digits, and executing a carry adds still more steps (e.g., 23 + 14 vs. 29 + 14) to the solution process.

Single-Digit Arithmetic

A substantial portion of the research on mathematical cognition is focused on the processing of arithmetic problems, especially single-digit arithmetic. The pre-eminent result is termed the problem-size effect: problems with smaller operands and answers (e.g., 2 × 3, 5 + 2, 16 ÷ 2, 6 − 3) are solved more quickly and accurately than problems with larger operands and answers (e.g., 8 × 9, 7 + 6, 54 ÷ 9, 15 − 7; Campbell, 1994; LeFevre, Bisanz, Daley, Buffone, Greenham, & Sadesky, 1996; Miller, Perlmutter, & Keating, 1984). Number magnitude per se does not seem to be related to working memory demands, however. When participants used memory retrieval to solve single-digit problems, working memory demands were unrelated to changes in problem size (DeRammelaere et al., 1999, 2001; DeRammelaere & Vandierendonck, 2001; Hecht, 2002), in accord with the view that retrieval is based on automatic spreading activation (Ashcraft, 1985, 1992, 1995; Campbell, 1995; LeFevre, Bisanz, & Mrkonjic, 1988). The central executive demands implicated in retrieval of arithmetic facts, therefore, relate to some other aspect of the solution process that is not automatic (e.g., encoding, answer assembly, answer production).

In contrast, when participants used nonretrieval solution procedures such as counting (e.g., solving 9 + 3 by counting up 10, 11, 12), working memory demands increased in relation to the number of steps required to solve the problem. For example, Hecht (2002) found that the number of counts required to solve a problem was related to the extent to which articulatory suppression (i.e., saying the same alphabet letter over and over) caused interference in solution. Seyler et al. (2003) found that adults reported far more use of nonretrieval strategies on larger than on smaller simple subtraction problems and that larger problems were especially disrupted by a secondary letter-recall task. Thus, when participants used procedures other than direct retrieval, working memory requirements were related to problem complexity. The availability of working memory resources may help to explain the problem-size effect in simple arithmetic, at least to the extent that it can be attributed to the selection of nonretrieval procedures on larger problems (Campbell & Gunter, 2002; Campbell & Xue, 2001; Hecht, 1999, 2002; LeFevre, Bisanz et al., 1996; LeFevre, Sadesky, & Bisanz, 1996; Penner-Wilger, Leth-Steensen, & LeFevre, 2002).

MultiDigit Arithmetic

Research on multidigit problems also supports the view that working memory is related to the number of steps required to solve problems. Seitz and Schumann-Hengsteler (2000, 2002) reported evidence that working memory demands increase as the number of operands in the problem increases for addition and multiplication. Fürst and Hitch (2000) found that working memory demands were greater on carry problems (e.g., 459 + 876) than on non-carry problems (e.g., 452 + 241). Campbell and Charness (1990) examined the use of a complex algorithm for squaring two-digit numbers. They found that errors, especially those attributable to working memory failures, were most frequent at points in problem solution at which demands for retaining intermediate subgoals were highest. Ayres and colleagues reported a similar clustering of errors at points at which working memory load was expected to be highest on multistep tasks in algebra (Ayres, 2001) and geometry (Ayres, 1993; Ayres & Sweller, 1990). Thus, as problems increase in complexity—multiple digits, more complex algorithms, and therefore more steps—they are likely to require increased working memory resources.

Summary

Research on problem complexity and working memory suggests a direct relation between the number of steps required to solve an arithmetic problem and variation in working memory demands. Evidence for working memory as a source of the problem-size effect in retrieval, however, was not obtained, even though all arithmetic problems seemed to require working memory for some aspects of processing. These findings should be incorporated into models of arithmetic solution in order to link problem characteristics to mental processing. Working memory seems like a natural theoretical bridge between problem complexity (defined as a characteristic of the stimulus) and problem difficulty as reflected in the mental processes that influence performance.

CODE-SPECIFIC PROCESSING IN MATHEMATICAL COGNITION AND WORKING MEMORY

Mathematics encompasses a wide range of quantitative tasks, including arithmetic, geometry, algebra, and word problem solving. Although all of these mathematical tasks involve transformations of magnitude or calculations, the codes required for each one may vary because the tasks vary in the extent to which language, spatial processes, visualization, and potentially other cognitive abilities may influence performance. Research has shown, for example, that children's reading comprehension skills are an important correlate of their ability to solve math word problems (Aiken, 1972; Kail & Hall, 1999; Majumder, 2003; Muth, 1984). Computational skills are also important in word problems. Recent evidence suggests that working memory processes account for additional variability (Bull & Scerif, 2001; Majumder, 2003). Even simple arithmetic can activate different mental codes, depending upon contextual factors such as whether the problems are presented as words or digits (Campbell, 1994, 1998; Noël, Fias, & Brysbaert, 1997) or whether problems are presented vertically or horizontally (Heathcote, 1994; Trbovich & LeFevre, 2003). Such research seems likely to advance our understanding of the role of mental codes in working memory as well as in mathematical cognition.

Baddeley's multicomponent model of working memory provides the most obvious framework for understanding how different mental codes might be important in mathematical tasks. As reviewed by DeStefano and LeFevre (2004), phonological, visual, and spatial codes all seem to be implicated in mathematical tasks, albeit depending upon various conditions and situations. Evidence for a role for phonological codes in mathematics comes from research in which the duration of problems is varied (Fürst & Hitch, 2000; Heathcote, 1994). Heathcote (1994), for example, found that shorter durations of operands were more likely to result in the activation of phonological codes, suggesting the solvers use phonological codes to keep operands activated. Similarly, maintenance of interim results during complex calculations seems to be mediated by a phonological code (Fürst & Hitch, 2000; Heathcote, 1994; Logie, Gilhooly, & Wynn, 1994; Seitz & Schumann-Hengsteler, 2000, 2002). Such findings are consistent with a role for the phonological loop in short-term maintenance of verbal information. They do not preclude the possibility, however, that problem operands or other components of mathematical tasks may be temporarily stored in visual or spatial representations.

Evidence for a role for visual-spatial codes is weaker, although researchers have speculated that visual-spatial codes are central to mental calculation as well as to other mathematical tasks such as geometry. For example, Hayes (1973) argued that when participants are presented with a problem such as 789 − 45 in a horizontal orientation, they will attempt to visualize the problem with the digits aligned vertically so that they can apply a standard subtraction algorithm. He also noted that when no space was given below a vertically aligned problem to mentally "write" the answer, participants reported visualizing such a space, suggesting that they used a visual-spatial representation to manipulate the problem.

Surprisingly, little research has been done to pursue this issue since Hayes' (1973) observations. Trbovich and LeFevre (2003) found that participants showed evidence of using visual-spatial codes when problems (e.g., 34 + 9) were presented vertically but relied more on verbal codes when problems were presented horizontally (see also Heathcote, 1994). Such results suggest that the working memory codes involved in multi-digit arithmetic can vary with presentation format, although not necessarily in the ways proposed by Hayes (1973). Some correlational research also supports a role for visual-spatial codes in more complex mathematical tasks. The performance of adolescents (ages 15 to 16) on a math test that measured word problems, algebra, and geometry was correlated with their performance on mental rotation and visual pattern memory tasks (Reuhkala, 2001). In contrast, verbal short-term and working memory measures (word and reading span) did not predict significant variance in math scores. These results lend support to the notion that visual codes are used when the test requires advanced problem solving (e.g., geometry, word problems), but the use of a composite math measure makes it impossible to determine exactly what the relation is between particular math processes and visual-spatial codes.

Working memory codes may also vary with operation. For example, Lee and Kang (2002) found evidence that spatial and verbal loads differentially affected subtraction and multiplication of single-digit problems such as 4 × 5 or 9 − 3. Their results are not consistent, however, with the majority of other studies in which verbal loads were unrelated to participants' performance on simple addition or multiplication problems when the problems were solved via memory retrieval (DeRammelaere et al., 1999, 2001; Lemaire, Abdi, & Fayol, 1996).

Summary

Mathematical processes involve a variety of mental codes. Conclusions about the specific role of particular codes in mathematical tasks cannot be made, however, because the literature is very limited. Research is needed from a working memory perspective, but it should also be framed within a model of mathematical cognition such as Dehaene's triple-code model (Dehaene & Cohen, 1995; chapter 25, this volume) or Campbell's encoding-complex model (Campbell, 1994; chapter 20, this volume) in order to provide theoretical coherence to the research. Correlational research in which various mathematical outcome measures are related to various working memory measures would provide useful guidance. Recent brain-imaging research is consistent with the view that different mathematical tasks implicate different brain processes (e.g., Dehaene, Spelke, Pinel, Stanescu, & Tsivkin, 1999). In our view, working memory models seem likely to provide a useful theoretical link among these diverse findings.

INDIVIDUAL DIFFERENCES IN MATHEMATICAL COGNITION AND WORKING MEMORY

Accounting for individual differences on complex tasks such as reading has been one of the driving forces behind correlational research on working memory (Daneman & Carpenter, 1980; Just & Carpenter, 1992). Similarly, working memory has been proposed as one source of the difficulties shown by individuals with learning disabilities (Swanson, 1993). In research on mathematics, however, few researchers have collected data on the role of working memory as a source of individual differences in performance for normal adults (LeFevre, 2003). Hence, the bulk of evidence on working memory as a source of individual differences comes from two areas, research on the cognitive consequences of math anxiety among adults and research on math disabilities among children.

Math Anxiety and Working Memory

Ashcraft and his colleagues (Ashcraft, 2002; Ashcraft & Faust, 1994; Ashcraft, Kirk, & Hopko, 1998; chapter 18, this volume) have identified math anxiety as a unique phenomenon, separate from, although related to, other forms of anxiety. Ashcraft suggests that the worry and intrusive thoughts of math-anxious adults interfere with their ability to perform math tasks (Hopko, Ashcraft, Gute, Ruggiero, & Lewis, 1998) by functioning as a secondary task during mathematical processing and consuming working memory resources. In this view, when working memory is required in math tasks, individuals who are high in math anxiety will show degradation of performance in the form of longer reaction times, increased errors, or both. Evidence in support of this view was reported by Ashcraft and Faust (1994). They demonstrated that math anxiety is related to performance on addition problems (e.g., 14 + 25). The less-anxious individuals took a significantly more efficient approach to verifying false problems involving the carry operation than did their more-anxious peers. Although in general participants showed a pattern of increasing reaction times and error rates with increasing anxiety levels, the most-anxious participants tended to complete all complex arithmetic tasks quickly but at the cost of sharp increases in errors.

Ashcraft and Kirk (2001) showed that operation span was correlated with math anxiety. They also tested the hypothesis that math anxiety operates through working memory with a memory-load paradigm (Experiment 2). Adults completed a production task that included simple through more complex addition (i.e., two-digit with and without carrying) while performing a secondary task (i.e., keeping either two or six random letters in memory for later recall). In the error analysis, the larger memory load had a more disruptive effect on arithmetic performance than the smaller load. This effect was greater for carry than no-carry problems. Most important for their hypothesis, the cost of carrying increased with math anxiety. Ashcraft and Kirk concluded that math anxiety taps into at least some of the same cognitive resources as the carry operation and possibly arithmetic procedures in general.

Math Disabilities and Working Memory

Math disabilities have been linked to deficits in working memory (Hitch & McAuley, 1991; McLean & Hitch, 1999; Siegel & Linder, 1984; Siegel & Ryan, 1989; Swanson, 1993; Keeler & Swanson, 2001; Wilson & Swanson, 2001). Some researchers have suggested that individuals with math disabilities have a deficit in some aspect of central executive processing that is domain-general (Bull & Johnston, 1997; Geary, Hoard, & Hamson, 1999; Passolunghi & Siegel, 2001; Keeler & Swanson, 2001). Researchers have also found that children with math disabilities may have domain-specific deficits, showing reduced ability to process information that is specifically numerical (Bull & Johnston, 1997; Dark & Benbow, 1991; Geary et al., 1999; Koontz & Berch, 1996). A role for a variety of possible links between math disability and working memory is supported by the multi-dimensional nature of math disabilities (Geary, 1993; 1994; Hanich, Jordan, Kaplan, & Dick, 2001; Jordan, 1995; Jordan, Hanich, & Kaplan, 2003a,b; Jordan & Montani, 1997).

Children with arithmetic disabilities have been shown to have particular difficulty with task switching (Rourke, 1993) and with inhibiting irrelevant information (e.g., Passolunghi & Siegel, 2001). In a sample of children who varied in math ability, measures of executive functioning, such as the Wisconsin Card Sorting Task and the Trails task, have been shown to predict significant variance in math performance, even after reading ability and IQ were partialed out (Bull, Johnston, & Roy, 1999; Bull & Scerif, 2001; Majumder, 2003). Bull and Scerif (2001) suggested that children with lower math ability had difficulty inhibiting a learned strategy and switching to a new strategy (cf. Bull et al., 1999).

Wilson and Swanson (2001) explored the role of working memory in predicting mathematical performance in a group that included both math-disabled and normally achieving individuals ranging in age from 11 to 52 years. They used verbal and visual-spatial working memory spans to predict mathematics performance on a standardized computation test. They assumed that verbal span reflects domain-general demands on working memory, whereas visual-spatial span reflects domain-specific processes (following Siegel & Ryan, 1989). Wilson and Swanson found that both verbal span and visual-spatial span accounted for significant unique variance in math performance across the age range, suggesting that both domain-general and domain-specific aspects of working memory will be important in understanding the relation between working memory and math performance (see also Bull & Scerif, 2001; Geary et al., 1999; Keeler & Swanson, 2001; Swanson & Sachse-Lee, 2001).

As was suggested in the previous section, mathematics may involve a variety of different mental codes. Thus, the definition of a "domain-specific" working memory measure for a mathematical task may depend upon the processes and codes required by that task. Hanich et al. (2001; Jordan et al., 2003b) demonstrated that children who had both math and reading disabilities showed a different pattern of deficiencies than children who had only math disabilities. The former had profound problems that were probably linked to their phonological processing deficits, whereas the latter appeared to have specific difficulties with numerical magnitudes and visual-spatial processing. Although such findings are consistent with a role of domain-specific working memory in math disabilities, more research linking working memory processes to math performance is needed.

Many children with math disabilities have particular difficulty memorizing arithmetic facts (Geary, 1993, 1994; Hanich et al., 2001; Jordan & Hanich, 2000), and these difficulties persist over time (Jordan et al., 2003b; Ostaad, 1997, 1998). One speculation is that working memory limitations are a potential source of this difficulty. According to Siegler's model of arithmetic development, children initially use procedural solutions to solve arithmetic problems (e.g., solving 3 + 2 by counting up 4, 5). Successful solution of a problem with a procedural solution will increase the strength of the association between 3 + 2 and the answer 5 in the child's associative network. Over time, this association leads to a predominance of retrieval solutions over procedural solutions (Shrager & Siegler, 1998; Siegler, 1988; Siegler & Shrager, 1984). Geary, Brown, and Samaranayake (1991) suggested that working memory deficits may have contributed to the failure of children with math disabilities to develop representations of basic facts. The initial problem information may decay so quickly that the answer fails to become associated with the problem, even after extensive practice. Thus, children with math disabilities may continue to rely on procedural (especially counting-based) solutions, even though these solutions are more demanding than retrieval. Other research is consistent with the view that children with math disabilities find speeded math tasks particularly difficult (Jordan et al., 2003b; Jordan & Montani, 1997).

Summary

Research on the role of individual differences in working memory for mathematical performance suggests that variations in both domain-general aspects of working memory (e.g., overall efficiency and capacity) and in domain-specific aspects (e.g., speed of access to arithmetic facts) may be important. Research on math anxiety from a cognitive perspective is consistent with the view that anxiety consumes working memory resources, negatively affecting math performance. Children with math disabilities have a diverse set of difficulties with mathematics that may involve both central executive and domain-specific limitations. Although it seems likely that research on individual differences in working memory will have important implications for understanding mathematical cognition, considerably more research needs to be done that encompasses a wider range of participants and tasks. Routine inclusion of individual difference measures in experimental studies provides one way to facilitate the process.

DEVELOPMENTAL CHANGES IN MATHEMATICAL COGNITION AND WORKING MEMORY

Working memory is positively correlated with children's math ability (Adams & Hitch, 1997; Gathercole & Pickering, 2000; Klein & Bisanz, 2000), and with the amount of math learning over a 1-year period (Hitch et al., 2001). Domain-general changes in working memory, such as increased functional capacity with age (cf. Case, 1985), and domain-specific changes, such as availability of more efficient solution procedures (Shrager & Siegler, 1998; Siegler & Shrager, 1984), both help to explain the connections between mathematical development and working memory processes.

Domain-General Changes in Working Memory during Development

Speed of processing increases with age and enhances performance on many cognitive measures, including short-term and working memory span tasks (Case et al., 1982; Kail, 1991; Kail & Park, 1994). The relation between working memory and math performance is partly explained by the relation between working memory and general speed, as measured by such perceptual tasks as crossing out identical figures (for discussions of the relation between working memory spans and speed, see Ackerman, Beier, & Boyle, 2002; and Hitch et al., 2001). Bull and Johnston (1997) reported that general processing speed accounted for 8% of the variance in mathematics ability in 7-year-old children, over-and-above the 45% accounted for by reading ability. Speed of number identification and a composite of memory measures (counting, digit, and word spans) did not account for unique variance, suggesting that processing speed, and not domain-specific number skills or working memory capacity, is crucial to understanding math performance. Kail and Hall (1999) reported parallel results for children aged 8 to 12. Reading skill and general processing speed accounted for unique variance in word problem performance, but working memory measures did not. Thus, general processing speed accounts for some variance in math performance, perhaps because speed enables efficient activation of representations in long-term memory, such as retrieval of arithmetic facts (cf. Bull & Johnston, 1997).

Various explanations of the relation of speed to span have been proposed (Case et al., 1982; Hitch et al., 2001). Speed may relate to span in that faster processing is linked to faster rehearsal of information. Increases in memory span during development have been linked specifically to age-related increases in articulation rate, which reflect the speed of rehearsal in the phonological loop (Hitch, Halliday, & Littler, 1989). With faster rehearsal, more items can be kept active within a limited-capacity system (Baddeley, Lewis, & Vallar, 1984), and it is less likely that items will decay in a given time period (Hitch et al., 2001). The rapid decay of items in working memory has been shown to limit reading and operation spans (Hitch et al., 2001).

Math ability has also been correlated with speed on tasks that involve numerical information (Adams & Hitch, 1997; Case et al., 1982; Koontz & Berch, 1996). In studies of young children using the counting span task, Case et al. (1982) showed that speed of counting was the best predictor of counting span. Adams and Hitch (1997) demonstrated a linear relation between speed on simple addition problems and the complexity of addition problems that children (aged 7 to 11 years) could solve. Children who were slower on basic addition were less successful on more complex addition problems, perhaps because they were unable to process the parts of the problem quickly enough to coordinate them. This result suggests a role for general memory limitations in arithmetic problem solving.

A second domain-general increase in working memory is the growth of storage capacity (Case, 1985). Case (1985) argued that children's operations become more efficient during development, leaving more of the total processing space available for storage and thus increasing functional capacity. Research consistently shows that storage capacity is a factor in mathematics performance. Performance on working memory measures such as counting span and operation span increases with age (Case et al., 1982; Hitch et al., 2001). Accordingly, smaller short-term memory spans, as measured by forward digit and letter spans, are related to lower arithmetic scores in children (Geary et al., 1991; Webster, 1979). For older children and adults tested on more complex math, however, short-term storage capacity does not predict math performance (LeFevre, 2003; Reuhkala, 2001).

Children may fail on some problems due to capacity limitations, despite adequate conceptual knowledge (Adams & Hitch, 1997; Klein & Bisanz, 2000). Klein and Bisanz (2000) investigated the role of working memory in mental arithmetic with preschoolers. Children watched as the experimenter added and subtracted poker chips to a temporarily hidden set and then tried to make their set of chips "the same as" the experimenter's set. The problems varied in the number of units that needed to be represented. For example, the problem 5 – 3 has a *representational set size* (RSS) of 5 because the largest number of units that needed to be mentally represented at one time was 5. In contrast, the problem 3 – 1 has an RSS of 3, therefore requiring less working memory capacity than 5 – 3. Consistent with the view that working memory capacity predicts performance on these problems, Klein and Bisanz found that representational set size was the best predictor of accuracy and accounted for unique variability in error rates when combined in regression analyses with any other single predictor (i.e., first operand, second operand, sum, correct answer, and operation). These results are consistent with the view that even when children possess adequate concepts and procedures (e.g., they know how to add 2 to 3 chips), their performance is limited by memory constraints. Thus, a role for interactions between developing storage capacity and processing efficiency, and consequent changes in working memory capacity is supported for mathematical cognition, but considerably more research is needed to explore these relations.

Domain-Specific Changes in Working Memory during Development

Through experience, children learn to manipulate domain-specific representations (number representations and concepts) and to execute specific procedures (e.g., counting, representing problems). In young children, domain-specific representations are critical to mathematical ability. Accordingly, Griffin and Case (1997) recommended that educators and caregivers emphasize counting and quantity in their proposal for redesigning primary school math curricula. Empirical research has supported the view that familiarity with number representations is important for early math performance. Bull and Johnston (1997) reported that speed of identifying numbers is related to children's performance on tests of math ability at age 7, suggesting that children with high math ability may have more accessible long-term representations of numbers than children with low ability (see also Dark & Benbow, 1991. for supporting results from a study of mathematically precocious adolescents). Representations that are more stable or better organized may require less working memory to activate.

As children acquire factual knowledge about numbers, working memory demands may decrease because more inefficient strategies such as counting all items for addition are replaced by more efficient strategies, such as counting up or fact retrieval (Geary et al., 1991; Hiebert, Carpenter, & Moser, 1982; Lemaire & Siegler, 1995; Siegler & Shrager, 1984). Geary et al. (1991) studied addition performance and working memory in a short-term longitudinal study of first and second graders. Children showed increased reliance on retrieval and decreased use of counting across grades. This shift in strategies may result in decreased working memory demands for problems on which the children use retrieval. Even adults show greater working memory demands when they use counting as compared to when they use retrieval or derived-fact solutions on simple arithmetic problems (Hecht, 2002). In a sample of adolescents, the use of strategies, such as placing the numbers from a word problem into an equation, has been linked to mathematical talent (Dark & Benbow, 1990). This type of strategy could be used to isolate and structure problem-relevant information, reducing the total working memory load and decreasing interference from irrelevant words in the problem. Thus, changes in the mixture of solution procedures on arithmetic problems is likely to be one source of the improvements in performance with age that is related to working memory.

The evidence reviewed here suggests that experience with numbers and math leads to domain-specific changes in the working memory demands of arithmetic. Children recognize and activate numbers more quickly with experience. This faster access to representations in long-term memory can alleviate working memory constraints because there is less time for items being held in working memory to decay. Working memory demands also decrease as procedures for manipulating number representations become more automated through practice. For example, counting becomes less effortful and the count-on strategy for addition is replaced by efficient retrieval. Thus, there is clear theoretical support for the view that working memory changes will be important in understanding how mathematical knowledge and skill develop.

Summary

Our review supports the view that the availability of short-term and working memory across development constrains mathematical performance. According to Case's (1985) model of cognitive development, children fail on problems when they cannot manage all the information at once or when they fail to represent the problem appropriately. Thus, working memory measures could be used to predict difficulty in math and signal the need for intervention. We propose that studying the contributions of working memory demands to math performance is an important complement to research on conceptual demands that have become the focus of curriculum-oriented research.

DIRECTIONS FOR FUTURE RESEARCH

Despite the consensus view that working memory is important to understanding mathematics, many questions remain unexplored. One area of ignorance that seems particularly relevant is the role of working memory within models of numerical cognition. None of the "big three" models of numerical cognition, that is, Dehaene's triple-code model (chapter 25, this volume; Dehaene & Cohen, 1995), McCloskey's abstract code model (McCloskey et al., 1985; McCloskey, 1992; McCloskey & Macaruso, 1994; McCloskey, Sokol, & Goodman, 1986), and Campbell's encoding-complex model (Campbell, 1994; chapter 20, this volume) has explicitly defined a role for working memory in numerical processing. Anderson and Lebiere (1998) proposed a model of simple arithmetic that is implemented with the ACT-R architecture and that includes working memory processes. Their model is limited to simple arithmetic, however, and is not intended as a general model of numerical processing.

The task of integrating working memory into any of the models of numerical cognition is complicated by the problem of selecting which working memory perspective to choose. Some combinations seem at least superficially plausible, whereas other combinations seem unworkable. For example, McCloskey's abstract code model, in which all encoded information is transformed into an internal abstract code, seems most consistent with models of working memory that assume a that working memory is a domain-general pool of cognitive resources. In contrast, Dehaene's triple-code model and Campbell's encoding-complex model both postulate the existence of multiple internal codes for numerical information and thus appear to be more compatible with working memory theories such as Baddeley's multiple-code model, in which different tasks are associated with different internal representations. More generally, none of the models of numerical cognitions include explicit mention of the control processes necessary to accomplish mathematical tasks or of the mechanisms that account for variations in efficiency among adults or for developmental changes.

Connecting models of numerical cognition with models of working memory is clearly necessary to enhance theoretical development in mathematical cognition. This research endeavor is also likely to facilitate the further development of the working memory models. Mathematics seems to activate and require a variety of mental codes. Research suggests that these mental codes can be differentially activated, depending upon such factors as presentation format (e.g., words vs. digits or horizontal vs. vertical), while holding other factors (such as number size) constant (e.g., Trbovich & LeFevre, 2003). Combining such manipulations with working memory paradigms should allow researchers to explore a variety of interesting questions about both domains. In particular, the resulting evidence may be very useful in understanding the conditions under which different working memory "capacities" (i.e., phonological, visual, or spatial) are required or activated as well as expanding research on domain-specific processing beyond verbal and reading-related processes.

CONCLUSIONS

Our examination of issues related to mathematical cognition and working memory supports the assumption that mathematics and working memory are intimately connected. Working memory is useful in understanding effects of problem complexity, in particular, why problems with more steps might be more difficult than those with fewer steps. Similarly, because mathematics requires multiple mental codes, models of working memory that allow for code-specific components are helpful in understanding the inter-relations among the processes involved in math problems. Further, working memory appears to be central in understanding individual and developmental differences in math. Many children with math disabilities may have a deficit in the central executive component of working memory; however, variations in domain-specific aspects of working memory also seem to be relevant for understanding variability in math performance. Finally, the development of math abilities is likely to be tied closely to children's development of short-term and working memory capacity and to acquisition of domain-specific knowledge that results in increases in functional capacity. Thus, existing research reaffirms the assumption that working memory and math are closely connected. Nevertheless, our review also highlighted the many areas in which only minimal information about the relation between working memory and mathematics is available.

REFERENCES

Ackerman, P. L., Beier, M. E., & Boyle, M. D. (2002). Individual differences in working memory within a nomological network of cognitive and perceptual speed abilities. *Journal of Experimental Psychology: General, 131,* 567–589.

Adams, J. W., & Hitch, G. J. (1997). Working memory and children's mental addition. *Journal of Experimental Child Psychology, 67,* 21–38.

Aiken, L. R., Jr. (1972). Language factors in learning mathematics. *Review of Educational Research, 42,* 359–385.

Anderson, J. R., & Lebiere, C. (1998). *The atomic components of thought.* Mahwah, NJ: Erlbaum.

Ashcraft, M. H. (1985). Is it farfetched that some of us remember our arithmetic facts? *Journal for Research in Mathematics Education, 16,* 99–105.

Ashcraft, M. H. (1992). Cognitive arithmetic: A review of data and theory. *Cognition, 44,* 75–106.

Achcraft, M. H. (1995). Cognitive psychology and simple arithmetic: A review and summary of new directions. *Mathematical Cognition, 1,* 3–34.

Ashcraft, M. H. (2002). Math anxiety: Personal, educational, and cognitive consequences. *Current Directions in Psychological Science, 11,* 181–185.

Ashcraft, M. H., & Faust, M. W. (1994). Mathematics anxiety and mental arithmetic performance: An exploratory investigation. *Cognition and Emotion, 8,* 97–125.

Ashcraft, M. H., & Kirk, E. P. (2001). The relationships among working memory, math anxiety, and performance. *Journal of Experimental Psychology: General, 130,* 224–237.

Ashcraft, M. H., Kirk, E. P., & Hopko, D. (1998). On the cognitive consequences of mathematics anxiety. In C. Donlan (Ed.), *The development of mathematical skills* (pp. 175–196). Hove, UK: Psychology Press.

Ayres, P. L. (1993). Why goal-free problems can facilitate learning. *Contemporary Educational Psychology, 18,* 224–381.

Ayres, P. L. (2001). Systematic mathematical errors and cognitive load. *Contemporary Educational Psychology, 26,* 227–248.

Ayres, P., & Sweller, J. (1990). Locus of difficulty in multistage mathematics problems. *American Journal of Psychology, 103,* 167–193.

Baddeley, A. D. (1986). *Working memory.* New York, NY: Clarendon Press/Oxford University Press.

Baddeley, A. D. (1996). Exploring the central executive. *Quarterly Journal of Experimental Psychology: Human Experimental Psychology, 49A,* 5–28.

Baddeley, A. D. (2002). Is working memory still working? *European Psychologist, 7,* 85–97.

Baddeley, A. D., & Hitch, G. J. (1974). Working memory. In G.H. Bower (Ed.), *The psychology of learning and motivation* (pp. 47–90). New York: Academic Press.

Baddeley, A. D., Lewis, V., & Vallar, G. (1984). Exploring the articulatory loop. *Quarterly Journal of Experimental Psychology: Human Experimental Psychology, 36A,* 233–252.

Baddeley, A. D., & Logie, R. H. (1999). Working memory: The multiple-component model. In A. Miyake & P. Shah (Eds.), *Models of working memory: Mechanisms of active maintenance and executive control* (pp. 28–61). Cambridge: Cambridge University Press.

Baddeley, A., & Wilson, B. (2002). Prose recall and amnesia: Implications for the structure of working memory. *Neuropsychologia, 40,* 1737–1743.

Barnard, P. J. (1999). Interacting cognitive subsystems: Modeling working memory phenomena within a multiprocessor architecture. In A. Miyake & P. Shah (Eds.), *Models of working memory: Mechanisms of active maintenance and executive control* (pp. 298–339). Cambridge: Cambridge University Press.

Bull, R., & Johnston, R. S. (1997). Children's arithmetical difficulties: Contributions from processing speed, item identification, and short-term memory. *Journal of Experimental Child Psychology, 65,* 1–24.

Bull, R., Johnston, R. S., & Roy, J. A. (1999). Exploring the roles of the visual-spatial sketch pad and central executive in children's arithmetical skills: Views from cognition and developmental neuropsychology. *Developmental Neuropsychology, 15,* 421–442.

Bull, R., & Scerif, G. (2001). Executive functioning as a predictor of children's mathematics ability: Inhibition, switching, and working memory. *Developmental Neuropsychology, 19,* 273–293.

Campbell, J. I. D. (1994). Architectures for numerical cognition. *Cognition, 53,* 1–44.

Campbell, J. I. D. (1995). Mechanisms of simple addition and multiplication: A modified network-interference theory and simulation. *Mathematical Cognition, 1,* 121–164.

Campbell, J. I. D. (1998). Notational and linguistic influence in cognitive arithmetic: Comment on Noël, Fias, and Brysbaert (1997). *Cognition, 67*, 353–364.

Campbell, J. I. D., & Charness, N. (1990). Age-related declines in working memory skills: Evidence from a complex calculation task. *Developmental Psychology, 26*, 879–888.

Campbell, J. I. D., & Gunter, R. (2002). Calculation, culture, and the repeated operand effect. *Cognition, 86*, 71–96.

Campbell, J. I. D., & Xue, Q. (2001). Cognitive arithmetic across cultures. *Journal of Experimental Psychology: General, 130*, 299–315.

Case, R. (1985). *Intellectual development: Birth to adulthood.* Orlando, FL: Academic Press.

Case, R., Kurland, D. M., & Goldberg, J. (1982). Operational efficiency and the growth of short-term memory span. *Journal of Experimental Child Psychology, 33*, 386–404.

Cocchini, G., Logie, R. H., Della Sala, S., MacPherson, S. E., & Baddeley, A. D. (2002). Concurrent performance of two memory tasks: Evidence for domain-specific working memory systems. *Memory and Cognition, 30*, 1086–1095.

Conway, A. R. A., & Engle, R. W. (1994). Working memory and retrieval: A resource-dependent inhibition model. *Journal of Experimental Psychology: General, 123*, 354–373.

Cowan, N. (1999). An embedded-processes model of working memory. In A. Miyake & P. Shah (Eds.), *Models of working memory: Mechanisms of active maintenance and executive control* (pp. 62–101). Cambridge: Cambridge University Press.

Daneman, M., & Carpenter, P. A. (1980). Individual differences in working memory and reading. *Journal of Verbal Learning and Verbal Behavior, 19*, 450–466.

Daneman, M., & Carpenter, P. A. (1983). Individual differences in integrating information between and within sentences. *Journal of Experimental Psychology: Learning, Memory, and Cognition, 9*, 561–583.

Daneman, M., & Merikle, P. M. (1996). Working memory and language comprehension: A meta-analysis. *Psychonomic Bulletin and Review, 3*, 422–433.

Dark, V. J., & Benbow, C. P. (1990). Enhanced problem translation and short-term memory: Components of mathematical talent. *Journal of Educational Psychology, 82*, 420–29.

Dark, V. J., & Benbow, C. P. (1991). Differential enhancement of working memory with mathematical versus verbal precocity. *Journal of Educational Psychology, 83*, 48–60.

De Rammelaere, S., Stuyven, E., & Vandierendonck, A. (1999). The contribution of working memory resources in the verification of simple mental arithmetic sums. *Psychological Research/Psychologische Forschung, 62*, 72–77.

De Rammelaere, S., Stuyven, E., & Vandierendonck, A. (2001). Verifying simple arithmetic sums and products: Are the phonological loop and the central executive involved? *Memory and Cognition, 29*, 267–273.

De Rammelaere, S., & Vandierendonck, A. (2001). Are executive processes used to solve simple arithmetic production tasks? *Current Psychology Letters: Behavior, Brain and Cognition*, 79–90.

Dehaene, S., & Cohen, L. (1995). Towards an anatomical and functional model of number processing. *Mathematical Cognition, 1*, 83–120.

Dehaene, S., Spelke, E., Pinel, P., Stanescu, R., & Tsivkin, S. (1999). Sources of mathematical thinking: Behavioral and brain-imaging evidence. *Science, 284*, 970–974.

DeStefano, D., & LeFevre, J., (2004). The role of working memory in mental arithmetic. *European Journal of Cognitive Psychology, 16*, 353–386.

Engle, R. W., Cantor, J., & Carullo, J. J. (1992). Individual differences in working memory and comprehension: A test of four hypotheses. *Journal of Experimental Psychology: Learning, Memory, and Cognition, 18*, 972–992.

Engle, R. W., Carullo, J. J., & Collins, K. W. (1991). Individual differences in working memory for comprehension and following directions. *Journal of Educational Research, 84*, 253–262.

Engle, R. W., Tuholski, S. W., Laughlin, J. E., & Conway, A. R. A. (1999). The effect of memory load on negative priming: An individual differences investigation. *Memory and Cognition, 27*, 1042–1050.

Ericsson, K. A., & Delaney, P. F. (1999). Long-term working memory as an alternative to capacity models of working memory in everyday skilled performance. In A. Miyake & P. Shah (Eds.), *Models of working memory: Mechanisms of active maintenance and executive control* (pp. 257–297). New York: Cambridge University Press.

Ericsson, K. A., & Kintsch, W. (1995). Long-term working memory. *Psychological Review, 102*, 211–245.

Fürst, A. J., & Hitch, G. J. (2000). Separate roles for executive and phonological components of working memory in mental arithmetic. *Memory and Cognition, 28*, 774–782.

Gathercole, S. E., & Pickering, S. J. (2000). Assessment of working memory in six- and seven-year-old children. *Journal of Educational Psychology, 92*, 377–390.

Geary, D. C. (1993). Mathematical disabilities: Cognitive, neuropsychological, and genetic components. *Psychological Bulletin, 114*, 345–362.

Geary, D. C. (1994). *Children's mathematical development: Research and practical applications.* Washington, DC: American Psychological Association.

Geary, D. C., Brown, S. C., & Samaranayake, V. A. (1991). Cognitive addition: A short longitudinal study of strategy choice and speed-of-processing differences in normal and mathematically disabled children. *Developmental Psychology, 27*, 787–797.

Geary, D. C., Hoard, M. K., & Hamson, C. O. (1999). Numerical and arithmetical cognition: Patterns of functions and deficits in children at risk for a mathematical disability. *Journal of Experimental Child Psychology, 74*, 213–239.

Griffin, S., & Case, R. (1997). Rethinking the primary school math curriculum: An approach based on cognitive science. *Issues in Education, 3*, 1–65.

Hambrick, D. Z., & Engle, R. W. (2002). Effects of domain knowledge, working memory capacity, and age on cognitive performance: An investigation of the knowledge-is-power hypothesis. *Cognitive Psychology, 44*, 339–387.

Hanich, L. B., Jordan, N. C., Kaplan, D., & Dick, J. (2001). Performance across different areas of mathematical cognition in children with learning difficulties. *Journal of Educational Psychology, 93*, 615–626.

Hayes, J. R. (1973). On the function of visual imagery in elementary mathematics. In W. Chase (Ed.), *Visual*

Information Processing (pp. 177–214). New York: Academic Press.

Heathcote, D. (1994). The role of visuo-spatial working memory in the mental addition of multi-digit addends. *Cahiers de Psychologie Cognitive/Current Psychology of Cognition, 13,* 207–245.

Hecht, S. A. (1999). Individual solution processes while solving addition and multiplication math facts in adults. *Memory and Cognition, 27,* 1097–1107.

Hecht, S. A. (2002). Counting on working memory in simple arithmetic when counting is used for problem solving. *Memory and Cognition, 30,* 447–455.

Hiebert, J., Carpenter, T. P., & Moser, J. M. (1982). Cognitive development and children's solutions to verbal arithmetic problems. *Journal for Research in Mathematics Education, 13,* 83–98.

Hitch, G. J. (1978). The role of short-term working memory in mental arithmetic. *Cognitive Psychology, 10,* 302–323.

Hitch, G. J., Halliday, M. S., & Littler, J. E. (1989). Item identification time and rehearsal rate as predictors of memory span in children. *Quarterly Journal of Experimental Psychology: Human Experimental Psychology, 41,* 321–337.

Hitch, G. J., & McAuley, E. (1991). Working memory in children with specific arithmetical learning difficulties. *British Journal of Psychology, 82,* 375–386.

Hitch, G. J., Towse, J. N., & Hutton, U. (2001). What limits children's working memory span? Theoretical accounts and applications for scholastic development. *Journal of Experimental Psychology: General, 130,* 184–198.

Hopko, D. R., Ashcraft, M. H., Gute, J., Ruggiero, K. J., & Lewis, C. (1998). Mathematics anxiety and working memory: Support for the existence of a deficient inhibition mechanism. *Journal of Anxiety Disorders, 12,* 343–355.

Jordan, N. C. (1995). Clinical assessment of early mathematics disabilities: Adding up the research findings. *Learning Disabilities Research and Practice, 10,* 59–69.

Jordan, N. C., & Hanich, L. B. (2000). Mathematical thinking in second-grade children with different forms of LD. *Journal of Learning Disabilities, 33,* 567–578.

Jordan, N. C., Hanich, L. B., & Kaplan, D. (2003a). Arithmetic fact mastery in young children: A longitudinal investigation. *Journal of Experimental Child Psychology, 85,* 103–119.

Jordan, N. C., Hanich, L. B., & Kaplan, D. (2003b). A longitudinal study of mathematical competencies in children with specific mathematics difficulties versus children with comorbid mathematics and reading difficulties. *Child Development, 74,* 834–850.

Jordan, N. C., & Montani, T. O. (1997). Cognitive arithmetic and problem solving: A comparison and children with specific and general mathematics difficulties. *Journal of Learning Disabilities, 30,* 624–634.

Just, M. A., & Carpenter, P. A. (1992). A capacity theory of comprehension: Individual differences in working memory. *Psychological Review, 99,* 122–149.

Kail, R. (1991). Processing time declines exponentially during childhood and adolescence. *Developmental Psychology, 27,* 259–266.

Kail, R., & Hall, L. K. (1999). Sources of developmental change in children's word-problem performance. *Journal of Educational Psychology, 91,* 660–668.

Kail, R., & Hall, L. K. (2001). Distinguishing short-term memory from working memory. *Memory and Cognition, 29,* 1–9.

Kail, R., & Park, Y. (1994). Processing time, articulation rate, and memory span. *Journal of Experimental Child Psychology, 57,* 281–291.

Kane, M. J., Bleckley, M. K., Conway, A. R. A., & Engle, R. W. (2001). A controlled-attention view of working-memory capacity. *Journal of Experimental Psychology: General, 130,* 169–183.

Keeler, M. L., & Swanson, H. L. (2001). Does strategy knowledge influence working memory in children with mathematical disabilities? *Journal of Learning Disabilities, 34,* 418–434.

Kieras, D. E., Meyer, D. E., Mueller, S., & Seymour, T. (1999). Insights into working memory form the perspective of the EPIC architecture for modeling skilled perceptual-motor and cognitive human performance. In A. Miyake & P. Shah (Eds.), *Models of working memory: Mechanisms of active maintenance and executive control* (pp. 183–223). Cambridge: Cambridge University Press.

Kintsch, W., Healy, A. F., Hegarty, M., Pennington, B. F., & Salthouse, T. A. (1999). Models of working memory: Eight questions and some general issues. In A. Miyake & P. Shah (Eds.), *Models of working memory: Mechanisms of active maintenance and executive control* (pp. 412–441). Cambridge: Cambridge University Press.

Klein, J. S., & Bisanz, J. (2000). Preschoolers doing arithmetic: The concepts are willing but the working memory is weak. *Canadian Journal of Experimental Psychology, 54,* 105–116.

Koontz, K. L., & Berch, D. B. (1996). Identifying simple numerical stimuli: Processing inefficiencies exhibited by arithmetic learning disabled children. *Mathematical Cognition, 2,* 1–23.

Leather, C. V., & Henry, L. A. (1994). Working memory span and phonological awareness tasks as predictors of early reading ability. *Journal of Experimental Child Psychology, 58,* 88–111.

Lee, K. M., & Kang, S. Y. (2002). Arithmetic operation and working memory: Differential suppression in dual tasks. *Cognition, 83,* B63–B68.

LeFevre, J. (2003). *Individual differences in working memory and arithmetic.* Unpublished manuscript.

LeFevre, J., Bisanz, J., Daley, K. E., Buffone, L., Greenham, S. L., & Sadesky, G. S. (1996). Multiple routes to solution of single-digit multiplication problems. *Journal of Experimental Psychology: General, 125,* 284–306.

LeFevre, J., Bisanz, J., & Mrkonjic, L. (1988). Cognitive arithmetic: Evidence for obligatory activation of arithmetic facts. *Memory and Cognition, 16,* 45–53.

LeFevre, J., Sadesky, G. S., & Bisanz, J. (1996). Selection of procedures in mental addition: Reassessing the problem-size effect in adults. *Journal of Experimental Psychology: Learning, Memory, and Cognition, 22,* 216–230.

Lemaire, P., Abdi, H., & Fayol, M. (1996). The role of working memory resources in simple cognitive arithmetic. *European Journal of Cognitive Psychology, 8,* 73–103.

Lemaire, P., & Siegler, R. S. (1995). Four aspects of strategic change: Contributions to children's learning of multiplication. *Journal of Experimental Psychology: General, 124,* 83–97.

Logie, R. H., Gilhooly, K. J., & Wynn, V. (1994). Counting on working memory in arithmetic problem solving. *Memory and Cognition, 22*, 395–410.

Majumder, S. (2003). *Factors in mathematical word problem solving.* Unpublished doctoral thesis, York University, Toronto, Canada.

McCloskey, M. (1992). Cognitive mechanisms in numerical processing: Evidence from acquired dyscalculia. *Cognition, 44*, 107–157.

McCloskey, M., & Macaruso, P. (1995). Representing and using numerical information. *American Psychologist, 50*, 351–363.

McCloskey, M., Sokol, S. M., & Goodman, R. A. (1986). Cognitive processes in verbal-number production: Inferences from the performance of brain-damaged subjects. *Journal of Experimental Psychology: General, 115*, 307–330.

McLean, J. F., & Hitch, G. J. (1999). Working memory impairments in children with specific arithmetic learning difficulties. *Journal of Experimental Child Psychology, 74*, 240–260.

Miyake, A. (2001). Individual differences in working memory: Introduction to the special section. *Journal of Experimental Psychology: General, 130*, 163–168.

Miyake, A., Friedman, N. P., Emerson, M. J., Witzki, A. H., Howerter, A., & Wager, T. D. (2000). The unity and diversity of executive functions and their contributions to complex "frontal lobe" tasks: A latent variable analysis. *Cognitive Psychology, 41*, 49–100.

Miyake, A., Friedman, N. P., Rettinger, D. A., Shah, P., & Hegarty, M. (2001). How are visuospatial working memory, executive functioning, and spatial abilities related? A latent-variable analysis. *Journal of Experimental Psychology: General, 130*, 621–640.

Miyake, A., & Shah, P. (1999). Toward unified theories of working memory: Emerging general consensus, unresolved theoretical issues, and future research directions. In A. Miyake & P. Shah (Eds.), *Models of working memory: Mechanisms of active maintenance and executive control* (pp. 442–481). Cambridge: Cambridge University Press.

Miller, K., Perlmutter, M., & Keating, D. (1984). Cognitive arithmetic: Comparison of operations. *Journal of Experimental Psychology: Learning, Memory, and Cognition, 10*, 46–60.

Muth, K. D. (1984). Solving arithmetic word problems: Role of reading and computational skills. *Journal of Educational Psychology, 76*, 205–210.

Noël, M. P., Fias, W., & Brysbaert, M. (1997). About the influence of the presentation format on arithmetical-fact retrieval processes. *Cognition, 63*, 335–374.

Oberauer, K., Süß, H.-M., Schulze, R., Wilhelm, O., & Wittmann, W. W. (2000). Working memory capacity—facets of a cognitive ability construct. *Personality and Individual Differences, 29*, 1017–1045.

Ostad, S. A. (1997). Developmental differences in addition strategies: A comparison of mathematically disabled and mathematically normal children. *British Journal of Educational Psychology, 67*, 345–357.

Ostad, S. A. (1998). Developmental differences in solving simple arithmetic word problems and simple number-fact problems: A comparison of mathematically normal and mathematically disabled children. *Mathematical Cognition, 4*, 1–19.

Passolunghi, M. C., & Siegel, L. S. (2001). Short-term memory, working memory, and inhibitory control in children with difficulties in arithmetic problem solving. *Journal of Experimental Child Psychology, 80*, 44–57.

Penner-Wilger, M., Leth-Steensen, C., & LeFevre, J. (2002). Decomposing the problem-size effect: A comparison of response time distributions across cultures. *Memory and Cognition, 30*, 1160–1167.

Reuhkala, M. (2001). Mathematical skills in ninth-graders: Relationship with visuo-spatial abilities and working memory. *Educational Psychology, 21*, 387–399.

Rourke, B. P. (1993). Arithmetic disabilities, specific and otherwise: A neuropsychological perspective. *Journal of Learning Disabilities, 26*, 214–226.

Salthouse, T. A., & Babcock, R. L. (1991). Decomposing adult age differences in working memory. *Developmental Psychology, 27*, 763–776.

Seitz, K., & Schumann-Hengsteler, R. (2000). Mental multiplication and working memory. *European Journal of Cognitive Psychology, 12*, 552–570.

Seitz, K., & Schumann-Hengsteler, R. (2002). Phonological loop and central executive processes in mental addition and multiplication. *Psychologische Beitrage, 44*, 275–302.

Seyler, D. J., Kirk, E. P., & Ashcraft, M. H. (2003). Elementary subtraction. *Journal of Experimental Psychology: Learning, Memory, and Cognition, 29*, 1339–1352.

Shrager, J., & Siegler, R. S. (1998). SCADS: A model of children's strategy choices and strategy discoveries. *Psychological Science, 9*, 405–410.

Siegler, R. S. (1988). Strategy choice procedures and the development of multiplication skill. *Journal of Experimental Psychology: General, 117*, 258–275.

Siegel, L. S., & Linder, B. A. (1984). Short-term memory processes in children with reading and arithmetic learning disabilities. *Developmental Psychology, 20*, 200–207.

Siegel, L. S., & Ryan, E. B. (1989). The development of working memory in normally achieving and subtypes of learning disabled children. *Child Development, 60*, 973–980.

Siegler, R. S., & Shrager, J. (1984). Strategy choice in addition and subtraction: How do children know what to do? In C. Sophian (Ed.), *Origins of cognitive skills* (pp. 229–293). Hillsdale, NJ: Erlbaum.

Swanson, H. L. (1993). Working memory in learning disability subgroups. *Journal of Experimental Child Psychology, 56*, 87–114.

Swanson, H. L. (2001). Research on interventions for adolescents with learning disabilities: A meta-analysis of outcomes related to higher-order processing. *Elementary School Journal, 101*, 331–348.

Swanson, H. L., & Sachse-Lee, C. (2001). A subgroup analysis of working memory in children with reading disabilities: Domain-general or domain-specific deficiency? *Journal of Learning Disabilities, 34*, 249–263.

Trbovich, P. L., & LeFevre, J. (2003). Phonological and visual working memory in mental addition. *Memory and Cognition, 31*, 738–745.

Turner, M. L., & Engle, R. W. (1989). Is working memory capacity task dependent? *Journal of Memory and Language, 28*, 127–154.

Webster, R. E. (1979). Visual and aural short-term memory capacity deficits in mathematics disabled students. *Journal of Educational Research, 72*, 277–283.

Wilson, K. M., & Swanson, H. L. (2001). Are mathematics disabilities due to a domain-general or a domain-specific working memory deficit? *Journal of Learning Disabilities, 34*, 237–248.

22

Mathematical Problem Solving
The Roles of Exemplar, Schema, and Relational Representations

James A. Dixon

Human mathematical abilities are a deep and somewhat underappreciated mystery in cognitive science. How can we explain the apparent fact that humans develop a set of relational representations that are completely portable and abstract? Much of the power of mathematics stems from the fact that it can be divorced from context and applied across an unlimited range of situations. However, our experiences, mathematical or otherwise, are contextually bound; everything occurs in some rich and textured environment. It is not clear how abstract, relational representations could arise from context-rich experience or what the nature of those representations might be. Therefore, how mathematical representations might come into being poses a serious and important theoretical puzzle. Viewed this way, mathematical representations constitute a prime instance of this classic problem in cognitive science, the problem of abstraction.

In this chapter, I review research on mathematical problem solving, the ability to apply mathematics to novel situations, with an emphasis on what this body of work suggests about the representation of mathematical relations and how such representations might come to reside in memory. Representations in memory must, of course, support reasoning and problem solving, as well as performance on recall, recognition, and categorization tasks. Mathematical problem solving may be particularly useful for investigating abstract representations because it involves interpreting a contextually rich problem (Kintsch & Greeno, 1985) and generating a mathematical solution that instantiates the appropriate structural relations. Because one can manipulate the surface or contextual features of the presented problem independently of its underlying mathematical structure, it is possible to evaluate the degree to which mathematical structure has been disembedded from context.

First, I consider the case against the existence of an abstract representation of mathematics. Under this hypothesis, mathematical relations are not abstracted; rather, each mathematical operation is represented by the set of problems one has previously solved with that operation. Next, I consider the hypothesis that problem schemas, summary representations that contain both contextual and structural features, develop over the course of experience with multiple problems. Finally, I propose an alternative, complementary representation and propose that two processes operate on different representations during mathematical problem solving. Given the extensive literature on this topic, my review is illustrative rather than comprehensive.

It is also worth noting at the outset that the mathematics addressed in this area is largely limited to foundational operations in arithmetic and algebra.

THE EXEMPLAR HYPOTHESIS:
MATHEMATICAL RELATIONS ARE NOT ABSTRACTED

A classic view in theorizing about problem solving is that previous examples or experiences are accessed and used to help solve a current problem (Duncker, 1945; Spearman, 1923). A large body of work has shown that people refer to previously solved problems in mathematical problem solving, even when the solution procedure is presented with the current problem (Anderson & Thompson, 1989; Ross, 1987; Rumelhart, 1989). Therefore, it seems reasonable to suppose that perhaps the set of previously solved problems stored in memory is a powerful representation of mathematical structure.

Detecting Problem Structure

Work by Reed (1987) addressed important aspects of the exemplar account. The logic of his approach was straightforward. If stored exemplars form the representation of mathematical relations, then people must compare the current problem (i.e., the problem they are trying to solve) to an exemplar stored in memory. Finding appropriate, structurally analogous exemplars will be crucial, because only those exemplars will be linked to the correct mathematical solution. In order to find an appropriate exemplar, one must be able to detect, and ultimately map, the structure of the current problem to that of the stored problem. To assess whether this was a reasonable explanation of mathematical problem solving, Reed tested whether people could detect and map structure across pairs of presented problems, forgoing temporarily the additional difficulties of recalling the stored problems in detail.

Reed applied structure-mapping theory (Gentner, 1983) to the process of solving word problems with mathematics. According to structure-mapping theory, the mapping process is influenced by the structural similarity between the base and target problem. Mapping is also influenced by transparency, the degree to which relations in the base problems are easily identifiable as relevant to the target problem (e.g., have similar surface features).

One straightforward implication of structure-mapping theory is that structural similarity and transparency should affect people's perceptions of problem similarity. If people are supposed to be selecting previously solved problems from a collection of exemplars in memory, then it seems necessary for them to discriminate relevant from irrelevant exemplars. To test this prediction, Reed asked participants to rate how useful it would be to know the solution to one problem (i.e., the base) for solving another problem (i.e., the target). In Experiment 1, Reed constructed 10 problems from a class of mixture problems with the general mathematical form: $P_1 \times A_1 + P_2 \times (A_2 - A_1) = P_3 \times A_2$. He manipulated whether problems were structurally isomorphic and whether they shared surface features. For example, consider the following three problems:

Chemist: A chemist mixes a 20% alcohol solution with a 30% alcohol solution. How many pints of each are needed to make 10 pints of a 22% alcohol solution?

Nurse: A nurse mixes a 6% boric acid solution with a 12% boric acid solution. How many pints of each are needed to make 4.5 pints of an 8% boric acid solution?

Auto: An automobile radiator contains 16 quarts of a 20% solution of antifreeze. How much of the original solution must be drawn off and replaced with 80% antifreeze to make a solution of 25% antifreeze?

The first two problems, Chemist and Nurse, are structurally isomorphic. They have the same mathematical structure. The third problem, Auto, has a different mathematical structure, despite being from the same general class of mixture problems. This is most easily shown by noting that the first two problems require computing two quantities, but the third problem only requires one. All three problems have strong surface similarity in that they involve mixing liquid solutions with different concentrations. Other problems in the set involved mixing dry items (e.g., candy) or interest rates and, therefore, had different surface features.

For all possible pairs of problems, college students were asked to evaluate how much knowing the solution to the first problem would help them solve the second problem. All problems occurred as both base and target.

Reed found that participants' ratings were influenced by surface similarity but not by structural similarity. Participants' insensitivity to problem structure in this situation is surprising, because the problems appear substantially different in structure. Requiring one or two quantities as an answer is not a subtle difference in problem structure, and these differences make a difference when college students are asked to solve problems (Reed, Dempster, & Ettinger, 1985).

Reed suggested that the mixture problems might have been too similar for the participants to notice the differences. In Experiment 2, he used the same procedure with a new category of mathematical problem, work problems. As in the first experiment, he varied both the structure and surface similarity of the problems. Consider these two structurally isomorphic examples:

Hose: A small hose can fill a swimming pool in 6 hours and a large one can fill it in 3 hours. How long will it take to fill the pool if both hoses are used at the same time?

Paint: Bob can paint a room in 6 hours and Fred can paint it in 4 hours. How long will it take them if they both work together?

These problems have different surface features but the same mathematical structure. The following problem shares surface features with the hose problem but has a different mathematical form.

Tank: A small pipe can fill a water tank in 20 hours and a large pipe can fill it in 15 hours. Water is used at a rate that would empty a full tank in 40 hours. How long will it take to fill the tank when both pipes are used at the same time, assuming that water is being used as the tank is filled?

Reed found that participants were sensitive to both the surface and structural features of these problems. As in the first experiment, problems with similar story contexts were judged as being more informative. However, in contrast to the first experiment, participants also rated problems with the same mathematical structure as more informative. It appears that the structural differences among this set of problems were sufficient for participants to detect.

In a third experiment, Reed presented students with either mixture or work problems and asked them to write the correct solution equation. They were given an example solution that was structurally isomorphic to two of the four target problems. Participants generated correct equations for target problems that were structurally isomorphic to the example much more frequently than for problems that were not isomorphic.

Reed's work established an important prerequisite for the hypothesis that stored exemplars serve as mathematical representations: participants can, at least sometimes, detect structural commonalities. A further, more stringent test of this hypothesis would require that participants solve a problem through comparison to an exemplar stored in memory.

Utilizing Stored Exemplars

Research by Novick and Ross illustrates some of the difficulties with accessing and mapping stored problems to a current one. Novick (1988) showed that participants could transfer a mathematical solution from a single example (i.e., the base problem) stored in memory to an ostensibly unrelated target problem presented at a later time. In the first experiment, the base problem, presented as one of four pretest problems for a later experiment, had either the same mathematical structure as the the target problem or an unrelated structure. In both conditions, the surface features of the base and target problems were largely dissimilar. Half the participants were expert at mathematics (i.e., had scores above 690 on the quantitative portion of the SAT), the other half were less expert (had scores between 500 and 650 on the SAT). The expert group showed strong transfer, but the novice group did not.

In a second experiment using the same procedure, Novick changed the base problem such that in one condition it was structurally unrelated to the target problem but shared many surface features (e.g., both problems involved people and rows). In the other condition, the base problem was unrelated to the target both structurally and superficially. Despite the fact that the base and target did not share a common mathematical structure, both experts and novices showed transfer of the inappropriate mathematical solution when the base and target problem shared surface features.

In a third experiment, Novick included two potentially relevant base problems: the structurally matching problem from Experiment 1 and the superficially matching, but structurally unrelated, problem from Experiment 2. She found that experts were more likely to transfer the mathematical solution from the structurally similar base problem than were novices. Novices transferred the inappropriate solution from the superficially related problem more often, although a substantial percentage of the experts did so as well (46%).

These experiments show that single examples can be retrieved spontaneously from memory and that the solution procedures from them can be applied to new problems. It is also clear from this work that both the structural and surface features of problems are involved in this process. Interestingly, regardless of their degree of mathematical skill, participants in Novick's second experiment transferred an inappropriate solution to the target problems. Experiment 3 replicates this result that both experts and novices transferred the inappropriate solution, although the novices did so more often. If one assumes that participants had an adequate understanding of the relations in both the base and target problems, then a somewhat uncomfortable conclusion follows: people readily transfer solutions across mismatched structures.

The Role of Surface Similarity

Novick's results highlight the possibility that nonstructural features play a role in accessing and mapping previously solved problems. Ross and his colleagues have extensively investigated this issue. For example, Ross (1989) showed that one type of surface similarity, whether the story lines in the base and target problems shared common features, strongly affected access to the base problem but did not affect mapping. Another type of surface similarity, whether similar objects occupy similar roles in the base and target problems, affects mapping. Even when the solution operation (i.e., appropriate formula) was provided with the target problem, participants who had studied an example that had reversed object correspondences relative to the current problem (e.g., mechanics assigned to cars versus cars assigned to mechanics) tended to assign the items in the problems to the wrong variables.

In later work, Ross and Kilbane (1997) showed that the effect of object correspondence on analogical mapping depends on how the original mathematical operation was presented and whether the story line was similar. In their first experiment, each of four probability principles was first presented as an abstract, mathematical concept, followed immediately by a completed example. Participants were then asked to solve problems with each principle; the mathematical formula, but not the example, was presented along with each new problem. Half the target problems had story lines that were highly similar to the appropriate base problem, and the remaining problems had story lines that differed from the base problem. For problems that had highly similar story lines, object correspondence had strong effects; participants often reversed assignment of items to variables in the equations. There were significantly fewer reversals when the story lines were not identical.

In a second experiment, Ross and Kilbane introduced the probability principles in the context of examples and then described the general mathematical principle. Under this instructional condition, the effect of similarity between the base and target story lines was the opposite to that found in Experiment 1. Problems with highly similar story lines showed fewer reversals than those with dissimilar story lines.

The studies discussed above show that people can retrieve stored examples and use the mathematical solution learned with that example as a means for solving the current problem. In this way, a person's repertoire of stored problem exemplars might be considered as a representation of the mathematical operations used to solve those examples. Accessing a stored exemplar allows the individual to bring the related mathematical operation to bear on the current problem. Although the work reported above demonstrates that people can sometimes do this, the results also raise some doubts about this process as a comprehensive explanation of mathematical problem solving.

Summary

Reed (1987) showed that people were sometimes insensitive to differences in mathematical structure, even when the problems were presented side by side. Participants were unable to detect substantial differences in mathematical structure among the mixture problems. The ability to recognize isomorphisms seems crucial to an exemplar-based account. The structural similarity between the current and base problem has to drive the mapping; otherwise, it is not possible to identify which stored problem is appropriate. If people cannot detect structure, then only stored problems that are also similar in other ways (i.e., share surface features) will be useful for solving a particular problem with mathematics. Although surface and structural features may be correlated to some degree, it seems evident that mathematical operations are not tied to particular domains.

Second, and relatedly, the strong and complex effects of surface similarity raise questions about the ability of problem solvers to access the appropriate stored example and map that example to the current problem. Recall that Novick found that, even among high-ability students (those with SAT scores above 690), surface similarity between the base and target facilitated transfer of a structurally inappropriate mathematical solution. Ross showed that the effects of surface similarity are quite complex. Surface similarity at a thematic or story-line level affects access, and surface similarity at an object-correspondence level affects mapping. Further, the effect of object correspondence appears to depend jointly on the method of instruction and on the similarity of the story-lines. It is not clear how one could overcome these effects so as to reliably access and map structurally appropriate exemplars in memory.

THE SCHEMA HYPOTHESIS: MATHEMATICAL RELATIONS ARE INDUCED FROM EXAMPLES

If individual problem exemplars stored in memory do not appear to provide a satisfactory account of the representation of mathematics, perhaps higher-order relational structure, induced from summarizing across multiple examples, would serve.

Schema Induction through Comparison

A powerful account of schema induction has been proposed by a number of researchers (Novick & Holyoak, 1991; Ross & Kennedy, 1990; Kotovsky & Gentner, 1996; see also Hintzman,

1986; Reeves & Weisberg, 1994). In this account, schema induction occurs incrementally, as a result of comparing individual problems with identical or highly similar structures. For example, Ross and Kennedy (1990) proposed that as a consequence of making an analogy between a base and a target problem, people construct generalizations about underlying commonalities. Eventually, these represented commonalities become more structural and less superficial in nature.

Ross and Kennedy (1990) presented evidence for schema induction via this type of comparison process. In their first experiment, participants studied four probability principles and a completed example problem. For each principle, two test problems were presented. None of the test problems were superficially similar to the study problems, despite being structurally isomorphic. The crucial manipulation was whether participants were explicitly cued to think back to the study problem while solving the first test problem. Each participant was cued to recall the study problem (on presentation of the first test problem) for two of the four principles. Ross and Kennedy predicted that cueing recall of the study problem should facilitate making an analogy between it and the first test problem. As a result of making the analogy, participants should be more likely to form a schema for problems of that type (i.e., have that structure). In this situation, the second test problem with that structure should show an advantage. Ross and Kennedy found that participants solved the second test problem more accurately if they had been cued at the first test problem.

Although this is a clever paradigm, providing strong evidence for a schema is quite difficult. Ross and Kennedy acknowledged that the observed effects could be explained by hypothesizing that cued recall of the study problem, at the presentation of the first test problem, may simply make the study problem more available later. Recalling the study problem once makes it easier to recall when the second problem is presented. In a final set of experiments, Ross and Kennedy addressed this issue effectively by showing that cueing the study problem at first test eliminated the object correspondence effect. Recall that Ross (1989) showed that reversing the correspondence between objects in the problem and the variables in the equation had strong effects on problem solving, particularly mapping. This effect should be dependent on recalling the original problem. In order for the difference in object correspondence to affect the current mapping, the original object–variable correspondence must be recalled. Ross and Kennedy showed that cueing recall of the first test problem eliminated the object correspondence effect for the second problem. These results are difficult to explain if cueing the study problem at first test is supposed to increase the probability of recalling it at the second test. Clearly, this should lead to poorer, rather than better, performance because of the object correspondence reversals.

Novick and Holyoak (1991) presented additional evidence regarding the induction of mathematical problem schemas. They first instructed college students on how to solve a multistep mathematical word problem. The solution involved using an efficient procedure that included finding the number that was lowest common multiple for three divisors and that satisfied a number of other constraints (henceforth the LCM procedure). Participants were later given a target problem with the same mathematical structure under one of 4 "hint" conditions: no-hint, retrieval, concept-mapping, and numerical-mapping. In the no-hint condition, the target problem was presented without any indication that the base problem would be useful. In the retrieval condition, the relevant base problem was identified. In the concept-mapping condition, the base problem was identified and the item correspondences were explained (e.g., the band members in the current problem are like the plants in the previous problem). In the numerical-mapping condition, the base problem was also identified, but the numerical correspondences rather than conceptual correspondences were explained (e.g., the 12 in the band problem is like 10 in the garden problem). After participants completed the target problem, they were asked to write down all the similarities between the solutions of the target and base problems. Finally, they were given a generalization problem that could be solved by the LCM procedure, although some modifications were necessary (e.g., there were 4 divisors in the generalization problem, whereas the base and target problems had 3).

Novick and Holyoak found that participants who received the numerical-mapping hint showed the best transfer performance as measured by use of the LCM strategy (other less efficient strategies were also used to accurately solve the target problem). The conceptual-mapping and retrieval hints were equally effective at producing transfer; both conditions showed more evidence of the LCM strategy than the no-hint condition.

Novick and Holyoak used participants' description of the similarities between the solutions of the base and target problems as a measure of schema induction. Schema quality was significantly related to transfer of the base problem to the target problem and to the generalization problem.

Summary

These studies, taken together with recent work that demonstrates that relational representations can be induced through comparison (e.g., Dixon & Bangert, 2004; Kotovsky & Gentner, 1996; Loewenstein & Gentner, 2001; Namy & Gentner, 2004), suggest that schemas for mathematical operations can be induced by comparing structurally isomorphic problems. Schemas for mathematical operations might contain increasingly more structural and less superficial or content information, as has been suggested by a number of researchers (e.g., Medin & Ross, 1989; Reeves & Weisberg, 1994). Superficial features that are maintained in a schema may be those that have some predictive value given the corpus of problems the person has experienced. For example, Bassok, Chase, and Martin (1998) demonstrated that, in the absence of information about the transformation on two sets of objects, people prefer to use addition with sets of like objects and division with sets of unrelated objects. They argued that this preference results from aligning semantic relations contained in one's knowledge about the sets with semantic information contained in one's schemas for these operations. This type of semantic information in the schema is not strictly structural. It is, of course, possible to add sets of objects that do not share any strong semantic commonalities. However, because addition is most often performed when there is a thematic relation between the two sets, this semantic feature is part of the schema.

LIMITATIONS OF THE SCHEMA ACCOUNT

Despite their obvious utility, schemas also have a number of limitations as representations of mathematics. First, schemas, if we are to take their representational form seriously, are compiled representations; they place arguments in a specific relational structure (see Halford, Bain, Maybery, & Andrews [1998] for discussion the properties of schemas). Specifically, schemas are often considered to have slots that take arguments. The slots bind the arguments into the appropriate relations. For example, assume that a child has developed a schema that represents the following equation: $(a + b)/c$. This schema would have three slots, for a, b, and c; placing a value into a slot binds it into the relational structure. A set of procedures would run on the completed structure, yielding a result. Note that the relations among the individual items and between each individual item and the result are not explicitly represented here. For example, the fact that increasing the value of c will decrease the value of the result is not part of this representation. Similarly, the fact that a and b form a total is not part of the representation. Both these facts can, of course, be derived from this representation, if one has the appropriate knowledge about the consequences of increasing a divisor and summing two numbers. But note that computing these facts results from the actions of an independent and knowledgeable cognizer on this representation; they are not an intrinsic part of the representation itself. A consequence of this compiled representational structure is that schemas are of tremendous utility when the relational structure of the problem perfectly matches that of the schema, but they are of considerably less utility when the relational structure is even slightly different. For example, if the relational structure above were applied to a problem with a fourth term, d, it contains no knowledge relevant to dealing with the new item, regardless of whether the item requires a trivial adaptation (e.g., an additional item to be summed) or radical restructuring (e.g., each term must be raised to the d power).

Catrambone's (1996) work on learning subgoals demonstrates this point. For example, in one experiment Catrambone (1996) trained students how to use the Poisson distribution to approximate binomial probabilities. The average value of the distribution is required for this calculation. In the three training examples Catrambone presented, the average value could be computed as a weighted average. Participants were assigned to one of three conditions. One group received the training examples with no label applied to the first step in computing the weighted average, finding the total number of items in the distribution. For a second group, this first step was meaningfully labeled (e.g., "total number of briefcases"). For the final group, this step was labeled with an arbitrary symbol (i.e., "Ω"). All three groups then solved two problems that were isomorphic to the training problem, two in which the total number of items was given in the problem, and two that required finding the total number of items by the simple summing of frequencies, as opposed to computing the weighted sum as in the training problems. Note that the latter two types of problems require slight modifications to the original schema. Catrambone found that all three groups performed equivalently on the isomorphic problems. However, the two groups who saw labels performed significantly better on the problems that required modifying the original schema. One interpretation of this result is that the labeling helped participants create two hierarchically related schemas. The result of the "Find the total number of items" schema becomes an argument in the "find the average value" schema. Participants with a single, compiled schema showed less flexibility in their problem solving (see Hummel & Holyoak [1997] for a relevant discussion).

I suggest that schemas are a useful and important form of representing mathematics but that they are limited in their flexibility. Therefore, they will be quite effective for isomorphic matches but less so for problems with an even moderately novel structure. In this way, schemas do not seem to capture one important property of mathematics, its generativity. Just as we can generate new combinations of elements of language to describe new situations, we can generate new combinations of mathematical elements to represent new relational structures. This would seem to require a more flexible representational system than that offered by the standard account of schemas (see Reed, 1999, for an alternative view).

Representations of Functional Relations: The Structure of Mathematical Regularities

My colleagues and I have proposed an alternative representation that would allow for the generative use of mathematics. This representation is based on the idea that people detect the relational structure of each mathematical operation as they use it. This relational structure eventually becomes part of the representation of the mathematical operation. Rather than reaching a mathematical operation through a linkage with previous problem exemplars or schemas, the representation of the relational structure of the problem is mapped directly to a representation of the relational structure of the operations.

Two lines of research led us to this hypothesis. First, my colleagues and I found that children and adults expressed very different understanding of a problem depending on whether we asked them to estimate the answers to problems or solve the problems with mathematics (Ahl, Moore, & Dixon, 1992; Moore, Dixon, & Haines, 1991). Although their pattern of estimates was systematically related to the mathematics they generated, the relationship was not what a schema-based theory would predict (I discuss the nature of this relationship in more detail below). To understand why the dissociation between estimates and mathematics is contrary to a schema-based account, consider the process of accessing mathematical operations via schemas in a bit more detail. First, students are assumed to interpret the structure of the presented problem (Kintsch & Greeno, 1985). If this structure can be mapped to the structure of a stored schema, the mathematical operation that goes with that structure (and instantiates those relationships mathematically) should be accessed. Because students are accessing the mathematical operation based on a match between the structure of the current problem and that of a stored schema, the interpreted structure and the mathematical structure should agree. Therefore, the same relations should be observed regardless of whether participants estimate and use mathematics.

Second, we have evidence from a number of different sources that the problem representation consists of domain-specific principles, which we call the intuitive representation (Ahl et al., 1992; Dixon & Moore, 1996, 1997; Dixon & Tuccillo, 2001; Moore et al., 1991; Reed & Evans, 1987). The principles that comprise the intuitive representation specify relations between variables in the domain. For example, if two containers of water, each at a different temperature, are mixed together, the range principle specifies that temperature of the combined water must be between the original temperatures. Dixon and Tuccillo (2001) showed that fifth-grade, eighth-grade, and college students transferred individual principles from familiar properties, such as sweetness and weight, to a novel property, "hemry." The conclusion that children and adults represent problem domains with individual relational principles led us to fundamentally reconsider how mathematical problem solving might proceed.

Patterns of Estimates Are Related to Mathematical Solutions

As a first step in investigating this issue, we assessed the principles that comprise the intuitive representation of temperature mixture with an estimation task and subsequently asked children to solve the same problems with mathematics (Dixon & Moore, 1996). Students from the 2nd, 5th, 8th, and 11th grades, as well as college students, first estimated the answers to a series of temperature-mixture problems. Each temperature-mixture problem showed two containers of water. The quantity and temperature of the water in each container was presented pictorially and no numerical information was given. Later, students were asked to solve temperature-mixture problems using mathematics; for these problems, numbers were given for each variable. The appropriate solution for this problem is to take the average temperature of the water, weighted by the quantity of water in each container. Note that even the youngest children make estimates very easily but generate mathematics (even inappropriate mathematics) much more slowly and with considerable effort.

Each participant's pattern of estimates was scored for consistency with each of four principles that govern the temperature-mixture task. Each of the four principles specifies a different aspect of the judgment pattern. For example, the "range" principle specifies the relationship between the initial temperatures and the final temperature (i.e., the final temperature must be between the two initial temperatures). To the extent that a participant's judgment pattern was consistent with the aspect specified by the principle, the participant received a high score for that principle.

The mathematics participants generated to solve temperature-mixture problems were systematically related to the measures of the intuitive principles. Only participants who understood a principle (as defined by having 75% of the maximum score for that principle) generated a mathematical operation consistent with the principle in the mathematical task. However, understanding a principle did not prevent participants from generating a mathematical solution that violated it. Understanding a principle was necessary, but not sufficient, to arrive at a solution consistent with that principle.

Based on these results, we proposed that the intuitive representation was used in a structure-mapping process in which participants search for a mathematical operation that contains the same (or maximally similar) relational structure. For example, consider a child who applied an inappropriate range principle to the temperature-mixture task. Rather than place his or her estimates between the combined temperatures, he or she systematically estimated the final temperature to be greater than the initial temperatures. According to this hypothesis, which we call Operation Mapping, the child would search for a mathematical operation that instantiated this same relation (i.e., answer > operands). However, in order for Operation Mapping to be tenable, people must represent mathematical relations that are analogous to the intuitive principles.

A Relational Representation of the Arithmetic Operations

We proposed that Operation Mapping was accessing represented regularities that are a consequence of performing each of the arithmetic operations: addition, subtraction, multiplication, and division. Although mathematics is often considered as a means for generating objectively correct answers, another important aspect of mathematical operations is that they each produce a signature pattern. Given a particular class of number (e.g., positive integers), the pattern that results from the operation has a set of invariant relational features, regardless of the values selected. The left-hand panels of Figure 22.1 show the signature pattern for each arithmetic operation. For example, the pattern for addition shows increasing values of the answer as either operand increases. The right-hand panels of Figure 22.1 present descriptions of each of four principles for the various arithmetic operations for positive integers. Each principle takes a value for each operation.

To test whether these relations were represented, we asked college participants to rate sets of completed arithmetic problems supposedly generated by a student just learning how to perform the given arithmetic operation (Dixon, Deets, & Bangert, 2001). Figure 22.2 shows four trials for the addition operation; each panel represents a single trial. Participants were told that each trial was the attempt of a different student. Participants were asked to rate how good or bad the student's attempt was overall. We independently manipulated whether or not the presented pattern of answers violated one of the principles and the average distance of the presented answers from the correct answers. The top two panels of Figure 22.2 show examples of problem sets that respect all the principles for addition. The bottom two panels violate the principle called "direction-of-effect." For addition, the direction-of-effect principle specifies that as the size of the operands increases, the size of the answers increases. Figure 22.2 also shows the amount-wrong manipulation. The two panels on the left side have an average amount wrong of 9, and the panels of the right side have an average amount wrong of 19. We predicted that participants would rate patterns of answers that violated principles as worse attempts at the operation and that they would rate patterns that were further from the correct answers as worse attempts.

We also predicted that we would observe effects of participants' developmental history with the arithmetic operations. For example, addition is introduced as a mathematical operation in first grade and later used as a model for explaining subtraction. Multiplication and division are usually not introduced until third grade; multiplication is introduced first and used to help explain division (National Council of Teachers of Mathematics, 2000).

Consistent with the predictions above, we found that participants rated problems that violated a principle as worse attempts at the arithmetic operation but that this effect depended jointly on the developmental history of operations and principles. For example, violations of all four principles were detected for addition, but violations of the slopes principle were not detected for multiplication and only violations of the monotonicity principle were detected for division. Importantly, the amount-wrong manipulation had effects for all four operations. Although participants appeared to represent different sets of principles for different opera-

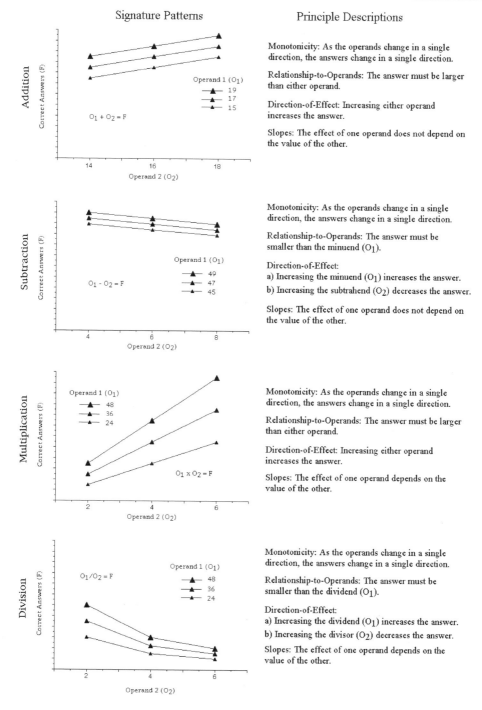

Figure 22.1. The "signature" patterns for the four arithmetic operations are shown in the four panels. Answers (F) are plotted as a function of the second operand (O_2), with a separate curve for each value of the first operand (O_1). The first operand is abbreviated as O_1, the second operand as O_2, and the answer as F. The principles for each operation are described on the right. (Adapted from Dixon et al., 2001.)

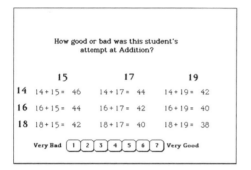
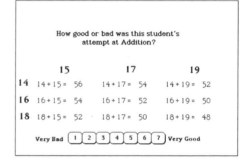

Figure 22.2. Each panel shows a different trial for addition. The rating scale is shown at the bottom of each display. For each panel, participants were asked to rate the hypothetical student's attempt at math. The upper two panels show problems that are incorrect but do not violate any principles. The lower two panels show problems that violate the Direction-of-Effect principle. Panels on the left side are equally wrong; the presented answers are an average absolute distance of 9 units from the correct answers. Panels on the right side are also equally wrong, 19 units from the correct answers. (From Dixon et al., 2001.)

tions, they were quite capable of utilizing information about the distance from the correct answers. This strongly suggests that the observed between-operation effects were not due to an inability to estimate what the answers should be.

We replicated and extended these results in a second experiment with an additional sample of college students and a sample of eighth graders. We predicted that eighth graders would have less-developed principle representations than college students and that this developmental difference would be observable across operations and principles. As predicted, eighth-grade students had less extensive principle representations and, as with the college students, operations that were introduced earlier had better principle representations than those introduced later.

It is worth noting that the between-operation differences make a number of alternative accounts inconsistent with the observed data. For example, one might suggest that participants did not represent the principles but rather induced the relationships during task. However, given that the operations are all equally regular with regard to the principles, this position has difficulty explaining the systematic between-operation differences. (In a third experiment, not discussed here, we addressed this issue more directly).

COMPLEMENTARY REPRESENTATIONS OF MATHEMATICS

Based on the work reviewed above, I propose that two representational systems are at work in mathematical problem solving, an exemplar-schema representation and a relational representation (see Figure 22.3). Each is a consequence of a particular developmental history and has a unique developmental course. The exemplar-schema representation begins as a set of stored problem examples. Each time a new problem is solved with an operation, that problem becomes part of the set of stored exemplars and, to the degree that the problem is compared to previous examples, contributes to the developing problem schema. As the diversity of the examples increases and more comparisons are made, the schema may become increasingly structural. For example, the left side of Figure 22.3 shows two hypothetical exemplar-schema representations. The representation for "Combining Discrete Sets" is highly schematic; structural and semantic features are at the top of the stack, although surface features remain part of the schema. The representation of "Change in Discrete Sets" is less schematic; superficial features are higher in the stack.

The relational representation, shown on the right side of Figure 22.3, develops as mathematical operations are executed, regardless of whether they are embedded in a problem context. The functional regularities that are a consequence of the operation are detected, just as other relations in the environment are. For example, each time a child solves a problem with addition (using positive integers, as is standard practice in early grade school), he or she will be exposed to the fact that the answer is greater than either operand, the relationship-to-operands relation. The right side of Figure 22.3 shows relationship-to-operands for operand 1 (O_1) and operand 2 (O_2). The relationship is represented as a fuzzy set in which numerical values (horizontal axis) have differing degrees of membership (vertical axis) in the set of potential answers. I propose that these relations are detected as children use arithmetic operations and that adults detect similar regularities for more complex mathematics (see Ross, 1996). Consistent with this idea, the hypothesized membership functions for O_1 and O_2 are not identical because larger numbers tend to be placed in the O_1 position and smaller numbers in the O_2 position (Greer, 1997). In this way, I propose that the membership functions are empirically, rather than logically, derived. For example, from a logical perspective, addition and multiplication would have identical membership functions for all the presented principles, but empirically the distribution of answers for these operations differ radically.

The exemplar-schema representation is used in a process I call Domain Mapping. Domain Mapping involves accessing and aligning the current problem with stored exemplars or problem schemas. A solution operation (shown in bold in Figure 22.3) is linked to each exemplar/schema in memory. If Domain Mapping is successful, the solution operation can be applied to the current problem. Consistent with the work on analogical problem solving discussed above, I assume that Domain Mapping follows the principles of structure mapping theory (Gentner, 1983; Gentner & Markman, 1997).

The relational representation is used in the process I call Operation Mapping. In Operation Mapping, the intuitive principle representation (shown toward the center of Figure 22.3) is mapped directly to the relational representations of the mathematical operations. The intuitive principles are shown as fuzzy sets. Different values of temperature (horizontal axis) have differing degrees of membership (vertical axis). For example, the range principles presented in the figure represent a common misunderstanding of temperature mixture. Temperatures that are greater than the initial temperatures (T_L and T_R) have membership in the set of potential final temperatures. Operation Mapping structurally aligns the intuitive principles with their counterparts in the mathematical relation representations. The best-matching operation is chosen as the solution operation.

I propose that both these processes are used in problem solving. Domain Mapping should be most heavily used early in the developmental history of a new operation. Operation Mapping will become the predominant route as children gain extensive experience with the operation. Further, the two processes should be complementary. If a problem cannot be solved through one process, the other may be used. For example, a student who does not understand the relationship-to-operands principle for addition may not be able to use Operation Mapping.

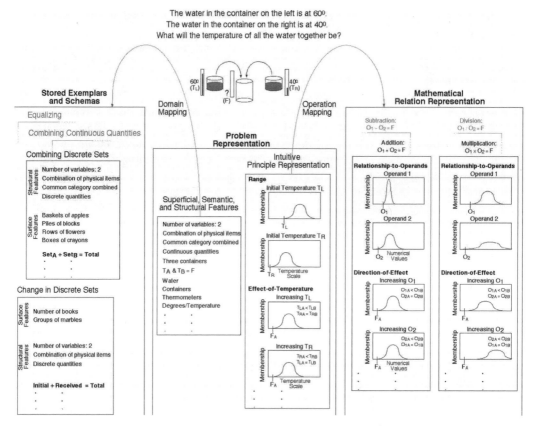

Figure 22.3. The figure shows an example of the representations involved in Domain Mapping and Operation Mapping. A simple temperature-mixture problem is presented as text at the top of the figure, along with a schematic drawing of the problem. A hypothetical problem representation appears in the middle of the figure. It consists of two major components, a collection of superficial, semantic, and structural features, and a representation of the intuitive principles. Each intuitive principle is expressed as a fuzzy set. The temperature scale is represented on the horizontal axis. The degree of membership in the set of potential answers is shown on the vertical axis. The curve shows the degree to which different values of temperature are potential answers according to that principle. The range principles specify membership in the set of answers relative to the initial temperatures on the left (T_L) and right (T_R). The effect-of-temperature principles specify membership in the set of answers relative to the answer from another problem, F_A, that differs in T_L (upper panel) or T_R (lower panel). The mathematical relation representation (on the right side) shows analogous fuzzy sets for the relationship-to-operands and direction-of-effect relations for addition and multiplication. Similar sets of relations are represented for other operations (e.g., subtraction and division) but are not displayed. Operation Mapping involves aligning the intuitive principles and mathematical relations. The representation of the stored exemplars and schemas (on the left side) contains superficial and structural features of previously solved problems. Examples of these types of features are shown for two problem types, combining discrete sets and change in discrete sets. Solution procedures are shown in bold. Other problem types are also represented but not displayed. Domain Mapping involves aligning the features of the current problem with those of the stored exemplars and schemas.

Therefore, he or she may search more extensively for a relevant example stored in memory. Use of Domain Mapping should depend on the degree to which the current problem cues relevant stored problems and whether the problems can be adequately aligned. Use of Operation Mapping should depend on the strength of the representation of the relational principles for the operations.

Recent evidence from our laboratory supports the hypothesis that Domain Mapping and Operation Mapping are complementary processes (Dixon & Bangert, 2003). We assessed the intuitive principle representation of children (aged 8 to 14 years) for two multiplicative and divisible problem domains. We also assessed their representation of the mathematical relations shown in Figure 22.3 for addition, subtraction, multiplication, and division. The match between intuitive principles and mathematical relations predicted the mathematical operations participants generated when asked to solve the problems mathematically. However, the effect of the match depended on whether participants reported recalling a problem from memory (i.e., engage in Domain Mapping). Participants who reporting recalling a problem were just as likely to arrive at an appropriate solution, but their solutions were not predicted by the intuitive–mathematical match.

CONCLUSIONS

Past research shows that people can and do access previously solved problems when asked to generate a mathematical solution to a new problem. In this way, stored exemplars can act as a representation of mathematical structure. However, the successful use of exemplars depends heavily on the problem solver's ability to map the structure of the current problem to that of the stored problem.

Comparing stored problems to one another or to current problems during problem solving may give rise to schemas that represent their common relational structure. This type of representation is thought to become increasingly structural as the diversity of examples on which it has been computed increases. Relational schemas will be very useful for situations in which the current problem maps directly onto an available schema. Problems that are structurally isomorphic to ones that have been solved previously and for which a schema has developed can be classified as instances of that schema. Schemas will be less useful for problems that are structurally novel. Because schemas simply bind arguments in relations, even small structural changes in a problem may result in a failure to apply the schema. Knowledge from outside the schema will be required to modify it appropriately.

We proposed an alternative representation of mathematical relations which consists of the functional regularities of each operation. In previous work, we provided evidence for this representation and suggested that it develops through repeated exposure to these regularities. We also suggested that during problem solving, this representation is mapped directly to a structurally analogous representation of relations for that particular problem (i.e., the intuitive representation). The representation of mathematical relations may take considerable time to develop. This may be especially true of higher-level relations that can only be detected by examining how changes in the answers are related to changes in the operands (e.g., direction-of-effect). Therefore, children and adults may need a good deal of experience in order to effectively use the relations in problem solving.

Based on these previous lines of work, we proposed that two representations of mathematical relations may be available for use in problem solving: an exemplar-schema representation and a relational representation. A process we call Domain Mapping works to align the current problem with stored exemplars and schemas. A second process, which we call Operation Mapping, creates a structure mapping between the intuitive representation of the problem and the representation of mathematical relations.

One important implication of this hypothesis is that the cognition underlying mathematical problem solving will depend on the status of these two representations and the relation of the current problem to them. For example, problems that strongly remind one of a stored example, either correctly or erroneously, may result in very fast Domain Mapping. Conversely, problems that are highly similar in structure to well-learned, stored examples, but do not cue those examples, may result in Operation Mapping. Of course, failures in Operation Mapping may lead to Domain Mapping. If one's intuitive representation of the problem does not adequately match any of the relational representations for mathematics, participants may search memory more extensively for a matching example. In summary, human abilities in mathematical problem solving can utilize a contextually rich, problem-specific representation, a more structural schema representation, or a strictly relational representation, depending on the dynamics of the representation and problem situation.

REFERENCES

Ahl, V., Moore, C. F., & Dixon, J. A. (1992). Development of intuitive and numerical proportional reasoning. *Cognitive Development, 7*, 81–108.

Anderson, J. R., & Thompson, R. (1989). Use of analogy in a production system architecture. In S. Vosniadou & A. Ortony (Eds.), *Similarity and analogical reasoning* (pp. 267–297). Cambridge: Cambridge University Press.

Bassok, M., Chase, V. M., & Martin, S. A. (1998). Adding apples and oranges: Alignment of semantic and formal knowledge. *Cognitive Psychology, 35*, 99–134.

Catrambone, R. (1996). Generalizing solution procedures from learned examples. *Journal of Experimental Psychology: Learning, Memory, and Cognition, 22*, 1020–1031.

Dixon, J. A., & Bangert, A. S. (2004). On the spontaneous discovery of a mathematical relation during problem solving. *Cognitive Science, 28*, 433–449.

Dixon, J. A., & Bangert, A. S. (2004). *The development of representations and mapping processes in mathematical problem solving.* Manuscript submitted for publication.

Dixon, J. A., Deets, J. K., & Bangert, A. (2001). The representations of the arithmetic operations include functional relationships. *Memory & Cognition, 29*, 462–477.

Dixon, J. A., & Moore, C. F. (1996). The developmental role of intuitive principles in choosing mathematical strategies. *Developmental Psychology, 32*, 241–253.

Dixon, J. A., & Moore, C. F. (1997). Characterizing the intuitive representation in problem solving: Evidence from evaluating mathematical strategies. *Memory & Cognition, 25*, 395–412.

Dixon, J. A., & Tuccillo, F. (2001). Generating initial models for reasoning. *Journal of Experimental Child Psychology, 78*, 178–212.

Duncker, K. (1945). On problem-solving. *Psychological Monographs, 58*(5, Whole No. 270).

Gentner, D. (1983). Structure-mapping: A theoretical framework for analogy. *Cognitive Science, 7*, 155–170.

Gentner, D., & Markman, A. B. (1997). Structure mapping in analogy and similarity. *American Psychologist, 52*, 45–56.

Greer, B. (1997). Modeling reality in mathematics classrooms: The case of word problems. *Learning and Instruction, 7*, 293–307.

Halford, G. S., Bain, J. D., Maybery, M. T., & Andrews, G. (1998). Induction of relational schemas: Common processes in reasoning and complex learning. *Cognitive Psychology, 35*, 201–245.

Hintzman, D. L. (1986). "Schema Abstraction" in a multiple-trace memory model. *Psychological Review, 4*, 411–428.

Hummel, J. E., & Holyoak, K. J. (1997). Distributed representations of structure: A theory of analogical access and mapping. *Psychological Review, 3*, 427–466.

Kintsch, W., & Greeno, J. G. (1985). Understanding and solving word arithmetic problems. *Psychological Review, 92*, 109–129.

Kotovsky, L., & Gentner, D. (1996). Comparison and categorization in the development of relational similarity. *Child Development, 67*, 2797–2822.

Loewenstein, J., & Gentner, D. (2001). Spatial mapping in preschoolers: Close comparisons facilitate far mapping. *Journal of Cognition and Development, 2*, 189–219.

Medin, D. L., & Ross, B. H. (1989). The specific character of abstract thought: Categorization, problem solving, and induction. In R. J. Sternberg (Ed.), *Advances in the psychology of human intelligence* (Vol. 5, pp. 189–223). Hillsdale, NJ: Erlbaum.

Moore, C. F., Dixon, J. A., & Haines, B. A. (1991). Components of understanding in proportional reasoning: A fuzzy set representation of developmental progression. *Child Development, 62*, 441–459.

Namy, L. L., & Gentner, D. (2002). Making a silk purse out of two sow's ears: Young children's use of comparison in category learning. *Journal of Experimental Psychology: General, 131*, 5–15.

National Council of Teachers of Mathematics (2000). *Principles and standards for school mathematics.* Reston, VA: Author.

Novick, L. R. (1988). Analogical transfer, problem similarity, and expertise. *Journal of Experimental Psychology: Learning, Memory, and Cognition, 14*, 510–520.

Novick, L. R., & Holyoak, K. J. (1991). Mathematical problem solving by analogy. *Journal of Experimental Psychology: Learning, Memory, and Cognition, 17*, 398–415.

Reed, S. K. (1987). A structure-mapping model for word problems. *Journal of Experimental Psychology: Learning, Memory, and Cognition, 13*, 124–139.

Reed, S. K. (1999). *Word problems*. Mahwah, NJ: Erlbaum.

Reed, S. K., Dempster, A., & Ettinger, M. (1985). Usefulness of analogous solutions for solving algebra word problems. *Journal of Experimental Psychology: Learning, Memory, and Cognition, 11*, 106–125.

Reed, S. K., & Evans, A. C. (1987). Learning functional relations: A theoretical and instructional analysis. *Journal of Experimental Psychology: General, 116*, 106–118.

Reeves, L. M., & Weisberg, R. W. (1994). The role of content and abstract information in analogical transfer. *Psychological Bulletin, 115*, 381–400.

Ross, B. H. (1987). This is like that: The use of earlier problems and the separation of similarity effects. *Journal of Experimental Psychology: Learning, Memory, and Cognition, 13*, 629–639.

Ross, B. H. (1989). Distinguishing types of superficial similarities: Different effects on access and use of earlier problems. *Journal of Experimental Psychology: Learning, Memory, and Cognition, 15*, 456–468.

Ross, B. H. (1996). Category representations and the effects of interacting with instances. *Journal of Experimental Psychology: Learning, Memory, and Cognition, 22*, 1249–1265.

Ross, B. H., & Kennedy, P. T. (1990). Generalizing from the use of earlier examples in problem solving. *Journal of Experimental Psychology: Learning, Memory, and Cognition, 16*, 42–55.

Ross, B. H., & Kilbane, M. C. (1997). Effects of principle explanation and superficial similarity on analogical mapping in problem solving. *Journal of Experimental Psychology: Learning, Memory, and Cognition, 23*, 427–440.

Rumelhart, D. E. (1989). Toward a microstructural account of human reasoning. In S. Vosniadou & A. Ortony (Eds.), *Similarity and analogical reasoning* (pp. 298–312). Cambridge: Cambridge University Press.

Spearman, C. (1923). *The nature of "intelligence" and the principles of cognition*. London: Macmillan.

23

Aging and Mental Arithmetic

Sandrine Duverne
Patrick Lemaire

Mental arithmetic, or the ability to find solutions to problems like 4 × 7 or 238 + 567, has been one of the most frequently investigated mathematical abilities by cognitive aging researchers. Overall, like many other types of cognitive performance, both simple and complex arithmetic performance have been shown to decline with age (Allen, Ashcraft, & Weber, 1992; Allen, Smith, Jerge, & Vires-Collins, 1997; Charness & Campbell, 1988; Geary, Frensch, & Wiley, 1993; Geary & Lin, 1998; Geary & Wiley, 1991; Salthouse & Coon, 1994; Sliwinski, Buschke, Kuslansky, Senior, & Scarisbrick, 1994; Verhaeghen, Kliegl, & Mayr, 1997; see Geary et al., 1997; Geary, Salthouse, Chen, & Fan, 1996, for exceptions). However, when analyzed in detail, age-related changes in adults' arithmetic performance show a fascinating set of patterns, with some aspects declining and others remaining unimpaired with age. The goal of the present chapter is to review findings on aging and mental arithmetic. We pursue this goal by reviewing studies that have precisely analyzed age-related differences in arithmetic performance. We report empirical evidence observed in classic experimental tasks of arithmetic problem solving (i.e., strategies, latencies, and error rates in verification and production tasks) rather than those observed in standardized tests of mental arithmetic (e.g., Addition and Subtraction/ Multiplication subtests of the French Kit; French, Ekstrom, & Price, 1963) that do not provide such specific information. First, we look at strategic changes in adults' arithmetic. Then we consider how age-related changes in processing resources account for some of the age-related changes in mental arithmetic. Third, data on the impact of Alzheimer's disease on arithmetic are reviewed. Finally, we provide general conclusions and suggestions for future research. This review of aging and mental arithmetic will highlight how research on aging contributes to our further understanding of both general and specific cognitive processes of arithmetic performance.

STRATEGIC CHANGES IN ADULTS' ARITHMETIC

Following Lemaire and Siegler's (1995) conceptual framework regarding strategic aspects of cognitive performance, age-related differences and similarities in strategy repertoire, execution, and selection are reviewed. Strategy repertoire concerns which strategies are used and how often each strategy is used. Strategy execution refers to relative levels of speed and accuracy of strategies. And strategy selection concerns the mechanism by which strategies are chosen and the determinants of these strategy choices.

Age-Related Differences in Strategy Use

For any given cognitive tasks, we want to know how people accomplish these tasks or which strategies they use. Many definitions of strategies have been given in cognitive psychology. They all view a strategy as "a procedure or a set of procedures for achieving a higher level goal or task" (Lemaire & Reder, 1999, p. 365). Changes in strategy repertoire involve both acquisition of new strategies and abandonment of old ones. Strategy distribution concerns the relative frequencies of each strategy (Lemaire & Siegler, 1995).

Geary and Wiley (1991) collected verbal reports of younger and older adults in a simple addition production task (e.g., 8 + 7 = ?) and observed differences in strategy repertoire. Both populations predominantly reported use of retrieval (i.e., direct access to the correct solution in memory) and decomposition strategies (i.e., decomposing the problem into subproblems like doing 7 + 3 + 2 to solve 7 + 5). A third strategy, the verbal counting strategy (e.g., doing 7 + 1 + 1 + 1 + 1 to solve 7 + 4), was used by younger adults in 5% of problems but was almost never used by older adults. Moreover, the distribution of retrieval and decomposition strategies differed across age groups, with younger adults decomposing problems into easier problems more frequently than older adults (7% vs. 2%, in younger and older adults, respectively). Older adults used retrieval more often than younger adults (98% vs. 88% in older and younger adults, respectively).

The same type of results were observed on simple (e.g., 9 − 3 = ?) and complex (i.e., 47 − 9 = ?) subtraction production tasks, showing differences in strategy repertoire and distribution across age groups (Geary et al., 1993; Geary & Lin, 1998). In simple subtractions, contrary to younger adults, older adults did not use a count-down strategy (e.g., doing 9 − 1 − 1 − 1 to solve 9 − 3; Geary et al., 1993). Moreover, they used an addition-reference strategy (e.g., doing 8 + 4 = 12 to solve 12 − 8) less frequently and a retrieval strategy more often. In complex subtraction, older adults almost always used columnar retrieval and almost never used counting-down, decomposition, and rules (Geary et al., 1993).

Overall, studies in simple and complex addition and subtraction tasks revealed age-related differences in strategy repertoire and distribution, with older adults using retrieval strategy more frequently than young adults. However, such findings may be related to cohort differences: younger adults may be less likely to have memorized correct answers than older adults; consequently, they may use more frequently other strategies than direct retrieval of correct answers. In more complex arithmetic problems that could not be simply solved by means of direct retrieval, such as multiplication of two-digit operands (e.g., 26 × 14 = ?), age-related differences in strategy distribution were not observed (Siegler & Lemaire, 1997; see also Lemaire & Lecacheur, 2001, for similar results in currency-conversion tasks from French Francs to Euros and vice versa). Siegler and Lemaire (1997) used the choice/no-choice method to analyze unbiased strategic aspects of arithmetic performance and asked participants to use mental calculation or a calculator to solve two-digit operand multiplication problems. Surprisingly, older adults used both strategies as frequently as younger adults, both age groups being equally biased toward using mental calculation. Therefore, when participants cannot rely on retrieval, such as in complex arithmetic tasks, younger and older adults are equally biased in using the most direct calculation strategy, which is mental calculation, instead of a calculator.

Finally, one study demonstrated that acquisition of new strategies can occur during adulthood. Charness and Campbell (Campbell & Charness, 1990; Charness & Campbell, 1988) tested the ability to acquire skills in mental calculation in adulthood. Younger, middle-age, and older adults were asked to square one- and two-digit numbers with an algorithm that involved number-rounding, addition, subtraction, and multiplication procedures. Participants were tested during seven sessions. Results revealed that, despite overall age-related differences (e.g., younger adults were faster in all sessions), both age groups had no problems in acquiring the squaring strategy. At the end of the experiment, older adults were approximately equivalent to the initial level of performance of younger adults in terms of latencies (Charness & Campbell, 1988) and calculation errors (Campbell & Charness, 1990). However, Touron and her colleagues (Touron, Hoyer, & Cerella, 2001) have recently tested the abilities to learn arithmetic algorithms in a simpler alphabet arithmetic task (e.g., 3 + A = ?). They showed that the rates of learning in older adults were slower than in younger adults and that prolonged practice would not bring them to the same level of performance reached by younger adults. Moreover, using the two-digit number-squaring task, Sanders and his colleagues (Sanders, Gonzalez, Murphy, Pesta, & Bucur, 2002) have revealed that, contrary to younger adults', older adults' learning rates did not change as a function of training conditions. Overall, older adults appeared able to learn new arithmetic algorithms but less efficiently than their younger peers.

Age-Related Differences in Strategy Execution

Strategy execution refers to quantitative features of performance when using a given strategy. Such features include how fast and accurate people are with each strategy. They also include variants of a given strategy. For example, when people use repeated addition to solve multiplications like 3 × 4, they add the first operand the number of times indicated by the second operand—add 3 four times—or do the reverse—add 4 three times.

In an addition production task, Geary and Wiley (1991) found that younger adults were faster than older adults when using retrieval (833 ms vs. 930 ms) and that both groups were equally fast when using decomposition strategies (1189 ms and 1271 ms for each age group, respectively). Decomposition was executed with fewer errors by older adults than by younger adults. However, such results must be interpreted with caution, since very few problems were solved with a decomposition strategy, especially in older adults. Similar results were obtained with simple- and complex-subtraction production tasks. For simple subtractions, older adults were significantly slowed only when using retrieval but not when using addition reference (Geary et al., 1993). However, the failure to find a reliable difference in addition-reference latencies across groups may also be due to the smaller number of addition-reference trials in older adults. For complex subtractions, younger adults retrieved in 1874 ms and older adults in 1990 ms (Geary et al., 1993). Overall, this set of results suggests that execution of arithmetic strategies is differently affected by age.

Arithmetic fact retrieval appeared to be the only strategy to be impaired with age in simple arithmetic problems. It is also the most documented strategy in the arithmetic literature in terms of which cognitive processes it involves (e.g., Ashcraft, Donley, Halas, & Vakali, 1992; Campbell & Graham, 1985; Geary, 1996; Groen & Parkman, 1972; Miller, Perlmutter, & Keating, 1984; Stazyk, Ashcraft, & Hamann, 1982; Widaman, Geary, Cormier, & Little, 1989; Widaman & Little, 1992). As a consequence, several studies have focused on determining which processes specifically involved in retrieval were affected by aging.

To further understand the locus of aging effects on fact retrieval, analyses of performance were based on a distinction, proposed in the cognitive aging literature, between central and peripheral processes (Cerella, 1985, 1990). In arithmetic, central processes refer to specific processes that are necessary for arithmetic problem solving and that largely vary with information structures like problems' or tasks' characteristics (Manly & Spoehr, 1999). Examples of central processes are retrieval and calculation processes that vary with problem difficulty in simple problems. In complex arithmetic, central processes in addition to fact retrieval may be required, such as coordination and integration of partial results (Fuerst & Hitch, 2000; Hitch, 1978; Lemaire & Lecacheur, 2001, 2002; Pesenti et al., 2001). Peripheral processes refer to all other processes that are common to all problems and that are expected to remain more or less constant across task structure, like encoding, decision-making, and responding (Allen et al., in press; Allen et al., 1997; Geary et al., 1993; Geary & Lin, 1998; Geary & Wiley, 1991; Salthouse & Coon, 1994).

The statistical techniques most often used to assess central and peripheral processes in arithmetic problem verification and production tasks are individual regression analyses. These techniques consist of assessing the rate of problem solving for each individual by using a problem characteristic as a predictor. This problem characteristic, such as the size of the correct answer, reflects processes of finding the correct solution (e.g., Allen et al., 1997; Geary, 1996; Geary & Wiley, 1991; Miller et al., 1984; Widaman et al., 1989). Therefore, retrieval processes can be assessed with slopes, and peripheral processes (e.g., encoding operands, responding) with intercepts in individual regression equations predicting solution times from problem characteristics such as the size of the correct product. Analyses of variance across age groups, performed on each individual's slope and intercept indices, allow examination of age-related differences in arithmetic peripheral and central processes.

Studies in simple arithmetic problem production and verification tasks have found that peripheral processes, but not central processes, are impaired with age (Allen et al., 1992; Allen et al., 1997; Geary et al., 1993; Geary & Lin, 1998; Geary & Wiley, 1991; Oberauer, Demmrich, Mayr, & Kliegl, 2001; Verhaeghen et al., 1997). These studies showed parallel slopes across age groups (Allen et al., 1992, 1997; Geary & Wiley, 1991), and some of them showed even flatter slopes in older adults than in younger adults (see Geary et al., 1993; Geary & Lin, 1998). Larger intercepts were found in older adults and suggested that age-related decreases in arithmetic retrieval execution were essentially accounted for by impairments in processes that do not vary with problem difficulty. Geary and his collaborators (Geary et al., 1993; Geary et al., 1997; Geary & Lin, 1998; Geary et al., 1996; Geary & Wiley, 1991) suggested that spared or even improved central processes with age may stem from older adults' compensating age-related decrements in central processes due to higher arithmetic skills and/or good formal training during elementary school. Such compensatory mechanisms have already been reported in the aging literature in areas such as problem solving (e.g., Charness, 1981; Charness & Campbell, 1988) or reading (e.g., Soederberg Miller & Stine-Morrow, 1998).

Findings on age-related differences in execution of arithmetic processes in complex problems are more ambiguous. Some studies revealed that central, as well as peripheral, processes were affected by aging (Charness & Campbell, 1988; Salthouse & Coon, 1994). Salthouse and Coon (1994; Experiment 2) performed individual-regression analyses on performance in a multi-operand problem verification task (i.e., a task composed of problems with 0–7 operands, like $5 + 3 - 1 - 3 + 4 - 1 = 6$). They performed individual-regression analyses on performance using the number of operations as a predictor of problem difficulty. The authors found that participants' rates of retrieval (i.e., slopes) largely increased as problem complexity increased, more so for older than for younger adults. The results of Charness and Campbell (1988) in a multi-digit number-squaring task were consistent with the results of Salthouse and Coon (1994) and showed an interaction between age and problem difficulty. That is, older adults had poorer performance for squaring the most difficult problems (i.e., multi-digit numbers that did not involve a 0 in the unit digit). This set of results suggests that central processes required in complex arithmetic problem solving (e.g., retrieval, coordination, and integration of partial results) are affected by aging.

As Salthouse and Coon concluded, such age-related decreases in central processes may be revealed with more powerful manipulations of problem complexity. Verhaeghen and his collaborators (1997) used a multiple-operand single-digit problem-solving task, similar to that used by Salthouse and Coon (1994) except that it was a production task instead of a verification task. They performed individual exponential equations to derive a time-accuracy function for each participant that allowed specific processes to be assessed independently of coordinative demands, a dimension that is necessarily involved in tasks that need several procedures to be solved. They found that the parameter that assessed retrieval processes did not vary with age.

As proposed by Verhaeghen and his collaborators (1997), Salthouse and Coon's (1994) results concerning central processes probably reflected differences in the ability to coordinate several procedures. Salthouse and Coon (1994) used the number of operations to predict the speed of calculation processes. Such a structural variable may reflect the number of procedures that had to be executed rather than the ability to execute a given procedure. Sliwinski and his collaborators (Sliwinski et al., 1994) tested the hypothesis of age-related changes in the ability to coordinate several procedures. In this study, a two-digit number was presented, and participants were asked to copy the number or to add another number (i.e., 1, 2, or 3) that was previously presented. Therefore, task demands were manipulated in two ways, first, by introducing an additional process (adding instead of just copying) and, second, by increasing the number of times the additional process had to be performed (increasing the addend size). Sliwinski et al. found that the effects of age were larger in the initiation of new processes than in the repetition of counting processes. Such a result is more consistent with larger age-related decrements in coordinating several processes than with age-related decrements in executing mental calculation processes.

Age-Related Differences in Strategy Selection

Strategy selection concerns the mechanisms by which strategies are chosen on each problem. Choosing among strategies on each problem, rather than choosing a strategy for the whole set of problems, leads to better performance because some strategies work better than others on some problems.

In an addition production task, Geary and Wiley (1991) found both age-related similarities and differences regarding the impact of problem features on strategy choices. Both younger and older adults tended to choose among strategies according to problem features such that both groups chose back-up strategies more often on harder problems. Geary and Wiley (1991) also found that younger adults preferentially used the decomposition strategy on harder problems (70% of decomposition trials occurred when the digit 9 was presented), whereas older adults did not show as strong a tendency to use this strategy on the harder problems (45% of decomposition trials occurred on problems that involved 9). Since older adults used the fastest and easiest retrieval strategy on most of the problems, they did not need to calibrate their strategy choices according to problem features like younger adults.

In a simple subtraction task, younger and older adults were also shown to rely on problem structural features to choose retrieval (i.e., use of retrieval decreased in both groups as the value of the minuend increased; Geary et al., 1993). However, a different pattern of results was observed for complex subtractions (Geary & Lin, 1998): younger adults varied their strategy use according to problem features, such as the presence/absence of borrow procedure, and they selected strategies in order to avoid columnar retrieval on problems that required borrowing (e.g., 23 – 9), whereas older adults did not. As in addition tasks, older adults did not switch systematically across strategies because they almost always used the fastest and easiest columnar retrieval strategy. Note however that younger and older adults used each strategy with different frequencies on each type of problem, prevented determining whether strategy choices were related to problem features (e.g., presence of the digit 9) or to the efficiency of each strategy.

Siegler and Lemaire (1997) used a more complex arithmetic task and showed that strategy selection was affected by two types of variables: structural features of problems and performance characteristics of each strategy (see also Lemaire, Arnaud, & Lecacheur, 2003; Siegler and Lemaire 1997). A problem's structural features are inherent properties of the problem, such as the size of the correct answer, the left/right side of the larger operand, the parity status of operands, and the presence of specific digits like 5 or 0. Performance characteristics of each strategy represent the relative benefits in terms of speed and accuracy of a particular strategy over other strategies. Participants solved multi-digit operand multiplication problems under the choice/no-choice experimental protocol: first, they solved a set of problems using multiple strategies (i.e., a choice condition), and second, they solved an entire set of problems using only one strategy (i.e., no-choice condition). Analyses of performance in no-choice conditions allowed identification and comparison of performance characteristics for each strategy. The authors could also test the impact of the relative difference in strategy performance on strategy use for each problem. They found that both younger and older adults largely relied on strategy performance characteristics (i.e., the relative speed difference between each strategy) to choose among strategies. That is, they tended to choose a given strategy when that strategy was the fastest. Moreover, the percentage of use of a given strategy in the choice condition largely correlated with the latency difference yielded by each strategy in the no-choice condition for both younger ($r = .85$) and older adults ($r = .78$). These results suggest that predictors of strategy choices and the way they are used do not vary with age in complex arithmetic problems (see Lemaire & Lecacheur, 2001, for replication in between-currency conversion tasks, and Duverne & Lemaire, 2003, in problem verification tasks).

Summary

Strategy repertoire, distribution, execution, and choices were shown to be selectively impaired in adulthood. First, strategy repertoire and distribution change with age. In simple arithmetic problems, older adults use direct retrieval more often than younger adults and they almost never use less sophisticated strategies (e.g., counting, decomposition) that are used by younger adults. In more complex arithmetic problems, such as two-digit operand multiplications and squaring tasks, tasks that cannot be solved by means of direct retrieval of correct answers, age-related changes in strategy distribution were not found, and older adults were shown to be able to learn new arithmetic strategies.

Second, with regard to strategy execution, each strategy is differently affected by age. For instance, older adults retrieve correct answers more slowly than younger adults, but they execute the decomposition strategy as well as younger adults. More precisely, analyses of all types of cognitive processes involved in retrieval (i.e., peripheral vs. central processes) revealed that central retrieval processes are maintained in both simple and complex arithmetic tasks, due to compensatory mechanisms of arithmetic skills. Age-related impairments in retrieval execution are explained by declines in more peripheral processes like encoding, deciding, and responding. In more complex arithmetic tasks, an over-additive effect of age is observed because of impairments of other arithmetic processes such as coordination and integration of partial results.

Finally, with regard to strategy choices, younger and older adults rely on the same predictors to determine their strategy choices. However, studies disagree on whether younger and older adults' strategy choices are equally influenced by each predictor. Some studies revealed that older adults do not adapt their strategy choices to problem features as well as younger adults, whereas other studies showed that they were influenced by problem features and strategy characteristics. Yet, in most of these studies, contrary to younger adults, older adults were able to always use the fastest and easiest retrieval strategies and they did not need to switch across strategies according to problem features. Future research may help gain information about determinants of arithmetic strategy choices and the conditions of appearance of age-related declines. One of the determinants that has started to receive attention from researchers is processing resources.

THE ROLE OF PROCESSING RESOURCES AS MEDIATORS OF AGE-RELATED DIFFERENCES IN MENTAL CALCULATION

The main hypothesis proposed to account for age-related differences in cognitive tasks in general, and in arithmetic tasks in particular, concerns processing resources. That is, the effect of age on specific cognitive processes may be the result of decreased processing resources with age. Processing resources are thought to comprise three main types of capacities: processing speed, working memory, and inhibition capacities (e.g., Light, 1991; Salthouse, 1991). Each of these resource types has been hypothesized as a mediator of the effects of age. Processing speed is the most documented hypothesis and led to the processing-speed theories of cognitive aging (Cerella, 1985; Myerson, Hale, Wagstaff, Poon, & Smith, 1990; Salthouse, 1996). According to these theories, age-related differences in cognitive performance result from slowed triggering and execution of cognitive processes. Second, the working-memory hypothesis of aging proposes that a decrement of simultaneous storage and temporary processing may lead to age-related decline in general cognitive performance (Craik, 1986; Craik & Byrd, 1982; Craik & Jennings, 1992). Finally, the inhibition hypothesis proposes that older people have greater difficulty than younger adults in inhibiting irrelevant pieces of information, thereby creating more interference and disturbing cognitive functioning (Chiappe, Hasher, & Siegel, 2000; Hasher, Stoltzfus, Zacks, & Rypma, 1991; Hasher & Zacks, 1979; Kane, Hasher, Stoltzfus, Zacks, & Connelly, 1994; Lustig, May, & Hasher, 2001; Zacks, Radvansky, & Hasher, 1996). Research into the relation between age and arithmetic has focused primarily on the roles of working memory and processing speed.

The Role of Working Memory as Mediator of Age-Related Differences

In arithmetic, the first study to examine the mediating role of processing resources in age effects tested the impact of working memory (Salthouse & Babcock, 1991). The authors showed that arithmetic performance negatively correlated with age under arithmetic single- and dual-task conditions (rs = -.57 and -.66 in each condition, respectively), suggesting that working-memory loads interacted with age in arithmetic. In later research that further determined the impact of working-memory capacities, two studies (Salthouse & Coon, 1994; Verhaeghen et al., 1997) tested multioperand problems that did or did not include brackets and parentheses (e.g., [(5 + 3) – 1] - [3 + (4 – 1)]; 5 + 3 – 1 – 3 + 4 – 1). Presence of brackets and parentheses involves coordinative demands, since problems cannot be solved from left to right but innermost brackets have to be computed first and stored in working memory. Verhaeghen and his collaborators (1997) found that older adults were not impaired when solving problems without brackets but they were markedly impaired when solving problems with brackets. These results suggest that older adults are not slowed when performing simple mental arithmetic (see also Allen et al., 1992; Allen et al., 1997; Geary et al., 1993; Geary & Lin, 1998; Geary & Wiley, 1991) but they have specific deficits in access and coordination of information in working memory (Sliwinski et al., 1994).

Recently, Oberauer and his colleagues (Oberauer, 2002; Oberauer et al., 2001; Oberauer & Kliegl, 2001; Oberauer, Süb, Schulze, Wilhelm, & Wittmann, 2000; Oberauer, Süb, Wilhelm, & Wittman, 2003) further determined the locus of the mediation of age-related changes in performance by working memory. In one of these studies (Oberauer et al., 2001), the dual-task paradigm was used and manipulation of the task structure allowed coordination and access demands in working memory to be assessed independently. In a control condition, participants only had to solve multioperand problems (including addition and subtraction operators). In a coordination condition (i.e., a classic dual-task condition), participants had to solve arithmetic problems while remembering pairs of letters and numbers that had to be retrieved. In an access condition, the memory task was integrated with the arithmetic task, so that some operands of the arithmetic problems were replaced by letters that were paired with digits. In this condition, participants had to substitute the letters to the corresponding number in order to compute the intermediate results. Results showed that the additional memory load (coordination condition) had no impact on either accuracy or latency for both younger and older adults. Moreover, accuracy of mental arithmetic substantially decreased when access to memory was required (access condition). Surprisingly, older adults were not impaired in the access condition: their accuracy level was comparable to that of younger adults, and an age-related general proportional slowing factor (i.e., significant Age × Condition interaction showing larger effects of age in the most difficult conditions) was not observed. Overall, these results suggest that access to working memory represents a critical source of concurrent-load interference. However, access to working memory was shown to be insensitive to the effects of age. Working-memory capacity may not be the limiting processing resource underlying the relation between age and arithmetic performance.

The Role of Processing Speed as Mediator of Age-Related Differences

Salthouse and Coon (1994, Experiment 2) tested the impact of processing speed and working memory in a multioperand problem verification task. In this study, participants solved problems that did or did not include parentheses and brackets for each condition. The presence/absence of parentheses allowed them to manipulate the load of working-memory resources. Moreover, the authors collected for each individual independent measures of processing speed and working-memory capacities with paper-and-pencil tests. In order to assess the impact of both types of processing resources, they performed hierarchical regression analyses on the indices of arithmetic processes derived from individual-regression analyses (i.e., slopes representing retrieval processes and intercepts reflecting the other arithmetic processes such as encoding and responding). Hierarchical regression analyses involve first assessing the effects of age on a criterion variable and, second, assessing the effects of age on the criterion variable after partialling out the contribution of another variable. The difference between the effects of age assessed alone and after statistical control of the predictor variable represents the amount of unique age-related differences in the criterion variable mediated by the predictor variable.

Salthouse and Coon (1994) found that all types of arithmetic processes were affected by age, including central processes as assessed with slopes derived from individual-regression analyses. Therefore, the authors performed hierarchical regression analyses on central process indices (i.e., slopes assessing retrieval and coordination of partial results) and on peripheral process indices (i.e., intercepts assessing encoding, deciding, and responding). R^2s associated with age and the increment in R^2s associated with age after controlling for processing-speed and working-memory measures were calculated. The differences between both types of R^2s represent the amount of age-related variance mediated by processing resources. Age-related variance in central processes decreased by 27% after controlling for working-memory measures and by 91% after controlling for processing-speed measures. Age-related variance in peripheral processes decreased by 46% after controlling for working-memory measures and by 99% after controlling for processing-speed measures. Finally, Salthouse and Coon conducted a second set of hierarchical regression analyses, with the working-memory measures as the criterion variable, and showed that age-related variance in working-memory resources could be reduced by 94% after controlling for processing-speed measures.

Sliwinski and his collaborators (Sliwinski et al., 1994) tried to further determine the mechanisms responsible for the mediation of age-related differences in arithmetic processes by a processing-speed decrement. More precisely, they tested whether age-related slowing was proportional or additive: regressing older adults' mean latencies on younger adults' latencies should reveal a slope indicating proportional slowing and an intercept indicating additive slowing. The presence of proportional slowing may be taken as evidence for impaired elementary cognitive processes. A proportional slowing was found uniformly across the entire distribution of older individuals. Such proportional slowing was sufficient to account for differences between younger and older adults and was not moderated by practice effects.

Sliwinski et al. (1994) also found task-specific effects with different functions describing the proportional slowing for the addition and copy conditions. The amount of slowing did not show a statistically reliable increase as addend size increased in the addition condition. This suggests that what is considered as generalized slowing of basic cognitive processes is mainly attributable to a specific slowing in the initiation of certain cognitive processes but not in the repetition of these processes. Such an argument is also consistent with other findings that suggest that aging is associated with specific impairments of some arithmetic processes rather than general impairments of all processes (Allen et al., 1992; Allen et al., in press; Allen et al., 1997; Geary et al., 1993; Geary & Lin, 1998; Geary & Wiley, 1991; Verhaeghen et al., 1997).

Summary

In spite of previous research in arithmetic that showed effects of working-memory load in arithmetic performance (e.g., Ashcraft et al., 1992; Ashcraft & Kirk, 2001; De Rammelaere, Stuyven, & Vandierendonck, 1999, 2001; Fuerst & Hitch, 2000; Hecht, 2002; Hitch, 1978; Lemaire, Abdi, & Fayol, 1996; Logie, Gilhooly, & Wynn, 1994; Seitz & Schumann-Hengsteler, 2000), working memory contributes little unique variance to age-related differences in arithmetic performance. All effects of age on calculation processes, on central as well as on peripheral processes, are completely eliminated after controlling basic processing speed, suggesting that a general slowing is responsible for age-related differences in arithmetic performance. Such a generalized slowing appears proportional and related to the initiation of cognitive processes. Overall, the studies suggest that the more promising explanation of age-related differences in arithmetic is a combination of both general and specific slowing processes.

ALZHEIMER'S DISEASE–RELATED DIFFERENCES IN MENTAL ARITHMETIC

Alzheimer's disease (AD) is a complex progressive and generalized dementia syndrome that generally appears in adulthood and whose primary and main characteristic is a profound episodic-memory loss in its early clinical course (APA, 1994; McKhann et al., 1984). The development of the disease involves impairments of several cognitive functions, mainly executive functions, language, and visuo-spatial functions, as well as neuropsychiatric syndromes such as hallucinations or delusions in the late stages of the disease. Results from several studies suggest that arithmetic disruption is an early sign of dementia (Deloche et al., 1995; Grafman, Kampen, Rosemberg, Salazar, & Boller, 1989; Mantovan, Delazer, Ermani, & Denes, 1999; Marterer, Danielczyk, Simanyi, & Fischer, 1996; Parlato et al., 1992; Pesenti, Seron, & Van Der Linden, 1994). Data showed that decreased arithmetic scores correlated with increased degree of dementia (Deloche et al., 1995; Mantovan et al., 1999; Marterer et al., 1996; Rosselli et al., 1998). Many authors have suggested that arithmetic impairment may represent a reliable hallmark for the diagnosis of AD (Carlomagno et al., 1999; Deloche et al., 1995; Kaufmann et al., 2002; Mantovan et al., 1999; Marterer et al., 1996; Rosselli et al., 1998).

However, heterogeneous patterns of preserved/impaired arithmetic processes have been observed in demented patients (Carlomagno et al., 1999; Crutch & Warrington, 2001; Deloche et al., 1995; Girelli, Luzzatti, Annoni, & Vecchi, 1999; Grafman et al., 1989; McGlinchey-Berroth, Milberg, & Charness, 1989). For instance, numerical knowledge is preserved in the early stages of AD (Grafman et al., 1989; Kaufmann et al., 2002). Further, Kaufmann and his collaborators (2002) compared performance of 19 probable AD patients and control healthy adults on several numerical and arithmetic tasks (e.g., number writing and reading, dot counting, number comparison, mental calculation). They repeatedly observed in one third of patients dissociations between basic numerical knowledge and arithmetic performance, with preserved numerical knowledge and impaired arithmetic performance. In the present section, we review previous findings on AD-related differences in mental arithmetic and, more precisely, on strategic aspects of AD arithmetic performance.

Alzheimer's Disease–Related Differences in Retrieval Processes

Concerning arithmetic problem solving tasks, very few studies have precisely examined the effects of AD in order to identify the loci of AD effects. The most documented effects of AD in arithmetic concern the execution of arithmetic fact-retrieval processes. Data appear contradictory concerning which specific arithmetic processes involved in retrieval are impaired.

A set of studies suggested that specific retrieval of arithmetic facts in memory was affected in AD patients. Kaufmann et al. (2002) showed that activities such as number comparison and subitizing were not affected in AD, but arithmetic fact retrieval processes were impaired. Two single-case studies showed the same type of results (Grafman et al., 1989; Pesenti, Seron, & Van, 1994). Grafman and his collaborators (Grafman et al., 1989) analyzed the performance of a 60-year-old patient and observed deteriorated calculation procedures, whereas numerical knowledge and number comparison remained intact over two years. However, not all calculation procedures declined: multiplication and division procedures were inaccessible, but addition and subtraction procedures remained maintained in the early stage of dementia. Similar results were obtained by Pesenti et al. (1994). They studied a 39-year-old patient who had early onset dementia. In simple arithmetic tasks, this patient had difficulties with specific calculation procedures, such as sum and product retrieval, but maintained performance in a subtraction task. Note, however, that given the diversity in symptoms and in distributions of plaques and tangles across AD patients, it is hard to generalize results of case studies to the entire population.

Duverne and her collaborators (Duverne, Lemaire, & Michel, 2003) further examined which processes involved in retrieval procedures were affected in AD. The authors tested 16 healthy younger adults, 16 healthy older adults, and 16 probable AD patients who completed an addition/number comparison task (e.g., 7 + 8 or 13, which item is larger?). The authors performed individual-regression analyses on latencies of small-split problems (small distance between the correct sum of addition and the proposed number) in which participants mainly used a retrieval strategy (see Ashcraft & Stazyk, 1981; De Rammelaere et al., 2001; Duverne & Lemaire, 2003; El Yagoubi, Lemaire, & Besson, 2003). They showed that indices of both retrieval processes (slopes) and more peripheral arithmetic processes (intercepts) increased in AD patients. In addition to impairments of encoding and response processes, arithmetic fact-retrieval processes were slowed in AD patients.

Another set of studies argues for arithmetic fact-retrieval processes being maintained in the early stages of AD. Mantovan et al. (1999) tested the performance of 12 AD patients in simple arithmetic tasks (one-digit or multidigit additions, multiplications, and subtractions). AD patients showed a moderate decline in arithmetic fact retrieval. Of the 12 patients, 5 had no difficulties in arithmetic fact retrieval. However, all AD patients were markedly impaired in calculation procedures, which are more demanding in terms of processing resources. Such a pattern of results was also observed in single-case studies of people with AD (Girelli et al., 1999; McGlinchey-Berroth et al., 1989). For example, McGlinchey-Berroth et al. (1989) used the complex arithmetic skill learning task of squaring two-digit numbers (see Charness & Campbell, 1988) in a single amnesic AD patient. Their results revealed a dissociation between preserved abilities to learn and execute the individual steps of the algorithm and impaired abilities to combine the steps of the algorithm. Those findings suggest that dementia-related differences in arithmetic may be accounted for by deficits in some components of working memory (like monitoring several pieces of information), while arithmetic fact knowledge may be preserved.

Consistent with a spared retrieval processes hypothesis, Allen et al. (in press) performed individual-regression analyses on production and verification multiplication latencies. Slopes were of equal magnitude across healthy younger adults, healthy older adults, and probable AD patients. The authors suggested that semantic processes, like fact retrieval, are stable in AD, but that nonsemantic cognitive components assessed with intercepts, such as encoding problems or responding, may account for decline in arithmetic performance with AD.

Alzheimer's Disease-Related Differences in Multiple-Strategy Use

To our knowledge, only three studies have tried to shed light on AD-related changes in multiple-strategy use (i.e., strategy repertoire, distribution, and choices) (Allen et al., in press; Duverne et al., 2003; Mantovan et al., 1999). Mantovan and his collaborators (1999) analyzed performance on multiplication problems involving 0 and showed that AD patients had severe difficulties with an extremely high incidence of $N \times 0 = N$ errors. Note that problems involving 0 as an operand may be solved via the rule $N \times 0 = 0$ (LeFevre, Bisanz, Daley, Buffone, & Sadesky, 1996; McCloskey, Aliminosa, & Sokol, 1991). Allen et al. (in press) used single-digit multiplication verification and production tasks and more precisely analyzed the effects of AD on multiple-strategy use. Results revealed a decreased ability to accurately and adaptively use the $N \times 0 = 0$ rule as well as the $N \times 1 = N$ rule and very high error rates on problems involving 0 and 1 as an operand (mean percent errors of 6%, 18%, and 40% in healthy younger adults, healthy older adults, and AD patients, respectively). Unfortunately, none of those studies specifically analyzed the pattern of error types. Therefore, we do not know whether errors on problems involving 0 and 1 resulted from the failure to access and use arithmetic rules or from the failure to inhibit interference rules such as $N + 0 = N$.

Duverne and her collaborators (Duverne et al., 2003) analyzed split effects, an indicator of the ability to calibrate strategy use to problem structure, in healthy younger and older adults and probable AD patients in the addition/number comparison task. Split effects reflect the better performance in large-split problems (i.e., problems whose proposed solution is far from the correct solution; e.g., $6 + 5 = 19$) than in small-split problems (i.e., problems whose proposed solution is close to the correct solution; e.g., $6 + 5 = 13$). These performance variations have been interpreted in terms of multiple-strategy use (Ashcraft & Stazyk, 1981; De Rammelaere et al., 2001; El Yagoubi et al., 2003; see, however, Geary, Widaman, & Little, 1986; Manly & Spoehr, 1999; Zbrodoff & Logan, 1990, for alternative explanations), such that small-split problems are solved by means of complete calculation strategies, whereas large-split problems are solved by means of incomplete calculation strategies. Analyses of z-score latencies showed decreased split effects between healthy younger and older adults but equal split effects in healthy older adults and AD patients. Contrary to Mantovan et al.'s (1999) and Allen et al.'s (in press) findings, these results suggest that age-related changes in multiple-strategy use were not amplified in AD patients who were able to switch between strategies from trial to trial. Multiple-strategy use appeared maintained in the early stage of AD, at least in a simple addition/number comparison task, but it seemed impaired in more complex production tasks in which people could use more sophisticated rules such as $N \times 0 = 0$ or $N \times 1 = N$.

Summary

Previous results on effects of AD on specific arithmetic processes, such as retrieval of arithmetic facts in memory, are contradictory. Some research showed impairments of arithmetic retrieval in dementia, whereas other research showed moderate impairments of these processes, but all of them agree in showing impairments of more peripheral processes such as encoding and responding. Findings concerning AD-related changes in strategy distribution and choices are also ambiguous. Two studies suggest that people with AD used arithmetic rules less well than control adults, whereas another study suggests a maintained ability to switch across complete and incomplete calculation strategies from trial to trial. Such inconsistencies may just reveal task-specific effects and may be resolved in future research with direct evidence (e.g., verbal protocols) of strategy use.

CONCLUSIONS AND FUTURE DIRECTIONS

Previous research on mental arithmetic and aging has yielded a number of important findings to understand both arithmetic and aging. In arithmetic, this research brought further evidence that (a) people use different strategies and vary in strategic aspects of their performance (i.e., strategy repertoire, distribution, execution, and selection at all points during adult development), (b) some processes (e.g., retrieval of arithmetic facts from memory) are more resistant to aging when well trained or heavily practiced throughout life, and (c) arithmetic performance is influenced by a number of different types of variables, namely characteristics of individuals (like their age or cognitive status), task constraints (e.g., necessity to respond quickly and/or accurately), and problem characteristics (e.g., problem size). In aging, previous research in arithmetic brought further evidence that (a) not all cognitive processes are negatively affected by age (e.g., automatic retrieval of information from memory may be spared), (b) aging has more negative effects on the most difficult problems (like in other cognitive domains), and (c) some strategic aspects of participants' performance are more affected than others throughout life (e.g., strategy distribution vs. strategy execution or selection).

Future research will advance our knowledge on aging and mental arithmetic. To do this, research will ask new questions and deepen our understanding of already addressed issues. A few examples of research questions that have begun to be explored include the roles of aging on strategy-selection mechanisms (e.g., are older and young adults equally able to select strategies optimally so as to choose the best strategy on each problem?), on strategy execution (e.g., what are the characteristics of strategies the execution of which are more affected by aging than others?), and on strategy repertoire/distribution (e.g., does the number of arithmetic strategies used by individuals vary with age?).

Future research on aging will advance our knowledge on domains of mathematical cognition other than mental arithmetic. For instance, the effects of age on basic numerical activities, like number processing and quantification, have been very rarely investigated (see, however, Geary & Lin, 1998; Kotary & Hoyer, 1995; Nebes, Brady, & Reynolds, 1992; Sliwinski, 1997; Trick, James, & Brodeur, 1996; Watson, Maylor, & Manson, 2002, for primary studies). However, it is necessary to know how older people read, write, transcode, quantify, comprehend, and represent numbers to understand how they do mental calculation. As examples of research questions with no answer now, we can mention: do young and older adults represent numbers with similar (logarithmic, linear, or exponential) scales? Do young and older adults use the same processes to transcode numbers (e.g., transform Arabic numbers into verbal numbers)? Are the quantification processes affected by aging?

Like research on aging and quantification processes or on aging and mental arithmetic, research on the effects of aging on other mathematical activities (e.g., numerical estimation, number transcoding) would also illustrate the usefulness of research in older adults for understanding mathematical cognition and for investigating general issues about cognitive aging. A few examples of other new questions that future research will include concern the roles of individual characteristics of older adults on math performance. More precisely, analyses of individual characteristics such as, among others, math anxiety (e.g., does the performance of math anxious participants decline with age faster than that of non-math-anxious participants?) or different levels of schooling (e.g., are aging effects more important in less-educated older adults?) may help in better understanding the impact of such variables in cognitive aging and in arithmetic cognition. Another direction for future research could be to analyze age-related changes in neural substrates of mathematical cognition (e.g., do these neural substrates of mental arithmetic change with age?). Of course, advances on both new and not-so-new questions will be made if researchers are inventive in designing new tasks, investigating new domains, or using new research techniques (e.g., brain-imaging or eye-movement techniques).

REFERENCES

Allen, P. A., Ashcraft, M. H., & Weber, T. A. (1992). On mental multiplication and age. *Psychology and Aging, 7,* 536–545.

Allen, P. A., Bucur, B., Lemaire, P., Duverne, S., Ogrocki, P., & Sanders, R. E. (in press). Influence of probable Alzheimer's disease on multiplication verification and production. *Aging, Neuropschology, and Cognition.*

Allen, P. A., Smith, A. F., Jerge, K. A., & Vires-Collins, H. (1997). Age differences in mental multiplication: Evidence for peripheral but not central decrements. *Journal of Gerontology: Psychological Sciences, 52b*(2), 81–90.

American Psychological Association. (1994). *Diagnostic and statistical manual of mental disorders* (4th ed.). Washington, DC: Author.

Ashcraft, M. H., Donley, R. D., Halas, M. A., & Vakali, M. (1992). Working memory, automaticity, and problem difficulty. In J. I. D. Campbell (Ed.), *The nature and origins of mathematical skills* (pp. 301–329). Oxford, U.K.: North-Holland.

Ashcraft, M. H., & Kirk, E. P. (2001). The relationships among working memory, math anxiety, and performance. *Journal of Experimental Psychology: General, 130,* 224–237.

Ashcraft, M. H., & Stazyk, E. H. (1981). Mental addition: A test of three verification models. *Memory and Cognition, 9*(2), 185–196.

Campbell, J. I. D., & Charness, N. (1990). Age-related declines in working-memory skills. Evidence from a complex calculation task. *Developmental Psychology, 26*(6), 879–888.

Campbell, J. I. D., & Graham, D. J. (1985). Mental multiplication skill: Structure, process, and acquisition. *Canadian Journal of Psychology, 39,* 338–366.

Carlomagno, S., Iavarone, A., Nolfe, G., Bourene, G., Martin, C., & Deloche, G. (1999). Dyscalculia in the early stages of Alzheimer's disease. *Acta Neurologia Scandinavia, 99,* 166–174.

Cerella, J. (1985). Information processing rates in the elderly. *Psychological Bulletin, 98*(1), 67–83.

Cerella, J. (1990). Age and information-processing rate. In J. E. Birren & K. W. Schaie (Eds.), *Handbook of the psychology of aging* (3rd ed., pp. 201–233). San Diego, CA: Academic Press.

Charness, N. (1981). Search in chess: Age and skill differences. *Journal of Experimental Psychology: Human Perception and Performance, 7,* 467–476.

Charness, N., & Campbell, J. I. D. (1988). Acquiring skill at mental calculation in adulthood: A task decomposition. *Journal of Experimental Psychology: General, 117,* 115–129.

Chiappe, P., Hasher, L., & Siegel, L. S. (2000). Working memory, inhibitory control, and reading disability. *Memory & Cognition, 28*(1), 8–17.

Craik, F. I. M. (1986). A functional account of age differences in memory. In F. Klix & H. Hagendorf (Eds.), *Human Memory and Cognitive Abilities* (Vols. 409–422). Amsterdam: Elsevier.

Craik, F. I. M., & Byrd, M. (1982). Aging and cognitive deficits: The role of attentional resources. In F. I. M. Craik & S. Trehub (Eds.), *Aging and cognitive processes* (pp. 191–211). New York: Plenum.

Craik, F. I. M., & Jennings, J. M. (1992). Human memory. In F. I. M. Craik & T. A. Salthouse (Eds.), *The handbook of aging and cognition* (pp. 51–110). Hillsdale, NJ: Erlbaum.

Crutch, S. J., & Warrington, E. K. (2001). Acalculia: deficits of operational and quantity number knowledge. *Journal of International Neuropsychology Society, 7,* 825–834.

De Rammelaere, S., Stuyven, E., & Vandierendonck, A. (1999). On the contribution of working memory resources in the verification of simple mental arithmetic sums. *Psychological Research, 62,* 72–77.

De Rammelaere, S., Stuyven, E., & Vandierendonck, A. (2001). Verifying simple arithmetic sums and products: Are the phonological loop and the central executive involved? *Memory and Cognition, 29,* 267–274.

Deloche, G., Hannequin, D., Carlomagno, S., Angiel, A., Dordain, M., Pasquier, F., Pellat, J., Denis, P., Desi, M., Beauchamp, D., Metz-Lutz, M. N., Cesaro, P., & Seron, X. (1995). Calculation and number processing in mild Alzheimer's disease. *Journal of Clinical Experimental Neuropsychology, 17,* 634–639.

Duverne, S., & Lemaire, P. (2003). *Age-related differences in arithmetic problem verification strategies.* Manuscript submitted for publication.

Duverne, S., Lemaire, P., & Michel, B. F. (2003). Alzheimer's disease disrupts arithmetic facts retrieval processes but not arithmetic strategy selection. *Brain and Cognition, 52,* 302–318.

El Yagoubi, R., Lemaire, P., & Besson, M. (2003). Different brain mechanisms mediate two strategies in arithmetic: Evidence from visual event-related brain potentials. *Neuropsychologia, 41,* 855–862.

French, J. W., Ekstrom, R. B., & Price, I. A. (1963). *Kit of reference tests for cognitive factors.* Princeton, NJ: Educational Testing Service.

Fuerst, A. J., & Hitch, G. J. (2000). Separate roles for executive and phonological components of working memory in mental arithmetic. *Memory & Cognition, 28*(5), 774–782.

Geary, D. (1996). The problem-size effect in mental addition: Developmental and cross-national trends. *Mathematical Cognition, 2*(1), 63–93.

Geary, D. C., Frensch, P. A., & Wiley, J. G. (1993). Simple and complex mental subtraction: Strategy choice and speed-of-processing differences in younger and older adults. *Psychology and Aging, 8,* 242–256.

Geary, D. C., Hamson, C. O., Chen, G. P., Liu, F., Hoard, M. K., & Salthouse, T. A. (1997). Computational and reasoning abilities in arithmetic: Cross-generational change in China and the United States. *Psychonomic Bulletin & Review, 4*(3), 425–430.

Geary, D. C., & Lin, J. (1998). Numerical cognition: Age-related differences in the speed of executing biologically primary and biologically secondary processes. *Experimental Aging Research, 24*(2), 101–138.

Geary, D. C., Salthouse, T. A., Chen, G. P., & Fan, L. (1996). Are East Asian versus American differences in arithmetic ability a recent phenomenon? *Developmental Psychology, 32,* 254–262.

Geary, D. C., Widaman, K. F., & Little, T. D. (1986). Cognitive addition and multiplication: Evidence for a single memory network. *Memory and Cognition, 14,* 478–487.

Geary, D. C., & Wiley, J. G. (1991). Cognitive addition: Strategy choices and speed-of-processing differences in young and elderly adults. *Psychology and Aging, 6*(3), 474–483.

Girelli, L., Luzzatti, C., Annoni, G., & Vecchi, T. (1999). Progressive decline of numerical skill in Alzheimer type dementia: A case study. *Brain & Cognition, 40,* 132–136.

Grafman, J., Kampen, D., Rosemberg, J., Salazar, A. M., & Boller, F. (1989). The progressive breakdown of number processing and calculation ability: A case study. *Cortex, 25,* 121–133.

Groen, G. J., & Parkman, J. M. (1972). A chronometric analysis of simple addition. *Psychological Review, 79*(4), 329–343.

Hasher, L., Stoltzfus, E. R., Zacks, R. T., & Rypma, B. (1991). Age and inhibition. *Journal of Experimental Psychology: Learning, Memory, and Cognition, 17,* 163–169.

Hasher, L., & Zacks, R. T. (1979). Automatic and effortful processes in memory. *Journal of Experimental Psychology: General, 108,* 356–388.

Hecht, S. A. (2002). Counting on working memory in simple arithmetic: When counting is used for problem solving. *Memory & Cognition, 30*(3), 447–455.

Hitch, G. J. (1978). The role of short-term working memory in mental arithmetic. *Cognitive Psychology, 10*(3), 302–323.

Kane, M. J., Hasher, L., Stoltzfus, E. R., Zacks, R. T., & Connelly, L. S. (1994). Inhibitory attentional mechanisms and aging. *Psychology & Aging, 9*(1), 103–112.

Kaufmann, L., Montanes, P., Jacquier, M., Matallana, D., Eibl, G., & Delazer, M. (2002). About the relationship between numerical processing and arithmetics in early Alzheimer's disease—a follow-up study. *Brain & Cognition, 48,* 398–405.

Kotary, L., & Hoyer, W. (1995). Age and the ability to inhibit distractor information in visual selective attention. *Experimental Aging Research, 21,* 159–171.

LeFevre, J., Bisanz, J., Daley, K. E., Buffone, L., & Sadesky, G. S. (1996). Multiple routes to solution of single-digit multiplication problems. *Journal of Experimental Psychology: General, 125,* 284–306.

Lemaire, P., Abdi, H., & Fayol, M. (1996). The role of working memory resources in simple cognitive arithmetic. *European Journal of Cognitive Psychology, 8*(1), 73–103.

Lemaire, P., Arnaud, L., & Lecacheur, M. (2003). Adults' age-related differences in computational estimation strategies. Manuscript submitted for publication.

Lemaire, P., & Lecacheur, M. (2001). Older and younger adults' strategy use and execution in currency conversion tasks: Insights from French Franc to Euro and Euro to French Franc conversions. *Journal of Experimental Psychology: Applied, 3,* 195–206.

Lemaire, P., & Lecacheur, M. (2002). Children's strategies in computational estimation. *Journal of Experimental Child Psyshology, 82,* 281–304.

Lemaire, P., & Reder, L. (1999). What affects strategy selection in arithmetic? The example of parity and five effects on product verification. *Memory and Cognition, 27*(2), 364–382.

Lemaire, P., & Siegler, R. S. (1995). Four aspects of strategic change: Contributions to children's learning of multiplication. *Journal of Experimental Psychology, 124*(1), 83–97.

Light, L. L. (1991). Memory and aging: Four hypotheses in search of data. *Annual Review of Psychology, 42,* 333–376.

Logie, R. H., Gilhooly, K. J., & Wynn, V. (1994). Counting on working memory in arithmetic problem solving. *Memory and Cognition, 22,* 395–410.

Lustig, C., May, C. P., & Hasher, L. (2001). Working memory span and the role of proactive interference.

Journal of Experimental Psychology: General, 130(2), 199–207.

Manly, C. F., & Spoehr, K. T. (1999). Mental multiplication: Nothing but the facts? *Memory & Cognition, 27*(6), 1087–1096.

Mantovan, M. C., Delazer, M., Ermani, M., & Denes, G. (1999). The breakdown of calculation procedures in Alzheimer's disease. *Cortex, 35,* 21–38.

Marterer, A., Danielczyk, W., Simanyi, M., & Fischer, P. (1996). Calculation abilities in dementia of Alzheimer's type and in vascular dementia. *Archives of Gerontology Geriatrics, 23,* 189–197.

McCloskey, M., Aliminosa, D., & Sokol, S. M. (1991). Facts, rules and procedures in normal calculation: Evidence from multiple single patient studies of impaired arithmetic fact retrieval. *Brain and Cognition, 17,* 377–397.

McGlinchey-Berroth, R., Milberg, W. P., & Charness, N. (1989). Learning of a complex arithmetic skill in dementia: Further evidence for a dissociation between compilation and production. *Cortex, 25,* 695–705.

McKhann, G., Drachmann, D. A., Folstein, M. F., Katzman, R., Price, D. L., & Stadlan, E. (1984). Clinical diagnosis of Alzheimer's disease: Report of the NINCDS-ADRDA work group under the auspices of the Department of Health and Human Services task force on Alzheimer's disease. *Neurology, 34,* 939–944.

Miller, K. F., Perlmutter, M., & Keating, D. (1984). Cognitive arithmetic: Comparison of operations. *Journal of Experimental Psychology: Learning, Memory, and Cognition, 10,* 46–60.

Myerson, J., Hale, S., Wagstaff, D., Poon, L. W., & Smith, G. A. (1990). The information-loss model: A mathematical theory of age-related cognitive slowing. *Psychological Review, 97*(4), 475–487.

Nebes, R. D., Brady, C. B., & Reynolds, C. F. (1992). Cognitive slowing in Alzheimer's disease and geriatric depression. *Journal of Gerontology: Psychological Sciences, 47,* 331–336.

Oberauer, K. (2002). Access to information in working memory: Exploring the focus of attention. *Journal of Experimental Psychology: Learning, Memory, and Cognition, 28,* 411–421.

Oberauer, K., Demmrich, A., Mayr, U., & Kliegl, R. (2001). Dissociating retention and access in working memory: An age-comparative study of mental arithmetic. *Memory & Cognition, 29,* 18–33.

Oberauer, K., & Kliegl, R. (2001). Beyond resources: Formal models of complexity effects and age differences in working memory. *European Journal of Cognitive Psychology, 13*(1/2), 187–215.

Oberauer, K., Süb, H.-M., Schulze, R., Wilhelm, O., & Wittmann, W. W. (2000). Working memory capacity-facets of a cognitive construct. *Personality and Individual Differences, 29,* 1017–1045.

Oberauer, K., Süb, H.-M., Wilhelm, O., & Wittman, W. W. (2003). The multiple faces of working memory: Storage, processing, supervision, and coordination. *Intelligence, 31,* 167–193.

Parlato, V., Lopez, O. L., Panisset, M., Iavarone, A., Grafman, F., & Boller, F. (1992). Mental calculation in mild Alzheimer's disease: A pilot study. *International Journal of Geriatric Psychiatry, 7,* 599–602.

Pesenti, M., Seron, X., & Van Der Linden, M. (1994). Selective impairment as evidence for mental organisation of arithmetical facts: BB, a case of preserved subtraction? *Cortex, 30*(4), 661–671.

Pesenti, M., Zago, L., Crivello, F., Mellet, E., Samson, D., Duroux, B., Seron, X., & Mazoyer, B. (2001). Mental calculation in a prodigy is sustained by right prefrontal and medial-temporal areas. *Nature Neuroscience, 4*(1), 103–107.

Rosselli, M., Ardila, A., Arvizu, L., Kretzmer, T., Standish, V., & Liebermann, J. (1998). Arithmetical abilities in Alzheimer disease. *International Journal of Neurosciences, 96*(141–148).

Salthouse, T. A. (1991). *Theoretical perspectives on cognitive aging*. Hillsdale, NJ: Erlbaum.

Salthouse, T. A. (1996). The processing-speed theory of adult age differences in cognition. *Psychological Review, 103*, 403–428.

Salthouse, T. A., & Babcock, R. L. (1991). Decomposing adult age differences in working memory. *Developmental Psychology, 27*(5), 763–776.

Salthouse, T. A., & Coon, V. E. (1994). Interpretation of differential deficits: The case of aging and mental arithmetic. *Journal of Experimental Psychology: Learning, Memory, and Cognition, 20*, 1172–1182.

Sanders, R. E., Gonzalez, D. J., Murphy, M. J., Pesta, B. J., & Bucur, B. (2002). Training content varability and the effectiveness of learning: An adult age assessment. *Aging, Neuropsychology, & Cognition, 9*, 157–174.

Seitz, K., & Schumann-Hengsteler, R. (2000). Mental multiplication and working memory. *European Journal of Cognitive Psychology, 12*, 552–570.

Siegler, R. S., & Lemaire, P. (1997). Older and younger adults' strategy choices in multiplication: Testing predictions of ASCM using the choice/no-choice method. *Journal of Experimental Psychology: General, 126*(1), 71–92.

Sliwinski, M. (1997). Aging and counting speed: Evidence for process-specific slowing. *Psychology and Aging, 12*, 38–49.

Sliwinski, M., Buschke, H., Kuslansky, G., Senior, G., & Scarisbrick, D. (1994). Proportional slowing and addition speed in old and young adults. *Psychology and Aging, 9*(1), 72–80.

Soederberg Miller, L. M., & Stine-Morrow, E. A. L. (1998). Aging and the effects of knowledge on on-line reading strategies. *Journal of Gerontology: Psychological Sciences, 53B*(4), 223–233.

Stazyk, E. H., Ashcraft, M. H., & Hamann, M. S. (1982). A network approach to mental multiplication. *Journal of Experimental Psychology: Learning, Memory, & Cognition, 8*(4), 320–335.

Touron, D. R., Hoyer, W. J., & Cerella, J. (2001). Cognitive skill acquisition and transfer in younger and older adults. *Psychology and Aging, 16*, 555–563.

Trick, L. M., James, T. E., & Brodeur, D. A. (1996). Lifespan changes in visual enumeration: The number discrimination task. *Developmental Psychology, 32*, 925–932.

Verhaeghen, P., Kliegl, R., & Mayr, U. (1997). Sequential and coordinative complexity in time-accuracy functions for mental arithmetic. *Psychology & Aging, 12*(4), 555–564.

Watson, D. G., Maylor, E. A., & Manson, N. J. (2002). Aging and enumeration: A selective deficit for the subitization of targets among distractors. *Psychology and Aging, 17*, 496–504.

Widaman, K. F., Geary, D. C., Cormier, P., & Little, T. D. (1989). A componential model for mental addition. *Journal of Experimental Psychology: Learning, Memory, & Cognition, 15*(5), 898–919.

Widaman, K. F., & Little, T. D. (1992). The development of skill in mental arithmetic: An individual differences perspective. In J. I. D. Campbell (Ed.), *The nature and origins of mathematical skills* (pp. 189–253). Amsterdam: Elsevier Science Publishers.

Zacks, R. T., Radvansky, G., & Hasher, L. (1996). Studies of directed forgetting in older adults. *Journal of Experimental Psychology: Learning, Memory, & Cognition, 22*(1), 143–156.

Zbrodoff, N. J., & Logan, G. D. (1990). On the relation between production and verification tasks in the psychology of simple arithmetic. *Journal of Experimental Psychology: Learning, Memory, and Cognition, 16*(1), 83–97.

24

Calculation Abilities in Expert Calculators

Mauro Pesenti

EXCEPTIONAL CALCULATION ABILITIES

Could you, in a few seconds, mentally multiply two arbitrarily chosen multi-digit numbers, divide two prime numbers and give the answer, say, to 20 decimals, or raise any 2- or 3-digit number to the fifth power (e.g., $675 \times 486 = ?$, $31:61 = ?$, $98^5 = ?$)? If yes, then you may be one of the very few people known as "calculating prodigies," "lightning calculators," or simply "expert calculators," who possess exceptional calculating abilities. Calculating prodigies are individuals able to mentally solve complex calculations that most people would be unable to solve without much time and effort. Such prodigies can add, multiply, subtract, or divide multi-digit numbers, raise to powers, extract roots, calculate sines, and much more. They can be found among great mathematicians and scientists but also among individuals, some with developmental delay, intellectual, neurological, or neuropsychiatric disorders, who exhibit out-standing focal calculating abilities without exceptional mathematical talent. Calculating prodigies have always been a source of puzzlement for their contemporaries. On the one hand, famous scientists and mathematicians impress because their expertise is usually thought to stem from some rare, high level of intellectual efficiency. On the other hand, mnemonists and calculators with developmental delay raise the question of whether or not they really possess exceptional capacities or are simply playing some ingenious tricks.

Defining and studying calculating abilities in experts is not an easy task, and there have been very few attempts to link research on calculating prodigies and current work on nonexpert subjects. This chapter summarizes what is known about calculating prodigies and reviews the findings suggesting that calculation expertise relies on a perfect knowledge of basic arithmetic operations and complex calculation algorithms as well as increased number-specific short- and long-term memory capacities. Behavioral and neuroanatomical data collected in healthy people and individuals with neurological or neuropsychiatric disorders are reviewed and implications for the study of nonexpert subjects are drawn.

ANECDOTES FROM THE PAST

Most of what is known about past calculating prodigies comes from anecdotal reports and summary investigations (see Insert 24.1 for examples). Very few prodigies were tested in

Insert 24.1 Some Calculating Prodigies from the Past
and Their Amazing Calculation Expertise

Jedediah Buxton (1702–1772), an English farmer with a slight developmental delay, could solve problems like *"In a body whose three sides are 23,145,789 yards, 5,642,732 yards, and 54,965 yards, how many cubical eights of an inch are there?"* and was used to estimating lengths or sizes of objects and fields. He was relatively slow at calculation but had an exceptional long-term memory for figures. He was once able to square a 39-digit number, but it took him about two and a half months.

Zerah Colburn (1804–1840), the son of an American farmer, started to give public exhibitions when he was 6 years old. At that time, he was able to multiply multi-digit numbers, extract roots of exact squares and cubes, and calculate the number of minutes or seconds in durations (e.g., *How many minutes in 219,000 hours? Answer: 13,140,000*) faster than could be done on paper. He was also extremely fast at factoring multi-digit numbers (e.g., *What two numbers multiplied together produce 1242? Answer: 54 and 23, 9 and 138, 27 and 46, 3 and 414, 6 and 207, 2 and 261*). He usually found it easier to multiply small numbers by large ones than to multiply numbers with the same amount of digits. For example, at the age of 8 years, he squared *999,999* by first multiplying *37,037* by itself, and the product twice by *27*, then multiplying the answer (*999,998,000,001*) twice by *49*, and this answer (*2,400,995,198,002,401*) by *25* to give the final product, *60,024,879,950,060,025*.

George Parker Bidder (1806–1878) was one of the most brilliant engineers in England in the 19th century. At the age of 10 years, he was able to solve calculations such as *dividing 468,592,413,563 by 9,076*, or:

$$\frac{5280^3 \times 12^3}{120 \times 282 \times 60 \times 24 \times 365}$$

Johann Martin Zacharias Dase (1824–1861), a German calculating prodigy, did not know much about mathematics. However, by the time he was 15, he was given the formula to compute *pi* ($\pi/4 = \tan^{-1} 1/2 + \tan^{-1} 1/5 + \tan^{-1} 1/8$), worked on the problem for two months, and gave a result with about 200 correct decimals, the best result ever reached at that time. At about 20 years of age, he performed calculations such as multiplying two 8-digit numbers in less then 1 minute, two 20-digit numbers in 6 minutes, and two 100-digit numbers in 8 and a half hours, or extracting the square root of a 100-digit number in 52 minutes. He later worked under the supervision of the mathematician C.F. Gauss to make the tables of factors and prime numbers for the 7th and 8th millions, which occupied him for about 11 years.

Henri Mondeux (1826–1862) and *Vito Mangiamele (1827–?)*, two illiterate French and Italian shepherds, learned the basics of arithmetic alone by arranging and playing with pebbles, discovered algorithms by themselves, and exhibited outstanding calculating abilities at an early age. For example, at the age of 10, Mangiamele answered correctly the question, *"What number has the following peculiarity, that if its cube is added to five times its square, and from the result 42 times the number and 40 is subtracted, the remainder is nothing? Answer: 5"* in less than one minute. *Jacques Inaudi (1867–1950)*, another young illiterate Italian shepherd, started to calculate mentally when he was 6 years old and soon acquired exceptional calculating abilities. At the age of 12, he went to Paris where he was presented at the Société d'Anthropologie by neurologist Paul Broca. He learned to read and write at about age 20 and was later tested by psychologist Alfred Binet. He lived as a professional calculator performing public exhibitions, during which he typically subtracted 21-digit numbers, added several 6-digit numbers, squared 4-digit numbers, completed division problems, extracted of the cube root of 9-digit numbers and the fifth root of 12-digit numbers, and did calendar calculation. He had an excellent memory for figures, as evidenced by his ability to repeat up to 36 digits after a single hearing, to report in order all the numbers he had used in an exhibition within 1 or 2 days after the event, and to recall large tables of numbers he had just learned.

Pericled Diamandi (1868–), the son of a Greek merchant, is one of the few late-developing prodigies, as his abilities seemed to have developed when he was about 16 years old. Besides good calculation abilities and memory capacities for figures, Diamandi was also able to speak five languages and was a great reader.

Shakuntala Devi (1920), a young Indian lady, is one of the very few known women exhibiting calculation expertise. She could multiply long numbers, extract roots, and make calendar calculations. For example, she would add *25,842,278, 111,201,721, 370,247,830* and *55,551,315*, then multiply the result by *9,878*, and correctly answer *5,559,369,456,432* in about 20 seconds.

(For more cases and fuller descriptions, see Barlow, 1952, and Smith, 1983.)

standardized situations by competent experimenters; thus, the reported results and response times must be viewed with caution, as they may have been distorted, exaggerated, or even underestimated. Despite the poor experimental conditions in which these data were collected, some elements can nevertheless be noted from earlier studies.

Types of Calculators

Calculating prodigies are usually divided into two groups, referred to as "early/auditory" and "late/visual" prodigies, depending on when they started to develop their exceptional abilities and how they mentally represent numbers. Auditory calculators "hear" the numbers in their head when calculating, and their calculation is often associated with some verbalization or exaggerated motor activity. Their abilities evolve at an early age, long before they learn written numeration, and they are therefore sometimes called *early* or *natural* calculators. They use typical left-to-right calculation methods (see below and Table 24.1A) that they all discover by themselves independently. By contrast, visual calculators "see" the numbers mentally, in their own handwriting or as they are displayed to them, and stay relatively quiet when calculating. They usually learn to calculate after reading and writing; some of them only start to develop their abilities during their teenage years and are therefore called *late* calculators. Their resolution strategies tend to be more similar to written calculation, for example, using cross-multiplication (see below and Table 24.1B). Finally, a few calculating prodigies do not fall into either of these groups, as the representations they use are neither visual nor verbal but tactile or motor (they move their fingers while counting) or unrelated to any sensory modality. It is, however, worth noting that these distinctions as a function of the type of representations used when calculating are mainly based on self-reports, and, hitherto, firm experimental demonstration is still lacking.

Calculation Methods

Calculating prodigies are not all alike, as each of them has his own specific domain of expertise and personal calculation methods. Describing all these methods is beyond the scope of this chapter, in which we only briefly mention the kinds of tasks that constitute the core of calculating activities in most prodigies.

Although their basic competencies varied greatly, virtually all past calculating prodigies mastered the four arithmetical operations. Adding and subtracting long series of multi-digit numbers are tasks frequently performed by professional calculators, but as addition and subtraction do not lead to interesting shortcuts, these activities are usually not favored. On the contrary, various shortcuts can be invented and used when multiplying multi-digit numbers, and most of the calculating prodigies consider multiplication as the most important operation, underlying and making more complex calculations possible. For these reasons, multiplication is often the most trained and developed operation in expert calculators. Table 24.1 shows two typical multiplication algorithms. The first one, called *left-to-right multiplication*, goes from the leftmost to the rightmost digit, summing the intermediate results at each step (see Table 24.1A). The main advantage of this method is that only one piece of information must be kept in working memory at any time since intermediate results are immediately added to the previous one. This algorithm is also referred to as the *natural method*, for it is often used by early-age calculators who learned algorithms by themselves during their childhood, sometimes before becoming literate. The second method, called *cross multiplication*, is closer to the usual written method taught at school. Cross multiplication goes from right to left and is particularly advantageous if the response can be written as the problem is being worked out because once a digit is found, it can be written and then ignored, which decreases the memory load (see Table 24.1B). Moreover, the intermediate multiplications are usually easier because they only

Table 24.1

Two Methods for a 2- by 2-Digit Number Multiplication (e.g., 64 × 83)

Formalization AB × CD = R	A. Left-to-right method		B. Cross method	
	Steps	Intermediate results	Steps	Intermediate results
A × C = E	60 × 80 =	4,800	4 × 3 =	12	2
A × D = F	60 × 3 =	180	carry	1	2
E + F = G	sum	4,980	4 × 8 =	32	2
B × C = H	4 × 80 =	320	3 × 6 =	18	2
G + H = I	sum	5,300	sum	51	12
B × D = J	4 × 3 =	12	carry	5	12
I + J = R	sum	5,312	6 × 8 =	48	12
			sum	53	5,312

involve single-digit numbers. However, if the response cannot be written progressively, the memory load is greater since several pieces of information must be kept in mind at the same time. Whatever the method considered, the number of steps to reach the solution obviously increases with the number of digits in the multipliers. The main purpose of shortcuts is to decrease the memory load.

Raising numbers to powers (or *involution*) is a complex calculation task generally restricted to squaring or cubing up to 5-digit numbers or raising to higher powers 2-digit numbers, an operation which can be performed using algebraic equations. For example, cubes can be computed as $[a+1] \times [a (a-1)+1] -1$ (e.g., $39^3 = 40 \times (39 \times 38 + 1) - 1 = 59,319$). *Factoring* an integer consists of finding those integers by which the target number can be divided without remainder (for example, 3, 7, 561, and 1,309 are factors of 3,927). *Decimalization of fraction* or division of two integers, usually prime numbers, is also a frequently performed task (e.g., 1/39 or 13/17). *Extracting roots* from integers (or *evolution*) is another typical calculation performed by prodigies.[1] Note that the difficulty of root extraction is not related to the size of the power but to the number of digits in the root (i.e., the answer). A final common calculation performed by professional calculators is *calendar calculation*, which involves giving the day of the week on which a date falls (e.g., Which day was January 12, 1897? A Tuesday). Various algorithms exist for this kind of calculation, some of them requiring the memorization of tables of codes for centuries, years, or months that are used at various steps in the calculation.

CALCULATION EXPERTISE IN THE SAVANT SYNDROME AND OTHER NEUROLOGICAL DISORDERS

The terms *savant syndrome* and *mono-savant* refer to individuals who exhibit an exceptional mental ability along with pervasive intellectual limitations.[2] There have been several reports of autistic individuals or individuals suffering from neurological disorders with such special high-level abilities in a background of developmental delay. These exceptional abilities include artistic and musical talent; drawing ability; verbal, musical, and visual memory; and mechanical, mathematical, reading, and motor abilities (Treffert, 1988). A series of studies reported such cases with some very specific numerical abilities. For example, autistic mono-savants usually excel in calendar calculation (Hermelin & O'Connor, 1986; Ho, Tsang, & Ho, 1991; Howe & Smith, 1988; Hurst & Mullhall, 1988; O'Connor & Hermelin, 1984). One of the most typical of these studies was carried out with twin mono-savant calendar calculators (Horwitz, Kestenbaum, Person, & Jarvik, 1969; Horwitz, Deming, & Winter, 1969). Charles and George were 24-year-old autistic individuals with IQs below 70 who had a range of competence in calendar computation of about 40,100 years. No details are provided regarding the speed of responses, but both calculators were said to "answer in a flash." Surprisingly, they were unable to answer simple additions, subtractions, multiplications and divisions correctly. Some studies occasionally reported other calculation abilities such as multi-digit calculation or factoring in autistic individuals (Hermelin & O'Connor, 1990; Kelly, Macaruso, & Sokol, 1997). Calendar calculation ability was also observed in non-autistic individuals, as in MC, a 17-year-old man suffering from Gilles de la Tourette syndrome (Moriarty, Ring, & Robertson, 1993); AC, an 18-year-old man suffering from Asperger's syndrome (Stevens & Moffit, 1988); and RD, an 18-year-old man who had a complete left hemispherectomy to relieve intractable seizures (Dorman, 1991). Interference tasks suggested that RD was using visual and verbal strategies when calculating. Selective preservation of exceptional calculating abilities with impairment of other cognitive function is also described in a patient suffering from dementia of the Alzheimer's type (DAT) (Remond-Besuchet et al., 1999).

There has been considerable debate as to whether mono-savants possess true calculating skills or only exceptional memory skills and whether or not these calculation abilities, if any, are related to intelligence. In the context of calendar calculation, interpretations have been proposed in terms of rote or eidetic memory (Horwitz et al., 1965, 1969) or rule-based algorithmic strategies (O'Connor & Hermelin, 1984).[3] Given the intrinsic difficulty of obtaining detailed self-reports from autistics about their own mental strategies, it is difficult to determine which of the above interpretations is more likely. However, it seems that memory alone probably cannot explain the wide range of dates some calculators are able to compute and that at least some of the autistic calculators were sensitive to, and frequently made use of, some of the rules producing calendar regularities. Concerning the relationship between such skills and intelligence, a recent study confirmed that calendar calculation was possible in individuals with very low IQs (around 50) but also showed that accuracy correlated positively with general intelligence (O'Connor, Cowan, & Samella, 2000).[4]

CALCULATION EXPERTISE IN ABACUS CALCULATORS

Imported from China centuries ago, the Japanese abacus (or *soroban*) is a wooden framed instrument made of 23 columns of beads (Hatano, Miyake, & Binks, 1977; Stigler, 1984). Numbers are represented in a base-10 system, with each column having an arbitrarily chosen value of *ones, tens, hundreds, thousands,* and so on. Each column is divided into an upper part containing one bead and a lower part containing five beads. The value of the upper bead is 5 when pushed down to the dividing bar and 0 when pushed up; conversely, the lower bead's value is 1 when pushed up and 0 when pushed down. By pushing different combinations of beads toward the dividing bar, each digit from 0 to 9 can be represented in any single column (see Figure 24.1).[5] In Japan and Taiwan, children are trained in mental calculation using the abacus, both at school and in extracurricular programs. With practice, abacus calculators learn to perform complex calculation very quickly. For example, they can add up a series of five 3-digit numbers in less than 4 seconds and a series of five 5-digit numbers in less than 8 seconds or find the product of two 5-digit numbers in less than 10 seconds. When the expert level is reached, they start calculating mentally using the same strategies without any actual abacus, which further increases their speed and decreases their error rate. Abacus users then report constructing a mental image of an abacus and performing mental calculation by moving the beads mentally, just as they would on a real abacus, reading off the answers when they are done. They can sometimes be seen moving their fingers during mental calculation as if they were actually fingering an abacus. Although their short-term memory span is not unusual for items such as letters of the alphabet or the names of fruits, abacus "grand masters" can accurately recall 13 to 16 digits both backward and forward (Hatano & Osawa, 1983).

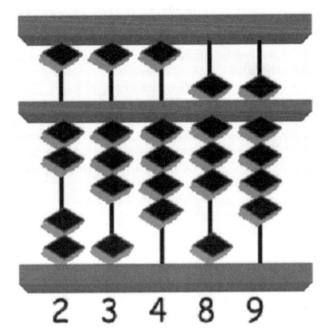

Figure 24.1. Representation of numbers 2, 3, 4, 8, and 9 on an abacus. If the upper bead is pushed down, its value is 5 (such as in 8 and 9); if the upper bead is pushed back up, its value is 0 (as in 2, 3, and 4). Lower bead's value is I when pushed up.

BASIC COMPONENTS OF CALCULATION EXPERTISE

The exceptional ability of calculating prodigies basically involves several components (Smith, 1988). First, calculating prodigies have a good conceptual knowledge of the basic arithmetical operations. Second, they perfectly know complex iterative algorithms that make use of the basic operations. Third, most of them know large sets of memorized data (e.g., squares, or prime numbers). This extensive declarative knowledge can then be used in algorithms, decreasing the short-term memory load of complex calculation. Finally, they seem to possess a very efficient working memory, at least for intermediate results that serve as the input for further stages of the algorithms.

In a recent study, my colleagues and I described the basic and exceptional calculation abilities of Rüdiger Gamm, a young German calculating prodigy whose performance in single- and multi-digit number multiplication, numerical comparison, raising of powers, and short-term memory tasks was investigated (Pesenti, Seron, Samson, & Duroux, 1999). This study is one of the very few experimental investigations carried out with a calculating prodigy with standard timed arithmetical tasks currently used in cognitive arithmetic research and for which the pattern of performance in nonexpert subjects is already well established. Parts of this study are presented in the following paragraphs.

Basic Arithmetical Operations

Calculating prodigies perfectly master not only arithmetical facts[6] but also the properties of the operations (commutability, transitivity, etc.) and basic decomposition rules. Yet, this conceptual knowledge is not absolutely necessary to acquire a specific calculation ability, as shown by some autistic individuals who exhibit exceptional abilities for different types of complex calculation while at the same time being very poor at simple arithmetic.

Evidence from studies on arithmetical facts in children, normal adults, and brain-damaged individuals supports the view that, in normal adults, the dominant solution strategy is retrieval from memory. Arithmetical facts are stored as declarative knowledge in semantic networks or associative structures reflecting the associative strength between a given problem, its correct solution, and competing false solutions. When memory retrieval fails to produce a satisfactory answer, compensatory procedural strategies (counting, decomposing into known problems, etc.) enable one to compute it.

How do calculating prodigies perform basic operations? Do they differ from nonexperts only because of the way they deal with complex calculations or because they also perform basic operations in a different way? Arithmetical fact retrieval is easy for educated adults and has been extensively studied in the literature (see chapters 18 and 19 for details). As there are very few records of prodigies' performances in basic arithmetical tasks, we investigated Gamm's performance in simple multiplication and in numerical comparison (Pesenti et al., 1999). Gamm was asked several times to answer all multiplications tables as quickly and accurately as possible. Problems were presented on a computer and response latencies were recorded to the nearest millisecond. In this task, Gamm appeared faster than control subjects, but his patterns of responses did not really differ from those usually observed in non-expert subjects. He presented the classic distinction between rule-based and fact-based problems, the usual problem-size/difficulty effect, and the specific pattern of speed and flat slope of response latencies for ties problems.[7] Thus, except for his speed, Gamm did not fundamentally differ from normal subjects in basic tasks. Most of the classic effects were observed, suggesting that he globally uses the same procedures as nonexperts, and the small differences may be attributed to individual differences, disappearing when group performances are analyzed. It is worth noting here that Gamm is probably a late calculating prodigy. His exceptional abilities manifested themselves around the age of 20 years. He is likely to have learned basic operations like any other child and to have used the same procedures and strategies. It is, thus, not surprising that his patterns of performance are very close to those of nonexpert subjects. Nevertheless, he appears to be faster, and one can hypothesize that his speed in solving complex calculation stems, at least partly, from cumulative faster performance in the basic subcomponents of computation.

Complex Calculation and Algorithms

The knowledge of algorithms, that is, the steps leading to the solution, for many different types of problems is the most likely main advantage that calculating prodigies possess over nonexpert subjects. When confronted with a problem, they usually know where to begin and in what order intermediate calculation steps must be taken to find the solution. Even more, they can imagine and derive new algorithms from their previous knowledge of related problems. With calculation intensive practice, most of these algorithms become automated and can thus be applied very rapidly and accurately. Algorithms can be derived from algebra or can simply express the optimal chronological order in which problems must be processed. Most of these algorithms, which the calculators either found by themselves or learned from books, are designed to minimize the short-term memory load of mental calculations by reducing the number of steps or the number of pieces of information to be kept in mind at one time. For some problems, different algorithms can be used successfully, and actual strategies can thus differ from one calculator to another. Describing and understanding these algorithms used to be a main concern in past investigations. Although some calculating prodigies are reluctant to explain their personal algorithms, either because they are not able to access them consciously and explain them or because they want to keep them secret, others can and are willing to do so. Insert 24.2 shows two such algorithms described by two calculating prodigies to solve the same multi-digit multiplication.

Algorithms are not intrinsically difficult, and as such, they are accessible to nonexperts, as shown by a training study investigating in detail how two nonexpert university students reached expertise in mental multi-digit multiplication through extensive practice (Staszewski, 1988).

Insert 24.2. Algorithms for Multiplying Two 4-Digit Numbers

The left-to-right method presented in Table 24.1A can be extended to any multiplication using the general formula: $(a_1 + a_2 + \ldots + a_n) \times (b_1 + b_2 + \ldots + b_m) = (a_1b_1 + a_1b_2 + \ldots + a_1b_m + a_2b_1 + a_2b_2 + \ldots + a_2b_m + \ldots a_nb_1 + a_nb_2 + \ldots + a_nb_m)$. However, calculating prodigies often develop their own algorithms and shortcuts. Here are two examples of alternative algorithms.

Wim Klein (1912–1986), an early calculating prodigy from the Netherlands, became one of the best and fastest calculators in history, working as a "living computer" in various mathematical institutes and at the European Center for Nuclear Research during the 1950s and 1960s. His interest in calculation began at the age of 8 when he was taught factoring at school. As his interest and experience grew, he progressively acquired and stored in long-term memory the multiplication tables up to 100 by 100, the squares of integers up to 1,000, the cubes of numbers up to 100, and all prime numbers below 10,000. Here is how he would multiply 6,241 by 3,635 (remember that he simply retrieved products of two 2-digit numbers from memory):

		Partial results:	
41 × 25 =	1,435	35
Carry	14	
41 ×36 =	1,476	
Sum =	1,490	
62 × 35 =	2,170	
Sum =	3,660	6,035
Carry	36	
62 × 36 =	2,232	
Sum =	2,268	
Final product =	22,686,035	

Gottfried Rückle (1879–?) was a German calculating prodigy and mathematician, one of whose most developed and fastest abilities was to reduce 5-digit numbers to the sum of four squares (e.g., $18,111 = 134^2 + 9^2 + 7^2 + 5^2$, a response given in about 25 seconds; Müller, 1911). To multiply two 4-digit numbers, Rückle used the following formula:

$$((a-b)/2 + b)^2 - ((a-b)/2)^2$$

which, if $a = 6,241$ and $b = 3,635$, gives:

6,241 – 3,635 =	2,606
2,606/2 =	1,303
3,635 + 1,303 =	4,938
4,938² =	24,383,844
1,303² =	1,697,809
Sum =	22,686,035

(Both examples adapted from Smith, 1987.)

After being taught the left-to-right method, they practiced mental multiplication up to 2- by 5-digit numbers (e.g., 25 × 65,849), accumulating, respectively, about 175 and 300 hours of training over 3 and 4 years. At the end of their training, both subjects could maintain their error rates below 10% and solve problems between 5 and 10 times more quickly than they could at the beginning of the study. Moreover, their level of performance was similar to that of AB, a professional calculating prodigy who had practiced mental calculation on a daily basis for more than 15 years (Chase & Ericsson, 1982). However, their expertise was limited to the types of problems they had learned and did not much extend beyond that range. In another study, a general algorithm for squaring 2-digit numbers derived from the equation $(a+b)^2 = a^2 + 2ab + b^2$ (e.g., $53^2 = 50^2 + 2 \times 50 \times 3 + 3^2$) was taught to young and aging subjects. Participants reduced their response speed by a factor of 2 (from 20s to 10s for the young and from 40s to 20s for the aging participants) after only five 1-hour training sessions (Charness

& Campbell, 1988). Finally, the same algorithm was taught to an 82-year-old patient suffering from DAT, who managed to improve the application of each single step but failed to integrate all the steps into a whole algorithm, which shows the critical role played by algorithmic knowledge in calculation expertise (McGlinchey-Berroth, Milberg, & Charness, 1989).

During the course of our investigation with Gamm, we examined his performance in multi-digit number multiplication because it required algorithms he was not used to applying. Multi-digit number multiplication was out of Gamm's domain of expertise, and he had never practiced it nor paid much attention to it before we asked him to do so. Before he was tested in timed tasks, we asked him to describe how he would resolve 2- by 2-digit number multiplications. He thought for a while and then described an algorithm he suspected to be the most efficient. This algorithm was the exact application of the left-to-right method presented in Table 24.1A. For larger multiplication problems (3- by 3-, 4- by 4-digit number multiplications), he rapidly derived algorithms based on the same logic. He then started to practice this algorithm, and after a few months of self-training, he was twice as fast for 2- by 2-digit number multiplication and decreased his response latency from about 4 minutes to less than 1 for 4- by 4-digit number multiplication. This clearly confirmed the prominent role played by the knowledge of algorithms in exceptional abilities.

Arithmetical Data Stored in Long-Term Memory

In the traditional literature devoted to calculating prodigies, memory constitutes a controversial criterion for separating "real" calculating prodigies from "simple mnemonists." The latter are usually thought only to play tricks simulating the calculation ability because no real calculation is involved, whereas the former, it is said, actually possess calculation abilities going beyond simple memorization (Barlow, 1952). Recently, researchers examined whether calendar calculators just relied on memorized images of calendars or on computation (O'Connor & Hermelin, 1984). The distinction, however, is actually much fuzzier since even great calculators know memorized data and easy shortcuts (Smith, 1983). Most great calculators report knowing large sets of memorized data. For example, they know the squares, cubes, products, and roots of numerous multi-digit numbers as well as lists of numbers with interesting properties (e.g., numbers that are the products of several problems, the powers of several numbers). This extensive declarative knowledge can easily be used during complex calculations. If, for example, squaring a multi-digit number is part of a complex calculation, the short-term memory load can be reduced if this intermediate result is retrieved from long-term memory without explicit computation (see Insert 24.2 for an example of how Klein's knowledge of the multiplication tables up to 100×100 helped him decrease the complexity of multi-digit multiplications). Some calculating prodigies strategically decided to learn large sets of data by heart but, in most of the cases, these new facts were progressively acquired by multiple exposures during training and practice. With such expertise, some multi-digit numbers acquire a specific status and are immediately recognized by experts. Indeed, although their quantitative meaning can be extracted rapidly and almost accurately, multi-digit numbers usually do not have a specific mathematical meaning for most people. For example, some strings of digits can call brands to mind, whereas famous dates, phone numbers, or zip codes can be recognized quite easily, but very few people can instantly say that 5,329, 389,017 and 28,398,241 are, respectively, the square, cube, and fourth power of 73. In contrast, most calculating prodigies can spontaneously give or recognize powers, roots, and the like in multi-digit numbers, suggesting that these pieces of information have become, with learning and practice, part of their long-term declarative knowledge. Some of them also reported personal associations related to numbers,[8] but this is not specific to prodigies, as shown by a study on nonexpert subjects (Seron, Pesenti, Noël, Cornet, & Deloche, 1992).

This aspect of calculation expertise was also investigated with Gamm by testing his ability to raise numbers to given powers (Pesenti et al., 1999). Actually, Gamm did not perform raising 2-digit numbers up to the 5th power by computation but by direct memory retrieval, as the answers to squares, cubes, 4th and 5th powers were learned and stored as associations. It turned out that Gamm was able to easily recognize and identify multi-digit numbers corresponding to powers of 2- and 3-digit numbers, demonstrating that these numbers were stored as declarative knowledge and were readily available to him. This was confirmed when he was asked to raise 2-digit numbers to various powers. He answered quickly and made very few errors, which were all immediately corrected, whatever the power. His averaged latencies ranged from 710 ms for squares to 1,120 ms for the 5th power. Yet, even many 5th powers were given in less than 1 second. For example, the largest 5th power (99^5) was given on average in about 830 ms. This strongly supports the idea that answers were directly retrieved from memory.

Short-Term Memory Capacities

Short-term memory is supposed to be involved in the intermediate stages of calculation in expert as well as in nonexpert calculators. For example, if no shortcuts are used, multiplying two 2-digit numbers with the algorithms presented in Table 24.1 involves seven different steps. At each one, earlier intermediate results must be kept in mind while the next step is computed. Both storage and processing are thus continuously and simultaneously involved during calculation, and many strategies of mental calculators aim at minimizing the short-term memory load of complex problems. Moreover, complex calculation often requires very large numbers to be handled in short-term memory.

Because of the speed at which they solve problems, as well as the size of the numbers they are able to keep in mind, calculating prodigies are often implicitly assumed to possess a larger short-term memory storage capacity than normal subjects, which enables them to perform complex calculations. However, little is known about short-term memory capacity of calculating prodigies except for anecdotal data stating that some of them are able to report very long lists of numbers randomly proposed by their audience. For example, the famous calculating prodigy Jacques Inaudi (see Insert 24.1) was said to be able to repeat 200 to 300 numbers in one of his public performances (Mitchell, 1907; see also reports in Barlow, 1952; Smith, 1983). Comparison of memory span in auditory (J. Inaudi) and visual (P. Diamandi; see Insert 24.1) prodigies showed the superiority of the latter in storing, manipulating, and recalling learned material in various orders (Binet, 1894). When reporting their case of an autistic calendar calculator, Ho and colleagues (1991) mentioned an auditory forward digit span of 7 and of 12 in the visual modality. Evidence from the few healthy calculating prodigies who were submitted to more formal testing reveals an auditory digit span usually ranging between 12 and 20, and suggests that the most common strategy is to recode the series of digits into chunks of a higher order (e.g., to encode the series 529 as five hundred and twenty-nine) and to link them to a specific meaning where possible (e.g., 529 is 23^2; Ericsson, 1985). However, this increased storage capacity is almost always domain specific: short-term memory spans are much greater for digits than for non-numerical material, for which calculating prodigies are usually no better than nonexperts (Pesenti et al., 1999). In this context, the effect of interfering tasks is not clear. Several calculating prodigies are said to be able to carry out their calculation while at the same time talking or even telling jokes to their audience or doing their work. Once again, however, these reports lack the experimental control needed to validate them. Let us note that when assessed in a controlled situation, Gamm's short-term memory capacities were negatively affected by concurrent tasks (Pesenti et al., 1999).

SHORT-TERM VERSUS LONG-TERM WORKING MEMORY

Educated adults are able to solve computation-based problems, but only with much time and effort because of the high short-term memory demand of the task. In contrast, calculating prodigies solve complex mental calculations quickly and accurately. Does this reflect specific working memory processes?

In the Skilled Memory Theory, it is proposed that expert-level performance depends upon the efficient use of a vast domain-specific knowledge base. Through practice, experts acquire knowledge structures and procedures for efficiently encoding and retrieving specific information in long-term memory. Developing highly efficient long-term memory encoding and retrieval processes enables experts to circumvent the limited capacity of short-term memory and the slowness of long-term encoding. Using episodic encoding-retrieval cues decreases the storage retrieval times in long-term memory and prevents proactive interference caused by prior storage of similar information. Moreover, contrary to general long-term memory processes, such skilled memory mechanisms apply specifically to each domain of expertise. In the case of calculation expertise, it was proposed that, instead of being simply kept in short-term memory, intermediate results and numerical information in general are rapidly encoded in long-term memory with cues that facilitate efficient and accurate retrieval, hence improving performances by decreasing the short-term demands (Chase & Ericsson, 1982; Ericsson & Lehmann, 1996; Ericsson & Kintsch, 1995; Ericsson & Staszewski, 1988). Until recently, however, this proposal lacked a strong empirical demonstration. Our experimental investigation with Gamm showed how, at a behavioral level, his highly efficient episodic memory processes (i.e., long-term memory storage and retrieval) critically contributed to his expertise, as demonstrated by his ease in storing novel numerical information. For instance, he was able to correctly recognize multi-digit numbers corresponding to products that he had computed several hours before, in tests involving long series of problems (Pesenti et al., 1999). This was further confirmed when we looked at his cerebral activity during mental calculation using brain-imaging techniques (see below).

Neural Correlates of Calculation Expertise

Much psychological research has been devoted to studying the modifications of cognitive processes resulting from domain-specific expertise (Ericsson & Kintsch, 1993; Ericsson, Krampe, & Tech-Romer, 1995). To date, the investigation of extensive learning-related cerebral changes has largely focused on motor and/or visuo-perceptive skill acquisition, with little attention paid to higher-level cognitive expertise in general and calculation expertise in particular. From a functional point of view, solving computation-based problems requires numbers to be held and manipulated on a short-term representational medium while the dedicated resolution algorithm is applied. This involves the sequential control of the various steps, the decomposition of the stimuli according to their semantic meaning (for example, whether digits correspond to units or tens), the memory retrieval of intermediate results, their short-term storage, and the application of basic arithmetical rules. Intermediate results must be kept in mind until required but must then be forgotten to keep the memory load at a minimum. The whole process thus involves various working memory mechanisms (such as updating) that are under the control of the central executive, the attentional control system responsible for strategy selection and for control and coordination of the mechanisms involved in short-term storage and processing tasks (Baddeley, 1986). As noted above, expert calculators circumvent the short-term memory limitations by using a long-term working memory sustained by dedicated encoding and retrieval episodic processes. However, the nature of the cerebral networks underlying this skilled process was not known before we decided to look at Gamm's cerebral activity in a Positron Emission Tomography study. In this study, we contrasted computation with retrieval-based problems to isolate the calculation processes (Pesenti et al., 2001). Computation-based problems were multiplications of two 2-digit numbers (e.g., $68 \times 76 = 5,168$), whereas retrieval-based problems were squares of 2-digit numbers (e.g., $73 \times 73 = 5,329$) that were not computed but stored in long-term memory by Gamm. Subtracting the cerebral activity observed during the resolution of retrieval-based problems from the activity observed during the resolution of computation-based problems allowed us to isolate the mental processes strictly related to calculation. These processes involved left frontal and bilateral parietal and occipital areas that were also observed in nonexpert subjects performing complex calculation (Zago et al., 2002) and that reflect visuo-spatial short-term memory and visual mental imagery processes. However, several right frontal foci of activation were observed in the expert only. These areas are part of the long-term memory network and reflect processes related to episodic memory, including the encoding of new pieces of information into new memory traces, the storage and consolidation of these traces in time, and their retrieval. Activation observed in the right frontal, parahippocampal, and anterior cingulate cortices (ACC) fit with the encoding and retrieval of intermediate results. Moreover, the ACC is known to participate in executive processes such as evaluating cognitive states for detecting response competition conflicts and representing the knowledge that strategic processes need to be engaged (Carter et al., 2000), monitoring performance for detecting errors (MacDonald, Cohen, Stenger, & Carter, 2000), and interacting with the lateral prefrontal cortex before compensatory mechanisms can be implemented (Gehring & Knight, 2000). This role of cognitive processing regulation devoted to the upper part of the ACC (Bush, Luu, & Posner, 2000) clearly reflects expertise in adapting behavior to complex situations and errors, and is also consistent with the consciousness an expert possesses of his own performance and his ability to detect and immediately self-correct his occasional calculation errors. Finally, medial-temporal structures (the hippocampal, parahippocampal, and close regions) are known to be involved in the visuo-spatial aspects of episodic memory, with the right parahippocampal region being in charge of the storing and maintenance of stimuli representations across long delays (Young, Otto, Fox, & Eichenbaum, 1997). Similar results were observed in abacus experts who, when compared to controls, exhibited significantly enhanced activity in visuo-spatial posterior parietal areas during calculation (Hanakawa, Honda, Okada, Fukuyama, & Shibasaki, 2003).

These brain-imaging results thus perfectly fit the assumed functional components of computation-based calculation and showed, for the first time in an expert calculator, the neural network for complex mental calculation beyond problem encoding, fact retrieval, and response production processes. Most importantly, they also gave neuroanatomical support to the idea that high-level cognitive expertise is not only accounted for by an acceleration of existing processes and by local modulation of activations, but that it also involves new processes relying on different brain areas. In the case of calculation expertise, these new processes corresponded to switching from strictly short-term effortful storage strategies to highly efficient episodic memory encoding and retrieval ones involved the application of automated resolution algorithms and implied careful monitoring and control of such algorithmic resolution. Along with our behavioral investigation of Gamm's performance, these neuroanatomical results thus supported the theoretical framework of long-term working memory. Moreover, they clearly show that calculation expertise results in processes and brain activations not present in non-experts and that it is partly accounted for by the use of long-term episodic mechanisms to expand the limitation of short-term working memory. Neuroanatomically, long-term working memory mechanisms thus recruit the same brain areas as long-term episodic memory.

ORIGIN OF CALCULATION EXPERTISE

Taken together, the results of the behavioral and brain-imaging studies we carried out with Gamm support Smith's (1988) claims about the components of calculation expertise. With regard to the basic arithmetical operations, Gamm was slightly faster than nonexpert subjects in standard timed tasks but globally exhibited the same patterns of effects, suggesting that he was using the same procedures as nonexpert subjects. Mastery of a previously unknown algorithm for multi-digit number multiplication allowed him to reach expertise in multi-digit calculation that was previously outside his domain of expertise. Our investigation further revealed that he had many arithmetical data readily available from long-term memory and that he could access them very quickly. Finally, his pattern of performance in short-term memory tasks showed a domain-specific storage capacity: his short-term memory spans were much better for digits than for non-numerical material, and they were also negatively affected by concurrent tasks. This study shows how the four investigated components relate together to contribute to calculation expertise; however, it does not establish whether these components are either necessary or sufficient to explain it fully. Further work is required to investigate each component and also to identify other possible components.

Innate Gift Versus Intensive Practice

In this search for underlying components, a long-standing dispute opposes the advocates of some genetic factors and those favoring the role of extensive practice to account for the expertise of calculating prodigies.

In healthy experts, calculation skills emerging at an unusually early age are often taken as evidence of an innate gift. Among individual mono-savants, a distinction has been made between *talented savants* and *prodigious savants* (Treffert, 1988). Because of their background of poor mental functioning, the former are said to lack the inventiveness and flexibility evident in normal experts; their success is attributed to constant repetition and practice in which they acquire rote procedures that are applied automatically. On the contrary, the latter are considered to be endowed with genetic factors that allow them to perform like true experts (Hermelin & O'Connor, 1986, 1990).

Others have argued that motivation and practice are the crucial elements in expertise (Ericsson & Faivre, 1988; Ericsson et al., 1993; Howe, Davidson, & Sloboda, 1998;[9] Pesenti et al., 1999; Smith, 1983). For example, a behavioral study of the Indian calculation expert Shakuntala Devi (see Insert 24.1) showed that her exceptional speed in mental calculation was not accompanied by an exceptional speed in elementary information processing (Jensen, 1990). On the contrary, Devi's unexceptional response latencies to basic cognitive tasks indicated that her calculation expertise depended on specific processes rather than on any unusual basic capacities and suggested that prolonged interest and practice of calculation played a main role in exceptional performance. Other studies of renowned healthy experts have demonstrated that expertise is invariably related to deliberate practice, often starting at an early age and continuing for many years (Ericsson & Charness, 1994). Similarly, mono-savants who achieve expert-like success are known to be preoccupied almost exclusively with their domain of specialization and practice it extensively (Charness, Clifton, & MacDonald, 1988). For mono-savants, dedication to a particular skill may be facilitated by social isolation and life circumstances that pose relatively few outside demands. Smith (1983) suggested that experts are not special in any real sense; rather, they excel because they devote much time and effort to perfecting skills in their area of interest. He claimed that just as every healthy child becomes a language-expert adult by extensive practice of speech, any child could become a calculating prodigy, were they motivated enough and had the opportunity and time to train properly. Finally, it is worth noting that early ability is not evidence of innate talent unless it emerges in the absence of special opportunities to learn (Howe et al., 1998).

Since details of Gamm's childhood are unavailable, we cannot, of course, determine the extent to which his exceptional skills may have originated from genetic factors. However, the late development of his expertise as well as the way it developed seems to us to be more in agreement with an interpretation in terms of practice rather than innate gift. The brain-imaging results also support this view. Indeed, although specific brain activities absent in non-experts were observed, it does not mean that Gamm's brain is different nor that he is using it differently. An analogy will help clarify this point. Imagine two points, A and B, distant from each other by one mile, and assume that all nonexpert people, all over the world, would go from point A to point B by walking. Now, imagine that Gamm does not walk from point A to point B but, rather, he runs. Would this imply that he is using the muscles of his legs differently? Certainly not, as we are all able to run, and we all use the same muscles for that. Simply, we do not run—hence, we do not use the "running" muscles—when going from A to B. Similarly, we all have an episodic memory taking place in the same cerebral areas as those observed in Gamm, and we all use this episodic memory to store and retrieve personal facts, but we are not able to use this type of memory when calculating. What makes Gamm—and, presumably, other experts—really an expert is that he is able to use his episodic memory when calculating, which leads to a pattern of brain activations different from the one observed in nonexperts. However, the dedicated role of these areas (i.e., episodic memory) is not fundamentally different and thus does not support the idea of a genetically different brain. Therefore, as long as no results from a strong anatomical or functional brain study support the innate/genetical factor, it seems safer to favor the practice interpretation.

Calculation Expertise, Mathematical Talent, and Intelligence

Another source of debate and confusion is the question of the possible mathematical talent and level of intelligence of calculating prodigies. Mathematical talent refers to the capacity of understanding, finding, or developing mathematical proofs, theorems, and models—in other words, understanding what lies behind arithmetic. For some authors, only those expert calculators who exhibit mathematical talent—great mathematicians or healthy calculators able to discover or derive personal algorithms—should be considered as "true" calculating prodigies. Similarly, as expert calculators can be found at every level of intelligence, only those with outstanding intellectual abilities are said to be prodigies. Such statements, however, stem from confusion between three different factors: calculation expertise, mathematical talent, and intelligence. There is, of course, little doubt that calculators who were also brilliant mathematicians (e.g., A. G. Aitken, A. M. Ampère, C. F. Gauss, etc.) possessed these three elements. However, these abilities represent three different aspects that can clearly dissociate: not all mathematicians are expert at mental calculation, not all intelligent people are good at mathematics, and not all good calculators are intelligent.[10] Where numerical abilities within normal range are considered, it is not uncommon to observe a selective deficit (or preservation) of calculation procedures along with preservation (or deficit) of mathematical conceptual knowledge after brain damage. For example, BE, a patient who had suffered a cerebral stroke affecting the basal ganglia, was no longer able to solve simple arithmetical facts but could compute the answer using complex decomposition back-up strategies based on mathematical rules such as commutability, transitivity, and the like (Hittmair-Delazer, Semenza, & Denes, 1994; for the reverse dissociation, see Delazer & Benke, 1997). If these aspects dissociate in nonexpert individuals, it follows that they can dissociate in experts as well. One can easily imagine that they can evolve differently, with one aspect reaching an expert level whereas the other just falls within normal range, or even below normal range, as is the case for experts with developmental delay. Calculation expertise, mathematical talent, and intelligence must thus be considered separately, and calculation expertise should be assessed independently from mathematical talent and general intelligence. Anyone who can carry out mentally complex calculations in a short time can thus qualify as a calculating expert, but the number and range of tasks in which this ability expresses itself varies from one calculator to another.

CONCLUSIONS

This chapter reviewed past and recent data about calculation expertise. Facts and calculating methods of healthy calculators as well as calculators with developmental delay or neurological disorders were presented and discussed. The data reviewed support the idea that calculation expertise is not an innate gift present in very few blessed, outstanding, mathematicians but that it relies on a conjunction of four elements, namely perfect knowledge of basic arithmetic operations, perfect knowledge of complex calculation algorithms, increased number-specific short-term capacities, and increased number-specific long-term memory capacities. I also argued that the brain-imaging results observed in Gamm give neuroanatomical support to the idea that high-level cognitive expertise cannot simply be accounted for by an acceleration of existing processes or by local modulation of activations. Rather, expertise involves new processes relying on different brain areas. In the case of calculation expertise, these new processes include switching from strictly short-term effortful storage strategies to highly efficient episodic memory encoding and retrieval ones, involve application of automated resolution algorithms, and imply careful monitoring and control of such algorithmic resolution. These processes do not operate in nonexperts; however, they could be acquired with practice and training. Future work will show if such learning will lead to the same cerebral recruitment.

When computers did not yet rule the earth, some calculating experts played an important role by working as "human computers" for mathematicians and physicists. Such a role, of course, is no longer topical. However, by studying calculating prodigies, one can clarify some theoretical problems that are difficult to solve with nonexperts only. Insert 24.3 shows two such examples. There are still a lot of topics to be investigated regarding prodigies to get a better understanding not only of their ability but also of every nonexpert calculator. Scientists just have to ask the right questions.

Insert 24.3. What can be learned from calculating prodigies?

The problem size/difficulty effect in arithmetical fact retrieval

In nonexpert subjects, the time needed to multiply two numbers increases with their size, a phenomenon called the *problem-size/difficulty effect*. The interpretation of this highly robust result is still under debate because the influence of structural, learning, and strategy choice variables cannot be completely disentangled. Rüdiger Gamm (*b.* 1971) is a young German calculating prodigy who trained himself and developed exceptional calculating abilities (raising to powers, root extraction, calendar calculation, etc.). He also memorized all the squares, cubes, and 4th and 5th powers of 2-digit numbers keeping differences in practice at a minimum. The problem-size/difficulty effect was present in simple multiplications but absent in raising to power: within each power, latencies were not affected by item or response size (see Fig. 24.2). Although magnitude *per se* of course still constituted a structural variable of the numbers involved in raising to powers, it did not affect the performance. Learning and practice thus seem to contribute much more to the effect.

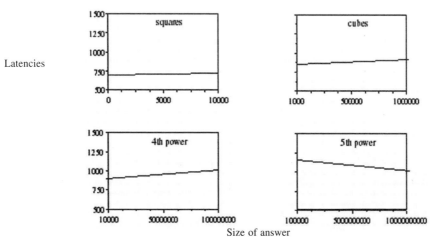

Figure 24.2. Regression lines relating latencies and size of the answers as a function of power in the raising to power task (from Pesenti et al., 1999; © Psychology Press).*Cerebral circuits for complex calculation*

Insert 24.3. Continued

The nature of the processes used by adults to mentally solve complex calculation was a matter of debate as findings suggested that verbal strategies might be used, whereas others suggested visual strategies. Gamm's cerebral activity showed that expert and nonexpert calculators use the same visual strategies in mental calculation, implemented in left frontal and bilateral parietal and temporal areas (green areas in Fig. 24.3; see also Zago et al., 2001). However, in non-experts, it is intrinsically not possible to perfectly match simple (e.g., 2×3=6) and complex problems (e.g., 37×14= 518) in terms of visual complexity of the problems. More visual processing of complex problems might thus have induced more visual activations. The strength of our study with Gamm is that, as simple and complex problems were perfectly matched in terms of visual complexity, activations of visual processing and visual short-term memory areas are clearly not related to such a bias. Moreover, we also overcame problems such as differences in verbal complexity of the answers, in response latencies, in error rates, in motivation, and in math anxiety.

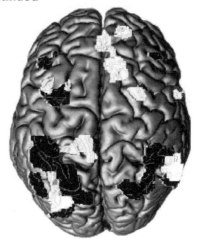

Figure 24.3. Brain areas activated during complex calculation (Green: common to expert and non-experts; Red: expert only. Adapted from Pesenti et al., 2001; image courtesy of N. Tzourio-Mazoyer.) A color version of this figure can be viewed at www.psypress.com/campbell.

NOTES

1. In 1978, Wim Klein (see Insert 24.2) extracted the 73rd root of a 500-digit number in 2 minutes, 43 seconds (Smith, 1983).
2. These people are also often called *idiot savants*. The prevalence of this diagnosis has been estimated at 0.06% of the institutionalized population with developmental delay in the United States (Hill, 1977).
3. Organic explanations, such as left–right asymmetry in brain organization, that have been proposed for some types of expertise (Brink, 1980) have not been extended to calculation.
4. Hence, the authors concluded that calendar calculation is *dependent* on intelligence—an erroneous conclusion, given the correlative nature of the link.
5. For example, if the upper bead is pushed down and three lower beads pushed up, the digit 8 is represented; if the upper bead is pushed back up but the lower beads left in place, then number 3 is represented.
6. Arithmetic facts are basic arithmetical problems for which answers are not computed but are directly retrieved from long-term memory (e.g., 2 + 2, 2 × 3, 3 × 6.).
7. Rule-based problems are problems potentially solvable by rules (e.g., the N × 0 = 0 rule refers to the fact that *Any number multiplied by 0 equals 0*; other rules involving 0 and 1 are *N × 1 = N, N + 0 = N*, etc.; McCloskey, 1992), whereas fact-based problems require complete retrieval from long-term memory (see note 5). The *problem size/difficulty effect* refers to the fact that problems involving large operands (and hence large answers) show longer reaction times and higher error rates. The effect is found for simple addition, subtraction, multiplication, and division, in production as well as in verification tasks, and ranges from children to adults and the elderly (Ashcraft & Battaglia, 1978; Campbell, 1987; Campbell & Graham, 1985; Groen & Parkman, 1972; Miller, Perlmutter, & Keating, 1984; Siegler, 1987, 1988). There exist, however, some exceptions to this rule. Ties (e.g., 2 × 2, 3 × 3) and five-multiple problems (e.g., 2 × 5, 3 × 5) are usually answered much faster and do not present the expected regression slope as do other size-related problems. The term *problem difficulty* is now often used and sometimes preferred to *problem size*, because confounded variables, such as the frequency of number words or problems and strength of storage, also appear to be actually as critical as the size *per se*. Effects not compatible with size (such as the rapid processing of large tie problems: 9 × 9) are more easily accounted for by the strength of association (Campbell & Graham, 1985; Hamann & Ashcraft, 1986).
8. For example, Hans Eberstark, a contemporary calculating prodigy, associated specific affective qualities to numbers. He wrote: "[...] the horny-handed, rough-and-tough bully 8 or the sinister 64 or the arrogant, smug, self-satisfied 36 [...] the ingenious, adventurous 26, the magic versatile 7, the helpful 37, the fatherly, reliable (if somewhat stodgy) 76..." (in Smith, 1983, p. xiii).
9. This article and its open peer commentary evaluate the pros and cons of the idea of innate talents.
10. As Smith (1988, p. 36) pointed out, if calculating ability were to be taken as evidence of intelligence, we would be compelled to grant intelligence to computers, pocket calculators, and old mechanical calculating machines as well.

REFERENCES

Ashcraft, M. H., & Battaglia, J. (1978). Cognitive arithmetic: Evidence for retrieval and decision processes in mental addition. *Journal of Experimental Psycholology: Human Learning and Memory, 4*(5), 527–538.

Baddeley, A. D. (1986). *Working memory*, Oxford: Clarendon Press.

Barlow, F. (1952). *Mental prodigies*. New York: Greenwood Press.

Binet, A. (1894). *Psychologie des grands calculateurs et joueurs d'échecs*. Paris: Hachette.

Brink, T. L. (1980). Idiot savant with unusual mechanical ability: An organic explanation. *American Journal of Psychiatry, 137*, 250–251.

Bush, G., Luu, P., & Posner, M I. (2000). Cognitive and emotional influences in anterior cingulate cortex. *Trends in Cognitive Sciences, 4*(6), 215–222.

Dorman, C. (1991). Exceptional calendar calculation ability after early left hemispherectomy. *Brain & Cognition, 15*, 26–36.

Campbell, J. I. D. (1987). Network interference and mental multiplication. *Journal of Experimental Psychology: Learning, Memory and Cognition, 13*(1), 109–123.

Campbell, J .I .D., & Graham, J.D. (1985). Mental multiplication skills: Structure, process, acquisition. *Canadian Journal of Psychology, 39*, 338–366.

Carter, C. S., MacDonald, A. W., Botvinick, M., Ross, L L., Stenger, V. A., Noll, D., & Cohen, J. D. (2000). Parsing executive processes: Strategic vs. evaluative functions of the anterior cingulate cortex. *Proceedings of the National Academy of Sciences, 97*(4), 1944–1948.

Chase, W. G., & Ericsson, K. A. (1982). Skill and working memory. In G.H. Bower (Ed.), *The psychology of learning and motivation* (vol. 16, pp. 1–58). New York: Academic Press.

Charness, N., & Campbell, J. I. D. (1988). Acquiring skill at mental calculation in adulthood: A task decomposition. *Journal of Experimental Psychology: General, 11*(2), 115–129.

Charness, N., Clifton, J., & MacDonald, L. (1998). Case study of a musical "mono-savant": A cognitive-psychological focus. In L. K. Obler & D. Fein (Eds.), *The exceptional brain* (pp. 277–293). New York: Guilford.

Delazer, M., & Benke, T. (1997). Arithmetic facts without meaning. *Cortex, 33*, 697–710.

Dorfman, C. (1991). Exceptional calendar calculation ability after early left hemispherectomy. *Brain and Cognition, 15*(1), 26–36.

Ericsson, K. A. (1985). Memory skill. *Canadian Journal of Psychology, 3*(2), 188–231.

Ericsson, K. A., & Charness, N. (1994). Expert performance: Its structure and acquisition. *American Psychologist, 49*, 725–747.

Ericsson, K. A., & Faivre, I. A. (1988). What's exceptional about exceptional abilities? In L.K. Obler & D. Fein (Eds.), *The exceptional brain* (pp. 435–473). New York: Guilford.

Ericsson, K. A., & Lehmann, A. C. (1996). Expert and exceptional performance: Evidence of maximal adaptation to task constraints. *Annual Review of Psychology, 47*, 273–305.

Ericsson, K. A., & Staszewski, J. J. (1989). Skilled memory and expertise: Mechanisms of exceptional performance. In D. Klahr & K. Kotovski (Eds.), *Complex information processing. The impact of Herbert A. Simon* (pp. 235–267). Hillsdale, NJ: Erlbaum.,

Ericsson, K . A. & Kintsch, W. (1995). Long-term working memory. *Psychological Review, 10*(2), 211–245.

Ericsson, K. A., Krampe, R. T., & Tesh-Romer, C. (1993). The role of deliberate practice in the acquisition of expert performance. *Psychological Review, 100*(3), 363–406.

Gehring, W. J., & Knight, R. T. (2000). Prefrontal-cingulate interactions in action monitoring. *Nature Neuroscience, 3*(5), 516–520.

Groen, G. J., & Parkman, J. M. (1972). A chronometric analysis of simple addition. *Psychological Review, 79*(4), 329–343.

Hamann, M. S., & Ashcraft, M. H. (1986). Textbook presentations of basic addition facts. *Cognition and Instruction, 3*(3), 173–192.

Hanakawa, T., Honda, M., Okada, T., Fukuyama, H., & Shibasaki, H. (2003). Neural correlates underlying mental calculation in abacus experts: A functional magnetic resonance imaging study. *NeuroImage, 19*, 296–307.

Hermelin, B., & O'Connor, N. (1986). Idiot savant calendrical calculators: Rules and regularities. *Psychological Medecine, 16*, 885–893.

Hermelin, B., & O'Connor, N. (1990). Factors and primes: A specific numerical ability. *Psychological Medicine, 16*, 885–893.

Hill, A. L. (1977). Idiot savants: Rate of incidence. *Perceptual and Motor Skill, 44*, 161–162.

Hitano, G., Miyake, Y., & Binks, M. G. (1977). Performance of expert abacus operators. *Cognition, 5*(1), 47–55.

Hitano, G., & Osawa, K. (1983). Digit memory of grand experts in abacus-derived mental calculation. *Cognition, 15*(1–3), 95–110.

Hittmair-Delazer, M., Semenza, C., & Denes, G. (1994). Concepts and facts in calculation. *Brain, 117*, 715–728.

Ho, E. D. R., Tsang, A. K. T., & Ho, D. Y. F. (1991). An investigation of calendar calculation ability of a chinese calendar savant. *Journal of Autism and Develomental Disorders, 21*(3), 315–327.

Horwitz, W. A., Deming, W. E., & Winter, R. F. (1969). A futher account of the idiots savants, experts with the calendar. *American Journal of Psychiatry, 126*, 160–163.

Horwitz, W. A., Kestembaum, C., Person, E., & Jarvik, L. (1965). Identical twin—"idiot savant"—calendar calculators. *American Journal of Psychiatry, 121*, 1075–1079.

Howe, M. J. A., Davidson, J. W., & Sloboda, J.A. (1998). Innate gifts and talents: Reality or myth? *Behavioral and Brain Sciences, 21*, 399–442.

Howe, M. J. A., & Smith, J. (1988). Calendar calculating in "idiots savants": How do they do it? *British Journal of Psychology, 79*, 371–386.

Hurst, L. C., & Mulhall, D. J. (1988). Another calendar savant. *British Journal of Psychiatry, 152*, 274–277.

Jensen, A. R. (1990). Speed of information processing in a calculating prodigy. *Intelligence, 14*, 259–274.

Kelly, S. J., Macaruso, P., & Sokol, S. M. (1997). Mental calculation in an autistic savant: A case study. *Journal of Clinical and Experimental Neuropsychology, 19*(2), 172–184.

MacDonald, A. W., Cohen, J. D., Stenger, V. A., & Carter, C. S. (2000). Dissociating the role of the dorsolateral prefrontal and anterior cingulate cortex in cognitive control. *Science, 288*, 1835–1838.

McCloskey, M. (1992). Cognitive mechanisms in numerical processing: Evidence from acquired dyscalculia. *Cognition, 44,* 107–157.

McGlinchey-Berroth, R., Milberg, W. P., & Charness, N. (1989). Learning of a complex arithmetic skill in dementia: Further evidence for a dissociation between compilation and production. *Cortex, 25,* 697–705.

Miller, K., Perlmutter, M., & Keating, D. (1984). Cognitive arithmetic: Comparison of operations. *Journal of Experimental Psychology: Learning, Memory and Cognition, 10 (1),* 46–60.

Mitchell, F. D. (1907). Mathematical prodigies. *American Journal of Psychology, 18,* 61–143.

Moriarty, J., Ring, H. A., & Robertson, M. M. (1993). An idiot savant calendrical calculator with Gilles de la Tourette syndrome: Implication for an understanding of the savant syndrome. *Psychology Medecine, 23,* 1019–1021.

O'Connor, N., & Hermelin, B. (1984). Idiot savant calendrical calculators: Maths or memory? *Psychological Medicine, 14,* 801–806.

O'Connor, N., Cowan, R., & Samella, R. (2000). Calendrical calculation and intelligence. *Intelligence, 28*(1), 31–48.

Pesenti, M., Seron, X., Samson, D., & Duroux, B. (1999). Basic and exceptional calculation abilities in a calculating prodigy: A case study. *Mathematical Cognition, 5*(2), 97–148.

Pesenti, M., Zago, L., Crivello, F., Mellet, E., Samson, D., Duroux, B., Seron, X., Mazoyer, B., & Tzourio-Mazoyer, N. (2001). Mental calculation in a prodigy is sustained by right prefrontal and medial-temporal areas. *Nature Neuroscience, 4,* 1–6.

Remond-Besuchet, C., Noël, M.-P., Seron, X., Thioux, M., Aspe, A., & Brun, M. (1999). Selective preservation of exceptional arithmetical knowledge in a demented patient. *Mathematical Cognition, 5*(1), 41–63.

Seron, X., Pesenti, M., Noël, M.-P., Deloche, G., & Cornet, J. A. (1992). Images of numbers, or "When 98 is upper left and 6 sky blue." *Cognition, 44,* 159–196.

Siegler, R. S. (1987). The peril of averaging data over strategies: An example from children's addition. *Journal of Experimental Psychology: General, 106*(3), 250–264.

Siegler, R. S. (1988). Strategy choice procedures and the development of multiplication skill. *Journal of Experimental Psychology: General, 117,* 82–138.

Smith, S. B. (1983). *The great mental calculators. The psychology, methods, and lives of calculating prodigies, past and present.* New York: Columbia University Press.

Smith, S. B. (1987). Les calculateurs prodiges. *La Recherche, 18*(185), 160–169.

Smith, S. B. (1988). Calculating prodigies. In L. K. Obler & D. Fein (Eds.), *The exceptional brain* (pp. 19–47). New York: Guilford.

Staszewski, J .J. (1988). Skilled memory and expert mental calculation. In M. T. H. Chi, R. Glaser, & M. J. Farr (Eds.), *The nature of expertise.* Hillsdale: Erlbaum.

Stevens, D. E., & Moffit, T. E. (1988). Neuropsychological profile of an Asperger's syndrome case with exceptional calculating ability. *The Clinical Neuropsychologist, 2*(3), 228–238.

Stigler, J. W. (1984). "Mental abacus": The effect of abacus training on Chinese children's mental calculation. *Cognitive Psychology, 16*(2), 145–176.

Treffert, D. A. (1988). The idiot savant: A review of the syndrome. *American Journal of Psychiatry, 145*(5), 563–572.

Young, B. J., Otto, T., Fox, G. D., & Eichenbaum, H. (1997). Memory representation within the parahippocampal region. *The Journal of Neuroscience, 17*(13), 5183–5195.

Zago, L., Pesenti, M., Mellet, E., Crivello, F., Mazoyer, B., & Tzourio-Mazoyer, N. (2001). Neural correlates of simple and complex mental calculation. *NeuroImage, 13,* 314–327.

Part 5

Neuropsychology of Number Processing and Calculation

25

Three Parietal Circuits
for Number Processing

Stanislas Dehaene
Manuela Piazza
Philippe Pinel
Laurent Cohen

INTRODUCTION

Did evolution endow the human brain with a predisposition to represent dedicated domains of knowledge? We have previously argued that the number domain provides a good candidate for such a biologically determined semantic domain (Dehaene, 1997; Dehaene, Dehaene-Lambertz, & Cohen, 1998a). Three criteria for domain specificity suggest that number and arithmetic are more than just cultural inventions and may have their ultimate roots in brain evolution. First, a capacity to attend to numerosity and to manipulate it internally in elementary computations is present in animals, even in the absence of training (Hauser, Carey, & Hauser, 2000). Second, a similar capacity for elementary number processing is found early on in human development, prior to schooling or even prior to the development of language skills (Spelke & Dehaene, 1999; Xu & Spelke, 2000). This suggests that numerical development follows a distinct developmental trajectory based on mechanisms with a long prior evolutionary history.

Third, it has been suggested that number processing rests on a distinct neural circuitry, which can be reproducibly identified in different subjects with various neuroimaging, neuropsychological, and brain-stimulation methods (Dehaene et al., 1998a). The present chapter focuses on the latter issue, taking into account the considerable progress that has recently been made in neuroimaging methods. The involvement of parietal cortex in number processing was initially discovered on the basis of lesion data (Gerstmann, 1940; Hécaen, Angelergues, & Houillier, 1961; Henschen, 1919). Subsequently, a systematic activation of the parietal lobes, together with precentral and prefrontal cortices, during calculation was discovered using single-photon emission tomography (SPECT) (Roland & Friberg, 1985) and extensively replicated with positron emission tomography (PET) (Dehaene et al., 1996; Pesenti, Thioux, Seron, & De Volder, 2000; Zago et al., 2001) and later functional magnetic resonance imaging (fMRI) (Burbaud et al., 1999; Rueckert et al., 1996). On this basis, some of us proposed that the parietal lobe contributes to the representation of numerical quantity on a mental "number line" (Dehaene & Cohen, 1995). Unfortunately, due to poor spatial resolution and limits on experimental designs, those studies did not permit a finer exploration of the regions involved in different kinds of numerical tasks. This has become critical, however, because recent behavioral studies have made clear that mental arithmetic relies on a highly composite set of processes, many of which are probably not specific to the number domain. For instance, studies of language interference in normal subjects suggest that language-based processes play an important role in exact but not approximate calculation (Spelke & Tsivkin, 2001). Likewise, concurrent performance of a spatial task interferes with subtraction but not multiplication, whereas concurrent performance of a language task interferes with multiplication but not subtraction (Lee & Kang, 2002). Such behavioral dissociations suggest that the neural bases of calculation must be heterogeneous.

The triple-code model of number processing predicts that, depending on the task, three distinct systems of representation may be recruited: a quantity system (a nonverbal semantic representation of the size and distance relations between numbers, which may be category specific), a verbal system (in which numerals are represented lexically, phonologically, and syntactically much like any other type of word), and a visual system (in which numbers can be encoded as strings of Arabic numerals) (Dehaene, 1992; Dehaene & Cohen, 1995). We initially proposed that the parietal activations during number processing reflected solely the contribution of the quantity system. However, it is now clear that this hypothesis requires further elaboration. First, the left perisylvian language network clearly extends into the inferior parietal lobe. Second, the posterior superior parietal lobes are strongly engaged in visual attention processes that may contribute to the visual processing of numbers. It is thus crucial to distinguish, within the parietal lobe, which activation sites, if any, are associated with a semantic representation of numerical quantity and which correspond to nonspecific verbal or visual/attentional systems.

Fortunately, fMRI has recently allowed finer-grained studies of the neuro-anatomy of number processing, using paradigms adapted from cognitive psychology. The present review focuses entirely on the parietal lobe activations identified by those recent neuro-imaging studies. We use three-dimensional visualization software to visualize how the parietal activations reported by various studies relate to one another in cortical space. On this basis, we propose that three circuits coexist in the parietal lobe and capture most of the observed differences between arithmetic tasks: a bilateral intraparietal system associated with a core quantity system, a region of the left angular gyrus associated with verbal processing of numbers, and a posterior superior parietal system of spatial and non-spatial attention.

It should be emphasized that our description provides only a tentative model. Although it is based on a synthesis of the existing literature, this model remains speculative and will require further validation by direct experimentation. For each postulated circuit, we first examine the relevant neuroimaging literature and then consider how those brain-imaging results impinge on our understanding of neuropsychological impairments of number processing. Our account predicts that depending on lesion localization, three different categories of numerical impairments should be observed: genuine semantic impairments of the numerical domain following intraparietal lesions; impairments of verbal fact retrieval following lesions to the left perisylvian cortices, including the left angular gyrus; and impairments of spatial attention on the number line following lesions to the dorsal parietal attention system.

THE BILATERAL HORIZONTAL SEGMENT OF THE INTRAPARIETAL SULCUS AND QUANTITY PROCESSING

Neuroimaging Evidence

The horizontal segment of the intraparietal sulcus (hereafter HIPS) is a major site of activation in neuroimaging studies of number processing. As shown in Figure 25.1A, this region lies

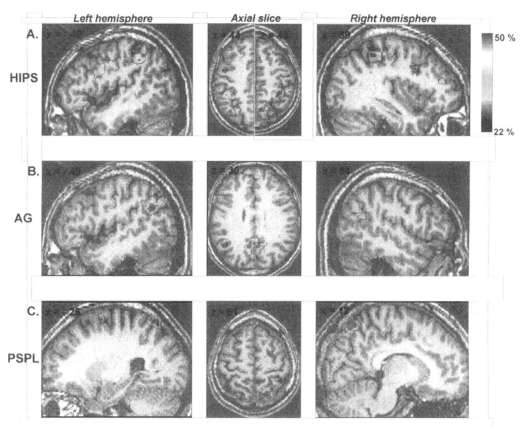

Figure 25.1. Regions of overlapping activity for three groups of studies, superimposed on axial and sagittal slices of a normalized single-subject anatomical image. The overlap was calculated by averaging binarized contrast images indicating which voxels were significant for a given contrast (studies and contrasts are listed in Table 25.1). The color scale indicates the percentage of studies showing activation in a given voxel. The same color scale (from 22 to 50% of overlap) is applied to all images. Although no single voxel was shared by 100% of studies in a group, probably due to variability across groups of subjects, laboratories, and imaging methods, Table 25.1 revealed a high consistency of activations. **(A)** The **horizontal segment of the intraparietal sulcus (HIPS)** was activated bilaterally in a variety of contrasts sharing a component of numerical quantity manipulation. The barycenter of the region of maximum overlap (> 50%) was at Talairach Coordinates (TC) 41, −42, 49 in the left hemisphere and −48, −41, 43 in the right hemisphere. Activation overlap is also visible in the precentral gyrus. **(B)** The **angular gyrus (AG)** was activated with a strong left lateralization (TC −48, −59, 30) and activated in 4/5 studies. Posterior cingulate as well as superior frontal regions also show some degrees of overlap. **(C)** The **posterior superior parietal lobule (PSPL)** was activated bilaterally in a few numerical tasks (left and right barycenters at TC −26, −69, 61 and 12, −69, 61; and see Table 25.1). To emphasize the nonspecificity of this region, the image shows the intersection of the overlap between four numerical tasks with an image of posterior parietal activity during a non-numerical visual attention shift task (Simon et al., 2002). A color version of this figure can be viewed at www.psypress.com/campbell.

at the intersection of the activations observed in many different number processing tasks (see Table 25.1). What seems to be common to those tasks is the requirement to access a semantic representation of the quantity that the numbers represent. We propose that a nonverbal representation of numerical quantity, perhaps analogous to a spatial map or "number line," is present in the HIPS of both hemispheres. This representation would underlie our intuition of

Table 25.1
Three Parietal Regions Activtated during Neuroimaging Studies of Number Processing

Reference	Contrast	Coordinates of maxima	
		Left x y z	Right x y z
Horizontal segment of Intraparietal Sulcus (HIPS)			
Chochon et al. (1999)	Comparison of one-digit numbers vs. letter naming	−45 −42 39	39 −42 42
Chochon et al. (1999)	Subtraction of one-digit numbers from 11 vs. Comparison	−42 −48 48	39 −42 42
Dehaene et al. (1999)	Approximate vs. exact addition of one-digit numbers	−56 −44 52	44 −36 52
Lee (2000)	Subtraction vs. multiplication of one-digit numbers	−31 −52 49	28 −54 52
Naccache et al. (2001)	Subliminal quantity priming across notations	−44 −56 56	36 −44 44
Piazza et al. (2002)	Numerosity estimation vs. physical matching	n.s.	44 −56 54
Pinel et al. (2001)	Distance effect in comparison of two-digit numbers	−40 −44 36	44 −56 48
Simon et al. (2002)	Subtraction of one-digit numbers from 11 vs. letter naming	−48 −44 52	52 −44 52
Stanescu-Cosson et al. (2000)	Size effect in exact addition of one-digit numbers	−44 −52 48	n.s.
	Mean	**−44 −48 47**	**41 −47 48**
	SD	7 5 6	7 7 5
Angular gyrus (AG)			
Chochon et al. (1999)	Multiplication vs. comparison of one-digit numbers	−30 −69 39	n.s.
Dehaene et al. (1999)	Exact vs. approximate addition of one-digit numbers	−44 −72 36	40 −76 20
Lee (2000)	Multiplication vs. subtraction of one-digit numbers	−49 −54 31	n.s.
Simon et al. (2002)	Intersection of subtraction and phoneme detection tasks	−31 −70 43	n.s.
Stanescu-Cosson et al. (2000)	Inverse size effect in exact addition of one-digit numbers	−52 −68 32	n.s.
	Mean	**−41 −66 36**	
	SD	9 6 4	
Posterior Superior Parietal Lobule (PSPL)			
Dehaene et al. (1999)	Approximate vs. exact addition of one-digit numbers	−32 −68 56	20 −60 60
Lee (2000)	Subtraction vs. multiplication of one-digit numbers	−29 −64 69	21 −61 65
Naccache et al. (2001)	Subliminal quantity priming across notations	n.s.	12 −60 48
Pinel et al. (2001)	Distance effect in comparison of two-digit numbers	−4 −72 44	8 −72 52
	Mean	**−22 −68 56**	**15 −63 56**
	SD	15 4 12	6 6 8

Note. Studies and contrasts that were used to isolate the three parietal regions in Figures 25.1 and 25.2. In each case, we report the coordinates of activation maxima, their mean, and their standard deviation (n.s. = not significant). Stars (*) indicate two studies in which we report the coordinates of activation subpeaks not reported in the original papers, which only reported a single global maximum for each activation cluster.

what a given numerical size means and of the proximity relations between numbers. In support of this view, several features of its responsiveness to experimental conditions are worth noting.

Mental Arithmetic

The HIPS seems to be active whenever an arithmetic operation that needs access to a quantitative representation of numbers is called for. For example, it is more active when subjects calculate than when they merely have to read numerical symbols (Burbaud et al., 1999; Chochon, Cohen, van de Moortele, & Dehaene, 1999; Pesenti et al., 2000; Rickard et al., 2000), suggesting that it plays a role in the semantic manipulation of numbers. Its activation increases, at least in the right hemisphere, when subjects have to compute two addition or subtraction operations instead of one (Menon, Rivera, White, Glover, & Reiss, 2000). Furthermore, even within calculation, the HIPS is more active when subjects estimate the approximate result of an addition problem than when they compute its exact solution (Dehaene, Spelke, Stanescu, Pinel, & Tsivkin, 1999). Finally, it shows greater activation for subtraction than for multiplication (Chochon et al., 1999; Lee, 2000). Multiplication tables and small exact addition facts can be stored in rote verbal memory and hence place minimal requirements on quantity manipulation. Contrariwise, although some subtraction problems may be stored in verbal memory, many are not learned by rote and therefore require genuine quantity manipulations. In another study, relative to five different visuo-spatial and phonological non-numerical tasks, subtraction was the only task that led to increased activation of the HIPS (Simon, Cohen, Mangin, Bihan, & Dehaene, 2002).

Number Comparison

The HIPS is also active whenever a comparative operation that needs access to a numerical scale is called for. For instance, it is more active when comparing the magnitudes of two numbers than when simply reading them (Chochon et al., 1999). The systematic contribution of this region to number comparison processes has been replicated in many paradigms using tomographic imaging (Le Clec'H et al., 2000; Pesenti et al., 2000; Pinel, Dehaene, Riviere, & LeBihan, 2001; Thioux, Pesenti, Costes, De Volder, & Seron, 2002) as well as scalp recordings of event-related potentials (Dehaene, 1996). Parietal activation in number comparison is often larger in the right than in the left hemisphere (Chochon et al., 1999; Dehaene, 1996; Pinel et al., 2001). This may point to a possible right-hemispheric advantage in comparison and in other tasks requiring an abstraction of numerical relations (Langdon & Warrington, 1997; Rosselli & Ardila, 1989). However, the parietal activation during comparison, although it may be asymmetric, is always present in both hemispheres, compatible with the observation that numerical comparison is accessible to both hemispheres in split-brain patients (Cohen & Dehaene, 1996; Seymour, Reuter-Lorenz, & Gazzaniga, 1994).

Specificity for the Number Domain

Several studies have reported greater HIPS activation when comparing numbers than when comparing other categories of objects on non-numerical scales (such as comparing the ferocity of animals, the relative positions of body parts, or the orientation of two visually presented characters) (Le Clec'H et al., 2000; Pesenti et al., 2000; Thioux et al., 2002). Event-related potentials have also revealed greater parietal activation for numbers than for other categories of words such as action verbs, names of animals, or names of famous persons (Dehaene, 1995). In this study, the first point in time in which category-specific semantic effects emerge during visual word processing was found to be 250–280 ms following stimulus onset.

One study directly tested the specificity of the HIPS for the numerical domain in multiple tasks (Thioux et al., 2002). Subjects were presented with number words and names of animals matched for length. The HIPS showed greater activation, bilaterally, to numbers than to animal names. This was true whether subjects were engaged in a comparison task (larger or smaller than 5; more or less ferocious than a dog), a categorization task (odd or even; mammal or bird), or even a visual judgment of character shape. Thus, the HIPS shows category-specificity independently of task context. Further research will be needed, however, to decide whether it is strictly specific for numbers or whether it extends to other categories that have a strong spatial or ordinal component (e.g., the alphabet, days, months, spatial prepositions).

Parametric Modulation

Parametric studies have revealed that the activation of the HIPS is modulated by semantic parameters such as the absolute magnitude of the numbers and their value relative to a reference point. Thus, intraparietal activity is larger and lasts longer during operations with large numbers than with small numbers (Kiefer & Dehaene, 1997; Stanescu-Cosson et al., 2000). It is also modulated by the numerical distance separating the numbers in a comparison task (Dehaene, 1996; Pinel et al., 2001). On the other hand, the activation of the HIPS is independent of the particular modality of input used to convey the numbers. Arabic numerals, spelled-out number words, and even nonsymbolic stimuli like sets of dots or tones can activate this region if subjects attend to the corresponding number (Le Clec'H et al., 2000; Piazza, Mechelli, Butterworth, & Price, 2002a; Piazza, Mechelli, Price, & Butterworth, 2002b; Pinel et al., 2001). In one study, subjects attended either to the numerosity or to the physical characteristics (color, pitch) of series of auditory and visual events. The right HIPS was active whenever the subjects attended to number, regardless of the modality of the stimuli (Piazza et al., 2002b). In another study, the activation of the bilateral HIPS was found to correlate directly with the numerical distance between two numbers in a comparison task, and this effect was observed whether the numbers were presented as words or as digits (Pinel et al., 2001). Those parametric studies are all consistent with the hypothesis that the HIPS codes the abstract quantity meaning of numbers rather than the numerical symbols themselves.

Unconscious Quantity Processing

Quantity processing and HIPS activation can be demonstrated even when the subject is not aware of having seen a number symbol (Dehaene et al., 1998b; Naccache & Dehaene, 2001). In this experiment, subjects were asked to compare target numbers to a fixed reference of 5. Unbeknownst to them, just prior to the target, another number, the prime, was briefly present in a subliminal manner. FMRI revealed that the left and right intraparietal regions were sensitive to the unconscious repetition of the same number. When the prime and target corresponded to the same quantity (possibly in two different notations, such as ONE and 1), less parietal activation was observed than when the prime and target corresponded to two distinct quantities (e.g., FOUR and 1). This result suggests that this region comprises distinct neural assemblies for different numerical quantities, so that more activation can be observed when two such neural assemblies are activated than when only one is. It also indicates that this region can contribute to number processing in a subliminal fashion.

Taken together, this data suggests that the HIPS is essential for the semantic representation of numbers as quantities. This representation may provide a foundation for our "numerical intuition," our immediate and often-unconscious understanding of where a given quantity falls with respect to others, and whether or not it is appropriate to a given context (Dehaene, 1992; Dehaene, 1997; Dehaene & Marques, 2002).

Neuropsychological Evidence

Neuropsychological observations confirm the existence of a distinct semantic system for numerical quantities and its relation to the vicinity of the intraparietal sulcus. Several single-case studies indicate that numbers doubly dissociate from other categories of words at the semantic level. On the one hand, spared calculation and number comprehension abilities have been described in patients with grossly deteriorated semantic processing ("semantic dementia"; Butterworth, Cappelletti, & Kopelman, 2001; Cappelletti, Butterworth, & Kopelman, 2001; Thioux et al., 1998). In those patients, the lesions broadly affected the left temporo-frontal cortices while sparing the intraparietal region. On the other hand, Cipolotti, Butterworth, and Denes (1991) reported a striking case of a patient with a small left parietal lesion and an almost-complete deficit in all aspects of number processing, sparing only the numbers 1 through 4, in the context of otherwise largely preserved language and semantic functions.

Although such a severe and isolated degradation of the number system has never been replicated, other cases confirm that small parietal lesions can severely impact on the understanding of numbers and their relations while sparing other aspects of language and semantics (e.g., Dehaene & Cohen, 1997; Delazer & Benke, 1997). In many cases, the deficit can be extremely incapacitating. Patients may fail to compute operations as simple as $2 + 2$, $3 - 1$, or 3×9. Several characteristics indicate that the deficit arises at an abstract, notation-independent level of processing. First, patients may remain fully able to comprehend and to produce numbers in all formats. Second, they show the same calculation difficulties whether the problem is presented to them visually or auditorily and whether they have to respond verbally or in writing or even merely have to decide whether a proposed operation is true or false. Thus, the calculation deficit is not due to an inability to identify the numbers or to produce the operation result. Third, the deficit often extends to tasks outside of calculation *per se*, such as comparison or bisection. For instance, patient MAR (Dehaene & Cohen, 1997) showed a mild impairment in deciding which of two numbers was the larger (16% errors) and was almost totally unable to decide what number fell in the middle of two others (bisection task: 77% errors). He easily performed analogous comparison and bisection tasks in non-numerical domains such as days of the week, months, or the alphabet (What is between Tuesday and Thursday? February and April? B and D?). This type of deficit seems best described as a category-specific impairment of the semantic representation and manipulation of numerical quantities (Dehaene & Cohen, 1997) rather than with the mere clinical label of "acalculia."

In such patients, calculation impairments often co-occur with other deficits, forming a cluster of deficits called Gerstmann's syndrome (Benton, 1992; Gerstmann, 1940), which comprises agraphia, finger agnosia, and left–right distinction difficulties (to which one may often add constructive apraxia). The lesions that cause acalculia of the Gerstmann's type are typically centered in the depth of the left intraparietal sulcus (Mayer et al., 1999; Takayama, Sugishita, Akiguchi, & Kimura, 1994). This is compatible with the above brain-imaging results showing intraparietal activation during various numerical manipulation tasks independently of language. Results from a recent brain-imaging study (Simon et al., 2002) shed some light on why the various elements of Gerstmann's syndrome often co-occur following left intraparietal lesions. In this study, fMRI was used to compare, in the same subjects, the localization of parietal activations during a number subtraction task with those observed during various tasks that also involve the parietal lobe, such as eye or attention movements, finger pointing, hand grasping, and a language task of phoneme detection. The results revealed a systematic topographical organization of activations and their intersections. In particular, the intraparietal sulcus appears to contain a "four-corners" region in which four areas of activation are juxtaposed: calculation only, calculation and language, manual tasks only, and an area activated during the four visuo-spatial tasks (eye and attention movements, pointing, and grasping). The simultaneous lesion of those four areas would predictably result in joint impairments of calculation, word processing (possibly including agraphia), finger knowledge and movement, and high-level spatial reference (possibly including understanding of left–right coordinates). Such a joint lesion might be frequent because this cortical territory is jointly irrigated by a branch of the middle cerebral artery, the angular gyrus artery. Inter-individual variability in the boundaries between cortical territories as well as in the branching patterns of this artery would explain that the different elements of Gerstmann's syndrome can be dissociated (Benton, 1961; Benton, 1992). Note that this interpretation implies that, contrary to a frequent speculation, Gerstmann's syndrome does not result from a homogeneous impairment to a single representation that would somehow intermingle fingers, numbers, and space (Butterworth, 1999; Gerstmann, 1940; Mayer et al., 1999). Rather, the syndrome may represent a happenstance conjunction of distinct but dissociable deficits that frequently co-occur due to a common vascularization and that are only loosely connected at the functional level due to the overarching spatial and sensorimotor functions of the parietal lobe.

Electrophysiology

How might a specific numerical quantity be represented in the HIPS? The metaphor of a "number line" suggests that quantities are represented mentally as distributions of activation over a numerical continuum. This is merely a metaphorical model, however. How might a population of neurons represent such a "number map"? Dehaene and Changeux (1993) speculatively described a neural network of elementary number processing, in which it was demonstrated that numerosity information could be extracted in parallel from a display of objects and could be represented by a population of neurons, each tuned to a particular approximate numerical quantity. Recently, two independent groups have reported direct electrophysiological evidence that the numerosity-detector neurons postulated by the model do indeed exist. In one study (Sawamura, Shima, & Tanji, 2002), macaque monkeys were trained to perform an action exactly five times and then switch to another action. The timing of the actions was varied to ensure that the animals were responding to number rather than to other temporal parameters. In a small area on the dorsal bank of the intraparietal sulcus, neurons were tuned to a particular number of actions. Distinct populations were tuned to 1, 2, 3, 4, or 5 actions. Sawamura et al. report that number neurons were observed in a well-delimited parietal area and were much less numerous in other parietal and prefrontal regions. The location that they describe in the macaque brain seems to be a plausible homolog of the HIPS in humans (see Figure 25.2; Simon et al., 2001).

A second study also reported neurons tuned to number (Nieder, Freedman, & Miller, 2002). Macaque monkeys were trained to perform a match-to-sample task on successively presented visual displays containing between 1 and 5 randomly arranged items. During training, number was confounded with other visual parameters such as total area. However, after training, the monkeys spontaneously generalized to novel displays in which all of the relevant non-numerical variables were unconfounded, suggesting that they were attending to number. Indeed, a large proportion of number-coding neurons were recorded in the prefrontal cortex. Each neuron was tuned to a specific numerosity between 1 and 5 (the maximal numerosity that was tested). Several detailed predictions of the Dehaene-Changeux model of numerosity detection were upheld in this electrophysiological experiment. The neurons' firing latency was short (about 120 ms) and independent of the number being represented, suggesting parallel numerosity extraction rather than serial counting. The tuning curves were broad, suggesting approximate coding, and their breadth was proportional to the neuron's preferred number, supporting Weber's law. Finally, the tuning curves were asymmetrical and became bell shaped only when plotted on a logarithmic scale, suggesting a compressive logarithmic internal encoding of numerical quantity (Dehaene, 2001).

Intensive training may explain why many prefrontal neurons became sensitive to number in Nieder and Miller's study. One intriguing discrepancy between the two data sets, however, is that Nieder and Miller (2002) report finding only a small proportion of number-coding neurons in the parietal cortex (about 7%). Systematic studies will be needed to ensure that the same parietal sites are sampled. If confirmed, the figure of 7% would have important consequences for human neuroimaging studies. It might imply that the intraparietal cortex contains a patchwork of intermingled representations, with neural populations coding for numbers intermixed with others coding, e.g., for space or movement-related parameters. In that case, although there would be high specificity at the single-neuron level, functional imaging with voxels containing millions of neurons might only reveal a weak or partial selectivity for the number domain. It is important to keep in mind that neuroimaging experiments provide only a very coarse image of neuronal coding. The claim that fMRI in humans has a high spatial resolution, in particular, seems exaggerated given that most fMRI studies cannot resolve the genuine coding elements of the nervous system (single neurons and cortical columns).

THE LEFT ANGULAR GYRUS AND VERBAL NUMBER MANIPULATIONS

Neuroimaging Evidence

The left angular gyrus (hereafter AG) is also often activated in neuroimaging studies of number processing (see Figure 25.1b and Table 25.1). This region is left lateralized and located posterior and inferior to the HIPS (see Figure 25.2 for their respective locations). A closer

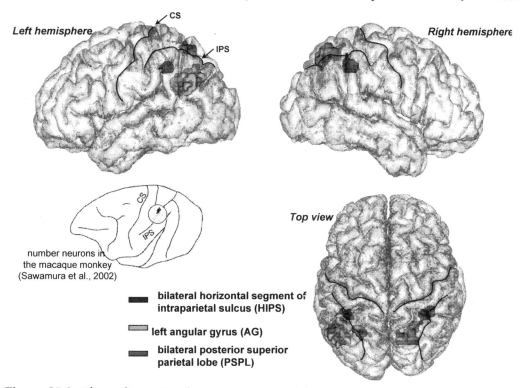

Figure 25.2. Three-dimensional representation of the parietal regions of interest. For a better visualization of each maximal overlap, the clusters show all parietal voxels activated in at least 40% of studies in a given group. Note that this is a transparent brain view and that the HIPS clusters are actually located deep in the intraparietal sulcus. The inset shows the localization of the intraparietal site where number neurons were identified in the macaque monkey and which may be homologous to the human HIPS. CS, central sulcus; IPS, intraparietal sulcus. A color version of this figure can be viewed at www.psypress.com/ campbell.

look at the types of numerical tasks that activate this region, detailed below, reveals that its functional properties are very different from the properties of the HIPS. The left AG does not seem to be concerned with quantity processing, but shows increasingly greater activation as the task puts greater requirements on verbal processing. We therefore propose that this region is part of the language system and contributes to number processing only inasmuch as some arithmetic operations, such as multiplication, make particularly strong demands on a verbal coding of numbers.

In support of this hypothesis, the left AG is not merely involved in calculation, but in different types of language-mediated processes such as reading or verbal short-term memory tasks (for reviews, see Fiez & Petersen, 1998; Paulesu, Frith, & Frackowiak, 1993; Price, 1998). In Simon et al.'s (2002) fMRI study of six different tasks, the left AG was the only parietal site where there was overlapping activity for calculation and phoneme detection but no activation during the other four visuo-spatial tasks. This clearly indicates that the left AG is not specific for calculation but jointly recruited by language and calculation processes.

Even within calculation, several studies indicate a modulation of AG activation in direct proportion to the verbal requirements of the task. First, the AG is more active in exact calculation than in approximation (Dehaene et al., 1999). This fits with behavioral data that indicate that exact arithmetic facts are stored in a language-specific format in bilinguals, whereas approximate knowledge is language independent and shows the classical numerical distance effect associated with the nonverbal quantity system (Spelke & Tsivkin, 2001). Second, within exact calculation, the left AG shows greater activation for operations that require access to a rote verbal memory of arithmetic facts, such as multiplication, than for operations that are not stored and require some form of quantity manipulation. For instance, the left AG shows increased activation for multiplication relative to both subtraction and number comparison (Chochon et al., 1999; Lee, 2000), for multiplication and division relative to a letter substitution control (Gruber, Indefrey, Steinmetz, & Kleinschmidt, 2001), and for multidigit multiplication relative to a digit-matching control (Fulbright et al., 2000).

Even within a given operation such as single-digit addition, the left AG is more active for small problems with a sum below 10 than for large problems with a sum above 10 (Stanescu-Cosson et al., 2000). This probably reflects the fact that small addition facts, just like multiplication tables, are stored in rote verbal memory, whereas behavioral evidence indicates that larger addition problems are often solved by resorting to various semantic elaboration strategies (Dehaene & Cohen, 1995; Lefevre, 1996).

In summary, the contribution of the left AG in number processing may be related to the linguistic basis of arithmetical computations. Its contribution seems essential for the retrieval of facts stored in verbal memory but not for other numerical tasks (like subtraction, number comparison, or complex calculation) which call for a genuinely quantitative representation of numbers and relate more to the intraparietal sulcus.

Neuropsychological Evidence: Dissociations between Operations

The finding that the intraparietal sulcus and the AG exhibit functionally differentiated properties can shed light on the neuropsychology of acalculia. One of the most striking findings is the occurrence of sharp dissociations between arithmetic operations. It is not rare for a patient to be much more severely impaired in multiplication than in subtraction (Cohen & Dehaene, 2000; Dagenbach & McCloskey, 1992; Dehaene & Cohen, 1997; Lampl, Eshel, Gilad, & Sarova-Pinhas, 1994; Lee, 2000; Pesenti, Seron, & van der Linden, 1994; van Harskamp & Cipolotti, 2001) while other patients are much more impaired in subtraction than in multiplication (Dehaene & Cohen, 1997; Delazer & Benke, 1997; van Harskamp & Cipolotti, 2001). Some have proposed that such dissociations reflect random impairments in a system with distinct stores of arithmetic facts for each operation (Dagenbach & McCloskey, 1992). Here, however, we would like to show that there is much more systematicity behind those observations. Our views suggest that dissociations between operations reflect a single, basic distinction between over-learned arithmetic facts such as the multiplication table, which are stored in rote verbal memory, and the genuine understanding of number meaning that underlies nontable operations such as subtraction (Dehaene & Cohen, 1997; Delazer & Benke, 1997; Hittmair-Delazer, Sailer, & Benke, 1995).

According to this interpretation, multiplication requires the integrity of language-based representations of numbers, because multiplication facts are typically learned by rote verbal memorization. Subtraction, on the other hand, is typically not learned by rote. Although the mechanisms by which simple subtraction problems are resolved are not understood yet, it is likely that some form of internal manipulation of nonverbal quantities on the internal number line is involved, as attested by the fact that very simple subtractions are accessible to preverbal infants (Wynn, 1992) and nonhuman primates (Hauser et al., 2000).

We would like to emphasize that the proposed dissociation between multiplication and subtraction is quantitative rather than qualitative. There is no doubt that some subtraction facts are stored in rote memory and that some multiplication facts are occasionally retrieved by semantic strategies in cases when direct retrieval fails. On average, however, we postulate that subtraction puts more emphasis on the internal manipulation of quantities and multiplication on the verbal coding of numbers. Note also that by verbal coding, we do not imply a low-level phonological coding of the string of number words. Phonological coding was clearly rejected by an experiment that showed that two patients who failed to retrieve the phonological form of number words, for instance, erroneously reading "2×4" as "five times three," nevertheless succeeded at solving the original problem ($2 \times 4 = 8$) (Whalen, McCloskey, Lindemann, & Bouton, 2002). The triple code model therefore postulates that multiplication facts are stored as a sequence of abstract word identities or "lemmas," as postulated in some models of language production (Levelt, 1989). This is compatible with studies of bilinguals, which indicate that exact arithmetic facts are coded internally using a language-specific representation (Spelke & Tsivkin, 2001).

Support for this "dual-route" view of multiplication and subtraction comes from several lines of research. First, as noted earlier, imaging studies in normals confirm that distinct sites of activation underlie performance in simple multiplication and subtraction (Chochon et al., 1999; Cohen, Dehaene, Chochon, Lehéricy, & Naccache, 2000; Lee, 2000). Second, all patients in whom subtraction was more impaired than multiplication had left parietal lesions and/or atrophy, most often accompanied by Gerstmann's syndrome (Dehaene & Cohen, 1997; Delazer & Benke, 1997; van Harskamp & Cipolotti, 2001; van Harskamp, Rudge, & Cipolotti, 2002). This is compatible with an impairment to the left HIPS. In one patient (van Harskamp et al., 2002), it was specifically claimed that the lesion localization was incompatible with our anatomical hypotheses. However, no Talairach coordinates were presented, whereas the MR images showed clearly an encroachment of the lesion into the banks of the anterior intraparietal sulcus (van Harskamp et al., 2002, Figure 1b), highly compatible with a HIPS lesion, and comparatively little or no lesion of the more lateral and inferior cortex of the angular gyrus.

Conversely, although this is not always thoroughly documented, patients in whom multiplication is more impaired than subtraction typically have associated aphasia (e.g., Cohen et al., 2000; Dehaene & Cohen, 1997). Furthermore, the lesions often spare the intraparietal cortex and can affect multiple regions known to be engaged in language processing, such as the left perisylvian cortices including the inferior parietal lobule (Cohen et al., 2000), the left parieto-temporal carrefour (Lampl et al., 1994), or the left basal ganglia (Dehaene & Cohen, 1997). The evidence clearly shows that multiple sites, not just the left AG, contribute to a distributed network supporting rote verbal knowledge and may cause multiplication impairments when lesioned. Multiplication impairments with spared subtraction have also been reported in two patients with reading deficits in whom the lesion affected access to the language system from visual symbols (Cohen & Dehaene, 2000; McNeil & Warrington, 1994). Amazingly, one of those patients was able to subtract better than she could read the same problems (Cohen & Dehaene, 2000). This confirms the relative independence of subtraction, but not multiplication, from the language system.

It is sometimes claimed that selective impairments in subtraction cannot be attributed to a lesion of the quantity representation because many of those patients do not exhibit much impairment of the semantic processing of quantities outside subtraction (e.g., van Harskamp et al., 2002). For instance, number comparison and proximity judgement are often largely preserved. However, the HIPS representation is bilateral, and there is evidence that number comparison, but not subtraction, can be performed by a single disconnected right hemisphere (Cohen & Dehaene, 1996; Gazzaniga & Smylie, 1984; Seymour et al., 1994). Thus, the preservation of the most elementary quantity-processing tasks might be due to the fact that none of the patients to date had bilateral intraparietal lesions. At present, the putative role of the right hemisphere in quantity processing remains largely untested by neuropsychological methods (but see Langdon & Warrington, 1997).

Perhaps the best evidence for a dissociation between quantity processing in the HIPS and verbal number processing in the left AG comes from two studies of the temporary calculation impairments caused by electrical brain stimulation. In one patient with strips of subdural electrodes arranged over the left inferior parietal, superior temporal, and posterior frontal regions, a single electrode site was found whose stimulation systematically disrupted multiplication performance much more than addition performance (27% correct vs. 87% correct; subtraction was not tested) (Whalen, McCloskey, Lesser, & Gordon, 1997). Although limited information is available on localization, this electrode was located in the left inferior parietal region, apparently close to the AG. Interestingly, multiplication performance was worse when the responses were given orally (27% correct) than when they were typed with a key pad (64% correct), suggesting that stimulation also interfered with the verbal coding of numbers.

A second case presented a double dissociation between subtraction and multiplication (Duffau et al., 2002). Cortical stimulation was performed intraoperatively during the resection of a parieto-occipital glioma. Two neighboring sites were found within the left parietal lobe. The first, located within the AG proper (approximate Talairach coordinates –50, –60, +30), disrupted multiplication but not subtraction when stimulated. The second, located more superiorily and anteriorily within the intraparietal sulcus (TC –45, –55, 40), disrupted subtraction but not multiplication. An intermediate location was also found where stimulation disrupted both operations. The reported coordinates, although imprecise given the distortions possibly induced by the glioma and the surgery, are highly compatible with the dissociated areas of activation observed in functional brain imaging (Chochon et al., 1999; Lee, 2000).

To close on the issue of dissociations between operations, we briefly consider the case of addition (see also Cohen & Dehaene, 2000). Addition is complex because it can be solved in at least two ways. It is similar to multiplication in that many people have memorized most of the basic addition table (single-digit addition facts with a sum below 10). However, addition is also similar to subtraction in that simple addition problems can also be solved by quantity manipulation strategies, something that would be utterly impractical with multiplication. This redundancy makes addition performance hard to predict. Indeed, in our experience, it varies considerably across patients or even within patients, depending on the strategy that they adopt. It might be thought that patients would always adopt the optimal strategy that remains available to them. For instance, a patient with impaired arithmetic fact retrieval and impaired multiplication but not subtraction should always perform well in addition, because he would be able to rely on his preserved abilities for quantity processing. However, this is not the case (e.g., Dagenbach & McCloskey, 1992). Rote retrieval seems to be the default strategy for addition in many subjects, especially elderly subjects who received extensive school training in addition and multiplication tables. Several patients whom we have observed insist on attempting to use retrieval because they believe that they should know the answer and feel that using finger counting or other strategies to solve problems as simple as 2 + 3 would be inappropriate for an educated adult. Thus, failure to perform correctly in the addition task may result from the selection of a suboptimal strategy. Note that this interpretation predicts that acalculic patients with impaired addition should improve sharply if encouraged to use alternative strategies. Unfortunately, there is no indication that this was attempted in the published cases to date.

Given this state of affairs, the only clear prediction from our model is that addition performance cannot dissociate from *both* subtraction and multiplication together (Cohen & Dehaene, 2000). That is to say, a patient cannot be impaired in addition but not in subtraction nor in multiplication (since the latter would imply that both the verbal and the quantity circuits are intact), nor can a patient show preserved addition with impaired subtraction and multiplication (since the latter would imply that both systems are impaired).

If dissociations between operations followed a chance pattern, this prediction should be violated in about one third of cases. In fact, however, it is confirmed by essentially all patients to date (11 out of 12 patients; Cohen & Dehaene, 2000; Dagenbach & McCloskey, 1992; Dehaene & Cohen, 1997; Delazer & Benke, 1997; Lampl et al., 1994; Lee, 2000; Pesenti et al., 1994; van Harskamp & Cipolotti, 2001; van Harskamp et al., 2002). The only exception (patient FS; van Harskamp & Cipolotti, 2001) is worth discussing. Overall, this patient was 96.3% correct (156/162) in single-digit subtraction and multiplication but only 61.7% correct (100/162) in single-digit addition, thus superficially qualifying as a straightforward violation of our hypothesis. However, the pattern of errors in this patient was quite different from other cases of acalculia. Eighty-seven percent of his addition errors consisted in selecting the wrong operation (he almost always solved the corresponding multiplication problem, e.g., 3 + 3 = 9). This is very different from the other two patients reported in the same paper: patient DT, who was impaired in subtraction, made only 12.5% operation errors, and patient VP, who was impaired in multiplication, made only 3.5% operation errors.

In a reanalysis, we excluded patient FS's operation errors and analyzed only the remaining trials, in which he was presumably really attempting to add the operands. In this way, we can estimate patient FS's conditional success rate in addition, given that he is really trying to add. This success rate is 92.6% correct (100/108), a value which does not differ from the performance observed in the other two operations (96.3% correct). Thus, it can be argued that patient FS experiences little difficulty with arithmetic operations *per se* but exhibits a selective deficit in choosing the appropriate operation. Specifically, a compact description of FS's performance is that he cannot avoid to multiply when the task requires to add. Why would FS do this? According to Miller and Paredes (1990), as children acquire the multiplication table, there is a temporary decrease in addition performance, reflecting increasing interference in arithmetic memory. Even adults are much more likely to give a correct multiplication result to an addition problem than the converse, suggesting a need to inhibit automatic multiplication fact retrieval when attempting to solve an addition problem. It seems that this inhibition process was impaired in FS, perhaps related to the deficit he was exhibiting in non-numerical tasks sensitive to frontal lobe dysfunction. We would like to argue that deficits affecting this task-control level should be kept conceptually distinct from other genuine impairments in arithmetical computation itself.

In summary, a review of neuropsychological dissociations between arithmetic operations indicates that it is not necessary to postulate as many brain circuits as there are arithmetical operations (Dagenbach & McCloskey, 1992). Rather, most if not all cases so far can be accommodated by the postulated dissociation between a quantity circuit (supporting subtraction and other quantity-manipulation operations) and a verbal circuit (supporting multiplication and other rote memory-based operations).

THE POSTERIOR SUPERIOR PARIETAL SYSTEM
AND ATTENTIONAL PROCESSES

Neuroimaging Evidence

A third region, observed bilaterally in the posterior superior parietal lobule (hereafter PSPL), with a frequent mesial extension into the precuneus, is also active in several tasks requiring number manipulations. This region is posterior to the HIPS and occupies a location superior and mesial to the AG in the superior parietal lobule (see Figure 25.1c and Figure 25.2). It is active during number comparison (Pesenti et al., 2000; Pinel et al., 2001), approximation (Dehaene et al., 1999), subtraction of 2 digits (Lee, 2000), and counting (Piazza et al., 2002a). It also appears to increase in activation when subjects carry out two operations instead of one (Menon et al., 2000). However, this region is clearly not specific to the number domain. Rather, it also plays a central role in a variety of visuo-spatial tasks including hand reaching, grasping, eye and/or attention orienting, mental rotation, and spatial working memory (Corbetta, Kincade, Ollinger, McAvoy, & Shulman, 2000; Culham & Kanwisher, 2001; Simon et al., 2002). For example, Wojciulik and Kanwisher (1999) have observed overlapping activations in this region in three tasks that all shared a component of attention orienting. Similarly, Simon et al. (2002) observed that this region was activated during eye movement, attention movements, grasping, and pointing.

The contribution of this region to spatial attention and/or eye orienting probably explains its activation during counting, in which subjects are sequentially attending to the enumerated objects. However, spatial attention does not seem to explain its activation during purely numerical operations of comparison, approximation, or subtraction. In all of those tasks, number-related activation in the PSPL was observed relative to a control that used the same spatial distribution of stimuli on screen as well as a very similar motor response.

Obviously, any reconciliation of those sparse and disparate data sets must remain tentative. The hypothesis that we would like to propose is that this region, in addition to being involved in attention orienting in space, can also contribute to attentional selection on other mental dimensions that are analogous to space, such as time (Coull & Nobre, 1998; Wojciulik & Kanwisher, 1999) or number. Psychological experiments indicate that the core semantic representation of numerical quantity can be likened to an internal "number line," a quasi-spatial representation on which numbers are organized by their proximity (Dehaene, Bossini, & Giraux, 1993; Moyer & Landauer, 1967). It is then conceivable that the same process of covert attention that operates to select locations in space can also be engaged when attending to specific quantities on the number line. Such number-based attention would be particularly needed in tasks that call for the selection of one among several quantities, for instance, when deciding which of two quantities is the larger (Pesenti et al., 2000; Pinel et al., 2001) or which of two numbers approximately fits an addition problem (Dehaene et al., 1999).

Neuropsychological Evidence: Joint Impairments
of Attention and Number Processing

Only a few neuropsychological and brain stimulation findings provide some support for our admittedly speculative theory. In a recent study using transcranial magnetic stimulation with normal subjects, Gobel et al. (2001) first located left and right dorsal posterior parietal sites where stimulation interfered with performance in a visual serial search task. Indeed, the coordinates of those regions correspond to those of the bilateral posterior parietal regions found active in neuroimaging studies of eye and attention orienting (Corbetta et al., 2000; Simon et al., 2002; Wojciulik & Kanwisher, 1999). They then tested the effect of magnetic stimulation at those locations on a two-digit number-comparison task. On stimulated trials, comparison performance was significantly slower. Interestingly, the numerical distance effect itself was still present and relatively unchanged (although stimulation on the left tended to interfere more with numbers close to the reference, particularly those that were larger than the reference). This suggests that the stimulation did not directly interfere with a core representation of numerical quantity but, rather, with the response decision process itself. At the very least, this experiment confirms that spatial attention orienting and numerical comparison both engage this parietal region, thus confirming previous brain-imaging evidence (Pinel et al., 2001).

Further support for a close interplay between the representations of space and numbers is provided by a study with unilateral neglect patients (Zorzi, Priftis, & Umilta, 2002). It is a well-known and, indeed, almost defining feature of those patients that they perform poorly in spatial bisection tests. When asked to locate the middle of a line segment, neglect patients with right parietal lesions tend to indicate a location further to the right, consistent with their failure to attend to the left side of space. Zorzi et al. tested their performance in a *numerical* bisection task, in which they were asked to find the middle of two orally presented numbers. Strikingly, patients erred systematically, often selecting a number far larger than the correct answer (e.g., what number falls in between 11 and 19? 17). This suggests that spatial attention can be oriented on the left-to-right oriented number line and that this attention orienting process contributes to the resolution of simple arithmetic problems such as the bisection test. Interestingly, these patients were said not to be acalculic and did not show any deficit in other numerical tasks such as in simple arithmetic fact retrieval. Indeed, Vuilleumier and Rafal (1999) demonstrated on a different group of patients with neglect that a posterior parietal lesion did not impair the mere quantification of small numbers of items. Neglect patients were able to estimate numerosity with sets of up to 4 objects, even when some of enumerated items fell in the neglected field. Again, this suggests that attentional and numerical systems are dissociable. However, Zorzi et al.'s finding of "representational neglect" on the numerical continuum indicates that spatial attention processes do contribute to some numerical tasks.

DEVELOPMENTAL DYSCALCULIA AND
THE ONTOGENY OF NUMBER REPRESENTATIONS

Whether or not our functional characterization of three parietal subsystems is correct, it is an anatomical fact that those activations sites are strikingly reproducible. It is remarkable that the HIPS, AG, and PSPL are systematically activated in different subjects, often from different countries, with different educational strategies and achievements in mathematics (Stevenson & Stigler, 1992), and with a diversity of linguistic schemes for expressing number (Hurford, 1987). Even the fine dissociation between subtraction and multiplication is reproducible with French versus Korean subjects (Chochon et al., 1999; Lee, 2000). Such systematicity in the anatomical organization of parietal numerical processes must be reconciled with the obvious fact that arithmetic is, in part, a recent cultural invention.

Our hypothesis is that the cultural construction of arithmetic is made possible by pre-existing cerebral circuits that are biologically determined and are adequate to support specific subcomponents of number processing (Dehaene, 1997). This hypothesis supposes an initial prespecialization of the brain circuits that will ultimately support high-level arithmetic in adults. It implies that it should be possible to identify precursors of those circuits in infancy and childhood. Indeed, quantity processing is present at a very young age. Infants in their first year of life can discriminate collections based on their numerosity (Dehaene et al., 1998a; Starkey & Cooper, 1980; Wynn, 1992), even when the numbers are as large as 8 versus 16 (Xu & Spelke, 2000). Although no brain-imaging evidence is available in infants yet, we speculate that this early numerical ability may be supported by a quantity representation similar to adults' (Dehaene, 1997; Spelke & Dehaene, 1999). This representation would serve as a foundation for the construction of higher-order arithmetical and mathematical concepts.

The hypothesis of an early emergence of quantity, verbal, and attentional systems leads to the following predictions concerning normal and impaired number development.

Brain Activation in Infancy and Childhood

A precursor of the HIPS region should be active in infants and young children during numerosity manipulation tasks. At present, this prediction has only been tested with 5-year-old children in a number comparison task (Temple & Posner, 1998). Event-related potentials revealed the scalp signature of a numerical distance effect, with a topography similar to adults, common to numbers presented as Arabic numerals or as sets of dots. There is a clear need to replicate those data at an earlier age and with a greater anatomical accuracy.

Developmental Dyscalculia and the Parietal Lobe

Deficits of number processing should be observed in the case of early left parietal injury or disorganization. Developmental dyscalculia is relatively frequent, affecting 3–6% of children (Badian, 1983; Kosc, 1974; Lewis, Hitch, & Walker, 1994). We predict that a fraction of those children may suffer from a core conceptual deficit in the numerical domain. Indeed, a "developmental Gerstmann syndrome" has been reported (Benson & Geschwind, 1970; Kinsbourne & Warrington, 1963; Spellacy & Peter, 1978; Temple, 1989; Temple, 1991). In those children, dyscalculia is accompanied by most or all of the following symptoms: dysgraphia, left–right disorientation, and finger agnosia, which suggest a neurological involvement of the parietal lobe. Interestingly, even in a sample of 200 normal children, a test of finger knowledge appears to be a better predictor of later arithmetic abilities than is a test of general intelligence (Fayol, Barrouillet, & Marinthe, 1998).

Two recent reports directly relate developmental dyscalculia to an underlying left parietal disorganization. Levy et al. (1999) report the case of an adult with lifelong isolated dyscalculia together with superior intelligence and reading ability, in whom the standard anatomical MRI appeared normal yet MR spectroscopy techniques revealed a metabolic abnormality in the left inferior parietal area. Similarly, Isaacs et al. (2001) used voxel-based morphometry to compare gray matter density in adolescents born at equally severe grades of prematurity, half of whom suffered from dyscalculia. They found a single region of reduced gray matter in the left intraparietal sulcus. The Talairach coordinates of this region (–39, –39, +45) are quite close to the coordinates of the HIPS.

Subtypes of Developmental Dyscalculia

As in adult acalculia, at least two subtypes of developmental dyscalculia should be observed, and those should be traceable to a differential impairment of quantity versus language-processing circuits. Although several distinctions between subtypes of developmental dyscalculia have been proposed (e.g., Ashcraft, Yamashita, & Aram, 1992; Geary, Hamson, & Hoard, 2000; Rourke & Conway, 1997; Temple, 1991), most are based on group studies and standardized batteries of tests, which are inappropriate for testing the predicted subtle distinctions between e.g., subtraction and multiplication. One exception is the single-case study of patient HM (Temple, 1991), who suffered from developmental phonological dyslexia. His deficit in arithmetic was mostly limited to multiplication facts, whereas he experienced no difficulty solving simple addition and subtraction problems with numbers of the same size. Our view predicts that the association of language and multiplication impairments observed in this study should be generalizable. Multiplication deficits should be present in cases of dyscalculia accompanied by dysphasia and/or dyslexia, whereas subtraction and quantity-manipulation deficits should be present in patients with dyscalculia but without any accompanying dyslexia or language retardation. Although this proposal remains largely untested, Geary et al. (2000) do report interesting differences between developmental dyscalculics with or without associated dyslexia. When faced with the same simple addition problems, nondyslexics tend to use fact retrieval much more often than do dyslexics, who instead use finger-counting strategies. This is consistent with the hypothesis that an impairment of rote verbal memory is partially responsible for dyscalculia in children with dyslexia.

Genetics of Developmental Dyscalculia

If the biological predisposition view is correct, specific combinations of genes should be involved in setting up the internal organization of the parietal lobe and, in particular, the distinction between quantity and language circuits. Thus, it should be possible to identify dyscalculias of genetic origin. The available data, indeed, indicates that when a child is dyscalculic, other family members are also frequently affected, suggesting that genetic factors may contribute to the disorder (Shalev et al., 2001). Although the search for dyscalculias of genetic origin has only very recently begun, the possibility that Turner syndrome may conform to this typology has recently attracted attention. Turner syndrome is a genetic disorder characterized by partial or complete absence of one X chromosome in a female individual. The disorder occurs in approximately 1 girl in 2,000 and is associated with well-documented physical disorders and abnormal estrogen production and pubertal development. The cognitive profile includes deficits in visual memory, visual-spatial and attentional tasks, and social relations, in the context of a normal verbal IQ (Rovet, 1993). Most interestingly in the present context is the documentation of a mild to severe deficit in mathematics, particularly clear in arithmetic (Mazzocco, 1998; Rovet, Szekely, & Hockenberry, 1994; Temple & Marriott, 1998).

Anatomically, the data suggest possible bilateral parieto-occipital dysfunction in Turner syndrome. A positron emission tomography study of 5 adult women demonstrated a glucose hypometabolism in bilateral parietal and occipital regions (Clark, Klonoff, & Hadyen, 1990). Two anatomical MR studies, one with 18 and the other with 30 affected women, demonstrated bilateral reductions in parieto-occipital brain volume together with other subcortical regions (Murphy et al., 1993; see also Reiss et al., 1993; Reiss, Mazzocco, Greenlaw, Freund, & Ross, 1995). Interestingly, the phenotype of Turner syndrome can differ depending on whether the remaining X chromosome is of paternal or maternal origin (Xm or Xp subtypes) (Bishop et al., 2000; Skuse, 2000; Skuse et al., 1997). Such a genomic imprinting effect was first demonstrated on tests of social competence (Skuse et al., 1997). It will be interesting to see if a similar effect exists in the arithmetic domain.

CONCLUSION

We have reviewed the evidence for a subdivision of calculation-related processes in the parietal lobe. A broader discussion of the specificity of the number-processing system should also consider the satellite systems that serve as inputs and outputs to calculation processes. At the visual identification level, pure alexic patients who fail to read words often show a largely preserved ability to read and process digits (Cohen & Dehaene, 1995; Déjerine, 1891; Déjerine, 1892). Conversely, a case of impaired number reading with preserved word reading is on record (Cipolotti, Warrington, & Butterworth, 1995). In the writing domain, severe agraphia and alexia may be accompanied by a fully preserved ability to write and read Arabic numbers (Anderson, Damasio, & Damasio, 1990). Even within the speech production system, patients who suffer from random phoneme substitutions, thus resulting in the production of an incomprehensible jargon, may produce jargon-free number words (Cohen, Verstichel, & Dehaene, 1997). These dissociations, however, need not imply a distinct semantic system for number. Rather, they can probably be explained by considering that the particular syntax of number words and the peculiarities of the positional notation for Arabic numerals place special demands on visual recognition, speech production, and writing systems.

Even within the parietal lobe, our review of number-related activations suggests that much of the human capacity for number processing relies on representations and processes that are not specific to the number domain. At least two of the parietal circuits that we have described, the posterior superior parietal attention system and the left angular verbal system, are thought to be associated with broader functions than mere calculation. The third circuit, in the bilateral horizontal intraparietal region (HIPS), is a more plausible candidate for domain specificity. As reviewed above, it is systematically activated during mental arithmetic; it is more activated by number words than by other words such as names of animals; and its activation increases with the amount or duration of quantity manipulation required, but is completely independent of the notation used for numbers. Still, we are reluctant to use the term "category-specific" for this brain region, and prefer the terms "core quantity system" or "number-essential" region instead. For a purely empirical point of view, deciding whether a given region is "specific" for numbers seems an extremely difficult enterprise. Testing for specificity would seem to require a systematic comparison of the target category (e.g., number) against a potentially infinite list of alternatives. It is also complicated by the limited resolution of brain-imaging techniques, which cannot yet resolve the fine-grained neuronal and columnar organization of human cortex. Comparison of group studies, as was done here, may overestimate the amount of overlap between tasks. Studies of multiple tasks within the same subjects will be required to examine whether the very same voxels can be activated by multiple quantity-related paradigms, and whether those voxels cannot be activated by any other non-numerical operation. Because such studies are still lacking (although see Simon et al., 2002), it is still premature to conclude for or against category specificity in number semantics.

REFERENCES

Anderson, S. W., Damasio, A. R., & Damasio, H. (1990). Troubled letters but not numbers. Domain specific cognitive impairments following focal damage in frontal cortex. *Brain, 113,* 749–766.

Ashcraft, M. H., Yamashita, T. S., & Aram, D. M. (1992). Mathematics performance in left and right brain-lesioned children and adolescents. *Brain and Cognition, 19,* 208–252.

Badian, N. A. (1983). Dyscalculia and nonverbal disorders of learning. In H. R. Myklebust (Ed.), *Progress in learning disabilities* (Vol. 5, pp. 235–264). New York: Stratton.

Benson, D. F., & Geschwind, N. (1970). Developmental Gerstmann syndrome. *Neurology, 20,* 293–298.

Benton, A. L. (1961). The fiction of the Gerstmann syndrome. *Journal of Neurology, 24,* 176–181.

Benton, A. L. (1992). Gerstmann's syndrome. *Archives of Neurology, 49,* 445–447.

Bishop, D. V., Canning, E., Elgar, K., Morris, E., Jacobs, P. A., & Skuse, D. H. (2000). Distinctive patterns of memory function in subgroups of females with Turner syndrome: evidence for imprinted loci on the X-chromosome affecting neurodevelopment. *Neuropsychologia, 38*(5), 712–721.

Burbaud, P., Camus, O., Guehl, D., Bioulac, B., Caille, J. M., & Allard, M. (1999). A functional magnetic resonance imaging study of mental subtraction in human subjects. *Neuroscience Letters, 273*(3), 195–199.

Butterworth, B. (1999). *The mathematical brain.* London: Macmillan.

Butterworth, B., Cappelletti, M., & Kopelman, M. (2001). Category specificity in reading and writing: the case of number words. *Nature Neuroscience, 4*(8), 784–786.

Cappelletti, M., Butterworth, B., & Kopelman, M. (2001). Spared numerical abilities in a case of semantic dementia. *Neuropsychologia, 39*(11), 1224–1239.

Chochon, F., Cohen, L., van de Moortele, P. F., & Dehaene, S. (1999). Differential contributions of the left and right inferior parietal lobules to number processing. *Journal of Cognitive Neuroscience, 11,* 617–630.

Cipolotti, L., Butterworth, B., & Denes, G. (1991). A specific deficit for numbers in a case of dense acalculia. *Brain, 114,* 2619–2637.

Cipolotti, L., Warrington, E. K., & Butterworth, B. (1995). Selective impairment in manipulating arabic numerals. *Cortex, 31,* 73–86.

Clark, C., Klonoff, H., & Hadyen, M. (1990). Regional cerebral glucose metabolism in Turner syndrome. *Canadian Journal of Neurological Sciences, 17,* 140–144.

Cohen, L., & Dehaene, S. (1995). Number processing in pure alexia: the effect of hemispheric asymmetries and task demands. *NeuroCase, 1,* 121–137.

Cohen, L., & Dehaene, S. (1996). Cerebral networks for number processing: Evidence from a case of posterior callosal lesion. *NeuroCase, 2,* 155–174.

Cohen, L., & Dehaene, S. (2000). Calculating without

reading: unsuspected residual abilities in pure alexia. *Cognitive Neuropsychology, 17*(6), 563–583.

Cohen, L., Dehaene, S., Chochon, F., Lehéricy, S., & Naccache, L. (2000). Language and calculation within the parietal lobe: A combined cognitive, anatomical and fMRI study. *Neuropsychologia, 38*, 1426–1440.

Cohen, L., Verstichel, P., & Dehaene, S. (1997). Neologistic jargon sparing numbers: a category specific phonological impairment. *Cognitive Neuropsychology, 14*, 1029–1061.

Corbetta, M., Kincade, J. M., Ollinger, J. M., McAvoy, M. P., & Shulman, G. L. (2000). Voluntary orienting is dissociated from target detection in human posterior parietal cortex. *Nature Neuroscience, 3*(3), 292–297.

Coull, J. T., & Nobre, A. C. (1998). Where and when to pay attention: the neural systems for directing attention to spatial locations and to time intervals as revealed by both PET and fMRI. *Journal of Neuroscience, 18*(18), 7426–7435.

Culham, J. C., & Kanwisher, N. G. (2001). Neuroimaging of cognitive functions in human parietal cortex. *Current Opinions in Neurobiology, 11*(2), 157–163.

Dagenbach, D., & McCloskey, M. (1992). The organization of arithmetic facts in memory: Evidence from a brain-damaged patient. *Brain and Cognition, 20*, 345–366.

Dehaene, S. (1992). Varieties of numerical abilities. *Cognition, 44*, 1–42.

Dehaene, S. (1995). Electrophysiological evidence for category-specific word processing in the normal human brain. *NeuroReport, 6*, 2153–2157.

Dehaene, S. (1996). The organization of brain activations in number comparison: Event-related potentials and the additive-factors methods. *Journal of Cognitive Neuroscience, 8*, 47–68.

Dehaene, S. (1997). *The number sense*. New York: Oxford University Press.

Dehaene, S. (2001). Subtracting pigeons: logarithmic or linear? *Psychologicial Science, 12*, 244–246.

Dehaene, S., Bossini, S., & Giraux, P. (1993). The mental representation of parity and numerical magnitude. *Journal of Experimental Psychology: General, 122*, 371–396.

Dehaene, S., & Changeux, J. P. (1993). Development of elementary numerical abilities: A neuronal model. *J. Cognitive Neuropsychology, 5*, 390–407.

Dehaene, S., & Cohen, L. (1995). Towards an anatomical and functional model of number processing. *Mathematical Cognition, 1*, 83–120.

Dehaene, S., & Cohen, L. (1997). Cerebral pathways for calculation: Double dissociation between rote verbal and quantitative knowledge of arithmetic. *Cortex, 33*, 219–250.

Dehaene, S., Dehaene-Lambertz, G., & Cohen, L. (1998a). Abstract representations of numbers in the animal and human brain. *Trends in Neuroscience, 21*, 355–361.

Dehaene, S., & Marques, J. F. (2002). Cognitive Euroscience: Scalar variability in price estimation and the cognitive consequences of switching to the Euro. *Quarterly Journal of Experimental Psychology, 55*(3), 705–731.

Dehaene, S., Naccache, L., Le Clec'H, G., Koechlin, E., Mueller, M., Dehaene-Lambertz, G., van de Moortele, P. F., & Le Bihan, D. (1998b). Imaging unconscious semantic priming. *Nature, 395*, 597–600.

Dehaene, S., Spelke, E., Stanescu, R., Pinel, P., & Tsivkin, S. (1999). Sources of mathematical thinking: Behavioral and brain-imaging evidence. *Science, 284*, 970–974.

Dehaene, S., Tzourio, N., Frak, V., Raynaud, L., Cohen, L., Mehler, J., & Mazoyer, B. (1996). Cerebral activations during number multiplication and comparison: a PET study. *Neuropsychologia, 34*, 1097–1106.

Déjerine, J. (1891). Sur un cas de cécité verbale avec agraphie suivi d'autopsie. *Mémoires de la Société de Biologie, 3*, 197–201.

Déjerine, J. (1892). Contribution à l'étude anatomo-pathologique et clinique des différentes variétés de cécité verbale. *Mémoires de la Société de Biologie, 4*, 61–90.

Delazer, M., & Benke, T. (1997). Arithmetic facts without meaning. *Cortex, 33*(4), 697–710.

Duffau, H., Denvil, D., Lopes, M., Gasparini, F., Cohen, L., & Capelle, L. (2002). Intraoperative mapping of the cortical areas involved in multiplication and subtraction: an electrostimulation study in a patient with a left parietal glioma. *Journal of Neurology, Neurosurgery, and Psychiatry, 73*(16), 733–738.

Fayol, M., Barrouillet, P., & Marinthe, X. (1998). Predicting arithmetical achievement from neuropsychological performance: A longitudinal study. *Cognition, 68*, B63–B70.

Fiez, J. A., & Petersen, S. E. (1998). Neuroimaging studies of word reading. *Proceedings of the National Academy of Sciences USA, 95*(3), 914–921.

Fulbright, R. K., Molfese, D. L., Stevens, A. A., Skudlarski, P., Lacadie, C. M., & Gore, J. C. (2000). Cerebral activation during multiplication: a functional MR imaging study of number processing. *American Journal of Neuroradiology, 21*(6), 1048–1054.

Gazzaniga, M. S., & Smylie, C. E. (1984). Dissociation of language and cognition: A psychological profile of two disconnected right hemispheres. *Brain, 107*, 145–153.

Geary, D. C., Hamson, C. O., & Hoard, M. K. (2000). Numerical and arithmetical cognition: a longitudinal study of process and concept deficits in children with learning disability. *Journal of Experimental Child Psychology, 77*(3), 236–263.

Gerstmann, J. (1940). Syndrome of finger agnosia, disorientation for right and left, agraphia, and acalculia. *Archives of Neurology: Psychiatry, 44*, 398–408.

Gobel, S., Walsh, V., & Rushworth, M. F. (2001). The mental number line and the human angular gyrus. *Neuroimage, 14*(6), 1278–1289.

Gruber, O., Indefrey, P., Steinmetz, H., & Kleinschmidt, A. (2001). Dissociating neural correlates of cognitive components in mental calculation. *Cerebral Cortex, 11*(4), 350–359.

Hauser, M. D., Carey, S., & Hauser, L. B. (2000). Spontaneous number representation in semi-free-ranging rhesus monkeys. *Proceedings of the Royal Society of London: Biological Sciences, 267*(1445), 829–833.

Hécaen, H., Angelergues, R., & Houillier, S. (1961). Les variétés cliniques des acalculies au cours des lésions rétro-rolandiques: Approche statistique du problème. *Review of Neurology, 105*, 85–103.

Henschen, S. E. (1919). Uber Sprach- Musik—un Rechenmechanismen und ihre Lokalisationen im Grosshirn. *Zeitschrift für die desamte Neurologie und Psychiatrie, 52*, 273–298.

Hittmair-Delazer, M., Sailer, U., & Benke, T. (1995). Impaired arithmetic facts but intact conceptual knowledge—A single case study of dyscalculia. *Cortex, 31*, 139–147.

Hurford, J. R. (1987). *Language and number.* Oxford: Basil Blackwell.

Isaacs, E. B., Edmonds, C. J., Lucas, A., & Gadian, D. G. (2001). Calculation difficulties in children of very low birthweight: A neural correlate. *Brain, 124*(9), 1701–1707.

Kiefer, M., & Dehaene, S. (1997). The time course of parietal activation in single-digit multiplication: Evidence from event-related potentials. *Mathematical Cognition, 3,* 1–30.

Kinsbourne, M., & Warrington, E. K. (1963). The developmental Gerstmann syndrome. *Archives of Neurology, 8,* 490.

Kosc, L. (1974). Developmental dyscalculia. *Journal of Learning Disabilities, 7,* 165–177.

Lampl, Y., Eshel, Y., Gilad, R., & Sarova-Pinhas, I. (1994). Selective acalculia with sparing of the subtraction process in a patient with left parietotemporal hemorrhage. *Neurology, 44,* 1759–1761.

Langdon, D. W., & Warrington, E. K. (1997). The abstraction of numerical relations: A role for the right hemisphere in arithmetic? *Journal of International Neuropsychological Society, 3,* 260–268.

Le Clec'H, G., Dehaene, S., Cohen, L., Mehler, J., Dupoux, E., Poline, J. B., Lehericy, S., van de Moortele, P. F., & Le Bihan, D. (2000). Distinct cortical areas for names of numbers and body parts independent of language and input modality. *Neuroimage, 12*(4), 381–391.

Lee, K. M. (2000). Cortical areas differentially involved in multiplication and subtraction: A functional magnetic resonance imaging study and correlation with a case of selective acalculia. *Annals of Neurology, 48,* 657–661.

Lee, K. M., & Kang, S. Y. (2002). Arithmetic operation and working memory: differential suppression in dual tasks. *Cognition, 83*(3), B63–68.

Lefevre, J.-A. (1996). Selection of procedures in mental addition: Reassessing the problem-size effect in adults. *Journal of Experimental Psychology: Learning, Memory, and Cognition, 22,* 216–230.

Levelt, W. J. M. (1989). *Speaking: From intention to articulation.* Cambridge, MA: MIT Press.

Levy, L. M., Reis, I. L., & Grafman, J. (1999). Metabolic abnormalities detected by H-MRS in dyscalculia and dysgraphia. *Neurology, 53,* 639–641.

Lewis, C., Hitch, G. J., & Walker, P. (1994). The prevalence of specific arithmetic difficulties and specific reading difficulties in 9- and 10-year-old boys and girls. *Journal of Child Psychology and Psychiatry, 35,* 283–292.

Mayer, E., Martory, M. D., Pegna, A. J., Landis, T., Delavelle, J., & Annoni, J. M. (1999). A pure case of Gerstmann syndrome with a subangular lesion. *Brain, 122*(6), 1107–1120.

Mazzocco, M. M. (1998). A process approach to describing mathematics difficulties in girls with Turner syndrome. *Pediatrics, 102*(2 Pt 3), 492–496.

McNeil, J. E., & Warrington, E. K. (1994). A dissociation between addition and subtraction with written calculation. *Neuropsychologia, 32*(6), 717–728.

Menon, V., Rivera, S. M., White, C. D., Glover, G. H., & Reiss, A. L. (2000). Dissociating prefrontal and parietal cortex activation during arithmetic processing. *Neuroimage, 12*(4), 357–365.

Miller, K. F., & Paredes, D. R. (1990). Starting to add worse: Effects of learning to multiply on children's addition. *Cognition, 37*(3), 213–242.

Moyer, R. S., & Landauer, T. K. (1967). Time required for judgments of numerical inequality. *Nature, 215,* 1519–1520.

Murphy, D. G., DeCarli, C., Daly, E., Haxby, J. V., Allen, G., White, B. J., McIntosh, A. R., Powell, C. M., Horwitz, B., Rapoport, S. I., et al. (1993). X-chromosome effects on female brain: a magnetic resonance imaging study of Turner's syndrome [see comments]. *Lancet, 342*(8881), 1197–2000.

Naccache, L., & Dehaene, S. (2001). The priming method: Imaging unconscious repetition priming reveals an abstract representation of number in the parietal lobes. *Cerebral Cortex, 11*(10), 966–974.

Nieder, A., Freedman, D. J., & Miller, E. K. (2002). Representation of the quantity of visual items in the primate prefrontal cortex. *Science. 297*(5587), 1708–1711.

Paulesu, E., Frith, C. D., & Frackowiak, R. S. J. (1993). The neural correlates of the verbal component of working memory. *Nature, 362,* 342–345.

Pesenti, M., Seron, X., & van der Linden, M. (1994). Selective impairment as evidence for mental organisation of arithmetical facts: BB, a case of preserved subtraction? *Cortex, 30*(4), 661–71.

Pesenti, M., Thioux, M., Seron, X., & De Volder, A. (2000). Neuroanatomical substrates of Arabic number processing, numerical comparison, and simple addition: A PET study. *Journal of Cognitive Neuroscience, 12*(3), 461–79.

Piazza, M., Mechelli, A., Butterworth, B., & Price, C. J. (2002a). Are subitizing and counting implemented as separate or functionally overlapping processes? *Neuroimage, 15*(2), 435–46.

Piazza, M., Mechelli, A., Price, C., & Butterworth, B. (2002b). The quantifying brain: functional neuroanatomy of numerosity estimation and counting. Submitted for publication.

Pinel, P., Dehaene, S., Riviere, D., & LeBihan, D. (2001). Modulation of parietal activation by semantic distance in a number comparison task. *Neuroimage, 14*(5), 1013–26.

Price, C. (1998). The functional anatomy of word comprehension and production. *Trends in Cognitive Science, 2,* 281–288.

Reiss, A. L., Freund, L., Plotnick, L., Baumgardner, T., Green, K., Sozer, A. C., Reader, M., Boehm, C., & Denckla, M. B. (1993). The effects of X monosomy on brain development: monozygotic twins discordant for Turner's syndrome. *Annals of Neurology, 34*(1), 95–107.

Reiss, A. L., Mazzocco, M. M., Greenlaw, R., Freund, L. S., & Ross, J. L. (1995). Neurodevelopmental effects of X monosomy: a volumetric imaging study. *Annals of Neurology, 38*(5), 731–8.

Rickard, T. C., Romero, S. G., Basso, G., Wharton, C., Flitman, S., & Grafman, J. (2000). The calculating brain: an fMRI study. *Neuropsychologia, 38*(3), 325–335.

Roland, P. E., & Friberg, L. (1985). Localization of cortical areas activated by thinking. *Journal of Neurophysiology, 53,* 1219–1243.

Rosselli, M., & Ardila, A. (1989). Calculation deficits in patients with right and left hemisphere damage. *Neuropsychologia, 27,* 607–617.

Rourke, B. P., & Conway, J. A. (1997). Disabilities of arithmetic and mathematical reasoning. Perspectives from neurology and neuropsychology. *Journal of Learning Disabilities, 30,* 34–46.

Rovet, J., Szekely, C., & Hockenberry, M. N. (1994). Specific arithmetic calculation deficits in children with Turner syndrome. *Journal of Clinical and Experimental Neuropsychology, 16*(6), 820–39.

Rovet, J. F. (1993). The psychoeducational characteristics of children with Turner syndrome. *Journal of Learning Disabilities, 26*(5), 333–41.

Rueckert, L., Lange, N., Partiot, A., Appollonio, I., Litvar, I., Le Bihan, D., & Grafman, J. (1996). Visualizing cortical activation during mental calculation with functional MRI. *NeuroImage, 3*, 97–103.

Sawamura, H., Shima, K., & Tanji, J. (2002). Numerical representation for action in the parietal cortex of the monkey. *Nature, 415*(6874), 918–922.

Seymour, S. E., Reuter-Lorenz, P. A., & Gazzaniga, M. S. (1994). The disconnection syndrome: basic findings reaffirmed. *Brain, 117*, 105–115.

Shalev, R. S., Manor, O., Kerem, B., Ayali, M., Badichi, N., Friedlander, Y., & Gross-Tsur, V. (2001). Developmental dyscalculia is a familial learning disability. *Journal of Learning Disabilities, 34*, 59–65.

Simon, O., Cohen, L., Mangin, J. F., Bihan, D. L., & Dehaene, S. (2002). Topographical layout of hand, eye, calculation and language-related areas in the human parietal lobe. *Neuron, 33*, 475–487.

Skuse, D. H. (2000). Imprinting, the X-chromosome, and the male brain: explaining sex differences in the liability to autism. *Pediatric Research, 47*(1), 9–16.

Skuse, D. H., James, R. S., Bishop, D. V., Coppin, B., Dalton, P., Aamodt-Leeper, G., Bacarese-Hamilton, M., Creswell, C., McGurk, R., & Jacobs, P. A. (1997). Evidence from Turner's syndrome of an imprinted X-linked locus affecting cognitive function [see comments]. *Nature, 387*(6634), 705–708.

Spelke, E., & Dehaene, S. (1999). On the foundations of numerical thinking: Reply to Simon. *Trends in Cognitive Science, 3*, 365–366.

Spelke, E. S., & Tsivkin, S. (2001). Language and number: a bilingual training study. *Cognition, 78*(1), 45–88.

Spellacy, F., & Peter, B. (1978). Dyscalculia and elements of the developmental Gerstmann syndrome in school children. *Cortex, 14*, 197–206.

Stanescu-Cosson, R., Pinel, P., van de Moortele, P.-F., Le Bihan, D., Cohen, L., & Dehaene, S. (2000). Cerebral bases of calculation processes: Impact of number size on the cerebral circuits for exact and approximate calculation. *Brain, 123*, 2240–2255.

Starkey, P., & Cooper, R. G. (1980). Perception of numbers by human infants. *Science, 210*, 1033–1035.

Stevenson, H. W., & Stigler, J. W. (1992). *The learning gap.* New York: Simon & Schuster.

Takayama, Y., Sugishita, M., Akiguchi, I., & Kimura, J. (1994). Isolated acalculia due to left parietal lesion. *Archives of Neurology, 51*, 286–291.

Temple, C. M. (1989). Digit dyslexia: A category-specific disorder in development dyscalculia. *Cognitive Neuropsychology, 6*, 93–116.

Temple, C. M. (1991). Procedural dyscalculia and number fact dyscalculia: Double dissociation in developmental dyscalculia. *Cognitve Neuropsychology, 8*, 155–176.

Temple, C. M., & Marriott, A. J. (1998). Arithmetic ability and disability in Turner's syndrome: A cognitive neuropsychological analysis. *Developmental Neuropsychology, 14*, 47–67.

Temple, E., & Posner, M. I. (1998). Brain mechanisms of quantity are similar in 5-year-olds and adults. *Proceedings of the National Academy of Sciences, USA, 95*, 7836–7841.

Thioux, M., Pesenti, M., Costes, N., De Volder, A., & Seron, X. (2002). Dissociating category-specific and task related cerebral activation during semantic processing. *Neuroimage*, submitted.

Thioux, M., Pillon, A., Samson, D., de Partz, M.-P., Noel, M.-P., & Seron, X. (1998). The isolation of numerals at the semantic level. *NeuroCase, 4*, 371–389.

van Harskamp, N. J., & Cipolotti, L. (2001). Selective impairments for addition, subtraction and multiplication. implications for the organisation of arithmetical facts. *Cortex, 37*(3), 363–88.

van Harskamp, N. J., Rudge, P., & Cipolotti, L. (2002). Are multiplication facts implemented by the left supramarginal and angular gyri? *Neuropsychologia, 40*(11), 1786–1793.

Vuilleumier, P., & Rafal, R. (1999). "Both" means more than "two": localizing and counting in patients with visuospatial neglect. *Nature Neuroscience, 2*(9), 783–784.

Whalen, J., McCloskey, M., Lesser, R. P., & Gordon, B. (1997). Localizing arithmetic processes in the brain: Evidence from transient deficit during cortical stimulation. *Journal of Cognitive Neuroscience, 9*(3), 409–417.

Whalen, J., McCloskey, M., Lindemann, M., & Bouton, G. (2002). Representing arithmetic table facts in memory: Evidence from acquired impairments. *Cognitve Neuropsychology, 19*(6), 505–522

Wojciulik, E., & Kanwisher, N. (1999). The generality of parietal involvement in visual attention. *Neuron, 23*(4), 747–64.

Wynn, K. (1992). Addition and subtraction by human infants. *Nature, 358*, 749–750.

Xu, F., & Spelke, E. S. (2000). Large number discrimination in 6-month-old infants. *Cognition, 74*(1), B1–B11.

Zago, L., Pesenti, M., Mellet, E., Crivello, F., Mazoyer, B., & Tzourio-Mazoyer, N. (2001). Neural correlates of simple and complex mental calculation. *Neuroimage, 13*(2), 314–27.

Zorzi, M., Priftis, K., & Umilta, C. (2002). Brain damage: Neglect disrupts the mental number line. *Nature, 417*(6885), 138–9.

26

Developmental Dyscalculia

Brian Butterworth

Severe difficulties in learning about numbers and arithmetic are probably as widespread as disorders of literacy development (dyslexia). The best prevalence estimates for each lie between 3.6% and 6.5% (see Table 26.1). Studies in the U.K. have revealed that poor mathematical skills are more of a handicap in the workplace than poor literacy skills (Bynner & Parsons, 1997). However, there has been much less research on dyscalculia than on dyslexia, and it is a much less widely recognized type of learning disability. In the U.K., its existence was first recognized by the Department of Education in 2001 (DfES, 2001).

In this chapter, I argue for a highly selective and specific deficit of a very basic capacity for understanding numbers, which leads to a range of difficulties in learning about number and arithmetic. This proposal is based on the idea that we are born with a capacity specialized for recognizing and mentally manipulating numerosities (cardinal values) and that this capacity is likely to be embodied in specialized neural circuits. Recent findings show that infants, even in the first week of life, are sensitive to the numorosity of a visual display (see below for further details). This capacity functions as a kind of starter kit for understanding numbers and arithmetic. Selective deficits will arise, on this view, when the specialized capacity, or "number module" (Butterworth, 1999), fails to develop normally. I shall call this "the defective number module hypothesis."

However, many researchers, as will be discussed, argue that difficulties in learning mathematics are due to a single impairment or combination of impairments in more general or more basic cognitive systems, and, as can be seen in chapters 8 and 25 in this volume, there is an alternative view about the basis of numerical abilities. According to some students of infant capacities (e.g., Carey & Spelke, in press; Gallistel & Gelman, 2000) and of functional neuroimaging (e.g., Dehaene, Spelke, Pinel, Stanescu, & Tsivkin, 1999), we are born not with a capacity for recognizing and mentally manipulating discrete numerosities but, rather, with a capacity for representing continuous quantities plus knowledge of the "integer list" (number words) which enables the development of representations for discrete numerosities above four. According to this view, linguistic disturbances can be critical for the development of numeracy, whereas in the first view, understanding numerosities and language are quite independent.

Some support for the defective number module hypothesis comes from studies of neurological patients who can show a sharp dissociation between those with severe acalculia but spared language and those with severely defective language but spared calculation. An example of spared language is the patient CG, who performed normally on all language tests (though she could no longer read) but was able to count only to four and was quite unable to handle any task at all involving numbers larger than four (Cipolotti, Butterworth, & Denes, 1991). It is much rarer to see patients with calculation selectively spared despite defective language, but patient IH was able to carry out single and multidigit calculations almost flawlessly while performing at chance at spoken word comprehension and close to zero on most tests of naming (Cappelletti, Butterworth, & Kopelman, 2001; Cappelletti, Kopelman, & Butterworth, 2002). This dissociation suggests that the language and the number circuits in the adult brain are distinct. However, it may still be the case that to develop a sense of numbers, including its recursive character, requires learning the integer list in the first place.

It is worth noting at the outset that there are several problems in studying this topic. First, there are many reasons for being bad at mathematics, including inappropriate teaching, behavioral problems, anxiety, and missing lessons. This makes identifying a specific endogenous condition difficult. Second, many educational authorities, many parents, and many children believe that difficulty in acquiring the basic skills is due to stupidity or laziness. This is reminiscent of the way in which difficulties in learning to read were treated 20 or 30 years ago. Third, there is a striking comorbidity with deficits in literacy. Table 26.1 shows that this comorbidity occurs across languages (Norwegian, Hebrew, and English) and orthographies. This has led several authors and dyslexia organizations to attribute dyscalculia, or at least some of its symptoms, to the dyslexic condition itself, as will be discussed below. Of course, language difficulties will affect learning of all kinds, and no doubt the child with problems understanding what the teacher says will be at a disadvantage.

Finally, mathematics, even in the early grades of schooling, comprise a wide variety of skills, including counting, estimating, retrieving arithmetical facts (number bonds, multiplication tables), understanding arithmetical laws such as commutativity of addition and multiplication (but not subtraction and division), knowing the procedures for carrying and borrowing in multidigit tasks, being able to solve novel word problems, and so on. Perhaps as a consequence, even standardized tests of arithmetical abilities show wide differences in the mathematics that compose the tests.

It is therefore perhaps unsurprising that there are no agreed-upon criteria for diagnosing

Table 26.1
Prevalence Estimates and Co-Occurrence with Literacy Disorder

Study Location	Estimate of Learning Disability	Criterion	Percentage of Sample with Literacy Disorder
Badian(1983) USA	6.4% "Developmental dyscalculia"	Stanford Achievement Test 43%	Low reading achievement
DSM-IV	1% "Developmental dyscalculia"	Standard mathematics score discrepant with IQ	N/A
Gross-Tsur et al. (1996) Israel	6.5% "Dyscalculia"	Two grades below Chronological Age on standardized battery	17% Reading disorder
Kosc (1974) Czechoslovakia	6.4% "Developmental dyscalculia"	Special test battery	N/A
Lewis et al. (1994) England	3.6% "Specific arithmetic difficulties"	< 85 on arithmetic test, > 90 on NVIQ	64% Reading difficulties
Ostad (1998) Norway	10.9% "Math disabled"	Registered for special long-term help	51% Spelling disorder

the deficit. This is apparent from the prevalence studies listed in Table 26.1.

One problem about using standardized tests of arithmetic attainment is that poor performance can, of course, have many causes. If a subject cannot solve a multiplication is this because he has a poor capacity for learning multiplication, or that his teacher failed to explain it properly, or even that the child was ill during the weeks when the fundamentals of multiplication were first taught and he still has not caught up? It seems to me vital to distinguish tests of attainment from tests of capacity. In general, without the capacity, high levels of attainment will not be achievable, but even with the capacity, attainment can depend on many factors. If one is interested in the capacity to learn arithmetic, his use of attainment tests will inevitably lead to an overestimation of rates of dyscalculia.

DEFINING DYSCALCULIA

The first systematic study of specific deficits in learning about numbers and arithmetic was published by Czechoslovakian psychologist Ladislav Kosc (1974), who introduced the term "developmental dyscalculia." This is also the term used by Shalev and colleagues, to distinguish it from the acquired kind, in many papers (Gross-Tsur, Manor, & Shalev, 1996; Shalev & Gross-Tsur, 1993, 2001; Shalev, Manor, & Gross-Tsur, 1997; Shalev et al., 2001). In this chapter, I shall use the term developmental dyscalculia, abbreviated to DD. However, other studies of selective deficits in numeracy acquisition have used other terminology. For example, Koontz and Berch (1996) prefer "arithmetic learning disabilities," whereas Hitch and colleagues use both "specific arithmetic difficulties" (Lewis et al., 1994) and "specific arithmetic learning difficulties" (McLean & Hitch, 1999).

Studies of DD need to be distinguished from experimental studies of the causes of difficulties with learning mathematics. As can be seen from Table 26.2, some studies use 20th, 25th, 30th, or even the 35th percentiles of standardized math attainment tests, whereas prevalence estimates suggest that only the lowest 5–7% of children should be so classified. By taking one quarter to one third of a cohort, these studies are likely to include children whose mathematics difficulties are caused by a very wide range of factors. Since these authors use similar terminology to those listed above, this can lead to confusion. For example, Geary and colleagues refer to "mathematical disabilities" (Geary, 1993; Geary et al., 1999, 2000) and, in a recent paper, to "arithmetic deficits"; Jordan and colleagues use the term "mathematics difficulties" (Jordan, Kaplan, & Hanich, 2002).

These differences in terminology are compounded by differences in criteria for assigning children to the category. Traditional definitions (e.g., *DSM-IV*) state that the child must substantially underachieve on a standardized test relative to the level expected given age, education, and intelligence and must experience disruption to academic achievement or daily living. Most of the studies have used this kind of discrepancy criterion or at least set lower bounds on intelligence and literacy before assignment. In Table 26.2, I list some of the many criteria that have been used.

However, standardized math tests are not sufficient for prevalence studies, as any a priori criterion will simply define a particular proportion of the population as DDs if the criterial dimension is normally distributed. Thus, a criterion of one standard deviation below the population mean (which is equivalent to a standard score of less than 85) entails that approximately 16% of those tested will be classified as DD. When a minimum IQ level is used to create a discrepancy criterion, for example, 90 or above, this means that about 12% of those tested will meet the criterion. (Notice that these are the criteria used by Lewis et al. (1994), and, strangely, they found not 12% of their cohort with "specific arithmetical difficulties" but only 3.4%.). Therefore, a different approach needs to be found.

An alternative approach is to take a qualitative criterion, which is the approach taken by the U.K. Department for Education and Skills. It defines dyscalculia as:

Table 26.2
Criteria for Dyscalculia

Study	Name	Test	Criteria	Exclusions	Age	N (+RD)
Butterworth, 2003	Dyscalculia	Item-timed tests of enumeration and number comparison	Bottom 2 stanines		6–14	
Geary et al., 1999	Mathematical disabilities (MD)	Woodcock Johnson Mathematics Reasoning	30th percentile	IQ < 80	1st grade, 6;10	15 (25)
Geary et al., 2000	Mathematical disabilities (MD)	Woodcock Johnson Mathematics Reasoning	35th percentile		1st and 2nd grades	12 (16)
Jordan et al., 2002; Jordan et al., 2003a,b	Mathematics difficulties (MD)	Woodcock Johnson Broad Mathematics Composite	35th percentile		2nd grade	46 (42)
Koontz & Berch, 1996	Arithmetic learning disabilities	Iowa Tests of Basic Skills	25th percentile	Below 30th percentile on reading or below normal IQ	10;4 yrs.	32
Landerl et al., in press	Developmental dyscalculia	Item-timed arithmetic and teacher's classification	3 SD below mean	50th + percentile IQ	8–9 yrs.	10 (10)
McLean & Hitch, 1999	Specific arithmetic learning difficulties	Graded Arithmetic-Mathematics Test	25th percentile	Mid-50% on Primary Reading Test	9 yrs.	12
Shalev et al., 1997	Developmental dyscalculia	Standardized arithmetic battery	2 grades below CA	IQ < 80	5th grade	104 (35)
Temple & Sherwood, 2002	Number fact disorder	WOND numerical operations	12 mths below CA		11–12 yrs.	10

Note: N means the number classified as DD in the sample. (RD) is the number of those found to have a literacy difficulty also.

A condition that affects the ability to acquire arithmetical skills. Dyscalculic learners may have difficulty understanding simple number concepts, lack an intuitive grasp of numbers, and have problems learning number facts and procedures. Even if they produce a correct answer or use a correct method, they may do so mechanically and without confidence. (DfES, 2001, p. 2)

Using a qualitative approach, the problem becomes one of trying to operationalize the criterion, which will depend on the core characteristics of DD as discovered empirically.

CHARACTERISTICS OF DYSCALCULIA

Whereas researchers have adopted a variety of terms and criteria for DD, there is a consensus about the basic behavioral characteristics for DD. It is generally agreed that children with dyscalculia have difficulty in learning and remembering arithmetic facts (Geary, 1993; Geary & Hoard, 2001; Ginsburg, 1997; N. Jordan & Montani, 1997; Kirby & Becker, 1988; Russell &

Ginsburg, 1984; Shalev & Gross-Tsur, 2001) and in executing calculation procedures. Landerl, Bevan, and Butterworth (2004), in a study of ten 9-year-old DDs and 18 matched controls, found that the DDs were less accurate in single-digit subtraction and multiplication than controls and also significantly slower on addition, subtraction, and multiplication.

DDs also depend much more on "immature strategies," such as counting on their fingers to solve problems (Butterworth, 1999; Ostad, 1999). Generally, one can fail to diagnose dyscalculia when only accuracy is considered, since percent correct will not reveal whether the subject is using immature strategies like counting in addition, whereas normal children will simply retrieve the answer from memory (Jordan & Montani, 1997).

The majority of DD children have problems with both knowledge of facts and knowledge of arithmetical procedures (Russell and Ginsburg, 1984), although Temple (1991) has demonstrated, using case studies, that knowledge of facts and grasp of procedures and strategies are dissociable in developmental dyscalculia (Temple, 1991; Temple & Sherwood, 2002).

Difficulty with basic arithmetic is a common characteristic, but dyscalculics appear to have a more fundamental problem in that they perform poorly on tasks requiring an understanding of basic numerical concepts, especially the concept of numerosity. This affects even very simple tasks such as counting or comparing numerical magnitudes. Koontz & Berch (1996) found that dyscalculic children appeared to be counting to three rather than subitizing in a dot-matching task, suggesting that this very fundamental capacity could be tied to the child's understanding of numerosity. Certainly, it has been argued that it underpins the acquisition of counting skills (Fuson, 1988). Geary, Hamson, and Hoard (2000) found small but systematic group differences between first-grade dyscalculic children and controls in magnitude comparison.

One recent study showed reliable reaction time differences between dyscalculic children and math-normal children (including a group with dyslexia) on tests of dot counting and of number magnitude comparison (Landerl et al., in press). In extreme cases such as "Charles" (Butterworth, 1999), DDs can show a reverse distance effect. That is, it takes them longer to decide that 9 is larger than 2 than that 9 is larger than 8. This seems to be due to some kind of counting strategy in which it takes longer to count from 2 to 9 than from 8 to 9.

Tasks such as dot counting and number comparison depend very little on experience of formal education, as children are able to do them even before they begin school (Fuson, 1988; Gelman & Gallistel, 1978). This suggests that poor performance is unlikely to be due to those exogenous factors that are known to affect school attainment, including inappropriate teaching, missing lessons, and lack of motivation and attention. They are more likely to be due to weak intuitive grasp of numbers and difficulties with understanding basic numerical concepts. Indeed, this is how DD children describe their difficulties. In a focus group study by Bevan and Butterworth, (forthcoming), 9-year-old DD children consistently reported that they did not understand what the teacher was saying.

Child 5: Oh, there's this really hard thing, about when you're doing times—Miss S_____ says you can't take away this number, but I keep on taking away, I don't understand one single bit of it.

Child 2: I sometimes don't understand whatever she (the teacher) says.

Child 2: I don't forget it, I don't even know what she's saying.

Even when they think they understand something, the slightest distraction causes them to lose track:

Child 3: When you listen to the teacher, then you turn your head and you don't know nothing . . . If I remember something, and then the teacher says "stop for a second, just listen to me" then as soon as she talks, yeah, and we come back, we do work, and I say "what do I have to do?" I always forget.

According to the defective number module hypothesis, the other problems faced by dyscalculic learners stem from the lack of an intuitive grasp of number. Thus, poor memory for arithmetical facts and the use of incorrect, immature, or inefficient calculation procedures may all be due to poor understanding of the basic ideas of the cardinality of sets, or what Butterworth (1999) has termed "numerosity."

IS DYSCALCULIA SECONDARY TO MORE GENERAL OR BASIC COGNITIVE DEFICITS?

Many researchers suggest that dyscalculia is secondary to more general or more basic cognitive abilities. The critical issue in this area, put crudely, is this: is dyscalculia a due to a defective number module, or is it the consequence of deficits in domain-general cognitive abilities, such as memory, reasoning, or spatial abilities?

Perhaps the most influential answer to this question comes from a review by Geary (1993). In this paper, Geary notes that DD "children show two basic functional, or phenotypic, numerical deficits":

1. "The use of developmentally immature arithmetical procedures and a high frequency of procedural errors" (p. 346)
2. "Difficulty in the representation and retrieval of arithmetic facts from long-term semantic memory" (p. 346)

Geary assembles evidence to demonstrate that the causes are deficits in long-term semantic memory and in two aspects of working memory, speed of processing and rate of decay of items being retained.

The role of long-term semantic memory is premised on the idea that there is a developmental progression from calculation strategies, such as counting on, to established associations between problems and their solutions (e.g., Siegler, 1988; Siegler & Shrager, 1984). "Mastery of elementary arithmetic is achieved when all basic facts can be retrieved from long-term memory without error ... [which in turn] appears to facilitate the acquisition of more complex mathematical skills" (Geary, 1993, p. 347). According to Geary, laying down these associations in long-term memory depends on maintaining the problem elements (for example, two addends, intermediate results, and solution) in working memory. Additionally, the use of immature or inefficient calculation strategies will risk decay of crucial information in working memory.

Memory span in children with "mathematical disability" (MD; lowest 25–33% of the age group in the following studies) is one digit fewer than controls, and their span is negatively correlated with calculation errors. MD children also seem to count more slowly when carrying out calculation procedures (see Geary, 1993, for review). The implication is that MD children will put a greater load on an already somewhat defective working memory, and this, in turn, will impair long-term storage of basic arithmetical facts. In a more recent study, Koontz and Berch (1996) tested children with and without dyscalculia (more strictly defined) using both digit and letter span (the latter being a measure of phonological working memory capacity which is not confounded with numerical processing). This study found that dyscalculic children performed below average on both span tasks, though IQ was not controlled.

However, the evidence is by no means unequivocal about the role of working memory in learning arithmetic. McLean and Hitch (1999) found no difference on a non-numerical task testing phonological working memory (non–word repetition), suggesting that dyscalculic children do not have reduced phonological working memory capacity in general, although they may have a specific difficulty with working memory for numerical information. Temple and Sherwood (2002) found no differences between groups on any of the working memory measures (forward and backward digit span, word span, and the Corsi blocks) and no correlation between the working memory measures and measures of arithmetic ability. Thus, although various forms of working memory difficulty may well co-occur with math difficulties, there is no convincing evidence implicating any form of working memory as a causal feature in dyscalculia. Landerl, Bevan, and Butterworth (in press) found no difference on forward or backward digit span between DD children and matched controls, though dyslexic children were significantly affected on this task.

Rourke (1993) has argued that DD is essentially due to a defective representation of space. More specifically, Geary (1993) noted that "a disruption of the ability to spatially represent numerical information . . . appears to affect both functional skills (e.g., columnar alignment in complex arithmetic problems) and the conceptual understanding of the representations (e.g., place value)" (p. 346). The idea that space and number are cognitively related has had many supporters, and the role of the parietal lobes in both space and number has been noted by researchers since Gerstmann (1940).

The representation of numerical magnitudes spatially as a kind of a mental number line has frequently been proposed (e.g., Dehaene, Piazza, Pinel, & Cohen, 2003; Fias, Lammertyn, Reynvoet, Dupont, & Orban, 2003; Seron, Pesenti, Noël, Deloche, & Cornet, 1992; Spalding & Zangwill, 1950), and it would seem plausible that deficits in spatial representation ability could affect a sense of numerical magnitude (but see Zorzi, Priftis, & Umiltà, 2002). However, there is no convincing evidence to show that spatial deficits in themselves lead to DD. Being able to maintain mental representations of multidigit numbers in the correct columns has been suggested as another potential contribution of spatial abilities to arithmetic (Dehaene & Cohen, 1995; Hécaen, Angelergues, & Houillier, 1961). In fact, Hécaen et al. (1961) proposed a special category of acquired secondary acalculia they term "spatial acalculia." Such a condition has been rarely, if ever, reported as a pure symptom and does not appear to affect the grasp of basic numerical concepts.

Finally, it is clear that DD is a persistent condition for many and perhaps all of its sufferers. "Charles," an intelligent and industrious graduate, was 30 years old when we first tested him, but despite his best efforts, he was several times slower than controls on single-digit addition and subtraction, was quite unable to do multiplications involving numbers above 5, could not do two-digit subtraction at all, and was severely disabled on dot counting and number comparison. Like other dyscalculics, Charles relied very heavily on finger counting to solve even very simple problems (Butterworth, 1999). We have since tested several other intelligent and well-educated adults who show similar disabilities. Ostad (1999) also notes the persistence of this condition. However, longitudinal studies have not yet been carried out to characterize the long-term development of DD.

THE PROBLEM OF COMORBIDITY

Although there is a high comorbidity between numeracy and literacy disabilities (see Table 26.2), it is unclear why this should be. One possible line of argument here is that there will be a range of numerical and arithmetical tasks that depend on language, and that dyslexia is usually a deficit in language abilities that affects phonological processing (Paulesu et al., 1996), which is known to reduce working memory capacity (Nation, Adams, Bowyer-Crane, & Snowling, 1999), which in turn may affect lexical learning as well (Gathercole, 1995). These considerations imply that dyslexics should have difficulty with fact retrieval, if these are stored in verbal form, and with multidigit arithmetic with high working memory load. The problem with this line of argument, as discussed above, is that, as we have seen, dyscalculics do not have reduced working memory span. Moreover, Shalev, Manor, and Gross-Tsur (1997) found no qualitative difference between children with both reading and math disability and children with math disability only. No quantitative differences on tests of arithmetic, or on simple number tasks such as counting and magnitude comparison, were found between dyscalculic children and those with both dyslexia and dyscalculia when the groups were matched for IQ (Landerl et al., in press).

Rourke (1993) has suggested that those suffering a double deficit will have a left hemisphere problem associated with the linguistic deficit in dyslexia, whereas the pure dyscalculics will have a right hemisphere abnormality affecting spatial abilities, which he believes lies at the root of dyscalculia. However, evidence reviewed here does not support this suggestion.

Other conditions that have been associated with DD are ADHD (Badian, 1983; Rosenberg, 1989; Shalev et al. 2001), poor hand–eye coordination (Siegel & Ryan, 1989), and poor memory for non-verbal material (Fletcher, 1985). Shalev and Gross-Tsur (1993) examined a group of seven children with developmental dyscalculia who were not responding to intervention. All seven were suffering from additional neurological conditions, ranging from petit mal seizures through dyslexia for numbers, attention deficit disorder, and developmental Gerstmann's syndrome, in which dyscalculia goes along with finger agnosia, agraphia, and left–right disorientation. However, it is clear from these studies that the majority of DDs do not have comorbid cognitive, physical, or affective problems.

In summary, although it is clearly the case that dyscalculia is frequently comorbid with other disabilities, causal relationships between the disorders have not been proven. In addition, the utility of subtyping dyscalculics according to neuropsychological or cognitive correlates will not be clear until it has been shown that the different subtypes display qualitatively different patterns of numerical deficit.

THE ORIGINS OF NUMERICAL ABILITIES

Psychologists from Piaget (1952) to Gelman and Gallistel (1978), who traced the ontogeny of numerical concepts, have stressed the child's increasing understanding of why two sets have the same numerosity—one-to-one correspondence between set members—and the kinds of manipulation that will and will not affect numerosity (Piaget's "conservation" experiments). It is also important for the child to understand how to map the set of objects to be counted one to one with the counting words (Gelman & Gallistel, 1978). There is evidence that infants in the first six months of life have an ability to discriminate between sets of visible, even moving, objects on the basis of numerosity (Antell & Keating, 1983; Starkey & Cooper, 1980; Van Loosbroek & Smitsman, 1990) and can mentally represent and manipulate objects no longer visible (Wynn, 1992). This may form the innate basis of a sense of numerosity, which in dyscalculics may be defective.

If this proposal is correct, then there is no reason why dyscalculic children should not be able to learn aspects of mathematics that do not depend crucially on a sense of numerosity, such as geometry, topology, or algebra.

IS THERE A SPECIFIC NEUROANATOMICAL SYSTEM?

The defective number module hypothesis suggests, though it does not entail, that there should be an anatomically discernible system in the brain, which is abnormal in DDs. There is some evidence for a specialized number-processing network in the brain. Functional neuroimaging reveals that the parietal lobes–especially the intraparietal sulci (IPS)–are active in numerical processing and arithmetic (Dehaene et al., 2003); and studies of brain-lesioned patients (Cipolotti & van Harskamp, 2001) have identified the left IPS and the angular gyrus as critical to normal arithmetical performance. Simpler numerical capacities, such as the ability to estimate the numerosity of small sets, appear to be specialized in the right IPS (Piazza, Giacomini, Le Bihan, & Dehaene, 2003; Piazza, Mechelli, Butterworth, & Price, 2002).

To date, it is not known whether the intraparietal sulci underpin infant capacities; hence, their role in subsequent development is far from clear. However, a recent voxel-based morphometric study of the brains of adolescents with poor arithmetic presents intriguing evidence. Isaacs, Edmonds, Lucas, and Gadian (2001) studied two groups of adolescents with very low birth-weight. One group was cognitively normal, whereas the second had a deficit just on the numerical operations subtest of the Wechsler Objective Numerical Dimensions (WOND; Wechsler, 1996). When the brains of these two groups were compared, those with arithmetical impairment had less grey matter in the left IPS.

Another source of evidence comes from reports of a developmental version of Gerstmann's Syndrome (e.g., Kinsbourne & Warrington, 1963). Gerstmann's Syndrome combines the symptom of acquired dyscalculia with finger agnosia (a disability in mental representation of fingers), dysgraphia and left-right disorientation (Gerstmann, 1940). This condition arises following damage to the left angular gyrus, which suggests, on analogy with the acquired version, that some cases of DD may be due damage to the left angular gyrus.

Is There a Specific Genetic Basis?

The defective number module hypothesis suggests that there should be a genetic basis to DD. (Kosc, 1974), in one of the earliest systematic studies of DD, proposed a role for heredity. A recent twin study showed that for DD probands, 58% of monozygotic co-twins and 39% of dizygotic co-twins were also DD and that the concordance rates were 0.73 and 0.56, respectively (Alarcon, Defries, Gillis Light, & Pennington, 1997). In a family study, Shalev et al. (2001) found that approximately half of all siblings of children with DD are also dyscalculic, with a 5–10-times greater risk than for the general population.

Children with Williams Syndrome, who have relatively spared language abilities despite severely impaired cognitive abilities, show abnormalities on simple numerosity tasks such as number comparison and are also much worse on simple numerical tasks such as seriation, counting, and single-digit arithmetic than chronological-age- and mental-age-matched controls and children with Down's Syndrome (Paterson, Girelli, Butterworth, & Karmiloff-Smith, submitted).

Some abnormalities of the X chromosome appear to affect numerical capacities more severely than other cognitive abilities. This is particularly clear in Turner's Syndrome, in which subjects can be at a normal or superior level on tests of IQ, language, and reading, but are severely disabled in arithmetic (Butterworth et al., 1999; Rovet, Szekely, & Hockenberry, 1994; Temple & Carney, 1993; Temple & Marriott, 1998).

However, this is not to rule out the possibility that dyscalculia can also arise through environmental disturbances of neural growth.

Math Anxiety and Dyscalculia

It is now well established that mathematical activities can cause anxiety (Ashcraft, 1995; Hembree, 1990; Richardson & Suinn, 1972) and that these are specific to mathematics and not just to any difficult task (Faust et al., 1996). Anxiety itself is known to have effects on a wide range of cognitive functions, including those that may affect mathematics performance, such as working memory (Eysenck & Calvo, 1992). However, the emotional effects, both long term and short term, of struggling with mathematics tasks that your peers find very easy are, as yet, unknown. A recent focus group study of 9-year-old children (Bevan & Butterworth, forthcoming) revealed that 9-year-old DDs suffered considerable anguish during the daily mathematics lesson:

Focus group 1
Child 5: It makes me feel left out, sometimes.
Child 2: Yeah.

Child 5: When I like—when I don't know something, I wish that I was like a clever person and I blame it on myself—

Child 4: I would cry and I wish I was at home with my mum and it would be—I won't have to do any maths.

Focus group 2

Moderator: How does it make people feel in a math lesson when they lose track?

Child 1: Horrible.

Moderator: Horrible? . . . Why's that?

Child 1: I don't know.

Child 3 (whispers): He does know.

Moderator: Just a guess.

Child 1: You feel stupid.

More able children, of course, are well aware of this and often tease or stigmatize DD classmates:

Child 1: She's like—she's like all upset and miserable, and she don't like being teased.

Child 4: Yeah, and then she goes hide in the corner—nobody knows where she is and she's crying there.

There is no evidence currently, however, that anxiety is causal in DD, though anxiety in math classes is unlikely to lead to improved learning; but it is clear that DD causes considerable anguish to its young sufferers.

CONCLUSIONS

Developmental dyscalculia is a condition with an estimated prevalence similar to dyslexia and which adversely affects school and working life.

DDs show strikingly poor performance on very simple tasks such as number comparison and counting small numbers of dots. It is likely that this is a symptom of a deficit in the capacity to represent and process numerosities. Indeed, young DDs report great difficulty in understanding basic number concepts and quickly find themselves losing track in daily math lessons.

DD does not seem to be a consequence of impairments to domain-general or more basic cognitive abilities such as semantic memory, working memory, spatial abilities, or linguistic abilities. There is well-established evidence for specialized neural circuits for numerical processing in the parietal lobes of the brain, especially the left and right intraparietal sulci and the left angular gyrus, and these areas are neuroanatomically distinct from the regions subserving these other functions. There is some evidence also that adolescents with poor basic numbers skills (possibly DD, though this was not explicitly tested) have reduced grey matter (or increased white matter) in the left IPS (Isaacs et al., 2001).

Dyscalculia appears to be heritable, on the basis of twin studies, and studies of genetically abnormal populations have suggested a possible locus on the X chromosome, though this does not mean that all cases of dyscalculia are inherited.

This combination of highly selective deficits to basic capacities, identifiable specialized neural circuitry, and likely heritability is consistent with the "defective number module hypothesis." A dyscalculia screener has been developed based on this hypothesis, which uses reaction time tasks of counting dots and magnitude comparison to measure basic numerical capacities. It is standardized for U.K. children from 6 to 14 years (Butterworth, 2003).

Compared with dyslexia, DD has been the focus of relatively little research. For dyslexia there is now widespread agreement about criteria, good evidence about the brain systems implicated (Paulesu et al., 1996; Paulesu et al., 2001), and indications of the genes that might be involved (Fisher & DeFries, 2002). For a comparable understanding of DD, we need to establish agreed upon diagnostic criteria, to discover differences in the structure and function of DD brains, and to identify genes that could lead to these differences.

Unlike dyslexia, DD is not widely recognized by governments or by educators. It is still confused, as dyslexia used to be, with stupidity. Using agreed criteria will help with recognition, and also with establishing reliable prevalence estimates that are needed for a proper needs analysis.

Finally, only with better understanding of the nature of developmental dyscalculia can we devise effective ways of helping the millions of our fellow citizens whose lives are blighted by it.

ACKNOWLEDGMENTS

My research into dyscalculia has been supported by the European Union and the U.K. Department of Education and Skills. I am grateful to Anna Bevan, Fulvia Castelli, Eva Ebner, Cres Fernandes of Nelson; Alessia Granà, Karin Landerl, and Lindsay Peer of the British Dyslexia Association; Manuela Piazza, David Skuse, and Dorian Yeo, my collaborators in dyscalculia research. Jamie Campbell was lavish with wise and detailed advice on this chapter: many thanks to him.

REFERENCES

Alarcon, M., Defries, J., Gillis Light, J., & Pennington, B. (1997). A twin study of mathematics disability. *Journal of Learning Disabilities, 30*, 617–623.

Antell, S. E., & Keating, D. P. (1983). Perception of numerical invariance in neonates. *Child Development, 54*, 695–701.

Ashcraft, M. (1995). Cognitive psychology and simple arithmetic: A review and summary of new directions. *Mathematical Cognition, 1*, 3–34.

Badian, N. A. (1983). Arithmetic and nonverbal learning. In H. R. Myklebust (Ed.), *Progress in learning disabilities* (Vol. 5, pp. 235–264). New York: Grune and Stratton.

Bevan, A., & Butterworth, B. (forthcoming). Fractions or friction? The responses of students and teachers to maths disabilities within the National Numeracy Strategy.

Butterworth, B. (1999). *The mathematical brain*. London: Macmillan.

Butterworth, B. (2003). *Dyscalculia Screener*. London: Nelson Publishing Company Ltd.

Butterworth, B., Granà, A., Piazza, M., Girelli, L., Price, C., & Skuse, D. (1999). Language and the origins of number skills: karyotypic differences in Turner's syndrome. *Brain & Language, 69*, 486–488.

Bynner, J., & Parsons, S. (1997). *Does numeracy matter?* London: The Basic Skills Agency.

Cappelletti, M., Butterworth, B., & Kopelman, M. (2001). Spared numerical abilities in a case of semantic dementia. *Neuropsychologia, 39*, 1224–1239.

Cappelletti, M., Kopelman, M., & Butterworth, B. (2002). Why semantic dementia drives you the dogs (but not to the horses): A theoretical account. *Cognitive Neuropsychology, 19*(6), 483–503.

Carey, S., & Spelke, E. (in press). Bootstrapping the integer list: Representations of number. In J. Mehler & L. Bonatti (Eds.), *Developmental cognitive science*. Cambridge, MA: MIT Press.

Cipolotti, L., Butterworth, B., & Denes, G. (1991). A specific deficit for numbers in a case of dense acalculia. *Brain, 114*, 2619–2637.

Cipolotti, L., & van Harskamp, N. (2001). Disturbances of number processing and calculation. In R. S. Berndt (Ed.), *Handbook of neuropsychology* (2nd. ed., Vol. 3). Amsterdam: Elsevier Science.

Dehaene, S., & Cohen, L. (1995). Towards an anatomical and functional model of number processing. *Mathematical Cognition, 1*, 83–120.

Dehaene, S., Piazza, M., Pinel, P., & Cohen, L. (2003). Three parietal circuits for number processing. *Cognitive Neuropsychology, 20*, 487–506.

Dehaene, S., Spelke, E., Pinel, P., Stanescu, R., & Tsivkin, S. (1999). Sources of mathematical thinking: Behavioral and brain-imaging evidence. *Science, 284*(5416), 970–974.

DfES. (2001). *Guidance to support pupils with dyslexia and dyscalculia* (No. DfES 0512/2001). London: Department of Education and Skills.

Eysenck, M. W., & Calvo, M. G. (1992). Anxiety and performance - the processing efficiency theory. *Cognition & Emotion, 6*(6), 409–434.

Faust, M. W., Ashcraft, M. H., & Fleck, D. E. (1996). Mathematics anxiety effects in simple and complex addition. *Mathematical Cognition, 2*(1), 25–62.

Fias, W., Lammertyn, J., Reynvoet, B., Dupont, P., & Orban, G. A. (2003). Parietal representation of symbolic and nonsymbolic magnitude. *Journal of Cognitive Neuroscience, 15*, 47–56.

Fisher, S., & DeFries, J. (2002). Developmental dyslexia: Genetic dissection of a complex cognitive trait. *Nature Review of Neuroscience*, 767–780.

Fletcher, J. F. (1985). Memory for verbal and nonverbal

stimuli in learning disabled subgroups: Analysis by selective reminding. *Journal of Experimental Child Psychology, 40,* 244–259.

Gallistel, C. R., & Gelman, R. (2000). Non-verbal numerical cognition: From reals to integers. *Trends in Cognitive Sciences, 4*(2), 59–65.

Gathercole, S. (1995). Nonword repetition: More than just a phonological output task. *Cognitive Neuropsychology, 12*(8), 857–861.

Geary, D. C. (1993). Mathematical disabilities: Cognition, neuropsychological and genetic components. *Psychological Bulletin, 114,* 345–362.

Geary, D. C., Hamson, C. O., & Hoard, M. K. (2000). Numerical and arithmetical cognition: A longitudinal study of process and concept deficits in children with learning disability. *Journal of Experimental Child Psychology, 77,* 236–263.

Geary, D. C., & Hoard, M. K. (2001). Numerical and arithmetical deficits in learning-disabled children: Relation to dyscalculia and dyslexia. *Aphasiology, 15*(7), 635–647.

Gelman, R., & Gallistel, C. R. (1978). *The child's understanding of number* (1986 ed.). Cambridge, MA: Harvard University Press.

Gerstmann, J. (1940). Syndrome of Finger Agnosia: disorientation for right and left, agraphia and acalculia. *Archives of Neurology and Psychiatry, 44,* 398–408.

Ginsburg, H. P. (1997). Mathematics learning disabilities: A view from developmental psychology. *Journal of Learning Disabilities, 30,* 20–33.

Gross-Tsur, V., Manor, O., & Shalev, R. S. (1996). Development dyscalculia: Prevalence and demographic features. *Developmental Medicine and Child Neurology, 38,* 25–33.

Hécaen, H., Angelergues, R., & Houillier, S. (1961). Les variétés cliniques des acalculies au cours des lésions rétro-rolandiques: Approche statistique du problème. *Revue Neurologique, 105,* 85–103.

Hembree, R. (1990). The nature, effects and relief of mathematics anxiety. *Journal for Research in Mathematics Education, 21*(1), 33–46.

Isaacs, E. B., Edmonds, C. J., Lucas, A., & Gadian, D. G. (2001). Calculation difficulties in children of very low birthweight: A neural correlate. *Brain, 124,* 1701–1707.

Jordan, N. C., Kaplan, D., & Hanich, L. B. (2002). Achievement growth in children with learning difficulties in mathematics: Findings of a two-year longitudinal study. *Journal of Educational Psychology, 96,* 586–597.

Jordan, N., & Montani, T. (1997). Cognitive arithmetic and problem solving: A comparison of children with specific and general mathematics difficulties. *Journal of Learning Disabilities, 30*(6), 624–634.

Jordan, N. C., Kaplan, D., & Hanich, L. B. (2002). Achievement growth in children with learning difficulties in mathematics: Findings of a two-year longitudinal study. *Journal of Educational Psychology, 96,* 586–597.

Kinsbourne, M., & Warrington, E. K. (1963). The developmental Gerstmann Syndrome. *Annals of Neurology, 8,* 490-501.

Kirby, J. R., & Becker, L. D. (1988). Cognitive components of learning problems in arithmetic. *Remedial and Special Education, 9,* 7–16.

Koontz, K. L., & Berch, D. B. (1996). Identifying simple numerical stimuli: processing inefficiencies exhibited by arithmetic learning disabled children. *Mathematical Cognition, 2*(1), 1–23.

Kosc, L. (1974). Developmental dyscalculia. *Journal of Learning Disabilities, 7,* 159–162.

Landerl, K., Bevan, A., & Butterworth, B. (in press) Developmental dyscalculia and basic numerical capacities. A study of 8-9 year old students. *Cognition*

Lewis, C., Hitch, G., & Walker, P. (1994). The prevalence of specific arithmetic difficulties and specific reading difficulties in 9- and 10-year-old boys and girls. *Journal of Child Psychology and Psychiatry, 35,* 283–292.

McLean, J. F., & Hitch, G. J. (1999). Working memory impairments in children with specific arithmetical difficulties. *Journal of Experimental Child Psychology, 74,,* 240–260.

Nation, K., Adams, J. W., Bowyer-Crane, C. A., & Snowling, M. J. (1999). Working memory deficits in poor comprehenders reflect underlying language impairments. *Journal of Experimental Child Psychology, 73*(2), 139–158.

Ostad, S. E. (1999). Developmental progression of subtraction studies: a comparison of mathematically normal and mathematically disabled childre. *European Journal of Special Needs Education, 14*(1), 21–36.

Paterson, S. J., Girelli, L., Butterworth, B., & Karmiloff-Smith, A. *Are numerical impairments syndrome specific? Evidence from Williams Syndrome and Down's Syndrome.* Manuscript submitted for publication.

Paulesu, E., Démonet, J.-F., Fazio, F., McCrory, E., Chanoine, V., Brunswick, N., et al. (2001). Dyslexia: Cultural diversity and biological unity. *Science, 291*(5511), 2165.

Paulesu, E., Frith, U., Snowling, M., Gallagher, A., Morton, J., Frackowiak, R., et al. (1996). Is developmental dyslexia a disconnection syndrome? Evidence from PET scanning. *Brain, 119*(1), 143–157.

Piaget, J. (1952). *The child's conception of number.* London: Routledge & Kegan Paul.

Piazza, M., Giacomini, E., Le Bihan, D., & Dehaene, S. (2003). Single-trial classification of parallel pre-attentive and serial attentive processes using functional magnetic resonance imaging. *Proceedings of the Royal Society B, 270*(1521), 1237–1245.

Piazza, M., Mechelli, A., Butterworth, B., & Price, C. (2002). re subitizing and counting: Implemented as separate or functionally overlapping processes? *NeuroImage, 15*(2), 435–446.

Richardson, F. C., & Suinn, R. M. (1972). The Mathematics Anxiety Rating Scale. *Journal of Counseling Psychology, 19,* 551–554.

Rosenberg, P. B. (1989). Perceptual-motor and attentional correlates of developmental dyscalculia. *Annals of Neurology, 26,* 216–220.

Rourke, B. P. (1993). Arithmetic disabilities, specific and otherwise: A neuropsychological perspective. *Journal of Learning Disabilities, 26,* 214–226.

Rovet, J., Szekely, C., & Hockenberry, M.-N. (1994). Specific arithmetic calculation deficits in children with Turner Syndrome. *Journal of Clinical and Experimental Neuropsychology, 16,* 820–839.

Russell, R. L., & Ginsburg, H. P. (1984). Cognitive analysis of children's mathematical difficulties. *Cognition & Instruction, 1,* 217–244.

Seron, X., Pesenti, M., Noël, M.-P., Deloche, G., & Cornet, J.-A. (1992). Images of numbers, or "When 98 is upper left and 6 sky blue." *Cognition, 44,* 159–196.

Shalev, R. S., & Gross-Tsur, V. (1993). Developmental dyscalculia and medical assessment. *Journal of Learning Disabilities, 26*, 134–137.

Shalev, R. S., & Gross-Tsur, V. (2001). Developmental dyscalculia. Review article. *Pediatric Neurology, 24*, 337–342.

Shalev, R. S., Manor, O., & Gross-Tsur, V. (1997). Neuropsychological aspects of developmental dyscalculia. *Mathematical Cognition, 3*(2), 105–120.

Shalev, R. S., Manor, O., Kerem, B., Ayali, M., Badichi, N., Friedlander, Y., et al. (2001). Developmental dyscalculia is a family learning disability. *Journal of Learning Disabilities, 34*(1), 59–65.

Siegel, L. S., & Ryan, E. B. (1989). The development of working memory in normally achieving and subtypes of learning disabled children. *Child Development, 60*, 973–980.

Siegler, R. S. (1988). Strategy choice procedures and the development of multiplication skill. *Journal of Experimental Psychology: General, 117*, 258–275.

Siegler, R. S., & Shrager, J. (1984). Strategy choices in addition and subtraction: How do children know what to do? In C. Sophian (Ed.), *Origins of Cognitive Skills*. Hillsdale, NJ: Erlbaum.

Spalding, J. M. K., & Zangwill, O. L. (1950). Disturbance of number-form in a case of brain injury. *Journal of Neurology, Neurosurgery and Psychiatry, 13*, 24–29.

Starkey, P., & Cooper, R. G., Jr. (1980). Perception of numbers by human infants. *Science, 210*, 1033–1035.

Temple, C. M. (1991). Procedural dyscalculia and number fact dyscalculia: Double dissociation in developmental dyscalculia. *Cognitive Neuropsychology, 8*, 155–176.

Temple, C. M., & Carney, R. A. (1993). Intellectual functioning in children with Turner's syndrome: A comparison of behavioural phenotypes. *Developmental Medicine and Child Neurology, 35*, 691–698.

Temple, C. M., & Marriott, A. J. (1998). Arithmetical ability and disability in Turner's syndrome: A cognitive neuropsychological analysis. *Developmental Neuropsychology, 14*, 47–67.

Temple, C. M., & Sherwood, S. (2002). Representation and retrieval of arithmetical facts: Developmental difficulties. *Quarterly Journal of Experimental Psychology, 55A*, 733–752.

Van Loosbroek, E., & Smitsman, A. W. (1990). Visual perception of numerosity in infancy. *Developmental Psychology, 26*, 916–922.

Wechsler, D. (1996). Wechsler Objective Numerical Dimensions (WOND). London: The Psychological Corporation.

Wynn, K. (1992). Addition and subtraction by human infants. *Nature, 358*, 749–751.

Zorzi, M., Priftis, K., & Umilta, C. (2002). Brain damage: Neglect disrupts the mental number line. *Nature, 417*(6885) 138–139.

27

Rehabilitation of Acquired Calculation and Number Processing Disorders

Aliette Lochy
Frank Domahs
Margarete Delazer

INTRODUCTION

There is general agreement that patients affected by deficits in number processing are severely handicapped in everyday life. Indeed, number processing is an essential part of our culture. Numbers are used for counting, measuring, comparing, for putting things in a certain order, for distinguishing objects, or for doing simple and complex calculations. Nonetheless, acquired deficits in arithmetic processing are frequently ignored after brain lesions and targeted rehabilitation approaches are still rare (Girelli & Seron, 2001).

What are the aims of rehabilitation in the field of number processing? Though it seems trivial at a first glance, agreement between patients, families, and therapists on the goals is a crucial precondition for successful intervention. As in other fields of rehabilitation, not only the impairment level has to be considered but also the resulting disability and handicap in daily life. Definition at an operational level (i.e., considering the daily handicap) makes numerical rehabilitation meaningful to the patient. For example, a patient might not be very motivated to work on numerical transcoding at an abstract level. However, once he realizes that regained numerical competence will enable him to check his bank account, rehabilitation will become more relevant. In the past, success was mostly measured in cognitive terms, but it has become increasingly clear that rehabilitation outcome should also be defined at an operational level.

At the cognitive level, the aim of intervention should be adaptive expertise (Hatano, 1988), which allows a subject to apply meaningful knowledge to familiar and to unfamiliar tasks (Baroody, 2003; Hatano, 1988). On the contrary, routine expertise is knowledge memorized by rote that can be used effectively with familiar tasks but not with novel ones. Thus, rehabilitation is not very successful if a patient learns to retrieve simple multiplication tables from memory but is unable to apply this knowledge in new situations, such as in complex calculation. Although most people agree on this general aim, less agreement is found on how it can be reached, and it is rarely assessed in daily life improvement. In the literature on mathematics instruction, traditionally two opposing views put emphasis either on skill learning and memory retrieval or on conceptual understanding and active problem solving. However, there are also several approaches that try to integrate rote skill learning and active problem solving.

As will be outlined in this chapter, studies on numerical rehabilitation increasingly take into account cognitive-processing models, but until now they did not bridge the gap between learning theories developed in experimental and developmental psychology on one side and neuropsychological application in brain-lesioned patients on the other. Though numerical rehabilitation has to consider these theories, one should be cautious not to draw parallels that are too simple between teaching children and rehabilitation of acquired deficits. Indeed, there are major differences between these domains due to the specificity of acquired deficits. Contrary to developmental disabilities, such deficits occur in a mature and previously well-organized and stable system, may be highly specific, and concern only one component in the complex numerical system. Such a clear fractionation is not the rule in developmental disabilities, in which the numerical system is by definition unstable and changing.

In the next sections, we focus on calculation and transcoding. In each, we briefly review basic assumptions and evidence stemming from single-case studies. Then we review the main studies of rehabilitation and attempt to integrate some data from learning theories. In a conclusion section, we highlight the main benefits of each described approaches. We then discuss principles of rehabilitation in the number-processing domain and propose perspectives for future research.

CALCULATION

Basic Assumptions and Evidence in Calculation

Arithmetic Facts Are Stored in Long-Term Memory and Can Be Selectively Impaired

In 1982, Warrington reported patient DRC, a consultant physician who, after suffering a left posterior intracerebral hematoma, was no longer able to retrieve answers to simple addition, subtraction, or multiplication problems from memory. Despite these severe problems with arithmetic facts, DRC showed a relatively preserved performance in additional tasks including complex calculation, estimation, approximation, and definition of arithmetic operations. The distinction between fact knowledge and general arithmetic processing has been incorporated into all neuropsychological models of calculation proposed later.

Arithmetic Fact-Retrieval Deficits May Be Operation Specific

Though multiplication is often the most compromised operation (McCloskey, 1992), a simple effect of operation difficulty cannot account for the observed error patterns across patients. Indeed, selectively preserved multiplication with impaired addition and subtraction was reported (Dehaene & Cohen, 1997; Delazer & Benke, 1997). In some patients subtraction has been found to be better preserved than multiplication and addition (Dagenbach & McCloskey, 1992). In other cases, operation-specific deficits interacted with modality-specific deficits (McNeil & Warrington, 1994).

Arithmetic Facts and Rules May Dissociate

In simple multiplication, McCloskey and coworkers (e.g., McCloskey, 1992) distinguished between three subsets of problems on the basis of error patterns after brain damage: 0s problems (all problems involving 0 as operand), 1s problems (all problems involving 1 as operand) and 2–9 problems (2×2 through 9×9). Whereas the first two subsets are thought to be answered by a stored rule, only the problems of the last subset are thought to be stored and retrieved from memory individually.

Arithmetic Facts and Arithmetic Procedures May Dissociate

Beyond the broad distinction between procedures and facts, recent studies attempt to demonstrate dissociations within the procedural component of the calculation system. In some case studies, patients' difficulties with multi-digit calculation were demonstrated to result from distorted knowledge of procedures (Girelli & Delazer, 1996), whereas in other cases (Semenza, Miceli, & Girelli, 1997) difficulties seemed to arise from deficient monitoring of the calculation procedures' execution.

Arithmetic Fact Knowledge and Conceptual Knowledge May Dissociate

Double dissociations between fact knowledge and conceptual knowledge (e.g., commutativity) point to the independence of these components within the cognitive system. Some patients may lose all conceptual understanding of arithmetic but preserve part of the memorized fact knowledge, whereas others show severe deficits in retrieving facts despite excellent conceptual knowledge (Delazer, 2003).

Approximate and Exact Processing May Dissociate

The dissociation between impaired exact calculation and preserved approximate processing observed by Warrington (1982) was later replicated in a neuropsychological case study by Dehaene and Cohen (1991). This patient erred even with the simplest calculation problems (e.g., $2 + 2 = 3$). In multiple-choice tasks, however, he easily rejected distant false results ($2 + 2 = 9$), whereas he accepted false results close in magnitude to the correct one ($2 + 2 = 5$). Dehaene and Cohen thus suggested two distinct systems in number processing—one for exact symbols and the other for approximate magnitudes.

The above-outlined characteristics of the number-processing system and its possible impairments after acquired deficits illustrate the necessity of a detailed and theoretically driven assessment. It should focus on all components of number processing, including counting, parity and magnitude judgments, arithmetic fact knowledge, complex mental calculation, approximate calculation, written calculation, arithmetic reasoning, and conceptual knowledge. Importantly, assessment should not focus only on the number of correct responses but also on how these responses were reached. Answers to simple calculation problems may be retrieved from memory or, alternatively, they may be reached via back-up strategies like counting or decomposing the problem into several steps. Such strategies may be more or less efficient, they may be conceptually based, or they may be executed as a stored procedure (Delazer, 2003). Importantly, the nature of errors should be carefully analyzed. For example, the error $7 \times 8 = 63$ is table-related and is produced also quite often by normal individuals, but the error $2 \times 8 = 73$ points to a more severe deficit: it indicates not only a deficit in retrieving arithmetic facts but also difficulties in monitoring, plausibility judgment, and approximation.

In the next section, studies on the rehabilitation of arithmetic abilities will be reviewed. Due to space limitations, we will focus on simple arithmetic.

REHABILITATION OF SIMPLE ARITHMETIC USING DRILL

The majority of attempts to regain the skill of simple calculation have relied on drill (i.e., extensive repetition). In most cases, problems were frequently presented to the patient who was asked to answer them, getting instant feedback about his results. The rationale for this method relies on associative-learning principles, shared by most current models of arithmetical facts (Ashcraft, 1995; Campbell, 1987; Siegler, 1988), and supposes that traces of arithmetical facts in declarative memory have different levels of activation that determine their rate and probability of being retrieved. All these models converge on the idea that (a) skilled performance reflects retrieval from memory; (b) in a retrieval attempt, multiple facts become active and their activation level depends on the similarities they share with the problem; and (c) all active representations then compete in an interactive-activation-like process until one representation reaches a sufficient level of activation to be selected as the answer. These assumptions are based on strong empirical data such as associative confusion errors (operation, operand, or table related), priming or interference effects.

The principle of errorless learning (Glisky, Schacter, & Tulving, 1986), applied in rehabilitation by providing instant feedback or by learning problems together with their answers in order to prevent erroneous associations from being established or strengthened, converges with associative learning theories. In the developmental domain, the *distribution of associations model* (Siegler, 1988) proposes that each solution of a problem (including incorrect ones) leads to the storage of an association in long term memory (LTM). This generates different distributions of associations between terms and answers, "peaked" on the correct answer for problems that provoked very few errors (i.e., easy problems) and "flat" for problems that gave rise to more errors. In the latter case, the correct answer will be less strongly associated since more false associations are stored. Errorless learning might be of capital importance, particularly in the case of memory-impaired subjects, as it has been shown that amnesic patients are more disturbed by errors than are healthy subjects (Glisky et al., 1986). To reach this goal, it might at first sight seem safer to train patients by asking them to rote-memorize problems along with the correct answer (e.g., $3 \times 4 = 12$) with a high exposure to the same facts in order to reach the frequency criterion. If asking the patient to solve a presented problem (e.g., $3 \times 4 = ?$), priming data from normal subjects (Campbell, 1987) suggest to prime the correct answer before presenting the problem in order to increase the probability of its retrieval and diminish the generation of errors.

Kashiwagi, Kashiwagi, and Hasegawa (1987) used drill to reestablish the retrieval of simple arithmetic facts in eight chronic aphasic subjects. All patients showed preserved addition and subtraction but severely impaired multiplication and division. Exercises addressed in four sets the tables of two successive multiplicands from 2 and 3 to 8 and 9, respectively, and a stable success criterion of 80% accuracy had to be achieved before starting with the following set. After 1 or 2 months of daily training and additional homework, all participants improved significantly in the retrieval of multiplication facts. However, this was only true for the visual-written route, targeted by the intervention. The auditory-verbal route, on the other hand, virtually exclusively used in healthy Japanese subjects, did not improve. Thus, a successful reorganization of fact retrieval had taken place; the auditory-verbal route affected by aphasia was replaced by the visual-written route, relatively preserved.

As Warrington (1982) stated, impaired calculation performance may also manifest itself in increased response latencies. Hittmair-Delazer, Semenza, and Denes (1994) used drill to regain the retrieval of multiplication facts in BE, a 45-year-old accountant, who revealed a highly selective deficit affecting the retrieval of multiplication or division facts from memory. Although back-up strategies mostly led to the correct result, they were effortful and time consuming. Accordingly, the therapy aimed at a reduction of BE's response latencies by training under time pressure. Guessing was discouraged and errors instantly corrected. All problems that BE could not retrieve from memory were divided into two sets, and each was trained separately in an ABACA design, A denoting test sessions, B training of one set, and C training of the other. Training comprised sessions of about 1 hour, twice weekly, over 4 weeks for each set. Improvement turned out to be specific to the trained problems. No significant transfer was observed for nontrained problems, including the complements of the trained set (e.g., 3 × 4; complement: 4 × 3). Such highly specific improvement could be interpreted as evidence for a separate representation of arithmetic facts in memory. Interestingly, BE was able to apply the relearned simple multiplication problems in complex written calculation as well as in division problems.

A comparable method of training was used by Girelli, Delazer, Semenza, and Denes (1996) for TL and ZA, who had almost completely lost the multiplication tables (9% and 19% correct, respectively). Calculation training took place twice weekly over 8 weeks. Problems were presented visually and at the same time read aloud by the therapist. The patients were allowed to answer in their preferred modality. Instant feedback was provided and errors were discussed with the patients if necessary.

Training led to long-lasting improvements, evidenced by accuracy rates of more than 90%. Remediation effects were stronger for trained compared to nontrained problems, but some overall generalization took place, too. Interestingly, the quality of errors also changed substantially, errors becoming more plausible. While TL produced mainly nontable errors before training (e.g., 2 × 9 = 44), close operand errors became characteristic afterward (e.g., 6 × 3 = 21). The error pattern of ZA changed from dominating nontable errors and omissions to close-miss errors (e.g., 5 × 6 = 31). Girelli et al. (1996) explained the different kinds of errors typical for each patient after training as resulting from different back-up strategies: whereas reciting the multiplication table triggered operand errors in TL, calculation errors in repeated addition, which was used as back-up strategy by ZA, caused close-miss answers (e.g., 4 × 5 = 5 + 5 + 5 + 5 = 21). The patients were able to apply the newly gained knowledge in new contexts as simple divisions or text problems.

Whetstone (1998) described the rehabilitation of a specific impairment for the retrieval of multiplication facts for MC, a 42-year-old computer programmer who had undergone surgical removal of a brain tumor. Trained problems were divided into three matched sets, trained in one specific format only (spoken verbal, written verbal, and Arabic format). Problems were presented together with their results for training; thus, no actual production but, instead memorizing was required. However, each training session was preceded and followed by a test in which the solution should be produced without feedback. In terms of accuracy, this intervention resulted in a stable performance, reaching the normal range (97% correct). A closer look at MC's response latencies, however, revealed a match effect: he was faster to respond to problems presented in the trained format (match condition) than in a nontrained format (nonmatch condition).

Domahs, Lochy, Eibl, and Delazer (2004) reported the rehabilitation of simple multiplication in ME, a 38-year-old man who had suffered from a traumatic brain injury three years before their study. At the time of the examination, ME was able to work part-time in a purchasing department but complained about difficulties in calculation. Indeed, although his basic numerical knowledge and transcoding were mainly preserved, his performance in multiplication and division was clearly disturbed. Again, this disturbance was not evidenced in accuracy (98.0% and 93.3% correct, respectively) but in dramatically increased response latencies of up to 90 seconds. During training, problems were initially presented in colors indicating the second digit of the result. For example, problems 4 × 3, 6 × 2, and 9 × 8 were all presented in yellow, because yellow indicated a "2" in the unit position of the result. This colored presentation was able to facilitate retrieval by increasing speed and accuracy. After all, the patient was able to produce his answers significantly faster even without colored cues. Although there was transfer of this improvement to complements of trained problems (e.g., 4 × 3 and 3 × 4) and even to nontrained multiplication problems, no improvement was observed for other basic operations of arithmetic (e.g., subtraction).

The studies reviewed up to this point have used drill to regain access to facts. In this approachl in which errorless memorization and higher efficiency in retrieva are the aim, some other suggestions from learning theories may be useful in rehabilitation.

For instance, is there an ideal number of facts to be trained at once? Actually, data diverge. Although learning rate was the same whatever the number of facts to be learned (e.g., 6, 12, or 18) when assessed per presentation rate of each item in Logan and Klapp's study (1991), other authors found that the acquisition of skill was faster the fewer the number of different addends given in one session (Haider & Kluwe, 1994).

Similarly, Graham (1987) and Campbell and Graham (1985) favor the idea that the context in which facts are learned, i.e., the number of facts, their similarity, and their presentation order, is an important key to their memorizability. In a training study of children on multiplication facts (Graham, 1987), the order in which problems were learned influenced greatly their retrieval times, even overriding the classical size effect. The authors stress the importance of emphasizing accuracy and reducing possible confusion between problems. They propose to reduce times-table relations by not training the facts in the context of tables and to enhance the distinctiveness of the learned facts (e.g., different operands, products differing in magnitude, no problems that share the same result). They suggest to divide the facts into sets of maximum six items, to train the most difficult problems first, and to adopt a strict performance criterion before moving to any new set. Also, any explicit heuristic to limit the amount of false candidates should be used (e.g., all answers to 5 × problems end in 0 or 5). Obviously, some of these propositions (e.g., difficult items first) contrast with problem-solving approaches of arithmetic acquisition, which assume that better competence is developed if facts are acquired by discovering regularities and relationships between problems.

REHABILITATION OF SIMPLE ARITHMETIC USING CONCEPTUAL TRAINING

Simple calculation can be perceived as a complex interaction between simple retrieval from memory, execution of procedures, and application of conceptual knowledge (Delazer, 2003). Thus, in addition to drill, the rehabilitation of simple calculation can, in principle, also concentrate on the improvement of procedural or conceptual knowledge. We are not aware of any neuropsychological investigation focusing exclusively on the former aspect, but comparison of efficiency in retrieval reached by rote-memorizing problems or solving problems with the execution of given procedures has been investigated in experimental studies with healthy subjects. Logan and Klapp (1991) contrasted learning by doing and learning by remembering alphabet–arithmetic facts (e.g., A + 2 = C). Subjects reached the same automaticity criterion (i.e., a zero-slope increment as a function of the addend size) in 1-hour rote memorizing as with extensive practice. With the latter method, a shift from algorithmic solution to memory retrieval required approximately 60 presentations of each fact. Thus, both training methods may lead to automaticity and could be considered in rehabilitation.

Not only skill learning and efficient fact retrieval, but also conceptual learning, should be taken into account in planning rehabilitation. There have been at least two studies using such an approach.

In a recent investigation, Girelli, Bartha, and Delazer (2002) addressed the reactivation of conceptual knowledge. FS, a 64-year-old retired bank employee, showed a consistent deficit in multiplication. Remarkably, FS failed to use back-up strategies by himself, even when he was encouraged to work out the solution and to emphasize accuracy over speed. Given that pattern, a targeted training was planned, based on the strategic use of his residual knowledge and explicit reference to principles that underlie simple arithmetic (e.g., commutativity, decomposition). This should enable FS to derive unknown solutions from the problems he could still answer automatically and at the same time reduce the amount of information to be memorized. For each problem the patient was taught a specific back-up strategy (e.g., $2 \times 4 = 4 \times 2$; $3 \times 4 = 3 \times 3 + 3$; $3 \times 9 = 3 \times 10 - 3$). He trained a first set of problems during 1 week twice a day and a second set of different problems during another week. Both sets were matched for pre-training accuracy and problem size. After the first week, accuracy increased for both the trained and the untrained set, although less pronounced for the latter. After the second week of training, FS improved to ceiling. Moreover, he applied strategies to problems that differed from the ones taught to him. Both good generalization and the creative use of strategies demonstrate the high flexibility of conceptual knowledge.

A direct comparison between conceptual training and drill was reported by Domahs, Bartha, and Delazer (2003). HV, a 87-year-old former manager, presented with a severe loss of his mathematical abilities. He answered simple multiplication problems slowly and reluctantly and was only 5.3% correct. Obviously, he had not only lost access to multiplication facts in memory but also conceptual knowledge about this operation. Therefore, during the initial five sessions, HV was explained the principle of multiplication as repeated addition, an operation which was relatively well preserved. To illustrate this principle, the multiplication results were symbolized by figures on a computer screen, ordered in lines and columns according to the two operands (see Figure 27.1). A second step consisted in six sessions of traditional verbal repetition. Tasks were presented visually and verbally, and instant feedback was provided. After rehabilitation, a general improvement was observed in HV's multiplication performance: he reached 63.6% accuracy after the conceptual training and 70.0% accuracy after the verbal repetition training. Crucially, conceptual training led to a benefit to both the trained and the untrained sets, whereas after drill HV improved only for the trained problems. A qualitative error analysis revealed that errors (operation and far-miss pretraining) became much more plausible (operand errors).

Thus, conceptual rehabilitation approaches to simple calculation have proven quite successful after relatively few sessions. Importantly, conceptual knowledge, explained with only a selection

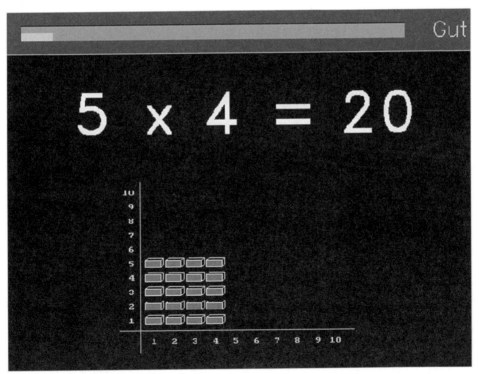

Figure 27.1. Visualization of a multiplication task (5 × 4) as repeated addition as used for patient HV (Domahs et al., 2003); software: R-PLAET 5.4 (Traeger-Verlag, Lotte, Germany, 1994, reproduction with kind permission).

of problems or problem-strategy associations, was flexibly applied to new contexts. Even when accuracy failed to reach ceiling, the patient's errors became more plausible due to newly applied strategies. As developmental research also suggests, different kinds of knowledge (declarative, procedural, and conceptual) should not be emphasized in isolation but, rather, should be regarded as iterative or intertwined (for a review, see Baroody, 2003).

DISCUSSION

This overview shows that arithmetic disorders are sensitive to intervention, even under unfavorable circumstances (e.g., patients in the chronic stage, with severe impairments, with accompanying deficits, or in an advanced age). In studies focusing on accuracy, patients improved by at least 40% or to a normal level of performance. Quantitative improvements were often paralleled by a qualitative change of the error pattern, from highly implausible to more plausible errors. Finally, significantly faster responses were reached in all reported studies focusing on fluency. However, consequences concerning the patients' handicap in daily life have almost never been reported.

In the evaluation of specific intervention strategies, assessment of transfer and generalization effects are of importance. This issue has been addressed in some rehabilitation studies but also in several training studies with healthy subjects using repetition and drill (Campbell, 1987; Fendrich, Healy, & Bourne, 1993; Rickard, Healy, & Bourne, 1994). Generally, training problems are presented in one order (6 × 8) and transfer to other problems is assessed (complementary order [8 × 6], other operation [48:8; 48:6], new problems [4 × 5]). Transfer to new problems does rarely occur, which supports the claim that skilled performance in arithmetic is based on retrieval of individual facts rather than application of a procedure. Even a negative effect has been observed on untrained problems immediately after training (Campbell, 1987), probably reflecting the higher interference due to competition among multiple facts during retrieval. Little or no transfer is observed between arithmetic operations but well between complement problems (Fendrich et al., 1993; Rickard et al., 1994), suggesting that they access a common representation unit. Findings of rehabilitation studies converge with the mentioned training studies: drill produced relatively specific effects (i.e., little generalization or flexible application to other problems), in particular when improvement was measured in terms of latency. When accuracy was the critical variable, slightly better generalization effects were reported. In contrast, conceptual training allowed better transfer and generalization to untrained problems and new situations.

The choice of the method in rehabilitation, either conceptually based or emphasizing drill and repetition, will depend on the goals, abilities, and limitations of the patient. Conceptual training will provide better understanding and adaptive knowledge. Indeed, patients are then able to develop back-up strategies and show good generalization effects. However, solving problems via strategies requires executive functions (e.g., working memory, planning, and monitoring) and may be effortful and time consuming. On the other hand, repeated exposure to the problem will be the appropriate method if the aim is a more efficient retrieval. But in most cases of calculation deficits, pure drill will not lead to well-connected and meaningful knowledge. Importantly, skills not supported by concepts remain error prone and inflexible.

However, skills and concepts should not be seen as opposite poles. As findings from developmental research suggest, advances in skills and conceptual knowledge may be seen in an iterative relation (Baroody, 2003). Conceptual knowledge may lead to advances in procedures, the application of which can lead to improved knowledge and so forth. Adopting this iterative view, intervention in one domain may lead to benefits in the other.

Rehabilitation studies summarized in this chapter are concerned with numerical deficits and their remediation and do not specifically consider other neuropsychological deficits. However, numerical deficits are frequently associated with other cognitive impairments, such as lack of monitoring and planning, aphasia, visuo-spatial problems, or reduced working memory. Main guidelines regarding accompanying deficits may be proposed for rehabilitation attempts. In the case of aphasia, assessment should use visually presented material and nonverbal answer modalities (e.g., multiple-choice tasks). Similarly, rehabilitation of calculation deficits may be based on nonverbal routines first and involve verbal comprehension and production later on. In the case of working memory impairment, a patient may not be able to elaborate mental back-up strategies relying on working memory resources (e.g., for the problem 8×7: $5 \times 8 = 40$, $2 \times 8 = 16$, $40 + 16 = 56$). Strategies require planning, retrieval of facts, storage of intermediate results, and constant updating. Thus, patients with limited working memory capacities and fact-retrieval deficits should particularly profit from a training aiming at direct retrieval of arithmetic facts.

Finally, the importance of self-monitoring processes or strategies should not be neglected, as they are important aspects in rehabilitation. For instance, access to arithmetic facts themselves might be impaired, but not the approximation and magnitude system (Dehaene & Cohen, 1991). If a patient shows preserved abilities in nonexact quantity-based manipulations, a specific training to use this knowledge in exact calculation might be of great help in self-correcting implausible results and lead to a more autonomous life with an acquired deficit.

TRANSCODING

Besides calculation, numerical processing implies the ability to transcode, i.e., to transform a number presented in one input format (e.g., verbal, such as "twenty five") into another output format (e.g., Arabic such as "25").

Basic Assumptions and Evidence in Transcoding

Transcoding Deficits May Be Selective for Production or Comprehension

Patients showing a dissociation between intact comprehension and impaired production processes have been repeatedly described, as well as the reverse dissociation (e.g., Benson & Denckla, 1969). Comprehension and production processes are measured through the ability to understand or produce a given number format in a context other than transcoding. For instance, if a patient commits errors in writing Arabic numbers to dictation but is able to understand verbally presented numbers to compare their size, then his impairment most probably stems from production rather than comprehension processes.

Transcoding Deficits May Concern One or More Numerical Formats

Specific deficits for the verbal or Arabic format have been observed in comprehension as well as in production (McCloskey & Caramazza, 1987; Noël & Seron, 1993). A patient may have intact comprehension (for both formats) but selective deficits in producing numbers in Arabic format (Cipolotti, Butterworth, & Warrington, 1994; Noël & Seron, 1995). Within the verbal format, dissociations between modalities have also been evidenced in lexical processing (McCloskey, 1992).

Transcoding Deficits May Be Specific for One Processing Stage, Such as Lexical or Syntactic Processing

Lexical processing involves comprehension or production of the individual elements in a number, whereas syntactic processing involves processing of relations among the elements in order to comprehend or produce a numeral as a whole. Typical errors would be to produce 58 for 56

at a lexical level and 5,004 for 504 at a syntactic level. Dissociation between these two mechanisms has also been repeatedly found (e.g., Noël & Seron, 1995).

Transcoding May Be Influenced by the Meaning of a Numeral

Neuropsychological case studies (Cipolotti & Butterworth, 1995; Cohen, Dehaene, & Verstichel,
1994; Delazer & Girelli, 1997) suggest that the production of a verbal numeral may be facilitated when a specific meaning is attributed to this numeral (e.g., encyclopedic knowledge such
as 1918, or within a calculation task). This effect has been attributed to facilitation at the
semantic level (Delazer & Girelli, 1997), to a separate transcoding route accessing a numerical
visual input lexicon (Cohen et al., 1994), or to multiple semantic and asemantic routes (Cipolotti
& Butterworth, 1995).

REHABILITATION OF TRANSCODING

Few studies have attempted to perform a well-controlled rehabilitation of transcoding deficits.
We report two detailed examples hereunder, based on different theoretical perspectives of
transcoding, an asemantic one (Deloche & Seron, 1982; Seron & Deloche, 1983) and a semantic
one (McCloskey, 1992). These two perspectives lead to very different views of rehabilitation of
transcoding; hence, we present a training study of a developmental disorder within McCloskey's
model, as there is, to our knowledge, no rehabilitation of acquired deficit realized within this
perspective until now. We then discuss some data from the neuropsychological and developmental
domain that may suggest directions for future rehabilitation studies.

RULES AND ALGORITHMS

A first rehabilitation study of transcoding processes (Deloche, Seron, & Ferrand, 1989) reported
two treatment programs (from the verbal-to-Arabic code and vice versa) framed according to
the asemantic model of Deloche and Seron (1987). In this view, transcoding is considered as an
algorithm operating on the input format to produce the output format without elaboration of
the quantity represented.

The programs were designed according to errorless learning and vanishing cues principles.
Prevention of errors was ensured by giving facilitating information and constraining the
action of the patient, to lower the probability of committing an error. The programs were also
modular in the sense that they worked on separate aspects of transcoding separately (e.g.,
parsing the input form vs. applying rules on it). Also, high experimental constraints were
introduced, such as reaching a 90% accuracy criterion before moving on to a further step. The
programs were strictly designed into separate levels devoted to specific transcoding patterns
(e.g., first level: 2-digit numbers, second level: numbers with "hundred," etc). Each level was
further subdivided into steps focusing on a specific rule and its associated exceptions. Any
new level introduced only one new rule, and stimuli were designed to imply only known rules
that had to be integrated in a new context (e.g., inserting a teen within a 3-digit number).
Finally, each step involved training under several experimental conditions applying the method
of vanishing cues. An example is depicted in Figure 27.2.

At the beginning of a new step, the patient was given a list of correspondences (Arabic
numbers and verbal names) with different colors associated with positions (see Figure 27.2).
The frame where the patient had to write the answer was labeled with the same color code.
These cues were taken away in successive steps, at each of which the patient had to reach 90%
accuracy. The first program, from Arabic-to-verbal numbers, lasted for 25 sessions (three per
week for 2 months). Performance was assessed 1 and 7 months posttraining. Improvement was
substantial (from 45% of errors to 0% at post1) and remained stable (6% at post2). Effects of

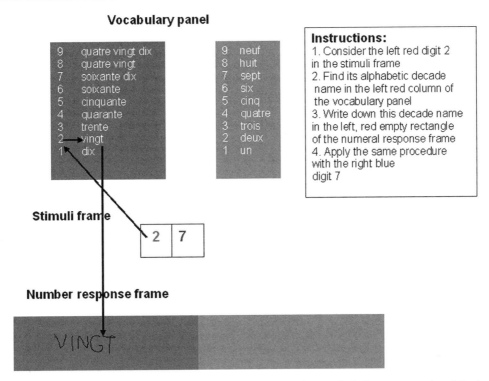

Figure 27.2. Example of frames used in the transcoding rehabilitation study of Deloche, Seron, and Ferrand (1989). At this level, the writing of decade-units is trained (see explanation in text).

training were not item specific, and they generalized also to a nontrained modality (from tokens to verbal). The second program, from verbal-to-Arabic numbers, consisted of 17 sessions and lasted for 8 weeks. The posttests took place 1 and 12 months after training. Improvement was observed in the trained modality (from 29% of errors to 2% at post1 and 0% at post2) but also in an untrained one (verbal to tokens, 35% to 5% of errors). Again, training generalized to new items and was stable in time.

These two cases are successful examples of therapies using the general principles of programmed learning, consisting of training procedures or rules in a logically organized manner, after a detailed analysis of the different steps required to perform the task. Results are consistent with the asemantic and procedural perspective of transcoding, as both patients reacquired successfully the transcoding operations without ever training the comprehension of underlying quantities and showed generalization of rules to untrained problems.

BUILDING FRAMES BASED ON SEMANTICS FOR WRITING NUMBERS

The second study involved a 13-year-old young man, CM, who presented with developmental dyscalculia (Sullivan, Macaruso, & Sokol, 1996) and committed errors when required to transcode numbers mostly from verbal to Arabic format (50% accuracy). Errors were mostly of the syntactic type, as they changed the overall size of the number, which contained too many or too few zeros (e.g., "three thousand five hundred two" written 30502; or "sixty six thousand one hundred five" written 6615). Sullivan et al. (1996) designed the rehabilitation program based on the theoretical propositions of McCloskey's model as concerns verbal-to-Arabic transcoding (see Figure 27.3).

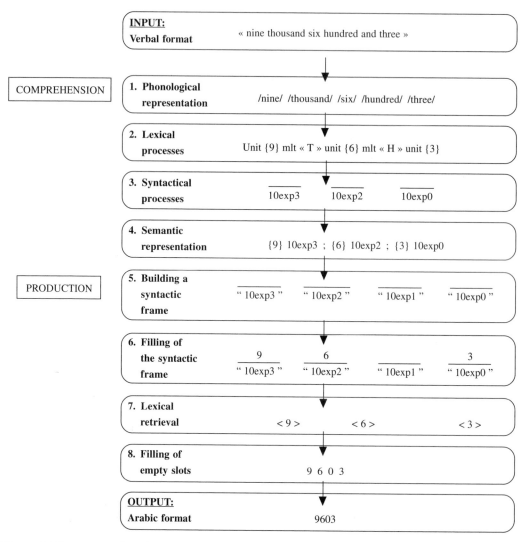

Figure 27.3. Transcoding from the verbal to the Arabic format in McCloskey's model (derived from Sullivan et al., 1996). The first three steps belong to the comprehension system and lead to the building of a semantic representation; the last four steps are part of the production processes specific for the Arabic format. Mlt H and T mean "multipliers" for hundred and thousand, respectively.

CM performed normally in tasks such as verbal number comparison, thus showing intact comprehension and access to semantic representation. In McCloskey's model, this representation holds number-basic values and their associated power of tens (e.g., "three thousand five hundred two" is <3>10exp3; <5>10exp2; <2>10exp0), and it is the basis for production processes. In the case of Arabic writing, the highest power of ten generates a syntactic frame containing empty slots to be filled in (see Figure 27.3). CM's impairment is located at this level: in his case, the frame would not contain the adequate number of slots. At further production steps, intact lexical processes correctly retrieve the digits corresponding to the represented basic quantities and place them into the frame. Finally, remaining empty slots are filled with the digit 0. An incorrect number of zeros are produced because the frame does not contain the correct number of slots.

The remediation program consisted of two training sessions of 45 minutes each in which CM was required to write 120 Arabic numbers from the written verbal modality. The spoken verbal modality was not trained, in order to examine if benefits of the program generalize to both formats.

Training consisted of teaching the patient to create frames containing the correct number of slots based on the size of the verbal number, derived from multiplier words, and to place quantities at appropriate slots within it. Very explicitly, the authors taught him to write down three slots when the word "hundred" is encountered, four slots for "thousand," and so on. Then they taught him to detect and recognize decades, teens, etc., and to place them in correct positions.

Effects of training were assessed at two sessions, 2 and 4 weeks posttraining. Error rates diminished first greatly (50% to 25% for the trained modality and 50% to 10% for the nontrained one) but then increased again (30% errors in both modalities). Syntactic errors diminished more in the trained modality (-33%, ratio of 2.8) than in the nontrained modality (-12%, ratio of 2.1). Finally, lexical errors also decreased, although this aspect of processing was not trained explicitly and suggests a benefit of the training situation in itself (being confronted with numerical material).

To sum up, this study shows benefits of a fast training program on syntactic mechanisms at the Arabic output level, which, however, do not seem to be very stable in time. Maybe some careful repetitive training would be able to stabilize the acquired knowledge.

NEUROPSYCHOLOGICAL AND DEVELOPMENTAL DATA AS CUES FOR REHABILITATION

Semantics and Monitoring

Some case studies highlight the role of monitoring and context in transcoding tasks, which could be cues for future rehabilitation research. For instance, DM, a 56-year-old man, produced syntactic errors in writing Arabic numbers (Cipolotti et al., 1994). At the end of the second testing session, he realized that he was committing mistakes and spontaneously self-corrected himself afterward. At the third session, his performance was suddenly perfect. This points to the role of awareness and monitoring in writing numbers, which could be raised simply by asking the patient to read aloud his own productions—of course, if the reading of Arabic numbers has been proven to function normally.

Two striking case studies evidence the potential positive role of a semantic context in transcoding. The first patient, ZA, committed approximately 30% of errors (most of the lexical type) in reading aloud Arabic numbers (Delazer & Girelli, 1997). However, when ZA was required to read the same numbers in semantic contexts (Alpha Romeo - 164) or to think about semantic properties of the number before reading it, his performance became better. The second case showing sensitivity to context was reported in an Alzheimer patient, YC (Thioux, Ivanoiu, Turconi, & Seron, 1999). Although more and more shift errors (i.e., intrusion of the verbal format into writing Arabic numbers, such as "4hundred20" for 420) were observed with the progress of the disease, the Arabic format was significantly better preserved when numbers were to be written in a calculation context.

These results suggest that transcoding numbers is not an all-or-none process but that different levels of processing may influence performance. The current data cannot disentangle two possible interpretations about the exact way a semantic context helps transcoding: either it activates another (semantic) transcoding route or it enhances the required activation level to apply the transcoding algorithm. In any case, these observations strongly suggest testing of transcoding abilities in several tasks, implying different types of processing or knowledge (encyclopedic knowledge, quantity-based processing, meaningful context such as calculation or prices vs. direct/without context transcoding). If the patient shows better performance in some tasks, a possible direction for rehabilitation could then lie in teaching strategies such as activating a supporting context in a transcoding situation.

DRILL IN TRANSCODING?

In another view, data from the developmental field suggest possible benefits of a drill approach in transcoding. Indeed, when learning to transcode, children have particular difficulties at the syntactical level, especially with sum relationships (Seron & Fayol, 1994), which manifest by errors such as "one hundred two" written 1002. Comparison of kinematics data from children and adults in handwriting Arabic numbers (Lochy, 2001) shows that such numbers, when written correctly, involve costly composition procedures at the beginning of the learning process, whereas in adulthood they do not necessitate complex procedures anymore. Frequency of processing could lead either to storage and retrieval of some numbers in an Arabic output lexicon or to automatization of specific procedures. In any case, this perspective could be useful in rehabilitation attempts.

DISCUSSION

Rehabilitation studies of transcoding abilities illustrated here were based on two different approaches directly driven by the underlying theoretical models. The first approach required a detailed analysis of each single step from one format to the other, leading to a strictly designed, hierarchical learning program. This type of program invested a lot of time but yielded long-lasting effects, presumably because it reached the goal of reestablishing clearly identified procedures. On the other hand, a very short training program, teaching explicitly to identify correspondences between some categories of words, size of number, and an appropriate frame also led to improved performance but was not stable for the long term. Also, differences between the trained and nontrained input modality (written) were observed and question the model, since the damaged syntactic component targeted by the training is supposed to be the same, whatever the modality of input. However, some peculiarities in these effects could also stem from the fact that CM was a developmental case of transcoding impairment. It would be worth applying some of these methods in acquired deficits in the future.

Finally, examples of possible hints for rehabilitation were given through case studies showing a complete recovery after awareness of errors, which illustrates the role of monitoring based on remaining transcoding abilities in rehabilitation. Also, far better performance was observed when a semantic meaning was given to the numbers, pointing to a possible benefit of activating different types of representations in transcoding. Besides semantic contexts, working with analogical material that mimics the verbal or the Arabic format may also be a direction of future rehabilitation studies. For instance, the use of tokens representing the lexical primitives of the verbal system (units, tens, hundreds) is common, but to our knowledge none has ever used material representing the Arabic base-ten positional system and the placeholder role of 0 (source of most difficulties in Arabic production deficits).

Finally, acquisition of transcoding by children suggests that some frequently processed numbers could be stored and retrieved as a whole in lexicons or lead to automatic application of procedures or, in any case, to possible benefits of a drill-like approach.

CONCLUDING REMARKS

This chapter reviewed rehabilitation studies in the numerical domain and attempted to integrate data from some developmental as well as learning theories on healthy individuals, although the specificity of acquired deficits was highlighted. Patients very often present a highly specific impairment and also often suffer from associated neuropsychological deficits, essential to assess and to take into account.

In rehabilitation of simple arithmetic, studies using drill versus conceptual training were reviewed, and the benefits as well as some criterion to choose one of these methods were discussed. In the transcoding domain, two studies were chosen to illustrate different theoretical models, and possible directions for future rehabilitation, such as monitoring, semantic context, and drill, were derived from the neuropsychological and developmental literature.

General principles of rehabilitation actually also apply for numerical disorders. A careful evaluation of the patient's abilities and impairments can result in different decisions: (a) to restore a certain function (e.g., fact retrieval), (b) to reorganize a certain function (e.g., fact retrieval from a verbal to a visual route in aphasic patients), or (c) to compensate for the loss of a certain function (e.g., using a pocket calculator). A systematic structure of the intervention program, with clearly defined steps of increasing difficulty and appropriate accuracy criteria, is always desirable. Furthermore, rehabilitation of more basic abilities (e.g., fact retrieval, transcoding two-digit numbers) should precede more complex abilities (e.g., complex calculation, transcoding larger numbers like three- or four-digit numbers).

Future research should better evaluate new developments in the methods used (e.g., errorless learning, method of vanishing cues), not only empirically but also by linking them with their theoretical foundations. Also, the relation between deficits in simple calculation or number processing and other numerical or non-numerical skills, until now, has been largely neglected and should be addressed. It usually remains unclear whether treatment of one deficit affects other parts of the number-processing domain. This issue seems important both for efficacy comparisons and for the assessment of theoretical models of number processing and calculation. Moreover, the impact of additional cognitive deficits on the treatment of calculation abilities has yet to be examined in a systematic way.

The present review focused on simple numerical tasks, in particular, on the remediation of arithmetic facts and on simple transcoding. This choice was motivated by the practical relevance of simple arithmetic in everyday life, as opposed to complex written calculation that may be substituted by a pocket calculator. Deficits of more basic numerical processes, on the other hand, such as impairments in processing quantities, were not discussed since they are rare and, to our knowledge, no specific rehabilitation studies concerning such deficits have been reported.

Overall, this short review of rehabilitation and numerical deficits shows that neuropsychological interventions may be rewarding and successful in the number domain if targeted training is provided. It also shows, however, that there are several issues to be addressed in future research.

REFERENCES

Ashcraft, M. (1995). Cognitive arithmetic: A review of data and theory. *Mathematical cognition, 1,* 3–34.

Baroody, A. J. (2003). The development of adaptive expertise and flexibility: The integration of conceptual and procedural knowledge. In A. J. Baroody & A. Dowker (Eds.), *The development of arithmetic concepts and skill: Constructing adaptive expertise* (pp. 1–34). Hillsdale, NJ: Erlbaum.

Benson, D. F., & Denckla, M. B. (1969). Verbal paraphasia as a source of calculation disturbance. *Archives of Neurology, 21,* 96–102.

Campbell, J. I. D. (1987). Production, verification, and priming of multiplication facts. *Memory and Cognition, 15,* 349–364.

Campbell, J. I. D., & Graham, D. J. (1985). Mental multiplication skill: Structure, process, and acquisition. *Canadian Journal of Psychology, 39,* 338–366.

Cipolotti, L., & Butterworth, B. (1995). Toward a multiroute model of number processing: Impaired number transcoding with preserved calculation skills. *Journal of Experimental Psychology, 124,* 375–390.

Cipolotti, L., Butterworth, B., & Warrington, E. K. (1994). From one thousand nine hundred and forty five to 1000,945. *Neuropsychologia, 32,* 503–509.

Cohen, L., Dehaene, S., & Verstichel, P. (1994). Number words and number non-words. A case of deep dyslexia extending to Arabic numerals. *Brain, 117,* 267–279.

Dagenbach, D., & McCloskey, M. (1992). The organization of arithmetic facts in memory: Evidence from a brain-damaged patient. *Brain and Cognition, 20,* 345–366.

Dehaene, S. (1992). Varieties of numerical abilities. *Cognition, 44,* 1–42.

Dehaene, S., & Cohen, L. (1991). Two mental calculation systems: A case study of severe acalculia with preserved approximation. *Neuropsychologia, 29*, 1045-1074.

Dehaene, S., & Cohen, L. (1995). Towards an anatomical and functional model of number processing. *Mathematical Cognition, 1*, 83-120.

Dehaene, S., & Cohen, L. (1997). Cerebral pathways for calculation: Double dissociation between rote verbal and quantitative knowledge of arithmetic. *Cortex, 33*, 219-250.

Delazer, M. (2003). Neuropsychological findings on conceptual knowledge of arithmetic. In A. J. Baroody & A. Dowker (Eds.), *The development of arithmetic concepts and skill: Constructing adaptive expertise* (pp. 385-408). Hillsdale, NJ: Erlbaum.

Delazer, M., & Benke, T. (1997). Arithmetic facts without meaning. *Cortex, 33*, 697-710.

Delazer, M., & Girelli, L. (1997). When "Alpha Romeo" facilitates 164: Semantic effects in verbal number production. *Neurocase, 3*, 461-475.

Delazer, M., Bodner, T., & Benke, T. (1998). Rehabilitation of arithmetical text problem solving. *Neuropsychological Rehabilitation, 8*, 401-412.

Delazer, M., Girelli, L., Semenza, C., & Denes, G. (1999). Numerical skills and aphasia. *Journal of the International Neuropsychological Society, 5*, 213-221.

Deloche, G., Seron, X., & Ferrand, I. (1989). Reeducation of number transcoding mechanisms: A procedural approach. In X. Seron & G. Deloche (Eds.), *Cognitive approach in neuropsychological rehabilitation* (pp. 247-271). Hillsdale, NJ: Erlbaum.

Deloche, G., & Seron, X. (1982). From one to 1 : An analysis of a transcoding process by means of neuropsychological data. *Cognition, 12*, 119-149.

Deloche, G., & Seron, X. (1987). Numerical transcoding: A general production model. In G. Deloche & X. Seron (Eds.), *Mathematical disabilities: A cognitive neuropsychological perspective* (pp. 137-170). Hillsdale, NJ: Erlbaum.

Domahs, F., Lochy, A., Eibl, G., & Delazer, M. (2004). Adding color to multiplication: Rehabilitation of arithmetic fact retrieval in a case of traumatic brain injury. *Neuropsychological Rehabilitation*.

Domahs, F., Bartha, L., & Delazer, M. (2003): Rehabilitation of arithmetic abilities: Different intervention strategies for multiplication. *Brain and Language, 87*, 165-166.

Fendrich, D. W., Healy A. F., & Bourne, L. E. (1993). Mental arithmetic: Training and retention of multiplication skills. In Izawa (Ed.), *Applied cognitive psychology: Application of cognitive theories and concepts.* Mahwah, NJ: Erlbaum.

Girelli, L., & Delazer, M. (1996). Subtraction bugs in an acalculic patient. *Cortex, 32*, 547-555.

Girelli, L., & Seron, X. (2001). Rehabilitation of number processing and calculation skills. *Aphasiology, 15*, 695-712.

Girelli L., Delazer, M., Semenza, C., & Denes G. (1996). The representation of arithmetical facts: Evidence from two rehabilitation studies. *Cortex, 32*, 49-66.

Girelli, L., Bartha, L., & Delazer, M. (2002). Strategic learning in the rehabilitation of semantic knowledge. *Neuropsychological rehabilitation, 12*, 41-61.

Glisky, E. L., Schacter, D. L., & Tulving, E. (1986). Learning and retention of computer-related vocabulary in amnesic patients: Method of vanishing cues. *Journal of Clinical and Experimental Neuropsychology, 8*, 292-312.

Graham, D.J. (1987). An associative retrieval model of arithmetic memory: How children learn to multiply. In J. Sloboda & D. Rogers (Eds.), *Cognitive processes in mathematics* (pp. 123-141). Oxford: Oxford University Press.

Haider J., & Kluwe, R. H. (1994). Acquisition of cognitive skills: an experimental test of Logan (1988) instance theory. *Zeitschrift für experimentelle und angewandte Psychologie, 41*, 39-77.

Hatano, G. (1988). Social and motivational bases for mathematical understanding. In G.B. Saxe & M. Gearhart (Eds.), *Children's mathematics* (pp. 55-70). San Francisco: Jossey-Bass.

Hittmair-Delazer, M., Semenza, C., & Denes G. (1994). Concepts and facts in calculation. *Brain, 117*, 715-728.

Jackson, M., & Warrington, E.K. (1986). Arithmetic skills in patients with unilateral cerebral lesions. *Cortex, 22*, 611-620.

Kashiwagi, A., Kashiwagi, T., & Hasegawa, T. (1987). Improvement of deficits in mnemonic rhyme for multiplication in Japanese aphasics. *Neuropsychologia, 25*, 443-447.

Lochy, A. (2001). *L'écriture des nombres Arabes: Une étude à la table digitalisante.* Unpublished doctoral thesis, Université Catholique de Louvain, Louvain-La-Neuve.

Lochy, A., Domahs, F., & Delazer, M. (2004). A case-study of access deficit to stored multiplication facts: Discrepancy between explicit and implicit tasks. *Cortex, 40*(1), 153-154.

Logan, G. D., & Klapp, S. T. (1991). Automatizing alphabet arithmetic: is extended practice necessary to produce automaticity? *Journal of Experimental Psychology: Learning, Memory and Cognition, 17*, 179-195.

McCloskey, M. (1992). Cognitive mechanisms in numerical processing: Evidence from acquired dyscalculia. *Cognition, 44*, 107-157.

McCloskey, M., & Caramazza, A. (1987). Cognitive mechanisms in normal and impaired number processing. In G. Deloche & X. Seron (Eds.), *Mathematical disabilities: A cognitive neuropsychological perspective* (pp. 201-219). Hillsdale, NJ: Erlbaum.

McCloskey, M., Caramazza, A., & Basili, A. (1985). Cognitive mechanisms in number processing and calculation: Evidence from dyscalculia. *Brain and Cognition, 4*, 171-196.

McNeil, J. E., & Warrington, E.K. (1994). A dissociation between addition and subtraction with written calculation. *Neuropsychologia, 32*, 717-728.

Miceli, G., & Capasso, R. (1991). *I disturbi del calcolo. Diagnosi e riabilitazione.* Milano: Masson.

Noël, M. P., & Seron, X. (1993). Arabic number reading deficit: A single case study or when 236 is read (2306) and judged superior to 1258. *Cognitive Neuropsychology, 10*, 317-339.

Noël, M. P., & Seron, X. (1995). Lexicalization errors in writing Arabic numerals: A single-case study. *Brain and Cognition, 29*, 151-179.

Rickard, T. C., Healy A. F., & Bourne, L. E. (1994). On the cognitive structure of basic arithmetic skills: Operation, order, and symbol transfer effects. *Journal of Experimental Psychology: Learning, Memory, and Cognition, 20*, 1139-1153.

Semenza, C., Miceli, G., & Girelli, L. (1997). A deficit for arithmetical procedures: Lack of knowledge or lack of monitoring? *Cortex, 33,* 483–498.

Seron, X., & Deloche, G. (1983). From four to 4, a supplement to "from three to 3." *Brain, 106,* 735–744.

Seron, X., & Fayol, M. (1994). Number transcoding in children: A functional analysis. *British Journal of Developmental Psychology, 12,* 281–300.

Siegler, R. (1988). Strategy choice procedure and the development of multiplication skills. *Journal of Experimental Psychology: General,* 117, 258–275.

Sullivan, K. S., Macaruso, P., & Sokol, S. M. (1996). Remediation of Arabic numeral processing in a case of developmental dyscalculia. *Neuropsychological rehabilitation, 6,* 27–53.

Thioux, M., Ivanoiu, A., Turconi, E., & Seron, X. (1999). Intrusion of the verbal code during the production of Arabic numerals: A single case study in a patient with probable Alzheimer's disease. *Cognitive Neuropsychology, 16,* 749–773.

Warrington, E. K. (1982). The fractionation of arithmetical skills: A single case study. *Quarterly Journal of Experimental Psychology,* 34, 31–51.

Whetstone, T. (1998). The representation of arithmetic facts in memory: Results from retraining a brain-damaged patient. *Brain and Cognition. 36,* 290–309.

Author Index

Subject Index

and language, 112, 433
and math
   and base-ten, 170
   and disorders, 255
   and fingers, 18, 303
   and language effects, 165, 167–168, 173, 176
   and math disability/deficits, 300, 303, 307, 470
   and social influences on, 165, 176, 236
   and universal features of, 176
   and working memory, 370
   cross-cultural comparisons, 176
   delayed/abnormal, 50
   disorders, 270, 303, 479; *see also* Dyscalculia

developmental, 179, 193, 447–449, 455–465, 479
Dyslexia, 448–449, 455–456, 459, 461–462, 464–465

E
Education/educational
   and cognitive development, 163
   and math avoidance, 315
   and math phobias, 324
   and numerosities, 23
   assessment, 144, 159
   background, 340

experience, 341, 343
formal, 23, 164, 173, 176, 324, 459
goal of, 332
informal, 173
mathematics, 114, 173, 197, 324
practices, 164, 174, 340
strategies, 447
Encoding complex hypothesis, 349–358, 368, 373
Error priming, 336–337, 356
Estimation
   computational, 198–205
   non-numerical, 198
   number line, 197–199, 208, 209–211
   numerical, 131, 197–198, 207, 211, 302, 408
   numerosity, 198, 204–207, 209, 211, 436
Evaluation apprehension, 241
Executive function, 261, 273, 275–277, 282, 284, 369,
      405, 476; *see also* Working Memory
Expertise, 362, 413–421, 423–427, 469, 501

F
Fechner's law, 72
Fingers, 48, 151, 179, 192, 215, 261, 417, 448
   agnosia, 43, 192, 439, 448, 462–463
   and adding, 333
   and base-ten, 28
   and counting, 15, 28, 47, 51, 77, 150, 152, 191, 257–
      259, 303, 305, 308, 338, 415, 445, 449, 459,
      461
      acquisition of, 15
   and external representations, 151, 159
   and number representations, 15–16, 18, 150, 338,
      440
      in the parietal lobe, 303
   and verbal system, 18
Format effects, 12, 348, 350–357
Fractions, 171–172, 197, 207, 216, 219–220, 230–231,
      274, 320, 323, 416
Fragile X syndrome, 269–273, 278–286, 291–293, 300
Functional magnetic resonance imaging (fMRI), 81,
      100, 192, 433–434, 438–439, 441–442

G
Gender and math, 235–236, 238–243, 318–319
Genetics or genetically, 245, 255, 261–262, 264, 425–
      426, 449, 463
Genetic disorders, 50, 193, 269, 284, 449
Geometry, 110, 112, 117, 122, 231, 253, 263, 273–274,
      280, 306–307, 366–367, 462
Gerstmann syndrome, 43, 192, 433, 439–440, 443,
      448, 461–463
Gesture, 112, 214, 221, 232
Goal-sketch filters, 153

H
Habituation, 4–5, 27, 87, 97, 132-136, 182
Heritability, 464

I
Ideomotor activity, 238–239
Intelligence, 175, 238, 241, 245, 280, 291, 302, 316,
      318, 417, 426, 448, 457
   implicit theories of, 245
Individual differences
   and cognitive skills, 310
   and executive control, 340
   and math stereotypes, 238, 246
   and working memory, 362, 364, 368, 370